WileyPLUS

S0-AFO-133

WileyPLUS is a research-based, online environment for effective teaching and learning.

The market-leading homework experience in *WileyPLUS* offers:

A Blank Sheet of Paper Effect

The *WileyPLUS* homework experience, which includes type-ahead for account title entry, imitates a blank sheet of paper format so that students use recall memory when doing homework and will do better in class, on exams, and in their professions.

A Professional Worksheet Style

The professional, worksheet-style problem layouts help students master accounting skills while doing homework that directly applies to the classroom and the real world.

The Opportunity to Catch Mistakes Earlier

Multi-part problems further help students focus by providing feedback at the part-level. Students can catch their mistakes earlier and access content-specific resources at the point of learning.

WileyPLUS includes a full ebook, interactive tutorials, assessment capabilities, and Blackboard integration.

STARR COMPANY
Trial Balance
June 30, 2014

	Debit	Credit
cal	$	
Cash		
Owner's Capital		
	$	$

Type-ahead feature for account title entry replaces drop-down menus.

www.wileyplus.com

WileyPLUS

ALL THE HELP, RESOURCES, AND PERSONAL SUPPORT YOU AND YOUR STUDENTS NEED!

www.wileyplus.com/resources

1st DAY OF CLASS ... AND BEYOND!

2-Minute Tutorials and all of the resources you and your students need to get started

WileyPLUS
Student Partner Program

Student support from an experienced student user

Wiley Faculty Network

Collaborate with your colleagues, find a mentor, attend virtual and live events, and view resources
www.WhereFacultyConnect.com

WileyPLUS
Quick Start

Pre-loaded, ready-to-use assignments and presentations created by subject matter experts

Technical Support 24/7
FAQs, online chat, and phone support
www.wileyplus.com/support

Your *WileyPLUS* Account Manager, providing personal training and support

ACCOUNTING PRINCIPLES

SIXTH CANADIAN EDITION

→ **Jerry J. Weygandt** *Ph.D., CPA*
University of Wisconsin—Madison

→ **Donald E. Kieso** *Ph.D., CPA*
Northern Illinois University

→ **Paul D. Kimmel** *Ph.D., CPA*
University of Wisconsin—Milwaukee

→ **Barbara Trenholm** *MBA, FCA*
University of New Brunswick—Fredericton

→ **Valerie A. Kinnear** *M.Sc. (Bus. Admin.), CA*
Mount Royal University

→ **Joan E. Barlow** *B.Comm., CA*
Mount Royal University

WILEY

To our students—past, present, and future

Library and Archives Canada Cataloguing in Publication

Accounting principles / Jerry Weygandt ... [et al.]. — 6th Canadian ed.

Includes indexes.
Issued also in a 2 vol. set.
ISBN 978-1-118-30678-9 (pt. 1).—ISBN 978-1-118-30679-6 (pt. 2).--
ISBN 978-1-118-30680-2 (pt. 3)

1. Accounting--Textbooks.   I. Weygandt, Jerry J

HF5636.A33 2012   657'.044   C2012-906476-9

Production Credits

Acquisitions Editor: Zoë Craig
Vice President and Publisher: Veronica Visentin
Vice President, Market Development: Carolyn Wells
Marketing Manager: Anita Osborne
Editorial Manager: Karen Staudinger
Production Manager: Tegan Wallace
Developmental Editor: Daleara Jamasji Hirjikaka
Media Editor: Channade Fenandoe
Editorial Assistant: Luisa Begani
Design: Interrobang Graphic Design, Inc.
Typesetting: Aptara
Cover Design: Sean Goodchild
Cover Photo: © John Foxx/Stockbyte/Getty
Printing and Binding: Friesens Corporation

Printed and bound in Canada
1 2 3 4 5 FP 17 16 15 14 13

John Wiley & Sons Canada, Ltd.
6045 Freemont Blvd.
Mississauga, Ontario L5R 4J3
Visit our website at: www.wiley.ca

BRIEF CONTENTS

CONTENTS – PART THREE

FINANCIAL REPORTING CONCEPTS

 THE **NAVIGATOR**

CONCEPTS FOR **REVIEW**

Before studying this chapter, you should understand or, if necessary, review:

a. The external users of accounting information and the objective of financial reporting. (Ch. 1, p. 6)

b. How accounting standards are set in Canada and internationally. (Ch. 1, pp. 9–10)

c. The definition of generally accepted accounting principles (GAAP). (Ch. 1, p. 9)

d. The economic entity concept and the accrual accounting and going concern assumptions. (Ch. 1, p. 11, and Ch. 3, p. 113)

e. The revenue recognition and expense recognition criteria. (Ch. 1, p. 13, and Ch. 3, p. 114)

HIGH STANDARDS FOR CANADIAN ACCOUNTING STANDARDS

TORONTO, Ont.—By now you're familiar with some of the accounting standards that Canadian companies must follow. But how are these standards set? In Canada, the Accounting Standards Board (AcSB) is responsible for the development of accounting standards for both private and public companies. The AcSB states that it "serves the public interest by establishing standards and guidance for financial reporting by all Canadian entities outside the public sector and by contributing to the development of internationally accepted financial reporting standards."

The AcSB responds to the needs and viewpoints of the entire economic community. The AcSB follows a rigorous process known as "due process" in developing and adopting accounting standards. This can include researching standards in other countries, issuing discussion papers to get preliminary input, and issuing exposure drafts to get feedback on proposed standards. "All of those stages involve a lot of consultation," says Rebecca Villmann, a senior AcSB principal. Before finalizing a standard, "We reach out to stakeholders, from holding one-on-one meetings to group discussions with entities in different industries, lenders, creditors, and investors to get a wide range of views that the board can consider." It can take about a year and half to amend an existing standard, and several years to develop a new one.

How does the AcSB develop or change a standard for private companies reporting under Accounting Standards for Private Enterprises (ASPE)? The AcSB begins the process when areas for improvement are identified. For example, stakeholders have pointed out that there is no standard under ASPE for the agriculture industry to account for "bearer biological assets," like a winery's grapevines. "That is an essential part of what you need to create your product, to grow the grapes, but there isn't specific guidance on how to account for that vine," says Ms. Villmann.

Throughout the process, the AcSB is guided by the financial statement concepts (or conceptual framework) outlined in the *CICA Handbook*. The conceptual framework sets out the objective of financial reporting; the characteristics the financial information needs in order to be useful; the definition of assets, liabilities, revenues, and expenses; and how items could be measured. For example, questions that need to be answered in developing a standard for accounting for agricultural assets such as vines are: Does the proposed standard satisfy the objective of financial reporting by providing useful information? Do the vines meet the definition of an asset? If the vines are reported as an asset, at what amount should they be reported?

How does the AcSB carry out its responsibility to develop standards for public companies reporting under International Financial Reporting Standards (IFRS)? The AcSB contributes to the International Accounting Standards Board's (IASB) standard-setting process, which is similar to the AcSB's process, including being guided by its conceptual framework. The AcSB participates in and monitors the IASB's due process to ensure that Canadians have the opportunity to discuss their views with the IASB and that the IASB considers these views when finalizing standards.

THE NAVIGATOR

>> STUDY **OBJECTIVES**

After studying this chapter, you should be able to:

1. Explain the importance of having a conceptual framework of accounting, and list the key components.

2. Identify and apply the objective of financial reporting, as well as the underlying assumption and cost constraint used by accountants.

3. Describe the fundamental and enhancing qualitative characteristics of financial reporting.

4. Identify and apply the basic recognition and measurement concepts of accounting.

THE NAVIGATOR

In the first 10 chapters, in Parts 1 and 2, you learned the process that leads to the preparation of a company's financial statements. You also learned that users make decisions based on financial statements, and that to be useful, these statements must communicate financial information to users in an effective way. This means that generally accepted accounting principles must be used. Otherwise, we would have to be familiar with each company's particular accounting and reporting practices in order to understand its financial statements. It would be difficult, if not impossible, to compare the financial results of different companies.

This chapter explores the conceptual framework that is used to develop generally accepted accounting principles. The chapter is organized as follows:

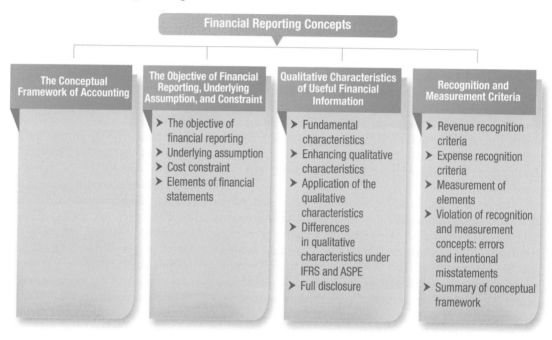

The Conceptual Framework of Accounting

» **STUDY OBJECTIVE 1**

Explain the importance of having a conceptual framework of accounting, and list the key components.

According to standard setters, the **conceptual framework of accounting** is "a coherent system of inter-related objectives and fundamentals that can lead to consistent standards and that prescribes the nature, function, and limits of financial accounting statements." In other words, the conceptual framework of accounting guides decisions about what to present in financial statements, how to report economic events, and how to communicate such information.

A conceptual framework ensures that we have a coherent set of standards. New standards are easier to understand and are more consistent when they are built on the same foundation as existing standards. As a foundation for accounting, the conceptual framework:

- ensures that existing standards and practices are clear and consistent
- provides guidance in responding to new issues and developing new standards
- assists accountants in the application of accounting standards
- increases financial statement users' understanding of and confidence in the financial statements

Alternative terminology Recall that, as we saw in Chapter 1, the words "standards" and "principles" mean the same thing in accounting.

It is impossible to create a rule for every situation. Canadian and international standards are therefore based mostly on general principles rather than specific rules. It is hoped that, with the help of a conceptual framework and their professional judgement, accountants will be able to quickly determine an appropriate accounting treatment for each situation.

Not every country uses the same conceptual framework and/or set of accounting standards. This lack of uniformity has arisen over time because of differences in legal systems, in processes for developing standards, in government requirements, and in economic environments. The International

Accounting Standards Board (IASB), the standard-setting body responsible for developing IFRS, was formed to try to reduce these areas of difference and unify global standard setting.

To promote global consistency and comparability, the IASB and its U.S. counterpart, the Financial Accounting Standards Board (FASB), agreed to work together to produce an updated common conceptual framework. At the time of writing, phase one of the project (regarding the objective of financial reporting, qualitative characteristics, and cost constraint) was finalized. The other phases had not yet been completed, so it is expected that there will continue to be changes to the IASB's conceptual framework.

Canada's Accounting Standards Board (AcSB) has committed to update the conceptual framework used in ASPE to be consistent with the IASB's conceptual framework used in IFRS. However, at the time of writing, the AcSB announced that it would defer updating the ASPE conceptual framework as it waited for further progress by IASB on its conceptual framework. This means that, although the conceptual frameworks for IFRS and ASPE are fundamentally similar, they are not identical. Differences between the two frameworks will be identified in the following sections of this chapter.

We describe the following key components of a conceptual framework in this chapter:

- objective of financial reporting
- underlying assumption
- cost constraint
- elements of financial statements
- qualitative characteristics of useful financial information
- recognition and measurement criteria

Helpful hint Accounting principles are affected by economic and political conditions, which change over time. As a result, accounting principles can and do change.

  BEFORE YOU GO ON...

Do It

Indicate if each of the following statements is true or false.

1. The specific rules for accounting for inventory are a component of the conceptual framework.
2. The use of a common conceptual framework will enhance the consistency and comparability of financial reporting in the global environment.
3. The conceptual framework eliminates the need for financial statement preparers to use professional judgement.
4. The conceptual framework includes recognition and measurement criteria.
5. The conceptual framework provides guidance in developing new standards.

Solution

1. F 2. T 3. F 4. T 5. T

Related exercise material: BE11–1.

Action Plan
- Review the purpose of the conceptual framework.
- Review the components of the conceptual framework.

THE NAVIGATOR

The Objective of Financial Reporting, Underlying Assumption, and Constraint

The first step in establishing accounting standards is to decide on the purpose or objective of financial reporting. Once this is established, then underlying assumptions and constraints can be determined.

THE OBJECTIVE OF FINANCIAL REPORTING

To decide what the objective of financial reporting should be, some basic questions need to be answered first: Who uses financial statements? Why? What information do the users need? How much do they know about business and accounting? How should financial information be reported so that it is best understood?

» STUDY OBJECTIVE 2

Identify and apply the objective of financial reporting, as well as the underlying assumption and cost constraint used by accountants.

The main objective of financial reporting is to **provide financial information that is useful to existing and potential investors and creditors in making decisions about a business.** You will recall from earlier chapters that financial statements are prepared for an economic or business unit that is separate and distinct from its owners. This is referred to as the economic entity concept. An economic (reporting) entity could be one company or a collection of companies consolidated under common ownership. We will learn more about consolidated companies in Chapter 16.

You will also recall from Chapter 1 that, although a wide variety of users rely on financial reporting, capital providers (investors and creditors) are identified as the main users of financial reporting. Capital providers play a fundamental role in the efficient functioning of the economy by providing capital (cash) to businesses. Businesses require cash to start up, maintain operations, and grow. Cash or capital comes from investors, lenders, and the company's revenue-generating activities.

To make decisions about allocating capital (such as about investing or lending), users look for information in the financial statements about a company's ability to earn a profit and generate future cash flows. To assess this ability, users read the financial statements to determine whether or not management acquired and used the company's resources in the best way possible. Consequently, financial statements must give information about the following:

1. Economic resources (assets) and claims on the economic resources (liabilities and equity)
2. Changes in economic resources and in claims on the economic resources
3. Economic performance

UNDERLYING ASSUMPTION

A key assumption, the going concern assumption, creates a foundation for the financial reporting process. You will recall from Chapter 1 that the going concern assumption assumes that the company will continue operating for the foreseeable future; that is, long enough to carry out its existing objectives and commitments. Although there are many business failures, most companies continue operating for a long time.

This assumption has important implications for accounting. If a company is assumed to be a going concern, then financial statement users will find it useful for the company to report assets, such as buildings and equipment, at their cost minus accumulated depreciation (carrying amount). If the company is not a going concern, then the carrying amount will not be relevant. Instead, the financial statement user would want to know what the assets can be sold for or their net realizable value. Furthermore, if the company is not a going concern, the classification of assets and liabilities as current or non-current would not matter. Labelling anything as non-current would be difficult to justify. The only time the going concern assumption should not be used is when liquidation is likely. If it cannot be assumed that the company is a going concern, this needs to be explicitly stated in the financial statements.

COST CONSTRAINT

The cost constraint is a pervasive constraint that ensures the value of the information provided is greater than the cost of providing it. That is, the benefits of financial reporting information should justify the costs. For example, in the section on the qualitative characteristics of useful financial information, we will recognize that to be useful, the financial information must be complete. To achieve completeness, accountants could record or disclose every financial event that occurs and every uncertainty that exists. However, providing this information increases reporting costs. The benefits of providing more information, in some cases, may be less than the costs.

The AcSB applied this constraint when it adopted IFRS for public companies and ASPE for private companies. As discussed in Chapter 1, users of private companies' financial statements generally require less information than users of public companies' financial statements. The board recognized that the cost to private companies of providing financial statements prepared under IFRS was greater than the benefits. Consequently, the board developed ASPE, which is simpler and requires less disclosure than IFRS.

Note that the ASPE conceptual framework refers to this constraint as the benefit versus cost constraint.

ELEMENTS OF FINANCIAL STATEMENTS

Elements of financial statements are the basic categories used in the financial statements to meet the objective of financial reporting. These elements include assets, liabilities, equity, revenues, and expenses.

Because these elements are so important, they must be precisely defined and applied in the same way by all reporting entities. Currently the definitions are being reviewed by the IASB and the FASB in their joint project to improve the conceptual framework. You have already been introduced to the definitions of assets, liabilities, equity, revenues, and expenses in earlier chapters. For your review, a summary of the definitions is provided in Illustration 11-1.

Element	Definition
Assets	An asset is a resource controlled by a business as a result of a past event that is expected to provide future economic benefits to the company.
Liabilities	A liability is a present obligation of the entity arising from past events, the settlement of which is expected to result in an outflow from the entity of resources embodying economic benefits.
Equity	Equity is the residual interest in the assets of the entity after deducting all its liabilities. (Assets − Liabilities = Equity)
Revenues	Revenue is an increase in assets or a decrease in liabilities that results in an increase in equity, other than those relating to contributions from owners. Under IFRS, revenue also includes gains. Revenue arises in the course of the company's ordinary activities, while gains may or may not arise from ordinary activities.
Expenses	Expenses are decreases in economic benefits during the accounting period in the form of outflows or depletions of assets or incurrences of liabilities that result in decreases in equity, other than those relating to distributions to owners. Under IFRS, expenses also includes losses. Expenses arise from the company's ordinary activities. Losses may or may not arise from the company's ordinary activities.

▶ **ILLUSTRATION**
Elements of financial statements

Under ASPE, gains and losses are defined in separate categories from revenues and expenses, but the basic definitions are similar to those under IFRS.

As indicated in the feature story, one of the questions that will need to be answered when the AcSB develops a standard for accounting biological products such as a winery's grapevines is: Do grapevines fit the definition of an asset? The AcSB will be guided by the key components of the definition of an asset as provided in the conceptual framework. Are the grapevines controlled by the company? Will the grapevines provide a future benefit?

 BEFORE YOU GO ON...

Do It

Presented below are two key concepts in financial reporting:

1. Going concern
2. Cost constraint

Identify the concept that applies to the following statements:

(a) _____ Private companies may follow ASPE, a simplified version of GAAP.
(b) _____ Assets and liabilities are classified as current or non-current.
(c) _____ A company expenses inexpensive office supplies when purchased to avoid the cost of tracking the use of supplies and determining the balance on hand at the balance sheet date.
(d) _____ Land is recorded at its cost.

Solution

(a) 2. (b) 1. (c) 2. (d) 1.

Related exercise material: BE11–2, BE11–3, BE11–4, E11–1, and E11–2.

Action Plan

- Recall that going concern is an underlying assumption in financial reporting.
- Recall that the cost constraint is a pervasive constraint on financial reporting.

THE **NAVIGATOR**

Qualitative Characteristics of Useful Financial Information

» **STUDY OBJECTIVE 3**

Describe the fundamental and enhancing qualitative characteristics of financial reporting.

How does a company like Reitmans (Canada) Limited decide how much financial information to disclose? In what format should its financial information be presented? How should assets, liabilities, revenues, and expenses be measured? Remember that the objective of financial reporting is to provide useful information for decision-making. Thus **the main criterion for judging accounting choices is decision usefulness.**

What makes information useful in decision-making? Accounting standard setters have decided that there are two fundamental characteristics that accounting information must have in order to be useful. In addition, there are other characteristics, complementary to the fundamental characteristics, that enhance the usefulness of accounting information. We discuss the qualitative characteristics in the following sections.

FUNDAMENTAL CHARACTERISTICS

In order for information to be useful in decision-making, accounting standard setters have agreed that the information should have two fundamental qualitative characteristics: relevance and faithful representation.

Relevance

Accounting information has **relevance** if it makes a difference in a decision. Relevant information has either predictive value or confirmatory value, or both. Predictive value helps users forecast future events. For example, the sales and profit reported by Reitmans in its comparative financial statements may be used along with other information to help predict future sales and profit. Confirmatory value confirms or corrects prior expectations. The sales and profit reported by Reitmans can also be used to confirm or correct previous predictions made by users.

Materiality is an important component of relevance. An item is material when it is likely to influence the decision of a reasonably careful investor or creditor. It is immaterial if including it or leaving it out has no impact on a decision maker. Materiality and relevance are both defined in terms of making a difference to a decision maker. A decision to not disclose certain information may be made because the users do not need that kind of information (it is not relevant) or because the amounts involved are too small to make a difference (they are immaterial). To determine the materiality of an amount, the accountant usually compares it with such items as total assets, total liabilities, gross revenues, cash, and profit.

Materiality is also related to the cost constraint, as illustrated in the following example. Assume that Yanik Co. purchases several inexpensive pieces of office equipment, such as wastepaper baskets. Although it is correct to capitalize these wastepaper baskets and depreciate them over their useful lives, they are usually expensed immediately instead. Immediate expensing is the easiest, and thus the least costly, method of accounting for these items and is justified because these costs are immaterial. Making depreciation schedules for these assets is costly and time-consuming. Expensing the wastepaper baskets will not make a material difference to total assets and profit.

In short, if the item does not make a difference in decision-making, GAAP does not have to be followed.

Faithful Representation

Once it is determined which information is relevant to financial statement users, then how the information is reported must be determined. To be useful, information must be a **faithful representation** of the economic reality of the events that it is reporting and not just the legal form. For example, a company may sign a lease agreement that requires periodic rental payments to be made over the life of the lease. If a company follows the legal form of the transaction, the periodic rental payments will be recorded as rent expense. However, for certain leases, the economic reality is that an asset is purchased and the periodic payments are loan payments. For these leases, it is necessary to record an asset and a liability to show the economic reality. You will learn more about the accounting for lease agreements in Chapter 15.

Faithful representation is achieved when the information is (1) complete, (2) neutral, and (3) free from material error, as explained below.

1. Accounting information is **complete** if it includes all information necessary to show the economic reality of the underlying transactions and events. If information is omitted, users will not be able to make appropriate resource allocation decisions. If Reitmans did not disclose when payments are due on its long-term debt, users would not have the necessary information to predict future cash flows. The concept of completeness is discussed further in this chapter in the section on full disclosure.

2. Accounting information is **neutral** if it is free from bias that is intended to attain a predetermined result or to encourage a particular behaviour. For example, accounting information would be biased if the income statement was prepared so that it resulted in a high enough level of profit that the management team received their bonuses.

3. If an error in accounting information could have an impact on an investor's or creditor's decision, then the error is a **material error**. There will always be some errors in accounting information because estimates, such as estimated useful life, are used. If accounting information is to be free from material error, estimates must be based on the best available information and be reasonably accurate. Accountants must use professional judgement and caution when using estimates in financial reporting.

The fundamental qualitative characteristics of accounting information are summarized in Illustration 11-2.

Relevance
1. Provides a basis for forecasts
2. Confirms or corrects prior expectations

Faithful Representation
1. Is complete
2. Is neutral
3. Is free from material error

▶ **ILLUSTRATION 11-2**
Fundamental qualitative characteristics of accounting information

ENHANCING QUALITATIVE CHARACTERISTICS

Enhancing qualitative characteristics complement the two fundamental qualitative characteristics: relevance and faithful representation. The enhancing characteristics are said to help users distinguish more useful information from less useful information. Comparability, verifiability, timeliness, and understandability are enhancing characteristics.

Comparability

Accounting information about a company is most useful when it can be compared with accounting information about other companies. There is **comparability** when companies with similar circumstances use the same accounting principles. Comparability enables users to identify the similarities and differences between companies.

Comparability is reduced when companies use different methods of accounting for specific items. For example, there are different methods of determining the cost of inventory, which can result in different amounts of profit. But if each company states which cost determination method it uses, the external user can determine whether the financial information for two companies is comparable.

Comparability is easier when accounting policies are used consistently. **Consistency** means that a company uses the same accounting principles and methods from year to year. For example, if a company selects FIFO as its inventory cost formula in the first year of operations, it is expected to use FIFO in subsequent years. When financial information has been reported consistently, the financial statements make it possible to do a meaningful analysis of company trends.

This does not mean, however, that a company can never change its accounting policies. Sometimes changes in accounting policies are required by standard setters. For example, when Canadian companies adopted either ASPE or IFRS in 2011, they were required to change some accounting policies. At other times, management may decide that it would be better to change to a new accounting policy. To do this, management must prove that the new policy will result in more relevant information in the statements.

In the year of a change in an accounting policy, the change and its impact must be disclosed in the notes to the financial statements. This disclosure makes users of the financial statements aware of the lack of consistency. In addition, the financial statements for past years must be restated as if the new accounting policy had been used in those years. We will learn more about accounting for, and reporting, changes in accounting policies in Chapter 14.

Verifiability

Verifiability helps assure users that the financial information shows the economic reality of the transaction. Information is verifiable if two knowledgeable and independent people would generally agree that it is faithfully represented. For example, the balance in a bank account can be directly verified by obtaining confirmation of the amount from the bank. Other types of information can be verified by checking inputs to a formula and recalculating the outputs. Information must be verifiable for external professional accountants to audit financial statements and to provide an opinion that the financial statements are presented fairly.

Timeliness

Timeliness means that accounting information is provided when it is still highly useful for decision-making. In other words, it must be available to decision makers before it loses its ability to influence decisions. Many people believe that by the time annual financial statements are issued—sometimes up to six months after a company's year-end—the information has limited usefulness for decision-making. Timely interim financial reporting is essential to decision-making.

Understandability

For the information in financial statements to be useful, users must be able to understand it. **Understandability** enables reasonably informed users to interpret and comprehend the meaning of the information provided in the financial statements. Users are expected to have a reasonable knowledge of business, economic, and financial activities, and of financial reporting. Users who do not have this level of understanding are expected to rely on professionals who do have an appropriate level of expertise. One of the benefits to Canadian public companies of using IFRS is that their financial statements will now be better understood by global users.

Understandability is greater when the information is classified, characterized, and presented clearly and concisely. In making decisions, users should review and analyze the information carefully.

The enhancing qualitative characteristics of accounting information are summarized in Illustration 11-3.

▶ **ILLUSTRATION 11-3**
Enhancing qualitative characteristics of useful financial information

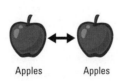

Comparability
1. Different companies use similar accounting principles.
2. A company uses the same accounting policies consistently from year to year.

Verifiability
3. Independent people agree that the economic reality is reported.

Timeliness
4. Information is provided when it is still useful.

Understandability
5. Information is understandable when it is understood by users who have a reasonable knowledge of accounting concepts and procedures.
6. Information is understandable when it is understood by users who have a reasonable knowledge of business and economic conditions.

APPLICATION OF THE QUALITATIVE CHARACTERISTICS

The qualitative characteristics are complementary concepts; that is, they work together. Nonetheless, they must be applied in a certain order. The qualitative characteristic of relevance should be applied first because it will identify the specific information that would affect the decisions of investors and creditors and that should be included in the financial report.

Once relevance is applied, faithful representation should be applied to ensure that the economic information faithfully represents the economic events being described. Taken together, relevance and faithful representation make financial reporting information decision useful.

Then the enhancing qualitative characteristics—comparability, verifiability, timeliness, and understandability—are applied. They add to the decision usefulness of financial reporting information that is relevant and representationally faithful. They must be applied after the first two characteristics because they cannot, either individually or together, make information useful if it is irrelevant or not faithfully represented.

DIFFERENCES IN QUALITATIVE CHARACTERISTICS UNDER IFRS AND ASPE

Earlier in the chapter, we noted that the IFRS and ASPE conceptual frameworks are fundamentally similar but not identical. While the conceptual framework for IFRS identifies two fundamental and four enhancing characteristics, the framework for ASPE identifies four principal qualitative characteristics: understandability, relevance, reliability, and comparability.

Note that both conceptual frameworks use relevance as a main characteristic. Faithful representation, identified as a fundamental qualitative characteristic under IFRS, is very similar to reliability, which is identified as a principal qualitative characteristic under ASPE. Under ASPE, information is considered reliable if it is a faithful representation of transactions and events, is verifiable, and is neutral. There is also a difference in how the two standards view understandability and comparability. Under IFRS, they are assigned a lower status because they are identified as enhancing qualitative characteristics, whereas under ASPE, they are considered to be as important as relevance and reliability.

ASPE also recognizes conservatism as a qualitative characteristic of financial information. The concept of conservatism means that, when preparing financial statements, accountants should choose the accounting treatment or estimate that will be the least likely to overstate assets, revenues, and gains and the least likely to understate liabilities, expenses, and losses. However, conservatism does not justify the deliberate understatement of assets, revenues, and gains or the deliberate overstatement of liabilities, expenses, and losses. It should be noted that the IASB eliminated the concept of conservatism when it updated the conceptual framework.

In summary, although at the time the text was written there were some differences between the conceptual frameworks, it is likely these differences will be eliminated because, as mentioned earlier, the AcSB intends to adopt the IASB's conceptual framework and incorporate it into ASPE.

FULL DISCLOSURE

Earlier in our discussion of the qualitative characteristic of faithful representation, we recognized that information provided in the financial statements must be complete. This requires that companies fully disclose circumstances and events that make a difference to financial statement users. It is important that investors be made aware of events that can affect a company's financial health.

Full disclosure is respected through two elements in the financial statements: the data they contain and the accompanying notes. For example, one of the notes in the statements summarizes the company's significant accounting policies. The summary includes the methods used by the company when there are alternatives in acceptable accounting principles. Reitmans' note on its significant accounting policies (see Note 3 in Appendix A at the end of this textbook) discloses that merchandise inventories are measured at the lower of cost (determined on an average basis using the retail method) and net realizable value.

The information that is disclosed in the notes to the financial statements generally falls into three additional categories. The information can:

1. Give supplementary detail or explanation (for example, a schedule of property, plant, and equipment).
2. Explain unrecorded transactions (for example, contingencies, commitments, and subsequent events).
3. Supply new information (for example, information about related party transactions).

Deciding how much disclosure is enough can be difficult. Accountants must use professional judgement in determining what information is relevant and material to users. Accountants must also consider the cost of providing the information versus the benefits.

ACCOUNTING IN ACTION
ALL ABOUT YOU INSIGHT

No doubt you have used a resumé to find a job. Your resumé is like a company's annual report, describing your recent accomplishments so others can evaluate your performance and try to predict how you will do in the future. Your resumé must be a faithful representation of your background, education, and experience. The temptation to overstate accomplishments is great, however—even at the highest levels of responsibility, as shown in the recent case of a former CEO of Yahoo, Scott Thompson. After just four months at the company's helm, Yahoo announced that Thompson had decided to step down. Although the company did not state the reasons, it was reported that the decision was partly to do with the fact that an activist hedge fund publicized the fact that Thompson had misrepresented his education on his resumé. His biography in the company's annual report stated that he had a degree in accounting and computer science, but his degree is in accounting only. Yahoo's annual report is a legal document filed with the U.S. Securities and Exchange Commission, in which CEOs must swear that all information is truthful. Yahoo said the statement was an "inadvertent error" and hired a lawyer to investigate the statement.

Sources: Michael J. de la Merced and Evelyn M. Rusli, "Yahoo's Chief to Leave as Company Strikes Deal with Loeb," *New York Times,* May 13, 2012; Julianne Pepitone, "Yahoo Confirms CEO Is Out after Resume Scandal," CNNMoney, May 14, 2012; Amir Efrati and Joann S. Lublin, "Yahoo CEO's Downfall," *Wall Street Journal,* May 15, 2012.

What may be the consequences to you if you misrepresent yourself on your resumé?

 BEFORE YOU GO ON...

Do It

Presented below are some of the qualitative characteristics of financial information.

1. Relevance
2. Faithful representation
3. Complete
4. Neutral
5. Comparability
6. Verifiability
7. Timeliness
8. Understandability

Match the qualitative characteristics to the following statements:

(a) _____ Information is available to decision makers before the information loses its ability to influence decisions.

(b) _____ Information is free from bias that is intended to attain a predetermined result.

(c) _____ Information makes a difference in a decision.

Action Plan
- Review the two fundamental qualitative characteristics.
- Review the enhancing qualitative characteristics.

(d) _____ Users are assured that the financial information shows the economic reality of the transaction.

(e) _____ All of the information necessary to show the economic reality of transactions is provided.

(f) _____ Accounting information about one company can be evaluated in relation to accounting information from another company.

(g) _____ Accounting information reports the economic reality of a transaction, not its legal form.

(h) _____ Accounting information is prepared on the assumption that users have a general understanding of general business and economic conditions and are able to read a financial report.

Solution

(a) 7. (b) 4. (c) 1. (d) 6. (e) 3. (f) 5. (g) 2. (h) 8.

Related exercise material: BE11–5, BE11-6, E11-3, and E11–4.

THE NAVIGATOR

Recognition and Measurement Criteria

You learned in earlier chapters that financial statements are prepared using the accrual basis of accounting. The **accrual basis of accounting** means that transactions affecting a company's financial statements are recorded in the period in which the events occur, rather than when the company receives cash or pays cash. Therefore accounting standards are necessary to help accountants answer two questions: (1) when should an event be recorded and (2) at what amount should it be recorded? **Recognition criteria help determine when an event should be recorded** in the financial statements. When an item is recorded in the financial statements, accountants say that it has been recognized. **Measurement criteria provide guidance on what amount should be recorded** for the event.

Generally an item will be included in the financial statements if it meets the definition of an asset, liability, equity, revenue, or expense; if it can be measured; and if a reasonable estimate of the amount can be made. The item is reported in the financial statements in a monetary amount. In Canada, the monetary unit used for financial reporting is generally the Canadian dollar.

There are two important concepts underlying the general criteria. The first concept is that for an asset to be recorded, it must be probable that there will be a future economic benefit, and for a liability to be recognized, it must be probable that economic resources will be given up. For example, a company does not have to be 100% certain that it will collect an account receivable to record the receivable; it just has to be probable that cash will be collected. The second concept is that estimates may be used to record dollar amounts if the precise dollar amount is not known.

Although the general recognition criteria provide guidance for recording events, it is necessary to have more specific criteria for when to recognize revenues and expenses. Should the revenue be recorded when the customer places an order with the company, or when the goods are delivered? How should the transaction be recorded if cash collection is uncertain? The revenue recognition criteria are discussed in the following section. Expense recognition will be discussed later in the chapter.

REVENUE RECOGNITION CRITERIA

In the opinion of many people, when to recognize revenue is the most difficult issue in accounting. And it is an issue that has been responsible for many of the accounting scandals of the past decade. For example, when Alexa Life Sciences, the manufacturer of Cold-FX, first started selling its products in the United States in 2006, it failed to recognize that there was considerable risk that a significant amount of the product would be returned by retailers. As a result, the company overstated its 2006 revenues (net sales) by $5.6 million.

» **STUDY OBJECTIVE 4**

Identify and apply the basic recognition and measurement concepts of accounting.

Why is revenue recognition such a difficult concept to apply? In some cases, revenue recognition has been intentionally abused in order to overstate profits. However, in most cases, revenue recognition is a difficult concept that requires professional judgement because the activities that generate revenues have become a lot more innovative and complex than in the past. These include "swap" transactions, "bill and hold" sales arrangements, risk-sharing agreements, complex rights of return, price-protection guarantees, and post-sale maintenance contracts—all topics that go beyond an introductory accounting course.

Basically, the **revenue recognition criteria** state that revenue is recognized when there has been an increase in an asset or a decrease in a liability due to ordinary profit-generating activities that results in an increase in owners' equity. The question that needs to be answered is, when have assets actually increased or liabilities decreased?

In the following sections, we will discuss revenue recognition criteria for the most common revenue-generating activities:

1. Sale of goods
2. Service contracts and construction contracts

Sale of Goods

Revenue from the sale of goods is recognized when all of the following conditions have been met:

1. The seller has transferred to the buyer the significant risks and rewards of ownership.
2. The seller does not have control over the goods or continuing managerial involvement.
3. The amount of the revenue can be reliably measured.
4. It is probable there will be an increase in economic resources (that is, cash will be collected).
5. Costs relating to the sale of the goods can be reliably measured.

For sales in a retail establishment, these conditions are generally met at the point of sale. Consider a sale by Reitmans for an item that is a final sale and cannot be returned. At the point of sale, the customer pays the cash and takes the merchandise. The company records the sale by debiting Cash and crediting Sales Revenue. In this example, there is no uncertainty about when or how much revenue should be recorded. Cash has been received and the customer has taken ownership of the goods. In the following paragraphs, we discuss common situations where there is more uncertainty as to when or how much revenue should be recognized.

When Goods Are Shipped. Typically, the risks and rewards of ownership are transferred when legal title passes and the customer is in possession of the goods. For goods that are shipped, the shipping terms determine when the legal title passes. Recall from Chapter 5 that, if the terms of the sale are FOB shipping point, then legal titles passes when the goods are shipped and the seller recognizes revenue on the date the goods are shipped. If the terms of the sale are FOB destination, then legal title passes when the goods arrive at their destination and revenue is recognized on the date the goods are delivered.

When Goods Are Sold on Credit. When merchandise is sold on credit, revenue is recognized at the point of sale as long as it is reasonably sure that the cash will be collected. If the sale were on credit rather than for cash, the company would record the sale by debiting Accounts Receivable and crediting Sales Revenue. Of course, not all accounts are actually collected. However, as we learned in Chapter 8, revenue can be recognized as long as an estimate can be made of any possible uncollectible accounts. Bad debt expense is recorded for the estimated uncollectible accounts and matched against revenue in the appropriate period.

When Goods May Be Returned for a Refund. If a company provides refunds to customers for goods returned, revenue is recognized at point of sale if the company is able to reliably estimate future returns. The company will report sales net of an allowance for the estimated returns and recognize a liability for the estimated returns in its financial statements. For example, Reitmans' note on significant accounting policy discloses that the sales reported in the income statement are net of returns and estimated possible returns (see Note 3 part I) in Appendix A at the end of the text). Note 12 to Reitmans' financial statements discloses that Reitmans recognized a $770,000 liability (provision) for estimated possible sales returns in its January 28, 2012, balance sheet

When Free Warranty Service Is Provided. Similarly, if a company provides free warranty service on its merchandise, revenue is recognized at point of sale if the company is able to reliably estimate the future warranty costs. You will recall from Chapter 10 that the estimated warranty expense is recorded and a warranty liability is recognized in its financial statements. If costs relating to the sale cannot be reliably measured, then the revenue cannot be recognized.

When the Sales Transaction Includes the Sale of Goods and a Service Component. Some sales transactions may include both the sale of goods and a service component. For example, assume a customer pays $3,250 cash for a large screen television and an extended warranty. The extended warranty normally sells for $250 as a separate warranty. The transaction must be recorded in the accounting records to reflect that the customer has paid for two items: the television and the extended warranty. Sales revenue of $3,000 is recorded for the sale of the television and $250 is recorded as unearned warranty revenue to recognize that the store has an obligation (liability) to provide warranty service in the future. Warranty revenue will be recognized when the company satisfies its obligation by providing warranty service.

Service Contracts and Construction Contracts

Generally, in businesses that provide services, revenue is recognized when the service has been provided and it is probable that the cash will be collected. To illustrate, assume your doctor gives you a routine checkup in September, bills the provincial health care plan in October, and receives payment in November. When should your doctor recognize the revenue? The revenue should be recognized in September because that was when the service was performed, the price would have been known, and the receivable was likely to be collected.

Revenue recognition becomes more difficult when the earnings process lasts several years. This happens in the case of long-term service contracts and construction contracts for large projects, such as building bridges, roads, and aircraft. For example, construction on "The Bow"—a large office tower in Calgary that is the second-tallest building in Canada—started in 2007 and was completed in 2012.

Assume that Warrior Construction Co. has a contract to build a dam for the Province of British Columbia for $400 million. Construction is estimated to take three years (starting early in 2012) at a cost of $360 million. If Warrior recognizes revenue only when the construction is complete, it will report no revenues and no profit in the first two years. When completion and sale take place, at the end of 2014, Warrior will report $400 million in revenues, costs of $360 million, and the entire profit of $40 million. Did Warrior really produce no revenues and earn no profit in 2012 and 2013? Obviously not.

In situations like this, if the costs to complete the project can be reasonably estimated, the percentage-of-completion method is typically used to recognize revenue. The **percentage-of-completion method** recognizes revenue on long-term projects as progress is made toward completion based on reasonable estimates of how much of the work has been performed to date.

Let's look at an illustration of the percentage-of-completion method. Assume that Warrior Construction has costs of $54 million in 2012, $180 million in 2013, and $126 million in 2014 on the dam project.

There are three steps in the percentage-of-completion method.

1. Progress toward completion is measured. One common method of measuring progress toward completion is to compare the costs incurred in a period with the total estimated costs for the entire project. This results in a percentage that indicates the percentage of the work that is complete. In the Warrior example, the project is 15% ($54 million ÷ $360 million) complete at the end of 2012.
2. This percentage is multiplied by the total revenue for the project, to determine the amount of revenue to be recognized for the period. Warrior will recognize revenue of $60 million (15% × $400 million) in 2012.
3. The costs incurred are then subtracted from the revenue recognized to arrive at the gross profit for the current period. Warrior will report gross profit of $6 million ($60 million − $54 million) for 2012. These three steps are presented in Illustration 11-4 (in millions).

▶ILLUSTRATION **11-4**
Percentage-of-
completion method

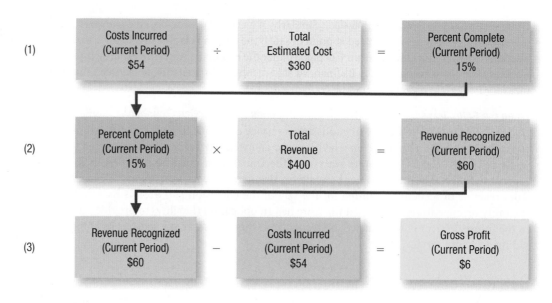

The portion of the $400 million of revenue and gross profit that Warrior will recognize in each of the three years is shown below (all amounts are in millions):

Year	Costs Incurred (Current Period)	÷	Total Estimated Cost	=	Percentage Complete (Current Period)	×	Total Revenue	=	Revenue Recognized (Current Period)	−	Costs Incurred (Current Period)	=	Gross Profit (Current Period)
2012	$ 54		$360		15%		$400		$ 60		$ 54		$ 6
2013	180		360		50%		400		200		180		20
2014	126		360		35%		400		140		126		14
Total	$360								$400		$360		$40

This example demonstrates the basic concepts followed in the percentage-of-completion method. However, the percentage-of-completion method can be fairly complex for companies to apply because the estimated cost to complete the project may change as the project progresses and more information becomes available. In addition, although costs incurred compared with costs to complete is a common method used to measure the project's progress, other measures may be more appropriate for some projects. Significant judgement is required to determine the best method of measuring progress.

The IASB has proposed a new standard for revenue recognition. This has been done in consultation with the FASB in the United States. The proposed standard is a "contract"-based approach. Under the proposed standard, a company would recognize revenue when it has transferred a promised good or service to a customer, which is when the customer obtains control of that good or service. The new standard is not expected to significantly change the way most companies recognize revenues but it may make a significant difference for those companies who have long-term service or construction contracts.

As indicated in the feature story, the development of a new standard can take years as the IASB must follow a due process, seeking input from the various stakeholders. After issuing a discussion paper on revenue recognition in 2008 and two exposure drafts seeking input from stakeholders, the IASB continued to deliberate on the proposed new revenue recognition standard in 2012 and planned to finalize the standard in 2013.

EXPENSE RECOGNITION CRITERIA

The basic **expense recognition criteria** state that expenses are recognized when there is a decrease in an asset or increase in a liability, excluding transactions with owners that result in a decrease in owners' equity. This is not necessarily when cash is paid. For example, as supplies are used, the asset Supplies is decreased and an expense is recognized. Alternatively, when a liability for salaries payable is recorded, salaries expense is recognized.

Expense recognition is tied to revenue recognition when there is a direct association between costs incurred and the earning of revenue. For example, there is a direct association between cost of goods sold and sales revenue. As we learned in Chapter 3, this process is commonly referred to as matching. Under matching, revenues and expenses that relate to the same transaction are recorded in the same accounting period. Other examples of expenses that relate directly to revenue are bad debt expense, warranty expense, and sales salaries.

Other costs are more difficult to directly associate with revenue. For example, it is difficult to match administrative salary expense or interest expense with the revenue they help to earn. Such costs are therefore expensed in the period when the liability arises.

Sometimes, however, there is no direct relationship between expenses and revenue. When it is hard to find a direct relationship and assets are expected to benefit several accounting periods, a rational and systematic allocation policy can sometimes be developed to allocate the cost of the asset to expense over time. For example, the cost of a long-lived asset can be allocated to depreciation expense over the life of the asset because it can be determined that the asset contributes in some way to revenue generation during its useful life. Allocation requires the accountant to use professional judgement in estimating the benefits that will be received from the asset and how the cost of the asset should be allocated to expense.

In other cases, when expenditures are made that do not qualify for the recognition of an asset, an expense is recognized immediately. For example, expenditures for research do not qualify for recognition of an asset as it is impossible to determine the future benefits arising from the research, so the research costs are expensed immediately. Another example is expenditures made for advertising, which are also expensed immediately.

Sometimes a previously recognized asset ceases to have future benefit, and the asset must be expensed. For example, inventory that is obsolete and cannot be sold is expensed when it becomes apparent it cannot be sold.

In summary, costs need to be analyzed to determine whether it is probable there is a future benefit to the company or not. If there is a direct relationship between the revenues recognized and costs, the costs are recognized as expenses (matched against the revenues) in the period when the revenue is recognized. If it is hard to determine a direct relationship, but the costs are expected to benefit several periods, then it might be appropriate to systematically and rationally allocate the cost to expense over the periods that are expected to benefit. If there is no future benefit, or if the benefit is uncertain, the costs should simply be expensed in the current period.

MEASUREMENT OF ELEMENTS

So far, we have looked at when items should be recognized or recorded in the accounting records. Now we will look at what dollar amounts should be used to record the items. There are a number of different measurements used in accounting. They include the following:

1. Cost
2. Fair value
3. Amortized cost

Assets are recorded at cost when they are acquired. Cost is used because it is both relevant and provides a faithful representation of the transaction. Cost represents the price paid, the assets sacrificed, or the commitment made at the date of acquisition. Cost is objectively measurable, factual, and verifiable. It is the result of an exchange transaction. Cost is relevant for reporting certain assets in the balance sheet because the assets are intended for use in the business and are not going to be sold.

Most companies use the cost model to report property, plant, and equipment where the carrying value on the balance sheet is cost less accumulated depreciation. However, you will recall from Chapter 9 that, under IFRS, companies can choose to account for their property, plant, and equipment under either the cost model or the revaluation model. Under the revaluation model, the carrying amount of property, plant, and equipment is its fair value less any accumulated depreciation less any subsequent impairment losses.

Alternative terminology Other common terms for *fair value* are *market value* and *realizable value*.

However, for some assets, it is more relevant to provide the assets' fair value: the amount of cash that is expected to be collected if the asset is sold. Users of financial information are better able to assess the impact of changes in fair value on the company's liquidity and solvency. For example, short-term or trading investments that are purchased for the purpose of resale are reported at their fair value in the financial statements. We will learn more about fair values used to report trading securities and some strategic long-term equity investments in Chapter 16.

Certain assets and liabilities, such as investments in bonds and bonds payable, are measured at amortized cost. We will learn more about amortized cost and investments in bonds and bonds payable in Chapters 15 and 16.

Cost is the most common basis used by companies in preparing their financial statements. Cost may be combined with other measurement bases. For example, you will recall from Chapter 6 that inventory is reported at the lower of cost and net realizable value.

VIOLATION OF RECOGNITION AND MEASUREMENT CONCEPTS: ERRORS AND INTENTIONAL MISSTATEMENTS

As we discussed earlier in the chapter, revenue recognition is considered the most difficult issue in accounting. In some cases, revenue recognition has been intentionally abused. Incorrect application of the expense and measurement criteria can also result in errors or intentional misstatement of the financial statements. In this section, we will discuss what situations might lead management and accountants to abuse accounting principles and potential misstatements that can be made in applying the recognition and measurement criteria.

Management may be under pressure to report a certain amount of profit to meet shareholders' (owners') expectations, or management's bonuses may be based on the company achieving a specified profit. In these situations, management may be inclined to overstate profits by overstating revenues or understating expenses. Alternatively, management of some private companies may want to reduce the amount of tax paid and consequently may be inclined to understate profits by understating revenues and overstating expenses. Ways in which revenues or expenses may be misstated in error or intentionally are as follows:

1. **Recognition of revenue or expense in the incorrect accounting period.** For example, the seller might recognize sales revenues for goods that are shipped FOB destination when the goods are shipped and not when the customer receives the goods. This would overstate revenues if the goods were shipped just prior to the company's fiscal year end and received by the customer after the year end. Alternatively, a company might delay recording an expense by recording as an asset an expenditure for which there is no future benefit.
2. **Misstatement of estimates.** Earlier in the chapter, we recognized that companies need to estimate potential returns and record an allowance that reduces net sales. If the allowance is understated, net sales will be overstated. Alternatively, management might understate the estimate for bad debt expense. Estimates do not need to be 100% accurate. However, professional judgement needs to be used in arriving at the estimate and the estimates need to be supported and verifiable.
3. **Misstatement of revenue or expense accruals.** In some cases, revenue has been earned or an expense incurred for which the exact amount is not yet known, and thus the accrual must be estimated. Again, professional judgement needs to be used in arriving at the estimate, and the estimate needs to be supported and verifiable. For example, a company may need to estimate the accrual for utilities expense because the bill has not been received. The accountant might use previous utility bills to arrive at a reasonable estimate.
4. **Failure to record a revenue or expense.** Due to poor internal controls and record keeping, the accountant may be unaware that revenue has been earned or an expense incurred.
5. **Failure to apply the correct measurement.** For example, a company may neglect to write down inventory to net realizable value. Or alternatively, land might be reported at fair value when the company is following the cost model for property, plant, and equipment.

It is important that accountants analyze transactions carefully to ensure that accounting principles are applied correctly and the financial statements are a faithful representation of the underlying economic events. When adjusting entries are prepared at the end of an accounting period, accountants must give careful attention to determining the appropriate accounting period that revenues and expenses should be recognized in, appropriate measurements and estimates, and if any economic events have occurred that need to be recorded. Accountants need to exercise professional judgement and ethical reasoning to guard against errors or abuse in applying accounting principles.

ACCOUNTING IN ACTION
ETHICS INSIGHT

One of the biggest accounting scandals in Canadian history involved former telecommunications giant Nortel Networks. The company was accused of accruing expenses that did not occur and then reversing these expenses in 2003 in order to turn a profit, after losing money in the 2001 dot-com bust. Nortel allegedly accrued millions of dollars in liabilities related to the company's downsizing, such as lawsuits from suppliers over cancelled contracts and employee severance packages. If the company overestimated the amounts of these liabilities, also known as accruals, reserves, or provisions, it would consider the savings as revenue in the period in which the settlement was reached. Three senior executives were charged with fraud, accused of manipulating earnings in 2003 to trigger millions of dollars in profitability bonuses for themselves. During a six-month trial in 2012, the Crown alleged that the executives ordered extra liabilities to be accrued in 2002, turning a profit into a loss, and then reversed the accruals in 2003, turning a loss into a profit. The Crown argued the accruals should have been reversed earlier. The company restated its financial information several times in the years thereafter, and filed for bankruptcy in 2009. At the time of writing, the fraud charges were before the court.

Sources: James Bagnall, "Were Senior Executives Scapegoats for Nortel's Demise?," Postmedia News, January 14, 2012; Jamie Sturgeon, "'Unsupportable' Reserves Remained on Nortel Books, Court Hears," *Financial Post,* March 5, 2012; Janet McFarland, "Nortel Releases $80-million in Accounting Reserves to Reach Profit Threshold: Witness," *Globe and Mail,* April 2, 2012; James Bagnall, "Nortel Witnesses Were 'Accomplices' to Fraud," *Ottawa Citizen,* August 7, 2012.

Accountants are often required to make estimates when preparing financial statements. What is the difference between what the three executives allegedly did at Nortel and what we would expect an accountant to do when estimating accruals for adjusting journal entries?

SUMMARY OF CONCEPTUAL FRAMEWORK

As we have seen, the conceptual framework for developing sound reporting practices starts with the objective of financial reporting. It then describes the underlying assumption, the elements of the financial statements, the qualitative (fundamental and enhancing) characteristics of accounting information, and the constraint on financial reporting. Finally, more detailed recognition and measurement criteria are provided. The conceptual framework is summarized in Illustration 11-5.

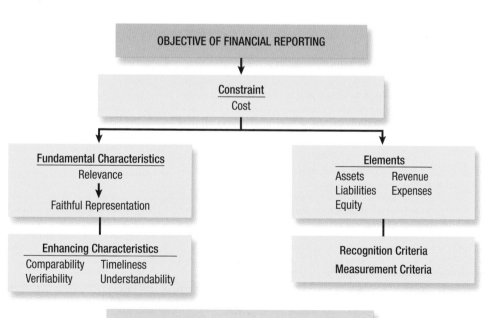

▶ **ILLUSTRATION 11-5**
Conceptual framework

As noted earlier in the chapter, the IASB and FASB continue to work on joint projects to improve the conceptual framework and the revenue recognition criteria. It is anticipated that there will be significant changes to GAAP in the next few years.

 BEFORE YOU GO ON...

Do It

1. For each of the following independent situations, indicate if the revenue should be recognized in 2013 or 2014 and explain why.
   (a) Customer orders widgets on December 15, 2013; widgets are shipped FOB destination on December 24, 2013; customer receives the goods on January 15, 2014.
   (b) Customer orders widgets on December 15, 2013; widgets are shipped FOB shipping point on December 14, 2013; customer receives the goods on January 15, 2014.
   (c) Customer signs a contract, on December 1, 2013, to receive monthly cleaning services. Cleaning services are provided each month from January to December 2014.
   (d) A company ships $100,000 of goods FOB shipping point in the month. The company has a 60-day return policy. Typically, 1% of goods are returned.

2. For each of the following independent situations, indicate if the expense should be recognized in 2013 or 2014 and explain why.
   (a) A company purchases office supplies in December 2013. The supplies are on hand at December 31, 2013, and will be used in 2014.
   (b) A company will pay employees on January 7, 2014, for work performed in December 2013.
   (c) Merchandise inventory with a cost of $50,000 was sold FOB destination on December 28, 2013. Customer received the merchandise on January 10, 2014.
   (d) Equipment with a cost of $75,000 was purchased and installed on December 15, 2013. The equipment has a five-year useful life with no residual value. The company started using the equipment on January 1, 2014.

Action Plan

- Determine when all the significant risks and rewards of ownership have been transferred to the customer.
- Determine when a service has been provided.
- Determine when an asset has decreased or liability increased that results in a decrease in owners' equity.
- Determine when revenues are recognized for those expenses that should be matched against revenues.
- Determine when the economic benefits are realized for long-lived assets that benefit more than one accounting period.

Solution

1. (a) Revenue should be recognized in 2014 as the seller retains ownership until the customer receives the goods.
   (b) Revenue should be recognized in 2013 as ownership of the goods is transferred to the customer when the goods are shipped.
   (c) Revenue should be recognized in 2014 each month as the cleaning service is provided.
   (d) Revenue should be recognized in 2013 as the ownership of the goods has transferred and the company is able to estimate returns. The company would record an allowance for the estimated sales returns and a corresponding liability.

2. (a) Supplies expense should be recognized in 2014 when the supplies are used. At December 31, 2013, the supplies should be reported as an asset because they will provide economic benefit in 2014.
   (b) The salary expense should be recorded in 2013 because the liability Salaries Payable must be recognized in 2013 as the employees provided the service to the company in 2013.
   (c) An expense, cost of goods sold, should be recognized in 2014 when the revenue is recognized. The revenue is recognized in 2014 because ownership transfers when the customer receives the merchandise.
   (d) Depreciation expense will not be recorded in 2013 because the company did not use the equipment during 2013. The economic benefits from the equipment will be realized over five years starting January 1, 2014.

Related exercise material: BE11–7, BE11–8, BE11–9, BE11–10, BE11–11, BE11–12, BE11–13, BE11–14, E11–5, E11–6, E11–7, E11–8, E11–9, E11–10, and E11–11.

THE **NAVIGATOR**

▮Comparing IFRS and ASPE ▮

Key Differences	International Financial Reporting Standards (IFRS)	Accounting Standards for Private Enterprises (ASPE)
Conceptual framework	Phase one of the IASB and FASB joint project is finalized and adopted (objectives and qualitative characteristics) Remaining phases are still under development	Deferring adoption of the joint project phase one improvements until further progress has been made by the IASB and FASB on the conceptual framework
Constraint	Uses the term "cost constraint"	Uses the term "benefit versus cost constraint"
Definition of elements: gains and losses	Defined as being part of revenues and expenses	Separate definitions for revenues and gains and for expenses and losses
Qualitative characteristics	Identifies two fundamental characteristics: relevance and faithful representation	Identifies four principal characteristics: understandability, relevance, reliability, and comparability Faithful representation is a component of reliability
Conservatism	Not recognized as a qualitative characteristic	Recognized as a qualitative characteristic

THE **NAVIGATOR**

Demonstration Problem

Several independent financial reporting situations follow:

1. Young Company recognized sales revenue for a customer order of merchandise inventory that had not yet been shipped.
2. In preparing its financial statements, Casco Company left out information about its depreciation policy.
3. Kenton Company amortized its patent over its legal life of 20 years instead of its estimated economic life of 5 years.
4. Taws Company, a private company reporting under ASPE, reported land that cost $50,000 at its fair value of $100,000.
5. Athwal Company used the cost model in its financial statements that were issued after the company had started liquidation procedures due to bankruptcy. The bankruptcy was not reported in the notes to the financial statements.
6. Yen Yeh Company capitalized the cost and recorded depreciation on its office wastepaper baskets.
7. Mayberry Company used a janitorial service in December to clean its offices. The company recorded the cost of the service when it paid the bill in the following February. Mayberry's year end is December 31.

Instructions

(a) For each of the above situations, indicate the concept (qualitative characteristic, assumption, constraint, recognition criteria, or measurement criteria) in the conceptual framework that has been violated. If there is more than one, list them.
(b) For each situation, provide a brief explanation of how the concept was violated.

ACTION PLAN

- Review the revenue recognition criteria for the sale of goods.
- Review the qualitative characteristics.
- Review the expense recognition criteria.
- Review the measurement criteria.
- Review the underlying assumption of going concern.

THE **NAVIGATOR**

Solution to Demonstration Problem

(a) Violation	(b) Explanation
1. Revenue recognition criteria	The risks and rewards of ownership have not been transferred to the customer as the goods have not been shipped. Revenue should be recognized when the customer has legal title of the goods.
2. Faithful representation: completeness and comparability	The company should fully disclose information that is relevant to the user. Users would require information on the depreciation policy to enhance comparability with other companies' financial statements. Understanding the depreciation policy may also help users make predictions about the company's future profitability.
3. Expense recognition: matching	The cost of the patent should be allocated to expense over the period for which the company will realize economic benefits.
4. Measurement criteria: cost	The company must use the cost model for financial reporting. The land should be reported at cost.
5. Going concern assumption	If the company is not a going concern, assets should be reported at net realizable value, not cost. There should be a note in the financial statements disclosing that the company is bankrupt.
6. Relevance: materiality	The carrying value of the wastepaper baskets is likely immaterial and therefore is not useful information to the user.
7. Expense recognition	The company has a liability at December 31 for services used during December.

▶ Summary of Study Objectives

1. **Explain the importance of having a conceptual framework of accounting, and list the key components.** The conceptual framework ensures that there is a consistent and coherent set of accounting standards. Key components of the conceptual framework are the: (1) objective of financial reporting; (2) underlying assumption; (3) cost constraint; (4) elements of financial statements; (5) qualitative characteristics of accounting information; and (6) recognition and measurement criteria.

2. **Identify and apply the objective of financial reporting, as well as the underlying assumption and cost constraint used by accountants.** The objective of financial reporting is to provide useful information for investors and creditors in making decisions in their capacity as capital providers. The underlying assumption is that, unless otherwise stated, the financial statements have been prepared using the going concern assumption. The cost constraint exists to ensure the value of the information provided is more than the cost of preparing it.

3. **Describe the fundamental and enhancing qualitative characteristics of financial reporting.** The fundamental qualitative characteristics are relevance and faithful representation. Accounting information has relevance if it makes a difference in a decision. Materiality is an important component of relevance. An item is material when it is likely to influence the decision of a reasonably careful investor or creditor. Information is faithfully represented when it shows the economic reality and is complete, neutral, and free from material error.

   The enhancing qualitative characteristics are comparability, verifiability, timeliness, and understandability. Comparability enables users to identify the similarities and differences between companies. The consistent use of accounting policies from year to year is part of the comparability characteristic. Information is verifiable if two knowledgeable and independent people would generally agree that it faithfully represents the economic reality. Timeliness means that accounting information is provided when it is still highly useful for decision-making. Understandability enables reasonably informed users to interpret and comprehend the meaning of the information provided in the financial statements.

4. ***Identify and apply the basic recognition and measurement concepts of accounting.*** The revenue recognition criteria require that revenue be recognized when assets have increased or liabilities have decreased as a result of a transaction with a customer. Expenses are recognized when there is a decrease in an asset or increase in a liability, excluding transactions with owners, which result in a decrease in owners' equity. Three measurements used in accounting are cost, fair value, and amortized cost. Incorrect application of the basic recognition and measurement concepts can lead to material misstatements in the financial statements. Incorrect application can be due to error or intentional misstatement.

THE NAVIGATOR

Flash cards

▶ Glossary

Accrual basis of accounting The method of accounting where revenues are recorded in the period when the transaction occurs and not when cash is received or paid. (p. 585)

Comparability An enhancing qualitative characteristic that accounting information has if it can be compared with the accounting information of other companies because the companies all use the same accounting principles. (p. 581)

Complete The characteristic of accounting information when it provides all information necessary to show the economic reality of the transactions. Completeness is part of the faithful representation fundamental qualitative characteristic of accounting information. (p. 581)

Conceptual framework of accounting A coherent system of interrelated elements that guides the development and application of accounting principles: it includes the objective of financial reporting, assumptions, cost constraint, elements of financial statements, qualitative characteristics of accounting information, and recognition and measurement criteria. (p. 576)

Consistency The use of the same accounting policies from year to year. Consistency is part of the comparability enhancing qualitative characteristic of accounting information. (p. 581)

Cost constraint The constraint that the costs of obtaining and providing information should not be more than the benefits that are gained. (p. 578)

Economic entity concept The concept that the accounting for an economic entity's activities be kept separate and distinct from the accounting for the activities of its owner and all other economic entities. (p. 578)

Elements of financial statements The basic categories in financial statements: assets, liabilities, equity, revenue, and expenses. (p. 579)

Expense recognition criteria The criteria that state that expenses should be recognized when there is a decrease in an asset or increase in a liability, excluding transactions with owners that result in a decrease in owners' equity. (p. 588)

Faithful representation A fundamental qualitative characteristic of accounting information that shows the economic reality of a transaction and not just its legal form. (p. 580)

Full disclosure The accounting concept that recognizes that financial statement information must be complete and requires the disclosure of circumstances and events that make a difference to financial statement users. (p. 583)

Going concern assumption The assumption that the company will continue operating for the foreseeable future; that is, long enough to meet its current objectives and carry out its current commitments. (p. 578)

Material error An error in the accounting information that could impact an investor's or creditor's decision. (p. 581)

Materiality An important component of relevance in which an item is considered material if it is likely to influence the decision of a reasonably careful investor or creditor. (p. 580)

Neutral The characteristic of accounting information when it is free from bias that is intended to attain a predetermined result or to encourage a particular behaviour. Neutrality is part of the faithful representation fundamental qualitative characteristic of accounting information. (p. 581)

Objective of financial reporting The goal of providing useful information for investors and creditors in making decisions in their capacity as capital providers. (p. 578)

Percentage-of-completion method A method of recognizing revenue on a long-term construction or service contract. When costs can be reliably estimated, a portion of the total revenue can be recognized in each period by applying a percentage of completion. This percentage can be determined by dividing the actual costs incurred by the estimated costs for the entire project. (p. 587)

Relevance A fundamental qualitative characteristic that accounting information has if it makes a difference in a decision. The information should have predictive and feedback value and be material. (p. 580)

Revenue recognition criteria The criteria that state that revenue should be recognized when there is an increase in assets or decrease in liabilities from profit-generating activities. (p. 586)

Timeliness An enhancing qualitative characteristic that accounting information has if it is provided when it is still highly useful to decision makers. (p. 582)

Understandability An enhancing qualitative characteristic of accounting information that enables reasonably informed users to interpret and comprehend the meaning of the information provided in the financial statements.

Understandability is greater when the information is classified, characterized, and presented clearly and concisely. (p. 582)

Verifiability An enhancing qualitative characteristic of accounting information that assures users that the information shows the economic reality of the transaction. (p. 582)

▶ Self-Study Questions
Answers are at the end of the chapter.

(SO 1) K 1. Which of the following is not a reason for having a conceptual framework for financial reporting?
(a) To provide specific rules for every situation in accounting
(b) To ensure that existing standards and practices are clear and consistent
(c) To provide guidance in responding to new issues and developing new standards
(d) To increase financial statement users' understanding of and confidence in the financial statements

(SO 1) K 2. Which of the following is not one of the components of the conceptual framework?
(a) Cost constraint
(b) Specific recommendations for financial statement presentation
(c) Qualitative characteristics
(d) Recognition and measurement concepts

(SO 2) K 3. Which of the following is not information that is required to meet the objective of financial reporting?
(a) Information about the economic resources and claims on the economic resources
(b) Information about the company management's personal economic resources
(c) Information about the changes in economic resources and in claims on the economic resources
(d) Information about the economic performance of the reporting entity

(SO 2) C 4. What is the assumption that financial statements are prepared under that recognizes that the business will continue to operate in the foreseeable future long enough to meet its objectives and carry out its commitments?
(a) Accrual basis of accounting
(b) Economic entity
(c) Going concern
(d) Fair value

(SO 3) K 5. Under IFRS, these qualitative characteristics should be applied in which order?
(a) Relevance, faithful representation, and understandability
(b) Relevance, understandability, and faithful representation
(c) Faithful representation, relevance, and understandability

(d) Understandability, relevance, and faithful representation

(SO 3) K 6. Accounting information faithfully represents an economic event when it is reported
(a) on a timely basis.
(b) on a comparable basis to other companies with the same economic events.
(c) on a consistent basis from year to year.
(d) in a way that portrays the economic reality and not just the legal form of the event.

(SO 3) C 7. An item is considered material when:
(a) it is more than $500.
(b) it affects profits.
(c) not reporting it would influence or change a decision.
(d) it occurs infrequently.

(SO 4) K 8. Which of the following is not a condition that must be met for revenue recognition on the sale of goods?
(a) The seller does not have control over the goods or continuing managerial involvement.
(b) The amount of the revenue can be reliably measured.
(c) Cash is collected.
(d) The seller has transferred to the buyer the significant risks and rewards of ownership.

(SO 4) C 9. Which of the following is not an appropriate time to recognize an expense?
(a) When cash is paid for the purchase of computer equipment
(b) When an expenditure is made that does not qualify for the recognition of an asset
(c) When the cost of computer equipment is allocated over its useful life
(d) When a previously recorded asset no longer has any future benefit

(SO 4) K 10. Which of the following statements about the cost basis of accounting is false?
(a) Cost is relevant for reporting certain assets in the balance sheet because the assets are intended for use in the business and are not going to be sold.
(b) Cost is relevant for reporting all assets on the balance sheet because it is measurable.
(c) Cost is measurable and verifiable.
(d) Cost is not relevant if the business is being liquidated.

THE NAVIGATOR

Questions

(SO 1) C 1. (a) Describe the conceptual framework of accounting and explain how it helps financial reporting. (b) Is the conceptual framework applicable to companies reporting under IFRS, under ASPE, or both?

(SO 2) K 2. (a) What is the main objective of financial reporting? (b) Although there are many users of financial statements, why does the objective identify the specific users?

(SO 2) C 3. (a) Explain the going concern assumption. (b) How does the going concern assumption support the use of the cost basis of accounting and the classification of assets and liabilities as current and non-current?

(SO 2) C 4. Describe the cost constraint on financial reporting.

(SO 2) C 5. Isabelle believes that the same GAAP should be used by every company, whether large or small and whether public or private. Do you agree? Explain.

(SO 3) K 6. Identify and explain the two fundamental qualitative characteristics of accounting information.

(SO 3) C 7. (a) Explain the concept of materiality. (b) How is materiality related to the qualitative characteristic of relevance?

(SO 3) K 8. Identify and explain the four enhancing qualitative characteristics of accounting information.

(SO 3) K 9. The qualitative characteristics should be applied in a certain order. Identify the order and explain why it matters.

(SO 3) C 10. Identify the differences between the qualitative characteristics identified in the conceptual framework for IFRS and the conceptual framework for ASPE.

(SO 2,3) C 11. Explain how the cost constraint relates to the quality of completeness.

(SO 3) C 12. The controller of Mustafa Corporation rounded all dollar figures in the company's financial statements to the nearest thousand dollars. "It's not important for our users to know how many pennies we spend," she said. Do you believe rounded financial figures can provide useful information for decision-making? Explain why or why not.

(SO 4) C 13. Why is revenue recognition a difficult concept to apply in practice?

(SO 4) K 14. Describe the general criteria for revenue recognition.

(SO 4) K 15. What are the five conditions that must be met for revenue to be recognized from the sale of goods?

(SO 4) A 16. A customer of JRT Company ordered merchandise inventory on December 15, 2013. The order was packed on December 31 and shipped on January 2, 2014. JRT's year end is December 31. Erin, the accountant, recorded the sales revenue in the December 31, 2013, income statement. She said, "We might as well recognize the revenue at December 31, we know the order was shipped. What difference do a couple of days make?" Do you agree? Explain.

(SO 4) A 17. On March 24, 2014, Greenthumb Landscaping Services received $10,000 for five months of landscaping service to be provided May through September 2014. Greenthumb's year end is April 30. (a) How should the $10,000 received be reported in the April 30, 2014, financial statements? Explain. (b) Assuming Greenthumb prepares monthly financial statements, how should the $10,000 be accounted for from May through September? Explain.

(SO 4) K 18. (a) How is revenue recognized in long-term service and construction contracts? (b) Describe the three steps in the percentage-of-completion method.

(SO 4) K 19. Explain how revenue should be recognized if a sales transaction includes both the sale of goods and a service component.

(SO 4) AP 20. A company has a return policy that allows customers to return goods within 30 days of purchase and receive a full refund. Should the company recognize revenue when the goods are sold or when the 30-day return period expires? Explain.

(SO 4) K 21. Describe when expenses should be recognized.

(SO 3, 4) C 22. Explain how the qualitative characteristics of relevance and faithful representation relate to the cost and fair value measurement bases of accounting.

(SO 4) K 23. Identify two situations that might lead management to overstate profits. Identify two ways the profit could be overstated by applying the recognition criteria incorrectly.

Brief Exercises

BE11–1 Indicate which of the following statements are true or false. (Write "T" or "F" beside each item.)

(a) _____ The conceptual framework includes recommendations on how to analyze financial statements.
(b) _____ The conceptual framework identifies the objective of financial reporting.
(c) _____ The conceptual framework is a temporary framework that provides guidance for accountants until standard setters can develop specific rules for every situation.
(d) _____ The conceptual framework defines assets, liabilities, owner's equity, revenue, and expenses.
(e) _____ The conceptual framework provides specific rules for financial statement presentation.

Identify items included in the conceptual framework.
(SO 1) K

(f) _____ The conceptual framework identifies qualitative characteristics of useful information.

(g) _____ The conceptual framework provides guidance for responding to new issues and developing new standards.

Identify violations of the going concern assumption. (SO 2) C

BE11–2   For each of the following situations, indicate if the going concern assumption has been violated. (Write "Yes" or "No" beside each item.)

(a) _____ A company that is going to continue to operate in the foreseeable future reports all of its assets on the balance sheet at the amount expected to be collected if the assets were sold.

(b) _____ A company that is being liquidated reports current assets, non-current assets, current liabilities, and non-current liabilities on its balance sheet.

(c) _____ A company that is going to operate in the foreseeable future reports its merchandise inventory at cost when the net realizable value is higher than cost.

Identify elements of financial statements. (SO 2) K

BE11–3   Here are the basic elements of financial statements that we learned about in earlier chapters:

1. Assets   4. Revenues
2. Liabilities   5. Expenses
3. Owner's equity

Each statement that follows is an important aspect of an element's definition. Match the elements with the definitions. *Note*: More than one number can be placed in a blank. Each number may be used more than once or not at all.

(a) _____ Increases in assets or decreases in liabilities resulting from the main profit-generating activities of the organization

(b) _____ Existing debts and obligations from past transactions

(c) _____ Resources owned by a business

(d) _____ Goods or services used in the process of earning revenue

(e) _____ A residual claim on total assets after deducting liabilities

(f) _____ The capacity to provide future benefits to the organization

Identify correct application of the cost constraint. (SO 2) AP

BE11–4   For each of the following situations, indicate if it is an example of applying the cost constraint correctly. (Write "Yes" or "No" beside each item.)

(a) _____ The company corrects its financial statements and reissues its annual report after discovering some minor errors in the financial statements.

(b) _____ Inventory is reported at cost when the fair value is higher.

(c) _____ The company expenses small inexpensive office equipment such as pencil sharpeners because of the high cost of tracking the equipment and recording depreciation on it.

Identify qualitative characteristics. (SO 3) K

BE11–5   The following selected items relate to the qualitative characteristics of useful information:

1. Comparability   7. Predictive value
2. Materiality   8. Consistency
3. Neutral   9. Understandability
4. Timeliness   10. Verifiability
5. Faithful representation   11. Complete
6. Feedback value

Match these qualitative characteristics to the following statements, using numbers 1 to 11.

(a) _____ Accounting information must be available to decision makers before the information loses its ability to influence their decisions.

(b) _____ Accounting information provides a basis to evaluate decisions made in the past.

(c) _____ Accounting information cannot be selected, prepared, or presented to favour one set of interested users over another.

(d) _____ Accounting information reports the economic substance of a transaction, not its legal form.

(e) _____ Accounting information helps reduce uncertainty about the future.

(f) _____ Accounting information must be provided in such a way that knowledgeable and independent people agree that it faithfully represents the economic reality of the transaction or event.

(g) _____ Accounting information about one company can be evaluated in relation to accounting information from another company.

(h) _____ Accounting information is provided in such a way that enables reasonably informed users to interpret and comprehend the meaning of the information provided in the financial statements.

(i) _____ Accounting information in a company is prepared using the same principles and methods year after year.

(j) _____ Accounting information that is insignificant and not likely to influence a decision does not need to be disclosed.

(k) _____ Accounting information includes all information necessary to show the economic reality of the transaction.

BE11–6 Here are some of the accounting concepts relating to the conceptual framework discussed in this chapter:

1. Going concern assumption
2. Economic entity concept
3. Full disclosure
4. Cost
5. Cost constraint
6. Materiality

Identify concepts in the conceptual framework. (SO 2, 3) C

Identify by number the accounting assumption, qualitative characteristic, concept, or constraint that describes each situation below. Do not use a number more than once.

(a) _____ is why land is not reported at its liquidation value. (Do not use item 4, cost.)
(b) _____ indicates that personal and business record-keeping should be kept separate.
(c) _____ ensures that all relevant financial information is reported.
(d) _____ requires that GAAP be followed for all significant items.
(e) _____ indicates the value at which an asset is recorded when acquired.

BE11–7 A list of accounting concepts follows:

1. Revenue recognition
2. Matching
3. Full disclosure
4. Cost
5. Expense recognition
6. Fair value

Identify concepts in the conceptual framework. (SO 2, 3, 4) C

Match these concepts to the following statements, using numbers 1 to 6.

(a) _____ The Hirjikaka Company reports information about pending lawsuits in the notes to its financial statements.
(b) _____ The Sudin Company reduces prepaid insurance to reflect the insurance that has expired.
(c) _____ The Joss Company recognizes revenue at the point of sale, not when the cash is collected.
(d) _____ The Rich Bank reports its short-term investments that are held for resale at market.
(e) _____ The Hilal Company reports its land at the price it paid for it, not at what it is now worth.
(f) _____ The law firm Thériault, Lévesque, and Picard records an accrual for legal services provided but not yet billed
(g) _____ The Nickel Company depreciates its mining equipment using the units-of-production method.

BE11–8 Howie, Price, and Liu operate an accounting firm. In March, their staff worked a total of 1,000 hours at an average billing rate of $250 per hour. They sent bills to clients in the month of March that totalled $150,000. They expect to bill the balance of their time in April. The firm's salary costs total $75,000 each month. How much revenue should the firm recognize in the month of March? How much salaries expense?

Determine revenue and expense to be recognized. (SO 4) AP

BE11–9 Mullen Manufacturing Ltd. sold $450,000 of merchandise on credit to customers in the month of September. All of the merchandise was sold FOB shipping point. At September 30, $45,000 of the merchandise was in transit. During September, the company collected $250,000 cash from its customers. The company estimates that about 2% of the sales will be returned by customers and that $4,500 of accounts receivable will not be collected. Mullen's allowance for doubtful accounts had a zero balance on September 1. How much revenue should the company recognize for the month of September? Describe how the uncollectible sales and returns by the customers should be accounted for.

Determine revenue to be recognized. (SO 4) AP

BE11–10 Abbotsford Ltd., a sports equipment wholesaler, sold $350,000 of merchandise to customers during November. The cost of the merchandise shipped was $200,000. All of the merchandise was shipped FOB destination. At November 30, $40,000 of the merchandise was in transit. The cost of the merchandise in transit was $23,000. During November, Abbotsford purchased $90,000 of merchandise inventory and made cash payments for merchandise inventory of $100,000. How much revenue should the company recognize for the month of November? What is the gross profit recognized in November?

Determine revenue and expenses to be recognized. (SO 4) AP

BE11–11 During December, Willow Appliance Company had sales of $425,000. Included in the sales was $25,000 for extended warranties purchased by customers. No warranty service was provided in December on the appliances sold during December. How much revenue should the company recognize for the month of December? Explain.

Determine revenue to be recognized. (SO 4) AP

BE11–12 Flin Flon Construction Company is under contract to build a commercial building at a price of $4.2 million. Construction begins in January 2013 and finishes in December 2015. Total estimated construction costs are $2.8 million. Actual construction costs incurred in each year are as follows: in 2013, $840,000; in 2014, $1,120,000; and in 2015, $840,000. Calculate the revenue and gross profit to be recognized in each year using the percentage-of-completion method.

Calculate revenue and gross profit—percentage-of-completion method. (SO 4) AP

BE11–13 Courtney Company reported total operating expenses of $55,000 on its adjusted trial balances for the year ended November 30, 2013. After the preliminary statements were prepared, the accountant became aware of the following situations:

Calculate expense. (SO 4) AP

1. The physical inventory count revealed that inventory costing $4,000 was damaged and needed to be scrapped.
2. Sales staff were owed $2,500 of sales commissions relating to November sales. The sales commissions were paid in December.

Calculate the total operating expenses that should be reported in the November 30, 2013, income statement.

Identify recognition and measurement violations. (SO 4) AP

BE11–14 The accountant for Ellery Co., a private company reporting under ASPE, recorded the following journal entries:

1. Land with a cost of $75,000 is reported at its fair value. The following entry was made:

Land	10,000	
Gain on Fair Value Adjustment of Land		10,000

2. Tickets for a musical production were sold in January and the production runs during March. The following entry was recorded in January.

Cash	5,000	
Admission Revenue		5,000

For each journal entry, indicate which recognition or measurement criterion has been violated. Explain.

▶ Exercises

Apply the objective of financial reporting, economic entity concept, and going concern assumption. (SO 2) AP

E11–1 The Skate Stop is owned by Marc Bélanger. It sells in-line skates and accessories. It shares rented space with another company, Ride Snowboards. Ride Snowboards is owned by Marc's wife, Dominique Maltais, who was an Olympic bronze medallist in snowboarding. Ride Snowboards sells snowboards and related accessories. The market for in-line skates is growing and Marc wants to expand the amount of inventory The Skate Stop carries. He has asked his bank for a loan to finance the inventory. The bank manager has requested financial statements that are prepared using GAAP.

Instructions

(a) Explain how financial statements will help the bank manager decide whether to loan Marc money for inventory.

(b) Why does the bank manager want the statements to be prepared using GAAP?

(c) Should Marc include Ride Snowboards' financial information in The Skate Stop's financial statements? Explain.

(d) Should Marc report all of the store's assets at cost or what they could be sold for? Explain.

Discuss financial reporting objective and cost constraint. (SO 2) C

E11–2 Susan began an office cleaning business by investing $5,000 cash and cleaning equipment. Her friend, Aristotelis, recommends that she prepare monthly financial statements.

Instructions

(a) Explain why Aristotelis recommends that she prepare monthly financial statements.

(b) Susan knows that, as a private company, she can choose to follow either ASPE or IFRS. Which one should she choose? Explain.

Identify qualitative characteristics. (SO 3) C

E11–3 Presented below are selected qualitative characteristics of accounting information.

1. Relevance	5. Faithful representation
2. Neutrality	6. Comparability
3. Verifiability	7. Understandability
4. Timeliness	

Instructions

For each of the following situations, indicate which qualitative characteristic was violated.

(a) _____ Allen Ltd. reported its merchandise inventory at a net realizable value of $25,000. The company's auditors disagree with this value and estimated the net realizable value to be $20,000.

(b) _____ Owens Corporation does not issue its annual financial statements for the year ended December 31, 2013, until December 2014.

(c) _____ Silver Mining Ltd. is the only company in the mining industry that uses the straight-line method to depreciate its mining equipment.

(d) _____ Chapman Ltd. switches inventory cost formulas from average to FIFO and back to average in a three-year period.

(e) _____ Enco Ltd. intentionally recorded revenue in 2013 for sales made in 2014 to ensure that management would receive their bonuses, which were based on profits.

(f) _____ World Talk Corporation used terminology in its financial statements and notes to the financial statements that is not commonly used in financial reporting and did not provide explanations of the terminology.

(g) _____ Precise Ltd., a multinational drilling company, reported separately its paper, paper clips, and pens in the balance sheet rather than reporting a single line item for office supplies. Total office supplies were $5,000.

(h) _____ Community Health Foods Ltd. signed a legal agreement to finance the purchase of equipment. The agreement required annual payments of $15,000 for five years. The agreement referred to the payments as rental payments. The company records rent expense when the annual payments are made.

E11–4 Here are some concepts related to the conceptual framework discussed in this chapter:

Identify concepts related to the conceptual framework. (SO 2, 3) C

1. Going concern assumption
2. Economic entity concept
3. Completeness
4. Cost
5. Cost constraint
6. Materiality

Instructions

Identify by number the concept that describes each situation below. Do not use a number more than once.

(a) _____ Barb Denton runs her accounting practice out of her home. She separates her business records from her household accounts.
(b) _____ The cost to provide financial information should not be more than the benefits.
(c) _____ Significant accounting policies are reported in the notes to the financial statements.
(d) _____ Assets are not stated at their liquidation value. (*Note:* Do not use number 4 Cost)
(e) _____ Dollar amounts on financial statements are often rounded to the nearest thousand.
(f) _____ Land is recorded at its cost of $100,000 rather than at its market value of $150,000.

E11–5 Several reporting situations follow:

Identify violations of the concepts in the conceptual framework. (SO 2, 3, 4) AP

1. Tercek Company recognizes revenue during the production cycle. The price of the product and how many items will be sold are not certain.
2. In preparing its financial statements, Seco Company left out information about its cost flow assumption for inventories.
3. Martinez Company amortizes patents over their legal life of 20 years instead of their economic life, which is usually about five years.
4. Ravine Hospital Supply Corporation reports only current assets and current liabilities on its balance sheet. Long-term assets and liabilities are reported as current. The company is unlikely to be liquidated.
5. Barton Company reports inventory on its balance sheet at its current market value of $100,000. The inventory has an original cost of $110,000.
6. Bonilla Company is in its third year of operations and has not yet issued financial statements.
7. Watts Company has inventory on hand that cost $400,000. Watts reports inventory on its balance sheet at its current market value of $425,000.
8. Steph Wolfson, president of the Download Music Company, bought a computer for her personal use. She paid for the computer with company funds and debited the computer account.
9. Sagoo Company decided not to implement a perpetual inventory system that would save $40,000 annually because the cost of the system was $100,000 and it was estimated to have a 10-year life.

Instructions

For each of the above, list what concept in the conceptual framework has been violated, if any.

E11–6 Business transactions for Ellis Company and East Air follow:

Identify violation of conceptual framework and correct entries. (SO 2, 4) AN

1. Merchandise inventory worth $50,000 is acquired at a cost of $42,000 from a company going out of business. The following entry is made:

Merchandise Inventory	50,000	
Cash		42,000
Cost of Goods Sold		8,000

2. The president of Ellis Company, Evan Ellis, purchases a computer for personal use and charges it to his expense account. The following entry is made:

Office Expense	13,000	
Cash		13,000

3. An asset was for recorded for the cost of advertising that appeared on television the previous month. The following entry is made:

Prepaid Advertising	5,000	
Cash		5,000

4. Merchandise inventory with a cost of $280,000 is reported at its fair value of $255,000. The following entry is made:

Cost of Goods Sold	25,000	
Merchandise Inventory		25,000

5. A coffee machine costing $50 is being depreciated over five years. The following adjusting entry is made:

Depreciation Expense	10	
Accumulated Depreciation—Equipment		10

6. East Air sells an airline ticket for $650 in February for a trip scheduled in April. The following entry is made:

Cash	650	
Service Revenue		650

Instructions

In each of the situations above, identify the concept that has been violated, if any. If a journal entry is incorrect, give the correct entry.

Identify point of revenue recognition. (SO 4) C

E11–7 The following situations require professional judgement to determine when to recognize revenue from the transactions:

1. Flamingo Airlines sells you a non-refundable airline ticket in September for your flight home at Christmas.
2. Cygman Furniture sells you a home theatre on a no money down, no interest, and no payments for one year promotional deal.
3. The Blue Hawks sell season tickets to their games on-line. Fans can purchase the tickets at any time, although the season doesn't officially begin until April. It runs from April through October.
4. Babineau Company sells merchandise with terms of 2/10, n/30, FOB destination.
5. In September, Confederation College collects tuition revenue for the term from students. The term runs from September through December.
6. The College Bookstore has the following return policy for textbook sales: "Textbooks (new and used) may be returned for seven calendar days from the start of classes. After that time, textbooks (new and used) may be returned within 48 hours of purchase."
7. Computer Company sells computer software. Included in the price of the software is a three-year service contract to update the customer's software.

Instructions

Identify when revenue should be recognized in each of the above situations.

Determine amount of revenue to be recognized. (SO 4) C

E11–8 Over the winter months, the Lush Lawns Co. pre-sells fertilizing and weed control lawn services to be performed from May through September, inclusive. If payment is made in full by April 1, a 5% discount is allowed. In March, 350 customers took advantage of the discount and purchased the summer lawn service package for $760 each. In June, 300 customers purchased the package for $800, and in July, 100 purchased it for the same price. For customers who pay after May 1, service starts in the month the customer makes the payment.

Instructions

How much revenue should be recognized by the Lush Lawns Co. in each of the months of March, April, May, June, July, August, and September? Explain.

Determine amount of revenue to be recognized. (SO 4) AP

E11–9 Consider the following transactions of the Mitrovica Company, a diversified manufacturing and construction company, for the year ended December 31, 2014:

1. Leased office space to a tenant for a one-year period beginning October 1. Four months of rent at $2,000 per month was received in advance.
2. Received a sales order for merchandise that cost $9,000. It was sold for $16,000 on December 28 to Warfield Company. The goods were shipped FOB shipping point on December 31. Warfield received them on January 3, 2015.
3. Signed a long-term contract to construct a building at a total price of $2 million. The total estimated cost of construction is $1.4 million. During 2014, the company incurred $300,000 of costs and collected $175,000 in cash.
4. Mitrovica introduced a new product into the market. The company shipped new product costing $25,000 to its customers' retail outlets. The customers were billed $50,000 for the product. To promote the product, Mitrovica does not require payment until June 2015 and if Mitrovica's customers do not sell all of the product by June 2015, they can return the unsold product to Mitrovica. The product is new and Mitrovica is uncertain if it will sell.
5. Issued a $5,000, six-month, 4% note receivable on September 1, with interest payable at maturity.
6. Received a sales order from a new customer for $20,000 of merchandise that cost $10,000. The customer was required to prepay the invoice. On December 29, 2014, a cheque for $20,000 was received from the customer. The merchandise was shipped on January 4, 2015.

Instructions

For each item above, indicate the amount of revenue Mitrovica should recognize in 2014. Explain.

Calculate revenue and gross profit—percentage-of-completion method. (SO 4) AP

E11–10 Shen Construction Company had a long-term construction project that lasted three years. The project had a contract price of $150 million, with total estimated costs of $100 million. Shen used the percentage-of-completion method. At the end of construction, the following actual costs had been incurred:

	2012	2013	2014
Actual cost	$25 million	$55 million	$20 million

Instructions

Calculate the revenue and gross profit that were recognized for each year of the construction contract.

E11–11 Consider the following events for Byer's Innovations Co. that occurred during 2014.

Determine amount of expenses to be recognized. (SO 4) AP

1. Leased factory space from Whole Properties Company for a one-year period starting November 1, 2014. Six months of rent at $3,000 per month was paid in advance.
2. Incurred $35,000 of research costs for new products. No new products were developed but management believes the research will lead to new products.
3. Used power and water during December for manufacturing. Byer's Innovations Co. will receive the bill in January 2015 and pay it in February 2015. Power and water costs totalling $55,000 have been recorded for the period January 1 to November 30, 2014.
4. New packaging equipment costing $48,000 was installed during November 2014. The equipment was tested in December and will be used for packaging starting in January 2015. The equipment has an estimated useful life of four years and an estimated residual value of $4,000. The company uses straight-line depreciation.

Instructions

For each event, indicate the amount of expense that should be recognized in the 2014 income statement. (*Hint*: Use professional judgement to estimate expense where appropriate.)

Problems: Set A

P11–1A An excerpt from the financial statements of **Reitmans (Canada) Limited** appears in the table below. Note 18, Commitments in the financial statements provides the following information on the future cash payments under lease agreements: "As at January 28, 2012, financial commitments for minimum lease payments under operating leases for retail stores, offices, automobiles and equipment, as well as amounts pertaining to agreements to purchase goods or services that are enforceable and legally binding on the Company, exclusive of additional amounts based on sales, taxes and other costs are payable as follows:"

Comment on the objective of financial reporting and qualitative characteristics. (SO 2, 3) C

	Store and Office Operating Leases	Purchase Obligations	Other Operating Leases	Total
Within 1 year	$ 99,202	$102,637	$ 4,498	$206,337
Within 2 years	88,467	326	3,723	92,516
Within 3 years	77,563	117	2,672	80,352
Within 4 years	66,012	—	2,477	68,489
Within 5 years	49,802	—	8	49,810
Subsequent years	89,873	—	—	89,873
Total	$470,919	$103,080	$13,378	$587,377

Instructions

Explain why Reitmans is required to disclose the future cash payments under its commitments. Support your answer with reference to the objective of financial reporting and the qualitative characteristics.

TAKING IT FURTHER Refer to the Notes to Financial Statements for Reitmans (Canada) Limited in Appendix A and provide another example for which the company discloses required future cash payments.

P11–2A During the 2008 and 2009 global economic crisis, several large corporations in both Canada and the United States could not meet their financial commitments and filed for bankruptcy protection. Bankruptcy protection gives companies time to reorganize their operations and financial commitments and to develop a comprehensive restructuring plan, which will allow them to continue to operate. While bankruptcy protection is in place, creditors are prevented from taking any action against the company.

Assumptions and concepts—going concern, full disclosure. (SO 2, 3) AP

Instructions

(a) What is the potential effect on a company's financial statements if the company files for bankruptcy?
(b) Should companies under bankruptcy protection prepare their statements under the going concern assumption? Explain.

TAKING IT FURTHER Describe the dilemma that a company's management faces in disclosing that a company may not be able to continue as a going concern.

Comment on objective of financial reporting, qualitative characteristics, and constraints. (SO 1, 3, 4) C

P11–3A Calgary-based **Humpty's Restaurants International Inc.** announced on October 1, 2009, that on September 30, 2009, it had successfully finalized its previously announced plan to privatize the company. Up until this date, Humpty's was a public company and would have been required to adopt IFRS in 2011 if it had stayed public. When Humpty's announced its plan to go private, it stated that the company had not relied on issuing new shares for financing for many years.

Instructions

Explain why Humpty's owners might have decided to make it a private company before it was required to adopt IFRS. Support your answer with reference to the objective of financial reporting, qualitative characteristics, and the accounting constraints.

TAKING IT FURTHER A Canadian private company may choose to prepare its financial statements using IFRS or ASPE. In what circumstances might a Canadian private company choose to report under IFRS rather than ASPE?

Identify concept or assumption violated and prepare entries. (SO 2, 3, 4) AN

P11–4A Czyz and Ng are accountants at Kwick Kopy Printers. Kwick Kopy has not adopted the revaluation model for accounting for its property, plant, and equipment. The accountants are having disagreements over the following transactions during the fiscal year ended December 31, 2014:

1. Kwick Kopy bought equipment on January 1, 2014, for $80,000, including installation costs. The equipment has a useful life of five years. Kwick Kopy depreciates equipment using the double diminishing-balance method. "Since the equipment as installed in our system cannot be removed without considerable damage, it will have no resale value. It should not be depreciated but, instead, expensed immediately," Czyz argues.

2. Depreciation for the year was $43,000. Since the company's profit is expected to be low this year, Czyz suggests deferring depreciation to a year when there is higher profits.

3. Kwick Kopy purchased equipment at a fire sale for $36,000. The equipment would normally have cost $50,000. Czyz believes that the following entry should be made:

Equipment	50,000	
Cash		36,000
Gain on Fair Value Adjustment of Equipment		14,000

4. Czyz says that Kwick Kopy should carry its furnishings on the balance sheet at their liquidation value, which is $30,000 less than cost.

5. Kwick Kopy rented office space for one year, effective September 1, 2014. Six months of rent at $3,000 per month was paid in advance. Czyz believes that the following entry should be made on September 1:

Rent Expense	18,000	
Cash		18,000

6. Land that cost $41,000 was appraised at $60,000. Czyz suggests the following journal entry:

Land	19,000	
Gain on Fair Value Adjustment of Land		19,000

7. On December 15, Kwick Kopy signed a contract with a customer to provide copying services for a six-month period at a rate of $1,500 per month starting January 1, 2015. The customer will pay on a monthly basis. Czyz argues that the contract should be recorded in December because the customer has always paid its bills on time in the past. The customer is legally obligated to pay the monthly amount because a contract has been signed. Czyz believes the following entry should be recorded:

Accounts Receivable	9,000	
Service Revenue		9,000

Ng disagrees with Czyz in each of the situations.

Instructions

(a) For each transaction, indicate why Ng disagrees. Support your answer with reference to the conceptual framework definition of elements, qualitative characteristics, assumption, constraint, recognition, and measurement criteria.

(b) Prepare the correct journal entry to record each transaction.

TAKING IT FURTHER Discuss the circumstances in which it is appropriate to record property, plant, and equipment at its liquidation value.

P11–5A Business transactions for Durkovitch Company from the current year follow. The company has not adopted the revaluation model of accounting for its property, plant, and equipment. The company's year end is December 31.

Identify assumption or concepts and correct entries. (SO 2, 4) AN

1. On December 20, an order for $90,000 was received from a customer for products on hand. The customer paid a $10,000 deposit when the order was placed. The order is to be shipped on January 9. The following entry was made on December 20:

Cash	10,000	
Accounts Receivable	80,000	
Sales		90,000

2. Merchandise with a selling price of $78,000 was sold and the customers paid an additional $5,000 for extended warranties. The company did not provide any warranty service on this merchandise. The following entry was made:

Cash	83,000	
Sales		83,000

3. The current year had been a very successful one for the company and the company was going to report record high profits. The company recorded $60,000 in additional depreciation expense so that in future years when profits are lower, it can record less depreciation expense. The following entry was made:

Depreciation Expense	60,000	
Accumulated Depreciation		60,000

4. On December 31, merchandise purchased for resale was received. The following entry was made:

Cost of Goods Sold	78,000	
Accounts Payable		78,000

5. Land was purchased on April 30 for $230,000. The company plans to build a warehouse on the land. On December 31, the land would have cost $200,000. The following entry was made:

Loss on Fair Value Adjustment of Land	30,000	
Land		30,000

Instructions

(a) In each of the situations above, identify the assumption or concept that has been violated, if any.
(b) Prepare the journal entry to correct each incorrect transaction identified in (a), if necessary.

TAKING IT FURTHER   Would your answer for item 5. have been different if the Durkovitch Company was a real estate company and the land had been purchased for resale? Explain.

P11–6A   Santa's Christmas Tree Farm, a private company reporting under ASPE, grows pine, fir, and spruce trees. The company cuts and sells the trees for cash during the Christmas season. Most of the trees are exported to the United States. The remaining trees are sold to local tree lot operators.

Identify point of revenue recognition. (SO 4) C

It normally takes about 12 years for a tree to grow to a good size. The average selling price for a mature tree is $48. The owner of Santa's Christmas Tree Farm believes that the company should recognize revenue at the rate of $4 a year ($48 ÷ 12 years) for each tree that it cuts. The biggest cost of this business is the cost of fertilizing, pruning, and maintaining the trees over the 12-year period. These costs average $40 a tree and the owner believes they should also be spread over the 12-year period.

Instructions

Do you agree with the proposed revenue recognition policy for Santa's Christmas Tree Farm? Explain why or why not. Use the revenue recognition criteria to explain your argument for when the revenue should be recognized for this tree-farming business.

TAKING IT FURTHER   Explain how the costs of fertilizing, pruning, and maintaining the trees should be recorded.

P11–7A   Mustang Company reported $1,200,000 net sales and $635,000 cost of goods sold for the 11 months ended November 30, 2014. Mustang offers a full refund for any merchandise returned within 30 days of sale. Additional information for the month of December is as follows:

Calculate revenue, cost of goods sold, and gross profit. (SO 4) AP

1. Refunds paid to customers totalled $20,000. All merchandise was returned to inventory. The cost of the merchandise returned was $10,600.

2. Sales to customers were $125,000 and the cost of the merchandise sold was $66,250.

3. Included in the $125,000 of sales was $12,000 for merchandise shipped FOB destination on December 31, 2014. The customers received the goods on January 5, 2015. The cost of the merchandise shipped on December 31, 2014, was $6,300.

4. The company estimates that during January 2015, it will refund customers $11,000 and that the estimated cost of the inventory returned will be $5,800. These estimated returns relate to the December sales. Normally, returned merchandise is returned to inventory.

5. Mustang's year end is December 31 and the company prepares adjusting journal entries annually.

Instructions

Calculate the net sales, cost of goods sold, and gross profit that Mustang will report in its income statement for the year ended December 31, 2014.

TAKING IT FURTHER   How would your response change if the merchandise returned in December and anticipated to be returned in January is not returned to inventory for resale? Explain.

Revenue recognition
criteria—sale of goods.
(SO 4) AP

P11–8A   Dave's Deep Discount Furniture Store opened for business on October 1, 2012. To promote the store and develop a loyal customer base, customers could buy furniture with no money down and no payments for 12 months. Customers wishing to take advantage of the special promotion were required to pass a thorough credit check. Of the customers from October 1 to December 31, 2012, most of the customers took advantage of the special promotion; the other customers paid for the furniture in full when it was delivered. Total sales from October 1 to December 31, 2012, were $325,000, of which $250,000 was for customers who chose to delay payment for 12 months. Of the remaining $75,000 of sales, $60,000 worth had been delivered to the customers by December 31, 2012, and the remaining $15,000 would be delivered in January 2013. The accountant for the store made the following entry to record the sales.

Accounts Receivable	15,000	
Cash	60,000	
Sales		75,000

Dave, the owner, disagreed with the accountant and argued that sales revenue of $325,000 should be recorded in 2012.

Instructions

(a) Identify the revenue recognition criteria that must be met before revenue is recorded for the sale of goods.

(b) Identify the critical factors relating to the Dave's Deep Discount Furniture Store's sales transactions that should be considered in determining how much revenue should be recognized.

(c) Indicate the amount of revenue that should be recognized for the period October 1 to December 31, 2012.

TAKING IT FURTHER   Would your response to (c) be different if the customers were not required to pass a thorough credit check? Explain why or why not.

Calculate revenue, expense,
and gross profit for
percentage-of-completion
method. (SO 4) AP

P11–9A   Cosky Construction Company is involved in a long-term construction contract to build an office building. The estimated cost is $60 million and the contract price is $90 million. Additional information follows:

Year	Cash Collections	Actual Costs Incurred
2012	$18,000,000	$12,000,000
2013	30,000,000	20,000,000
2014	15,000,000	10,000,000
2015	27,000,000	18,000,000
	$90,000,000	$60,000,000

The project is completed in 2015 as scheduled and all cash collections related to the contract have been received.

Instructions

Prepare a schedule to determine the revenue, expense, and gross profit for each year of the contract using the percentage-of-completion method. Round calculations to two decimal places.

TAKING IT FURTHER   Assume instead that by the end of 2012, Cosky Construction had problems with the office building as it discovered that the foundation was leaking and it was not able to reliably estimate the costs to fix the foundation and complete the building. Would it still be appropriate to use the percentage-of-completion method? Explain.

P11–10A   Kamloops Company is a grocery wholesaler and is planning to expand its operations. The company has asked the bank for a loan to finance the expansion. Alphonzo, the company's manager, has prepared the preliminary financial statements. The preliminary financial statements for the year ended December 31, 2014, reported the following:

Objective of financial reporting, identifying elements, and revenue and expense recognition.
(SO 2, 4) AP

Current assets	$120,000
Current liabilities	80,000
Net sales	560,000
Cost of goods sold	252,000
Total operating expenses	106,000

The bank has requested that Kamloops have an independent professional accountant review the statements. You have been asked to review the statements and during your review you have discovered the following:

1. Kamloops's inventory supplier shipped $15,000 of inventory to Kamloops on December 31, 2014, FOB shipping point. Alphonzo indicated that he did not record the inventory for the year ended December 31, 2014, because it was not received until January 2, 2015.

2. Included in net sales and accounts receivable was $8,400 for merchandise ordered by a customer that was packed and in the warehouse. The customer indicated that they might pick it up on January 10, 2015. The customer will pay for the merchandise within 30 days of pick up. The cost of the merchandise was $4,300 and was included in inventory because the merchandise was still in Kamloops's warehouse.

3. Kamloops offers its customers a full refund for merchandise returned within 15 days of purchase. Sales recorded from December 17 to December 31 were $26,000. Typically, about 5% of sales are returned. The returned goods are scrapped and not returned to inventory. Alphonzo said, "that customers had not returned any merchandise from the December 17 to December 31 sales by the company's year end. Any returns from these sales will be recorded in January when the merchandise is returned and the company knows the exact amount of the returns."

4. During the last week of December, the company had run a promotional campaign in the local newspaper. The cost of the campaign was $3,500. Alphonzo recorded it as a prepaid expense because he anticipates that January 2015 sales will be higher as a result of the campaign.

Instructions

(a) Explain how financial statements help the bank with its decision on whether or not to lend money to Kamloops.

(b) Explain why the bank has requested an independent review of the financial statements.

(c) Calculate the correct amounts for current assets, current liabilities, net sales, cost of goods sold, and total operating expenses. Explain each of your corrections.

TAKING IT FURTHER   Calculate the current ratio based on (a) the preliminary financial statements and (b) the corrected amounts. Is the current ratio based on the corrected amounts better or worse? Does there appear to be bias in the types of errors that were made? Explain.

▶ Problems: Set B

P11–1B   Note 2, Basis of Presentation (part d), in **Reitmans (Canada) Limited's** financial statements states: "The preparation of the financial statements in accordance with IFRS requires management to make judgments, estimates and assumptions that affect the application of accounting policies and the reported amounts of assets, liabilities, the disclosure of contingent assets and contingent liabilities at the date of the financial statements and reported amounts of revenues and expenses during the period."

Comment on the objective of financial reporting, and qualitative characteristics.
(SO 2, 3) C

Instructions

Explain why Reitmans' management is required to use estimates in the company's financial statements. Support your answer with reference to the objective of financial reporting and the qualitative characteristics.

TAKING IT FURTHER   Which qualitative characteristics may be sacrificed when management is required to make estimates in the financial statements that may differ materially from actual results?

P11–2B   **Air Canada** reported a $1-billion loss for the year ended December 31, 2008. After financial restructuring in 2009, Air Canada continued to report losses, and it reported a $250-million loss for the year ended December 31, 2011. In June 2012, Air Canada was preparing to ask the Canadian government to allow it to

Comment on application of accounting assumptions and concepts. (SO 2, 3) AP

make reduced cash contributions to one of the company's pension plans as well as to reduce other financial pressures. Arbitrator Michel Picher stated, "It is of critical interest for the company to gain that relief now, thereby assuring its long-term solvency." Solvency refers to the company's ability to repay its long-term debt and survive over a long period of time.

Instructions

(a) Air Canada's December 31, 2011, financial statements were prepared using the cost model. What assumption did Air Canada make about its operations?

(b) With the uncertainty facing Air Canada, should the company's financial statements be prepared under the assumption that it will continue to operate for the foreseeable future? Explain.

TAKING IT FURTHER   Explain the implications of the full disclosure concept for Air Canada's financial statements in these circumstances.

Comment on the objective of financial reporting, qualitative characteristics, and constraints. (SO 1, 3, 4) C

P11–3B   As you learn more about accounting, you will learn that for certain economic events or transactions, companies reporting under ASPE can choose between alternative accounting methods. For example, corporations can choose between different methods for accounting for income tax and investments. Typically, if the company reporting under ASPE has a choice between alternative methods, one accounting method is much simpler to apply and requires less disclosure.

Instructions

Explain why it is appropriate that companies reporting under ASPE can choose between alternative accounting methods to report certain events or transactions. Include references to the objective of financial reporting and qualitative characteristics in your explanation.

TAKING IT FURTHER   Typically, when a company reporting under ASPE has a choice between alternative accounting methods, the alternative method that is more complex and requires more disclosure is consistent with the method required under IFRS. Why do you think some private companies reporting under ASPE might decide to use a method that is consistent with IFRS?

Identify elements, assumptions, constraints, and recognition and measurement criteria. (SO 2, 3, 4) AN

P11–4B   Jivraj and Juma are accountants at Desktop Computers. Desktop Computers has not adopted the revaluation model for accounting for its property, plant, and equipment. They disagree over the following transactions that occurred during the fiscal year ended December 31, 2013:

1. Desktop purchased equipment for $60,000 at a going-out-of-business sale. The equipment was worth $75,000. Jivraj believes that the following entry should be made:

Equipment	75,000	
Cash		60,000
Gain on Fair Value Adjustment of Equipment		15,000

2. Land costing $90,000 was appraised at $215,000. Jivraj suggests the following journal entry:

Land	125,000	
Gain on Fair Value Adjustment of Land		125,000

3. Depreciation for the year was $18,000. Since the company's profit is expected to be lower this year, Jivraj suggests deferring depreciation to a year when there is higher profit.

4. Desktop bought a custom-made piece of equipment for $54,000. This equipment has a useful life of six years. Desktop depreciates equipment using the straight-line method. "Since the equipment is custom-made, it will have no resale value," Jivraj argues. "So, instead of depreciating it, it should be expensed immediately." Jivraj suggests the following entry:

Miscellaneous Expense	54,000	
Cash		54,000

5. Jivraj suggests that the company building should be reported on the balance sheet at the lower of cost and fair value. Fair value is $15,000 less than cost, although it is expected to recover its value in the future.

6. On December 20, 2013, Desktop hired a marketing consultant to design and implement a marketing plan in 2014. The plan will be designed and implemented in three stages. The contract amount is $60,000, payable in three instalments in 2014 as each stage of the plan is completed. Jivraj argues that the contract must be recorded in 2013 because there is a signed contract. Jivraj suggests the following:

Advertising Expense	60,000	
Accounts Payable		60,000

7. On December 23, Desktop received a written sales order for 10 computers. The computers will be shipped in January when the required software is installed. Jivraj suggests the following entries:

Accounts Receivable	103,000	
Sales		103,000
Cost of Goods Sold	53,000	
Merchandise Inventory		53,000

Juma disagrees with Jivraj on each of the situations.

Instructions

(a) For each transaction, indicate why Juma disagrees. Support your answer with reference to the conceptual framework (definition of elements, qualitative characteristics, assumptions, constraints, and recognition and measurement criteria).

(b) Prepare the correct journal entry to record each transaction.

TAKING IT FURTHER   How would your response in (a) differ if Desktop adopted the revaluation model of accounting for its property, plant, and equipment?

P11–5B   Business transactions for SGI Company, a private company reporting under ASPE, in the current year follow:

1. The company used the average cost formula to determine that the cost of the merchandise inventory at December 31 was $65,000. On December 31, it would have cost $80,000 to replace the merchandise inventory, so the following entry was made:

Identify assumptions and concepts and correct entries. (SO 2, 4) AN

Merchandise Inventory	15,000	
Cost of Goods Sold		15,000

2. An order for $35,000 of goods on hand was received from a customer on December 27. The customer paid a $5,000 deposit when the order was placed. This order is to be shipped on January 9 next year. The following entry was made on December 27:

Cash	5,000	
Accounts Receivable	30,000	
Sales		35,000

3. On December 31, SGI Company's fiscal year end, a 12-month insurance policy for the following year was purchased. The following entry was made:

Insurance Expense	24,000	
Cash		24,000

4. At a fire sale, equipment worth $300,000 was acquired at a cost of $225,000. It had soot and smoke damage, but was otherwise in good condition. The following entry was made:

Equipment	300,000	
Cash		225,000
Gain on Fair Value Adjustment of Equipment		75,000

5. The cost of utilities used during December was $4,200. No entry was made for the utilities in December as the bill was not received until January and was paid in February.

Instructions

(a) In each of the situations, identify the assumption or concept that has been violated, if any.

(b) Prepare the journal entry to correct each incorrect transaction identified in (a).

TAKING IT FURTHER   Would your response to item 5. be different if you did not know the cost of the December utilities?

P11–6B   Superior Salmon Farm, a private company reporting under ASPE, raises salmon that it sells to supermarket chains and restaurants. The average selling price for a mature salmon is $6. Many people believe that the selling price will increase in the future, because the demand for salmon is increasing as more people become aware of the health benefits of the omega-3 fatty acids in this fish.

Identify point of revenue recognition. (SO 4) C

It normally takes three years for the fish to grow to a saleable size. During that period, the fish must be fed and closely monitored to ensure they are healthy and free of disease. Their habitat must also be maintained. These costs average $4.50 per fish over the three-year growing period. The owner of Superior Salmon

Farm believes the company should recognize revenue at a rate of $2 a year ($6 ÷ 3 years) for each fish that it harvests.

Instructions

Do you agree with the proposed revenue recognition policy for Superior Salmon Farm? Explain why or why not. Use the revenue recognition criteria to explain when you believe the revenue should be recognized for this salmon-farming business.

TAKING IT FURTHER   Explain how the costs of feeding, monitoring, and maintaining healthy fish and a proper habitat should be recorded.

Calculate revenue, cost of goods sold, and gross profit. (SO 4) AP

P11–7B   Corvette Company, a window and door manufacturer, reported the following for the 11 months ended November 30, 2014:

Net sales	$2,500,000
Cost of goods sold	1,500,000
Warranty revenue	15,000
Service revenue	100,000
Unearned revenue	75,000

Additional information for the month of December is as follows:

1. The service revenue is for revenue earned on installation and the unearned revenue is for any unearned warranty revenue.
2. Provided $10,000 of warranty service to customers.
3. Window and doors sales to customers were $230,000 and the cost of the windows and doors sold was $138,000.
4. In addition, customers paid $6,000 for extended warranties and $9,500 for installation services.
5. Included in the December sales was $10,500 for windows and doors delivered to the customer by December 31, 2014, which still required installation. The customers prepaid $1,200 for installation when the windows and doors were ordered. The windows and doors will be installed during January 2015.
6. Corvette's year end is December 31 and the company prepares adjusting journal entries annually.

Instructions

Calculate the net sales, cost of goods sold, installation revenue, and warranty revenue that Corvette will report in its income statement for the year ended December 31, 2014.

TAKING IT FURTHER   Assume that Corvette pays its sales staff a 5% commission on all window and door sales. The sales staff is paid their commission when the company is paid by the customer. At December 31, 2014, the company's accounts receivable for windows and doors are $190,000 and the company estimates that 2% of the accounts receivable will not be collected. Calculate the commission expense for the year ended December 31, 2014.

Determine when to recognize revenue when revenues are uncertain. (SO 4) AP

P11–8B   Vitamins R Us developed a new 100%-organic multivitamin, Vita X, which is more easily absorbed by the body. Vita X is significantly more expensive than other vitamins on the market. In order to promote the product, Vitamins R Us shipped 50,000 bottles of Vita X, FOB destination, to retailers during December 2013. Retailers can return any Vita X not sold by March 31, 2014. As an added incentive, the retailers do not have to pay Vitamins R Us for any bottles of Vita X that they do not return to Vitamins R Us until March 31, 2014.

The selling price of the vitamins to the retailers is $45 per bottle. Vitamins R Us has not had previous promotions of this nature. Vitamins R Us has a December 31 fiscal year end.

The company's bookkeeper recognized the revenue on the vitamins when the vitamins were shipped to the retailers and made the following entry:

Accounts Receivable	2,250,000	
Sales		2,250,000

Instructions

(a) Indicate whether you agree or disagree with the bookkeeper's decision to recognize revenue when the vitamins were shipped. Support your answer with reference to the revenue recognition criteria.
(b) Indicate when the revenue for Vita X should be recognized.

TAKING IT FURTHER   Would your answers to (a) and (b) be different if Vitamins R Us had previously used the same promotion for Vita X and only 10% of the product was returned to Vitamins R Us? Explain your answer.

P11–9B   MacNeil Construction Company has a long-term construction contract to build a shopping centre. The centre has a total estimated cost of $120 million, and a contract price of $152 million. Additional information follows:

Calculate revenue and gross profit for percentage-of-completion method. (SO 4) AP

Year	Cash Collections	Actual Costs Incurred
2012	$ 32,000,000	$ 24,000,000
2013	24,000,000	18,000,000
2014	46,000,000	30,000,000
2015	50,000,000	48,000,000
	$152,000,000	$120,000,000

The shopping centre is completed in 2015 as scheduled. All cash collections for the contract have been received.

Instructions

Prepare a schedule to determine the revenue, expense, and gross profit for each year of the long-term construction contract, using the percentage-of-completion method.

TAKING IT FURTHER   Assume that late in 2012, MacNeil Construction discovered that it made a mistake when preparing the bid for the contract. The estimated costs used in the proposed bid were understated by such a large amount that MacNeil is now unsure that it will make any profit on the job, because the total costs cannot be readily determined. Is it still appropriate to use the percentage-of-completion method for the remaining years of the contract? Explain.

P11–10B   Eugene Company is a small private company that sells computers and provides consulting services. The owner of the company, Eugene, wants to expand and has asked you to become his business partner. Eugene has prepared financial statements for the year ended December 31, 2014. These financial statements reported the following:

Objective of financial reporting, identifying elements, and revenue and expense recognition. (SO 2, 4) AP

Current assets	$ 90,000
Current liabilities	65,000
Net sales and consulting revenue	650,000
Cost of goods sold	475,000
Total operating expenses	106,000

You are trying to decide if you will invest in the business and you are reviewing the financial statements. During your review, you have discovered the following:

1. On December 1, 2014, Eugene signed a $24,000, one-year consulting contract with a new customer starting December 1. Eugene reported the $24,000 in net sales and consulting revenue because the customer paid the full amount on December 1.
2. During 2014, Eugene started a new warranty program. Under this program, customers can buy a five-year extended warranty for $500 and 20 customers purchased the warranty. Eugene reported the warranty sales in net sales and consulting revenue. No warranty service was provided in 2014.
3. Included in net sales is $55,000 for computers that the customer had paid for but had not picked up from the company by December 31, 2014. The customer was picking up the computers on January 2. The cost of these computers is $35,000 and Eugene included this cost in inventory because the computers were still in the warehouse.
4. During the last week of December, the company ran a promotional campaign in the local newspaper. The cost of the campaign was $4,800. Eugene recorded it as a prepaid expense because he anticipates that January 2015 sales will be higher as a result of the campaign.

Instructions

(a) Explain how financial statements help you with your decision on whether or not to invest in the company.
(b) Calculate the correct amounts for current assets, current liabilities, net sales and consulting revenue, cost of goods sold, and total operating expenses. Explain each of your corrections.

TAKING IT FURTHER   Based on your review of the financial statements, would you invest in Eugene Company? Explain. What other information might help with your decision?

▶ Continuing Cookie Chronicle

(*Note:* This is a continuation of the Cookie Chronicle from Chapters 1 through 10.)

Natalie's high school friend, Katy Peterson, has been operating a bakery for approximately 10 months, which she calls The Baker's Nook. Natalie and Katy usually meet once a month to catch up and discuss problems they have encountered while operating their respective businesses. Katy wishes to borrow from her bank so she can purchase a new state-of-the-art oven. She recognizes that the bank will be evaluating her financial statements.

Katy has recently negotiated a one-year contract with Coffee to Go to provide 1,500 cinnamon buns every week. Coffee to Go, upon receipt of a monthly invoice, will send Katy a cheque by the 15th of the following month. Katy has decided that, because she has signed this contract, she is able to record as revenue in her financial statements the contracted revenue that she is about to earn over the next 12 months.

When Katy negotiated the contract with Coffee to Go, she purchased additional baking supplies to meet the increased demand for cinnamon buns. She has decided that she will not record the purchase of these supplies until the invoice is due, which is in about 30 days. She argues that the amount to be paid for the purchase of baking supplies is relatively small and the amount won't really make much of a difference to the bank when it makes its decision.

Katy assures Natalie that this is the right way to account for this revenue and the purchase of additional baking supplies. She is now sure that the bank will lend her the money that she needs to purchase this new oven.

Natalie is confused and comes to you with the following questions:

1. Is Katy accounting for this revenue correctly?
2. Is Katy accounting for the purchase of the baking supplies correctly?
3. What other information will the bank be considering when deciding whether or not to extend the loan to Katy?
4. Do you think that Katy is being honest when she identifies this revenue as being earned on her income statement?

Instructions

(a) Answer Natalie's questions.
(b) How should Katy be recording this revenue? Why?
(c) How should Katy be recording the purchase of baking supplies? Why?
(d) How could Katy ensure that the bank is aware of this contractual arrangement with Coffee to Go when it reads her financial statements?

Cumulative Coverage—Chapters 6 to 11

Johan Company and Nordlund Company are competing businesses. Both began operations six years ago and they are quite similar. The current balance sheet data for the two companies are as follows:

	Johan Company	Nordlund Company
Cash	$ 70,300	$ 48,400
Accounts receivable	309,700	312,500
Allowance for doubtful accounts	(13,600)	0
Merchandise inventory	463,900	520,200
Property, plant, and equipment	255,300	257,300
Accumulated depreciation	(112,650)	(189,850)
Total assets	$972,950	$948,550
Current liabilities	$440,200	$436,500
Non-current liabilities	78,000	80,000
Total liabilities	518,200	516,500
Owner's equity	454,750	432,050
Total liabilities and owner's equity	$972,950	$948,550

You have been hired as a consultant to do a review of the two companies. Your goal is to determine which one is in a stronger financial position. Your review of their financial statements quickly reveals that the two companies have not followed the same accounting policies. The differences, and your conclusions, are summarized below:

1. Johan Company has had good experience in estimating its uncollectible accounts. A review shows that the amount of its write offs each year has been quite close to the allowances the company provided.

   Nordlund Company has been somewhat slow to recognize its uncollectible accounts. Based on an aging analysis and review of its accounts receivable, it is estimated that $20,000 of its existing accounts will become uncollectible.

2. Johan Company has determined the cost of its merchandise inventory using the average inventory cost formula. The result is that its inventory appears on the balance sheet at an amount that is slightly below its current replacement cost. Based on a detailed physical examination of its merchandise on hand, the current replacement cost of its inventory is estimated at $477,000.

   Nordlund Company has used the FIFO inventory cost formula. The result is that its ending inventory appears on the balance sheet at an amount that is close to its current replacement cost.

3. Johan Company estimated a useful life of 12 years and a residual value of $30,000 for its property, plant, and equipment, and has been depreciating them on a straight-line basis. Nordlund Company has the same type of property, plant, and equipment. However, it estimated a useful life of 10 years and a residual value of $10,000. It has been depreciating its property, plant, and equipment using the double diminishing-balance method.

   Based on engineering studies of these types of property, plant, and equipment, you conclude that Nordlund's estimates and method for calculating depreciation are more appropriate.

Instructions

(a) Where would you find the above information on the two companies' accounting policies? Be specific about what information would be available and where you would find it.

(b) Using similar accounting policies for both companies, revise the balance sheets presented above.

(c) Has preparing the revised statements in (b) improved the quality of the accounting information for the two companies? If so, how?

BROADENING YOUR PERSPECTIVE | CHAPTER 11

▶ Financial Reporting and Analysis

Financial Reporting Problem

BYP11–1   Refer to the Notes to Consolidated Financial Statements for **Reitmans (Canada) Limited** in Appendix A.

Instructions

(a) Subsection b) of Note 2, Basis of Presentation, states that the financial statements have been prepared on the historical cost basis except for available for sale financial assets and derivative instruments and the pension liability. Reitmans' available for sale financial assets are short-term investments in marketable securities classified as current assets. Why does Reitmans report these investments at fair value?

(b) Subsection l) of Note 3, Significant Accounting Policies, describes Reitmans' revenue recognition policy. When does Reitmans recognize revenue for gift cards and loyalty points and awards? Does this policy seem reasonable to you given the nature of gift cards and loyalty point programs? Explain why or why not, referring to the appropriate revenue recognition criteria and concepts in the conceptual framework.

(c) Note 23, Credit Facility, discloses that Reitmans had unsecured operating lines of credit available up to $125 million. Do you think this additional disclosure was necessary? Explain why or why not, referring to the appropriate concepts or items from the conceptual framework of accounting in your answer.

(d) Reitmans' independent auditors' report is provided in Appendix A with the company's financial statements. What is the purpose of an independent audit? What did Reitmans' auditors say about the company's financial statements?

Interpreting Financial Statements

BYP11–2   McCain Foods Limited is a large multinational private company with $6 billion in sales. It produces both frozen and non-frozen food products and makes one-third of the frozen French fries produced worldwide. It has manufacturing operations in 18 countries, sales operations in over 100 countries, and employs more than 20,000 people. Most private companies in Canada have chosen to follow ASPE; however, some private companies like McCain have chosen to follow IFRS. "We believe that we are exactly the type of company for whom IFRS was developed," McCain told the IASB in a letter of comment responding to the IASB's preliminary views on financial statement presentation.

Instructions

(a) Other than the owners of McCain, who might be the users of McCain's financial statements?
(b) McCain has numerous subsidiaries located throughout the globe. How would this type of multinational structure motivate McCain to follow IFRS?
(c) What are the benefits to the users of its financial statements of McCain reporting under IFRS?

▶ Critical Thinking

Collaborative Learning Activity

Note to instructor: Additional instructions and material for this group activity can be found on the Instructor Resource Site and in *WileyPLUS*.

BYP11–3   In this group activity, you will be given a set of financial statements and a list of items that might need correcting. You will be required to (a) decide if an adjusting journal entry is required, (b) justify your decision by referring to the conceptual framework (including revenue and expense recognition criteria), and (c) calculate profit. Your decisions may have an impact on the annual bonuses that senior management members hope to receive.

Communication Activity

BYP11–4   Junk Grrlz (Junk) is a wholesale distributor of goods. Junk purchases goods that are not selling from manufacturers and other wholesalers and sells them to discount retail outlets. You are a professional accountant and are preparing Junk's financial statements for the year ended September 30, 2014. The company had $300,000 of real animal fur coats in inventory that were not selling. Junk has not had an order for real fur coats for over a year. The president is reluctant to write off the inventory and consequently signed a sales agreement with Cheap But Good (Cheap). Cheap agreed to buy the coats for $350,000 and could return any coats that it had not sold by December 31, 2014. In addition, Cheap was not required to pay Junk for the coats until December 31, 2014. The coats were shipped to and received by Cheap on September 29, 2014.

Instructions

Write a memo to the president of Junk Grrlz answering the following questions:

(a) When should revenue be recognized on the fur coats sold to Cheap But Good? Explain.
(b) How should the fur coats be reported in Junk's financial statements for the year ended September 30, 2014? Explain.

Ethics Case

BYP11–5   When the IASB and AcSB issue new accounting recommendations, the required implementation date (the date when a company has to start applying the recommendations) is usually 12 months or more after the date of publication. For example, in October 2010, the IASB issued new recommendations for classifying and reporting investments: companies are required to implement the new recommendations for fiscal years starting January 1, 2015. This allows companies some time to change their accounting procedures. Nevertheless, early implementation is usually encouraged for those who are able to do so, because new rules are intended to provide better representation of the company's financial performance and position.

Carol DesChenes, an accountant at Grocery Online, discusses with her vice-president of finance the need for early implementation of a recently issued recommendation. She says it will result in a much more faithful representation of the company's financial position. When the vice-president of finance determines that early implementation will have a negative impact on the profits reported for the year, he strongly discourages Carol from implementing the recommendation until it is required.

Instructions

(a) Who are the stakeholders in this situation?
(b) What, if any, are the ethical considerations in this situation?
(c) What could Carol gain by supporting early implementation? Who might be affected by the decision against early implementation?

"All About You" Activity

BYP11–6   In the "All About You" feature, you learned about the importance of your personal resumé being a faithful representation of your personal background, education, and experience.

To apply this concept further, assume that you are applying for a car loan. The loan application requires that you prepare two reports: (1) a projected cash budget and (2) information about your assets and liabilities. The information in the loan application will be used to determine if the bank manager will approve the loan or not.

Instructions

(a) Why would a bank manager ask you to complete a projected cash budget and provide information about your assets and liabilities in order to decide whether or not to approve your loan? What is the bank manager trying to determine about you?

(b) Describe the qualitative characteristics the information you provide to the bank manager should have for this information to be useful to the bank manager.

(c) The cash budget will primarily be based on future cash inflow and outflows. How might a bank manager verify the reasonableness of the cash budget?

(d) What might be the consequences to you if the bank manager determines the information provided is misleading?

ANSWERS TO CHAPTER QUESTIONS

ANSWERS TO ACCOUNTING IN ACTION INSIGHT QUESTIONS

All About You, p. 584

Q: What may be the consequences to you if you misrepresent yourself on your resumé?

A: If it is determined that you have misrepresented yourself on your resumé, your credibility will be damaged. If your employer determines that you misrepresented yourself, you may lose your job, or at the very least your employer may always question your trustworthiness. You may also find yourself in a job for which you are not qualified and therefore your reputation will be damaged because of your inability to perform to the level required. In addition, it may be difficult for you to get a good reference from your employer when you apply for jobs in the future.

Ethics, p. 591

Q: Accountants are often required to make estimates when preparing financial statements. What is the difference between what the three executives allegedly did at Nortel and what we would normally expect an accountant to do when estimating accruals for adjusting journal entries?

A: When an accountant makes estimates in the financial statements, these estimates should be made using professional judgement and the best information available at the time to arrive at a reasonable estimate. Differences between these types of estimates and actual amounts are considered to be part of the accounting process. In the case of Nortel, the executives were accused of not using professional judgement to arrive at the best estimate but intentionally misstating the accruals in the financial statements for their personal benefit.

ANSWERS TO SELF-STUDY QUESTIONS

1. a   2. b   3. b   4. c   5. a   6. d   7. c   8. c   9. a   10. b

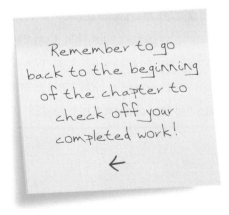

 THE **NAVIGATOR**

- ☐ Understand *Concepts for Review*
- ☐ Read *Feature Story*
- ☐ Scan *Study Objectives*
- ☐ Read *Chapter Preview*
- ☐ Read text and answer *Before You Go On*
- ☐ Review *Comparing IFRS and ASPE*
- ☐ Work *Demonstration Problem*
- ☐ Review *Summary of Study Objectives*
- ☐ Answer *Self-Study Questions*
- ☐ Complete assignments
- ☐ Go to *WileyPLUS* for practice and tutorials

CONCEPTS FOR **REVIEW:**

Before studying this chapter, you should understand or, if necessary, review:

a. The different forms of business organization. (Ch. 1, pp. 8–9)

b. The cost principle of accounting. (Ch. 1, p. 16)

c. The statement of owner's equity. (Ch. 1, pp. 24–25)

d. How to make closing entries. (Ch. 4, pp. 175–178)

e. The steps in the accounting cycle. (Ch. 4, p. 181)

f. The classified balance sheet. (Ch. 4, pp. 185–193)

JOINING FORCES FOR SUCCESS

TORONTO, Ont.—The benefit of strength in numbers is what leads some professionals to form partnerships to provide complementary skills to serve the market, and to gain a larger base of clients. A partnership agreement is crucial. It states how the partners, as part owners of the firm, will contribute time, expertise, and money and share in profits and losses. The agreement also states what will happen when a partner leaves the firm or the partnership is wound up.

Harris & Chong LLP is a Toronto-based accounting firm. The "LLP" stands for "limited liability partnership." The partners in a limited liability partnership are not personally liable for the negligent acts of another partner or an employee who is directly supervised by another partner, explains Sonja Chong.

Ms. Chong joined as a junior partner in 1991 when the firm was known as Braithwaite & Harris, after founding partners Bruce Braithwaite and Peter Harris. The firm has ranged from two to four partners, and has consisted of Mr. Harris and Ms. Chong since 2007. Each time a partner leaves or joins, the partnership agreement is amended to adapt to their circumstances. "Partnerships and partners are subject to change from time to time," Ms. Chong says. "You have to be flexible."

Under the firm's partnership agreement, generally a new partner does not have to contribute any equity, but may have to loan money to the partnership to meet operating needs until he or she starts to collect fees from clients. What most partners contribute is their list of clients, so if Harris & Chong admitted another partner, it would likely be a chartered accountant with a strong client base. The firm would also consider admitting junior partners if they had a different or complementary area of expertise the firm could expand upon, or hiring a senior accountant who could be groomed to eventually become a partner.

Peter Harris says that there are many ways of allocating partnership profits. Some partnerships share profits based on a predetermined percentage of the partnership's profit while others may allocate profits proportionately to the revenue each partner generates from their own clients. In the latter situation, costs for things such as rent and staff could be based on a formula that allocates costs in an equitable manner. Of course, formulas can be changed depending on the circumstances.

What happens when a partner leaves? "The most crucial thing that should exist in a partnership agreement is how to divvy things up when you part," Ms. Chong says. Generally, a departing partner would take his or her clients and the balance of his or her capital account represented by accounts receivable and work in progress relating to those clients, less a proportionate share of the firm's liabilities. They could also be required to pay a fair amount to the firm for any office equipment that they may wish to take upon leaving. "In an accounting firm, the most valuable asset is really your clients. Furniture and computers are generally not worth very much," Mr. Harris adds.

THE **NAVIGATOR**

>> STUDY **OBJECTIVES**

After studying this chapter, you should be able to:

1. Describe the characteristics of the partnership form of business organization.

2. Account for the formation of a partnership.

3. Allocate and record profit or loss to partners.

4. Prepare partnership financial statements.

5. Account for the admission of a partner.

6. Account for the withdrawal of a partner.

7. Account for the liquidation of a partnership.

THE **NAVIGATOR**

It is not surprising that Bruce Braithwaite and Peter Harris decided to use the partnership form of organization when they started their accounting practice. They saw an opportunity to combine their expertise and better leverage their resources. In this chapter, we will discuss why the partnership form of organization is often chosen. We will also explain the major issues in accounting for partnerships.

The chapter is organized as follows:

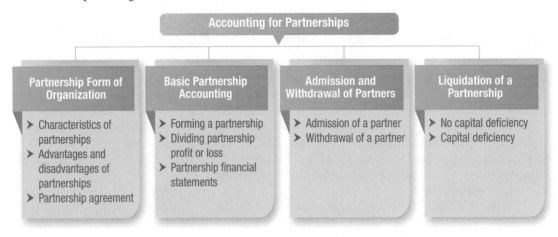

Accounting for Partnerships

Partnership Form of Organization	Basic Partnership Accounting	Admission and Withdrawal of Partners	Liquidation of a Partnership
➤ Characteristics of partnerships ➤ Advantages and disadvantages of partnerships ➤ Partnership agreement	➤ Forming a partnership ➤ Dividing partnership profit or loss ➤ Partnership financial statements	➤ Admission of a partner ➤ Withdrawal of a partner	➤ No capital deficiency ➤ Capital deficiency

Partnership Form of Organization

» **STUDY OBJECTIVE 1**

Describe the characteristics of the partnership form of business organization.

All provinces in Canada have a partnership act that sets out the basic rules for forming and operating partnerships. These acts define a **partnership** as a relationship between people who do business with the intention of making a profit. This does not necessarily mean that there must be a profit—just that profit is the objective. Partnerships are common in professions such as accounting, advertising, law, and medicine. Professional partnerships can vary in size from two partners to thousands.

CHARACTERISTICS OF PARTNERSHIPS

▶ **ILLUSTRATION 12-1**
Partnership characteristics

The main characteristics of the partnership form of business organization are shown in Illustration 12-1. They are explained after the illustration.

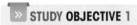

Association of Individuals

Unlimited Liability

Co-Ownership of Property

Division of Profit

Limited Life

Mutual Agency

Association of Individuals

The association of two or more individuals in a partnership can be based on an act as simple as a handshake. However, it is much better to have a legal, written agreement that outlines the rights and obligations of the partners, as in the feature story. Partners who have not put their agreement in writing have found that the absence of a written agreement can sometimes cause later difficulties. In fact, some partnership acts state that if you receive a share of profit from a business, you will be considered a partner in the business unless there is contrary evidence. If there is no formal agreement that says who the partners of a business are, you may be part of a partnership without knowing it!

A partnership is a legal entity for certain purposes. For instance, property (land, buildings, and equipment) can be owned in the name of the partnership. The firm can sue or be sued. A partnership is also an accounting entity for financial reporting purposes. Thus, the personal assets, liabilities, and transactions of the partners are kept separate from the accounting records of the partnership, just as they are in a proprietorship.

However, a partnership is not taxed as a separate entity. It must file an information tax return that reports the partnership's profit and each partner's share of that profit. Each partner must then report his or her share of the partnership profit on their personal income tax returns. The partner's profit is taxed at his or her personal income tax rate, and does not depend on how much money the partner withdrew from the partnership during the year.

Co-Ownership of Property

Partnership assets are owned jointly by the partners. If the partnership is dissolved, an asset does not legally return to the partner who originally contributed it. The assets are normally sold and the partners share any gain or loss on disposition according to their profit and loss ratios. After partnership liabilities are paid, each partner then has a claim on any cash that remains: the claim is equal to the balance in the partner's capital account.

Similarly, if, in doing business, a partner invests a building in the partnership that is valued at $100,000 and the building is later sold at a gain of $20,000, that partner does not receive the entire gain. The gain becomes part of the partnership profit, which is shared among the partners, as described in the next section.

Division of Profit

Just as property is co-owned, so is partnership profit (or loss). The partners specify how the partnership profit (loss) will be divided when they form the partnership. As explained in the feature story, this can be changed later depending on the circumstances. If the division is not specified, profit (loss) is assumed to be shared equally. We will learn more about dividing partnership profit in a later section of this chapter.

Limited Life

A partnership does not have an unlimited life. Any change in ownership ends the existing partnership. There is a **partnership dissolution** whenever a partner withdraws or a new partner is admitted. When a partnership is dissolved, this does not necessarily mean that the business ends. If the continuing partners agree, operations can continue without any interruption by forming a new partnership.

Mutual Agency

Mutual agency means that each partner acts for the partnership when he or she does partnership business. The action of any partner is binding on all other partners—in other words, the action cannot be cancelled by one of them. This is true even when partners exceed their authority, as long as the act looks appropriate for the partnership. For example, a partner of an accounting firm who purchases a building that is suitable for the business creates a binding contract in the name of the partnership. On the other hand, if a partner in a law firm decides to buy a snowmobile for the partnership, the act would not be binding on the partnership, because the purchase is unrelated to the business.

Unlimited Liability

Each partner is jointly and severally (individually) liable for all partnership liabilities. If one partner incurs a liability, the other partners are also responsible for it. For repayment, creditors first have claims on the partnership assets. If there are not enough assets to pay back the creditors, however, they can then claim the personal assets of any partner, regardless of that partner's equity in the partnership. Because each partner is responsible for all the debts of the partnership, each partner is said to have unlimited liability.

Unlimited liability and mutual agency can combine for disastrous results. An unethical or incompetent partner can commit the partnership to a deal that eventually bankrupts the partnership. The creditors may then be able to claim the partners' personal assets—the assets of all the partners, not just those of the partner who made the bad deal. Consequently, an individual must be extremely cautious in choosing a partner.

Because of concerns about unlimited liability, there are now special forms of partnership organization that modify liability. These include limited partnerships and limited liability partnerships, discussed in the next two sections.

Limited Partnerships (LP). In a **limited partnership**, or "LP," one or more of the partners have unlimited liability. This type of partner is called a *general partner*. A general partner normally contributes work and experience to the partnership and is authorized to manage and represent the partnership. The general partner's liability for the partnership's debts is unlimited.

The other partners have limited liability for the partnership's debts. This type of partner is called a *limited partner*. Limited partners normally give cash or assets to the partnership, but not services. The amount of debt that the limited partner is liable for in the partnership is limited to the amount of capital that he or she contributed to the partnership. In other words, a limited partner's personal assets cannot be sold to repay any partnership debt that is more than the amount that he or she contributed to the partnership.

A limited partnership is identified in its name with the words "Limited Partnership" or the abbreviation "LP." Limited partnerships are normally used by businesses that offer income tax shelters for investors, such as real estate investment trusts, rental properties, and sports ventures.

Limited Liability Partnerships (LLP). Most professionals, such as lawyers, doctors, and accountants, form a **limited liability partnership** or "LLP." As noted in the feature story, Harris & Chong operates as a limited liability partnership.

A limited liability partnership is designed to protect innocent partners from the acts of other partners that result in lawsuits against the partnership. That is, partners in an LLP continue to have unlimited liability for their own negligence but have limited liability for other partners' negligence. In addition to being liable for their own actions, partners are also liable for the actions of employees whom they directly supervise and control.

ADVANTAGES AND DISADVANTAGES OF PARTNERSHIPS

Why do people choose partnerships? Harris & Chong formed a partnership in part to provide complementary skills to serve the market, and to gain a larger base of clients. The two partners can also divide among themselves different areas of responsibility and expertise—assurance, taxation, and business valuation, for example.

A partnership is easily formed and is controlled by fewer government regulations and restrictions than a corporation is. Also, decisions can be made quickly on important matters that affect the firm. This is also true in a proprietorship, but not in a corporation, where some decisions have to be approved by the board of directors.

Partnerships also have some disadvantages: mutual agency, limited life, and unlimited liability in general partnerships. Unlimited liability is particularly troublesome. Many individuals fear they may lose not only their initial investment but also their personal assets if those assets are needed to pay partnership creditors. As a result, partnerships often have difficulty getting large amounts of investment capital. That is one reason why the largest businesses in Canada are corporations, not partnerships.

The advantages and disadvantages of the general partnership form of business organization are summarized below.

Advantages	Disadvantages
• Combines skills and resources of two or more individuals	• Mutual agency
• Easily formed	• Limited life
• Fewer government regulations and restrictions than corporations	• Unlimited liability
• Easier decision-making	

PARTNERSHIP AGREEMENT

Ideally, when two or more individuals agree to organize a partnership, their agreement should be expressed as a written contract. Called a **partnership agreement**, this contract contains such basic information as the name and main location of the firm, the purpose of the business, and the date of inception. In addition, relationships among the partners must be specified, such as:

1. The names and capital contributions of partners
2. The rights and duties of partners
3. The basis for sharing profit or loss
4. Provisions for a withdrawal of assets
5. Procedures for submitting disputes to arbitration
6. Procedures for the withdrawal, or addition, of a partner
7. The rights and duties of surviving partners if a partner dies
8. Procedures for the liquidation of the partnership

The importance of a written contract cannot be overemphasized. As discussed in our feature story, for Harris & Chong, a partnership agreement is crucial. If there is no partnership agreement, the provisions of the partnership act will apply, and they may not be what the partners want. For example, as previously discussed, profits and losses are shared equally in the absence of an agreement. The partnership agreement should be written with care so that it considers all possible situations, contingencies, and future disagreements between the partners.

Ethics note A partnership agreement that is carefully planned reduces ethical conflict among partners. It specifies, in clear language, the process for solving ethical and legal problems, which is especially important when the partnership is in financial distress.

BEFORE YOU GO ON...

Do It

Answer the following true or false questions:
1. A partnership may be based on a handshake.
2. A partnership is not an accounting entity for financial reporting purposes.
3. A partner pays income tax on the amount of money he or she withdrew from the partnership during the year.
4. Mutual agency means that each partner acts for the partnership when he or she does partnership business.
5. When a partner exceeds his or her authority, and the act looks appropriate for the partnership, the act is not binding on the other partners and the partnership.
6. A partnership has unlimited life.
7. Each partner is jointly and severally liable for all of the partnership liabilities.
8. In a limited partnership, the amount of partnership debt that a limited partner is liable for is limited to the amount of capital that he or she has contributed to the partnership.

Solution

1.	T	5.	F
2.	F	6.	F
3.	F	7.	T
4.	T	8.	T

Related exercise material: BE12–1 and E12–1.

Action Plan
• Review characteristics of partnerships.

THE **NAVIGATOR**

Basic Partnership Accounting

We now turn to the basic accounting for partnerships. Accounting for a partnership is very similar to accounting for a proprietorship. Just as most proprietorships will choose to use Accounting Standards for Private Enterprises (ASPE), many partnerships are private and will also choose to follow these accounting standards. On the other hand, Limited Partnerships are often public enterprises and these partnerships will follow International Financial Reporting Standards (IFRS). In addition, some large professional partnerships are international and these partnerships must also follow IFRS.

There are three accounting issues where there are some differences between partnerships and proprietorships: formation of a partnership, dividing the partnership profit or loss, and preparing partnership financial statements. There are no significant differences in the accounting for these issues between partnerships following ASPE or IFRS. We will examine each of these in the following sections.

FORMING A PARTNERSHIP

» **STUDY OBJECTIVE 2**

Account for the formation of a partnership.

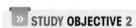

Each partner's initial investment in a partnership is entered in the partnership records. **These investments should be recorded at the assets' fair value at the date of their transfer to the partnership.** The values used must be agreed to by all of the partners.

To illustrate, assume that M. Gan and K. Sin combine their proprietorships on January 2 to start a partnership named Interactive Software. Gan and Sin each have the following assets before forming the partnership:

| | M. Gan | | K. Sin | |
	Book Value	Fair Value	Book Value	Fair Value
Cash	$ 8,000	$ 8,000	$ 9,000	$ 9,000
Accounts receivable			4,000	4,000
Allowance for doubtful accounts			(700)	(1,000)
Equipment	5,000	4,000		
Accumulated depreciation	(2,000)			
	$11,000	$12,000	$12,300	$12,000

The entries to record the investments in the partnership are:

A	=	L	+	OE
+8,000				+12,000
+4,000				

↑ Cash flows: +8,000

Investment of M. Gan

Jan. 2	Cash		8,000	
	Equipment		4,000	
	M. Gan, Capital			12,000
	To record investment of Gan.			

A	=	L	+	OE
+9,000				+12,000
+4,000				
−1,000				

↑ Cash flows: +9,000

Investment of K. Sin

2	Cash		9,000	
	Accounts Receivable		4,000	
	Allowance for Doubtful Accounts			1,000
	K. Sin, Capital			12,000
	To record investment of Sin.			

Helpful hint The fair value of the noncash assets at the date of acquisition becomes the cost of these assets to the partnership. The fair value is what the assets would have cost if they had been purchased at that time.

Note that neither the original cost of Gan's equipment ($5,000) nor its accumulated depreciation ($2,000) is recorded by the partnership. Instead, the equipment is recorded at its fair value of $4,000. Because the equipment has not yet been used by the partnership, there is no accumulated depreciation.

In contrast, Sin's gross claims on customers ($4,000) are carried into the partnership. The allowance for doubtful accounts is adjusted to $1,000 to arrive at a net realizable value of $3,000. A partnership may start with an allowance for doubtful accounts, because it will continue to track and collect existing accounts receivable and some of these are expected to be uncollectible. In addition, this procedure maintains the control and subsidiary relationship between Accounts Receivable and the accounts receivable subsidiary ledger that we learned about in Chapter 8.

After the partnership has been formed, the accounting for transactions is similar to the accounting for any other type of business organization. For example, all transactions with outside parties, such as the performance of services and payment for them, should be recorded in the same way for a partnership as for a proprietorship.

The steps in the accounting cycle that are described in Chapter 4 for a proprietorship are also used for a partnership. For example, a partnership journalizes and posts transactions, prepares a trial balance, journalizes and posts adjusting entries, and prepares an adjusted trial balance. However, there are minor differences in journalizing and posting closing entries and in preparing financial statements, as explained in the following sections. The differences occur because there is more than one owner.

 BEFORE YOU GO ON...

Do It

On June 1, Eric Brown and Erik Black decide to organize a partnership, E&E Painting. Eric Brown contributes equipment with a cost of $5,000 and $2,000 of accumulated depreciation. Erik Black contributes accounts receivable of $1,200. Eric and Erik agree that the equipment has a fair value of $2,500 and the accounts receivable a net realizable value of $1,000. Erik Black will also contribute the amount of cash required to make his investment equal to Eric Brown's. (a) How much cash must Erik Black contribute? (b) Prepare the journal entries to record their investments in the partnership.

Solution

(a) Fair value of equipment contributed by Eric Brown		$2,500
Less: fair value of accounts receivable contributed by Erik Black		1,000
Cash investment required from Erik Black		$1,500

(b)	July 1	Equipment	2,500	
		E. Brown, Capital		2,500
		To record investment of Eric Brown.		
	1	Cash	1,500	
		Accounts Receivable	1,200	
		Allowance for Doubtful Accounts		200
		E. Black, Capital		2,500
		To record investment of Erik Black.		

Action Plan
- Use fair values for the assets invested in the partnership.
- Each partner's equity is equal to the fair value of the net assets he invested in the partnership.

THE **NAVIGATOR**

Related exercise material: BE12–2, BE12–3, and E12–2.

DIVIDING PARTNERSHIP PROFIT OR LOSS

Partners are not employees of the partnership; they are its owners. If a partner works for the partnership, it is to earn profit, not to earn a salary. Thus, as in a proprietorship, when partners withdraw assets from the business, these amounts are called drawings, and are not expenses. In order to track each partner's equity in the business, it is necessary to create a separate drawings account for each partner.

To illustrate, assume that the partners of Interactive Software, M. Gan and K. Sin, had cash drawings of $8,000 and $6,000, respectively, for the year ended December 31, 2014. The journal entries (shown in summary format for the year) to record the partners' drawings are:

» **STUDY OBJECTIVE 3**

Allocate and record profit or loss to partners.

Dec. 31	M. Gan, Drawings	8,000	
	Cash		8,000
	Gan's withdrawal of cash for personal use.		
31	K. Sin, Drawings	6,000	
	Cash		6,000
	Sin's withdrawal of cash for personal use.		

A	=	L	+	OE
−8,000				−8,000

↓Cash flows: −8,000

A	=	L	+	OE
−6,000				−6,000

↓Cash flows: −6,000

Each partner's share of the partnership's profit or loss is determined according to the partnership's **profit and loss ratio**. This basis for division is usually the same for both profit and losses. As you will see in the following discussion, the profit and loss ratio can be a simple ratio or a more complicated calculation to recognize the different contributions of service and capital by each partner. If the profit and loss ratio is not specified in the partnership agreement, profit and losses are shared equally among the partners.

A partner's share of profit or loss is recognized in the accounts through closing entries. In the following sections, we will first review closing entries. We will then illustrate closing entries when profit and loss is shared equally. This is followed by more complex profit and loss ratios and the related closing entries.

Closing Entries

As in a proprietorship, there are four entries to prepare closing entries for a partnership:

1. To close revenue accounts: Debit each revenue account for its balance and credit Income Summary for total revenues.
2. To close expense accounts: Debit Income Summary for total expenses and credit each expense account for its balance.
3. To close Income Summary: Debit Income Summary for its balance (which should equal the profit amount) and credit each partner's capital account for his or her share of profit. Conversely, credit Income Summary and debit each partner's capital account for his or her share of a loss.
4. To close drawings: Debit each partner's capital account for the balance in that partner's drawings account, and credit each partner's drawings account for the same amount.

The first two entries are the same as in a proprietorship, as shown in Chapter 4, and are not shown in this chapter. The last two entries are different from those closing entries in a proprietorship because (1) it is necessary to divide profit (or loss) among the partners, and (2) there are two or more owners' capital and drawings accounts.

To illustrate the last two closing entries, we will assume that Interactive Software has a profit of $32,000 for the year and that the partners, M. Gan and K. Sin, share profit and loss equally. Recall that drawings for the year were $8,000 for Gan and $6,000 for Sin. The closing entries on December 31 are as follows:

A	=	L	+	OE			
				−32,000			
				+16,000			
				+16,000			

Cash flows: no effect

Dec. 31	Income Summary		32,000	
	M. Gan, Capital ($32,000 × 50%)			16,000
	K. Sin, Capital ($32,000 × 50%)			16,000
	To close profit to capital accounts.			

A	=	L	+	OE
				−8,000
				−6,000
				+8,000
				+6,000

Cash flows: no effect

31	M. Gan, Capital		8,000	
	K. Sin, Capital		6,000	
	M. Gan, Drawings			8,000
	K. Sin, Drawings			6,000
	To close drawings accounts to capital accounts.			

Recall from the previous section that both Gan and Sin had made investments in the partnership of $12,000 at the beginning of the year. After posting the closing entries, the capital and drawing accounts will appear as shown below:

M. Gan, Capital						**K. Sin, Capital**				
Dec. 31	Clos.	8,000	Jan. 2		12,000	Dec. 31	Clos.	6,000	Jan. 2	12,000
			Dec. 31	Clos.	16,000				Dec. 31 Clos.	16,000
			Dec. 31	Bal.	20,000				Dec. 31 Bal.	22,000

M. Gan, Drawings						**K. Sin, Drawings**				
Dec. 31		8,000	Dec. 31	Clos.	8,000	Dec. 31		6,000	Dec. 31 Clos.	6,000
Dec. 31	Bal.	0				Dec. 31	Bal.	0		

As in a proprietorship, the partners' capital accounts are permanent accounts, and their drawings accounts are temporary accounts.

Profit and Loss Ratios

As Peter Harris noted in our feature story, there are many ways of allocating partnership profits. The partners may share profit and loss equally, or the partnership agreement may specify a more complex basis for sharing profit or loss. The following are typical profit and loss ratios:

1. A fixed ratio, expressed as a proportion (2:1), a percentage (67% and 33%), or a fraction ($\frac{2}{3}$ and $\frac{1}{3}$)
2. A ratio based either on capital balances at the beginning or end of the year, or on average capital balances during the year
3. Salary allowances to partners and the remainder in a fixed ratio
4. Interest allowances on partners' capital balances and the remainder in a fixed ratio
5. Salary allowances to partners, interest allowances on partners' capital balances, and the remainder in a fixed ratio

In each case, the goal is to share profit or loss in a way that fairly reflects each partner's capital investment and service to the partnership.

A fixed ratio is easy to use, and it may be a fair basis in some circumstances. Assume, for example, that Hughes and Samfiru are partners. Each contributes the same amount of capital, but Hughes expects to work full-time in the partnership, while Samfiru expects to work only half-time. Accordingly, the partners agree to a fixed ratio of two-thirds to Hughes and one-third to Samfiru.

A ratio that is based on capital balances may be the right choice when the funds invested in the partnership are the critical factor. Capital balances may also be fair when a manager is hired to run the business and the partners do not plan to take an active role in daily operations.

The three remaining kinds of profit and loss ratios (items 3, 4, and 5 in the list above) recognize specific differences among the partners. These ratios give salary allowances for time worked and interest allowances for capital invested. Any remaining profit or loss is divided using a fixed ratio.

Salary allowances to partners and interest allowances on partners' capital balances are not expenses of the partnership. They are also **not** distributions of cash—partners' drawings are the distributions of cash or other assets. Salary and interest allowances are used only in the calculations that divide profit or loss among partners. In a partnership, as with other companies, salary expense is the cost of services performed by employees. Likewise, interest expense is the cost of borrowing from creditors. As owners, **partners are neither employees nor creditors.**

The only relationship between salary allowances and cash withdrawals is that under some partnership agreements, partners are allowed to make monthly cash withdrawals based on their salary allowance. But in such cases, as with all withdrawals, the withdrawals are debited to each partner's drawings account, not to salary expense.

Salaries, Interest, and Remainder in a Fixed Ratio

In three of the profit- and loss-sharing ratios, salary and/or interest allowances must be allocated before the remainder of the profit is divided according to a fixed ratio. This is true even if the salary and/or interest allowances are more than profit. It is also true even if the partnership has suffered a loss for the year. The same basic method of dividing (or allocating) profit or loss is used if there is only a salary allowance, or if there is only an interest allowance, or if both are used. In the illustration that follows, we will use a profit and loss ratio that includes both salary and interest allowances before allocating the remainder (see item 5 from the list of ratios above).

Assume that Sylvie King and Ray Lee are partners in the Kingslee Company. The partnership agreement specifies (1) salary allowances of $8,400 for King and $6,000 for Lee, (2) interest allowances of 5% on capital balances at the beginning of the year, and (3) the remainder to be allocated equally. Capital balances on January 1, 2014, were King $28,000 and Lee $24,000. In 2014, partnership profit is $22,000. The division of profit for the year is shown in Illustration 12-2.

Helpful hint It is often easier to work with fractions or percentages than proportions when allocating profit or loss. When converting to a fraction, determine the denominator for the fractions by adding the proportions, then use the appropriate proportion to determine each partner's fraction. For example, (2:1) converts to $\frac{2}{3}$ and $\frac{1}{3}$; (3:5) converts to 3/8 and 5/8; and for three partners using (3:2:1), these proportions convert to $\frac{3}{6}$, $\frac{2}{6}$, and $\frac{1}{6}$.

Helpful hint The total of the amounts allocated to each partner must equal the profit or loss.

▶ILLUSTRATION 12-2
Division of profit when
profit exceeds allowances

KINGSLEE COMPANY
Division of Profit
Year Ended December 31, 2014

	S. King	R. Lee	Total
Profit			$22,000
Salary allowance			
S. King	$ 8,400		
R. Lee		$6,000	
Total			14,400
Profit remaining for allocation			7,600
Interest allowance			
S. King ($28,000 × 5%)	1,400		
R. Lee ($24,000 × 5%)		1,200	
Total			2,600
Profit remaining for allocation			5,000
Fixed ratio (*remainder shared equally*)			
S. King ($5,000 × 50%)	2,500		
R. Lee ($5,000 × 50%)		2,500	
Total			5,000
Profit remaining for allocation			0
Profit allocated to the partners	$12,300	$9,700	$22,000

The entry to record the division of profit is:

A = L + OE
−22,000
+12,300
+9,700

Cash flows: no effect

Dec. 31	Income Summary		22,000	
	S. King, Capital			12,300
	R. Lee, Capital			9,700
	To transfer profit to partners' capital accounts.			

Let's now look at a situation where the salary and interest allowances are greater than profit. Assume that Kingslee Company reports profit of $14,000. In this case, the salary and interest allowances create a deficiency of $3,000 ($14,000 − $14,400 − $2,600). This deficiency is divided equally among the partners as in Illustration 12-3.

▶ILLUSTRATION 12-3
Division of profit when
allowances exceed profit

KINGSLEE COMPANY
Division of Profit
Year Ended December 31, 2014

	S. King	R. Lee	Total
Profit			$14,000
Salary allowance			
S. King	$8,400		
R. Lee		$6,000	
Total			14,400
Profit (deficiency) remaining for allocation			(400)
Interest allowance			
S. King ($28,000 × 5%)	1,400		
R. Lee ($24,000 × 5%)		1,200	
Total			2,600
Profit (deficiency) remaining for allocation			(3,000)

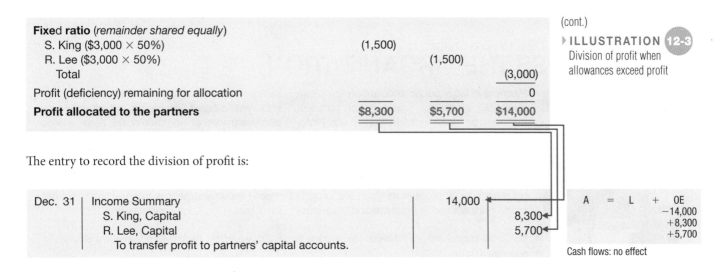

(cont.)

Fixed ratio (*remainder shared equally*)		
S. King ($3,000 × 50%)	(1,500)	
R. Lee ($3,000 × 50%)		(1,500)
Total		(3,000)
Profit (deficiency) remaining for allocation		0
Profit allocated to the partners	$8,300	$5,700	$14,000

▶**ILLUSTRATION 12-3**
Division of profit when allowances exceed profit

The entry to record the division of profit is:

Dec. 31	Income Summary	14,000	
	S. King, Capital		8,300
	R. Lee, Capital		5,700
	To transfer profit to partners' capital accounts.		

A = L + OE
−14,000
+8,300
+5,700

Cash flows: no effect

Let's now look at a situation where there is a loss. Assume that Kingslee Company reports a loss of $18,000. The salary and interest allowances are still allocated first. After the salary and interest allowances, there is a deficiency of $35,000 ($18,000 + $14,400 + $2,600). The deficiency is then divided equally among the partners as in Illustration 12-4.

▶**ILLUSTRATION 12-4**
Division of loss

	S. King	R. Lee	Total
KINGSLEE COMPANY			
Division of Loss			
Year Ended December 31, 2014			
Loss			$(18,000)
Salary allowance			
S. King	$ 8,400		
R. Lee		$6,000	
Total			14,400
Deficiency remaining for allocation			(32,400)
Interest allowance			
S. King ($28,000 × 5%)	1,400		
R. Lee ($24,000 × 5%)		1,200	
Total			2,600
Deficiency remaining for allocation			(35,000)
Fixed ratio (*remainder shared equally*)			
S. King ($35,000 × 50%)	(17,500)		
R. Lee ($35,000 × 50%)		(17,500)	
Total			(35,000)
Loss remaining for allocation			0
Loss allocated to the partners	$(7,700)	$(10,300)	$(18,000)

The salary and interest allowances are calculated first, as in the previous examples, whether the partnership reports a profit or a loss. Any remaining excess or deficiency is then allocated to the partners.

The journal entry to record the division of the loss would be as follows:

Dec. 31	S. King, Capital	7,700	
	R. Lee, Capital	10,300	
	Income Summary		18,000
	To transfer loss to partners' capital accounts.		

A = L + OE
−7,700
−10,300
+18,000

Cash flows: no effect

ACCOUNTING IN ACTION
ACROSS THE ORGANIZATION

Partners in large public accounting firms can make big incomes. A few senior partners may earn as much as $1 million a year. However, the average earnings of partners are more likely to be in the $300,000 range. The compensation of partners in most large partnerships is similar to the compensation of a proprietor in a proprietorship. Like proprietors, partners are not guaranteed an annual salary—compensation depends entirely on each year's operating results, which could be positive (profit) or negative (loss). Also, a large investment is required of each partner. This capital is at risk for the partner's entire career—often 25 to 30 years—and there is no rate of return on it. Upon leaving, the partner is simply repaid the investment without any adjustment for inflation or increase in value.

Source: QRI International, "CA Profession Compensation Survey 2011—Summary Report," Canadian Institute of Chartered Accountants, October 22, 2011.

How is the profit earned by a partner in an accounting partnership different from the earnings of a staff accountant in the same partnership?

 BEFORE YOU GO ON...

Do It

LeMay Company reports profit of $72,000 for the year ended May 31, 2014. The partnership agreement specifies (1) salary allowances of $30,000 for L. Leblanc and $24,000 for R. May, (2) an interest allowance of 4% based on average capital account balances, and (3) sharing any remainder on a 60:40 basis (60% to Leblanc, 40% to May). Average capital account balances for the year were $40,000 for Leblanc and $30,000 for May. (a) Prepare a schedule dividing the profit between the two partners. (b) Prepare the closing entry for profit.

Solution

(a)

		L. Leblanc	R. May	Total
			LEMAY COMPANY Division of Profit Year ended May 31, 2014	
Profit				$72,000
Salary allowance				
L. Leblanc		$30,000		
R. May			$24,000	
Total				54,000
Profit remaining for allocation				18,000
Interest allowance				
L. Leblanc ($40,000 × 4%)		1,600		
R. May ($30,000 × 4%)			1,200	
Total				2,800
Profit remaining for allocation				15,200
Fixed ratio (*remainder shared 60:40*)				
L. Leblanc (60% × $15,200)		9,120		
R. May (40% × $15,200)			6,080	
Total				15,200
Profit remaining for allocation				0
Profit allocated to the partners		$40,720	$31,280	$72,000

Action Plan

- First allocate the salary allowances and the interest allowances.
- Then apply the partners' fixed ratios to divide the remaining profit or the deficiency.
- In the closing entry, distribute profit or loss among the partners' capital accounts according to the profit and loss ratio.

(b)

May 31	Income Summary		72,000	
	L. Leblanc, Capital			40,720
	R. May, Capital			31,280
	To close profit to partners' capital accounts.			

Related exercise material: BE12–4, BE12–5, BE12–6, BE12–7, BE12–8, E12–3, and E12–4.

THE NAVIGATOR

PARTNERSHIP FINANCIAL STATEMENTS

The financial statements of a partnership are very similar to those of a proprietorship. The differences are due to the additional owners involved in a partnership.

The income statement for a partnership is identical to the income statement for a proprietorship. The division of the partnership profit or loss is not an additional financial statement. It is simply a schedule that shows how the profit or loss was allocated to the partners. It is often disclosed as a separate schedule or in a note to the statement.

The statement of equity for a partnership is called the **statement of partners' equity**. Its function is to explain the changes in each partner's capital account and in total partnership capital during the year. As in a proprietorship, changes in capital may result from three causes: additional investments by owners, drawings, and each partner's share of the profit or loss.

The statement of partners' equity for Kingslee Company is shown in Illustration 12-5. It is based on the division of $22,000 of profit in Illustration 12-2. The statement includes assumed data for the investments and drawings.

» **STUDY OBJECTIVE 4**

Prepare partnership financial statements.

▶ **ILLUSTRATION 12-5**
Statement of partners' equity

KINGSLEE COMPANY
Statement of Partners' Equity
Year Ended December 31, 2014

	S. King	R. Lee	Total
Capital, January 1	$28,000	$24,000	$52,000
Add: Investments	2,000	0	2,000
Profit	12,300	9,700	22,000
	42,300	33,700	76,000
Less: Drawings	7,000	5,000	12,000
Capital, December 31	$35,300	$28,700	$64,000

The statement of partners' equity is prepared from the income statement and the partners' capital and drawings accounts.

The balance sheet for a partnership is the same as for a proprietorship, except for the equity section. In a proprietorship, the equity section of the balance sheet is called owner's equity. A one-line capital account is reported for the owner. In a partnership, the capital balances of each partner are shown in the balance sheet, in a section called partners' equity. The partners' equity section in Kingslee Company's balance sheet appears in Illustration 12-6.

▶ **ILLUSTRATION 12-6**
Partners' equity section of a partnership balance sheet

KINGSLEE COMPANY
Balance Sheet (partial)
December 31, 2014

Liabilities and Partners' Equity		
Total liabilities (assumed amount)		$115,000
Partners' equity		
S. King, Capital	$35,300	
R. Lee, Capital	28,700	64,000
Total liabilities and partners' equity		$179,000

It is impractical for large partnerships to report each partner's equity separately. For reporting purposes, these amounts are usually aggregated in the balance sheet.

 BEFORE YOU GO ON...

Do It

The capital accounts of Mindy Dawson and Rania Alam, partners in the Best Skate Company, had balances of $80,000 and $95,000, respectively, on January 1, 2014. During the year, Dawson invested an additional $15,000 and each partner withdrew $50,000. Profit for the year was $150,000 and was shared equally between the partners. Prepare a statement of partners' equity for the year ended December 31, 2014.

Solution

Action Plan

- Each partner's capital account is increased by the partner's investments and profit, and decreased by the partner's drawings.
- Allocate profit between the partners according to their profit-sharing agreement.

THE **NAVIGATOR**

BEST SKATE COMPANY Statement of Partners' Equity Year Ended December 31, 2014			
	M. Dawson	R. Alam	Total
Capital, January 1	$ 80,000	$ 95,000	$175,000
Add: Investments	15,000	0	15,000
Profit	75,000	75,000	150,000
	170,000	170,000	340,000
Less: Drawings	50,000	50,000	100,000
Capital, December 31	$120,000	$120,000	$240,000

Related exercise material: BE12–9, E12–5, and E12–6.

Admission and Withdrawal of Partners

» **STUDY OBJECTIVE 5**

Account for the admission of a partner.

We have seen how the basic accounting for a partnership works. We now look at how to account for something that happens often in partnerships: the addition or withdrawal of a partner.

ADMISSION OF A PARTNER

The admission of a new partner legally dissolves the existing partnership and begins a new one. From an economic standpoint, the admission of a new partner (or partners) may have only a minor impact on the continuity of the business. For example, in large public accounting or law firms, partners are admitted without any change in operating policies. To recognize the economic effects, it is only necessary to open a capital account for each new partner. In most cases, the accounting records of the old partnership will continue to be used by the new partnership.

A new partner may be admitted by either (1) purchasing the interest of an existing partner, or (2) investing assets in the partnership. The purchase of a partner's interest involves only a transfer of capital among the partners who are part of the transaction: the total capital of the partnership is not affected. The investment of assets in the partnership increases both the partnership's net assets (total assets less total liabilities) and its total capital.

Purchase of a Partner's Interest

Helpful hint In a purchase of an interest, the partnership is not a participant in the transaction. No cash is contributed to the partnership.

The **admission by purchase of a partner's interest** is a personal transaction between one or more existing partners and the new partner. Each party acts as an individual, separate from the partnership entity. The price paid is negotiated by the individuals involved. It may be equal to or different from the partner's capital in the partnership's accounting records. The purchase price passes directly from the new partner to the partner who is giving up part or all of his or her ownership claims. Any money or other consideration that is exchanged is the personal property of the participants and not the property of the partnership.

Accounting for the purchase of an interest is straightforward. In the partnership, only the transfer of a partner's capital is recorded. The old partner's capital account is debited for the ownership claims that have been given up. The new partner's capital account is credited with the ownership interest purchased. Total assets, total liabilities, and total capital remain unchanged, as do all individual asset and liability accounts.

To illustrate, assume that on July 1, L. Carson agrees to pay $8,000 each to two partners, D. Arbour and D. Baker, for one-third of their interest in the ABC partnership. At the time of Carson's admission, each partner has a $30,000 capital balance. Both partners, therefore, give up $10,000 ($\frac{1}{3}$ × $30,000) of their capital. The entry to record the admission of Carson is as follows:

July 1	D. Arbour, Capital	10,000	
	D. Baker, Capital	10,000	
	L. Carson, Capital		20,000
	To record admission of Carson by purchase.		

A = L + OE
−10,000
−10,000
+20,000

Cash flows: no effect

Note that the cash paid by Carson is not recorded by the partnership because it is paid personally to Arbour and Baker. The entry above would be exactly the same regardless of the amount paid by Carson for the one-third interest. If Carson pays $12,000 each to Arbour and Baker for one-third of their interest in the partnership, the above entry is still made.

The effect of this transaction on the partners' capital accounts is as follows:

D. Arbour, Capital		**D. Baker, Capital**		**L. Carson, Capital**	
	Bal. 30,000		Bal. 30,000		
July 1 10,000		July 1 10,000			July 1 20,000
	Bal. 20,000		Bal. 20,000		Bal. 20,000

Each partner now has a $20,000 ending capital balance and total partnership capital is $60,000 ($20,000 + $20,000 + $20,000). Net assets (assets − liabilities) and total partners' capital remain unchanged. Arbour and Baker continue as partners in the firm, but the capital interest of each has been reduced from $30,000 to $20,000.

Investment of Assets in a Partnership

The admission of a partner by an investment of assets in the partnership is a transaction between the new partner and the partnership. It is sometimes referred to simply as **admission by investment**. This transaction increases both the net assets and the total capital of the partnership. Frequently a new partner will contribute cash, but a professional partnership, such as Harris & Chong in the feature story, may be more interested in having a new partner to contribute their clients to the partnership instead of cash.

To illustrate when cash is invested, assume that instead of purchasing a partner's interest as illustrated in the previous section, Carson invests $30,000 in cash in the ABC partnership for a one-third capital interest. In this case, the entry is:

July 1	Cash	30,000	
	L. Carson, Capital		30,000
	To record admission of Carson by investment.		

A = L + OE
+30,000   +30,000

↑Cash flows: +30,000

Both net assets and total capital increase by $30,000. The effect of this transaction on the partners' capital accounts is as follows:

D. Arbour, Capital		**D. Baker, Capital**		**L. Carson, Capital**	
	Bal. 30,000		Bal. 30,000		
					July 1 30,000
	Bal. 30,000		Bal. 30,000		Bal. 30,000

Remember that Carson's one-third capital interest might not result in a one-third profit and loss ratio. Carson's profit and loss ratio should be specified in the new partnership agreement. It may or may not be equal to the one-third capital interest.

The before and after effects of an admission by purchase of an interest or by investment are shown in the following comparison of the net assets and capital balances:

	Before Admission of Partner	After Admission of Partner	
		Purchase of a Partner's Interest	Investment of Assets in the Partnership
Net assets	$60,000	$60,000	$90,000
Partners' capital			
D. Arbour	$30,000	$20,000	$30,000
D. Baker	30,000	20,000	30,000
L. Carson		20,000	30,000
Total partners' equity	$60,000	$60,000	$90,000

When an interest is purchased, the partnership's total net assets and total capital do not change. In contrast, when a partner is admitted by investment, both the total net assets and the total capital increase by the amount of cash invested by the new partner.

In an admission by investment, complications occur when the new partner's investment is not the same as the equity in the partnership acquired by the new partner. When those amounts are not the same, the difference is considered a bonus to either (1) the old (existing) partners or (2) the new partner.

Bonus to Old Partners. The existing partners may want a bonus when admitting a new partner. In an established firm, existing partners may insist on a bonus as compensation for the work they have put into the partnership over the years. The fair value of the partnership's assets may exceed their carrying value. If a partnership has been profitable, goodwill may exist. Recall that internally generated goodwill is not recorded as part of the company's net assets. In such cases, the new partner is usually willing to pay a bonus to become a partner. The bonus is allocated to the existing partners based on their profit and loss ratios before the admission of the new partner.

To illustrate, assume that on November 1, the Peart-Huang partnership, owned by Sam Peart and Hal Huang, has total partnership capital of $120,000. Peart has a capital balance of $72,000; Huang has a capital balance of $48,000. The two partners share profits and losses as follows: Peart 60% and Huang 40%.

Peart and Huang agree to admit Lana Trent to a 25% ownership (capital) interest in exchange for a cash investment of $80,000. Trent's capital balance on the new partnership books of $50,000 and the bonus to the old partners are calculated as follows:

Partnership capital before Trent is admitted ($72,000 + $48,000)	$120,000
Trent's investment in the partnership	80,000
Partnership capital after Trent is admitted	$200,000
Trent's capital in the partnership ($200,000 × 25%)	$ 50,000
Bonus to the old partners ($80,000 − $50,000)	$ 30,000
The bonus is allocated to the old partners based on their profit and loss ratios:	
To Peart ($30,000 × 60%)	$ 18,000
To Huang ($30,000 × 40%)	12,000
Total bonus allocated to old partners	$ 30,000

The entry to record the admission of Trent on November 1 is:

A	=	L	+	OE
+80,000				+18,000
				+12,000
				+50,000

↑ Cash flows: +80,000

Nov. 1	Cash	80,000	
	S. Peart, Capital		18,000
	H. Huang, Capital		12,000
	L. Trent, Capital		50,000
	To record admission of Trent and bonuses to old partners.		

The before and after effects of the admission of a partner who pays a bonus to the old partners are shown in the following comparison of the net assets and capital balances:

| | **Bonus to Old Partners** | |
	Before Admission of Partner	**After Admission of Partner**
Net assets	$120,000	$200,000
Partners' capital		
S. Peart	$ 72,000	$ 90,000
H. Huang	48,000	60,000
L. Trent		50,000
Total capital	$120,000	$200,000

In summary, Lana Trent invests $80,000 cash in the partnership for a 25% capital interest of $50,000. The difference of $30,000 between these two amounts is a bonus that is allocated to the old partners based on their profit- and loss-sharing ratio as follows: $18,000 to Sam Peart and $12,000 to Hal Huang.

Bonus to New Partner. If a new partner has specific resources or special attributes that the partnership wants, the partnership may be willing to give a bonus to the new partner. For example, the new partner may be able to supply cash that is urgently needed for expansion or to meet maturing debts. Or the new partner may be a recognized expert or authority in a relevant field. Or the new partner may be a celebrity whose name will draw more customers to the business.

A bonus to a new partner decreases the capital balances of the old partners. The amount of the decrease for each partner is based on the profit and loss ratios before the admission of the new partner.

To illustrate, assume instead that on November 1, the Peart-Huang partnership admits Lana Trent to a 25% ownership (capital) interest in exchange for a cash investment of $20,000 (instead of $80,000 as in the previous illustration). Trent's capital balance on the new partnership books of $35,000 and allocation of the bonus from the old partners are calculated as follows:

Partnership capital before Trent is admitted ($72,000 + $48,000)	$120,000
Trent's investment in the partnership	20,000
Partnership capital after Trent is admitted	$140,000
Trent's capital in the partnership ($140,000 × 25%)	$ 35,000
Bonus to the new partner ($35,000 − $20,000)	$ 15,000

The bonus from the old partners is based on their profit and loss ratios:

From Peart ($15,000 × 60%)	$ 9,000
From Huang ($15,000 × 40%)	6,000
Total bonus allocated to the new partner	$ 15,000

The entry to record the admission of Trent on November 1 in this case is:

Nov. 1	Cash	20,000	
	S. Peart, Capital	9,000	
	H. Huang, Capital	6,000	
	L. Trent, Capital		35,000
	To record Trent's admission and bonus to new partner.		

A = L + OE
+20,000   −9,000
             −6,000
            +35,000

↑ Cash flows: +20,000

The before and after effects of the admission of a partner who is paid a bonus by the old partners are shown in the following comparison of the net assets and capital balances:

| | Bonus to New Partner | |
	Before Admission of Partner	After Admission of Partner
Net assets	$120,000	$140,000
Partners' capital		
S. Peart	$ 72,000	$ 63,000
H. Huang	48,000	42,000
L. Trent		35,000
Total capital	$120,000	$140,000

In summary, $20,000 cash was invested in the partnership by Lana Trent for a $35,000 capital credit, and the $15,000 bonus was allocated from the partners' capital accounts as follows: $9,000 from Sam Peart and $6,000 from Hal Huang.

Action Plan

- Recognize that the admission by purchase of a partnership interest is a personal transaction between one or more existing partners and the new partner.
- In an admission by purchase, no cash is received by the partnership and the capital credit for the new partner is not based on the cash paid.
- Recognize that the admission by investment of partnership assets is a transaction between the new partner and the partnership.
- In an admission by investment, determine any bonus to old or new partners by comparing the total capital of the new partnership with the new partner's capital credit. Allocate the bonus based on the old partners' profit and loss ratios.

BEFORE YOU GO ON...

Do It

I. Shandler and M. Rossetti have a partnership in which they share profit and loss equally. There is a $40,000 balance in each capital account. Record the journal entries on September 1 for each of the independent events below:

(a) Shandler and Rossetti agree to admit A. Rachel as a new one-fourth interest partner. Rachel pays $16,000 in cash directly to each partner.

(b) Shandler and Rossetti agree to admit A. Rachel as a new one-fourth interest partner. Rachel contributes $32,000 to the partnership.

Solution

(a) Sept. 1	I. Shandler, Capital	10,000	
	M. Rossetti, Capital	10,000	
	A. Rachel, Capital		20,000[1]
	To record admission of Rachel by purchase.		

(b) Sept. 1	Cash	32,000	
	I. Shandler, Capital ($4,000[2] × 50%)		2,000
	M. Rossetti, Capital ($4,000[2] × 50%)		2,000
	A. Rachel, Capital		28,000
	To record admission of Rachel by investment.		

[1]Total capital of partnership: $40,000 + $40,000 = $80,000
 Rachel's capital credit: $80,000 × ¼ = $20,000
[2]Total capital of partnership: $40,000 + $40,000 + $32,000 = $112,000
 Rachel's capital credit: $112,000 × ¼ = $28,000
 Bonus to old partners: $32,000 − $28,000 = $4,000 (shared equally)

Related exercise material: BE12–10, BE12–11, E12–7, and E12–8.

THE NAVIGATOR

WITHDRAWAL OF A PARTNER

STUDY OBJECTIVE 6

Account for the withdrawal of a partner.

Let's now look at the opposite situation, when a partner withdraws. A partner may withdraw from a partnership voluntarily, by selling his or her equity in the firm. He or she may withdraw involuntarily, by reaching mandatory retirement age, by expulsion, or by dying. The withdrawal of a partner, like the admission of a partner, legally dissolves the partnership. However, it is customary to record only the economic effects of the partner's withdrawal, while the partnership reorganizes itself and continues to operate.

As indicated earlier, the partnership agreement should specify the terms of withdrawal. Ms. Chong believes that the most crucial part of a partnership agreement is how to divide things up when a partner leaves. On the other hand, the withdrawal of a partner can also occur outside of the terms of the partnership agreement. For example, when the remaining partners are anxious to remove an uncontrollable partner from the firm, they may agree to pay the departing partner much more than was specified in the original partnership agreement.

The withdrawal of a partner may be done by a payment from partners' personal assets or a payment from partnership assets. Payment from personal assets affects only the remaining partners' capital accounts, not total capital. Payment from partnership assets decreases the total net assets and total capital of the partnership.

After a partner has withdrawn, profit and loss ratios for the remaining partners must be reviewed and specified again. If a new profit and loss ratio is not indicated in the partnership agreement, the remaining partners are assumed to share profit and losses equally.

Payment from Partners' Personal Assets

A **withdrawal by payment from partners' personal assets** is a personal transaction between the partners. It is the direct opposite of admitting a new partner who purchases a partner's interest. Payment to the departing partner is made directly from the remaining partners' personal assets. Partnership assets are not involved in any way, and total capital does not change. The effect on the partnership is limited to a transfer of the partners' capital balances.

To illustrate, assume that Javad Dargahi, Dong Kim, and Roberta Viau have capital balances of $25,000, $15,000, and $10,000, respectively. The partnership equity totals $50,000 ($25,000 + $15,000 + $10,000). Dargahi and Kim agree to buy out Viau's interest. Each agrees to personally pay Viau $8,000 in exchange for one-half of Viau's total interest of $10,000 on February 1. The entry to record the withdrawal is as follows:

Feb. 1	R. Viau, Capital	10,000	
	J. Dargahi, Capital		5,000
	D. Kim, Capital		5,000
	To record purchase of Viau's interest by other partners.		

A	=	L	+	OE
				−10,000
				+5,000
				+5,000

Cash flows: no effect

The effect of this transaction on the partners' capital accounts is as follows:

J. Dargahi, Capital		D. Kim, Capital		R. Viau, Capital	
	Bal. 25,000		Bal. 15,000		Bal. 10,000
	5,000		5,000	10,000	
	Bal. 30,000		Bal. 20,000		Bal. 0

Net assets of $50,000 remain the same and total partnership capital is also unchanged at $50,000 ($30,000 + $20,000 + $0). All that has happened is a reallocation of capital amounts. Note also that the $16,000 paid to Roberta Viau personally is not recorded because this is not partnership cash. Viau's capital is debited for only $10,000, not the $16,000 cash that she received. Similarly, both Javad Dargahi and Dong Kim credit their capital accounts for only $5,000, not the $8,000 they each paid. This is because we are showing the accounting for the partnership, not the partners' personal accounting.

Payment from Partnership Assets

A **withdrawal by payment from partnership assets** is a transaction that involves the partnership. Both partnership net assets and total capital are decreased. Using partnership assets to pay for a withdrawing partner's interest is the reverse of admitting a partner through the investment of assets in the partnership.

In accounting for a withdrawal by payment from partnership assets, asset revaluations should not be recorded. Recording a revaluation to the fair value of the assets at the time of a partner's withdrawal violates the cost principle, which requires assets to be stated at original cost. It would also ignore the going concern assumption, which assumes that the entity will continue indefinitely. The terms of the partnership contract should not dictate the accounting for this event.

To illustrate, assume that instead of Roberta Viau's interest being purchased personally by the other partners, as illustrated in the previous section, her interest is bought out by the partnership. In this case, the entry is:

A	=	L	+	OE
−10,000				−10,000

↓ Cash flows: −10,000

Feb. 1	R. Viau, Capital	10,000	
	Cash		10,000
	To record purchase of Viau's interest by partnership.		

Both net assets and total partnership capital decrease by $10,000. The effect of this transaction on the partners' capital accounts is as follows:

J. Dargahi, Capital			D. Kim, Capital			R. Viau, Capital		
	Bal.	25,000		Bal.	15,000		Bal.	10,000
						10,000		
	Bal.	25,000		Bal.	15,000		Bal.	0

The before and after effects of the withdrawal of a partner when payment is made from personal assets or from partnership assets are shown in the following comparison of the net assets and capital balances:

		After Withdrawal of Partner	
	Before Withdrawal of Partner	Payment from Partners' Personal Assets	Payment from Partnership Assets
Net assets	$50,000	$50,000	$40,000
Partners' capital			
J. Dargahi	$25,000	$30,000	$25,000
D. Kim	15,000	20,000	15,000
R. Viau	10,000	0	0
Total capital	$50,000	$50,000	$40,000

When payment is made from partners' personal assets, the partnership's total net assets and total capital do not change. In contrast, when payment is made from the partnership assets, both the total net assets and the total capital decrease.

In a payment from partnership assets, it is rare for the partnership to pay the partner the exact amount of his or her capital account balance, as was assumed above. When the amounts are not the same, the difference between the amount paid and the withdrawing partner's capital balance is considered a bonus to either (1) the departing partner, or (2) the remaining partners.

Bonus to Departing Partner. A bonus may be paid to a departing partner in any of these situations:

1. The fair value of partnership assets is more than their carrying amount.
2. There is unrecorded goodwill resulting from the partnership's superior earnings record.
3. The remaining partners are anxious to remove the partner from the firm.

The bonus is deducted from the remaining partners' capital balances based on their profit and loss ratios at the time of the withdrawal.

To illustrate a bonus to a departing partner, assume the following capital balances in the RST Partnership: Fred Roman, $50,000; Dee Sand, $30,000; and Betty Terk, $20,000. The partners share profit in the ratio of 3:2:1, respectively. Terk retires from the partnership on March 1 and receives a cash payment of $25,000 from the firm. The bonus to the departing partner and the allocation of the bonus to the remaining partners is calculated as follows:

Terk's capital balance in the partnership before departing	$20,000
Cash paid from partnership to Terk	25,000
Bonus paid to the departing partner—Terk	$ 5,000
Allocation of bonus from the remaining partners:	
From Roman ($5,000 × $^3/_5$)	$ 3,000
From Sand ($5,000 × $^2/_5$)	2,000
Total bonus to the departing partner—Terk	$ 5,000

The entry to record the withdrawal of Terk on March 1 is as follows:

Mar. 1	B. Terk, Capital	20,000	
	F. Roman, Capital	3,000	
	D. Sand, Capital	2,000	
	Cash		25,000
	To record withdrawal of, and bonus to, Terk.		

A   =   L   +   OE
−25,000   −20,000
                   −3,000
                   −2,000

↓ Cash flows: −25,000

The before and after effects of the withdrawal of a partner when a bonus is paid to the departing partner are shown in the following comparison of the net assets and capital balances:

	Bonus to Departing Partner	
	Before Withdrawal of Partner	**After Withdrawal of Partner**
Net assets	$100,000	$75,000
Partners' capital		
F. Roman	$ 50,000	$47,000
D. Sand	30,000	28,000
B. Terk	20,000	0
Total capital	$100,000	$75,000

In summary, both net assets and capital decreased by $25,000 when $25,000 cash was paid by the partnership to Betty Terk to purchase her $20,000 equity interest. The $5,000 bonus was allocated from the remaining partners' capital accounts according to their profit and loss ratios. Fred Roman and Dee Sand, the remaining partners, will recover the bonus given to Terk as the undervalued assets are used or sold.

Bonus to Remaining Partners. The departing partner may give a bonus to the remaining partners in the following situations:

1. Recorded assets are overvalued.
2. The partnership has a poor earnings record.
3. The partner is anxious to leave the partnership.

In such cases, the cash paid to the departing partner will be less than the departing partner's capital balance. The bonus is allocated (credited) to the capital accounts of the remaining partners based on their profit and loss ratios.

To illustrate, assume, instead of the example above, that Terk is paid only $16,000 for her $20,000 equity when she withdraws from the partnership on March 1. The bonus to the remaining partners is calculated as follows:

Terk's capital balance in the partnership before departing	$20,000
Cash paid from partnership to Terk	16,000
Bonus to the remaining partners	$ 4,000
Allocation of bonus to the remaining partners:	
To Roman ($4,000 × ³/₅)	$ 2,400
To Sand ($4,000 × ²/₅)	1,600
Total bonus to the remaining partners	$ 4,000

The entry to record the withdrawal on March 1 follows:

```
A     =   L   +   OE
−16,000          −20,000
                 +2,400
                 +1,600

↓ Cash flows: −16,000
```

Mar. 1	B. Terk, Capital	20,000	
	F. Roman, Capital		2,400
	D. Sand, Capital		1,600
	Cash		16,000
	To record withdrawal of Terk and bonus to remaining partners.		

The effect of a partner's withdrawal, when there is a bonus to the remaining partners, is shown in the following comparison of the net assets and capital balances:

	Bonus to Remaining Partners	
	Before Withdrawal of Partner	**After Withdrawal of Partner**
Net assets	$100,000	$84,000
Partners' capital		
F. Roman	$ 50,000	$52,400
D. Sand	30,000	31,600
B. Terk	20,000	0
Total capital	$100,000	$84,000

In summary, both net assets and capital decreased by $16,000 when $16,000 cash was paid by the partnership to Betty Terk to purchase her $20,000 equity interest. The $4,000 bonus was allocated to the remaining partners' capital accounts according to their profit and loss ratios.

Death of a Partner

The death of a partner dissolves the partnership. But there is generally a provision in the partnership agreement for the surviving partners to continue operations. When a partner dies, the partner's equity at the date of death normally has to be determined. This is done by (1) calculating the profit or loss for the year to date, (2) closing the books, and (3) preparing the financial statements.

The death of the partner may be recorded by either of the two methods described earlier in the section for the withdrawal of a partner: (1) payment from the partners' personal assets or (2) payment from the partnership assets. That is, one or more of the surviving partners may agree to use his or her personal assets to purchase the deceased partner's equity. Or, partnership assets may be used to settle with the deceased partner's estate. To make it easier to pay from partnership assets, many partnerships take out life insurance policies on each partner. The partnership is named as the beneficiary. The proceeds from the insurance policy on the deceased partner are then used to settle with the estate.

Action Plan
- Recognize that the withdrawal by sale of a partnership interest is a personal transaction between one or more remaining partners and the withdrawing partner.
- Recognize that the withdrawal by payment of partnership assets is a transaction between the withdrawing partner and the partnership.
- In a withdrawal by payment of partnership assets, determine any bonus to the departing or remaining partners by comparing the amount paid with the amount of the withdrawing partner's capital balance. Allocate the bonus based on the remaining partners' profit and loss ratios.

BEFORE YOU GO ON...

Do It

S. Hosseinzadeh, M. Bélanger, and C. Laurin have a partnership in which they share profit and loss equally. There is a $40,000 balance in each capital account. Record the journal entries on March 1 for each of the independent events below:

(a) Laurin withdraws from the partnership. Hosseinzadeh and Bélanger each pay Laurin $25,000 out of their personal assets.

(b) Laurin withdraws from the partnership and is paid $30,000 of partnership cash.

Solution

(a) Mar. 1	C. Laurin, Capital	40,000	
	S. Hosseinzadeh, Capital ($40,000 × ½)		20,000
	M. Bélanger, Capital ($40,000 × ½)		20,000
	To record purchase of Laurin's interest.		
(b) Mar. 1	C. Laurin, Capital	40,000	
	Cash		30,000
	S. Hosseinzadeh, Capital ($10,000[1] × ½)		5,000
	M. Bélanger, Capital ($10,000[1] × ½)		5,000
	To record withdrawal of Laurin by payment of partnership assets and bonus to remaining partners.		

[1]Bonus: $30,000 − $40,000 = $(10,000)

Related exercise material: BE12–12, BE12–13, E12–9, and E12–10.

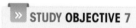

THE **NAVIGATOR**

Liquidation of a Partnership

The liquidation of a partnership ends the business. It involves selling the assets of the business, paying liabilities, and distributing any remaining assets to the partners. Liquidation may result from the sale of the business by mutual agreement of the partners or from bankruptcy. A **partnership liquidation** ends both the legal and the economic life of the entity.

» **STUDY OBJECTIVE 7**

Account for the liquidation of a partnership.

Before the liquidation process begins, the accounting cycle for the partnership must be completed for the final operating period. This includes preparing adjusting entries, a trial balance, financial statements, closing entries, and a post-closing trial balance. Only balance sheet accounts should be open when the liquidation process begins.

In liquidation, the sale of noncash assets for cash is called **realization**. Any difference between the carrying amount and the cash proceeds is called the gain or loss on realization. To liquidate a partnership, it is necessary to follow these steps:

1. Sell noncash assets for cash and recognize any gain or loss on realization.
2. Allocate any gain or loss on realization to the partners, based on their profit and loss ratios.
3. Pay partnership liabilities in cash.
4. Distribute the remaining cash to partners, based on their capital balances.

Each of the steps must be done in sequence, and creditors must be paid before partners receive any cash distributions.

It sometimes happens, when a partnership is liquidated, that all partners have credit balances in their capital accounts. This situation is called **no capital deficiency**. Alternatively, one or more of the partners' capital accounts may have a debit balance. This situation is called a **capital deficiency**.

To illustrate each of these situations, assume that Ace Company is liquidated on April 15, 2014, when its post-closing trial balance shows the assets, liabilities, and partners' equity accounts in Illustration 12-7. The profit and loss ratios of the partners are 3:2:1 for R. Aube, P. Chordia, and W. Elliott.

▶ILLUSTRATION  12-7
Account balances
before liquidation

ACE COMPANY Post-Closing Trial Balance April 15, 2014		
	Debit	**Credit**
Cash	$ 5,000	
Accounts receivable	33,000	
Equipment	35,000	
Accumulated depreciation—equipment		$ 8,000
Accounts payable		31,000
R. Aube, capital		15,000
P. Chordia, capital		17,800
W. Elliott, capital		1,200
Totals	$73,000	$73,000

NO CAPITAL DEFICIENCY

No capital deficiency means that all partners have credit balances in their capital accounts prior to the final distribution of cash. An example of the steps in the liquidation process with no capital deficiency follows:

1. Assume the noncash assets (accounts receivable and equipment) are sold on April 18 for $75,000. The carrying amount of these assets is $60,000 ($33,000 + $35,000 − $8,000). Thus, a gain of $15,000 is realized on the sale, and the following entry is made:

A = L + OE
+75,000   +15,000
+8,000
−33,000
−35,000

↑ Cash flows: +75,000

		(1)		
Apr. 18	Cash		75,000	
	Accumulated Depreciation—Equipment		8,000	
	Accounts Receivable			33,000
	Equipment			35,000
	Gain on Realization			15,000
	To record realization of noncash assets.			

2. The gain on realization of $15,000 is allocated to the partners based on their profit and loss ratios, which are 3:2:1 (or $\frac{3}{6}$, $\frac{2}{6}$, and $\frac{1}{6}$). The entry is:

A = L + OE
      −15,000
      +7,500
      +5,000
      +2,500

Cash flows: no effect

		(2)		
Apr. 18	Gain on Realization		15,000	
	R. Aube, Capital ($15,000 × $\frac{3}{6}$)			7,500
	P. Chordia, Capital ($15,000 × $\frac{2}{6}$)			5,000
	W. Elliott, Capital ($15,000 × $\frac{1}{6}$)			2,500
	To allocate gain to partners' capital accounts.			

3. Partnership liabilities consist of accounts payable, $31,000. Creditors are paid in full on April 23 by a cash payment of $31,000. The entry is:

A = L + OE
−31,000 −31,000

↓ Cash flows: −31,000

		(3)		
Apr. 23	Accounts Payable		31,000	
	Cash			31,000
	To record payment of partnership liabilities.			

Illustration 12-8 shows the account balances after the entries in the first three steps are posted. All of the accounts will have zero balances except for cash and the partners' capital accounts.

	Assets			= Liabilities	+ Partners' Equity		
Cash	Accounts Receivable	Equipment	Accum. Dep. Equipment	Accounts Payable	R. Aube, Capital	P. Chordia, Capital	W. Elliott, Capital
Account balances prior to liquidation: $ 5,000	$ 33,000	$ 35,000	$8,000	$31,000	$15,000	$17,800	$1,200
1. & 2. Sale of assets and share of gain +75,000	−33,000	−35,000	−8,000		+7,500	+5,000	+2,500
Balances 80,000	0	0	0	31,000	22,500	22,800	3,700
3. Payment of accounts payable −31,000				−31,000			
Balances 49,000	0	0	0	0	22,500	22,800	3,700
4. Distribution of cash to partners −49,000					−22,500	−22,800	−3,700
Final balances $ 0	$ 0	$ 0	$ 0	$ 0	$ 0	$ 0	$ 0

4. The remaining cash is distributed to the partners on April 25 based on their capital balances as shown in Illustration 12-8. The entry to record the distribution of cash on April 25 is:

Apr. 25	R. Aube, Capital	22,500	
	P. Chordia, Capital	22,800	
	W. Elliott, Capital	3,700	
	Cash		49,000
	To record distribution of cash to partners.		

▶ **ILLUSTRATION 12-8**
Partnership liquidation— no capital deficiency

A	=	L	+	OE
−49,000				−22,500
				−22,800
				−3,700

↓ Cash flows: −49,000

As shown in Illustration 12-8, after this entry is posted, all of the accounts have zero balances and the liquidation of the partnership is complete.

Two points to remember:

- Gains or losses on sale of assets are allocated to the partners based on the profit and loss ratio.
- **The final cash payment to the partners is based on the balances in the partners' capital accounts.**

CAPITAL DEFICIENCY

Capital deficiency means that at least one partner has a debit balance in his or her capital account before the final distribution of cash. This may be caused by recurring losses, excessive drawings, or losses from the realization during liquidation.

To illustrate, assume instead that Ace Company (see Illustration 12-7) is almost bankrupt. The partners decide to liquidate by having a going-out-of-business sale on April 18. Many of the accounts receivable cannot be collected, and the equipment is sold at auction at less than its fair value. Cash proceeds from the equipment sale and collections from customers total only $42,000. The loss on liquidation is $18,000 ($60,000 in carrying amount − $42,000 in proceeds). The steps in the liquidation process are as follows:

1. The entry for the realization of noncash assets is recorded on April 18:

	(1)		
Apr. 18	Cash	42,000	
	Accumulated Depreciation—Equipment	8,000	
	Loss on Realization	18,000	
	Accounts Receivable		33,000
	Equipment		35,000
	To record realization of noncash assets.		

A	=	L	+	OE
+42,000				−18,000
+8,000				
−33,000				
−35,000				

↑ Cash flows: +42,000

2. The loss on realization is allocated to the partners based on their profit and loss ratios of 3:2:1 and is recorded as follows:

A	=	L	+	OE
				−9,000
				−6,000
				−3,000
				+18,000

Cash flows: no effect

		(2)		
Apr. 18	R. Aube, Capital ($18,000 × 3/6)		9,000	
	P. Chordia, Capital ($18,000 × 2/6)		6,000	
	W. Elliott, Capital ($18,000 × 1/6)		3,000	
	Loss on Realization			18,000
	To allocate loss to partners' capital accounts.			

3. Partnership liabilities are paid on April 23 and recorded:

A	=	L	+	OE
−31,000		−31,000		

↓ Cash flows: −31,000

		(3)		
Apr. 23	Accounts Payable		31,000	
	Cash			31,000
	To record payment of partnership liabilities.			

After posting of the three entries, as shown in Illustration 12-9, there is $16,000 of cash remaining. Two of the partners' capital accounts have credit balances: R. Aube, Capital $6,000; and P. Chordia, Capital $11,800. The illustration shows W. Elliott's capital account as a negative number, which represents a debit balance or capital deficiency of $1,800.

▶**ILLUSTRATION 12-9**
Partnership liquidation—
capital deficiency

	Assets				= Liabilities	+ Partners' Equity		
	Cash	**Accounts Receivable**	**Equipment**	**Accum. Dep. Equipment**	**Accounts Payable**	**R. Aube, Capital**	**P. Chordia, Capital**	**W. Elliott, Capital**
Account balances prior to liquidation:	$ 5,000	$ 33,000	$ 35,000	$ 8,000	$31,000	$ 15,000	$17,800	$1,200
1. & 2. Sale of assets and share of loss	+42,000	−33,000	−35,000	−8,000		−9,000	−6,000	−3,000
Balances	47,000	0	0	0	31,000	6,000	11,800	−1,800
3. Payment of accounts payable	−31,000				−31,000			
Balances	16,000	0	0	0	0	6,000	11,800	−1,800

W. Elliott's capital deficiency of $1,800 means that he owes the partnership $1,800. R. Aube and P. Chordia have a legally enforceable claim for that amount against Elliott's personal assets. The final distribution of cash depends on how Elliott's deficiency is settled. Two alternatives for settling are presented next.

Payment of Deficiency

If the partner with the capital deficiency pays the amount owed to the partnership, the deficiency is eliminated. To illustrate, assume that W. Elliott pays $1,800 to the partnership on April 24. The entry to record this payment is as follows:

A	=	L	+	OE
+1,800				+1,800

↑ Cash flows: +1,800

		(4)		
Apr. 24	Cash		1,800	
	W. Elliott, Capital			1,800
	To record payment of capital deficiency by Elliott.			

As shown in Illustration 12-10, after posting this entry, the cash balance of $17,800 is now sufficient to pay the two remaining partners with credit balances in the capital accounts ($6,000 + $11,800).

▶ ILLUSTRATION 12-10
Payment of deficiency

	Assets =	Partners' Equity		
	Cash	R. Aube, Capital	P. Chordia, Capital	W. Elliott, Capital
Account balances after selling assets and paying liabilities:	$ 16,000	$6,000	$ 11,800	$−1,800
Payment of capital deficiency	+1,800			+1,800
Balances	17,800	6,000	11,800	0
Distribution of cash to partners	−17,800	−6,000	−11,800	
Final balances	$ 0	$ 0	$ 0	$ 0

Cash is distributed based on these balances on April 25. This was step 4 in the list when there was no capital deficiency. The following entry is made:

		(5)		
Apr. 25	R. Aube, Capital		6,000	
	P. Chordia, Capital		11,800	
	Cash			17,800
	To record distribution of cash to partners.			

A   =   L   +   OE
−17,800   −6,000
                       −11,800
↓ Cash flows: −17,800

As shown in Illustration 12-10, after this entry is posted, all accounts will have zero balances and the partnership liquidation is finished.

Nonpayment of Deficiency

If a partner with a capital deficiency is unable to pay the amount owed to the partnership, the partners with credit balances must absorb the loss. The loss is allocated based on the profit and loss ratios between the partners with credit balances. Recall that the profit and loss ratios of R. Aube and P. Chordia are 3:2 (or $^3/_5$ and $^2/_5$), respectively. The following entry would be made to remove W. Elliott's capital deficiency on April 25:

Helpful hint The profit and loss ratio changes when the partner with the capital deficiency is not included. When allocating the loss from the sale of the assets, the profit and loss ratio was divided among the three partners as 3:2:1 or $^3/_6$, $^2/_6$, and $^1/_6$. When Elliott is excluded, the profit and loss ratio is now 3:2 or $^3/_5$ and $^2/_5$.

		(4)		
Apr. 25	R. Aube, Capital ($1,800 × $^3/_5$)		1,080	
	P. Chordia, Capital ($1,800 × $^2/_5$)		720	
	W. Elliott, Capital			1,800
	To write off Elliott's capital deficiency.			

A   =   L   +   OE
                       −1,080
                       −720
                       +1,800
Cash flows: no effect

After posting this entry, the cash balance of $16,000 now equals the sum of the credit balances in the capital accounts ($4,920 + $11,080), as shown in Illustration 12-11:

▶ ILLUSTRATION 12-11
Nonpayment of deficiency

	Assets =	Partners' Equity		
	Cash	R. Aube, Capital	P. Chordia, Capital	W. Elliott, Capital
Account balances after selling assets and paying liabilities:	$16,000	$6,000	$ 11,800	$−1,800
Write off of capital deficiency	0	−1,080	−720	+1,800
Balances	16,000	4,920	11,080	0
Distribution of cash to partners	−16,000	−4,920	−11,080	
Final balances	$ 0	$ 0	$ 0	$ 0

The entry to record the final distribution of cash is:

A = L + OE
−16,000   −4,920
            −11,080

↓ Cash flows: −16,000

	(5)		
Apr. 25	R. Aube, Capital	4,920	
	P. Chordia, Capital	11,080	
	Cash		16,000
	To record distribution of cash to partners.		

After this entry is posted, all accounts will have zero balances, as shown in Illustration 12-11, but Aube and Chordia still have a legal claim against Elliott for the deficiency. If Elliott is able to make a partial payment, it would be split between Aube and Chordia 3:2 in the same way as the deficiency was split.

ACCOUNTING IN ACTION
ALL ABOUT YOU INSIGHT

Many successful businesses start as a simple partnership based on an inspiration, idea, or dream shared by a couple of friends. Bill Hewlett and David Packard became close friends after graduating with degrees in electrical engineering from Stanford University in 1934. Later they began working part-time on a product in a rented garage with $538 in cash and a used drill press. In 1939, the men formalized their partnership, using a coin flip to determine HP's now-iconic name.

In 1968, Bill Gates and Paul Allen met at a computer club meeting at Seattle's private Lakeside School. In Gates's dorm room at Harvard University in 1974, they devised and sold a BASIC platform for the Altair 8800. The university disciplined Gates for running a business in his dorm. A year later, Gates and Allen formed Microsoft, now the world's largest software company.

Larry Page and Sergey Brin met while working on their doctorates in computer science at Stanford in 1995. Working in their dorm rooms, they created a proprietary algorithm for a search engine on the Net that catalogued search results according to the popularity of pages. The result was Google, arguably the world's No. 1 Internet search engine.

Sources: Steve Lohr, "An 'Unvarnished' Peek Into Microsoft's History," *New York Times,* April 17, 2011; "Larry Page and Sergey Brin," *Entrepreneur,* October 16, 2008; Stacy Perman, "Historic Collaborations—Business Partnerships That Changed the World," *Business Week,* November 21, 2008.

If you and a friend wanted to start a partnership, how might you use a partnership agreement to ensure that your partnership becomes successful, instead of ending in an unhappy liquidation?

 BEFORE YOU GO ON...

Do It

S. Anders, J. Haque, and R. Smit, LLP, dissolved their partnership as of August 31. Before liquidation, the three partners shared profit and losses in the ratio of 3:2:4. After the books were closed on August 31, the following summary accounts remained:

Cash	$ 6,000	S. Anders, Capital	$30,000
Noncash assets	110,000	J. Haque, Capital	20,000
Accounts payable	25,000	R. Smit, Capital	41,000

On September 24, the partnership sold the remaining noncash assets for $74,000 and paid the liabilities. If there is a capital deficiency, none of the partners will be able to pay it. Prepare the journal entries to record (a) the sale of noncash assets, (b) the allocation of any gain or loss on realization, (c) the payment of liabilities, and (d) the distribution of cash to the partners.

Solution

(a) Sept. 24	Cash		74,000	
	Loss on Realization		36,000	
	Noncash Assets			110,000
	To record realization of noncash assets.			
(b) Sept. 24	S. Anders, Capital ($36,000 × $^{3}/_{9}$)		12,000	
	J. Haque, Capital ($36,000 × $^{2}/_{9}$)		8,000	
	R. Smit, Capital ($36,000 × $^{4}/_{9}$)		16,000	
	Loss on Realization			36,000
	To allocate loss to partners' capital accounts.			
(c) Sept. 24	Accounts Payable		25,000	
	Cash			25,000
	To record payment of liabilities.			
(d) Sept. 24	S. Anders, Capital ($30,000 − $12,000)		18,000	
	J. Haque, Capital ($20,000 − $8,000)		12,000	
	R. Smit, Capital ($41,000 − $16,000)		25,000	
	Cash ($6,000 + $74,000 − $25,000)			55,000
	To record distribution of cash to partners.			

Action Plan
- Calculate the gain or loss by comparing cash proceeds with the carrying amount of assets.
- Allocate any gain or loss to each partner's capital account using the profit and loss ratio.
- Allocate the capital deficiency, if there is one, using the profit and loss ratio of the other partners.
- Record the final distribution of cash to each partner to eliminate the balance in each capital account. Do not distribute cash using the profit and loss ratio.

Related exercise material: BE12–14, BE12–15, BE12–16, E12–11, E12–12, E12–13, and E12–14.

THE **NAVIGATOR**

■Comparing IFRS and ASPE ■

Key Differences	International Financial Reporting Standards (IFRS)	Accounting Standards for Private Enterprises (ASPE)
No significant differences.		

THE **NAVIGATOR**

Demonstration Problem

On January 1, 2013, the partners' capital balances in Hollingsworth Company are Lois Holly, $26,000, and Jim Worth, $24,000. For the year ended December 31, 2013, the partnership reports profit of $32,500. The partnership agreement specifies (1) salary allowances of $12,000 for Holly and $10,000 for Worth, (2) interest allowances on opening capital account balances of 5%, and (3) the remainder to be distributed equally. Neither partner had any drawings in 2013.

In 2014, assume that the following independent transactions occur on January 2:

1. Donna Reichenbacher purchases one-half of Lois Holly's capital interest from Holly for $25,000.
2. Marsha Mears is admitted with a 25% capital interest by a cash investment of $37,500.
3. Stan Keewatin is admitted with a 30% capital interest by a cash investment of $32,500.

Instructions
(a) Prepare a schedule that shows the distribution of profit in 2013.
(b) Journalize the division of 2013 profit and its distribution to the partners on December 31.
(c) Journalize each of the independent transactions that occurred on January 2, 2014.

Solution to Demonstration Problem

(a)

HOLLINGSWORTH COMPANY
Division of Profit
Year Ended December 31, 2013

	L. Holly	J. Worth	Total
Profit			$32,500
Salary allowance			
L. Holly	$12,000		
J. Worth		$10,000	
Total			22,000
Profit remaining for allocation			10,500
Interest allowance			
L. Holly ($26,000 × 5%)	1,300		
J. Worth ($24,000 × 5%)		1,200	
Total			2,500
Profit remaining for allocation			8,000
Fixed ratio (remainder shared equally)			
L. Holly ($8,000 × 50%)	4,000		
J. Worth ($8,000 × 50%)		4,000	
Total			8,000
Profit remaining for allocation			0
Profit allocated to the partners	**$17,300**	**$15,200**	**$32,500**

ACTION PLAN

- Allocate the partners' salaries and interest allowances, if any, first. Divide the remaining profit among the partners, based on the profit and loss ratio.
- Journalize the division of profit in a closing entry.
- Recognize the admission by purchase of a partnership interest as a personal transaction between an existing partner and the new partner.
- Recognize the admission by investment of partnership assets as a transaction between the new partner and the partnership.
- In an admission by investment, determine any bonus to old or new partners by comparing the total capital of the new partnership with the new partner's capital credit. Allocate the bonus based on the old partners' profit and loss ratios.

(b) 2013

Dec. 31	Income Summary		32,500	
	L. Holly, Capital			17,300
	J. Worth, Capital			15,200
	To close profit to partners' capital accounts.			

L. Holly, Capital				J. Worth, Capital		
	Bal.	26,000			Bal.	24,000
		17,300				**15,200**
	Bal.	43,300			Bal.	39,200

(c) 2014

1. Jan. 2	L. Holly, Capital ($43,300 × 50%)		21,650	
	D. Reichenbacher, Capital			21,650
	To record purchase of one-half of Holly's interest.			
2. Jan. 2	Cash		37,500	
	L. Holly, Capital ($7,500 × 50%)			3,750
	J. Worth, Capital ($7,500 × 50%)			3,750
	M. Mears, Capital			30,000
	To record admission of Mears by investment and bonus to old partners.			

Total capital after investment: ($43,300 + $39,200 + $37,500)	$120,000
Mears's capital in the partnership: (25% × $120,000)	$30,000
Bonus to old partners: ($37,500 − $30,000)	$7,500

3. Jan. 2	Cash	32,500	
	L. Holly, Capital ($2,000 × 50%)	1,000	
	J. Worth, Capital ($2,000 × 50%)	1,000	
	S. Keewatin, Capital		34,500
	To record admission of Keewatin by		
	investment and bonus to new partner.		

Total capital after investment: ($43,300 + $39,200 + $32,500)	$115,000
Keewatin's capital in the partnership: (30% × $115,000)	$34,500
Bonus to Keewatin: ($34,500 − $32,500)	$2,000

THE NAVIGATOR

Summary of Study Objectives

1. **Describe the characteristics of the partnership form of business organization.** The main characteristics of a partnership are (1) the association of individuals, (2) mutual agency, (3) co-ownership of property, (4) limited life, and (5) unlimited liability for a general partnership.

2. **Account for the formation of a partnership.** When a partnership is formed, each partner's initial investment should be recorded at the assets' fair value at the date of their transfer to the partnership. If accounts receivable are contributed, both the gross amount and an allowance for doubtful accounts should be recorded. Accumulated depreciation is not carried forward into a partnership.

3. **Allocate and record profit or loss to partners.** Profit or loss is divided based on the profit and loss ratio, which may be any of the following: (1) a fixed ratio; (2) a ratio based on beginning, ending, or average capital balances; (3) salaries allocated to partners and the remainder in a fixed ratio; (4) interest on partners' capital balances and the remainder in a fixed ratio; and (5) salaries allocated to partners, interest on partners' capital balances, and the remainder in a fixed ratio.

4. **Prepare partnership financial statements.** The financial statements of a partnership are similar to those of a proprietorship. The main differences are that (1) the statement of owners' equity is called the statement of partners' equity, and (2) each partner's capital account is usually reported on the balance sheet or in a supporting schedule.

5. **Account for the admission of a partner.** The entry to record the admission of a new partner by purchase of a partner's interest affects only partners' capital accounts. The entry to record the admission by investment of assets in the partnership (1) increases both net assets and total capital, and (2) may result in the recognition of a bonus to either the old partners or the new partner.

6. **Account for the withdrawal of a partner.** The entry to record a withdrawal from the firm when payment is made from partners' personal assets affects only partners' capital accounts. The entry to record a withdrawal when payment is made from partnership assets (1) decreases net assets and total capital, and (2) may result in recognizing a bonus to either the departing partner or the remaining partners.

7. **Account for the liquidation of a partnership.** When a partnership is liquidated, it is necessary to record (1) the sale of noncash assets, (2) the allocation of the gain or loss on realization based on the profit and loss ratio, (3) the payment of partnership liabilities, (4) the removal of any capital deficiency either by repayment or by allocation to the other partners, and (5) the distribution of cash to the partners based on their capital balances.

THE NAVIGATOR

Flash cards

Glossary

Admission by investment Admission of a partner by an investment of assets in the partnership. Both partnership net assets and total capital increase. (p. 631)

Admission by purchase of a partner's interest Admission of a partner through a personal transaction between one or more existing partners and the new partner. It does not change total partnership assets or total capital. (p. 630)

Capital deficiency A debit balance in a partner's capital account after the allocation of a gain or loss on liquidation of a partnership. Capital deficiencies can be repaid or allocated among the remaining partners. (p. 639)

Limited liability partnership (LLP) A partnership in which partners have limited liability for other partners' negligence. (p. 620)

Limited partnership (LP) A partnership in which one or more general partners have unlimited liability, and the other partners, known as limited partners, have limited liability for the obligations of the partnership. (p. 620)

Mutual agency The concept that the action of any partner is binding on all other partners. (p. 619)

No capital deficiency A situation where all partners have credit balances after the allocation of a gain or a loss on liquidation of a partnership. (p. 639)

Partnership An association of individuals who operate a business for profit. (p. 618)

Partnership agreement A written contract that expresses the voluntary agreement of two or more individuals in a partnership. (p. 621)

Partnership dissolution A change in the number of partners that dissolves (ends) the partnership. It does not necessarily end the business. (p. 619)

Partnership liquidation An event that ends both the legal and economic life of a partnership. (p. 639)

Profit and loss ratio The basis for dividing both profit and loss in a partnership. (p. 624)

Realization The sale of noncash assets for cash on the liquidation of a partnership. (p. 639)

Statement of partners' equity The equity statement for a partnership that shows the changes in each partner's capital balance, and in total partnership capital, during the year. (p. 629)

Withdrawal by payment from partners' personal assets Withdrawal of a partner by a personal transaction between partners. It does not change total partnership assets or total capital. (p. 635)

Withdrawal by payment from partnership assets Withdrawal of a partner by a transaction that decreases both partnership net assets and total capital. (p. 635)

▶ Self-Study Questions

Answers are at the end of the chapter.

(SO 1) K 1. Which one of the following is considered to be a disadvantage of the partnership form of organization?
 (a) Unlimited life
 (b) Limited liability
 (c) Mutual agency
 (d) Ease of formation

(SO 2) AP 2. Brianne and Stephen are combining their two proprietorships to form a partnership. Brianne's proprietorship has $6,000 of accounts receivable and an allowance for doubtful accounts of $1,000. The partners agree that the fair value of the accounts receivable is $4,800. The entry that the partnership makes to record Brianne's initial contribution includes a
 (a) debit to Accounts Receivable for $6,000.
 (b) debit to Accounts Receivable for $4,800.
 (c) debit to Bad Debts Expense for $200.
 (d) credit to Allowance for Doubtful Accounts for $200.

(SO 3) AP 3. The ABC Company reports profit of $60,000. Partners A, B, and C have a salary allowance of $10,000 each and a fixed ratio of 50%, 30%, and 20%, respectively. What is each partner's share of the profit?

	A	B	C
(a)	$20,000	$20,000	$20,000
(b)	$25,000	$19,000	$16,000
(c)	$30,000	$18,000	$12,000
(d)	$15,000	$ 9,000	$ 6,000

(SO 4) K 4. The purpose of the statement of partners' equity is to explain:
 (a) The salary and interest allowances allocated to each partner.
 (b) The initial contributions by each partner.

 (c) The fair value of each partner's claim on the net assets of the partnership.
 (d) The changes in each partner's capital account, and in total partnership capital, during the year.

(SO 5) AP 5. R. Ranken purchases 50% of L. Lars's capital interest in the Kim & Lars partnership for $20,000. The capital balances of Kim and Lars are $40,000 and $30,000, respectively. Ranken's capital balance after the purchase is:
 (a) $15,000.
 (b) $20,000.
 (c) $22,000.
 (d) $35,000.

(SO 5) AP 6. Capital balances in the DEA partnership are Delano, Capital $60,000; Egil, Capital $50,000; and Armand, Capital $40,000. The profit and loss ratio is 5:3:2. The DEAR partnership is formed by admitting Ramachandran to the firm with a cash investment of $60,000 for a 25% capital interest. The bonus to be credited to Delano, Capital, in admitting Ramachandran is:
 (a) $1,500.
 (b) $3,750.
 (c) $7,500.
 (d) $10,000.

(SO 6) AP 7. Capital balances in the Alouette partnership are Tremblay, Capital $50,000; St-Jean, Capital $40,000; and, Roy, Capital $30,000. The profit and loss ratio is 5:4:3. Roy withdraws from the partnership after being paid $16,000 personally by each of Tremblay

and St-Jean. St-Jean's capital balance after recording the withdrawal of Roy is:
(a) $46,000.
(b) $50,000.
(c) $55,000.
(d) $65,000.

(SO 6) AP 8. Capital balances in the TERM partnership are Takako, Capital $50,000; Endo, Capital $40,000; Reiko, Capital $30,000; and Maeda, Capital $20,000. The profit and loss ratio is 4:3:2:1. Maeda withdraws from the firm after receiving $29,000 in cash from the partnership. Endo's capital balance after recording the withdrawal of Maeda is:
(a) $36,000.
(b) $37,000.
(c) $37,300.
(d) $40,000.

(SO 7) AP 9. Fontaine and Tomah were partners in the AFN partnership, sharing profit and losses in a ratio of 3:2. Fontaine's capital account balance was $30,000 and Tomah's was $20,000, immediately before the

partnership liquidated on February 19. If noncash assets worth $60,000 were sold for $75,000, what were Fontaine and Tomah's capital account balances after the sale?

	Fontaine	Tomah
(a)	$21,000	$14,000
(b)	$30,000	$20,000
(c)	$39,000	$26,000
(d)	$66,000	$54,000

(SO 7) AP 10. Partners Aikawa, Ito, and Mori shared a profit and loss ratio of 2:1:3 in the AIM Company. After AIM was liquidated, $12,000 cash remained and the balances in the partners' capital accounts were as follows: Aikawa, $9,000 Cr.; Ito, $6,000 Cr.; and Mori, $3,000 Dr. How much cash would be distributed to Aikawa and Ito respectively, assuming Mori does not repay his capital deficiency?
(a) $7,000 and $5,000
(b) $7,500 and $4,500
(c) $8,000 and $4,000
(d) $9,000 and $6,000

THE NAVIGATOR

▶ Questions

(SO 1) C 1. K. Nasser and T. Yoko are considering a business venture. They ask you to explain the advantages and disadvantages of the partnership form of organization.

(SO 1) C 2. Gurprinder and Harjinder decided to form a partnership and operate a business together. Harjinder is much more cautious and concerned about keeping expenses to a minimum than Gurprinder. Harjinder also has significantly more personal assets than Gurprinder. Should Harjinder have any concerns about using the partnership form of business organization to operate this business? Explain.

(SO 1) K 3. Because of concerns over unlimited liability, there are now special forms of partnership organization that modify that characteristic. Describe these other forms of partnership.

(SO 1) K 4. (a) What items should be specified in a partnership agreement? (b) Why is it important to have this agreement in writing?

(SO 2) K 5. (a) For accounting purposes, when a partner invests assets in a partnership, how is the value of these assets determined? (b) Is this practice consistent with the cost principle? Explain.

(SO 2) K 6. When a partnership is formed, one or more of the partners may contribute equipment as part of their initial investment. How is the amount of accumulated depreciation to be recorded on this equipment determined?

(SO 2) K 7. Franca and Naheed are transferring $8,000 of accounts receivable from each of their sole proprietorships into a partnership. They have agreed that $7,000 of Franca's receivables is collectible but it is likely they will collect only $6,000 of the receivables

from Naheed's proprietorship. How should these receivables be recorded in the partnership? Explain why.

(SO 3) C 8. S. Hark and R. Green are discussing how profit and losses should be divided in a partnership they plan to form. They think they should wait to see who has worked the hardest before agreeing on how to share the profit. What are the advantages and disadvantages of doing this?

(SO 3) C 9. What is the relationship between (a) a salary allowance for allocating profit among partners and (b) partners' cash withdrawals?

(SO 3) C 10. What is the difference between a salary allowance for allocating profit among partners and salary expense? Between an interest allowance and interest expense?

(SO 4) C 11. What is included in a statement of partners' equity? How is it similar to, and different from, a statement of owner's equity?

(SO 4) C 12. The income statement of a partnership includes the details of how the profit or loss is divided among the partners. Do you agree or disagree? Explain.

(SO 4) C 13. The equity section of a partnership's balance sheet shows the total amount invested by the partners separate from the profit earned to date and retained in the business. Do you agree or disagree? Explain.

(SO 5) AP 14. How is the accounting for admission to a partnership by purchase of a partner's interest different from the accounting for admission by an investment of assets in the partnership? In your explanation, also include how the net assets and total capital change after the admission of a partner in each of these two ways.

(SO 5) C 15. R. Minoa decides to invest $25,000 in a partnership for a one-sixth capital interest. Will Minoa's capital balance be $25,000? Does Minoa also acquire a one-sixth profit and loss ratio through this investment?

(SO 5) C 16. What are some reasons why the existing partners may be willing to give a new partner a bonus for joining a partnership?

(SO 6) C 17. What is the impact on a partnership's balance sheet when (a) a partner withdraws by payment from partners' personal assets, and (b) a partner withdraws by payment from partnership assets?

(SO 6) C 18. Under what circumstances will a partner who is leaving a partnership give the remaining partners a bonus?

(SO 6) C 19. What is the purpose of a partnership's obtaining life insurance policies on each of the partners?

(SO 7) C 20. How is the liquidation of a partnership different from the dissolution of a partnership?

(SO 7) K 21. Identify the steps in liquidating a partnership.

(SO 7) C 22. What basis is used for making the final distribution of cash to the partners when there is a capital deficiency and the deficiency is paid? And when it is not paid?

(SO 7) C 23. Joe and Rajiv are discussing the liquidation of a partnership. Joe argues that all cash should be distributed to partners based on their profit and loss ratios. Is he correct? Explain.

▶ Brief Exercises

Identify partnership terminology. (SO 1) K

BE12–1 The following terms were introduced in this chapter:

1. Profit and loss ratio
2. Admission by investment
3. Partnership liquidation
4. Mutual agency
5. Salary allowance
6. Withdrawal by payment from partners' personal assets
7. Capital deficiency
8. Limited liability partnership
9. General partnership
10. Partnership dissolution

Match the terms with the following descriptions:

(a) _____ Partners have limited liability.
(b) _____ Partners have unlimited liability.
(c) _____ It is the basis for dividing profit and loss.
(d) _____ Partnership assets and capital increase with the change in partners.
(e) _____ Partnership assets and capital stay the same with the change in partners.
(f) _____ Actions of partners are binding on all other partners.
(g) _____ It is a compensation for differences in personal effort put into the partnership.
(h) _____ Partnership is changed by the addition or withdrawal of a partner.
(i) _____ There is a debit balance in a partner's capital account.
(j) _____ Partnership is ended.

Record formation of partnership. (SO 2) AP

BE12–2 R. Black and B. Rivers decide to organize the Black River Partnership. Black contributes $10,000 cash and equipment that originally cost $7,000. The accumulated depreciation on the equipment is $2,500 and the fair value is $4,000. Rivers contributes $2,400 of accounts receivable, of which the partners agree that $2,000 is collectible. Rivers will also contribute the amount of cash required so both partners have the same amount in their capital accounts. Prepare the entry to record each partner's investment in the partnership on July 1, 2014.

Prepare opening balance sheet. (SO 2) AP

BE12–3 Data for Black River Partnership are presented in BE12–2. (a) Prepare the assets section of the partnership's balance sheet at July 1, 2014. (b) What is the total amount of partners' equity on July 1, 2014?

Convert proportions into fractions and percentages. (SO 3) AP

BE12–4 Fixed profit and loss ratios can be expressed as proportions, fractions, or percentages. For each of the following proportions, determine the equivalent fractions or percentages:

	Proportions	Fractions	Percentages
(a)	2:1		
(b)	6:4		
(c)	3:8		
(d)	4:3:2		
(e)	1:2:1		

BE12–5 During the fiscal year ended November 30, 2014, the profit for Scrimger & Woods Partnership was $84,000. The partners, A. Scrimger, and D. Woods, share profit and loss in a 3:5 ratio, respectively. (a) Calculate the division of profit to each partner. (b) Prepare entries to close the income summary and drawings accounts assuming the partners withdrew $35,000 each during the year.

Calculate division of profit and record closing entries. (SO 3) AP

BE12–6 MET Co. reports profit of $70,000 for the current year. Partner salary allowances are J. Moses $24,000; T. Eaton $30,000; and M. Tung-Ching $5,000. The profit and loss ratio is 5:3:2. Calculate the division of profit to each partner.

Calculate division of profit. (SO 3) AP

BE12–7 The MillStone Partnership reported profit of $60,000 for the year ended February 28, 2014. Salary allowances are $45,000 for H. Mills and $25,000 for S. Stone. Interest allowances of 5% are calculated on each partner's opening capital account balance. Capital account balances at March 1, 2013, were as follows: H. Mills $72,000 (Cr.) and S. Stone $47,000 (Cr.). Any remainder is shared equally. Calculate the division of profit to each partner.

Calculate division of profit. (SO 3) AP

BE12–8 Tognazzini Company had a $15,000 loss for the year ended October 31, 2014. The company is a partnership owned by Lilia and Terry Tognazzini. Salary allowances for the partners are Lilia $25,000 and Terry $16,000. Interest allowances are Lilia $5,000 and Terry $9,000. The remainder is shared 75% by Lilia and 25% by Terry. (a) Calculate the loss to be allocated to each partner. (b) Prepare a journal entry to close the income summary account.

Calculate and record division of loss. (SO 3) AP

BE12–9 The medical practice of Dr. W. Jarratt and Dr. M. Bramstrup had the following general ledger account balances at April 30, 2014, its fiscal year end:

Prepare financial statements. (SO 4) AP

Accounts payable	$25,000	M. Bramstrup, drawings	$120,000
Accumulated depreciation—		Operating expenses	145,000
equipment	15,000		
Cash	35,000	Service revenue	375,000
Equipment	75,000	W. Jarratt, capital	35,000
M. Bramstrup, capital	50,000	W. Jarratt, drawings	125,000

(a) Calculate the profit or loss for the year.
(b) Prepare the statement of partners' equity and the balance sheet, assuming the doctors share profit or loss equally.

BE12–10 In ABC Co., the capital balances of the partners are A. Ali $30,000; S. Babson $25,000; and K. Carter $36,000. The partners share profit equally. On June 9 of the current year, D. Dutton is admitted to the partnership by purchasing one-half of K. Carter's interest for $20,000. (a) Journalize the admission of Dutton on June 9. (b) How would the entry change if Dutton had paid $20,000 to purchase one-half of A. Ali's interest instead of K. Carter's interest?

Record admission of partner. (SO 5) AP

BE12–11 In the EZ Co., the capital balances of the partners are J. Edie $48,000 and K. Zane $32,000. The partners share profit in a 5:3 ratio, respectively. On October 1 of the current year, when she invests $40,000 cash in the partnership, J. Kerns is admitted to the partnership with a 40% interest. (a) Journalize the admission of Kerns on October 1. (b) What would the journal entry be if Kerns had paid $60,000 for a 40% interest in the partnership?

Record admission of partner. (SO 5) AP

BE12–12 On December 31, 2014, capital balances of the partners in Manitoba Maple Co. are R. Neepawa $45,000; S. Altona $35,000; and T. Morden $25,000. The partners share profit in a 5:3:2 ratio, respectively. Morden decides that she is going to leave the partnership. Journalize the withdrawal of Morden assuming:

Record withdrawal of partner. (SO 6) AP

(a) Neepawa and Altona both pay Morden $17,000 from their personal assets to each receive 50% of Morden's equity.
(b) Neepawa and Altona both pay Morden $12,000 from their personal assets to each receive 50% of Morden's equity.
(c) Neepawa pays Morden $30,000 from her personal assets to receive 100% of Morden's equity.

BE12–13 Data for Manitoba Maple Co. are presented in BE12–12. Instead of a payment from personal assets, assume that Morden receives cash from the partnership when she withdraws from the partnership. Journalize the withdrawal of Morden if she receives (a) $35,000 cash, and (b) $20,000 cash.

Record withdrawal of partner. (SO 6) AP

BE12–14 On November 15 of the current year, the account balances in Greenscape Partnership were Cash $8,000; Other Assets $17,000; D. Dupuis, Capital $12,000; V. Dueck, Capital $10,000; and B. Veitch, Capital $3,000. The three partners share profit and losses equally. The other assets are sold for $20,000 cash. Prepare journal entries to (a) record the sale of the other assets, (b) distribute any resulting gain or loss to the capital accounts, and (c) record the final distribution of cash to the partners.

Record partnership liquidation. (SO 7) AP

BE12–15 Data for Greenscape Partnership are presented in BE12–14. Assume that the other assets were sold for $14,000 cash instead of $20,000. Prepare journal entries to (a) record the sale of the other assets, (b) distribute any resulting gain or loss to the capital accounts, and (c) record the final distribution of cash to the partners.

Record partnership liquidation. (SO 7) AP

<table>
<tr><td>Record partnership
liquidation. (SO 7) AP</td><td colspan="3">**BE12–16** Before the distribution of cash to the partners on April 30 of the current year, the accounts in LMN Enterprises are as follows:</td></tr>
</table>

	Debit	Credit
Cash	$40,000	
G. Lodge, Capital	4,000	
L. McDonald, Capital		$20,000
A. Norin, Capital		24,000

The profit and loss ratio is 4:3:2. (a) Assuming Lodge repays her capital deficiency, prepare the entry on April 30 to record (1) Lodge's payment of $4,000 in cash to the partnership, and (2) the distribution of cash to the partners. (b) Assuming Lodge is not able to repay her capital deficiency, prepare the entry on April 30 to record (1) the absorption of Lodge's capital deficiency by the other partners, and (2) the distribution of cash to the partners.

▶ Exercises

Determine form of
organization. (SO 1) AN

E12–1 Presented below are three independent situations:

1. Angelique Gloss and David Deutsch, two students looking for summer employment, decide to open a home meal replacement business. Each day, they prepare nutritious, ready-to-bake meals, which they sell to people on their way home from work.
2. Joe Daigle and Cathy Goodfellow own a ski repair business and a ski shop, respectively. They have decided to combine their businesses. They expect that in the coming year they will need a large amount of money to expand their operations.
3. Three business professors have formed a business to offer income tax services to the community. They expect to hire students during the busy season.
4. Myles Anawak would like to organize a company that buys and leases commercial real estate. Myles will need to raise a large amount of capital so that he can buy commercial property for lease.

Instructions

In each of the above situations, explain whether the partnership form of organization is the best choice for the business. Explain your reasoning.

Record formation of
partnership and prepare
partial balance sheet.
(SO 2) AP

E12–2 Hollis Sourman and Heidi Sweetgrass have each operated a proprietorship for several years. On January 1, 2014, they decide to form the Sour and Sweet Partnership and transfer the assets from their proprietorships to the partnership. The following information is available:

	Hollis Sourman		Heidi Sweetgrass	
	Book Value	Fair Value	Book Value	Fair Value
Cash	$10,000	$10,000	$7,000	$7,000
Accounts receivable			6,500	6,500
Allowance for doubtful accounts			(500)	(1,500)
Equipment	12,000	6,000		
Accumulated depreciation	(4,000)			

Instructions

(a) Prepare entries to record the partners' investment in the Sour and Sweet Partnership.
(b) Prepare the assets section of the balance sheet at January 1, 2014.

Calculate and record division
of profit. (SO 3) AP

E12–3 R. Huma and W. How have capital balances on July 1, 2014, of $60,000 and $55,000, respectively. The partnership profit-sharing agreement specifies (1) salary allowances of $30,000 for Huma and $22,000 for How, (2) interest at 5% on beginning capital balances, and (3) for the remaining profit or loss to be shared 60% by Huma and 40% by How.

Instructions

(a) Prepare a schedule showing the division of profit for the year ended June 30, 2015, assuming profit is
   (1) $70,000, and (2) $55,000.
(b) Journalize the allocation of profit in each of the situations in (a).

Calculate and record division
of loss. (SO 3) AP

E12–4 Daisey Brodsky and Jim Leigh began a partnership on February 1, 2014, by investing $62,000 and $88,000, respectively. They agree to share profit and losses by allocating yearly salary allowances of $60,000 to

Daisey and $40,000 to Jim, an interest allowance of 8% on their investments, and to split the remainder 55:45. During the year, Daisey withdrew $30,000 and Jim withdrew $22,000. The partnership recorded a loss of $15,000 in its first fiscal year.

Instructions

(a) Prepare a schedule showing the division of the loss for the year.

(b) Prepare the journal entry to close the income summary account at the end of the year.

(c) How much of the loss should be allocated to each partner if Daisey and Jim failed to agree on the method of sharing profit or loss?

E12–5 Copperfield Developments is a partnership owned by Alvaro Rodriguez and Elisabetta Carrieri. On December 31, 2013, the partners' capital balances are Alvaro $61,000 and Elisabetta $79,000. During 2014, Elisabetta invested $4,000 cash into the partnership; drawings were $32,000 by Alvaro and $55,000 by Elisabetta, and profit was $77,000. Alvaro and Elizabetta share profit based on a 3:4 ratio.

Prepare partial financial statements and closing entries. (SO 3, 4) AP

Instructions

(a) Prepare the statement of partners' equity for the year.

(b) Prepare the partners' equity section of the balance sheet at year end.

(c) Prepare entries to close the income summary and drawings accounts.

E12–6 Dr. J. Kovacik and Dr. S. Donovan have been operating a dental practice as a partnership for several years. The fixed profit and loss ratio is 60% for Dr. Kovacik and 40% for Dr. Donovan. The dental practice had the following general ledger account balances at November 30, 2014, its fiscal year end:

Prepare financial statements and closing entries. (SO 3, 4) AP

Cash	$ 32,000
Supplies	15,750
Equipment	175,500
Accumulated depreciation—equipment	41,250
Accounts payable	15,000
Note payable, due 2018	50,000
J. Kovacik, capital	58,000
J. Kovacik, drawings	140,000
S. Donovan, capital	32,000
S. Donovan, drawings	90,000
Fees earned	422,000
Salaries expense	78,500
Office expense	81,500
Interest expense	5,000

Instructions

(a) Prepare financial statements for the partnership.

(b) Prepare closing entries.

E12–7 A. Veveris and J. Rubenis share profit on a 2:1 basis, respectively. They have capital balances of $42,000 and $33,000, respectively, when S. Weiss is admitted to the partnership on September 1, 2014.

Record admission of partner. (SO 5) AP

Instructions

(a) Prepare the journal entry to record the admission of Weiss under each of the following independent assumptions:

    1. Weiss purchases 50% of Ververis's equity for $25,000.

    2. Weiss purchases 25% of Ververis's and Rubenis's equity for $15,000 and $10,000, respectively.

    3. Weiss invests $25,000 cash in the partnership for a 25% interest in the partnership.

(b) For each of these alternatives, indicate the balance in each partner's capital account and total partners' equity after Weiss is admitted to the partnership.

E12–8 Olive Oil Imports is a partnership owned by Magda Stavros and Giannis Metaxas. The partners share profit on a 3:2 basis, respectively. On January 1, 2014, they have capital balances of $95,000 and $65,000, respectively. On that day, Magda and Giannis agree to admit Iona Xanthos to the partnership in exchange for an investment of cash into the partnership.

Record admission of partner. (SO 5) AP

Instructions

(a) Prepare the journal entry to record the admission of Iona on January 1 under each of the following independent assumptions:

    1. Iona invests $65,000 cash for a 33⅓% ownership interest.

    2. Iona invests $95,000 cash for a 33⅓% ownership interest.

(b) For each of these alternatives, indicate the balance in each partner's capital account and total partners' equity after Iona is admitted to the partnership.

(c) Calculate the amount Iona would have to pay for a 33⅓% ownership interest where there would be no bonus to the old partners or to Iona.

Record withdrawal of partner. (SO 6) AP

E12–9 Julie Lane, Sara Miles, and Amber Noll have capital balances of $50,000, $40,000, and $30,000, respectively. The profit and loss ratio is 5:3:2. Assume Noll withdraws from the partnership on December 31 of the current year under each of the following independent conditions:

1. Lane and Miles agree to purchase Noll's equity by paying $17,500 each from their personal assets. Each purchaser receives 50% of Noll's equity.
2. Miles agrees to purchase all of Noll's equity by paying $35,000 cash from her personal assets.
3. Noll withdraws $30,000 cash from the partnership.
4. Noll withdraws $35,000 cash from the partnership.

Instructions

(a) Journalize the withdrawal of Noll under each of the above assumptions.

(b) Determine the balances in the partners' capital accounts and in total partners' equity after Noll has withdrawn, for conditions 1 and 4 above.

Record withdrawal of partner. (SO 6) AP

E12–10 Dale Nagel, Keith White, and Issa Mbango have capital balances of $95,000, $73,000, and $65,000, respectively. They share profit or loss on a 4:3:2 basis. White withdraws from the partnership on September 30 of the current year.

Instructions

(a) Journalize the withdrawal of White under each of the following assumptions.
   1. White is paid $85,000 cash from partnership assets.
   2. White is paid $68,000 cash from partnership assets.
   3. White sells his interest in the partnership to Emily Wolstenholme for $68,000 cash.

(b) Determine the balances in the partners' capital accounts and in total partners' equity after White has withdrawn from the partnership for conditions 2 and 3 above.

Calculate amounts paid on liquidation of partnership. (SO 7) AP

E12–11 Windl, Houghton, and Pesowski decided to liquidate their partnership on October 1. Before the noncash assets were sold, the capital account balances were Windl, $86,250; Houghton, $34,500; and Pesowski, $51,750. The partners divide profits and losses equally. After the noncash assets are sold and the liabilities are paid, the partnership has $172,500 of cash.

Instructions

(a) How much cash will each partner receive in the final liquidation?

(b) Assume instead that there is $139,500 of cash after the noncash assets are sold and the liabilities are paid. How much cash will each partner receive?

Calculate amounts paid on liquidation of partnership. (SO 7) AP

E12–12 At December 31, Baylee Company has cash of $40,000, equipment of $130,000, accumulated depreciation of $40,000, liabilities of $55,000, and the following partners' capital balances: H. Bayer $45,000 and J. Leech $30,000. The partnership is liquidated on December 31 of the current year and $100,000 cash is received for the equipment. Bayer and Leech share profits and losses equally.

Instructions

(a) How much is the gain or loss on the disposal of the noncash assets?

(b) How much of that gain or loss is allocated to each partner?

(c) How much cash will be paid to each of the partners when the company is liquidated on December 31?

Record partnership liquidation. (SO 7) AP

E12–13 Data for the Baylee Company partnership are presented in E12–12.

Instructions

Prepare the entries to record (a) the sale of the equipment, (b) the allocation to the partners of the gain or loss on liquidation, (c) the payment of creditors, and (d) the distribution of cash to the partners.

Record partnership liquidation. (SO 7) AP

E12–14 Ole Low, Arnt Olson, and Stig Lokum decided to liquidate the LOL partnership on December 31 of the current year, and go their separate ways. The partners share profit and losses equally. As at December 31, the partnership had cash of $15,000, noncash assets of $120,000, and liabilities of $20,000. Before selling their noncash assets, the partners had capital balances of $45,000, $60,000, and $10,000, respectively. The noncash assets were sold for $84,000 and the creditors were paid.

Instructions

(a) Calculate the loss on the sale of the noncash assets and the amount of cash remaining after paying the liabilities.
(b) Calculate the balance in each of the partners' capital accounts after allocating the loss from the sale of the noncash assets and paying the liabilities.
(c) Assume that all of the partners have the personal resources to cover a deficit in their capital accounts. Prepare journal entries to record any cash receipts from the partners to cover any existing deficit and to record the final distribution of cash.
(d) Now assume that the partners do not have the personal resources to cover a deficit in their capital accounts. Prepare journal entries to allocate any deficit to the remaining partners and to record the final distribution of cash.

▶ Problems: Set A

P12–1A Patricia Derbyshire and Ann Oleksiw are interested in starting a marketing company that will focus on branding for performers and musicians in the entertainment industry. Patricia is very creative and understands how the entertainment industry operates. Ann has exceptional administrative and customer relations skills.

Discuss advantages and disadvantages of partnerships and partnership agreements. (SO 1) C

Instructions

(a) What are the advantages and disadvantages for these two individuals of forming a partnership as opposed to setting up a corporation?
(b) Assuming they decide to form a partnership, what should be included in their partnership agreement? Be specific given the nature of their business and the two partners.

TAKING IT FURTHER How can a partnership agreement help reduce the effects of mutual agency?

P12–2A The trial balances of two proprietorships on January 1, 2014, follow:

Record formation of partnership and prepare balance sheet. (SO, 2, 4) AP

	Domic Company		Dasilva Company	
	Dr.	Cr.	Dr.	Cr.
Cash	$ 9,000		$10,000	
Accounts receivable	13,500		24,000	
Allowance for doubtful accounts		$ 3,000		$ 5,500
Merchandise inventory	11,500		15,500	
Equipment	40,000		31,000	
Accumulated depreciation—equipment		24,000		13,000
Accounts payable		11,000		34,000
I. Domic, capital		36,000		
P. Dasilva, capital				28,000
	$74,000	$74,000	$80,500	$80,500

Domic and Dasilva decide to form a partnership on January 1 and agree on the following valuations for the noncash assets that they are each contributing:

	Domic	Dasilva
Accounts receivable—net realizable value	$ 9,000	$21,000
Merchandise inventory	14,000	13,000
Equipment	18,000	15,000

All of the assets in each of the proprietorships will be transferred to the partnership. The partnership will also assume all the liabilities of the two proprietorships. Domic and Dasilva are also agreed that Dasilva will invest the amount of cash required so their investments in the partnership are equal.

Instructions

(a) Prepare separate journal entries to record the transfer of each proprietorship's assets and liabilities to the partnership on January 1.
(b) Journalize the additional cash investment.
(c) Prepare a balance sheet for the partnership at January 1.

TAKING IT FURTHER What are some of the advantages of two individuals such as Domic and Dasilva operating as a partnership instead of as two separate proprietorships?

Calculate and record division of profit. Prepare statement of partners' equity. (SO 3, 4) AP

P12–3A At the end of its first year of operations, on December 31, 2014, CDW Company's accounts show the following:

Partner	Drawings	Capital
J. Chapman-Brown	$10,000	$30,000
C. Duperé	8,000	40,000
H. Weir	6,000	50,000

The capital balance represents each partner's initial capital investment. No closing entries for profit (loss) or drawings have been recorded as yet.

Instructions

(a) Journalize the entry to record the division of profit for the year ended December 31, 2014, under each of the following independent assumptions:
   1. Profit is $40,000. Duperé and Weir are given salary allowances of $8,000 and $12,000, respectively. The remainder is shared equally.
   2. Profit is $40,000. Each partner is allowed interest of 5% on beginning capital balances. Chapman-Brown, Duperé, and Weir are given salary allowances of $15,000, $20,000, and $18,000, respectively. The remainder is shared in a ratio of 5:3:2.

(b) Journalize the entry to close each partner's drawings account.

(c) Prepare a statement of partners' equity for the year under assumption (2) in (a) above.

TAKING IT FURTHER Explain why partnerships such as CDW Company include an interest allowance in their profit- and loss-sharing arrangements.

Calculate division of profit or loss. Prepare income statement, statement of partners' equity, and closing entries. (SO 3, 4) AP

P12–4A Veda Storey and Gordon Rogers have a partnership agreement with the following provisions for sharing profit or loss:

1. A salary allowance of $30,000 to Storey and $40,000 to Rogers
2. An interest allowance of 4% on capital balances at the beginning of the year
3. The remainder to be divided between Storey and Rogers on a 2:3 basis

The capital balances on January 1, 2014, for Storey and Rogers were $80,000 and $100,000, respectively. For the year ended December 31, 2014, the Storey Rogers Partnership had sales of $340,000; cost of goods sold of $250,000; operating expenses of $130,000; V. Storey drawings of $24,000; and G. Rogers drawings of $32,000.

Instructions

(a) Prepare an income statement for Storey Rogers Partnership for the year.

(b) Prepare a schedule to show how the profit or loss will be allocated to the two partners.

(c) Prepare a statement of partners' equity for the year.

(d) Prepare closing entries at December 31.

TAKING IT FURTHER Assume that gross profit was lower than expected for 2014 because Rogers sold a significant amount of inventory to friends at substantially reduced prices. These arrangements were made without Storey's approval. She therefore argues that she should be allocated her salary allowance and the remaining loss should be allocated to Rogers. Is this reasonable?

Prepare financial statements and closing entries. (SO 3, 4) AP

P12–5A Below is an alphabetical listing of the accounts in the general ledger of the Kant-Adder accounting firm at the partnership's fiscal year end, March 31, 2014. Adjusting entries for the year have been posted and included in these balances.

Accounts payable	$ 12,500	Note payable	$ 50,000
Accounts receivable	61,000	Rent expense	36,000
Accumulated depreciation—equipment	12,000	Salaries expense	80,000
Cash	14,000	Salaries payable	8,000
Depreciation expense	8,000	Supplies	1,500
Equipment	42,000	Supplies expense	5,000
Fees earned	255,000	U. Adder, capital	30,000
I. Kant, capital	30,000	U. Adder, drawings	60,000
I. Kant, drawings	90,000	Unearned revenue	5,000
Interest expense	5,000		

Additional information:

1. The balance in Kant's capital account includes an additional $5,000 investment during the year.
2. $1,500 of the note payable is due within the next year.
3. Kant and Adder share profit in the ratio of 2:1, respectively.

Instructions

(a) Prepare an income statement, statement of partners' equity, and balance sheet.
(b) Journalize the closing entries.

TAKING IT FURTHER   Each partner's drawings are larger than their respective capital account balances. Is this a problem?

P12–6A   Tyler Gilligan and Matt Melnyk, two college friends, decided to set up a snow removal business called Ty & Matt Snow Removal Services. On January 1, 2014, they put their resources together, shook hands, and started their business. They each contributed the following to the business:

Prepare entries to form a partnership, allocate profit, and close temporary accounts; prepare financial statements. (SO 1, 2, 3, 4) AP

	Tyler Gilligan		Matt Melnyk	
	Original Cost	Fair Value	Original Cost	Fair Value
Cash	$ 2,000	$ 2,000	$ 1,000	$ 1,000
Equipment	3,000	2,000		
Vehicle			25,000	10,000

At the end of the first year of business, Tyler, who was studying accounting, provided the following information:

TY & MATT SNOW REMOVAL SERVICES		
Income Statement		
Year ended December 31, 2014		
Service revenue		$50,000
Expenses		
Supplies expense	$ 6,000	
Depreciation expense	2,400	
Salaries expense	30,000	38,400
Profit		$11,600

Additional information:

1. Salaries expense is $20,000 and $10,000 cash paid to Tyler and Matt, respectively, during the year.
2. All revenues were collected in cash.
3. All supplies were paid for in cash. At the end of the year, there were no supplies on hand.
4. Tyler estimates that the equipment and vehicle have five-year useful lives, with no residual value. He used the straight-line method to calculate depreciation expense.
5. There is $17,000 in the bank account at December 31, 2014.

Instructions

(a) Prepare the entries to record each partner's investment in the partnership on January 2, 2014.
(b) Prepare journal entries to correct the errors, if any, on the income statement.
(c) Calculate the correct profit and the amount to be allocated to each partner.
(d) Prepare a statement of partners' equity for the year ended December 31, 2014.
(e) Prepare a balance sheet at December 31, 2014.
(f) Prepare closing entries for 2014.

TAKING IT FURTHER   Tyler is not happy about how the profit was allocated. He says that he works twice as hard as Matt. Matt argues that he made a larger contribution to start the partnership. What should Tyler and Matt do to deal with their concerns?

P12–7A   At April 30 of the current year, partners' capital balances and the profit- and loss-sharing ratio in SOS Enterprises are as follows:

Record admission of partner. (SO 5) AP

Partner	Capital Balance	Profit and Loss Ratio
R. Sanga	$40,000	3
K. Osborne	$20,000	2
W. Sanga	$60,000	4

On May 1, the SOSO Company is formed by admitting N. Osvald to the firm as a partner.

Instructions

Journalize the admission of Osvald under each of the following independent assumptions:

(a) Osvald purchases 50% of W. Sanga's ownership interest by paying W. Sanga $32,000 cash.
(b) Osvald purchases 50% of Osborne's ownership interest by paying Osborne $13,000 cash.
(c) Osvald invests $70,000 cash in the partnership for a 40% ownership interest.
(d) Osvald invests $40,000 in the partnership for a 20% ownership interest.
(e) Osvald invests $30,000 in the partnership for a 20% ownership interest.

TAKING IT FURTHER   Why would a new partner be willing to pay a bonus to the existing partners in order to join a partnership? Give an example of a situation where this might happen.

Record withdrawal of partner. (SO 6) AP

P12–8A   On December 31, the capital balances and profit and loss ratios in the FJA Company are as follows:

Partner	Capital Balance	Profit and Loss Ratio
H. Fercho	$140,000	60%
P. Jiang	$ 60,000	30%
R. Antoni	$ 49,000	10%

Antoni is withdrawing from the partnership.

Instructions

Journalize the withdrawal of Antoni under each of the following independent assumptions:

(a) Each of the remaining partners agrees to pay $29,000 cash from personal funds to purchase Antoni's ownership equity. Each partner receives 50% of Antoni's equity.
(b) Jiang agrees to purchase Antoni's ownership interest for $58,000 cash.
(c) Antoni is paid $58,000 from partnership assets.
(d) Antoni is paid $38,200 from partnership assets.

TAKING IT FURTHER   What factors are important in deciding whether the withdrawing partner should be paid from the remaining partners' personal assets or from the partnership's assets?

Record withdrawal and admission of partners; allocate profit. (SO 3, 5, 6) AP

P12–9A   Triple A Accountants is a partnership with three partners. On February 28, 2014, the three partners, M. Kumar, H. Deol, and A. Kassam, have capital balances of $85,000, $72,000, and $43,000, respectively. The profit and loss ratio is 4:3:1. On March 1, 2014, Deol withdraws from the partnership and they agree to pay him $90,000 cash from the partnership assets.

After Deol leaves, Kumar and Kassam agree to a 4:2 profit ratio. During the year ended February 28, 2015, the partnership earns a profit of $24,000. Neither Kumar nor Kassam makes any withdrawals because the partnership is short of cash after paying Deol. On March 1, 2015, Kumar and Kassam agree to admit C. Mawani to the partnership with a 45% interest for $75,000 cash. After Mawani is admitted, the new profit ratio will be 4:2:5 for Kumar, Kassam, and Mawani, respectively.

Instructions

(a) Journalize the withdrawal of Deol from the partnership.
(b) What are the balances in Kumar's and Kassam's capital accounts after Deol leaves the partnership?
(c) Prepare the journal entry to close the income summary account on February 28, 2015.
(d) What is the total partnership capital on March 1, 2015, prior to admitting Mawani?
(e) Prepare the journal entry to record the admission of Mawani into the partnership.
(f) What is the balance in each of the partners' capital accounts after Mawani is admitted to the partnership?

TAKING IT FURTHER   Why would the remaining partners agree to pay a bonus to a partner who is withdrawing from the partnership?

Prepare and post entries for partnership liquidation. (SO 7) AP

P12–10A   The partners in Cottage Country Company decided to liquidate the company on April 30, 2014, when balances in the company's accounts were as follows:

Cash	$11,700	Accumulated depreciation	$16,800
Accounts receivable	23,500	Accounts payable	30,200
Allowance for doubtful accounts	1,700	A. Hoffer, capital	42,100
Inventory	47,100	K. Lonseth, capital	18,800
Equipment	28,600	D. Posca, capital	1,300

The partners share profit and loss 5:3:2 for Hoffer, Lonseth, and Posca, respectively. During the process of liquidation, the transactions below were completed in the sequence shown:

1. A total of $18,000 was collected from the accounts receivable on May 4.
2. The inventory and equipment were sold for $50,000 cash on May 6.
3. Liabilities were paid in full on May 7.
4. Posca paid his capital deficiency on May 9.
5. Cash was paid to the partners with credit balances on May 12.

Instructions

(a) Prepare the entries to record the transactions.
(b) Post the transactions to the cash and capital accounts.
(c) Assume instead that Posca is unable to repay his capital deficiency. Prepare the entry to record (1) the reallocation of his deficiency, and (2) the final distribution of cash.

TAKING IT FURTHER   When determining how the cash is distributed to partners in a liquidation, the profit and loss ratio should be used. Is this correct or incorrect? Why?

P12–11A   The three partners of Hawkdale Veterinary Clinic agree to liquidate their partnership on August 8, 2014. At that point, the accounting records show the following balances:

Record liquidation of partnership. (SO 7) AP

Cash	$150,000	H. Brumby, capital	$230,000
Supplies	400,000	R. Criolio, capital	170,000
Bank loan payable	125,000	A. Paso, capital	25,000

The three partners share profit and loss equally.

Instructions

(a) Journalize the liquidation of the partnership on August 8 under each of the following independent assumptions:
   1. The supplies are sold for $430,000 cash, the bank loan payable is paid, and the remaining cash is paid to the partners.
   2. The supplies are sold for $310,000 cash and the bank loan payable is paid. Assume that any partners with a debit capital balance pay the amount owed to the partnership.
(b) Refer to item 2 above. Assume instead that any partners with a debit capital balance are unable to pay the amount owed to the partnership. Journalize the reallocation of the deficiency and final distribution of cash to the remaining partners.

TAKING IT FURTHER   What can partners do when a partnership is first created to reduce the possibility that one of the partners will have a deficit (debit balance) when the partnership is liquidated?

P12–12A   On March 2, 2013, Zoe Moreau, Karen Krneta, and Veronica Visentin start a partnership to operate a personal coaching and lifestyle consulting practice for professional women. Zoe will focus on work-life balance issues, Karen on matters of style, and Veronica on health and fitness. They sign a partnership agreement to split profits in a 3:2:3 ratio for Zoe, Karen, and Veronica, respectively. The following are the transactions for MKV Personal Coaching:

Account for formation of a partnership, allocation of profits, and withdrawal and admission of partners; prepare partial balance sheet. (SO 2, 3, 4, 5, 6) AP

2013

Mar. 2 The partners contribute assets to the partnership at the following agreed amounts:

	Z. Moreau	K. Krneta	V. Visentin
Cash	$15,000	$10,000	$20,000
Furniture		17,000	
Equipment	18,000		13,000
Total	$33,000	$27,000	$33,000

They also agree that the partnership will assume responsibility for Karen's note payable of $5,000.

Dec. 20 Zoe, Karen, and Veronica each withdraw $30,000 cash as a "year-end bonus." No other withdrawals were made during the year.
   31 Total profit for 2013 was $110,000.

2014

Jan.   5   Zoe and Veronica approve Karen's request to withdraw from the partnership for personal reasons. They agree to pay Karen $15,000 cash from the partnership.

       6   Zoe and Veronica agree to change their profit-sharing ratio to 4:5, respectively.

Dec. 20   Zoe and Veronica withdraw $42,750 and $45,000 cash, respectively, from the partnership.

      31   Total profit for 2014 was $123,750.

2015

Jan.   4   Zoe and Veronica agree to admit Dela Hirjikaka to the partnership. Dela will focus on providing training in organizational skills to clients. Dela invests $31,000 cash for a 25% ownership in the partnership.

Instructions

(a) Record the above transactions. For the profit earned each year, calculate how it is to be allocated and record the closing of the income summary account.

(b) Prepare the partners' equity section of the balance sheet after Dela is admitted to the partnership.

TAKING IT FURTHER   Every time a new partner is admitted to a partnership or a partner withdraws from a partnership, it is necessary to completely close the accounting records of the existing partnership and start new accounting records for the new partnership. Do you agree or disagree? Explain.

▶ Problems: Set B

Discuss advantages and disadvantages of partnerships and partnership agreements. (SO 1) C

P12–1B   Max Reinholt and Rubin Stelmach are interested in starting a lawn and yard maintenance company that will operate under the name of Maximum Yard Maintenance. Max is very good at marketing and sales but isn't that fond of physical labour. Rubin excels at completing yard work on a timely basis but has limited people skills.

Instructions

(a) What are the advantages and disadvantages to Max and Rubin of operating this business as a partnership as opposed to a corporation?

(b) What other alternatives might they consider to setting up a partnership?

(c) Assuming they decide to form a partnership, what should be included in their partnership agreement? Be specific given the nature of the business and the two partners.

TAKING IT FURTHER   Should Max and Rubin consider forming a limited partnership or a limited liability partnership? Would either of these types of partnerships be of benefit in their particular situation? Explain.

Record formation of partnership and prepare balance sheet. (SO 2, 4) AP

P12–2B   Here are the post-closing trial balances of two proprietorships on January 1 of the current year:

	Visanji Company		Vanbakel Company	
	Dr.	Cr.	Dr.	Cr.
Cash	$ 9,500		$ 5,000	
Accounts receivable	15,000		20,000	
Allowance for doubtful accounts		$ 2,500		$ 4,000
Merchandise inventory	18,000		15,000	
Equipment	42,500		25,000	
Accumulated depreciation—equipment		22,000		14,000
Accounts payable		25,000		20,000
F. Visanji, capital		35,500		
P. Vanbakel, capital				27,000
	$85,000	$85,000	$65,000	$65,000

Visanji and Vanbakel decide to form the Varsity partnership and agree on the following fair values for the noncash assets that each partner is contributing:

	Visanji	Vanbakel
Accounts receivable	$11,500	$15,500
Merchandise inventory	20,000	15,000
Equipment	18,000	14,000

All of the assets in the two proprietorships will be transferred to the partnership on January 1. The partnership will also assume all the liabilities of the two proprietorships. Further, it is agreed that Vanbakel will invest the amount of cash required so her investment in the partnership is equal to Visanji's.

Instructions

(a) Prepare separate journal entries to record the transfer of each proprietorship's assets and liabilities to the partnership on January 1.

(b) Journalize the additional cash investment.

(c) Prepare a balance sheet for the partnership at January 1.

TAKING IT FURTHER What are some of the advantages of two individuals such as Visanji and Vanbakel operating their businesses as a partnership instead of as two separate proprietorships?

P12–3B At the end of its first year of operations, on December 31, 2014, LBG Company's accounts show the following:

Calculate and record division of profit. Prepare statement of partners' equity. (SO 3, 4) AP

Partner	Drawings	Capital
S. Little	$20,000	$65,000
L. Brown	15,000	45,000
P. Gerhardt	10,000	25,000

The capital balance represents each partner's initial capital investment on January 1, 2014. No closing entries have been recorded for profit (loss) or drawings as yet.

Instructions

(a) Journalize the entry to record the division of profit for the year ended December 31, 2014, under each of the following independent assumptions:

1. Profit is $55,000. Little, Brown, and Gerhardt are given salary allowances of $5,000, $25,000, and $10,000, respectively. The remainder is shared equally.

2. Profit is $25,000. Each partner is allowed interest of 5% on beginning capital balances. Brown and Gerhardt are given salary allowances of $15,000 and $20,000, respectively. The remainder is shared 3:2:1.

(b) Journalize the entry to close each partner's drawings account.

(c) Prepare a statement of partners' equity for the year under assumption (2) in (a) above.

TAKING IT FURTHER Explain why partnerships such as LBG Company include a salary allowance in their profit- and loss-sharing arrangements.

P12–4B Terry Lam and Chris Tan have a partnership agreement with the following provisions for sharing profit or loss:

Calculate division of profit or loss. Prepare income statement, statement of partners' equity, and closing entries. (SO 3, 4) AP

1. A salary allowance of $25,000 to Lam and $35,000 to Tan
2. An interest allowance of 6% on capital balances at the beginning of the year
3. The remainder to be divided between Lam and Tan on a 3:4 basis

The capital balances on February 1, 2013, for T. Lam and C. Tan were $110,000 and $130,000, respectively. For the year ended January 31, 2014, the Lam Tan Partnership had sales of $395,000; cost of goods sold of $275,000; operating expenses of $150,000; T. Lam drawings of $25,000; and C. Tan drawings of $35,000.

Instructions

(a) Prepare an income statement for the Lam Tan Partnership for the year.

(b) Prepare a schedule to show how the profit or loss is allocated to the two partners.

(c) Prepare a statement of partners' equity for the year.

(d) Prepare closing entries on January 31, 2014.

TAKING IT FURTHER In general, what is the relationship between the salary allowance specified in the profit and loss ratio and a partner's drawings?

P12–5B Below is an alphabetical listing of the accounts in the general ledger of Clay and Ogletree, LLP, at the partnership's fiscal year end, September 30, 2014. Adjusting entries for the year have been posted and included in these balances.

Prepare financial statements and closing entries. (SO 4) AP

Accounts payable	$ 21,500
Accounts receivable	105,000
Accumulated depreciation—equipment	12,000
Cash	13,500
Depreciation expense	12,000
Equipment	60,000
Fees earned	515,000

G. Clay, capital	75,000
G. Clay, drawings	150,000
Insurance expense	18,500
Interest expense	5,000
M. Ogletree, capital	37,500
M. Ogletree, drawings	100,000
Note payable	22,500
Prepaid insurance	3,500
Property tax expense	15,000
Salaries expense	225,000
Unearned revenue	24,000

Additional information:

1. The balance in Clay's capital account includes an additional investment of $10,000 made during the year.
2. $5,000 of the note payable is due within the next year.
3. Clay and Ogletree share profit and loss in the ratio of 3:2, respectively.

Instructions

(a) Prepare an income statement, statement of partners' equity, and balance sheet.
(b) Journalize the closing entries.

TAKING IT FURTHER   Should the two partners draw equal amounts each year? Both of them work full-time for the partnership.

Prepare entries to form a partnership, allocate profit, and close temporary accounts; prepare financial statements. (SO 1, 2, 3, 4) AP

P12–6B   Caitlin Maguire and Fiona Whelan, two college friends, decided to set up a house-cleaning business called Maguire & Whelan Cleaning Services. On January 1, 2014, they put their resources together, shook hands, and started their business. They each contributed the following to the business:

	Caitlin Maguire		Fiona Whelan	
	Original Cost	Fair Value	Original Cost	Fair Value
Cash	$ 1,000	$1,000	$ 750	$ 750
Equipment	2,000	1,500		
Vehicle			14,000	8,000

At the end of the first year of business, Caitlin, who was studying accounting, provided the following information:

MAGUIRE & WHELAN CLEANING SERVICES		
Income Statement		
Year ended December 31, 2014		
Service revenue		$35,000
Expenses		
Supplies expense	$ 3,000	
Depreciation expense	1,900	
Salaries expense	20,000	24,900
Profit		$10,100

Additional information:

1. Salaries expense is $12,000 and $8,000 cash paid to Caitlin and Fiona, respectively, during the year.
2. All revenues were collected in cash.
3. All supplies were paid for in cash. At the end of the year, there were no supplies on hand.
4. Caitlin estimates that the equipment and vehicle have five-year useful lives, with no residual value. She used the straight-line method to calculate depreciation expense.
5. There is $13,750 in the bank account at December 31, 2014.

Instructions

(a) Prepare the entries to record each partner's investment in the partnership on January 2, 2014.
(b) Prepare journal entries to correct the errors, if any, on the income statement.
(c) Calculate the correct profit and the amount to be allocated to each partner.
(d) Prepare a statement of partners' equity for the year ended December 31, 2014.
(e) Prepare a balance sheet at December 31, 2014.
(f) Prepare closing entries for 2014.

TAKING IT FURTHER   Caitlin is not happy about how the profit was allocated. She says that she works twice as hard as Fiona. Fiona argues that she made a larger contribution to start the partnership. What should Caitlin and Fiona do to deal with their concerns?

P12–7B   At September 30 of the current year, partners' capital balances and profit and loss ratios in NEW Company are as follows:

Record admission of partner. (SO 5) AP

Partner	Capital Balance	Profit and Loss Ratio
A. Nolan	$62,000	5
D. Elder	$48,000	4
T. Wuhan	$14,000	1

On October 1, the NEWS Company is formed by admitting C. Santos to the partnership.

Instructions

Journalize the admission of C. Santos under each of the following independent assumptions:

(a) Santos purchases 25% of Nolan's ownership interest by paying Nolan $20,000 cash.
(b) Santos purchases 33⅓% of Elder's ownership interest by paying Elder $20,000 cash.
(c) Santos invests $80,000 for a 30% ownership interest.
(d) Santos invests $36,000 for a 30% ownership interest.
(e) How much would Santos have to invest in the partnership for a 30% ownership interest so there is no bonus to the existing partners or the new partner?

TAKING IT FURTHER   Why would the existing partners be willing to give a bonus to the new partner? Give an example of a situation where this might happen.

P12–8B   On December 31, the capital balances and profit and loss ratios in the VKD Company are as follows:

Record withdrawal of partner. (SO 6) AP

Partner	Capital Balance	Profit and Loss Ratio
B. Vuong	$75,000	50%
G. Khan	50,000	30%
R. Dixon	37,500	20%

Instructions

Journalize the withdrawal of Dixon under each of the following independent assumptions:

(a) Each of the continuing partners agrees to pay $22,500 cash from personal funds to purchase Dixon's ownership equity. Each partner receives 50% of Dixon's equity.
(b) Khan agrees to purchase Dixon's ownership interest for $45,000 cash.
(c) Dixon is paid $47,500 from partnership assets.
(d) Dixon is paid $29,500 from partnership assets.

TAKING IT FURTHER   Assume that, instead of any of the above options, Dixon withdraws from the partnership by selling her interest to S. Meyers. Do Vuong and Khan need to approve it? Why or why not?

P12–9B   Ajax Architects is a partnership with three partners. On January 31, 2014, the three partners, Tova Radzik, Sela Kopel, and Etti Falkenberg, have capital balances of $98,000, $79,000, and $47,000, respectively. The profit and loss ratio is 4:3:1. On February 1, 2014, Radzik withdraws from the partnership and they agree to pay her $90,000 cash from the partnership assets.

Record withdrawal and admission of partners; allocate profit. (SO 3, 5, 6) AP

After Radzik leaves, Kopel and Falkenberg agree to a 2:1 profit ratio. During the year ended January 31, 2015, the partnership earns profit of $45,000. Neither Kopel nor Falkenberg makes any withdrawals because the partnership is short of cash after paying Radzik. On March 1, 2015, Kopel and Falkenberg agree to admit Devra Malkin to the partnership with a 45% interest for $110,000 cash. After Malkin is admitted, the new profit ratio will be 4:2:5 for Kopel, Falkenberg, and Malkin, respectively.

Instructions

(a) Journalize the withdrawal of Radzik from the partnership.
(b) What are the balances in Kopel's and Falkenberg's capital accounts after Radzik leaves the partnership?
(c) Prepare the journal entry to close the income summary account on January 31, 2015.
(d) What is the total partnership capital on February 1, 2015, prior to admitting Malkin?
(e) Prepare the journal entry to record the admission of Malkin into the partnership.
(f) What is the balance in each of the partners' capital accounts after Malkin is admitted to the partnership?

TAKING IT FURTHER Why might a partner who is withdrawing from a partnership agree to a cash payment that results in a bonus to the remaining partners?

Prepare and post entries for partnership liquidation. (SO 7) AP

P12–10B The partners in Omni Company decided to liquidate the company on May 31, 2014, when balances in the company's accounts were as follows:

Cash	$33,000	Accumulated depreciation	$ 6,600
Accounts receivable	30,000	Accounts payable	53,160
Allowance for doubtful accounts	1,200	L. Sciban, Capital	39,600
Inventory	41,400	V. Subra, Capital	25,200
Equipment	25,200	C. Werier, Capital	3,840

The partners share profit and loss 5:3:2 for Sciban, Subra, and Werier, respectively. During the process of liquidation, the transactions below were completed in the sequence shown:

1. A total of $20,000 was collected from the accounts receivable on June 2.
2. The inventory and equipment were sold for $48,000 cash on June 3.
3. Liabilities were paid in full on June 4.
4. Werier paid her capital deficiency on June 6.
5. Cash was paid to the partners with credit balances on June 9.

Instructions

(a) Prepare the entries to record the transactions.
(b) Post the transactions to the cash and capital accounts.
(c) Assume that Werier is unable to repay her capital deficiency. Prepare the entry to record (1) the reallocation of her deficiency, and (2) the final distribution of cash.

TAKING IT FURTHER In a liquidation, why are the liabilities paid before the partners?

Record liquidation of partnership. (SO 7) AP

P12–11B The three partners of Summer Springs Medical Clinic agree to liquidate their partnership on September 15, 2014. At that point, the accounting records show the following balances:

Cash	$100,000	M. Nokota, capital	$70,000
Supplies	110,000	S. Taishuh, capital	30,000
Accounts payable	90,000	A. Paso, capital	20,000

The three partners share profit and loss 50%, 25%, and 25%, for Nokota, Taishuh, and Paso, respectively.

Instructions

(a) Journalize the liquidation of the partnership on September 30 under each of the following independent assumptions:
   1. The supplies are sold for $130,000 cash, the liabilities are paid, and the remaining cash is paid to the partners.
   2. The supplies are sold for $25,000 cash and the liabilities are paid. Assume that any partners with a debit capital balance pay the amount owed to the partnership.
(b) Refer to item 2 in part (a) above. Assume instead that any partners with a debit capital balance are unable to pay the amount owed to the partnership. Journalize the reallocation of the deficiency and final distribution of cash to the remaining partners.

TAKING IT FURTHER For what reasons would a partnership decide to liquidate?

Account for formation of a partnership, allocation of profits, and admission and withdrawal of partners; prepare partial balance sheet. (SO 2, 3, 4, 5, 6) AP

P12–12B On February 14, 2013, Isabelle Moretti, Aida Kam, and Channade Fenandoe start a partnership to operate a marketing consulting practice. They sign a partnership agreement to split profits in a 2:3:4 ratio for Isabelle, Aida, and Channade, respectively. The following are transactions for MKF Marketing:

2013

Feb. 14 The partners contribute assets to the partnership at the following agreed amounts:

	I. Moretti	A. Kam	C. Fenandoe
Cash	$ 9,000	$12,000	$18,000
Furniture	15,000		
Equipment		24,000	40,000
Total	$24,000	$36,000	$58,000

They also agree that the partnership will assume responsibility for Channade's accounts payable of $10,000.

Dec. 20 The partners agree to withdraw a total of $72,000 cash as a "year-end bonus." Each partner will receive a share proportionate to her profit-sharing ratio. No other withdrawals were made during the year.

    31 Total profit for 2013 was $81,900.

2014

Jan. 5 The three partners agree to admit Carolyn Wells to the partnership. Carolyn will pay Channade $30,000 cash for 50% of her interest in the partnership. The profit-sharing ratio will be changed so that Carolyn is allocated 50% of what was previously allocated to Channade. The partnership's name is changed to MKFW Marketing.

Dec. 20 The partners agree to pay another "year-end bonus." The total amount withdrawn is $91,800. Each partner will receive a share proportionate to her profit-sharing ratio. No other withdrawals were made during the year.

    31 Total profit for 2014 was $103,050.

2015

Jan. 2 Channade withdraws from the partnership. The partners agree the partnership will pay her $25,550 cash. The partnership's name is changed to MKW Marketing.

Instructions

(a) Record the above transactions. For the profit earned each year, calculate how it is to be allocated and record closing the income summary account.

(b) Prepare the statement of partners' equity for 2014.

(c) Calculate the balance in each partner's capital account on January 2, 2015, after Channade has withdrawn.

TAKING IT FURTHER Every time a new partner is admitted to a partnership or a partner withdraws from a partnership, it is necessary to change the name of the partnership to reflect the fact that a new partnership has been formed. Do you agree or disagree? Explain.

▶ Continuing Cookie Chronicle

(*Note:* This is a continuation of the Cookie Chronicle from Chapters 1 through 11.)

Because Natalie has been so successful operating Cookie Creations, Katy would like to have Natalie become her partner. Katy believes that together they will create a thriving cookie-making business. Recall that Katy is Natalie's high school friend and has been operating her bakery for approximately 10 months.

Natalie is quite happy with her current business set-up. Up until now, she had not considered joining forces with anyone. From past meetings with Katy, however, Natalie has gathered the following information about Katy's business and compared it with her own results.

- The current fair values of the assets and liabilities of both businesses are as follows:

	The Baker's Nook	Cookie Creations
Cash	$ 1,500	$8,050
Accounts receivable	5,250	800
Merchandise inventory	500	1,200
Supplies	350	450
Equipment	7,500	1,500
Bank loan payable	10,000	0

All assets would be transferred into the partnership. The partnership would assume all of the liabilities of the two proprietorships. The Baker's Nook bank loan is due on October 31, 2015.

- Katy operates her business from leased premises. She has just signed a lease for 12 months. Monthly rent will be $1,000; Katy's landlord has agreed to draw up a new lease agreement that would be signed by both partners.
- Katy has no assets and has a lot of student loans and credit card debt. Natalie's assets consist of investments in Canada Savings Bonds. Natalie has no personal liabilities.
- Katy is reluctant to have a partnership agreement drawn up. She thinks it's a waste of both time and money. As Katy and Natalie have been friends for a long time, Katy is confident that all problems can be easily resolved over a nice meal.

Natalie believes that it may be a good idea to establish a partnership with Katy. She comes to you with the following questions:

1. Do I really need a formalized partnership agreement drawn up? What would be the point of having one if Katy and I agree on all major decisions? What type of information should the partnership agreement contain?

2. I would like to have Katy contribute the same amount of capital as I am contributing. How much additional cash, in addition to the amount in Katy's proprietorship, would Katy have to borrow to invest in the partnership so that she and I have the same capital balances?

3. Katy has a lot of personal debt. Should this affect my decision about whether or not to go forward with this business venture? Why or why not?

4. What other issues should I consider before I say yes or no to Katy?

Instructions

(a) Answer Natalie's questions.

(b) Assume that Natalie and Katy go ahead and form a partnership called Cookie Creations and More on August 1, 2014, and that Katy is able to borrow the additional cash she needs to contribute to the partnership. Prepare a balance sheet for the partnership at August 1.

CHAPTER 12 | BROADENING YOUR PERSPECTIVE

▶ Financial Reporting and Analysis

Financial Reporting Problem

BYP12–1 Reitmans (Canada) Limited, Canada's largest women's specialty retailer, was founded in 1926 by Herman and Sarah Reitman. Their traditional "general store" opened on Saint-Laurent Boulevard in Montreal and was run and managed by the Reitman family. The popularity of their clothing line prompted them to open their second store, which exclusively sold women's apparel. Over the last 85 years, Herman and Sarah's children and grandchildren have taken a family-operated business and transformed it into one of Canada's largest fashion retailers.

Instructions

(a) When Herman and Sarah Reitman opened their first store, they may have operated it as a partnership or they may have incorporated the business from the start. What factors might have influenced their decision?

(b) Regardless of its start, Reitmans is now organized as a corporation. What factors may have influenced this decision?

(c) Look at Reitmans (Canada) Limited's corporate financial statements reproduced in Appendix A at the back of this textbook. In what ways would the partnership financial statements have been different from these corporate statements?

Interpreting Financial Statements

BYP12–2 The Inter Pipeline Fund is a major petroleum, natural gas liquids extraction, and bulk liquid storage business operating in Western Canada and Europe. The balance sheet and notes to its financial statements include the following excerpts:

INTER PIPELINE FUND Balance Sheet (partial) December 31, 2011 (in thousands)	
Partners' equity	
Partners' equity	$1,452,066
Total reserves*	(32,280)
Total partners' equity	$1,419,786

*Normally called Accumulated other comprehensive income in a corporation.

> **INTER PIPELINE FUND**
> **Notes to the Financial statements (partial)**
> **December 31, 2011**
>
> **Structure of the Partnership**
>
> Inter Pipeline Fund (Inter Pipeline) was formed as a limited partnership under the laws of Alberta pursuant to a Limited Partnership Agreement (LPA) dated October 9, 1997. Inter Pipeline's Class A limited liability partnership units (Class A units) are listed on the Toronto Stock Exchange and are classified as partners' equity in the consolidated balance sheets. Pipeline Management Inc. (the General Partner) is required to maintain a minimum 0.1% interest in Inter Pipeline. Inter Pipeline is dependent on the General Partner for administration and management of all matters relating to the operation of Inter Pipeline.

The annual report also states:

"Class A unitholders generally do not have voting rights in relation to matters involving Inter Pipeline or the General Partner, including with respect to the election of directors of the General Partner. The General Partner manages and controls the activities of Inter Pipeline. Class A unitholders have no right to elect the General Partner on an annual or other ongoing basis and, except in limited circumstances, the General Partner may not be removed by the limited partners."

Instructions

(a) What are the advantages to the company of operating as a limited partnership rather than as a general partnership?

(b) Why might there be a restriction on the ability of the limited partners to be involved in matters involving the partnership or in determining who is the general partner?

▶ Critical Thinking

Collaborative Learning Activity

Note to instructor: Additional instructions and handout material for this group activity can be found on the Instructor Resource Site and in *WileyPLUS*.

BYP12–3 In this group activity, you will be given two independent scenarios: one involving the admission of a partner, and one involving the withdrawal of a partner. You will be required to determine the balance in the cash account and in each partner's capital account after the change in ownership.

Communication Activity

BYP12–4 You are an expert in forming partnerships. Dr. Konu Chatterjie and Dr. Sheila Unger want to establish a partnership to practise medicine. They will meet with you to discuss their plans. However, you will first send them a letter that outlines the issues they need to consider beforehand.

Instructions

Write a letter, in good form, discussing the different types of partnership organizations and the advantages and disadvantages of each type so that the doctors can start thinking about their needs.

Ethics Case

BYP12–5 Susan and Erin operate a spa as partners and share profits and losses equally. Their business has been more successful than they expected and is operating profitably. Erin works hard to maximize profits. She schedules appointments from 8 a.m. to 6 p.m. daily and she even works weekends. Susan schedules her appointments from 9 a.m. to 5 p.m. and does not work weekends. Susan regularly makes much larger withdrawals of cash than Erin does, but tells Erin not to worry. "I never make a withdrawal without you knowing about it," she says to Erin, "so it's properly recorded in my drawings account and charged against my capital at the end of the year." To date, Susan's withdrawals are twice as much as Erin's.

Instructions

(a) Who are the stakeholders in this situation?

(b) Identify the problems with Susan's actions. In what ways are they unethical?

(c) What provisions could be put in the partnership agreement so that the differences in Susan's and Erin's work and withdrawal habits are no longer unfair to Erin?

"All About You" Activity

BYP12–6 In the "All About You" feature, we learned about some famous partnerships. The Beatles and the Rolling Stones were popular music bands that started in the early 1960s. However, the Beatles broke up in 1970 after disagreements, including a disagreement on who should be their financial advisor. In contrast, the Rolling Stones have continued to play together.

You and a couple of friends have decided to form an "indie" band. An indie band records and publishes its music independently from commercial record labels, thus maintaining control over its music and career. You play the guitar and sing; your friends are a bass player and a keyboard player. You have written the lyrics to a couple of songs and the music for the lyrics was composed by the band. After the songs are recorded, the band intends to register the recordings with SOCAN. SOCAN sells access to music registered with it by collecting licence fees from anyone playing or broadcasting live or recorded music. SOCAN then pays the musicians a royalty.

The three of you have decided to get together and discuss some of the issues that may arise and what should be addressed in the band's agreement.

Instructions

(a) Is the band a partnership even if a partnership agreement is never created?

(b) Identify the different types of revenues that the band may earn.

(c) Identify the costs that the band will incur to earn these revenues.

(d) Identify issues that may arise when the band is determining how the revenues and costs should be shared by the members.

(e) Identify issues that may arise if one of the band members wants to leave the band. How might this be addressed in the agreement?

(f) Identify issues that may arise if a new member joins the band after the band has already successfully recorded music and is receiving royalties.

(g) Identify issues that may arise if one of the band members does a solo recording or performance.

(h) Identify issues that may arise if the band decides to split up.

ANSWERS TO CHAPTER QUESTIONS

Across the Organization, p. 628

Q: How is the profit earned by a partner in an accounting partnership different from the earnings of a staff accountant in the same partnership?

A: The earnings paid to a staff accountant is recorded as salaries expense, which reduces profit. This amount is fixed in advance. The profit earned by a partner varies depending on the partnership's earnings during the year and the profit-sharing arrangements among all the partners. A partner can receive cash payments in the form of withdrawals during the year, but these are recorded as reductions of capital and not as salary expense.

All About You, p. 644

Q: If you and a friend wanted to start a partnership, how might you use a partnership agreement to ensure that your partnership becomes successful, instead of ending in an unhappy liquidation?

A: A partnership agreement should include: Who are the partners? What is each partner contributing? What are each partner's duties? How is profit (loss) shared? How will disputes be resolved? Addressing these items in advance may assist in resolving issues that might arise as the partnership evolves.

ANSWERS TO SELF-STUDY QUESTIONS

1. c   2. a   3. b   4. d   5. a   6. b   7. c   8. b   9. c   10. a

Remember to go back to the beginning of the chapter to check off your completed work!

CHAPTER THIRTEEN
INTRODUCTION TO CORPORATIONS

 THE **NAVIGATOR**

- ☐ Understand *Concepts for Review*
- ☐ Read *Feature Story*
- ☐ Scan *Study Objectives*
- ☐ Read *Chapter Preview*
- ☐ Read text and answer *Before You Go On*
- ☐ Review *Comparing IFRS and ASPE*
- ☐ Work *Demonstration Problem*
- ☐ Review *Summary of Study Objectives*
- ☐ Answer *Self-Study Questions*
- ☐ Complete assignments
- ☐ Go to *WileyPLUS* for practice and tutorials

CONCEPTS FOR **REVIEW**

Before studying this chapter, you should understand or, if necessary, review:

a. The differences between the forms of business organization. (Ch. 1, pp. 8 and 14–15)

b. The content of the equity section of the balance sheet for the different forms of organization. (Ch. 1, p. 24 and Ch. 4, p. 189)

c. How to prepare closing entries for a proprietorship (Ch. 4, pp. 175–178) and for a partnership. (Ch. 12, p. 624)

WHEN INCORPORATING MAKES GOOD BUSINESS SENSE

MISSISSAUGA, Ont.—When you think of a Canadian corporation, companies such as Canadian Tire, Scotiabank, or Tim Hortons might come to mind. Most of the largest corporations are public—they issue shares to the public to raise money to grow the business. But in fact, in Canada there are also many private corporations, whose shares are owned by just a few people. Most of these private corporations are small and medium-sized enterprises.

The decision to incorporate is based on business, legal, and tax reasons, says Keith Doxsee, President of Doxsee & Co., a chartered accounting firm that among other things provides advice and help to businesses looking to incorporate. The business owners need to consider if they will earn enough money to justify the expense of incorporation, and how many people are going to be involved in running and profiting from the business.

One of the first things to consider is whether the business is a financial and legal liability risk. "If you do something, are you likely to be sued if anything goes wrong? If you are, then you need to consider incorporation," Mr. Doxsee says. That's because, in a corporation, the shareholders are usually only liable for any financial obligations such as lawsuits or debts up to the amount they invested in the business but directors have responsibility for other liabilities such as taxes and unpaid wages. "A corporation provides you with a shield against most liabilities that would arise," he says. With a sole proprietorship or partnership,

all the owners are liable for all the business's obligations, and their personal assets could be at stake.

There can be big tax advantages to incorporating, which allows corporations to defer paying income taxes so they can put more income toward growing the business. So any business that might be starting small but has a business plan for fast growth, such as one in the high-tech industry, could incorporate at the start in order to generate working capital. Corporations pay an average of 15% income tax on the first $500,000 in corporate profits (depending on the province), whereas individuals earning more than $133,000 pay about 47%, Mr. Doxsee says.

Corporations are also good structures for some family-run businesses. For example, with a husband and wife ownership team, one spouse could be a shareholder and director and one only a shareholder, limiting their personal liability to just the director. Or the spouse in the lower personal income tax bracket could own more shares than the other and earn higher dividends but pay lower taxes.

However, Mr. Doxsee advises against forming a corporation for sole proprietors who do not intend on leaving income in the business to grow. That's because "once you take money out of the company, you have to pay personal tax on that as a dividend or salary." In that case, there is no financial advantage to being incorporated, and the costs and administrative burden of incorporating and filing annual corporate income tax returns are not worth it, he says.

THE **NAVIGATOR**

>> STUDY **OBJECTIVES**

After studying this chapter, you should be able to:

1. Identify and discuss characteristics of the corporate form of organization.

2. Account for the issuance of common and preferred shares.

3. Prepare a corporate income statement.

4. Account for cash dividends.

5. Prepare a statement of retained earnings and closing entries for a corporation.

6. Prepare the shareholders' equity section of the balance sheet and calculate return on equity.

THE **NAVIGATOR**

Many incorporated companies start out as unincorporated proprietorships or partnerships and later incorporate. Because of its advantages, the corporation dominates as the most common form of business organization. In this chapter, we will explain the essential features of a corporation, issuing share capital, corporate income tax, cash dividends, and retained earnings. Financial statements for a corporation reporting under ASPE, including an income statement, statement of retained earnings, and the shareholders' equity section of a balance sheet, are also shown. In Chapter 14, we will look at additional topics for corporations and the different corporate financial statements required under IFRS.

The chapter is organized as follows:

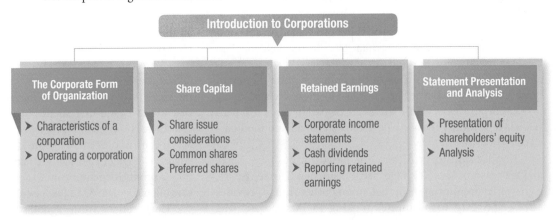

The Corporate Form of Organization

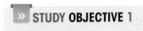
» STUDY OBJECTIVE 1

Identify and discuss characteristics of the corporate form of organization.

A **corporation** is a legal entity that is separate from its owners, who are known as shareholders. Corporations can be classified in a variety of ways. Two common classifications are by purpose and by ownership. For example, a corporation may be organized for the purpose of making a profit (such as Canadian Tire) or it may be **not-for-profit** (such as the Canadian Cancer Society).

In classification by ownership, there is a difference between public and private corporations. A **public corporation** is a corporation whose shares are available for purchase by the general public in an organized securities market, such as the Toronto Stock Exchange; it may have thousands of shareholders. All public corporations are "publicly accountable enterprises" and, as such, must follow International Financial Reporting Standards (IFRS). Most of the largest Canadian corporations are publicly held. Examples of publicly held corporations are Royal Bank of Canada, Magna International Inc., and, of course, Reitmans (Canada) Limited, as featured in Appendix A.

In contrast, a **private corporation**—often called a privately or closely held corporation—is a corporation whose shares are held by a few shareholders and are not available for the general public to purchase. Private companies are generally much smaller than publicly held companies, although there are notable exceptions, such as McCain Foods, The Jim Pattison Group, and the Irving companies. A private company has the choice of following IFRS or Accounting Standards for Private Enterprises (ASPE) unless it is considered a publicly accountable enterprise because, for example, it has bonds that are publicly held.

CHARACTERISTICS OF A CORPORATION

Regardless of the purpose or ownership of a corporation, there are many characteristics that make corporations different from proprietorships and partnerships. The most important ones are explained below.

Separate Legal Existence

As an entity that is separate from its owners, the corporation acts under its own name rather than in the name of its shareholders. A corporation may buy, own, and sell property. It may borrow money and enter into legally binding contracts in its own name. It may also sue or be sued, and it pays income tax as a separate legal entity.

Remember that in a proprietorship or partnership, the acts of the owners (partners) bind the proprietorship or partnership. In contrast, the acts of owners (shareholders) do not bind a corporation unless these individuals are also official agents of the corporation. For example, if you owned shares of Reitmans (Canada) Limited, you would not have the right to purchase or lease a new building unless you were an official agent of the corporation.

Limited Liability of Shareholders

Since a corporation is a separate legal entity, creditors have access to corporate assets only to have their claims repaid to them. The liability of each shareholder is limited to the amount that he or she invested in the shares of the corporation. This means that shareholders cannot be made to pay for the company's liabilities out of their personal assets, which can be done in the case of a proprietorship and a general partnership.

Limited liability is a significant advantage for the corporate form of organization, just as it is for a limited, or limited liability, partnership. However, in private corporations, creditors may demand a personal guarantee from a controlling shareholder. This makes the controlling shareholder's personal assets available, if required, for satisfying the creditor's claim—which eliminates or reduces the limited liability advantage. Also, as Keith Doxsee explains in our feature story, if a shareholder is also a director of the corporation, they are personally responsible for certain liabilities such as unpaid wages.

Transferable Ownership Rights

Ownership of a corporation is held in shares of capital. These are transferable units. Shareholders may dispose of part or all of their interest in a corporation simply by selling their shares. In a public corporation, the transfer of shares is entirely decided by the shareholder. It does not require the approval of either the corporation or other shareholders. However, in some private corporations, there may be a shareholders' agreement that limits how, and to whom, a shareholder can sell his or her shares.

The transfer of ownership rights between shareholders has no effect on the corporation's operating activities and it doesn't affect the corporation's assets, liabilities, and total equity. The transfer of these ownership rights is a transaction between individual shareholders. The company is only involved in the original sale of the share capital. Therefore, whenever a shareholder sells his or her shares to another investor, the company does not record a journal entry.

Ability to Acquire Capital

Corporations may issue shares in order to obtain capital (cash) for operations or new investments. Buying shares in a corporation is often attractive to an investor because a shareholder has limited liability and, in a public company, shares are easily transferable. Also, because only small amounts of money need to be invested, many individuals can become shareholders. For these reasons, a successful corporation's ability to obtain capital is almost unlimited.

Note that the "almost unlimited" ability of a corporation to acquire capital by issuing shares is only true for large, public corporations. Private corporations can have as much difficulty getting capital as any proprietorship or partnership.

Continuous Life

Corporations have an unlimited life. Since a corporation is a separate legal entity, its continuance as a going concern is not affected by the withdrawal, death, or incapacity of a shareholder, employee, or officer. As a result, a successful corporation can have a continuous and indefinite life. For example, the Hudson's Bay Company, the oldest commercial corporation in North America, was founded in 1670 and is still going strong. Its shareholders have changed over the years, but the corporation itself continues. In contrast, proprietorships end if anything happens to the proprietor and partnerships must reorganize if anything happens to one of the partners.

Government Regulations

Canadian companies may be incorporated federally, under the terms of the *Canada Business Corporations Act*, or provincially, under the terms of a provincial business corporations act. Federal and provincial laws specify the requirements for issuing shares, distributing income to shareholders, and reacquiring shares. Similarly, provincial securities commissions' regulations control the sale of share capital to the general public. When a corporation's shares are listed and traded on foreign securities markets, the corporation must also respect the reporting requirements of these exchanges. Respecting international, federal, provincial, and securities regulations increases costs and complexity for corporations.

Income Tax

Proprietorships and partnerships do not pay income tax as separate entities. Instead, each owner's (or partner's) share of profit from these organizations is reported on his or her personal income tax return. Income tax is then paid by the individual on this amount. In terms of income tax, it does not matter how much cash a proprietor or partner withdraws from the business. The owner is taxed on the profit, not on the cash withdrawals.

Corporations, on the other hand, must pay federal and provincial income tax as separate legal entities. Income tax rates vary based on the type of income and by province. In general, as Keith Doxsee explains in the feature story, corporate income tax rates are lower than the rate an individual would pay on the same amount of profit, especially in the case of small businesses.

In addition to the potential for reduced income tax, another advantage of incorporation is being able to delay personal income tax. The shareholders do not pay income tax on the profit, instead they pay income tax if they receive dividends or a salary from the corporation. Thus, some people argue that corporate income is taxed twice: once at the corporate level and again at the individual level when the dividend is received. This is not exactly true, however, as individuals receive a dividend tax credit to offset most of the tax paid at the corporate level.

To determine whether incorporating will result in more or less income tax for a proprietorship or partnership, it is wise to get expert advice. Income tax laws are complex, and careful tax planning is essential for any business venture.

The following list summarizes the advantages and disadvantages of the corporate form of business organization:

Advantages	Disadvantages
• Separate legal existence • Limited liability of shareholders • Potential for deferred or reduced income tax • Transferable ownership rights • Ability to acquire capital • Continuous life	• Increased cost and complexity to follow government regulations • Potential for additional income tax

OPERATING A CORPORATION

There are a few differences between operating a business using the corporate form of organization and using a partnership or proprietorship.

Forming a Corporation

Proprietorships and partnerships can be formed and begin operations without any formalities. On the other hand, the process of creating a corporation requires that the organizers submit articles of incorporation to the federal or provincial government for approval.

Articles of incorporation form the company's "constitution." They include information such as (1) the name and purpose of the corporation, (2) the number of shares and the kinds of shares to be authorized, and (3) the location of the corporation's head office. Anyone can apply to incorporate a company, as long as he or she is over the age of 18, of sound mind, and not bankrupt.

After receiving its articles of incorporation, the corporation sets its bylaws. The bylaws are the internal rules and procedures for operations. Corporations that operate interprovincially must also get a licence from each province they do business in. The licence ensures that the corporation's operating activities respect the laws of the province.

The costs of forming a corporation are called **organization costs**. These costs include legal fees, accounting fees, and registration costs. Under both ASPE and IFRS, these costs are recorded as expenses in the period when they are incurred.

Ownership Rights of Shareholders

Shareholders purchase ownership rights in the form of shares. Depending on the company's articles of incorporation, it may be authorized to issue different classes of shares, such as Class A, Class B, and so on. The rights and privileges for each class of shares are stated in the articles of incorporation. The different classes are often identified by the generic terms *common shares* and *preferred shares*. When a corporation has only one class of shares, this class has the rights and privileges of **common shares**. Each common share gives the shareholder the following ownership rights:

Vote: Shareholders have the right to vote on the election of the board of directors and appointment of external auditors. Each shareholder normally has one vote for each common share owned.
Dividends: Shareholders share in the distribution of the corporate profit through dividends, proportionate to the number of shares owned, if the board of directors declares a dividend.
Liquidation: Shareholders share in any assets that remain after liquidation, in proportion to the number of shares owned. This is known as a residual claim because shareholders are paid only if any cash remains after all the assets have been sold and the liabilities paid.

Corporation Management

Shareholders legally own the corporation. But as just explained, they have limited rights. They manage the corporation indirectly through the board of directors that they elect. The board, in turn, decides on the company's operating policies and selects officers—such as a chief executive officer (CEO) and other executive officers—to execute policy and to perform daily management functions. This structure is shown in Illustration 13-1.

▸ **ILLUSTRATION 13-1**
Authority structure in corporations

In a small private company, it is possible to have only one shareholder, who elects him- or herself to be the only person on the board of directors. In that capacity, he or she can appoint him- or herself as the CEO. On the other hand, the authority structure of a corporation makes it possible for it to hire professional managers to run the business, which is generally the case in public corporations.

Distribution of Profit—Dividends

Profits can be either reinvested by a company or distributed to its shareholders as dividends. A **dividend** is a pro rata distribution of a portion of a corporation's profits to its shareholders. "Pro rata" means that if you own, say, 10% of a corporation's shares, you will receive 10% of the total dividend paid to all shareholders. Dividends in corporations are somewhat similar to drawings in proprietorships or partnerships.

ACCOUNTING IN ACTION
ALL ABOUT YOU INSIGHT

If you are starting a business, you need to ask if it is better to use a proprietorship or to incorporate. The best form of organization for a business start-up may not be the best as the business's profits increase. When you start your business, a proprietorship is generally more advantageous because it involves relatively low start-up costs and low regulatory costs. Also, if your proprietorship suffers losses in its early years, these losses may be deducted against your other personal income, thus reducing your personal tax. As your business becomes profitable, there may be advantages if it is incorporated, especially in terms of tax savings. For example, some Canadian private corporations are eligible for a small business deduction that reduces the federal tax rate to 11% on the first $500,000 of taxable income. In comparison, your personal federal tax rate may be as high as 29% on taxable income over $132,406. Most owners of a corporation will need to take some income out of the business and must decide if it should be a salary or dividends. If the owner is paid a salary, it will reduce corporate income taxes, but the owner will pay personal income taxes on employment income. Personal income taxes paid on dividends are less than those on employment income. But if an individual only has dividend income, he or she cannot contribute to the Canada Pension Plan (CPP) or a Registered Retirement Savings Plan (RRSP). As you can see, deciding whether to incorporate or not is a complex matter.

Given the complexity of tax planning, and the impact that taxes could have on the advantages of incorporating, what should you do before deciding to incorporate your business?

BEFORE YOU GO ON...

Do It

Indicate if each of the following sentences is true or false:

_____ 1. Shareholders of a corporation have unlimited liability.
_____ 2. A corporation does not journalize the transfer of shares from one shareholder to another.
_____ 3. A corporation does not pay income tax on its profits.
_____ 4. Corporations are separate legal entities and continue to exist after the death of a shareholder.
_____ 5. The articles of incorporation contain information about the kinds of shares a corporation is authorized to issue.
_____ 6. The shareholders of a corporation have the right to declare a dividend.

Action Plan
• Review the characteristics and operation of a corporation.

THE NAVIGATOR

Solution

1. False   4. True
2. True   5. True
3. False   6. False

Related exercise material: BE13–1 and E13–2.

Share Capital

» STUDY OBJECTIVE 2

Account for the issuance of common and preferred shares.

You may recall from Chapters 1 and 4 that the shareholders' equity section of a balance sheet includes (1) share capital (contributed capital), and (2) retained earnings (earned capital). **Share capital** is amounts paid or contributed to the corporation by shareholders in exchange for shares of ownership. In the following section, we will look at issuing shares and the two main classes of shares—common shares and preferred shares. We will learn about retained earnings later in the chapter.

SHARE ISSUE CONSIDERATIONS

A corporation must determine how many different classes of shares it will issue, the specific rights and privileges of each class of shares, and how many of each class of shares can be sold to shareholders. It also has to decide how many to sell and at what price.

Authorized Share Capital

A corporation's **authorized shares**—the total number of each class of shares a corporation is allowed to sell—is indicated in its articles of incorporation. It may be specified as an unlimited number or a certain number (such as 500,000 shares authorized). Most corporations in Canada have an unlimited number of authorized shares. If a number is specified, the amount of authorized shares normally reflects the company's initial need for capital and what it expects to need in the future. The authorization of share capital does not result in a formal accounting entry, because the event has no immediate effect on either assets or shareholders' equity.

Issue of Shares

Issued shares are the authorized shares that have been sold. If a corporation has issued all of its authorized shares, it must get approval to change its articles of incorporation before it can issue additional shares. To find out how many shares can still be issued without changing the articles of incorporation, the total shares issued are subtracted from the total authorized.

A corporation can issue common shares in two ways: either directly to investors or indirectly through an investment dealer (brokerage house) that specializes in making potential investors aware of securities. Direct issue is typical in private corporations; indirect issue is typical for public corporations. The first time a corporation's shares are offered to the public, the offer is called an **initial public offering (IPO)**.

Once shares have been issued, investors can buy and sell them to each other, rather than buying them from the company. In public companies, the shares are traded on a **secondary market**, or stock exchange. When a company's shares are sold among investors, there is no impact on the company's financial position. The only change in the company records is the name of the shareholder, not the number of shares issued.

Market Value of Shares

The market value of a public company's shares changes according to the interaction between buyers and sellers on the secondary market. To some extent, the price follows the trend of a company's profit and dividends. The price also depends to some extent on how well the company is expected to perform in the future. Factors that a company cannot control (such as an embargo on oil, changes in interest rates, the outcome of an election, terrorism, and war) can also influence market prices.

For each listed security, the financial press reports the highest and lowest prices of the shares for the year; the annual dividend rate; the highest, lowest, and closing prices for the day; and the net change from the previous day. The total volume of shares traded on a particular day is also reported. Shares that are regularly bought and sold on the secondary market are considered to be actively traded. When shares are actively traded, the quoted market value of the share is considered to be a very good indication of the fair value of the shares.

Legal Capital

The distinction between share capital and retained earnings is important for both legal and financial reasons. Retained earnings can be distributed to shareholders as dividends or retained in the company for operating needs. On the other hand, share capital is **legal capital** that cannot be distributed to shareholders. Because shareholders have limited liability, legal capital must remain invested in the company for the protection of corporate creditors. In a proprietorship or a partnership, there is no such thing as legal capital. Proprietors or partners may withdraw whatever amount they choose because a company's creditor can access the owner's personal assets if the creditor suffers a loss.

Some countries, notably the United States, assign a par or stated value to shares to determine the amount of legal capital. The use of par value shares is rare in Canada, with fewer than 1% of publicly traded companies issuing par value shares. In fact, companies that are incorporated federally, as well as companies that incorporate in most Canadian provinces, are not allowed to issue shares with par values.

In Canada, **no par value shares**—shares that have not been assigned any specific value—are normally issued. When no par value shares are issued, all of the proceeds received from the sale of the shares are considered to be legal capital. In this text, we will assume that all of the shares in the examples and end of chapter material have no par value.

COMMON SHARES

All corporations must issue common shares. Some corporations also issue preferred shares, which have different rights and privileges than common shares. We will look at common shares in this section, and preferred shares in the next.

Issuing Shares for Cash

As discussed earlier, when no par value common shares are issued, the entire proceeds from the issue become legal capital. That means that the proceeds of the share issue are credited to the Common Share account. Most of the time, shares are issued in exchange for cash, particularly in large corporations.

To illustrate the issue of common shares for cash, assume that Hydroslide Inc., a private company, is authorized to issue an unlimited number of common shares. It issues 20,000 of these shares for $1 cash per share on January 2. The entry to record this transaction is as follows:

A = L + SE
+20,000   +20,000

↑ Cash flows: +20,000

Jan. 2	Cash	20,000	
	Common Shares		20,000
	To record issue of 20,000 common shares.		

Issuing Shares for Services or Noncash Assets

Helpful hint Fair value is the amount that would be agreed upon in an arm's-length transaction between knowledgeable, willing parties, or as the result of a bargaining process over the value of the good or service.

Although it is more usual to issue common shares for cash, shares are sometimes issued in exchange for services (such as compensation to lawyers or consultants) or for noncash assets (land, buildings, and equipment). When this happens, should the transaction be recorded at the fair value of the goods or services received, or at the fair value of the shares given up?

Under IFRS, the fair value of the goods or services received should be used, and it is presumed that this value can be determined except in rare cases. If the fair value of the goods or services received cannot be reliably determined, then the transaction is recorded at the fair value of the shares given in exchange. Under ASPE, the rules are more flexible; the transaction should be valued at whichever amount can be more reliably measured—the fair value of the goods or services received or the fair value of the shares issued. As a private company's shares are not widely traded, it can be very difficult to measure the fair value of the shares. Thus it is more likely that the value of the goods or services received will be used in recording the transaction.

To illustrate, assume that on February 25, the lawyer who helped Hydroslide incorporate billed the company $3,900 for her services. If Hydroslide has limited cash available, it may offer to issue common shares to the lawyer instead of cash. If the lawyer agrees, the challenge is to determine how many shares to offer in exchange for the legal services. As Hydroslide is a private company, its shares are not actively traded in a stock market. Therefore, it is difficult to determine the fair value per share, which in turn makes it difficult to know how many shares to issue.

Recall from the previous example that Hydroslide issued shares for $1 cash each at the beginning of the year. Therefore, it may offer the lawyer 3,900 share in exchange for the legal services. On the other hand, the lawyer may argue that she wants 4,000 shares because she is not getting paid in cash. The actual number of shares issued will be the result of a negotiation between the company and the lawyer. Regardless of the number of shares issued, the transaction is recorded at the fair value of the lawyer's services received, not at the value of the shares given up, because the fair value of the lawyer's services can be more reliably determined. For purposes of this example, we will assume that 4,000 shares are issued. Accordingly, the entry is recorded at $3,900 as follows:

Feb. 25	Legal Fees Expense	3,900	
	Common Shares		3,900
	To record issue of 4,000 common shares for legal services.		

A = L + SE
           −3,900
           +3,900
Cash flows: no effect

If shares are issued in exchange for land, buildings, or equipment, it is often necessary to use an appraiser to determine the fair value of the asset. Appraised values are often used as a reasonable estimate of the fair value of the asset, assuming the appraiser has the appropriate independence and expertise.

To illustrate, assume that FlexIt Ltd., a public company, issues 10,000 shares on October 1 to acquire refurbished bottling equipment. Assuming that an appraisal valued the equipment at $72,000, the following entry is made:

Helpful hint The asking or list price of land, buildings, or equipment is rarely the fair value of the asset. Asking or list prices are typically used only to start the bargaining process.

Oct. 1	Equipment	72,000	
	Common Shares		72,000
	To record issue of 10,000 common shares for equipment.		

A = L + SE
+72,000   +72,000
Cash flows: no effect

If the fair value of the equipment could not be determined, and if FlexIt's shares are actively traded with a market value of $7 per share, the equipment would be recorded at the fair value of the shares given up, $70,000 (10,000 × $7).

PREFERRED SHARES

A corporation may issue preferred shares in addition to common shares. **Preferred shares** have a preference, or priority, over common shares in certain areas. Typically, preferred shareholders have priority over (1) dividends (distributions of profit) and (2) assets if the company is liquidated. They generally do not have voting rights.

Like common shares, preferred shares may be issued for cash or for noncash assets or services. When a company has more than one class of shares, the transactions for each class should be recorded in separate accounts (e.g., Preferred Shares, Common Shares).

Unlike common shares, the annual dividend rate that the preferred shareholder may receive is specified in the articles of incorporation. The rate may be expressed as a percentage of the issue price or as a specific dollar amount. For example, if the annual dividend rate on the preferred shares is specified as $5 per share, these shares would be referred to as "$5 preferred shares." The dividend rate is always stated as an annual rate.

To illustrate, assume that Hydroslide Inc. issues 500, $5 preferred shares for $100 per share on July 7. The entry to record this transaction is as follows:

July 7	Cash (500 × $100)	50,000	
	Preferred Shares		50,000
	To record issue of 500, $5 preferred shares.		

A = L + SE
+50,000   +50,000
↑ Cash flows: +50,000

Some typical features of preferred shares, including dividend and liquidation preferences, are discussed next.

Dividend Preference

Preferred shareholders have the right to share in the distribution of dividends before common shareholders. For example, using the example of Hydroslide's $5 preferred shares explained above, the common shareholders will not receive any dividends in the current year until preferred shareholders have first received $5 for every share they own.

The first claim to dividends does not, however, guarantee that dividends will be paid. Dividends depend on many factors, such as having enough retained earnings and available cash. In addition, all dividends must be formally approved by the board of directors.

Preferred shares may have a **cumulative** dividend feature. This means that preferred shareholders must be paid dividends from the current year as well as any unpaid dividends from past years before common shareholders receive any dividends. When preferred shares are cumulative, preferred dividends that are not declared in a period are called **dividends in arrears**. Preferred shares without this feature are called **noncumulative**. A dividend on a noncumulative preferred share that is not paid in any particular year is lost forever. If a company has both cumulative and noncumulative preferred shares, the cumulative preferred shares will have priority over the noncumulative shares when dividends are declared.

To illustrate the cumulative dividend feature, assume that Hydroslide Inc.'s $5 preferred shares are cumulative. Hydroslide's annual total preferred dividend is $2,500 (500 × $5 per share). If dividends are two years in arrears, Hydroslide's preferred shareholders are entitled to receive the following dividends:

Dividends in arrears ($2,500 × 2)	$5,000
Current year dividends	2,500
Total preferred dividends	$7,500

No distribution can be made to common shareholders until this entire preferred dividend is paid. In other words, dividends cannot be paid on common shares while any preferred shares are in arrears.

Dividends in arrears are not considered a liability. There is no obligation to pay a dividend until one is declared by the board of directors. However, the amount of dividends in arrears should be disclosed in the notes to the financial statements. This allows investors to assess the potential impact of a future dividend declaration on the corporation's financial position.

Even though there is no requirement to pay an annual dividend, companies that do not meet their dividend obligations—whether cumulative or noncumulative—are not looked upon favourably by the investment community. When discussing one company's failure to pay its preferred dividend, a financial officer noted, "Not meeting your obligations on something like that is a major black mark on your record." The accounting entries for dividends are explained later in this chapter.

Liquidation Preference

In addition to having a priority claim on the distribution of income over common shares, preferred shares also have a priority claim on corporate assets if the corporation fails. This means that if the company is bankrupt, preferred shareholders will get money back before common shareholders do. The preference to assets can be for the legal capital of the shares or for a specified liquidating value. So, while creditors still rank above all shareholders in terms of preference, preferred shareholders rank above the common shareholders, and this is important as the money usually runs out before everyone gets paid.

Because of these two preferential rights—the right to dividends and assets—preferred shareholders generally do not mind that they do not have the voting right that common shareholders have.

Convertible Preferred

As an investment, preferred shares are even more attractive when there is a conversion privilege. Nearly half of the companies in Canada that report having preferred shares also have a conversion feature. **Convertible preferred shares** give preferred shareholders the option of exchanging their preferred shares for common shares at a specified ratio. They are purchased by investors who want the greater security of preferred shares but who also want the option of converting their preferred shares to common shares if the fair value of the common shares increases significantly.

To illustrate, assume that Ross Industries Inc. issues 1,000 convertible preferred shares at $100 per share. One preferred share is convertible into 10 common shares. The current fair value of the common shares is $9 per share. At this point, holders of the preferred shares would not want to convert, because they would exchange preferred shares worth $100,000 (1,000 × $100) for common shares worth only $90,000 (10,000 × $9). However, if the fair value of the common shares were to increase above $10 per share, it would be profitable for shareholders to convert their preferred shares to common shares.

When the shares are converted, the cost of the preferred shares is transferred to the Common Shares account. As it is seldom possible to determine the original cost of the preferred shares that are involved in the conversion, the average cost per share of the preferred shares is used instead. This is calculated by dividing the balance in the Preferred Shares account by the number of preferred shares issued immediately prior to the conversion.

To illustrate, assume that the 1,000 preferred shares of Ross Industries Ltd. with an average cost of $100 per share are converted into 10,000 common shares when the fair values of the two classes of shares are $101 and $12 per share, respectively, on June 10. The entry to record the conversion is:

June 10	Preferred Shares	100,000	
	Common Shares		100,000
	To record conversion of 1,000 preferred shares into 10,000 common shares.		

A = L + SE
−100,000
+100,000

Cash flows: no effect

Note that the fair value of the shares is *not* used by the corporation in recording the transaction because the total amount of share capital has not changed. But fair values are used by the preferred shareholders in their *decision* to convert.

Redeemable and Retractable Preferred

Many preferred shares are issued with a redemption or call feature. **Redeemable (or callable) preferred shares** give the issuing corporation the right to purchase the shares from shareholders at specified future dates and prices. The redemption feature gives a corporation some flexibility: it allows the corporation to eliminate the preferred shares when doing this will benefit it.

Often, shares that are redeemable are also convertible. Sometimes, companies will redeem or call their preferred shares to force investors to convert those preferred shares into common shares.

Retractable preferred shares are similar to redeemable preferred shares except that the shareholders can redeem shares at their option instead of the corporation redeeming the shares at its option. The retraction usually occurs at an arranged price and date.

When preferred shares are redeemable or retractable, the distinction between equity and debt is not clear. Redeemable and retractable preferred shares are similar in some ways to debt. They both offer a rate of return to the investor, and with the redemption or retraction of the shares, they both offer a repayment of the principal investment.

Recall from Chapter 11 that in order for accounting information to be useful, it must be presented in accordance with its economic substance rather than its form. Therefore, redeemable and retractable preferred shares may be presented in the *liabilities* section of the balance sheet rather than in the shareholders' equity section if, depending on the exact terms of the redemption or retraction, they have more of the features of debt than of equity. Accounting for these types of shares is left to an intermediate accounting course.

Helpful hint The two features benefit different parties. Redeemable shares are at the option of the corporation. Retractable shares are at the option of the shareholder.

ACCOUNTING IN ACTION
ACROSS THE ORGANIZATION

There are many reasons why some companies issue preferred shares to raise cash instead of borrowing or issuing common shares. Normally, companies pay a fixed dividend on preferred shares, but they aren't legally required to, so they can skip issuing dividends during tough times—something they can't do with interest payments on debt. Debt also has to be repaid at a certain time, whereas preferred shares do not normally have a maturity date. Preferred shares are considered equity and so do not show up on a company's books as a liability, which can help its credit rating. Since the fixed dividend is an attractive feature to some investors, issuing preferred shares can be a "win-win" arrangement.

While these are some financial reasons for companies to issue preferred shares, there is also an important strategic reason, particularly for private companies. Unlike common shareholders, preferred shareholders generally do not have voting rights, such as the right to elect members to the board of directors, so the common shareholders will not lose or reduce their voting control over business matters.

Sources: : Nick Louth, "Preference Shares Boast Yields of 7–10%," *Financial Times*, May 18, 2012; Mark Koba, "Preferred Stock: CNBC Explains," CNBC, January 5, 2012; David Aston, "Are Preferred Shares a Good Buy?", *MoneySense* magazine, November 2011; Alex Kocic, "Why Issue Preferred Shares?," eHow, retrieved on September 13, 2012, from http://www.ehow.com/about_7360408_issue-preferred-shares_.html.

Why might the "no maturity date" feature of preferred shares be useful to an organization?

BEFORE YOU GO ON...

Do It

Turin Corporation, a private company, was incorporated on March 1. The following are selected transactions over the next several months:

Mar. 15   Issued 120,000 common shares for cash at $8 per share.

Apr. 2   Issued 3,200 common shares to its lawyers in settlement of their bill for $25,000. Turin's president and the law firm agreed that the shares had a fair value of $8 each.

May 22   Issued 10,000 preferred shares for $90 each. Each share was convertible into 10 common shares.

Oct. 5   Preferred shareholders converted 2,000 of the preferred shares into common. At that point, it was estimated that the fair values of the common and preferred shares were $10 and $92, respectively.

Record the share transactions.

Action Plan

- Credit the Common Shares account for the entire proceeds.
- When shares are issued for services, use the fair value of what is received. If this amount cannot be determined, use the fair value of what is given up.
- Credit the Preferred Shares account for the entire proceeds of the share issue.
- Use the cost to record the conversion. Fair values are irrelevant.

Solution

Mar. 5	Cash	960,000	
	Common Shares (120,000 × $8)		960,000
	To record issue of 120,000 shares at $8 per share.		
Apr. 2	Legal Fees Expense	25,000	
	Common Shares		25,000
	To record issue of 3,200 shares for $25,000 of lawyers' fees.		
May 22	Cash	900,000	
	Preferred Shares (10,000 × $90)		900,000
	To record issue of 10,000 preferred shares at $90.		
Oct. 5	Preferred Shares (2,000 × $90)	180,000	
	Common Shares		180,000
	To record conversion of 2,000 preferred shares into 20,000 (2,000 × 10) common shares at an average cost of $90 per preferred share.		

THE NAVIGATOR

Related exercise material: BE13–2, BE13–3, BE13–4, BE13–5, BE13–6, E13–1, E13–3, E13–4, E13–5, and E13–6.

Retained Earnings

» **STUDY OBJECTIVE 3**

Prepare a corporate income statement.

Retained earnings are earned capital (cumulative profit or loss since incorporation) that has been retained in the company for future use. In other words, it is the cumulative profit that has not been distributed to shareholders. In the following sections, we will learn about two major components of retained earnings: (1) profit, and how it is reported on a corporation's income statement; and (2) cash distributions to owners (dividends) that reduce retained earnings. We will also learn how retained earnings are reported in the financial statements for companies following ASPE, and examine closing entries for a corporation.

CORPORATE INCOME STATEMENTS

In a corporation, unlike a proprietorship or partnership, income tax expense must be deducted when determining profit. Income tax expense is based on profit before income tax, which is calculated by subtracting all of the other expenses from total revenue. Although there are many complexities in corporate income tax, in this text we will keep it straightforward by simply multiplying profit before income tax by the income tax rate to determine income tax expense.

To illustrate, we will assume that Media General Limited had profit before income tax of $281,250 and a 20% income tax rate, which results in $56,250 ($281,250 × 20%) of income tax expense. Because income tax expense is based on profit before income tax, both of these amounts are shown on the income statement. Using assumed data for revenues and expenses, the condensed, multiple-step income statement for Media General Limited is shown in Illustration 13-2.

MEDIA GENERAL LIMITED **Income Statement** **Year Ended December 31, 2014**	
Sales	$800,000
Cost of goods sold	420,000
Gross profit	380,000
Operating expenses	94,000
Profit from operations	286,000
Interest expense	4,750
Profit before income tax	281,250
Income tax expense	56,250
Profit	$225,000

▶ILLUSTRATION 13-2
Corporate income statement

Income taxes affect not only the income statement (through the Income Tax Expense account) but also the balance sheet (through the Income Tax Payable account). Companies prepare a corporate income tax return (called a T2) annually to determine their taxable income and income tax payable. However, the Canada Revenue Agency requires income tax to be estimated in advance and paid (remitted to taxing authorities) in monthly instalments, rather than waiting until the end of the company's fiscal year.

After a company determines its total income tax payable at year end, it compares this amount with the total income tax instalments paid during the year. The difference between the income tax paid and income tax payable results in either an additional amount payable or a refund. Companies have six months after their fiscal year end to submit their corporate income tax return, or else they will incur late filing penalties on any balance due.

Once the additional liability (or receivable) has been determined, an adjusting entry is required. Assume Media General Limited had originally estimated that its taxable income would be $210,000. It has a 20% income tax rate, so its income tax was anticipated to be $42,000 ($210,000 × 20%). Media General remitted monthly instalments in the amount of $3,500 per month ($42,000 ÷ 12). At year end, Media General actually reports taxable income (profit before income tax) of $281,250. Its total income tax liability is $56,250 ($281,250 × 20%), and not $42,000 as estimated. Assuming it has already recorded and remitted $42,000 of income tax, the required adjusting entry is for $14,250 ($56,250 − $42,000) and is recorded as follows:

Dec. 31	Income Tax Expense	14,250	
	Income Tax Payable		14,250
	To adjust estimated income tax expense to actual.		

A = L + SE
+14,250 −14,250
Cash flows: no effect

Media General's income statement reports income tax expense of $56,250. The balance sheet reports a current liability of $14,250.

The Media General Limited example is typical of a private company following ASPE. In Chapter 14, we will learn about additional complexities that affect corporate income statements, including information required under IFRS.

BEFORE YOU GO ON...

Do It

For the year ended June 30, 2014, Viceron Inc. had service revenue of $350,000; operating expenses of $195,000; and interest expense of $14,000. The company has a 25% income tax rate. (a) Determine income tax expense. (b) Prepare an income statement. (c) Prepare the entry to record income tax, assuming that $30,000 had been previously accrued.

Action Plan

- Determine profit before income tax by deducting expenses from revenues.
- Calculate income tax expense by multiplying profit before income tax by the tax rate.
- Prepare the income statement, deducting income tax expense from profit before income tax.
- Deduct the income tax previously accrued from income tax expense to prepare the entry to record income tax.

THE NAVIGATOR

Solution

(a) Profit before income tax = $350,000 − $195,000 − $14,000 = $141,000
Income tax expense = $141,000 × 25% = $35,250

(b)

VICERON INC. Income Statement Year Ended June 30, 2014	
Service revenue	$350,000
Operating expenses	195,000
Profit from operations	155,000
Interest expense	14,000
Profit before income tax	141,000
Income tax expense	35,250
Profit	$105,750

(c)

June 30	Income Tax Expense ($35,250 − $30,000)	5,250	
	Income Tax Payable		5,250
	To adjust estimated income tax expense to actual.		

Related exercise material: BE13–7 and E13–7.

CASH DIVIDENDS

» **STUDY OBJECTIVE 4**

Account for cash dividends.

A **cash dividend** is a distribution of cash, on a pro rata basis, to shareholders. Cash dividends are the most common type of dividend in practice but stock dividends are also declared on occasion. We will learn about stock dividends in Chapter 14.

Necessary Conditions to Pay Cash Dividends

For a corporation to pay a cash dividend, it must have all three of the following:

1. **Enough cash.** A company must keep enough cash on hand to pay for its ongoing operations and to pay its bills as they come due. Under the *Canada Business Corporations Act*, a corporation cannot pay a dividend if it would then become unable to pay its liabilities. Therefore, a company must consider its ongoing cash needs before paying shareholders a cash dividend.

2. **The maintenance of legal capital.** As discussed earlier, in order to protect creditors, a company must maintain its legal capital. Under the *Canada Business Corporations Act*, a company must ensure that the dividend does not reduce the realizable value of its assets below the total of its liabilities and legal capital. Under some provincial legislation, a company must also have enough retained earnings before it can pay a dividend. In those cases, a corporation is not allowed to create or increase a deficit (negative retained earnings) by declaring the dividend.

In addition to maintaining legal capital, there may be specific **retained earnings restrictions** that make a portion of the Retained Earnings balance unavailable for dividends. For example, a company may have long-term debt contracts that restrict retained earnings as a condition of the loan. These restrictions are known as **debt covenants**, which, among other things, can limit the payment of dividends in order to make it more likely that the corporation will be able to meet required loan payments.

3. **A declaration of dividends by the board of directors.** A company cannot pay dividends unless its board of directors decides to do so, at which point the board "declares" the dividend to be payable. The board of directors has full authority to determine the amount of retained earnings to be distributed as a dividend and the amount to keep in the business. Dividends do not accrue like interest on a note payable. Even if the preferred shares are cumulative, dividends in arrears are not a liability until they are declared.

Entries for Cash Dividends

There are three important dates for dividends: (1) the declaration date, (2) the record date, and (3) the payment date. Normally, there are several weeks between each date and the next one. Accounting entries are required on two of the dates: the declaration date and the payment date.

On the **declaration date**, a company's board of directors formally declares (authorizes) the cash dividend and announces it to shareholders. Declaring a cash dividend commits the corporation to a legal obligation. The obligation is binding and cannot be rescinded (reversed). An entry is required to recognize the increase in Cash Dividends (which results in a decrease in Retained Earnings) and the increase in a current liability account, Dividends Payable. Cash dividends can be paid to preferred and common shareholders. If dividends are paid to the common shareholders, remember that preferred shareholders have to be paid first.

To illustrate a cash dividend, assume that on December 1, the directors of Media General Limited declare a $0.50-per-share quarterly cash dividend on the company's 100,000 common shares. Media does not have any preferred shares and thus does not need to pay them as well. The dividend totals $50,000 ($0.50 × 100,000) and is payable on January 23 to shareholders on December 30. The entry to record the declaration is as follows:

	Declaration Date		
Dec. 1	Cash Dividends—Common	50,000	
	Dividends Payable		50,000
	To record declaration of cash dividend.		

A   =   L   +   SE
        +50,000   −50,000
Cash flows: no effect

Note that the balance in Dividends Payable is a current liability. It will normally be paid within the next month or so. In the case of Media General, it will be paid on January 23. Also note that the Cash Dividends—Common account is similar to the owner's drawings accounts in proprietorships and partnerships.

Instead of debiting a Cash Dividends account, it is also acceptable to debit Retained Earnings when the dividends are declared because dividends reduce retained earnings. The only difference is that, if a Cash Dividends account is debited, then it will have to be closed at the end of the accounting period. While that is an extra step, the advantage of debiting a Cash Dividends account, instead of Retained Earnings, is that it is easier to keep track of the dividends declared during the period.

On the **record date**, ownership of the shares is determined so that the corporation knows who to pay the dividend to. These shareholders are known as the shareholders of record on that date. This date is particularly important for public corporations whose share ownership constantly changes as shares are bought and sold on the secondary market. For Media General, the record date is December 30. No entry is required on this date because the corporation's liability was recognized on the declaration date and is unchanged.

On the **payment date**, dividend cheques are mailed to shareholders and the payment of the dividend is recorded. The entry on January 23, the payment date, is as follows:

Helpful hint Between the declaration date and the record date, the number of shares remains the same. The purpose of the record date is to identify the persons or entities that will receive the dividend, not to determine the total amount of the dividend liability.

	Payment Date		
Jan. 23	Dividends Payable	50,000	
	Cash		50,000
	To record payment of cash dividend.		

A   =   L   +   SE
−50,000   −50,000
↓ Cash flows: −50,000

Note that the declaration of a cash dividend increases liabilities and reduces shareholders' equity. The payment of the dividend reduces both assets and liabilities, but has no effect on shareholders' equity. The cumulative effect of the declaration and payment of a cash dividend is to decrease both shareholders' equity (through the Retained Earnings account) and total assets (through the Cash account).

The key dates for dividends are shown in Illustration 13-3.

▸**ILLUSTRATION** **13-3**
Key dividend dates

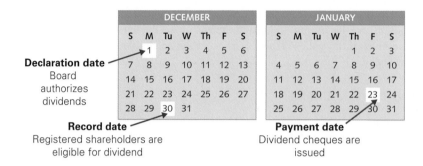

Dividends in a corporation are the equivalent of drawings in a proprietorship or a partnership. Dividends reduce shareholders' equity, just as drawings reduce owner's equity in a proprietorship and partners' equity in a partnership.

Action Plan
- Remember that as soon as a dividend is declared, the company has an obligation to pay it.
- The date of record is used to determine who will receive the dividend.
- On the payment date, there is no impact on shareholders' equity but assets and liabilities are reduced.

THE **NAVIGATOR**

BEFORE YOU GO ON...

Do It

The board of directors of the Blue Heron Corporation met on December 22 and voted in favour of declaring both the annual preferred share dividend and a $1 common share dividend to shareholders of record on January 1. The dividend will be paid on January 15. The company has 30,000, $4 noncumulative preferred shares and 150,000 common shares. Prepare the entries required on each of these dates.

Solution

Dec. 22	Cash Dividends—Preferred (30,000 × $4)	120,000	
	Cash Dividends—Common (150,000 × $1)	150,000	
	Dividends Payable ($120,000 + $150,000)		270,000
	To record declaration of cash dividend.		
Jan. 1	No journal entry		
Jan. 15	Dividends Payable	270,000	
	Cash		270,000
	To record payment of cash dividend.		

Related exercise material: BE13–8 and E13–8.

» **STUDY OBJECTIVE 5**

Prepare a statement of retained earnings and closing entries for a corporation.

ASPE

REPORTING RETAINED EARNINGS

Statement of Retained Earnings (ASPE)

All corporations are required to provide information on each of the transactions and events that changed retained earnings during the period and to show how ending retained earnings has been calculated. For companies following ASPE, this information is reported in a **statement of retained earnings**. In Chapter 14, you will learn how companies following IFRS include this information in a statement of changes in shareholders' equity.

A statement of retained earnings is similar to the statement of owner's equity prepared for a proprietorship. The income statement must be prepared before the statement of retained earnings in order to determine the profit that will be added to (or loss that will be deducted from) beginning retained earnings. As in the statement of owner's equity, the statement of retained earnings starts with the beginning balance, and then shows all of the changes in order to calculate the ending balance.

As cash dividends declared reduce retained earnings, this amount is shown as a deduction in the statement of retained earnings. This is similar to deducting drawings in a statement of owner's equity. However, it should be noted that **the statement of retained earnings reports the amount of dividends declared, not the amount of dividends paid.** Frequently these are the same amounts. But as we saw in the previous section, dividends can be declared in one year and paid in the next; thus dividends declared and dividends paid during the year are not always the same amounts.

To illustrate, assume that Media General Limited had $928,000 of retained earnings at January 1, 2014, and declared total cash dividends of $200,000 in 2014. Recall from Illustration 13-2 that the company had profit of $225,000 in 2014. Its statement of retained earnings for the year ended December 31, 2014, is shown in Illustration 13-4.

MEDIA GENERAL LIMITED Statement of Retained Earnings Year Ended December 31, 2014	
Retained earnings, January 1	$ 928,000
Add: Profit	225,000
	1,153,000
Less: Cash dividends	200,000
Retained earnings, December 31	$ 953,000

▶ **ILLUSTRATION 13-4**
Statement of retained earnings

Closing Entries for a Corporation

As in a proprietorship or partnership, it is necessary to close all of a corporation's temporary accounts at the end of the accounting period to get the accounts in the general ledger ready for the next period. It is also necessary to update the balance in the Retained Earnings account to its year-end balance.

Recall that recording closing entries and preparing a post-closing trial balance are the final steps in the accounting cycle. Also recall that in a proprietorship or partnership, each revenue and expense account (which combine to produce profit or loss) is closed to Income Summary, which is then closed to the owner's capital account, and drawings are also closed to the owner's capital account.

In a corporation, the process is the same, except that the income summary and the dividend accounts are closed to Retained Earnings. The closing process for a corporation is shown in Illustration 13-5.

▶ **ILLUSTRATION 13-5**
Closing process for a corporation

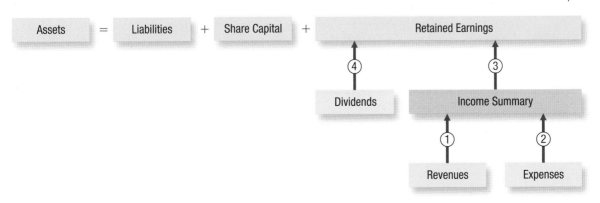

Notice that the closing process does not affect assets, liabilities, or share capital accounts.

To illustrate the closing journal entries, use the income statement accounts shown for Media General Limited in Illustration 13-2. Also recall from Illustration 13-4 that it declared dividends of $200,000 in 2014. The Cash Dividends account will also need to be closed. The closing entries follow:

A	=	L	+	SE				
				−800,000				
				+800,000				

Cash flows: no effect

A	=	L	+	SE
				−575,000
				+575,000

Cash flows: no effect

A	=	L	+	SE
				−225,000
				+225,000

Cash flows: no effect

A	=	L	+	SE
				−200,000
				+200,000

Cash flows: no effect

Dec. 31	Sales	800,000	
	Income Summary		800,000
	To close revenue to income summary.		
31	Income Summary	575,000	
	Cost of Goods Sold		420,000
	Operating Expenses		94,000
	Interest Expense		4,750
	Income Tax Expense		56,250
	To close expenses to income summary.		
31	Income Summary ($800,000 − $575,000)	225,000	
	Retained Earnings		225,000
	To close income summary to retained earnings.		
31	Retained Earnings	200,000	
	Cash Dividends—Common		200,000
	To close dividends to retained earnings.		

Posting the closing entries to the Income Summary and Retained Earnings accounts follows:

Income Summary					**Retained Earnings**		
Clos.	575,000	Clos.	800,000			Bal.	928,000
		Bal.	225,000	Clos.	200,000	Clos.	225,000
Clos.	225,000					Bal.	953,000
		Bal.	0				

Although not shown, after posting the closing entries, all of the revenue, expense, and dividend accounts will have a zero balance.

After these entries are posted, the Retained Earnings account (a permanent account) is updated in the general ledger to the December 31, 2014, balance of $953,000, previously shown in the statement of retained earnings. This ending balance is reported in the shareholders' equity section of the balance sheet. The normal balance of the Retained Earnings account is a credit. If total losses and dividends to date are greater than total profit to date, the Retained Earnings account will have a debit balance, which is called a **deficit**. The ending Retained Earnings balance becomes the opening balance for the next period.

 BEFORE YOU GO ON...

Do It

On January 1, 2014, SlopeBack Ltd. had a balance of $326,700 in its retained earnings account. During the year, it declared $100,000 cash dividends and paid $75,000. Its profit in 2014 was $115,000, calculated as follows:

Sales		$425,000
Cost of goods sold	$202,500	
Selling expenses	75,000	
Income tax expense	32,500	310,000
Profit		$115,000

(a) Prepare a statement of retained earnings.
(b) Prepare closing entries.
(c) Post closing entries to the income summary and retained earnings accounts.

Solution

(a)

SLOPEBACK LTD. Statement of Retained Earnings Year Ended December 31, 2014		
Retained earnings, January 1, 2014	$326,700	
Add: Profit	115,000	
	441,700	
Less: Cash dividends	100,000	
Retained earnings, December 31, 2014	$341,700	

(b)

Dec. 31	Sales		425,000	
		Income Summary		425,000
		To close revenue to income summary.		
31	Income Summary		310,000	
		Cost of Goods Sold		202,500
		Selling Expenses		75,000
		Income Tax Expense		32,500
		To close expenses to income summary.		
31	Income Summary		115,000	
		Retained Earnings		115,000
		To close income summary ($425,000 − $310,000) to retained earnings.		
31	Retained Earnings		100,000	
		Cash Dividends—Common		100,000
		To close dividends to retained earnings.		

(c)

Income Summary				Retained Earnings			
Clos.	310,000	Clos.	425,000			Bal.	326,700
		Bal.	115,000	Clos.	100,000	Clos.	115,000
Clos.	115,000					Bal.	341,700
		Bal.	0				

Related exercise material: BE13–9, BE13–10, E13–9, and E13–10.

Action Plan

- A statement of retained earnings shows the changes in the company's retained earnings. It starts with the previous year's retained earnings. Then profit is added and dividends declared are deducted to determine the ending balance.
- Dividends declared are shown on the statement of retained earnings.
- Closing entries are similar to proprietorships and partnerships except that the Income Summary and Cash Dividends accounts are closed to Retained Earnings.

THE NAVIGATOR

Statement Presentation and Analysis

In this section, we explain the preparation and presentation of the shareholders' equity section of the balance sheet and then learn how to use this information to calculate an important profitability measure—the return on equity ratio.

PRESENTATION OF SHAREHOLDERS' EQUITY

As explained earlier in the chapter, shareholders' equity always includes two parts: (1) share capital and (2) retained earnings. On the balance sheet, share capital may be shown as part of contributed capital, as explained below. Corporations following IFRS will also have a third section called accumulated other comprehensive income, illustrated in Chapter 14. Companies following ASPE do not have accumulated other comprehensive income.

» STUDY **OBJECTIVE 6**

Prepare the shareholders' equity section of the balance sheet and calculate return on equity.

Contributed Capital

Contributed capital is the total amount contributed by, or accruing to, the shareholders. Within contributed capital, there are two classifications shown on the balance sheet:

1. **Share capital.** This category consists of preferred and common shares. Because of the additional rights they possess, preferred shares are shown before common shares. The number of shares authorized, number of shares issued, and any particular share preferences (such as convertible) are reported for each class of shares either on the balance sheet or in a note to the financial statements.

    Private companies following ASPE are not required to disclose the number of shares authorized, only the number issued and their related rights and privileges.
2. **Contributed surplus.** This category includes other amounts contributed by shareholders (in addition to contributions for share capital), or amounts that accrue to shareholders from transactions such as reacquiring and retiring shares. Other situations not discussed in this textbook can also result in contributed surplus. If a company has a variety of sources of contributed surplus, it is important to distinguish each one. For many companies, there is no contributed surplus. In those situations, it is more common to use the category "share capital" instead of "contributed capital" on the balance sheet.

Alternative terminology Contributed surplus is also known as additional contributed capital.

Retained Earnings

Recall that retained earnings are the cumulative profit (or loss) since incorporation that has been retained (that is, not distributed to shareholders). The statement of retained earnings provides information on how the account changed during the year. On the balance sheet, the year-end balance in retained earnings is shown in shareholders' equity. A deficit is reported as a deduction from shareholders' equity, rather than as an addition.

Sample Shareholders' Equity Section

The shareholders' equity section of Zaboschuk Inc. is shown in Illustration 13-6. Zaboschuk's preferred shares dividend rate is $6 per year; 50,000 noncumulative preferred shares have been authorized; and 6,000 shares are issued for $770,000.

The company has authorized an unlimited number of common shares; at December 31, 2014, 400,000 shares are issued for $2.8 million. Zaboschuk's ending retained earnings is $1,050,000.

▸**ILLUSTRATION** 13-6
Shareholders' equity section

ZABOSCHUK INC. Balance Sheet (partial) December 31, 2014		
Shareholders' equity		
Share capital		
$6 noncumulative preferred shares, 50,000 shares authorized, 6,000 shares issued	$ 770,000	
Common shares, unlimited shares authorized, 400,000 shares issued	2,800,000	
Total share capital		$3,570,000
Retained earnings		1,050,000
Total shareholders' equity		$4,620,000

ANALYSIS

There are many ratios determined from the shareholders' equity section of the balance sheet. We will learn about return on equity here. In the next chapter, we will learn about earnings per share and the price-earnings and dividend payout ratios.

Return on Equity

Return on equity, also known as return on investment, is considered by many to be *the* most important measure of a company's profitability. This ratio is used by management and investors to evaluate how many dollars are earned for each dollar invested by the shareholders. It can be used to compare investment opportunities in the marketplace. The higher the ratio, the better.

Return on equity is a widely published figure. Illustration 13-7 calculates the return on equity ratio for Reitmans (Canada) Limited ($ in thousands).

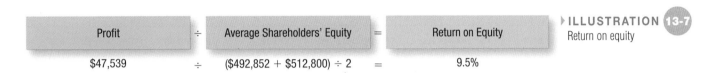

▶ **ILLUSTRATION 13-7**
Return on equity

Reitmans' return on equity, at 9.5%, is below the industry average, which was reported as 20.2% by Reuters. Return on equity can vary significantly by company and by industry.

Calculations can be done to produce a return on equity for common shareholders only. This is done by dividing profit available to common shareholders by the average common shareholders' equity. Profit available to common shareholders is profit less any preferred dividends. Common shareholders' equity is total shareholders' equity less the legal capital of any preferred shares. Recall that everything else belongs to the common, or residual, shareholders.

 **BEFORE YOU GO ON...**

Do It

The following information is available for Tanim's Sewing Goods for three recent years:

	2014	2013	2012
Total shareholders' equity	$659,200	$599,822	$558,850
Profit	79,170	54,630	40,620

Calculate return on equity for Tanim's Sewing Goods for 2014 and 2013 and comment on any trends.

Solution

	2014	2013
Average shareholders' equity	($659,200 + $599,822) ÷ 2 = $629,511	($599,822 + $558,850) ÷ 2 = $579,336
Return on equity	$12.6\% = \dfrac{\$79,170}{\$629,511}$	$9.4\% = \dfrac{\$54,630}{\$579,336}$

The increase in the return on equity indicates improved profitability over the two years.

Related exercise material: BE13–11, BE13–12, E13–11, and E13–12.

Action Plan
- Calculate average shareholders' equity using the total shareholders' equity at the beginning and end of the year.
- Divide profit by the average shareholders' equity for that year to calculate return on equity.
- Recall if it is better for return on equity to increase or decrease.

Comparing IFRS and ASPE

Key Differences	International Financial Reporting Standards (IFRS)	Accounting Standards for Private Enterprises (ASPE)
Issue of shares for noncash goods or services	Record the transaction at the fair value of the goods or services received. If this value cannot be reliably determined, then the fair value of the shares given up is used.	Record the transaction at the most reliable of the two values—the fair value of the goods or services received or the fair value of the shares. As private company shares are not traded, it is often difficult to measure their fair value. Thus, in practice, the fair value of the goods or services received is used more often.
Changes in retained earnings	Presented in a statement of changes in shareholders' equity.	Presented in a statement of retained earnings.
Accumulated other comprehensive income	Reported in shareholders' equity on the balance sheet.	Not required under ASPE.
Authorized share capital	Must present the number of shares authorized for each class of shares.	Not required under ASPE.

THE NAVIGATOR

Demonstration Problem

On January 2, 2014, Rolman Corporation began operations. Its articles of incorporation authorize it to issue an unlimited number of common shares and 500,000, $3 noncumulative preferred shares. In its first year, 2014, the company had the following selected transactions:

Jan. 2	Issued 50,000 common shares to Rowena Rolman for $10 cash per share.
Jan. 10	Issued 1,500 common shares to Rowena's brother in exchange for a used vehicle. The vehicle was appraised at $15,000.
June 30	Declared a $0.25 dividend to the common shareholders of record on July 1, payable July 5.
July 5	Paid the common share dividend.
Oct. 1	Issued 1,000 preferred shares to Rowena's grandmother at $60 per share.
Dec. 30	Declared the $0.75 quarterly preferred share dividend, and a $0.25 common share dividend. Both dividends are payable on January 5 to the shareholders of record on January 1.

During 2014, the company had Service Revenue of $240,000, and Operating Expenses of $180,000. The company has a 15% income tax rate and did not make any instalments during the year. Rowena has decided the company will use ASPE.

Instructions
(a) Journalize the transactions (ignore the revenues and expenses).
(b) Prepare an income statement and record the journal entry to record income tax expense.
(c) Prepare a statement of retained earnings and the shareholders' equity section of the balance sheet.
(d) Prepare closing entries.

Solution to Demonstration Problem

(a)

Jan. 2	Cash	500,000	
	Common Shares (50,000 × $10)		500,000
	To record issue of 50,000 common shares at $10.		
Jan. 10	Vehicles	15,000	
	Common Shares		15,000
	To record issue of 1,500 common shares for a vehicle.		
June 30	Cash Dividends—Common ($0.25 × 51,500)	12,875	
	Dividends Payable		12,875
	To record declaration of a $0.25 common share dividend.		
July 5	Dividends Payable	12,875	
	Cash		12,875
	To record payment of cash dividend.		
Oct. 1	Cash ($60 × 1,000)	60,000	
	Preferred Shares		60,000
	To record issue of 1,000 preferred shares at $60 per share.		
Dec. 30	Cash Dividends—Common ($0.25 × 51,500)	12,875	
	Cash Dividends—Preferred ($0.75 × 1,000)	750	
	Dividends Payable ($12,875 + $750)		13,625
	To record declaration of $0.75 quarterly preferred share dividend and $0.25 common share dividend.		

(b)

ROLMAN CORPORATION
Income Statement
Year Ended December 31, 2014

Service revenue	$240,000
Operating expenses	180,000
Profit before income tax	60,000
Income tax expense	9,000
Profit	$ 51,000

Dec. 31	Income Tax Expense ($60,000 × 15%)	9,000	
	Income Tax Payable		9,000
	To record 15% income taxes for 2014.		

(c)

ROLMAN CORPORATION
Statement of Retained Earnings
Year Ended December 31, 2014

Retained earnings, January 1		$ 0
Add: Profit for the year		51,000
		51,000
Less: Common share dividends	$25,750	
Preferred share dividends	750	26,500
Retained earnings, December 31		$24,500

ROLMAN CORPORATION
Balance Sheet (partial)
December 31, 2014

Shareholders' equity
   Share capital

Preferred shares, $3 noncumulative, 1,000 issued	$ 60,000		
Common shares, 51,500 issued	515,000[1]		
Total share capital		$575,000	
Retained earnings		24,500	
Total shareholders' equity		$599,500	

[1]500,000 + 15,000 = 515,000

(d)

Dec. 31	Service Revenue	240,000	
	Income Summary		240,000
	To close revenue to income summary.		
31	Income Summary	189,000	
	Operating Expenses		180,000
	Income Tax Expense		9,000
	To close expenses to income summary.		
31	Income Summary ($240,000 − $189,000)	51,000	
	Retained Earnings		51,000
	To close income summary to Retained Earnings.		
31	Retained Earnings	26,500	
	Cash Dividends—Common		25,750
	Cash Dividends—Preferred		750
	To close dividends to Retained Earnings.		

THE **NAVIGATOR**

▶ Summary of Study Objectives

1. *Identify and discuss characteristics of the corporate form of organization.* The major characteristics of a corporation are as follows: separate legal existence, limited liability of shareholders, transferable ownership rights, ability to acquire capital, continuous life, government regulations, and corporate income tax. Corporations must be incorporated federally or provincially, and may have shareholders of different classes. Each class of shares carries different rights and privileges. The rights of common share owners are restricted to the right to elect the board of directors, to receive a proportionate share of dividends, if declared, and to receive the remaining assets if the corporation is liquidated. Corporations are managed by the board of directors.

2. *Account for the issuance of common and preferred shares.* When shares are issued, the entire proceeds from the issue become legal capital and are credited to the Common Shares account. When shares are issued for noncash assets or services, the fair value of the consideration received is used if it can be determined. If not, the fair value of the

consideration given up is used. The accounting for preferred shares is similar to the accounting for common shares.

Preferred shares typically do not have voting rights but do have priority over common shares to receive (1) dividends, and (2) assets, if the company is liquidated. The dividend is specified and may be cumulative or noncumulative. Cumulative preferred shares must be paid dividends for the current year as well as any unpaid dividends from previous years before the common shares many receive dividends. Noncumulative preferred shares lose the right to unpaid dividends from prior years. In addition, preferred shares may be convertible, redeemable, and/or retractable. Convertible preferred shares allow their holder to convert them into common shares at a specified ratio. Redeemable preferred shares give the corporation the right to redeem the shares for cash; retractable give the shareholder the right to convert the shares to cash.

3. *Prepare a corporate income statement.* Corporate income statements are similar to the income statements for proprietorships and partnerships, with one exception. Income tax

expense must be reported in a separate section before profit in the corporation's income statement.

4. **Account for cash dividends.** Dividends are similar to drawings in that they are a distribution of profit to the owners (shareholders). Entries for cash dividends are required at the declaration date and the payment date. Cash dividends reduce assets and shareholders' equity (retained earnings).

5. **Prepare a statement of retained earnings and closing entries for a corporation.** Retained earnings are increased by profit, and decreased by losses and dividends. Companies reporting under ASPE are required to prepare a statement of retained earnings showing the beginning balance, changes during the year, and ending balance of retained

earnings. In a corporation, the income summary account and dividends accounts are closed to retained earnings.

6. **Prepare the shareholders' equity section of the balance sheet and calculate return on equity.** Within the shareholders' equity section of the balance sheet, all corporations will report contributed capital and retained earnings. Within contributed capital, two classifications may be shown if applicable: share capital and additional contributed surplus. Corporations reporting under IFRS will also have another component in shareholders' equity, which will be introduced in Chapter 14.

Return on equity is calculated by dividing profit by average shareholders' equity. It is an important measure of a company's profitability.

THE **NAVIGATOR**

▶ Glossary

Authorized shares The total number of each class of shares a corporation is allowed to sell, as indicated in its articles of incorporation. This amount may be specified or unlimited. (p. 677)

Cash dividend A pro rata (equal) distribution of cash to shareholders. (p. 684)

Common shares Shares where the owners have the right to (1) vote on the election of the board of directors, (2) share in the distribution of profit through dividends, and (3) share any assets that remain after all debts and shares with priority rights have been paid. If the corporation has only one class of shares, these are the common shares. (p. 675)

Contributed capital The total amount contributed by, or accruing to, the shareholders. Consists of share capital and contributed surplus. (p. 690)

Convertible preferred shares Preferred shares that the shareholder can convert into common shares at a specified ratio. (p. 680)

Corporation A business organized as a separate legal entity, with most of the rights and privileges of a person. Shares are evidence of ownership. (p. 672)

Cumulative A feature of preferred shares that entitles the shareholder to receive current dividends and unpaid prior-year dividends before common shareholders receive any dividends. (p. 680)

Debt covenant A restriction in a loan agreement that, among other things, may limit the use of corporate assets for the payment of dividends. (p. 685)

Declaration date The date when the board of directors formally declares a dividend and announces it to shareholders. (p. 685)

Deficit A debit balance in the Retained Earnings account created when total losses and dividends to date are greater than total profit to date; it is reported as a deduction from shareholders' equity. (p. 688)

Dividend A distribution of profit by a corporation to its shareholders on a pro rata basis. (p. 675)

Dividends in arrears Dividends on cumulative preferred shares that were not declared. (p. 680)

Initial public offering (IPO) The initial offering of a corporation's shares to the public. (p. 677)

Issued shares The authorized shares that have been sold. (p. 677)

Legal capital The share capital that must be retained in the business for the protection of corporate creditors. (p. 677)

No par value shares Share capital that has not been given a specific value. All the proceeds from the sale of no par value shares are treated as legal capital. (p. 678)

Noncumulative Preferred shares that are entitled to the current dividend, but not to any unpaid amounts from previous years. (p. 680)

Organization costs Costs incurred in the formation of a corporation. (p. 675)

Payment date The date when cash dividends are paid to shareholders. (p. 685)

Preferred shares Shares that have contractual preferences over common shares. (p. 679)

Private corporation A corporation that has only a few shareholders. Its shares are not available for sale to the general public. (p. 672)

Public corporation A corporation that may have thousands of shareholders. Its shares are usually traded on an organized securities market. (p. 672)

Record date The date when ownership of shares is determined for dividend purposes. (p. 685)

Redeemable (callable) preferred shares Preferred shares that give the issuer the right to purchase the shares from shareholders at specified future dates and prices. (p. 681)

Retained earnings Earned capital (cumulative profit less losses and amounts distributed to shareholders since incorporation) that has been retained for future use. If negative (i.e., a debit balance), it is called a *deficit*. (p. 682)

Retained earnings restrictions Circumstances that make a portion of retained earnings currently unavailable for dividends. (p. 685)

Retractable preferred shares Preferred shares that give the shareholder the right to sell the shares to the issuer at specified future dates and prices. (p. 681)

Return on equity A measure of profitability from the shareholders' point of view. It is calculated by dividing profit by average common shareholders' equity. (p. 691)

Secondary market A market where investors buy and sell shares of public companies from each other, rather than from the company. (p. 677)

Share capital The amount paid, or contributed, to the corporation by shareholders in exchange for shares of ownership. It can consist of preferred and common shares. (p. 676)

Statement of retained earnings A financial statement that shows the changes in retained earnings during the year, used only under ASPE. (p. 686)

▶ Self-Study Questions
Answers are at the end of the chapter.

(SO 1) K   1. An important characteristic unique to a corporation is that:
(a) it is separate and distinct from its owners.
(b) owner liability is unlimited.
(c) owners personally manage the company.
(d) ownership rights are not transferable.

(SO 1) AP   2. Ilona Schiller purchased 100 common shares of Tim Hortons Inc. on the Toronto Stock Exchange for $50 per share. Tim Hortons Inc. had originally issued these shares at $33. This transaction will have what impact on Tim Hortons Inc.'s Common Shares account?
(a) Increase of $1,700
(b) Increase of $3,300
(c) Increase of $5,000
(d) No effect

(SO 2) AP   3. ABC Corporation issues 1,000 common shares at $12 per share. In recording the transaction, a credit is made to:
(a) Gain on Sale of Shares for $12,000.
(b) Common Shares for $12,000.
(c) Investment in ABC Common Shares for $12,000.
(d) Cash for $12,000.

(SO 2) K   4. Which of the following is *not* true? Preferred shares:
(a) have priority over common shareholder dividends.
(b) have priority over common shareholders for assets in the event of liquidation.
(c) generally have voting rights.
(d) can be reacquired.

(SO 3) AP   5. In 2014, Westney Corp. had $420,000 of revenue and $206,000 of operating expenses. The company has a 15% income tax rate. What is the company's profit for the year?
(a) $32,100.
(b) $181,900.
(c) $214,000.
(d) $246,100.

(SO 4) K   6. The necessary conditions to pay a cash dividend include:
(a) approval from the shareholders, and enough cash to pay all current liabilities.
(b) total profit for the year must be in excess of the dividend.
(c) a declaration from the board, and enough cash to pay for its ongoing operations and pay its bills as they come due.
(d) all authorized shares have been issued.

(SO 4) K   7. The dates on which a corporation will record a journal entry with regard to a cash dividend are the:
(a) record date and payment date.
(b) declaration date and record date.
(c) declaration date, record date, and payment date.
(d) declaration date and payment date.

(SO 5) AP   8. Ajax Netscape Ltd. began operations on January 1, 2013, when common shares were issued for $285,000 cash. In 2013, the company had a loss of $57,000. In 2014, the company had a profit of $123,000. On December 31, 2014, the company declared a $30,000 cash dividend payable on January 8, 2015. The statement of retained earnings for 2014 will show which of the following amounts?

	Beginning retained earnings	Ending retained earnings
(a)	$ (57,000)	$ 36,000
(b)	228,000	321,000
(c)	(57,000)	66,000
(d)	0	93,000

(SO 6) C   9. The shareholders' equity section of a balance sheet for a company reporting under ASPE will never report:
(a) the total number of shares issued.
(b) accumulated other comprehensive income.

(c) a deficit (debit balance in Retained Earnings).
(d) cumulative preferred shares.

(SO 6) AP 10. If a company's profit is $50,000, its total assets $1 million, its average common shareholders'

equity $500,000, and its net sales $800,000, its return on equity is:
(a) 3.3%. (c) 6.25%.
(b) 5%. (d) 10%.

THE **NAVIGATOR**

▶ Questions

(SO 1) C 1. Corporations can be classified in different ways. For example, they may be classified by purpose (e.g., profit or not-for-profit) or by ownership (e.g., public or private). Explain the difference between each of these types of classifications.

(SO 1) C 2. Pat Kabza, a student, asks for your help in understanding the following characteristics of a corporation: (a) limited liability of shareholders, (b) transferable ownership rights, and (c) ability to acquire capital. Explain to Pat how these characteristics work together to create a significant advantage for the corporate form of organization.

(SO 1) C 3. What are the advantages and disadvantages of a corporation compared with a proprietorship or partnership? Explain why some of the advantages of the corporate form of organization may not apply to small, privately held corporations.

(SO 1) C 4. Explain the ownership rights of shareholders and the authority structure in a corporation.

(SO 2) C 5. Explain the difference between authorized and issued shares. For a corporation, why is the amount of authorized shares important? Of issued shares?

(SO 2) C 6. Paul Joyce purchases 100 common shares of TechTop Ltd. for $12 per share from the company's initial public offering. Later, Paul purchases 200 more TechTop Ltd. common shares for $20 each on the Toronto Stock Exchange, using his own online brokerage account. Explain the impact of each of these transactions on TechTop's assets, liabilities, and shareholders' equity.

(SO 2) C 7. Equipment with an estimated fair value of $25,000 is acquired by issuing 1,000 common shares. How should this transaction be recorded? Include in your explanation how this might be different for a company following IFRS or ASPE.

(SO 2) AP 8. Compare the rights of preferred shareholders with common shareholders. Include in your answer the areas in which preferred shares are given priority over common shares.

(SO 2) C 9. What is the difference between noncumulative and cumulative preferred shares? What are the differences among convertible, redeemable, and retractable preferred shares?

(SO 2) AP 10. Following two years of no dividend payments to either cumulative preferred or common shareholders,

management decides to declare a dividend for all shareholders. (a) Is the company required to pay all shareholders for the previous two years of missed dividends? (b) Should the company report a liability for the years of missed dividends or are there any other reporting requirements?

(SO 2) AP 11. A preferred shareholder converts her convertible preferred shares into common shares. What effect does this have on the corporation's (a) total assets, (b) total liabilities, and (c) total shareholders' equity?

(SO 3) C 12. What is the main difference between income statements for corporations and income statements for proprietorships and partnerships? Why does this difference exist?

(SO 4) K 13. A dividend is a "pro rata" distribution of retained earnings. Explain what "pro rata" means.

(SO 4) K 14. At what point does a cash dividend become a liability of a company? What entries are made for cash dividends on the declaration date, the record date, and the payment date?

(SO 4) C 15. Why is having enough retained earnings a requirement for paying a cash dividend, even if the company has sufficient cash to make the payment?

(SO 5) C 16. Explain what information is included in a statement of retained earnings. In what ways is it similar to a statement of owner's equity and in what ways is it different?

(SO 5) C 17. Explain how temporary accounts are closed in a corporation. In what ways are closing entries similar to those of a proprietorship and in what ways are they different?

(SO 6) K 18. The shareholders' equity is divided into major components. Identify and explain what each component represents.

(SO 6) C 19. Two independent companies have the same annual earnings ($100,000); however, the companies have different amounts of shareholders' equity. Average shareholders' equity for company 1 is $300,000 and for company 2 is $350,000. Which company would you consider a better investment and why?

(SO 6) C 20. Common shareholders may want a more precise measure of a company's performance. How could the return on equity formula be changed to meet this requirement?

▶ Brief Exercises

Distinguish between characteristics of different business organizations. (SO 1) C

BE13–1 For each characteristic listed, identify which type of business organization best fits the description. There may be more than one answer in some cases. The first one has been done for you as an example.

Characteristic	Proprietorship	Partnership	Corporation
1. Continuous life			X
2. Unlimited liability			
3. Ease of formation			
4. Separate legal existence			
5. Ability to acquire capital			
6. Shared skills and resources			
7. Fewer government regulations			
8. Separation of ownership and management			
9. Owners' acts are binding			
10. Easy transfer of ownership rights			

Record issue of common shares. (SO 2) AP

BE13–2 On August 5, Hansen Corporation issued 2,000 common shares for $12 per share. On September 10, Hansen issued an additional 500 shares for $13 per share. (a) Record the share transactions. (b) What is the average cost per share of the common shares following the last transaction?

Record issue of common shares in noncash transaction and provide rationale. (SO 2) AP

BE13–3 Juke Joint Ltd., a private company, began operations on March 12 by issuing 5,000 common shares for $20 cash per share. On September 10, the company issued 500 common shares in exchange for equipment with an appraised value of $9,500. (a) Assuming the company uses ASPE, prepare a journal entry to record the September 10 transaction and provide a rationale for the value. (b) How might your answer change if Juke Joint was a public company?

Record issue of preferred shares. (SO 2) AP

BE13–4 StarLight Ltd. is authorized to issue 10,000, $4 noncumulative preferred shares. On January 13, it issued 3,000 preferred shares for $90 cash per share. (a) Prepare a journal entry to record the transaction. (b) Determine the total amount of dividends that must be paid to the preferred shareholders prior to paying a dividend to common shareholders.

Determine dividends in arrears. (SO 2) AP

BE13–5 Beauce Incorporated had 45,000, $2.50 preferred shares issued. It did not pay a dividend to the preferred shareholders in 2013 and 2014. (a) What are the dividends in arrears, if any, at December 31, 2014, if the shares are cumulative and if they are noncumulative? (b) How are dividends in arrears reported in the financial statements?

Record conversion of preferred shares. (SO 2) AP

BE13–6 Progressive Parts Corporation issued 25,000 preferred shares on May 10 for $35 each. Each share is convertible into two common shares. On November 21, the preferred shares had a fair value of $37 each, and the common shares $19 each. On this day, 5,000 of the preferred shares are converted into common shares. (a) Journalize the issue of the preferred shares on May 10. (b) Journalize the conversion of the preferred shares on November 21.

Record income tax and prepare corporate income statement. (SO 3) AP

BE13–7 For the year ended June 30, 2014, Viceron Inc. had Service Revenue of $800,000 and Operating Expenses of $575,000. The company has a 15% income tax rate. It has not paid any income tax instalments or accrued for income tax expense. Prepare (a) the journal entry to record income tax, and (b) the income statement.

Record cash dividend. (SO 4) AP

BE13–8 On October 14, the board of directors of Celery Cede Corp. voted to declare the annual preferred share dividend to shareholders of record on November 1, payable on November 21. The company is authorized to issue 100,000, $5.25 noncumulative preferred shares; 25,000 have been issued. Prepare the required entries on each of these dates.

Prepare a statement of retained earnings. (SO 5) AP

BE13–9 For the year ending December 31, 2014, Grayfair Inc. reports profit of $175,000. During the year, the company declared a total of $120,000 cash dividends and paid $85,000 of these dividends. Prepare a statement of retained earnings for the year, assuming the balance in Retained Earnings on December 31, 2013, was $248,000.

Record closing entries and post to retained earnings. (SO 5) AP

BE13–10 For the year ended December 31, 2014, Huron Lake Enterprises Ltd. had the following revenues and expenses: Sales, $745,000; Cost of Goods Sold, $450,000; Operating Expenses $135,000; and Income Tax Expense, $35,000. The company also declared $25,000 of dividends to the common shareholders on each of June 30 and December 31. The dividend declared on December 31 will be paid on January 10, 2015. (a) Prepare closing entries. (b) Post the entries to the Retained Earnings account assuming the balance in that account on December 31, 2013, was $382,000.

BE13–11 True Green Nurseries Ltd. is a private company that follows ASPE. It is authorized to issue an unlimited number of both common and $6.50 cumulative preferred shares. On December 31, 2014, there were 15,000 common and 1,000 preferred shares issued with the following balances: Common Shares, $150,000; and Preferred Shares, $100,000. The statement of retained earnings showed retained earnings of $285,000 at December 31, 2014. The dividend on the preferred shares was two years in arrears. Prepare the shareholders' equity section of the balance sheet on December 31, 2014.

Prepare shareholders' equity section. (SO 6) AP

BE13–12 For the year ended December 31, 2011, **Canada Bread Company, Limited** reported (in thousands) net revenue $1,595,456; profit $51,951; beginning shareholders' equity $638,995; and ending shareholders' equity $663,602. (a) Calculate the return on equity. (b) Canada Bread has no preferred shares. Would its return on common shareholders' equity be the same as, or different from, its return on equity? Why?

Calculate return on equity. (SO 6) AP

Exercises

E13–1 Here are some of the terms discussed in the chapter:

Identify terminology. (SO 1, 2) K

1. Retained earnings
2. Issued shares
3. Legal capital
4. Liquidation preference
5. Authorized shares
6. Public corporation
7. Convertible
8. Retractable preferred shares
9. Cumulative
10. Initial public offering
11. Redeemable preferred shares
12. Secondary market

Instructions

For each description, write the number of the term it best matches.

(a) _____ Preferred shares that give the shareholder the right to redeem shares at their option
(b) _____ The type of corporation whose shares are traded in an organized security market, such as the Toronto Stock Exchange
(c) _____ Preferred shares that give the issuing corporation the right to repurchase the shares at a specified price and date
(d) _____ The maximum number of shares a corporation is allowed to sell
(e) _____ The number of shares a corporation has actually sold
(f) _____ The first time a corporation's shares are offered to the public
(g) _____ Where investors buy and sell shares from each other, rather than from the company
(h) _____ The element of shareholders' equity that is increased by profit and decreased by losses
(i) _____ A preference to get money back before common shareholders if the company is bankrupt
(j) _____ The share capital that must be retained in the business for the protection of corporate creditors
(k) _____ A feature that allows preferred shareholders to exchange their shares for common shares
(l) _____ A preference to collect unpaid dividends on preferred shares before common shareholders can receive a dividend

E13–2 As an accountant for the consulting firm Insite, you are asked by a client to provide advice on the form of organization her new business in the medical industry should take. After a brief conversation, you have learned the following about your client's needs:

Identify the characteristics of a corporation. (SO 1) C

1. The client has several children whom she expects to become involved in the business, and to whom she will want to transfer ownership in the future.
2. Companies in this industry tend to be sued frequently.
3. Profit (and taxable income) are expected to be significant in the early years.
4. The company is expected to grow significantly, and your client expects to need substantial funding in the next few years to manage this growth.

Instructions

Write a brief report to advise your client on why organizing as a corporation may, or may not, be the appropriate choice.

Record issue of shares in cash and noncash transactions. (SO 2) AP

E13–3 Santiago Corp., a private corporation, received its articles of incorporation on January 3, 2014. It is authorized to issue an unlimited number of common shares and $1 preferred shares. It had the following share transactions during the year:

Jan. 12   Issued 50,000 common shares for $5 per share.
     24   Issued 950 common shares in payment of a $4,500 bill for legal services.
July 11   Issued 1,000 preferred shares for $25 per share.
Oct. 1   Issued 10,000 common shares in exchange for land. The land's fair value was estimated to be $55,000. Santiago's accountant estimated that the fair value of the shares issued might be as high as $6 per share.

Instructions

(a) Journalize the share transactions.
(b) Calculate the average cost for the common shares.
(c) Assume instead that Santiago's shares trade on the TSX Venture Exchange. How might this affect the value assigned to the shares issued on October 1?

Record issue of shares in cash and noncash transactions. (SO 2) AP

E13–4 Southwest Corporation is authorized to issue an unlimited amount of common shares, and as at December 31, 2013, has 9,000 shares issued. Manji and MacDonald each own 4,500 of these shares. On December 31, 2013, the balances in Southwest's shareholders' equity are as follows:

Common Shares $18,000
Retained Earnings   35,000

On January 1, 2014, Mah bills Southwest Corporation $5,000 for legal services. As Southwest Corporation has a limited amount of cash, Manji and MacDonald suggest to Mah that the corporation issue shares in exchange for the legal services instead of paying the bill in cash. After a series of negotiations, Mah agrees but wants a 10% ownership interest in the corporation.

Instructions

(a) How many shares would Southwest Corporation need to issue to Mah in order for Mah to have a 10% ownership interest?
(b) Assuming Southwest uses ASPE, prepare the journal entry to record the issue of shares. Include an explanation for the value used in the journal entry.
(c) Why might Manji and MacDonald not want to issue shares to Mah?

Determine conversion date and record conversion of preferred shares. (SO 2) AP

E13–5 New Wave Pool Corporation is authorized to issue common and $3 convertible preferred shares. Each preferred share is convertible into four common shares. On July 2, the company issued 100,000 preferred shares for $110 per share. The common shares were trading at $25 on September 7, $27.50 on September 19, and $29 on September 28.

Instructions

(a) On which date or dates would the preferred shareholders consider converting their shares to common? Why?
(b) Journalize the conversion of the preferred shares using the date chosen in part (a).
(c) Assume also that the preferred shares are redeemable at $115 per share at the option of the company. How, if at all, will this affect the preferred shareholders' decision to convert?

Determine dividends in arrears. (SO 2) AP

E13–6 Windswept Power Corporation issued 150,000, $4.50 cumulative preferred shares to fund its first investment in wind generators. In its first year of operations, it paid $450,000 of dividends to its preferred shareholders. In its second year, the company paid dividends of $900,000 to its preferred shareholders.

Instructions

(a) What is the total annual preferred dividend supposed to be for the preferred shareholders?
(b) Calculate any dividends in arrears in years 1 and 2.
(c) Explain how dividends in arrears should be reported in the financial statements.
(d) If the preferred shares were noncumulative rather than cumulative, how much dividend would the company likely have paid its preferred shareholders in year 2?

Prepare income statement and entry to record income tax. (SO 3) AP

E13–7 Shrunk Inc. has recorded all necessary adjusting entries, except for income tax expense, at its fiscal year end, July 31, 2014. The following information has been taken from the adjusted trial balance:

Accounts payable	$ 25,500	Interest expense	$ 5,000
Cash dividends—common	60,000	Notes payable	100,000
Common shares	200,000	Retained earnings (Aug. 1, 2013)	352,000
Cost of goods sold	310,000	Salaries expense	140,000
Dividends payable	15,000	Sales	665,000
Income tax expense	30,000	Supplies expense	10,000
Income tax payable	3,000	Unearned revenue	12,000

All accounts have normal balances and total assets equal $817,500. Shrunk has a 20% income tax rate.

Instructions

Prepare a multiple-step income statement and the required journal entry to adjust income tax expense.

E13–8   Accentrics Limited has the following information available regarding its share capital at December 31, 2013:

Determine split between preferred and common shares and record cash dividend transactions. (SO 2, 4) AP

Preferred shares, $3.50 cumulative, 20,000 shares issued	$1,000,000
Preferred shares, $4.50 noncumulative, 10,000 shares issued	500,000
Common shares, 300,000 shares issued	1,500,000

The shares were issued when the corporation began operations on January 1, 2012. No dividends were declared during 2012 and 2013. On October 30, 2014, the board of directors declares the required preferred share dividends and a $0.50 dividend for each of the common shares. The dividends are payable on December 1, 2014, to the shareholders of record on November 16, 2014.

Instructions

(a) How much will be paid to each class of shares?
(b) Prepare journal entries on the appropriate dates for the 2014 dividends.
(c) Assume instead that the maximum cash dividend the company can pay in 2014 is $200,000. Determine the dividends in arrears, if any, at December 31, 2014.

E13–9   Refer to the data given in E13–7 for Shrunk Inc.

Prepare a statement of retained earnings and closing entries. (SO 5) AP

Instructions

(a) Prepare a statement of retained earnings.
(b) Prepare closing entries and post to the Income Summary and Retained Earnings accounts.

E13–10   Didsbury Digital Ltd. has a September 30 fiscal year end and a 15% income tax rate. The following information is available for its 2014 year end:

Record income tax; prepare an income statement and statement of retained earnings. (SO 3, 4, 5) AP

1. Earned $529,000 service revenue and incurred $442,000 operating expenses. Interest expense was $2,500.
2. Recorded and remitted $10,000 of income tax (related to the 2014 fiscal year) during the year.
3. On October 5, 2013, paid $50,000 of dividends that had been declared on September 25, 2013.
4. On September 28, 2014, declared $40,000 of dividends payable on October 8, 2014.
5. Retained earnings on September 30, 2013, were $237,500.
6. Issued common shares for $25,000 cash on July 2, 2014.

Instructions

(a) Prepare an income statement and record the adjustment to income tax.
(b) Prepare a statement of retained earnings.

E13–11   Raiders Limited is a private company that follows ASPE. It is authorized to issue an unlimited number of both common and $5 cumulative preferred shares. On December 31, 2014, there were 35,000 common and 1,000 preferred shares issued. The common shares had been issued at an average cost of $10 per share; the preferred shares at $105. The balance in the Retained Earnings account on January 1, 2014, was $287,000. During 2014, the company had profit of $125,000 and declared a total of $75,000 of dividends, of which $56,250 was paid during the year.

Prepare shareholders' equity section and calculate return on equity. (SO 6) AP

Instructions

(a) Prepare the shareholders' equity section of the balance sheet on December 31, 2014.
(b) Calculate return on equity for 2014. Assume there were no changes in the Common Shares account during the year.

Record share issue, dividends, and income tax; prepare partial income statement and balance sheet and statement of retained earnings. (SO 2, 3, 4, 5, 6) AP

E13-12 Ozabal Inc., a private company, is authorized to issue an unlimited number of common shares and 100,000 noncumulative $4 preferred shares. It began operations on January 1, 2014, and the following are selected transactions during 2014:

Jan. 1   Issued 300,000 common shares for $150,000 cash.
      2   Issued 30,000 preferred shares for $40 cash per share.
Dec. 1   Declared a total of $225,000 in dividends, payable on January 5, to shareholders of record on December 13.
      31 Determined that it had total revenues of $915,000 and operating expenses of $610,000.

Ozabal elected to report under ASPE. It has a 15% income tax rate and did not pay income tax instalments during the year.

Instructions

(a) Record the share issue and dividend transactions.
(b) Prepare a partial income statement starting with profit before income taxes and record an adjusting entry for income tax.
(c) Prepare a statement of retained earnings and the shareholders' equity section of the balance sheet.

▶ Problems: Set A

Determine form of business organization. (SO 1) AN

P13-1A   Presented below are five independent situations:

1. After passing their final accounting exam, four students put together plans to offer bookkeeping services to small companies. The students have signed an agreement that details how the profits of this new business will be shared.
2. Darien Enns has had so many people ask about the new solar and wind equipment he recently added to his home, he has decided to start a company that will offer planning, design, and installation of alternative power technology. To launch the business, Darien will need substantial funding to purchase a service truck, a special crane, and the solar- and wind-generating equipment. He expects the business to grow quickly and that he will have to hire additional employees and triple the number of trucks and cranes owned by the business. Darien has no way to provide funding for the start of the business, and he also understands that the expected growth will require large additional investments.
3. Joanna Hirsh lives 12 months a year on Look About Bay, where most of her neighbours have summer cottages. To generate income in her retirement, Joanna has decided to offer cottage inspection services for residents while they are away. Joanna will need a snowmobile to access the buildings in the winter. She also hopes to expand her service to surrounding areas. Expansion will require hiring more inspectors and purchasing additional snowmobiles.
4. After working in the construction industry for several years, Joel Pal has decided to offer his own roofing services to homeowners.
5. Frank Holton owns a small two-seater airplane to fly hunters and hikers to remote areas in northern Ontario. Demand for Frank's services has grown so much that he plans to hire additional pilots and purchase four larger planes. Frank will also purchase liability insurance in case of accidents, and plans to maintain control of the company.

Instructions

In each case, explain what form of organization the business is likely to take: proprietorship, partnership, or corporation. Give reasons for your choice.

TAKING IT FURTHER   Since a corporation is a separate legal entity, what gives employees the authority to complete a transaction on behalf of the company?

Record and post share transactions. Determine balances and answer questions. (SO 2) AP

P13-2A   Wetland Corporation, a private corporation, was organized on February 1, 2013. It is authorized to issue 100,000, $6 noncumulative preferred shares, and an unlimited number of common shares. The following transactions were completed during the first year:

Feb. 10   Issued 80,000 common shares at $4 per share.
Mar. 1   Issued 5,000 preferred shares at $115 per share.
Apr. 1   Issued 22,500 common shares for land. The asking price of the land was $100,000 and its appraised value was $90,000.
June 20   Issued 78,000 common shares at $4.50 per share.

July 7   Issued 10,000 common shares to lawyers to pay for their bill of $45,000 for services they performed in helping the company organize.

Sept. 1   Issued 10,000 common shares at $5 per share.

Nov. 1   Issued 1,000 preferred shares at $117 per share.

Instructions

(a) Journalize the transactions.

(b) Open general ledger accounts and post to the shareholders' equity accounts.

(c) Determine the number of shares issued and the average cost per share for both common and preferred shares.

(d) How many more shares is the company authorized to issue for each class of shares?

(e) If the preferred shares were cumulative instead of noncumulative, would this have changed the amount investors were willing to pay for the shares? Explain.

TAKING IT FURTHER   If Wetland was a public corporation, how might that affect the journal entry recorded for the April 1 and July 7 issues of common shares?

P13–3A   At the beginning of its first year of operations, Northwoods Limited has 5,000, $4 preferred shares and 50,000 common shares.

Allocate dividends between preferred and common shares. (SO 2) AP

Instructions

Using the format shown below, allocate the total dividend paid in each year to the preferred and common shareholders, assuming that the preferred shares are (a) noncumulative, and (b) cumulative.

		(a)		(b)	
Year	Dividend Paid	Noncumulative Preferred	Common	Cumulative Preferred	Common
1	$20,000				
2	15,000				
3	30,000				
4	35,000				

TAKING IT FURTHER   Why would an investor choose to invest in common shares if preferred share dividends have a higher priority?

P13–4A   Pro Com Ltd. issues 8,000, $5 cumulative preferred shares (convertible into two common shares apiece) at $66, and 15,000 common shares (at $30 each) at the beginning of 2012. During the years 2013 and 2014, the following transactions affected Pro Com's shareholders' equity accounts:

Allocate dividends between preferred and common shares and record conversion. (SO 2, 4) AP

2013

Jan. 10   Paid $12,000 of annual dividends to preferred shareholders.

2014

Jan. 10   Paid annual dividend to preferred shareholders and a $4,000 dividend to common shareholders.

Mar. 1   The preferred shares were converted into common shares.

Instructions

(a) Journalize each of the transactions.

(b) Are there any additional reporting requirements regarding preferred share dividends in either 2013 or 2014?

(c) What factors affect preferred shareholders' decision to convert their shares into common shares?

TAKING IT FURTHER   Why might investors be willing to pay more for preferred shares that have a conversion option?

P13–5A   Zurich Limited is a private corporation reporting under ASPE. At December 31, 2014, its general ledger contained the following summary data:

Record dividends; prepare income statement and statement of retained earnings. (SO 3, 4, 5) AP

Cost of goods sold	$1,225,000
Interest expense	35,000
Interest revenue	12,500
Operating expenses	210,000
Retained earnings, January 1	550,000
Sales	1,650,000

Additional information:

1. In 2014, common share dividends of $25,000 were declared on June 30 and December 31. The dividends were paid on July 8, 2014, and January 8, 2015, respectively.
2. The company's income tax rate is 20%.

Instructions

(a) Record the dividend transactions in 2014.
(b) Determine income tax expense and prepare a multiple-step income statement for 2014.
(c) Prepare a statement of retained earnings for 2014.

TAKING IT FURTHER Compare a statement of retained earnings with a statement of owner's equity.

Adjust income tax; prepare income statement, statement of retained earnings, and closing entries. (SO 3, 4, 5) AP

P13–6A Memphis Ltd. is a private corporation reporting under ASPE. It has recorded all necessary adjusting entries, except for income tax expense, at its fiscal year end October 31, 2014. The following information has been taken from the adjusted trial balance:

Accounts payable	$ 15,800	Interest expense	$ 4,500
Cash dividends—common	80,000	Notes payable	75,000
Common shares	100,000	Rent expense	28,800
Depreciation expense	34,375	Retained earnings (Nov. 1, 2013)	430,000
Dividends payable	20,000	Salaries expense	195,000
Income tax expense	25,000	Service revenue	445,000
Income tax payable	2,500	Unearned revenue	22,300
Insurance expense	6,900		

All accounts have normal balances and total assets equal $736,025. Memphis has a 20% income tax rate.

Instructions

(a) Record the entry to adjust income tax expense and prepare a multiple-step income statement for the year.
(b) Prepare a statement of retained earnings for the year.
(c) Prepare closing entries.
(d) Post the closing entries to the Income Summary and Retained Earnings accounts and compare with the financial statements.

TAKING IT FURTHER Why is the entry to adjust income tax expense usually the last adjusting entry prepared each year?

Record and post transactions; prepare shareholders' equity section. (SO 2, 4, 6) AP

P13–7A On January 1, 2014, Schipper Ltd. had the following shareholders' equity accounts:

Common shares (1,000,000 issued)	$1,500,000
Retained earnings	1,800,000

The company was also authorized to issue an unlimited number of $4 noncumulative preferred shares. As at January 1, 2014, none had been issued. During 2014, the corporation had the following transactions and events related to its shareholders' equity:

Jan. 2	Issued 100,000 preferred shares for $50 per share.
Apr. 1	Paid quarterly dividend to preferred shareholders.
July 1	Paid quarterly dividend to preferred shareholders.
Aug. 12	Issued 100,000 common shares for $1.70 per share.
Oct. 1	Paid quarterly dividend to preferred shareholders and a $0.25 per share dividend to the common shareholders.
Dec. 31	Loss for the year was $100,000.

Instructions

(a) Journalize the transactions and the entries to close dividends and the Income Summary account.
(b) Open general ledger accounts for the shareholders' equity accounts and post entries from (a).
(c) Prepare the shareholders' equity section of the balance sheet at December 31, 2014, including any required disclosures. Assume Schipper is reporting under ASPE.

TAKING IT FURTHER Schipper incurred a loss in 2014. Are companies allowed to declare and pay dividends during a year when they have a loss?

Record and post transactions; prepare shareholders' equity section. (SO 2, 4, 6) AP

P13–8A Cattrall Corporation is authorized to issue an unlimited number of $5 cumulative preferred shares and an unlimited number of common shares. On February 1, 2014, the general ledger contained the following shareholders' equity accounts:

Preferred shares (10,000 shares issued) $ 475,000
Common shares (70,000 shares issued)   1,050,000
Retained earnings   700,000

The following equity transactions occurred during the year ended January 31, 2015:

Feb. 28   Issued 5,000 preferred shares for $275,000.
Apr. 12   Issued 200,000 common shares for $3.2 million.
May 25   Issued 5,000 common shares in exchange for land. At the time of the exchange, the land was valued at $75,000.
Jan. 1   Paid dividend of $2.50 per share to preferred shareholders.
   31   A loss of $50,000 was incurred for the year.

Instructions

(a) Journalize the transactions and the entries to close dividends and the Income Summary account.
(b) Open general ledger accounts for the shareholders' equity accounts and post entries from (a).
(c) Prepare the shareholders' equity section of the balance sheet at January 31, 2015, including any required disclosures. Assume Cattrall is reporting under ASPE.

TAKING IT FURTHER   What are the difficulties in determining how many shares to issue in exchange for non-cash assets as well as how to value the transaction?

P13–9A   Choke Cherry Ltd. is a private company reporting under ASPE. Its adjusted trial balance at its fiscal year end, December 31, 2014, is shown below:

Prepare financial statements and closing entries.
(SO 3, 5, 6) AP

CHOKE CHERRY LTD.
Adjusted Trial Balance
December 31, 2014

	Debit	Credit
Cash	$ 28,000	
Inventory	26,500	
Supplies	5,000	
Equipment	300,000	
Accumulated depreciation—equipment		$ 65,000
Accounts payable		34,000
Income tax payable		8,985
Unearned revenue		21,000
Note payable ($12,000 is due in 2015)		30,000
Preferred shares ($4 noncumulative, 1,000 issued)		40,000
Common shares (120,000 issued)		60,000
Retained earnings		73,000
Cash dividends—preferred	4,000	
Cash dividends—common	50,000	
Sales revenue		515,000
Cost of goods sold	159,000	
Depreciation expense	20,000	
Income tax expense	14,385	
Insurance expense	8,200	
Interest expense	1,800	
Rent expense	32,600	
Salaries expense	185,000	
Supplies expense	12,500	
	$846,985	$846,985

Instructions

(a) Prepare an income statement, statement of retained earnings, and balance sheet.
(b) Journalize the closing entries.

TAKING IT FURTHER   What are the differences between dividends paid to owners of corporations and withdrawals by owners of proprietorships or partnerships?

Prepare financial statements and calculate return on equity. (SO 3, 5, 6) AP

P13–10A Northwood Architects Ltd. is a private company reporting under ASPE. It is authorized to issue an unlimited number of common and $3 cumulative preferred shares. The following is an alphabetical list of its adjusted accounts at March 31, 2014, its fiscal year end. All accounts have normal balances.

Accounts payable	$ 21,350	Income tax expense	16,535
Accounts receivable	38,700	Insurance expense	$ 6,550
Accumulated depreciation— equipment	23,650	Interest expense	3,000
Cash	54,600	Note payable	50,000
Cash dividends—common	40,000	Preferred shares	56,250
Cash dividends—preferred	4,500	Prepaid expenses	6,150
Common shares	75,000	Rent expense	35,800
Consulting revenue	404,500	Retained earnings	64,800
Depreciation expense	11,825	Salaries expense	245,400
Dividends payable	15,000	Salaries payable	2,310
Equipment	224,000	Supplies expense	25,800

The note payable is due in 2016. There are 1,500 preferred and 75,000 common shares issued.

Instructions

(a) Prepare an income statement, statement of retained earnings, and balance sheet.
(b) Calculate return on equity. Note: No shares were issued during the year.

TAKING IT FURTHER Why is it important that retained earnings be tracked and presented separately from share capital in the balance sheet?

Calculate return on assets and equity and comment. (SO 6) AP

P13–11A The following financial information (in millions) is for two major corporations for the three fiscal years ended December 31 as follows:

	2011	2010	2009
Canadian Pacific Railway Limited			
Profit	$ 570	$ 651	$ 550
Shareholders' equity	4,649	4,824	4,658
Total assets	14,110	13,676	14,155
Canadian National Railway Company			
Profit	$ 2,457	$ 2,104	$ 1,854
Shareholders' equity	10,680	11,284	11,233
Total assets	26,026	25,206	25,176

Instructions

(a) Calculate return on assets and return on equity for each company for 2011 and 2010. Comment on whether their ratios have improved or deteriorated.
(b) Compare Canadian Pacific's ratios with Canadian National's.
(c) The industry average for return on equity in 2011 was 5.33%. Compare the two companies' performance with the industry average.

TAKING IT FURTHER Using your findings in this question to illustrate, explain why it is important to use comparisons in evaluating ratios.

Record transactions and adjustments; prepare financial statements. (SO 2, 3, 4, 5, 6) AP

P13–12A Maple Corporation, a private company, is authorized to issue an unlimited number of common shares and 500,000, $2.50 cumulative preferred shares. It began operations on January 1, 2014, and the following transactions occurred in 2014:

Jan. 1   Issued 5,000 common shares for $50,000 cash.
     2   Issued 1,000 preferred shares for $35 cash per share.
Dec. 1   Declared a total of $12,500 in dividends, payable on January 5, to shareholders of record on December 13.

The following information is also available with respect to the company's operations during the year:

1. Collected $349,000 cash for consulting revenue earned.
2. Paid $184,200 salaries expense; $48,000 rent expense; and $15,000 office expense.
3. Purchased equipment for $150,000 cash.
4. At December 31, determined that the following adjustments were required:
   • Depreciation on the equipment, $15,000
   • Consulting revenue earned but not yet collected in cash, $16,000

- Accrued salaries expense, $5,800
- Income tax rate, 15%. No instalments were made during the year.

Maple elected to report under ASPE.

Instructions

(a) Record the share issue and dividend transactions.
(b) Record summary journal entries for transactions (1) to (3) and adjusting entries for items in (4).
(c) Open an account for Cash and post transactions.
(d) Prepare an income statement, statement of retained earnings, and balance sheet.

TAKING IT FURTHER   Why are common shareholders sometimes referred to as "residual owners"?

▶ Problems: Set B

P13–1B   Five independent situations follow:

1. Kevin Roberts, President and CEO of Hanley Tools Inc., has just been notified that his company has been sued due to the failure of one of its key products. Although the lawsuit is for several million dollars, Kevin is not concerned that he will have to sell his new house to pay damages if his company is unsuccessful in defending itself against the lawsuit.
2. Salik Makkar has just negotiated a borrowing agreement with a bank. The completed borrowing agreement is a contract between two parties: the bank and the company that Salik works for as the Treasurer.
3. Ping Yu is in the top personal tax bracket due to a significant amount of investment income she earns each year. Ping has just started a new company and has organized it as a publicly held corporation. Sales for the first few years are expected to make her new company eligible for tax incentives and deductions as an active small business.
4. Marion Kureshi incorporated her business, Kureshi Fine Furniture Corporation, in 1974. The business has grown steadily every year, and now employs over 2,000 people. Kureshi Fine Furniture's common shares trade on a public stock exchange. Marion is currently the President of the company; however, due to deteriorating health, Marion can no longer be active in the business. Fortunately, Marion has put plans in place for her daughter to assume her role as President.
5. Matthew Antoine has been working on a new technology to improve cell phone reception in remote rural locations. Matthew knows that a significant amount of funding will be required to purchase the production equipment and inventory to manufacture his new antenna. In order to launch his new business, Matthew plans to organize the business as a publicly held corporation and issue shares on the TSX Venture Exchange.

Identify and discuss major characteristics of a corporation. (SO 1) AN

Instructions

In each case, identify the characteristic being described in the situation that separates a corporation from a proprietorship or partnership, and explain how the situation might be different for a sole proprietor or partnership.

TAKING IT FURTHER   How does limited liability help investors sell shares in the secondary markets?

P13–2B   Highland Corporation was organized on January 1, 2014. It is authorized to issue 50,000, $3 noncumulative preferred shares, and an unlimited number of common shares. The following transactions were completed during the first year:

Record and post share transactions. Determine balances and answer questions. (SO 2) AP

Jan. 10	Issued 100,000 common shares at $2 per share.
Mar. 1	Issued 10,000 preferred shares at $42 per share.
Mar. 31	Issued 75,000 common shares at $3 per share.
Apr. 3	Issued 25,000 common shares for land. The land's appraised value was $74,000.
July 24	Issued 20,500 common shares for $60,000 cash and used equipment. The equipment originally cost $25,000. It now has a carrying amount of $15,000 and a fair value of $12,000.
Nov. 1	Issued 2,000 preferred shares at $48 per share.

Instructions

(a) Journalize the transactions.
(b) Open general ledger accounts and post to the shareholders' equity accounts.
(c) Determine the number of shares issued and the average cost per share for both common and preferred shares.
(d) How many more shares is the company authorized to issue for each class of shares?
(e) If the preferred shares were cumulative instead of noncumulative, would this have changed the amount investors were willing to pay for the shares? Explain.

TAKING IT FURTHER   If Highland was a public corporation, how might that affect the journal entry recorded for the April 3 and July 24 issues of common shares?

Allocate dividends between preferred and common shares. (SO 2) AP

P13–3B At the beginning of its first year of operations, Backwoods Limited has 3,000, $5 preferred shares and 50,000 common shares.

Instructions

Using the format shown below, allocate the total dividend paid in each year to the preferred and common shareholders, assuming that the preferred shares are (a) noncumulative, and (b) cumulative.

		(a)		(b)	
Year	Dividend Paid	Noncumulative Preferred	Common	Cumulative Preferred	Common
1	$15,000				
2	12,000				
3	27,000				
4	35,000				

TAKING IT FURTHER Why would an investor choose to invest in common shares if preferred share dividends have a higher priority?

Allocate dividends between preferred and common shares and record conversion. (SO 2, 4) AP

P13–4B Kari Corporation issues 5,000, $4 cumulative preferred shares (convertible into four common shares apiece) at $80, and 10,000 common shares (at $18 each) at the beginning of 2012. During the years 2013 and 2014, the following transactions affected the Kari Corporation's shareholders' equity accounts:

__2013__

Jan. 10   Paid $12,000 of annual dividends to preferred shareholders.

__2014__

Jan. 10   Paid annual dividend to preferred shareholders and a $4,000 dividend to common shareholders.
Mar. 1   The preferred shares were converted into common shares.

Instructions

(a) Journalize each of the 2013 and 2014 transactions.
(b) Are there any additional reporting requirements regarding preferred share dividends in either 2013 or 2014?
(c) What factors affect preferred shareholders' decision to convert their shares into common shares?

TAKING IT FURTHER Why might investors be willing to pay more for preferred shares that have a conversion option?

Record dividends; prepare income statement and statement of retained earnings. (SO 3, 4, 5) AP

P13–5B Hyperchip Limited is a private corporation reporting under ASPE. At December 31, 2014, its general ledger contained the following summary data:

Cost of goods sold	$ 950,000
Net sales	1,425,000
Operating expenses	270,000
Other expenses	30,000
Other revenues	45,000
Retained earnings, December 31, 2013	1,150,000

Additional information:

1. In 2014, common share dividends of $80,000 were declared on June 26 and December 26. The dividends were paid on July 9, 2014, and January 9, 2015, respectively.
2. The company's income tax rate is 20%.

Instructions

(a) Record the dividend transactions in 2014.
(b) Prepare a multiple-step income statement for 2014.
(c) Prepare a statement of retained earnings for 2014.

TAKING IT FURTHER Compare a statement of retained earnings with a statement of owner's equity.

Adjust income tax; prepare income statement, statement of retained earnings, and closing entries. (SO 3, 4, 5) AP

P13–6B Hayden Inc. is a private corporation reporting under ASPE. It has recorded all necessary adjusting entries, except for income tax expense, at its fiscal year end of November 30, 2014. The following information has been taken from the adjusted trial balance:

Accounts payable	$ 23,700	Interest expense	$ 7,500
Cash dividends—common	120,000	Notes payable	125,000
Common shares	150,000	Rent expense	43,500
Depreciation expense	51,650	Retained earnings (Dec. 1, 2013)	339,500
Dividends payable	30,000	Salaries expense	220,000
Income tax expense	15,000	Service revenue	425,000
Income tax payable	1,500	Unearned revenue	19,500
Insurance expense	10,350		

All accounts have normal balances and total assets equal $646,200. Hayden has a 15% income tax rate.

Instructions

(a) Record the entry to adjust income tax expense and prepare a multiple-step income statement for the year.
(b) Prepare a statement of retained earnings for the year.
(c) Prepare closing entries.
(d) Post the closing entries to the Income Summary and Retained Earnings accounts and compare with the financial statements.

TAKING IT FURTHER   Why is the entry to adjust income tax expense usually the last adjusting entry prepared each year?

P13–7B   On January 1, 2014, Conway Ltd. had the following shareholders' equity accounts:

Record and post transactions. Prepare shareholders' equity section. (SO 2, 4, 6) AP

Common shares, unlimited number of shares authorized, 1.5 million issued	$1,650,000
Retained earnings	400,000

It was also authorized to issue an unlimited number of $6 noncumulative preferred shares. During 2014, the corporation had the following transactions and events related to its shareholders' equity:

Jan. 2	Issued 100,000 preferred shares at $66 per share.
Mar. 31	Paid quarterly dividend to preferred shareholders.
Apr. 18	Issued 250,000 common shares at $1.30 per share.
June 30	Paid quarterly dividend to preferred shareholders.
Sept. 30	Paid quarterly dividend to preferred shareholders.
Dec. 31	Profit for the year was $160,000.

Instructions

(a) Journalize the transactions and the entries to close dividends and the Income Summary account.
(b) Open general ledger accounts for the shareholders' equity accounts and post transactions in (a).
(c) Prepare the shareholders' equity section of the balance sheet at December 31, 2014, including any required disclosures. Assume Conway reports under ASPE.

TAKING IT FURTHER   What is required to declare dividends? What was the maximum amount of dividends Conway could have declared on the common shares at December 31, 2014?

P13–8B   Largent Corporation is authorized to issue 200,000, $4 cumulative preferred shares and an unlimited number of common shares. On January 1, 2014, the general ledger contained the following shareholders' equity accounts:

Record and post transactions. Prepare shareholders' equity section. (SO 2, 4, 6) AP

Preferred shares (8,000 shares issued)	$ 440,000
Common shares (70,000 shares issued)	1,050,000
Retained earnings	800,000

During 2014, the following transactions occurred:

Jan. 1	Issued 10,000 preferred shares for $600,000.
Apr. 14	Issued 40,000 common shares for $560,000.
June 30	Paid a semi-annual dividend to the preferred shareholders.
Aug. 22	Issued 10,000 common shares in exchange for a building. At the time of the exchange, the building's fair value was $150,000.
Dec. 31	Profit for the year was $582,000.

Instructions

(a) Journalize the transactions and the entries to close dividends and the Income Summary account.
(b) Open general ledger accounts for the shareholders' equity accounts and post entries from (a).
(c) Prepare the shareholders' equity section of the balance sheet at December 31, 2014, including any required disclosures. Assume Largent is reporting under ASPE.

TAKING IT FURTHER   What are the difficulties in determining how many shares to issue in exchange for non-cash assets as well as how to value the transaction?

Prepare financial statements and closing entries. (SO 3, 5, 6) AP

P13–9B   Rupert Engineering Corp. is a private company reporting under ASPE. Its adjusted trial balance at its fiscal year end, March 31, 2014, is shown below:

RUPERT ENGINEERING CORP. Adjusted Trial Balance March 31, 2014		
	Debit	Credit
Cash	$ 65,400	
Accounts receivable	31,150	
Supplies	7,300	
Equipment	148,000	
Accumulated depreciation—equipment		$ 29,600
Accounts payable		14,200
Income tax payable		1,900
Unearned revenue		2,500
Note payable ($10,000 is due within the next year)		40,000
Preferred shares ($3.75 cumulative, 500 issued)		18,750
Common shares (35,000 issued)		50,000
Retained earnings		65,000
Cash dividends—preferred	1,875	
Cash dividends—common	53,125	
Consulting revenue		315,500
Depreciation expense	14,800	
Income tax expense	21,200	
Interest expense	2,400	
Rent expense	36,000	
Salaries expense	140,300	
Supplies expense	15,900	
	$537,450	$537,450

Instructions

(a) Prepare an income statement, statement of retained earnings, and balance sheet.

(b) Journalize the closing entries.

TAKING IT FURTHER   Are there any differences between the retained earnings account for corporations and the owner's capital account used for proprietorships?

Prepare financial statements and calculate return on equity. (SO 3, 5, 6) AP

P13–10B   Carlotta's Cakes Inc. is a private company reporting under ASPE. It is authorized to issue an unlimited number of common and $3 cumulative preferred shares. The following is an alphabetical list of its adjusted accounts at May 31, 2014, its fiscal year end. All accounts have normal balances.

Accounts payable	$ 38,500	Income tax expense	11,230
Accounts receivable	15,300	Insurance expense	$ 7,500
Accumulated depreciation—equipment	126,000	Interest expense	4,500
Cash	20,600	Inventory	70,220
Cash dividends—common	50,000	Note payable	75,000
Cash dividends—preferred	7,500	Preferred shares	150,000
Common shares	50,000	Rent expense	24,500
Cost of goods sold	277,475	Retained earnings	73,000
Depreciation expense	42,000	Salaries expense	67,800
Dividend payable	7,500	Sales revenue	504,500
Equipment	420,000	Supplies expense	5,875

The note payable is due in 2017.

Instructions

(a) Prepare an income statement, statement of retained earnings, and balance sheet.

(b) Calculate return on equity. Note: No shares were issued during the year.

TAKING IT FURTHER   Is the return on equity ratio useful when a company reports a loss?

Calculate return on assets and equity and comment. (SO 6) AP

P13–11B The following financial information (in millions) is for two major corporations for the three fiscal years ended December 31:

	2011	2010	2009
Husky Energy Inc.			
Profit	$ 2,224	$ 947	
Shareholders' equity	17,773	14,574	$13,716
Total assets	32,426	28,050	25,508
Suncor Energy Inc.			
Profit	$ 4,304	$ 3,829	
Shareholders' equity	38,600	35,192	$32,485
Total assets	74,777	68,607	67,799

Instructions

(a) Calculate return on assets and return on equity for each company for 2011 and 2010. Comment on whether their ratios have improved or deteriorated.
(b) Compare Husky's ratios with Suncor's.
(c) The industry average for return on equity in 2011 was 9.03%. Compare the two companies' performance with the industry average.

TAKING IT FURTHER Using your findings in this question to illustrate, explain why is it important to use comparisons in evaluating ratios.

Record transactions and adjustments; prepare financial statements. (SO 2, 3, 4, 5, 6) AP

P13–12B Nygren Corporation, a private company, is authorized to issue an unlimited number of common shares and 500,000, $5 cumulative preferred shares. It began operations on January 1, 2014, and the following transactions occurred in 2014:

Jan. 1 Issued 6,000 common shares for $60,000 cash.
    2 Issued 1,000 preferred shares for $62.50 cash per share.
Dec. 10 Declared a total of $17,000 in dividends, payable on January 3, to shareholders of record on December 23.

The following information is also available with respect to the company's operations during the year:

1. Collected $268,000 cash for consulting revenue earned.
2. Paid $164,000 salaries expense; $42,000 rent expense; and $12,000 office expense.
3. Purchased equipment for $130,000 cash.
4. At December 31, determined the following adjustments were required:
   • Depreciation on the equipment, $13,000
   • Consulting revenue earned but not yet collected in cash, $22,000
   • Accrued salaries expense, $4,200
   • Income tax rate, 15%. No instalments were made during the year.

Nygren elected to report under ASPE.

Instructions

(a) Record the share issue and dividend transactions.
(b) Record summary journal entries for transactions (1) to (3) and adjusting entries for items in (4).
(c) Open an account for Cash and post transactions.
(d) Prepare an income statement, statement of retained earnings, and balance sheet.

TAKING IT FURTHER Why are common shareholders sometimes referred to as "residual owners"?

⊙ Continuing Cookie Chronicle

(*Note:* This is a continuation of the Cookie Chronicle from Chapters 1 through 12.)

Recall (from Chapter 12) that Natalie had been considering forming a partnership with Katy, a high school friend. Natalie has concluded that she and Katy are not compatible to operate a business together and Natalie has continued on her own.

   Natalie's parents, Janet and Brian Koebel, have been operating Koebel's Family Bakery Ltd., a private corporation, for a number of years. They are very proud of Natalie and the success of Cookie Creations and have decided that it may be time to get Natalie involved with the operation of the family business.

   In anticipation of Natalie graduating, and in hopes of spending a little more time away from the bakery, they have discussed with Natalie the possibility of her becoming one of the shareholders of Koebel's Family Bakery Ltd.

In addition, once Natalie has graduated, Natalie would assume the full-time position of administrator. Natalie could continue to provide cookie-making lessons and sell mixers; however, that would be done by Koebel's Family Bakery in future rather than by Natalie's Cookie Creations.

The share capital and the retained earnings of Koebel's Family Bakery Ltd. at August 1, 2013, are as follows:

$6 cumulative preferred shares, 10,000 shares authorized, none issued	
Common shares, unlimited number of shares authorized, 200 shares issued	$ 200
Retained earnings	116,251

Profit before income tax for the year ended July 31, 2014, was $255,823. The company has an 18% income tax rate. A cash dividend of $85,000 was declared on July 15, 2014, to common shareholders of record on July 20, 2014, and was paid on July 30, 2014.

Based on the bakery's success, the Koebels would like to issue 10 shares to Natalie for $1,200 per share. Natalie would contribute the fair value of Cookie Creations' assets in exchange for the shares of Koebel's Family Bakery as follows:

	Cookie Creations
Cash	$8,050
Accounts receivable	800
Merchandise inventory	1,200
Supplies	450
Equipment	1,500

The sale of shares by Koebel's Family Bakery to Natalie is expected to take place on August 1, 2014. Currently, Janet and Brian each own 100 shares. Assume Koebel's Family Bakery reports using ASPE.

Instructions

(a) Prepare the journal entries required for the cash dividend declared on July 15 and paid on July 30, 2014. Who received the cash dividend, and for what amount?

(b) Prepare the statement of retained earnings for the year ended July 31, 2014.

(c) Prepare the shareholders' equity section of the balance sheet at July 31, 2014.

(d) Assume that Natalie purchases the shares of Koebel's Family Bakery Ltd. on August 1, 2014, in exchange for the fair value of assets held by Cookie Creations. Prepare the journal entries required by Koebel's Family Bakery Ltd.

(e) Determine the number of shares issued and the average cost per common share before and after Natalie purchases the shares of Koebel's Family Bakery. Why is there a significant change in value?

(f) How do you think a value of $1,200 per share was determined when Janet and Brian were attempting to come up with the number of shares to be sold to Natalie? Do you think that the number of shares Natalie received in exchange for the assets of Cookie Creations is fair? Why or why not?

CHAPTER 13 | **BROADENING YOUR PERSPECTIVE**

Financial Reporting and Analysis

Financial Reporting Problem

BYP13–1   The shareholders' equity section for **Reitmans (Canada) Limited** is shown in the consolidated balance sheet in Appendix A. You will also find data related to this problem in the notes to the financial statements.

Instructions

(a) How many classes of shares does Reitmans have? For each class of shares, specify how many shares are authorized and issued at January 28, 2012.

(b) Refer to note 16. What are the rights of each class of shares?

(c) Did Reitmans issue any additional shares in fiscal 2012? If so, specify how many were issued, for what dollar amount, and for what purpose.

(d) What was the average cost of each class of Reitmans' shares at the end of fiscal 2012?

(e) Did Reitmans declare any cash dividends in fiscal 2012? If yes, how much? If not, why might a company choose not to pay dividends?

(f) Reitmans' return on equity was calculated for fiscal 2012 in Illustration 13-7. Calculate the company's return on equity for fiscal 2011. Did this ratio improve or worsen from 2011 to 2012?

Interpreting Financial Statements

BYP13–2   Talisman Energy Inc., headquartered in Calgary, is a large international oil and gas producer. Talisman's authorized share capital includes an unlimited number of common shares and an unlimited number of two classes of preferred shares.

On December 5, 2011, Talisman issued 8 million cumulative redeemable Series 1 preferred shares at a price of $25 per share. The following information is also available for the years ended December 31, 2010 and 2011:

	2011	2010
Profit margin	9.4%	28.1%
Asset turnover	0.36 times	0.33 times
Return on assets	3.4%	4.5%
Return on equity	8.1%	10.5%
Common share market price per share	$12.98	$22.12
Preferred share market price per share	$24.34	Not applicable

Instructions

(a) Discuss the change in Talisman's profitability from 2010 to 2011.

(b) Is your assessment in (a) consistent with the change in market price per share? Explain.

(c) Talisman did not issue any common shares in 2011. Why might it have issued preferred shares instead?

(d) Total gross proceeds from the preferred share issue were $200 million ($25 × 8 million). However, Talisman credited its Preferred Share account $191 million because of underwriting fees of $9 million. Why is this fee recorded as a reduction of proceeds from the issue of shares as opposed to an expense?

(e) The preferred shareholders are entitled to receive a dividend of 4.2%. What is this in dollars per share? Why is this rate higher than the interest rate on savings accounts paid by banks?

(f) The preferred shares are redeemable for $25 per share (plus unpaid dividends) on December 31, 2016, and on December 31 every five years thereafter. Why might Talisman choose to redeem the shares?

▶ Critical Thinking

Collaborative Learning Activity

Note to instructor: Additional instructions and material for this group activity can be found on the Instructor Resource Site and in *WileyPLUS*.

BYP13–3   In this group activity, you will be forming a new corporation and making decisions about the number of shares to be issued to the founding shareholders as well as to an individual who becomes a shareholder at a later date. You will also prepare a corporate income statement and balance sheet for this corporation.

Communication Activity

BYP13–4   Your cousin owns 100% of the common shares of a corporation, Ghost River Back Country Limited, a retail company specializing in outdoor clothing and equipment. The company has the opportunity to purchase land and a building in a desirable location that would be used to operate a second store. Your cousin is very excited about this opportunity but is wondering about the best way to finance this purchase as the company currently does not have excess cash. She and the seller are currently considering the possibility of issuing new shares of Ghost River Back Country Limited to the seller to pay for the land and buildings.

Instructions

Write a memo to your cousin explaining some of the advantages and disadvantages to issuing either common or preferred shares, compared with borrowing money, to purchase the land and buildings. Also include in your discussion any issues in terms of recording the transaction if shares are issued.

Ethics Case

BYP13–5   The R&D division of Simplex Chemical Corp. has just developed a chemical to sterilize the voracious mountain pine beetles that are invading Western Canada's forests. The president of Simplex is anxious to get the new chemical to market and has already named it PinebeetleX101. Simplex's profits need a boost and the president's job is in jeopardy because of decreasing sales and profits. Simplex has an opportunity to sell this chemical in several Central American countries, where the laws about proving a product's safety before beginning to use it or sell it are much more relaxed than in Canada.

The director of Simplex's R&D division strongly recommends more laboratory testing for side effects of this chemical on other insects, birds, animals, plants, and even humans. He cautions the president, "We could be sued from all sides if the chemical has tragic side effects that we didn't even test for in the labs." The president answers,

"We can't wait an additional year for your lab tests. We can avoid losses from such lawsuits by creating a new separate corporation called Simplex Central America Inc., which will be 100% owned by Simplex Chemical Corp., to operate our business in those countries. We will invest just the patent covering this chemical in Simplex Central America Inc. That corporation will have limited liability so we can't lose any more than the assets that we put into it. Since we will own 100% of the shares of Simplex Central America Inc., we can put ourselves on its board of directors, and then we can make it pay dividends to Simplex Chemical Corp. when it makes a profit. We'll reap the benefits if the chemical works and is safe, and avoid the losses from lawsuits if it's a disaster."

The following week, Simplex Chemical Corp. creates the new 100%-owned corporation Simplex Central America Inc., sells it the chemical patent for PinebeetleX101 for $10, delivers a shipload of the chemicals, and watches the spraying begin.

Instructions

(a) Who are the stakeholders in this situation?
(b) Are the president's motives and actions ethical?
(c) Can Simplex Chemical Corp. be certain that it is protected against all losses related to the activities of Simplex Central America Inc.?

"All About You" Activity

BYP13–6   As you learned in the "All About You" feature, the decision to incorporate or not is complex. After you have completed your post-secondary business education, you may be an entrepreneur and may need to decide if and when to incorporate your business. And if you decide to incorporate, you will also need to know more about how.

Instructions

Go to the website of Corporations Canada, part of Industry Canada, at http://corporationscanada.ic.gc.ca. Click on "FAQs" (frequently asked questions).
(a) What are the benefits of incorporating with the federal government?
(b) What kinds of businesses can incorporate under the *Canada Business Corporations Act*?
(c) Who can form a corporation?
(d) Go to the FAQ "If I decide to incorporate, what next?" When are corporations formed? Describe the information required in the Articles of Incorporation (forms 1 and 2).
(e) What are the advantages of incorporating online?
(f) On the Corporations Canada homepage, go to "Incorporate a Business" and then click on the "Guide to Federal Incorporation." Go to Chapter 6, Other Obligations of the Corporation. Answer the following questions:
   1. By what date do the annual financial statements have to be prepared?
   2. The financial statements are required to be prepared in accordance with generally accepted accounting principles (GAAP). For Canadian corporations, where is GAAP set out?
   3. Does a company have to appoint auditors?
   4. What corporate records are required to be kept by a corporation?

ANSWERS TO CHAPTER QUESTIONS

ANSWERS TO ACCOUNTING IN ACTION INSIGHT QUESTIONS

All About You, p. 676

Q: Given the complexity of tax planning, and the impact that taxes could have on the advantages of incorporating, what should you do before deciding to incorporate your business?
A: The business owner should seek expert tax advice to ensure the benefits of incorporating are greater than the costs.

Across the Organization, p. 681

Q: Why might the "no maturity date" feature of preferred shares be useful to an organization?
A: The "no maturity date" feature can provide management with flexibility in terms of the timing of redeeming the preferred shares. With debt, a company cannot predict with certainty if it will have cash to repay the debt on the maturity date, which makes debt riskier to the company. With preferred shares, a company can include a redemption feature, which it is not required to act on if it doesn't have the cash.

ANSWERS TO SELF-STUDY QUESTIONS

1. a   2. d   3. b   4. c   5. b   6. c   7. d   8. a   9. b   10. d

Remember to go back to the beginning of the chapter to check off your completed work!
←

 THE **NAVIGATOR**

- ☐ Understand *Concepts for Review*
- ☐ Read *Feature Story*
- ☐ Scan *Study Objectives*
- ☐ Read *Chapter Preview*
- ☐ Read text and answer *Before You Go On*
- ☐ Review *Comparing IFRS and ASPE*
- ☐ Work *Demonstration Problem*
- ☐ Review *Summary of Study Objectives*
- ☐ Answer *Self-Study Questions*
- ☐ Complete assignments
- ☐ Go to *WileyPLUS* for practice and tutorials

CONCEPTS FOR **REVIEW**

Before studying this chapter, you should understand or, if necessary, review:

a. How to record cash dividends. (Ch. 13, p. 685–686)

b. How to account for share transactions. (Ch. 13, pp. 678–681)

c. The qualitative characteristics of accounting information. (Ch. 11, pp. 580–584)

d. How to prepare a statement of retained earnings. (Ch. 13, pp. 686–687)

e. The form and content of the shareholders' equity section of the balance sheet. (Ch. 13, pp. 689–690)

f. How to calculate return on equity. (Ch. 13, p. 691)

BREWING SHAREHOLDER RETURN

OAKVILLE, Ont.—Public corporations issue shares, but they can buy some of their shares back, as well. One reason why companies sometimes do this is that they may be sitting on a large amount of cash. For example, at the end of its 2011 fiscal year, Tim Hortons Inc., the iconic quick service restaurant franchise chain, had cash and cash equivalents of nearly $127 million.

With consistently healthy cash flows, a priority for Tim Hortons is to invest in the business. "We turn around and reinvest quite a bit of our free cash flow in capital expenditures, such as building new restaurants, renovating existing restaurants, and building new manufacturing facilities or distribution centres," says Diana Fife, Vice President, Financial Reporting.

If there is still money left over after making all its desired capital expenditures, then the company may want to make sure it has a solid balance sheet so it can weather any economic storms, like the 2008 global financial crisis, when Tim Hortons did not need to rely on banks for funding. Once the company is assured its balance sheet is strong, it really needs to return the rest to shareholders because to sit on cash idly is not a good investment decision. It doesn't earn you very much today with interest rates the way they are, and if the

cash coffer is built up too significantly, you could be subject to a takeover.

To return money to shareholders, Tim Hortons has considered the right balance between issuing dividends to existing shareholders and buying back some of its shares. As of 2012, the company had undergone six consecutive major share repurchase programs since it went public in 2006. For example, in early 2012, the company announced plans to start a new share repurchase program to buy up to $200 million in common shares.

Tim Hortons has a dividend policy whereby it commits to paying out a certain percentage of its profit to shareholders every year. Since becoming a public company, it increased its quarterly dividend six times, ranging from an 11% increase to a 31% increase.

The company also sets a target that it communicates to shareholders each year to achieve a certain earnings per share for the upcoming year. For 2012, that target was earnings per share of $2.65 to $2.75. If it achieves same-store sales growth and if it delivers the targeted number of new restaurants for the year, then that translates to earnings. It is a real partnership with the restaurant owners. If the restaurant owners are growing their businesses, then Tim Hortons is too.

THE **NAVIGATOR**

» STUDY **OBJECTIVES**

After studying this chapter, you should be able to:

1. Account for stock dividends and stock splits and compare their financial impact.

2. Account for the reacquisition of shares.

3. Prepare an income statement showing continuing and discontinued operations, and prepare a statement of comprehensive income.

4. Explain the accounting for different types of accounting changes and account for corrections of prior period errors.

5. Prepare a statement of changes in shareholders' equity.

6. Evaluate earnings and dividend performance.

THE **NAVIGATOR**

This chapter builds on the introduction to corporations in Chapter 13 and discusses issues that are either more complex or more likely to be encountered only by public companies. Financial statements required for a corporation reporting under IFRS—the statements of comprehensive income and changes in shareholders' equity—are also shown. The chapter is organized as follows:

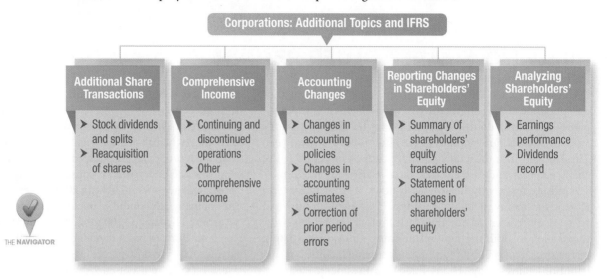

THE **NAVIGATOR**

Additional Share Transactions

Recall from Chapter 13 that shares can be issued for cash and for noncash assets or services, and that they can be issued when preferred shares are converted into common shares. Shares can also be issued as the result of stock dividends, stock splits, and stock options. Companies may also decide to reacquire previously issued shares.

STOCK DIVIDENDS AND STOCK SPLITS

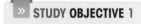

» STUDY OBJECTIVE 1

Account for stock dividends and stock splits and compare their financial impact.

Recall from Chapter 13 that a dividend is a pro rata distribution of a portion of a corporation's retained earnings to its shareholders. Cash dividends, covered in Chapter 13, are the most common type of dividend and are used in both private and public corporations.

Stock dividends are another type of dividend rarely used in private corporations; they are more common in public corporations. Stock splits are not dividends, but have some similarities with stock dividends and also are typically used only in public corporations.

Stock Dividends

A **stock dividend** is a distribution of the corporation's own shares to shareholders. Whereas a cash dividend is paid in cash, a stock dividend is distributed (paid) in shares. And while a cash dividend decreases assets and shareholders' equity, a stock dividend does not change either assets or shareholders' equity. A stock dividend results in a decrease in retained earnings and an increase in share capital, but there is no change in *total* shareholders' equity.

From the company's point of view, no cash has been paid, and no liabilities have been assumed. What are the purposes and benefits of a stock dividend? A corporation generally issues stock dividends for one or more of the following reasons:

1. To satisfy shareholders' dividend expectations without spending cash.
2. To increase the marketability of the corporation's shares. When the number of shares increases, the market price per share tends to decrease. Decreasing the market price makes it easier for investors to purchase the shares.
3. To emphasize that a portion of shareholders' equity has been permanently retained in the business and is unavailable for cash dividends.

The size of the stock dividend and the value to be assigned to each share are determined by the board of directors when the dividend is declared. It is common for companies to assign the fair value per share for stock dividends at the declaration date.

To illustrate the accounting for stock dividends, assume that on June 30, IBR Inc. declares a 10% stock dividend on its 50,000 common shares, to be distributed on August 5 to shareholders of record on July 20. This means 5,000 (10% × 50,000) shares will be issued. In recording the transaction, **the fair value at the declaration date is used**, not the fair value on the record or distribution dates.

Assuming the fair value of its shares on June 30 is $15 per share, the amount debited to Stock Dividends is $75,000 (5,000 × $15). The entry to record the declaration of the stock dividend is as follows:

Declaration Date		
June 30	Stock Dividends	75,000	
	Stock Dividends Distributable		75,000
	To record declaration of 10% stock dividend.		

A = L + SE
+75,000
−75,000
Cash flows: no effect

At the declaration date, the Stock Dividends account is increased by the fair value of the shares to be issued. This will result in a decrease in Retained Earnings, similar to cash dividends, when the Stock Dividends account is closed. Stock Dividends Distributable, a shareholders' equity account, is increased by the same amount. Stock Dividends Distributable is not a liability, because assets will not be used to pay the dividend. Instead, it will be "paid" with common shares. If a balance sheet is prepared before the dividend shares are issued, the Stock Dividends Distributable account is reported as share capital in the shareholders' equity section of the balance sheet.

As with cash dividends, no entry is required at the record date. When the dividend shares are issued on August 5, the **distribution date**, the account Stock Dividends Distributable is debited and the account Common Shares is credited:

> **Helpful hint** As with cash dividends, it is also acceptable to directly debit Retained Earnings. This eliminates the need to close the stock dividends account at the end of the year but might make it more difficult to track the amount of each type of dividend declared.

Distribution Date		
Aug. 5	Stock Dividends Distributable	75,000	
	Common Shares		75,000
	To record issue of 5,000 common shares in a stock dividend.		

A = L + SE
+75,000
−75,000
Cash flows: no effect

Note that neither of the above entries changes shareholders' equity in total. However, the composition of shareholders' equity changes because a portion of Retained Earnings is transferred to the Common Shares account. The number of shares issued has also increased. These effects are shown below for IBR Inc. using assumed data for Retained Earnings and Common Shares prior to the stock dividend:

	Before Stock Dividend	**After Stock Dividend**
Shareholders' equity		
Common shares	$500,000	$575,000
Retained earnings	300,000	225,000
Total shareholders' equity	$800,000	$800,000
Total number of common shares issued	50,000	55,000

In this example, the account Common Shares is increased by $75,000 and Retained Earnings is decreased by the same amount. Total shareholders' equity remains unchanged at $800,000, the total before and after the stock dividend.

Stock Splits

A **stock split**, like a stock dividend, involves the issue of additional shares to shareholders according to their percentage ownership. However, a stock split is usually much larger than a stock dividend.

The purpose of a stock split is to increase the shares' marketability by lowering the fair value per share. A lower fair value interests more investors and makes it easier for the corporation to issue additional shares. On the other hand, sometimes companies will decrease the number of shares outstanding by doing a **reverse stock split**. Instead of issuing two stocks for one, they issue one stock for two, to increase the fair value per share.

The effect of a split on fair value is generally inversely proportional to the size of the split. For example, in a 2-for-1 stock split, since there are twice as many shares, the fair value will normally decrease by half. Sometimes, due to increased investor interest, the share price will quickly rise beyond its split value.

In a stock split, the number of shares is increased by a specified proportion. For example, in a 2-for-1 split, one share is exchanged for two shares. A stock split does not have any effect on share capital, retained earnings, or shareholders' equity. Only the number of shares increases.

A stock split is illustrated below for IBR Inc.'s common shares. For the illustration, we assume that, instead of a 10% stock dividend, IBR splits its 50,000 common shares on a 2-for-1 basis.

	Before Stock Split	**After Stock Split**
Shareholders' equity		
Common shares	$500,000	$500,000
Retained earnings	300,000	300,000
Total shareholders' equity	**$800,000**	**$800,000**
Total number of common shares issued	50,000	100,000

Because a stock split does not affect the balances in any shareholders' equity accounts, it is not necessary to journalize it. Only a memo entry explaining the details of the split is needed.

Either common or preferred shares can be split. If preferred shares that have a stated dividend rate are split, then the dividend must also be adjusted for the effects of the split. For example, if 10,000, $6 preferred shares are split 3 for 1, then after the split there will be 30,000 preferred shares with a $2 annual dividend. The total dividend before and after the split remains unchanged at $60,000 (10,000 × $6 before and 30,000 × $2 after). After all, it is the same shareholders who held 10,000 shares before the split who now hold 30,000 shares.

Comparison of Effects

Significant differences among stock splits, stock dividends, and cash dividends (after payment) are shown below.

		Shareholders' Equity	
	Assets	**Share Capital**	**Retained Earnings**
Cash dividend	Decrease	No effect	Decrease
Stock dividend	No effect	Increase	Decrease
Stock split	No effect	No effect	No effect

Cash dividends reduce assets and shareholders' equity. Stock dividends increase share capital (the Common Shares or Preferred Shares account) and decrease retained earnings. Stock splits do not affect any of the accounts. However, both a stock dividend and a stock split increase the number of shares issued.

Note that since stock dividends and splits neither increase nor decrease the assets in the company, investors are not receiving anything they did not already own. In a sense, it is like having a piece of pie and cutting it into smaller pieces. They are no better or worse off, as they have the same amount of pie.

To illustrate a stock dividend or stock split for the common shareholders, assume that a shareholder owns 1,000 of IBR Inc.'s 50,000 common shares. If IBR declares a 10% stock dividend, the shareholder will receive 100 shares (10% × 1,000). On the other hand, if IBR splits its shares on a 2-for-1 basis, the shareholder will receive 1,000 shares. Will the shareholder's ownership interest change? As shown in Illustration 14-1, there is no change.

| | Stock Dividend | | | Stock Split | | |
| | Company | Shareholder | | Company | Shareholder | |
	Total Shares issued	# Shares	Ownership Interest	Total Shares issued	# Shares	Ownership Interest
Before	50,000	1,000	2%	50,000	1,000	2%
New shares issued	5,000	100		50,000	1,000	
After	55,000	1,100	2%	100,000	2,000	2%

▶ILLUSTRATION 14-1
Effect of stock dividend and stock split for shareholders

ACCOUNTING IN ACTION
ACROSS THE ORGANIZATION

Stock exchanges usually require publicly traded stocks to maintain a minimum value or they will be delisted, meaning a company's shares will no longer be traded. The New York Stock Exchange (NYSE), for example, requires shares to be worth a daily average of at least US$1 over a consecutive 30-day trading period. The shares of Toronto-based Kingsway Financial Services Inc., an insurance holding company, recently were at risk of dipping below that minimum. To avoid being delisted on the NYSE, it implemented a reverse stock split. As approved by shareholders at an annual meeting, Kingsway offered shareholders one share for every four that they owned, as at July 3, 2012. The consolidation reduced the number of common shares from approximately 52 million to about 13 million. By increasing the fair value per share, Kingsway could continue to trade on the NYSE, along with the Toronto Stock Exchange. In the months immediately after the 1-for-4 split, Kingsway's shares were consistently trading above $1.75.

There were other advantages, too. "The Company's Board believes a reverse stock split would have the additional benefit of attracting a broader range of institutional and other investors. The Board also believes that a higher share price will reduce per share transaction fees and certain administrative costs," Kingsway stated.

Sources: "Kingsway Implements Previously Announced Share Consolidation," company news release, July 3, 2012; Rick Aristotle Munarriz, "Reverse Splits Aren't All Bad," Motley Fool newsletter, March 20, 2012; "Kingsway Announces Reverse Stock Split," company news release, January 27, 2012; "Detailed Quote for Kingsway Financial Services Inc. (KFS)," QuoteMedia, http://www.newswire.ca/en/stock_chart/KFS, accessed September 17, 2012.

If a company announces a reverse stock split, is this considered a positive or negative sign about the future of the company?

BEFORE YOU GO ON...

Do It

Sing CD Corporation has had five years of high profits. Due to this success, the market price of its 500,000 common shares tripled from $15 to $45 per share. During this period, the Common Shares account remained the same at $2 million. Retained earnings increased from $1.5 million to $10 million. President Bill Zerter is considering either (a) a 10% stock dividend, or (b) a 2-for-1 stock split. He asks you to show the before-and-after effects of each option on the Common Shares and Retained Earnings accounts and on the number of shares.

Solution
(a) With a 10% stock dividend, 50,000 new shares will be issued (500,000 × 10%). The stock dividend amount is $2,250,000 (50,000 × $45). The new balance in Common Shares is $4,250,000 ($2,000,000 + $2,250,000). In Retained Earnings, it is $7,750,000 ($10,000,000 − $2,250,000).
(b) With a 2-for-1 stock split, 500,000 new shares will be issued. The account balances in Common Shares and Retained Earnings after the stock split are the same as they were before: $2 million and $10 million, respectively.

Action Plan
- Calculate the stock dividend effect on Retained Earnings by multiplying the stock dividend percentage by the number of existing shares to determine the number of new shares to be issued. Multiply the number of new shares by the shares' market price.
- A stock dividend increases the number of shares and affects both Common Shares and Retained Earnings.
- A stock split increases the number of shares but does not affect Common Shares and Retained Earnings.

BEFORE YOU GO ON continued...

The effects in the shareholders' equity accounts of each option are as follows:

	Original Balances	After Stock Dividend	After Stock Split
Common shares	$ 2,000,000	$ 4,250,000	$ 2,000,000
Retained earnings	10,000,000	7,750,000	10,000,000
Total shareholders' equity	$12,000,000	$12,000,000	$12,000,000
Total number of common shares issued	500,000	550,000	1,000,000

Related exercise material: BE14–1, BE14–2, BE14–3, E14–1, and E14–2.

THE NAVIGATOR

REACQUISITION OF SHARES

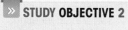

STUDY OBJECTIVE 2

Account for the reacquisition of shares.

Companies can purchase or reacquire their own shares from shareholders. Typically, the reasons for doing this will be different for a private company as opposed to a public company. Private companies reacquire shares when there is a change in business circumstances or a change in the needs of the shareholders. For example, a private corporation may have an agreement in which it must reacquire the shares owned by an employee if the employee leaves the company.

A public corporation may acquire its own shares for any number of reasons. For example, as explained in our feature story, Tim Hortons repurchases its shares as a way of returning cash to shareholders when the cash is not needed to grow the business. Other reasons a public corporation may reacquire shares include the following:

1. To increase trading of the company's shares in the securities market in the hope of increasing the company's fair value.
2. To reduce the number of shares issued, which will increase earnings per share.
3. To eliminate hostile shareholders by buying them out.
4. To have additional shares available so that they can be reissued to officers and employees through bonus and stock compensation plans, or can be used to acquire other companies.

For federally incorporated companies, and most provincially incorporated companies, the repurchased shares must be retired and cancelled. This restores the shares to the status of authorized but unissued shares. In some Canadian provinces, in the United States, and internationally, reacquired shares can also be held for subsequent reissue. If the shares are not retired and cancelled, they are referred to as **treasury shares.**

Whether the company is private or public, the following steps are required to record a reacquisition of common (or preferred) shares:

1. **Remove the cost of the shares from the share capital account:** Recall that, when a long-lived asset is retired, the cost of the asset must be deleted (credited) from the appropriate asset account. Similarly, the cost of the common shares that are reacquired and retired must be determined and this amount is then deleted (debited) from the Common Shares account.

   In order to determine the cost of the common shares reacquired, it is necessary to calculate an **average cost per share.** It is impractical, and often impossible, to determine the cost of each individual common share that is reacquired. An average cost per common share is therefore calculated by dividing the balance in the Common Shares account by the number of shares issued at the transaction date.

2. **Record the cash paid:** The Cash account is credited for the amount paid to reacquire the shares. Note that a public company has little choice in what it has to pay to reacquire the shares (it can only decide when to make the reacquisition). It must purchase the shares on the secondary market by paying the current market price on the date of purchase.

3. **Record the "gain" or "loss" on reacquisition:** The difference between the cash paid to reacquire the shares and their average cost is basically a "gain" or "loss" on reacquisition. However, because companies cannot realize a gain or suffer a loss from share transactions with their own shareholders, these amounts are not reported on the income statement. They are seen instead as an excess or deficiency that belongs to the shareholders. As a result, the amount is reported as an increase or decrease in the shareholders' equity section of the balance sheet.

The accounting for the reacquisition of shares differs depending on whether the shares are reacquired by paying less than the average cost or more than the average cost. We will examine each situation in the next two sections.

Reacquisition below Average Cost

When a company reacquires its shares for less than what the shareholder originally paid, the company has a "gain" on reacquisition. This "gain" is part of the contributed capital of the company because, effectively, the shareholder has made a contribution to the company equal to the difference between the original cost of the shares and the price the shareholder received when the shares were reacquired. It is recorded in the account Contributed Surplus—Reacquisition of Shares and is shown in the contributed capital section of the shareholders' equity section on the balance sheet, along with the share capital, to indicate the total capital contributed by the shareholders.

To illustrate the reacquisition of common shares at a price less than average cost, assume that Campagne Inc. has an unlimited number of common shares authorized, and a total of 75,000 common shares issued. It has a balance in its Common Shares account of $150,000. The average cost of Campagne's common shares is therefore $2 per share ($150,000 ÷ 75,000).

On September 23, Campagne reacquired 5,000 of its common shares at a price of $1.50 per share. Since the average cost of the shares is $0.50 ($2.00 − $1.50) more than the price paid to reacquire them there is an additional contribution to shareholders' equity. The entry is recorded as follows:

Sept. 23	Common Shares (5,000 × $2)	10,000	
	Contributed Surplus—Reacquisition of Shares		2,500
	Cash (5,000 × $1.50)		7,500
	To record reacquisition and retirement		
	of 5,000 common shares.		

A = L + SE
−7,500   −10,000
           +2,500

↓ Cash flows: −7,500

After this entry, Campagne still has an unlimited number of shares authorized, but only 70,000 (75,000 − 5,000) shares issued, and a balance of $140,000 ($150,000 − $10,000) in its Common Shares account. The average cost is still $2 per share ($140,000 ÷ 70,000).

Reacquisition above Average Cost

If shares are reacquired at a price greater than average cost, then the company has a "loss" on reacquisition and shareholders' equity will need to be reduced by the difference between these two amounts. If there is any balance in the contributed surplus account from previous reacquisitions, this amount would first be reduced (debited). However, contributed surplus cannot be reduced below zero. In other words, contributed surplus can never have a negative, or debit, balance. Instead, if the debit amount is greater than the balance in contributed surplus, the difference is recorded in Retained Earnings, which can go into a deficit (debit) position. The following two examples show how to record the reacquisition of shares with and without a balance in a contributed surplus account.

Balance in the Contributed Surplus Account. To illustrate, we will continue with the Campagne Inc. example. Assume that on December 5, Campagne Inc. reacquires an additional 10,000 shares, this time for $2.75 per share. Assuming no additional shares have been issued since September 23, the average cost of the shares is still $2.00, as previously shown. The result is a loss of $0.75 ($2.00 − $2.75) per share. The total loss is $7,500 (10,000 × $0.75). As there is only $2,500 in the Contributed Surplus account, the rest of the loss is recorded as a reduction of retained earnings as follows:

Dec. 5	Common Shares (10,000 × $2)	20,000	
	Contributed Surplus—Reacquisition of Shares	2,500	
	Retained Earnings ($7,500 − $2,500)	5,000	
	Cash (10,000 × $2.75)		27,500
	To record reacquisition and retirement of		
	10,000 common shares.		

A = L + SE
−27,500   −20,000
            −2,500
            −5,000

↓ Cash flows: −27,500

After this entry, Campagne still has an unlimited number of shares authorized, but only 60,000 (70,000 − 10,000) shares issued, and a balance of $120,000 ($140,000 − $20,000) in its Common Shares account. The average cost is still $2 per share ($120,000 ÷ 60,000).

No Balance in the Contributed Surplus Account. To illustrate, we will continue with the Campagne Inc. example. Assume that on December 27, Campagne Inc. reacquires an additional 2,000 shares, this time for $2.25 per share. Assuming no additional shares have been issued since the previous transaction on December 5, the average cost of the shares is still $2.00, as previously shown. The result is a loss of $0.25 ($2.00 − $2.25) per share. The total loss is $500 (2,000 × $0.25). As there is no balance in the Contributed Surplus account, the full amount of the loss is recorded as a reduction of retained earnings, as follows:

A	=	L	+	SE
−4,500				−4,000
				−500

↓ Cash flows: −4,500

Dec. 27	Common Shares (2,000 × $2)	4,000	
	Retained Earnings	500	
	Cash (2,000 × $2.25)		4,500
	To record reacquisition and retirement of 2,000 common shares.		

Note that the reductions to retained earnings on December 5 and 27 will never be reversed, even if the company later reacquires shares below cost.

In summary, the only difference in the accounting for a reacquisition at prices below or above the average cost has to do with recording the difference between the average cost of the shares and the amount of cash paid to reacquire them. If the shares are reacquired at a price below the average cost, the difference is always credited to a contributed surplus account. If the shares are reacquired at a price above their average cost, the difference is debited first to the contributed surplus account from any previous reacquisition below cost of the same class of shares, and then to the Retained Earnings account if there is no credit balance left in the contributed surplus account.

Action Plan

- Determine the average cost of the shares by dividing the balance in the Common Shares account by the number of shares issued.
- Reduce the Common Shares account by the number of shares reacquired times the average cost per share.
- Compare the cost of the shares reacquired with the cash paid to reacquire the shares.
- If the cost is less than the cash paid, the company has a "gain" and records it as contributed surplus.
- If the reacquisition price is above the average cost, debit the difference to Retained Earnings unless there is already a balance in a contributed surplus account from previous reacquisitions and retirements.

BEFORE YOU GO ON...

Do It

Ramsay Corporation reported having 25,000 common shares issued for a total share capital of $100,000 on its December 31, 2013, balance sheet. On February 15, 2014, it reacquired 4,000 of these shares. This is the first time Ramsay has reacquired any of its shares. Record the reacquisition of the shares assuming the company paid (a) $14,000, and (b) $18,000, to reacquire the shares.

Solution

(a)

Feb. 15	Common Shares (4,000 × $4.00)	16,000	
	Contributed Surplus—Reacquisition of Shares ($16,000 − $14,000)		2,000
	Cash		14,000
	To record reacquisition and retirement of 4,000 common shares at an average cost of $4.00 ($100,000 ÷ 25,000).		

(b)

Feb. 15	Common Shares (4,000 × $4.00)	16,000	
	Retained Earnings ($18,000 − $16,000)	2,000	
	Cash		18,000
	To record reacquisition and retirement of 4,000 common shares at an average cost of $4.00 ($100,000 ÷ 25,000).		

Related exercise material: BE14–4, BE14–5, and E14–3.

THE **NAVIGATOR**

Comprehensive Income

In Chapter 13, we introduced corporate income tax and how to prepare an income statement for a corporation. In the following section, we will build on those concepts and show how to prepare an income statement when a company has gains or losses from discontinued operations. We also introduce the concept of other comprehensive income for companies following IFRS and show how it is combined with profit to determine comprehensive income.

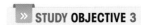

» **STUDY OBJECTIVE 3**

Prepare an income statement showing continuing and discontinued operations, and prepare a statement of comprehensive income.

CONTINUING AND DISCONTINUED OPERATIONS

Recall from Chapter 11 that investors need accounting information that is relevant in making decisions about such things as whether or not they should buy (or sell) shares of a company. Creditors need to know if they should lend to a company or not. Thus both investors and creditors use the income statement to evaluate a company's profitability and performance in the previous accounting period. But they are often even more interested in being able to predict or forecast how much profit the company may earn the following year. In order to provide this information, it is necessary to divide the company's profit or loss between its continuing and discontinued operations.

Continuing operations are the revenues, expenses, and profit or loss generated from the company's ongoing activities. **Discontinued operations** refer to the disposal or reclassification to "held for sale" of a component of an entity. A **component of an entity** is a separate major line of business or geographic area of operations. It must be possible to clearly separate operations and cash flows from the rest of the entity in order to be considered a component of an entity.

Many large corporations have multiple separate major lines of business. For example, Canadian Tire reports that it operates principally in two business segments: retail and financial services. Reitmans, as it operates only in the women's apparel retail sector, does not have separate business segments.

When a component of an entity is disposed of, the disposal is reported separately on the income statement as a nonrecurring item called discontinued operations. In order to fully separate profit earned (or losses incurred) in a company's continuing operations from its discontinued operations, it is necessary to also allocate income tax expense or savings to the two categories. This is known as **intraperiod tax allocation**. In intraperiod tax allocation, the income tax expense or saving is associated with certain items or categories, and the items are reported net of applicable income tax. The general concept is "let the tax follow the profit or loss."

The profit (or loss) reported in the discontinued operations section consists of two parts: the profit (loss) from these operations and the gain (loss) on disposal of the segment. Both items are presented net of applicable income tax.

To illustrate, assume Leads Inc. has a 30% income tax rate and that in 2014 it sold its unprofitable kayak manufacturing division. The following information is available:

1. Profit before income tax on its continuing operations (details shown in the income statement in Illustration 14-2) is $156,000.
2. The loss from operating the kayak manufacturing division during 2014 (prior to selling it) is $70,000.
3. The loss from selling the assets in the kayak manufacturing division is $50,000.

Note that the losses in the kayak manufacturing division will result in income tax savings, as opposed to income tax expense. Income tax expense (or savings) is allocated to each of these items and is calculated as follows:

1. Income tax expense on continuing operations is $46,800 ($156,000 × 30%).
2. The income tax savings on the loss from operating the kayak manufacturing prior to its sale is $21,000 ($70,000 × 30%).
3. The income savings on the loss on disposal of the assets in this division is $15,000 ($50,000 × 30%).

On the income statement, the losses of $70,000 and $50,000 from the two components of the discontinued operations are not shown. Instead, the losses are shown minus the income tax savings, and the income tax savings are shown as part of the description of the discontinued item. Deducting the income tax is referred to as "net of tax" and is calculated as follows: loss from the kayak manufacturing division operations is $49,000 ($70,000 − $21,000) and the loss on disposal of the kayak manufacturing division is $35,000 ($50,000 − $15,000).

Illustration 14-2 shows how the continuing and discontinued operations are reported in Leads' income statement.

ILLUSTRATION 14-2
Income statement presentation with discontinued operations

LEADS INC.
Income Statement
Year Ended December 31, 2014

Sales		$800,000	Continuing operations
Cost of goods sold		600,000	
Gross profit		200,000	
Operating expenses		40,000	
Profit from operations		160,000	
Other expenses		4,000	
Profit before income tax		156,000	
Income tax expense		46,800	
Profit from continuing operations		109,200	
Discontinued operations			Discontinued operations
Loss from kayak manufacturing operations, net of $21,000 income tax savings	**$49,000**		
Loss on disposal of kayak manufacturing division, net of $15,000 income tax savings	**35,000**	84,000	
Profit		$ 25,200	

Note that the captions "Profit from continuing operations" and "Discontinued operations" are used. This presentation clearly indicates the separate effects of continuing operations and discontinued operations on profit. This allows us to separate the effects of operations that are not relevant to the company's ongoing performance.

Companies reporting under IFRS and ASPE must both report discontinued operations separately from continuing operations.

OTHER COMPREHENSIVE INCOME

ASPE

Under IFRS, there are certain gains (and losses) that are not included in profit but are still added to (or deducted from) shareholders' equity. These gains and losses that are not included in profit are referred to as **other comprehensive income (loss)**. The total of profit plus other comprehensive income is referred to as comprehensive income. Thus **comprehensive income** includes all changes in shareholders' equity during a period except for changes that result from the sale or repurchase of shares or from the payment of dividends. Companies following ASPE do not report other comprehensive income or comprehensive income.

There are several types of gains or losses that are considered other comprehensive income. One example that we will learn about in Chapter 16 is gains and losses on certain types of equity investments. Gains and losses are recorded when investments are adjusted up or down to their fair value at the end of each accounting period and when they are sold. You will learn in Chapter 16 how to determine whether the gains and losses should be included in profit or in other comprehensive income. In this chapter, we will tell you how to classify these gains and losses.

Other comprehensive income is reported separately from profit for two important reasons: (1) it protects profit from sudden changes that could simply be caused by fluctuations in fair value, and (2) it informs the financial statement user of the cash that would have been received if the investment had actually been sold at year end because the investment is reported at its fair value.

Statement of Comprehensive Income

Companies reporting under IFRS must prepare a **statement of comprehensive income** that shows all of the items included in comprehensive income. There are two possible formats for this statement:

1. **All-inclusive format.** A statement of comprehensive income can include all components of profit or loss and other comprehensive income in a single statement. In this case, the traditional profit or loss is shown as a subtotal in arriving at comprehensive income. By showing all of the revenues and expenses and resulting profit or loss found in the traditional income statement, in combination with other sources of income, the statement of comprehensive income makes it easier to evaluate a company's profitability on an "all-inclusive" basis. If using this format, the company would not prepare a traditional income statement.

2. **Separate statement.** The other option is to present the traditional income statement, followed by a separate statement of comprehensive income. In this case, the statement of comprehensive income starts with the profit or loss that was reported on the income statement. Then the other comprehensive income gains or losses are added to, or deducted from, profit to calculate comprehensive income. Reitmans, as shown in Appendix A, has used this format.

Similar to discontinued operations, other comprehensive income must be reported net of income tax. Each other comprehensive income item can be shown net of income tax, or if a company has several items in other comprehensive income, it can show the total income tax on the other comprehensive items as one number. In this textbook, we will show each other comprehensive income item net of income tax.

To illustrate a comprehensive income statement, we will continue our example with Leads Inc. Recall that Leads Inc. has prepared a separate traditional income statement, with profit of $25,200, as shown in Illustration 14-2. Assume that Leads Inc. also has equity investments where the gains and losses are recognized as other comprehensive income and that in 2014 Leads had a loss on these equity investments of $5,000. This will be shown in the statement of comprehensive income net of $1,500 ($5,000 × 30%) of income tax at $3,500 ($5,000 − $1,500). This information is presented in Illustration 14-3 in a statement of comprehensive income for Leads Inc.

LEADS INC. Statement of Comprehensive Income Year Ended December 31, 2014	
Profit	$25,200
Other comprehensive income (loss)	
Loss on equity investments, net of $1,500 of income tax savings	(3,500)
Comprehensive income	$21,700

▶ **ILLUSTRATION 14-3**
Statement of comprehensive income

Accumulated Other Comprehensive Income

The cumulative amount of other comprehensive income and losses over the life of the company is reported as a separate component in shareholders' equity on the balance sheet, called **accumulated other comprehensive income**. Thus, every year, the other comprehensive income or loss is either added to, or deducted from, beginning Accumulated Other Comprehensive Income to determine ending Accumulated Other Comprehensive Income. Later in the chapter, we will illustrate how this is reported on the statement of changes in shareholders' equity.

However, profit is always added to (losses deducted from) retained earnings. This is still the case even if a company reports other comprehensive income. Thus it is always necessary to divide comprehensive income into profit (loss) and other comprehensive income (loss).

Using assumed data for beginning retained earnings and accumulated other comprehensive income, and assuming no dividends or other changes to retained earnings, the following diagram shows how Leads Inc.'s comprehensive income is allocated to these two shareholders' equity accounts.

Balance Sheet Account	Balance January 1, 2014	Allocation of Comprehensive Income		Balance December 31, 2014
Retained earnings	$338,500	Profit	$25,200	$363,700
Accumulated other comprehensive income	31,400	Other comprehensive income (loss)	(3,500)	27,900

BEFORE YOU GO ON...

Do It

Qu Ltd. reports comprehensive income in a single statement of comprehensive income. In 2014, the company reported profit before income tax of $400,000; a pre-tax loss on discontinued operations of $75,000; a pre-tax gain on the disposal of the assets from the discontinued operations of $30,000; and other comprehensive income from a gain on an unrealized foreign currency translation adjustment of $14,000 before tax. The company has a 25% income tax rate. Prepare a statement of comprehensive income, beginning with profit before income tax.

Action Plan

- Allocate income tax between income from continuing operations, income from discontinued operations, and other comprehensive income items.
- Separately disclose (1) the results of operations of the discontinued division, and (2) the disposal of the discontinued operation.
- A statement of comprehensive income presents other comprehensive income amounts, net of income tax, following the profit for the year.

Solution

QU LTD.
Statement of Comprehensive Income (partial)
Year Ended December 31, 2014

Profit before income tax		$400,000
Income tax expense		100,000[1]
Profit from continuing operations		300,000
Discontinued operations		
Loss from operations, net of $18,750[2] income tax savings	$56,250[3]	
Gain on disposal of assets, net of $7,500[4] income tax expense	22,500[5]	33,750
Profit		266,250
Other comprehensive income		
Unrealized gain on foreign currency translation adjustment, net of $3,500[6] income tax expense		10,500[7]
Comprehensive income		$276,750

[1] $400,000 × 25% = $100,000   [5] $30,000 − $7,500 = $22,500
[2] $75,000 × 25% = $18,750   [6] $14,000 × 25% = $3,500
[3] $75,000 − $18,750 = $56,250   [7] $14,000 − $3,500 = $10,500
[4] $30,000 × 25% = $7,500

THE NAVIGATOR

Related exercise material: BE14–6, BE14–7, BE14–8, E14–4, and E14–5.

Accounting Changes

» **STUDY OBJECTIVE 4**

Explain the accounting for different types of accounting changes and account for corrections of prior period errors.

In order to increase comparability between companies, there are specific accounting and reporting requirements that companies must follow when they have a change in accounting policies, a change in an estimate, or they need to correct an error made in a previous accounting period.

CHANGES IN ACCOUNTING POLICIES

To make comparisons from one year to the next easier, financial statements for the current period are prepared using the same accounting policies that were used for the preceding period. This improves comparability, an important characteristic of accounting information that we learned about in Chapter 11. An accounting policy used in the current year can be different from the one used in the previous year only if the change (1) is required by generally accepted accounting principles or (2) results in the financial statements providing more reliable and relevant information. This is called a **change in accounting policy**.

The change that all Canadian companies had to make in 2011 to either IFRS or ASPE is an example of a change in accounting policy because of a change in generally accepted accounting principles. **When there is a change in accounting policy, companies are required to retroactively apply the new standards** except if it is impractical to do so. That means the company must recalculate and restate all of the related accounts as if it had always followed the new policy. But, if significant estimates are required, or if the required information is not available, then it is not possible for prior financial statements to be restated for comparative purposes. Whether or not the prior periods are restated, companies must disclose the details of the change to the new policy in their notes to the financial statements.

If the company starts using a new accounting method because of a change in circumstances, this is not considered a change in accounting policy, and the company does not retroactively change prior periods as in the case of a change in accounting policy. For example, in Chapter 9, we explained that companies must review their choice of depreciation methods each year. If a change in circumstances indicates the depreciation method must be changed, then the company will simply start using the new method in the current and future periods.

CHANGES IN ACCOUNTING ESTIMATES

In accounting, estimates of future conditions and events are often made. For example, in order to calculate depreciation, it is necessary to estimate the useful life of the depreciable asset. Recording bad debt expense or warranty expense also requires estimates to be made. As time passes, it is very possible that there may be a change in circumstances or new information about the estimate is available that indicates the need for a **change in an accounting estimate**.

A change in an accounting estimate does not mean an error was made in the prior period. Since it is not an error, we do not go back and correct the prior periods. Instead, we use the new estimate to change our calculations in the current and future periods. In Chapter 9, an example of how to account for a change in an estimate was shown—the revision of depreciation when there was a change in the estimated useful life or residual value of the long-lived asset.

CORRECTION OF PRIOR PERIOD ERRORS

Suppose that a corporation's temporary accounts have been closed and the financial statements have been issued. The corporation then discovers that a material error has been made in a revenue or expense account in a prior year that misstated that year's profit. This also means that the Retained Earnings account is incorrect because the incorrect amount of revenue or expense was transferred to retained earnings in the closing entries. Thus the **correction of a prior period error** is made directly to Retained Earnings since the effect of the error is now in this account.

Alternative terminology Corrections of prior period errors are frequently called *prior period adjustments*.

Entries to Correct Prior Period Errors

The entry to correct a prior period error includes a debit or credit to Retained Earnings, net of income tax, a debit or credit to income tax payable for the change in income tax, and a debit or a credit to the related asset or liability account. To illustrate, assume that Graber Inc. discovers in 2014 that it overstated its cost of goods sold in 2013 by $10,000 as a result of errors in counting inventory. Because cost of goods sold (an expense account) was overstated, profit before income tax was understated by the same amount, $10,000. If we assume an income tax rate of 30%, income tax expense would also be understated by $3,000 ($10,000 × 30%). The overall effect on profit is to understate it by $7,000 ($10,000 − $3,000).

If profit is understated, then retained earnings at the end of 2013 would also be understated by the same amount, $7,000, which is referred to as the "after-tax difference" or the "error net of income tax."

The following table details the effect of this error on the prior year's income statement, using assumed data for revenues and expenses:

	Incorrect	Correct	Difference
Revenues	$900,000	$900,000	$ 0
Expenses	550,000	540,000	10,000
Profit before income tax	350,000	360,000	10,000
Income tax expense (30%)	105,000	108,000	3,000
Profit	$245,000	$252,000	$ 7,000

In addition to overstating cost of goods sold by $10,000, the error will result in merchandise inventory being understated by the same amount. You will recall that we learned about the pervasive impact of inventory errors in Chapter 6.

The entry for the correction of this error, discovered on February 12, 2014, is as follows:

A	=	L	+	SE
+10,000		+3,000		+7,000

Cash flows: no effect

Feb. 12	Merchandise Inventory	10,000	
	Income Tax Payable		3,000
	Retained Earnings		7,000
	To adjust for overstatement of cost of goods sold in a prior period.		

A credit to an income statement account, in this case Cost of Goods Sold, instead of Retained Earnings, would be incorrect because the error is for a prior year.

Presentation of Corrections of Prior Period Errors

Corrections of prior period errors must also be reported in the financial statements. They are added to (or deducted from, depending on the direction of the adjustment) the beginning Retained Earnings balance. They are also reported net of the related income tax in the same way that the correcting entry to retained earnings was net of tax. The method of reporting is similar to reporting gains or losses from discontinued operations or other comprehensive income, as shown earlier in the chapter.

To illustrate, using the adjustment we journalized above—the correction for the overstatement of cost of goods sold—assume that Graber had previously reported $750,000 of retained earnings at December 31, 2013, which is also the beginning balance in Retained Earnings on January 1, 2014. It is still necessary to show this as the beginning balance, even though we now know it is incorrect. The phrase "as previously reported" is added so users know this amount was reported as the ending balance in the previous year.

As the error was found in 2014, it is reported as a correction to beginning retained earnings in the 2014 financial statements. Also shown is the correct, or adjusted, beginning retained earnings balance. Illustration 14-4 shows how the correction of Graber's prior period error will be presented in its 2014 financial statements:

▶ **ILLUSTRATION 14-4**
Presentation of a correction of a prior period error

Retained earnings, January 1, 2014, as previously reported	$750,000
Add: Correction for overstatement of cost of goods sold in 2013, net of $3,000 income tax expense	7,000
Retained earnings, January 1, 2014, as adjusted	757,000

This is shown on the statement of retained earnings if the company is following ASPE. If the company is following IFRS, as we will see later in the chapter, it is shown in the retained earnings section of the statement of changes in shareholders' equity. The effects of the change should also be detailed and disclosed in a note to the statements. The prior year's financial statements are also corrected if they are shown for comparative purposes with the current year's statements.

The accounting for a change in accounting policy is similar to the correction of prior period errors. Opening retained earnings is adjusted for the cumulative effect of the change, net of the applicable income tax.

BEFORE YOU GO ON...

Do It

Vega Corporation reported retained earnings of $5,130,000 at December 31, 2013. In 2014, the company earns $2 million of profit and declares and pays a $275,000 cash dividend. On March 7, 2014, Vega found an error made in 2013 when it purchased land; the $275,000 cost of the land was debited to Legal Expense in error. Vega's income tax rate is 30%. (a) Prepare the journal entry to correct the error. (b) Prepare a statement of retained earnings for the year ended December 31, 2014.

Solution

(a)

Mar. 7	Land	275,000	
	Income tax payable ($275,000 × 30%)		82,500
	Retained Earnings ($275,000 − $82,500)		192,500
	To correct for overstatement of legal expenses in a prior period		

(b)

VEGA CORPORATION Statement of Retained Earnings Year Ended December 31, 2014	
Balance, January 1, 2014, as previously reported	$5,130,000
Add: Correction for overstatement of legal expenses in 2013, net of $82,500 income tax	192,500
Balance, January 1, 2014, as adjusted	5,322,500
Add: Profit	2,000,000
	7,322,500
Less: Cash dividend	275,000
Balance, December 31, 2014	$7,047,500

Related exercise material: BE14–9, BE14–10, E14–6, and E14–7.

THE **NAVIGATOR**

Action Plan

- Calculate the tax effect of the error by multiplying the error by the tax rate.
- If expenses were overstated in a prior year, that means income tax expense was understated. It also means that profit and retained earnings were understated by the difference between the error and the related tax.
- When reporting the correction of the error, begin with retained earnings as reported at the end of the previous year.
- Add or subtract corrections of prior period errors, net of applicable income tax, to arrive at the adjusted opening retained earnings balance.
- Add profit to and subtract dividends declared from the adjusted opening retained earnings balance to arrive at the ending balance in retained earnings.

Reporting Changes in Shareholders' Equity

>> STUDY **OBJECTIVE 5**

Prepare a statement of changes in shareholders' equity.

Companies reporting under IFRS are required to disclose all changes affecting shareholders' equity in a **statement of changes in shareholders' equity**. This statement shows the changes in total shareholders' equity during the year, as well as changes in each shareholders' equity account, including contributed capital, retained earnings, and accumulated other comprehensive income. Under ASPE, companies do not prepare a statement of changes in shareholders' equity. Instead they prepare a statement of retained earnings, with details about changes in other equity accounts disclosed in the notes to the statements.

In the following sections, we will first review the transactions that affect shareholders' equity and then show how to prepare a statement of changes in shareholders' equity.

Alternative terminology The statement of changes in shareholders' equity is also called the *statement of shareholders' equity* or *statement of changes in equity.*

SUMMARY OF SHAREHOLDERS' EQUITY TRANSACTIONS

In Chapter 13, and earlier in this chapter, you have learned several transactions and events that affect shareholders' equity accounts. These are summarized in Illustration 14-5.

It is important to review this summary and make sure you understand each of these transactions and their impact on the shareholders' equity accounts. This is the information that is included in the statement of changes in shareholders' equity.

▶ ILLUSTRATION **14-5**
Summary of
transactions affecting
shareholders' equity

Transaction	Impact on Shareholders' Equity Accounts
1. Issuance of share capital	1. Common or Preferred Shares is increased.
2. Reacquisition of share capital	2. Common or Preferred Shares is decreased. Contributed Surplus may be increased or decreased. Retained Earnings may be decreased.
3. Correction of a prior period error that affected the prior year's ending retained earnings	3. Opening Retained Earnings is either increased or decreased as required to make the correction.
4. Cumulative effect of a change in accounting policy on the prior year's ending retained earnings	4. Opening Retained Earnings is either increased or decreased as required to make the adjustment.
5. Profit (loss)	5. Retained Earnings is increased (decreased).
6. Other comprehensive income (loss)	6. Accumulated Other Comprehensive Income is increased (decreased).
7. Cash dividends are declared	7. Retained Earnings is decreased.
8. Stock dividends are declared	8. Retained Earnings is decreased and Stock Dividends Distributable is increased.
9. Stock dividends are distributed	9. Stock Dividends Distributable is decreased and Common Shares is increased.
10. Stock split	10. Number of shares issued increases; there is no effect on account balances.

STATEMENT OF CHANGES IN SHAREHOLDERS' EQUITY

To explain and illustrate the preparation of a statement of changes in shareholders' equity, we will use financial information from Tech International Inc. Illustration 14-6 presents Tech International's prior year shareholders' equity section of the balance sheet and its current year statement of comprehensive income.

▶ ILLUSTRATION **14-6**
Tech International's
financial information

TECH INTERNATIONAL INC.
Balance Sheet (partial)
December 31, 2013

Shareholders' equity	
Share capital	
Common shares, unlimited number authorized, 1,000,000 shares issued	$2,980,000
Contributed surplus—reacquired shares	20,000
	3,000,000
Retained earnings	190,000
Accumulated other comprehensive income	385,700
Total shareholders' equity	$3,575,700

TECH INTERNATIONAL INC.
Statement of Comprehensive Income
Year Ended December 31, 2014

Profit	$349,800
Other comprehensive income	
Gain on equity investments, net of $132,000 of income tax expense	198,000
Comprehensive income	$547,800

During 2014, Tech International entered into a number of transactions that affected its shareholders' equity accounts, as follows:

1. On January 21, Tech International reacquired 25,000 common shares for $115,000. As you learned previously in this chapter, Common Shares is decreased by $74,500 [($2,980,000 ÷ 1,000,000) × 25,000]. Contributed Surplus—Reacquired Shares is decreased by its balance of $20,000. Retained Earnings is decreased by $20,500 ($115,000 − $74,500 − $20,000).

2. On March 4, Tech International declared a 4% stock dividend to be distributed on April 10 to shareholders of record on March 20. The fair value of its shares on March 4 was $4.75. As the total shares issued at that point amounted to 975,000 (1,000,000 − 25,000), 39,000 shares are distributed (975,000 × 4%) at $185,250 (39,000 × $4.75).

3. On September 22, Tech International sold 50,000 common shares at $5 per share for a total of $250,000 cash.

4. On November 9, Tech International declared cash dividends of $100,000 to be paid on January 2, 2015, to shareholders of record on December 7, 2014.

It was also determined that cost of goods sold had been overstated by $70,000 in 2013. Tech International has an income tax rate of 40%. The income tax impact of the overstatement was $28,000 ($70,000 × 40%). The net impact of the error on opening retained earnings was $42,000 ($70,000 − $28,000).

In the statement of changes in shareholders' equity, this information is organized by shareholders' equity account. For each account, the beginning balance from the prior-year balance sheet is shown, followed by the increases and decreases during the year. The ending balance is calculated for each shareholders' equity account and then the overall total of shareholders' equity is determined.

Remember that comprehensive income is divided into profit and other comprehensive income in terms of its impact on shareholders' equity. Profit is added to Retained Earnings, and Other Comprehensive Income is added to Accumulated Other Comprehensive Income.

In Illustration 14-7, Tech International's statement of changes in equity for 2014 has been prepared using the above information.

▶ **ILLUSTRATION 14-7**
Statement of changes in shareholders' equity

TECH INTERNATIONAL INC. Statement of Changes in Shareholders' Equity Year Ended December 31, 2014	
Share capital, common shares	
Balance, January 1, 1,000,000 shares issued	$2,980,000
Reacquired 25,000 shares	(74,500)
Stock dividend issued, 39,000 shares	185,250
Issued for cash, 50,000 shares	250,000
Balance, December 31, 1,064,000 shares issued	3,340,750
Stock dividends distributable	
Balance, January 1	0
Stock dividend declared	185,250
Stock dividend distributed	(185,250)
Balance, December 31	0
Contributed surplus—reacquired shares	
Balance, January 1	20,000
Reacquired common shares	(20,000)
Balance, December 31	0
Retained earnings	
Balance, January 1, as previously reported	190,000
Correction for overstatement of cost of goods sold in 2013, net of $28,000 of income tax expense	42,000
Balance, January 1, as adjusted	232,000
Profit	349,800
Reacquired common shares	(20,500)
Stock dividends	(185,250)
Cash dividends	(100,000)
Balance, December 31	276,050
Accumulated other comprehensive income	
Balance, January 1	385,700
Other comprehensive income	198,000
Balance, December 31	583,700
Shareholders' equity, December 31	$4,200,500

Note that the end-of-year balances shown in the statement of changes in shareholders' equity are the amounts that are reported on the shareholders' equity section of the December 31, 2014, balance sheet.

 BEFORE YOU GO ON...

Do It

Grand Lake Corporation had the following shareholders' equity balances at January 1, 2014:

Common shares, unlimited number authorized, 500,000 issued	$1,000,000
Retained earnings	600,000
Accumulated other comprehensive income	100,000

The following selected information is available for the year ended December 31, 2014:

1. Issued 100,000 common shares for $300,000 cash.
2. Declared dividends of $50,000.
3. Reported profit of $360,000.
4. Reported a loss after tax on equity investments of $25,000 as other comprehensive loss.

Solution

Action Plan

- The statement of shareholders' equity covers a period of time, starting with the opening balances and ending with the ending balances for the period.
- Include all of the changes in each shareholders' equity account, as well as total shareholders' equity.
- Recall that comprehensive income consists of both profit and other comprehensive income.

THE NAVIGATOR

GRAND LAKE CORPORATION Statement of Changes in Shareholders' Equity Year Ended December 31, 2014	
Share capital, common shares	
Balance, January 1, 500,000 shares issued	$1,000,000
Issued for cash, 100,000 shares	300,000
Balance, December 31, 600,000 shares issued	1,300,000
Retained earnings	
Balance, January 1	600,000
Profit	360,000
Cash dividends	(50,000)
Balance, December 31	910,000
Accumulated other comprehensive income	
Balance, January 1	100,000
Other comprehensive loss	(25,000)
Balance, December 31	75,000
Shareholders' equity, December 31	$2,285,000

Related exercise material: BE14–11, BE14–12, E14–8, E14–9, and E14–10.

Analyzing Shareholders' Equity

» STUDY OBJECTIVE 6

Evaluate earnings and dividend performance.

Shares are generally purchased by investors for potential capital gains (increases in the shares' market price) or for potential income (dividends). Consequently, investors are interested in both a company's earnings performance and its dividend record.

EARNINGS PERFORMANCE

When shareholders want to analyze their investment in a company, they can measure the company's earnings performance, or profitability, in several different ways. We learned about one measure in Chapter 13: the return on equity ratio. Two other ratios are widely used by existing shareholders and potential investors: earnings per share and the price-earnings ratio.

Earnings per share is useful because shareholders usually think in terms of the number of shares they own—or plan to buy or sell—so determining profit per share makes it easier for the shareholder to understand the return on his or her investment. Some companies, such as Tim Hortons in our feature story, even communicate to their shareholders their targeted earnings per share for the upcoming year.

Investors and others also link earnings per share to the market price per share. This relationship produces the second ratio: the price-earnings ratio.

Earnings per Share

Earnings per share (EPS) indicates the profit earned by each common share. Thus, earnings per share is reported only for common shares. When a company has both preferred and common shares, the current year's dividend declared on preferred shares is subtracted from profit to determine the income available to common shareholders. Illustration 14-8 shows the formula for calculating EPS.

Profit Minus Preferred Dividends	÷	Weighted Average Number of Common Shares	=	Earnings per Share
($47,539 − $0)	÷	66,101	=	$0.72

▶ **ILLUSTRATION 14-8**
Earnings per share formula

To show the calculation of earnings per share, the illustration uses data (in thousands) from Reitmans' 2012 financial statements. Reitmans' profit, or net earnings as Reitmans calls it, of $47,539,000 is divided by the weighted average number of common shares, 66,101,000, to determine its earnings per share of $0.72.

In determining the numerator of the earnings per share calculation ($47,539,000), note that Reitmans had no preferred dividends to subtract from profit. If it did, any preferred dividends declared for the current year would be subtracted from profit to determine the income available for the common shareholders. In addition, note that if preferred shares are cumulative, the dividend is deducted whether or not it is declared.

For the denominator of the earnings per share calculation (66,101), the **weighted average number of shares** is used instead of the ending balance, or a straight average. If there is no change in the number of common shares issued during the year, the weighted average number of shares will be the same as the ending balance. If new shares are issued in the year, these shares are adjusted for the fraction of the year they are outstanding to determine the weighted average number of shares. This is done because the issue of shares during the period changes the amount of net assets that income can be earned on.

To illustrate the calculation of the weighted average number of common shares, assume that a company had 100,000 common shares on January 1. It reacquired and retired 7,500 shares on May 1, and issued an additional 10,000 shares on October 1. The weighted average number of shares for the year would be calculated as follows:

Date	Actual Number	Fraction of Year	Weighted Average
Jan. 1	100,000	$\times \, 12/12 =$	100,000
May 1	(7,500)	$\times \, 8/12 =$	(5,000)
Oct. 1	10,000	$\times \, 3/12 =$	2,500
	102,500		97,500

As illustrated, 102,500 shares were actually issued by the end of the year. Of these, 100,000 were outstanding at the beginning of the year and are allocated a full weight, 12 months out of 12. The 7,500 reacquired shares were only issued for four months (January 1 to April 30) and should be included for $4/12$ of the year. Consequently, a weighted average of 5,000 shares must be deducted for the portion of the year when they were no longer issued, May 1 to December 31, or $8/12$ of the year. As 10,000 of the shares have only been outstanding for three months (from October 1 to December 31), they are weighted for $3/12$ of the year, resulting in 2,500 weighted shares. In total, the company's weighted average number of shares is 97,500 for the year. In the next calendar year, the 102,500 shares would receive a full weight (unless some of these shares are repurchased) because all 102,500 shares would be outstanding for the entire year.

The disclosure of earnings per share is required for companies reporting under IFRS. This disclosure is so important that EPS must be reported directly on the statement of comprehensive income or income statement if presented separately, and it also has to be explained in the notes to the financial statements. It is the only ratio that is reported in this way. Companies using ASPE are not required to report EPS.

Complex Capital Structure. When a corporation has securities that may be converted into common shares, it has what is called a complex capital structure. One example of a convertible security is convertible preferred shares. When the preferred shares are converted into common shares, the additional common shares will result in a reduced, or diluted, earnings per share figure.

Two earnings per share figures are calculated when a corporation has a complex capital structure. The first earnings per share figure is called **basic earnings per share**. The earnings per share amount we calculated in Illustration 14-8, $0.72, is known as basic earnings per share, which is what Reitmans reported on its income statement for fiscal 2012.

The second earnings per share figure is called **fully diluted earnings per share**. This figure calculates *hypothetical* earnings per share as though *all* securities that can be converted into, or exchanged for, common shares have been (even though they really have not). Reitmans, which has other securities that can be converted into common shares (stock options, in this case), is considered to have a complex capital structure. It reports fully diluted earnings per share of $0.72 for fiscal 2012, which is identical to its basic earnings per share, because its stock options are *anti-dilutive*. That means if the stock options had been exercised, it would have increased earnings per share. As companies are not allowed to report fully diluted earnings per share higher than basic earnings per share, Reitmans reports the same amount for both figures.

The calculation of fully diluted earnings per share is complex. In addition, the determination of the weighted average number of shares for both basic and fully diluted earnings per share becomes more complicated when there are stock dividends and stock splits during the year. Further discussion of these and other earnings per share complexities is left to an intermediate accounting course.

Price-Earnings Ratio

Comparing the earnings per share amounts of different companies is not very helpful, because there are big differences in the numbers of shares in companies and in the share prices. In order to compare earnings across companies, we instead calculate the **price-earnings (PE) ratio**. The price-earnings ratio is a frequently quoted statistic that gives the ratio of the market price of each common share to its earnings per share.

To illustrate, we will calculate the price-earnings ratio for Reitmans (Canada) Limited. Reitmans' earnings per share for the year ended January 28, 2012, was $0.72, as shown in Illustration 14-8. Its market price per share for its Class A shares at year end was $14.64. Illustration 14-9 shows Reitmans' price-earnings ratio.

▶**ILLUSTRATION 14-9**
Price-earnings ratio formula

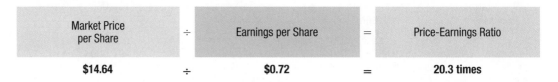

Market Price per Share	÷	Earnings per Share	=	Price-Earnings Ratio
$14.64	÷	**$0.72**	=	**20.3 times**

This ratio indicates that Reitmans' shares are trading at more than 20 times their earnings. The PE ratio reflects investors' assessment of a company's future earnings. The ratio of price to earnings will be higher if investors think that current income levels will continue or increase. It will be lower if investors think that income will decrease.

The price-earnings ratio is not relevant for private companies. Private companies will not have a readily available market price per share, and, as discussed above, if they follow ASPE, they also do not report earnings per share in their financial statements.

DIVIDENDS RECORD

In order to remain in business, companies must honour their interest payments to creditors, bankers, and debt holders. But the payment of dividends to shareholders is another matter. Many companies can survive, and even thrive, without such payouts. For example, high-growth companies generally do not pay dividends. Their policy is to retain all of their earnings to finance their growth.

On the other hand, some companies, such as Tim Hortons in our feature story, have a dividend policy where they commit to paying out a portion of their profit to shareholders every year. Presumably, investors who feel that regular dividends are important will buy shares in companies that pay periodic dividends, and those who feel that the share price is more important will buy shares in companies that retain earnings.

One way of assessing a company's dividend-paying policy is to calculate the **payout ratio**, which tells you what percentage of profit the company is distributing to its shareholders. The payout ratio is calculated by dividing cash dividends by profit. This ratio can also be expressed on a per-share basis by dividing dividends per share by earnings per share. The payout ratio can be calculated for total dividends, for common dividends, or for preferred dividends. The formula to calculate the payout ratio is shown in Illustration 14-10.

Cash Dividends	÷	Profit	=	Payout Ratio
$52,654	÷	$47,539	=	1.11

▶ **ILLUSTRATION 14-10**
Payout ratio

Reitmans' payout ratio is 1.11. This indicates that, for every dollar of profit earned during the fiscal year, the company has paid approximately $1.11 to the owners. As the company paid out more dividends than its profit, Reitmans' retained earnings are lower at the end of the year than at the beginning of the year.

Reitmans' payout ratio, at 1.11, is well above the industry average, which was reported as 0.38 by Reuters. A high payout ratio such as Reitmans' could be a warning signal—it could mean the company is failing to reinvest enough of its profit in its operations. On the other hand, it can also be caused when profits have dropped but the dividend payment has been left at a level that is fairly consistent from one year to the next. This is a common practice for public companies such as Reitmans. It provides a signal that management expects profits to recover the following year. It appears that this might be the case for Reitmans, as its dividends in 2012 were very close to its dividends in 2011, but its profit was approximately 45% lower in 2012 than 2011.

Like most ratios, the payout ratio varies with the industry. For example, utilities have high payout ratios. But companies that have high growth rates generally tend to have low payout ratios because they reinvest their profit in the company.

ACCOUNTING IN ACTION
ALL ABOUT YOU INSIGHT

Suppose you have some extra cash. Should you invest it in some shares of a public company or put in a savings account and earn interest? Buying shares in a company is a greater risk than putting the cash in a savings account. Investing in a company's shares carries neither a promise that your investment will be returned to you nor a guarantee that your investment will earn income. However, investing in shares can often provide higher income than a savings account. Shareholders can earn income by receiving dividends or by selling the shares at a price higher than what they paid for them. Share prices are determined by the interaction of the buyers and the sellers in the market. Share prices can be influenced by both objective factors, such as a company's profits, and subjective factors, such as future share price expectations, including unverified rumours. Nevertheless, if a company prospers, the price of its common shares will typically rise in the long run. If the company doesn't prosper, or if external factors such as the economy are negative, the share price will likely decline.

If you were thinking about investing in a company, where might you find information about the company's dividend policy, its profitability, and its share price?

BEFORE YOU GO ON...

Do It

Shoten Limited, a publicly traded company, reported profit of $249,750 on its October 31 year-end income statement. The shareholders' equity section of its balance sheet reported 3,000, $2 noncumulative preferred shares and 50,000 common shares. Of the common shares, 40,000 had been issued since the beginning of the year, 15,000 were issued on March 1, and 5,000 were repurchased on August 1. The preferred dividend was declared and paid during the year. The market price per share on October 31 was $40.
(a) Calculate Shoten's earnings per share.
(b) Calculate Shoten's price-earnings ratio.

Action Plan

- Subtract the preferred dividends from profit to determine the income available for common shareholders.
- Adjust the shares for the fraction of the year they were outstanding to determine the weighted average number of shares.
- Divide the income available for common shareholders by the weighted average number of shares to calculate the earnings per share.

Solution

(a) Preferred dividends: 3,000 preferred shares × $2 dividend per share = $6,000
    Income available to common shareholders: $249,750 − $6,000 = $243,750
    Weighted average number of common shares:

Date	Actual Number	Fraction of Year	Weighted Average
Nov. 1	40,000	× $^{12}/_{12}$ =	40,000
Mar. 1	15,000	× $^{8}/_{12}$ =	10,000
Aug. 1	(5,000)	× $^{3}/_{12}$ =	(1,250)
	50,000		48,750

Earnings per share: $\dfrac{\$243,750}{48,750} = \$5$

(b) Price-earnings ratio: $40 ÷ $5 = 8

> *Related exercise material:* BE14–13, BE14–14, BE14–15, E14–11, E14–12, and E14–13.

THE NAVIGATOR

Comparing IFRS and ASPE

Key Differences	International Financial Reporting Standards (IFRS)	Accounting Standards for Private Enterprises (ASPE)
Other comprehensive income and statement of comprehensive income	Required	Not required
Statement of changes in shareholders' equity	Required	Changes in retained earnings presented in the statement of retained earnings. Changes to other shareholders' equity accounts presented in the notes.
EPS	Required	Not required

THE NAVIGATOR

Demonstration Problem

On January 1, 2014, Fuso Corporation, a public company, had the following shareholders' equity accounts:

Common shares, unlimited number authorized, 260,000 issued	$3,120,000
Retained earnings	3,200,000
Accumulated other comprehensive income	75,000

During the year, the following transactions occurred:

Jan. 18   Reacquired 10,000 common shares for $13 per share.
Apr. 10   Discovered that it had understated its cost of goods sold in 2013 by $50,000.
June 1   Announced a 2-for-1 stock split of the common shares. Immediately before the split, the share price was $13.50 per share.
June 30   Declared a $0.40 cash dividend to common shareholders of record on July 16, payable August 1.
Aug. 1   Paid the dividend declared on June 30.
Nov. 30   Reacquired 40,000 common shares for $5.50 per share.
Dec. 30   Declared a 5% stock dividend to common shareholders of record on January 15, distributable January 31. On December 30, the share price was $5 per share. On January 15, it was $5.50 per share, and on January 31, it was $6 per share.

In addition, Fuso Corporation reported profit of $590,000 and a pre-tax loss on equity investments of $60,000, which is other comprehensive income (loss).

The company has a 30% income tax rate.

Instructions

(a) Record the transactions.
(b) Prepare a statement of comprehensive income.
(c) Prepare a statement of changes in shareholders' equity.
(d) Prepare the shareholders' equity section of the balance sheet.

Solution to Demonstration Problem

(a)

Jan. 18	Common Shares [($3,120,000 ÷ 260,000) × 10,000]	120,000	
	Retained Earnings ($130,000 − $120,000)	10,000	
	Cash ($13 × 10,000)		130,000
	Reacquired 10,000 common shares.		
Apr. 10	Retained Earnings ($50,000 − $15,000)	35,000	
	Income Tax Payable ($50,000 × 30%)	15,000	
	Merchandise Inventory		50,000
	To adjust for understatement of cost of goods sold in 2013.		
June 1	Memo entry only about 2-for-1 stock split. Now 500,000 [(260,000 − 10,000) × 2] common shares.		
30	Cash Dividend—Common	200,000	
	Dividend Payable		200,000
	To record cash dividend ($0.40 × 500,000).		
Aug. 1	Dividend Payable	200,000	
	Cash		200,000
	To record payment of cash dividend.		
Nov. 30	Common Shares [($3,000,000 ÷ 500,000) × 40,000]	240,000	
	Contributed Surplus—Reacquisition of Common Shares		20,000
	Cash ($5.50 × 40,000)		220,000
	Reacquired 40,000 common shares for $20,000 ($240,000 − $220,000) less than cost.		

Common Shares	Number	Cost
Jan. 1, Balance	260,000	$3,120,000
Jan. 18 reacquisition	(10,000)	(120,000)
June 1 2-for-1 split	250,000	0
Balance Nov. 30	500,000	$3,000,000

ACTION PLAN

- Keep a running total of the number of shares issued and total cost of shares.
- When shares are reacquired, reduce Common Shares by the cost of the shares. If reacquiring for less than cost, the gain is credited to a contributed surplus account. If reacquiring for more than cost, the loss is first debited to any previous contributed surplus, then to retained earnings.
- Errors from prior periods are corrected, net of income tax, to the retained earnings account.
- Adjust the number of shares for the stock split, but make no journal entry.
- Make journal entries for dividends on the declaration and payment dates, but not on the record date.
- Apply the stock dividend percentage to the number of shares issued. Multiply the new shares to be issued by the shares' fair value at the date of declaration.
- If not prepared on an all-inclusive basis, the statement of comprehensive income starts with profit. Other comprehensive income (loss) is add to (deducted from) profit on a net-of-tax basis.
- Recall that the statement of changes in shareholders' equity explains the changes for the period in the beginning and ending balances of each shareholders' equity account.
- The balance sheet reports shareholders' equity at the end of the period. These numbers are the ending balances on the statement of changes in shareholders' equity.

Dec. 30	Stock Dividend (23,000 × $5)			115,000	
	Stock Dividend Distributable				115,000
	To record stock dividend to common shareholders				
	(460,000 × 5% = 23,000)				
	Common Shares	Number	Cost		
	Balance Nov. 30	500,000	$3,000,000		
	Nov. 30 reacquisition	(40,000)	(240,000)		
	Balance Dec. 30	460,000	$2,760,000		

(b)

FUSO CORPORATION
Statement of Comprehensive Income
Year ended December 31, 2014

Profit	$590,000
Other comprehensive income (loss)	
Loss on equity investments, net of $18,000[1] of income tax savings	(42,000)[2]
Comprehensive income	$548,000

[1] $18,000 = $60,000 × 30%   [2] $42,000 = $60,000 − $18,000

(c)

FUSO CORPORATION
Statement of Changes in Shareholders' Equity
Year ended December 31, 2014

Common shares	
Balance, January 1, 260,000 common shares issued	$3,120,000
Reacquired 10,000 common shares	(120,000)
Issued 250,000 common shares in a 2-for-1 split	0
Reacquired 40,000 common shares	(240,000)
Balance, December 31, 460,000 common shares issued	2,760,000
Stock dividends distributable	
Balance, January 1	0
Common stock dividend declared, 23,000 shares	115,000
Balance, December 31, 23,000 shares	115,000
Contributed Surplus—Reacquisition of Common Shares	
Balance, January 1	0
Reacquired common shares	20,000
Balance, December 31	20,000
Retained earnings	
Balance, January 1, as previously reported	3,200,000
Less: Correction for understatement of cost of goods sold in 2013,	
net of $15,000 of income tax	(35,000)
Balance, January 1, as adjusted	3,165,000
Profit	590,000
Reacquired common shares	(10,000)
Cash dividends	(200,000)
Stock dividends	(115,000)
Balance, December 31	3,430,000
Accumulated other comprehensive income	
Balance, January 1	75,000
Other comprehensive income (loss)	(42,000)
Balance, December 31	33,000
Shareholders' equity, December 31	$6,358,000

(d)

FUSO CORPORATION
Balance Sheet (partial)
December 31, 2014

Shareholders' equity	
Contributed capital	
Common shares, unlimited number authorized, 460,000 issued	$2,760,000
Contributed surplus—reacquisition of common shares	20,000
Common stock dividend distributable, 23,000 shares	115,000
Total contributed capital	2,895,000
Retained earnings	3,430,000
Accumulated other comprehensive income	33,000
Total shareholders' equity	$6,358,000

THE **NAVIGATOR**

▶ Summary of Study Objectives

1. *Account for stock dividends and stock splits and compare their financial impact.* Entries for stock dividends are required at the declaration and distribution dates. There is no entry for a stock split. Stock dividends reduce retained earnings and increase common shares, but have no impact on total shareholders' equity. Both stock dividends and stock splits increase the number of shares issued. Stock dividends and splits reduce the fair value of the shares, but have no impact on the company's financial position.

2. *Account for the reacquisition of shares.* When shares are reacquired, the average cost is debited to the Common Shares account. If the shares are reacquired at a price below the average cost, the difference is credited to a contributed surplus account. If the shares are reacquired at a price above the average cost, the difference is debited first to a contributed surplus account if a balance exists, and then to the Retained Earnings account.

3. *Prepare an income statement showing continuing and discontinued operations, and prepare a statement of comprehensive income.* Gains or losses on discontinued operations must be presented net of income tax after profit (or loss) from continuing operations. Companies following IFRS must prepare a statement of comprehensive income that reports all increases and decreases to shareholders' equity during a period except changes resulting from the sale or repurchase of shares and from the payment of dividends. The statement of comprehensive income can be prepared on an all-inclusive basis, or can start with profit or loss as shown on a separate income statement.

4. *Explain the accounting for different types of accounting changes and account for corrections of prior period*

errors. A change in accounting policy, from the method used in the previous year, is allowed only when there is a change in GAAP or if it results in the financial statements providing more reliable and relevant information. These changes are applied retroactively when possible. A change in an accounting estimate is not an error and only the current and future periods are revised. If an error in a prior year's profit and retained earnings is found after the temporary accounts have been closed and the statements have been issued, then beginning retained earnings is adjusted. This is shown in the financial statements as a correction to beginning retained earnings net of the related income tax impact.

5. *Prepare a statement of changes in shareholders' equity.* A statement of changes in shareholders' equity explains all of the changes in each of the shareholders' equity accounts, and in total, for the reporting period. This includes changes in contributed capital (common shares, preferred shares, and any other contributed surplus accounts), retained earnings, and accumulated other comprehensive income. The statement is required for companies reporting under IFRS.

6. *Evaluate earnings and dividend performance.* Profitability measures that are used to analyze shareholders' equity include return on equity (discussed in Chapter 13), earnings per share, the price-earnings ratio, and the payout ratio. Earnings (loss) per share is calculated by dividing profit (loss) available to the common shareholders by the weighted average number of common shares and is reported only under IFRS. The price-earnings ratio is calculated by dividing the market price per share by the earnings per share. The payout ratio is calculated by dividing cash dividends by profit.

Flash cards

▶ Glossary

Accumulated other comprehensive income   The cumulative amount of other comprehensive income and losses over the life of the company reported as a separate amount in shareholders' equity. (p. 727)

Basic earnings per share   The profit (or loss) earned by each common share. It is calculated by subtracting any preferred dividends declared from profit and dividing the result by the weighted average number of common shares. (p. 736)

Change in accounting estimate   A change in an accounting estimate because of a change in circumstances or because new information about the estimate is available that indicates that the estimate needs to be changed. (p. 729)

Change in accounting policy   The use of a generally accepted accounting policy in the current year that is different from the one used in the preceding year. (p. 729)

Component of an entity   A separate major line of business or geographic area of operations. (p. 725)

Comprehensive income   All changes in shareholders' equity during a period except for changes resulting from the sale or repurchase of shares, or from the payment of dividends. (p. 726)

Continuing operations   The revenues, expenses, and profit or loss generated from a company's ongoing activities. (p. 725)

Correction of a prior period error   The correction of an error in previously issued financial statements. (p. 729)

Discontinued operations   A component of an enterprise that has been disposed of or is reclassified as "held for sale." (p. 725)

Distribution date   The date when stock dividends are distributed to shareholders. (p. 719)

Earnings per share (EPS)   The profit (or loss) earned by each common share. (p. 735)

Fully diluted earnings per share   Earnings per share adjusted for the maximum possible dilution that would occur if securities were converted, or changed, into common shares. (p. 736)

Intraperiod tax allocation   The procedure of associating income tax expense with the specific item that directly affects the income tax for the period. (p. 725)

Other comprehensive income (loss)   Gains and losses that are not included in profit but affect shareholders' equity. (p. 726)

Payout ratio   A ratio that measures the percentage of income distributed as cash dividends. It is calculated by dividing cash dividends by profit. (p. 737)

Price-earnings (PE) ratio   The ratio of the price of a common share to earnings per common share. (p. 736)

Reverse stock split   A decrease in the number of shares outstanding. A 1-for-3 reverse stock split would reduce the amount of shares owned by a shareholder to one for every three shares owned before the split. (p. 720)

Statement of changes in shareholders' equity   A statement that reports all increases and decreases to shareholders' equity during a period. (p. 731)

Statement of comprehensive income   A statement that reports all items included in comprehensive income during a period. (p. 727)

Stock dividend   A pro rata distribution of the corporation's own shares to shareholders. (p. 718)

Stock split   The issue of additional shares to shareholders in a multiple, such as 2 for 1. A 2-for-1 stock split means that two new shares are issued in exchange for one old share. (p. 719)

Treasury shares   A corporation's own shares that have been reacquired and not yet retired or cancelled. They are held in "treasury" for later reissue or cancellation. (p. 722)

Weighted average number of shares   The number of common shares outstanding during the year, with any shares purchased or issued during the year weighted by the fraction of the year that they have been outstanding. (p. 735)

▶ Self-Study Questions

Answers are at the end of the chapter.

(SO 1) K   1. Which of the following statements about stock dividends and stock splits is correct?

    (a) A stock dividend decreases total shareholders' equity; a stock split increases total shareholders' equity.

    (b) Both result in an increased percentage ownership for shareholders.

    (c) Both are recorded at the fair value of the shares on the declaration date.

    (d) Both result in no change in total shareholders' equity.

(SO 2) C   2. A company will buy back its own shares to:
(a) increase the share price.
(b) decrease the share price.
(c) increase the number of shares available for dividends.
(d) save cash.

(SO 2) AP 3. Common shares are repurchased for $150,000 by a company with Contributed Surplus—Reacquisition of Shares $75,000; and Retained Earnings $750,000. The repurchased shares have an average cost of $125,000. The journal entry to record the repurchase would include a:
(a debit to Retained Earnings of $25,000.
(b) credit to Contributed Surplus—Reacquisition of Shares of $25,000.
(c) debit to Contributed Surplus—Reacquisition of Shares of $25,000.
(d) debit to Common Shares of $150,000.

(SO 3) K   4. Discontinued operations:
(a) are reported as part of operating expenses on the income statement.
(b) are reported separately on the income statement as a nonrecurring item.
(c) are never presented net of applicable income tax.
(d) result in an entry to retained earnings directly.

(SO 3) K   5. A statement of comprehensive income:
(a) must include all components of profit and loss and other comprehensive income.
(b) does not include profit or loss from the traditional income statement.
(c) is required for companies reporting under IFRS and ASPE.
(d) is required for companies reporting under IFRS only.

(SO 4) K   6. Which of the following statements about changes in accounting policies is incorrect?
(a) Changing an accounting policy from the one used in the preceding period is allowed only if it is required by GAAP or results in more relevant information.
(b) When a change in an accounting policy is required, it must be applied on a retroactive basis, except if it is impractical to do so.

(c) If the company is able to make the change on a retroactive basis, it is not necessary to disclose the details of the change in the notes.
(d) A change in circumstances is not considered a change in accounting policy.

(SO 4) K   7. A correction of a prior period error is reported:
(a) in the income statement.
(b) directly in the shareholders' equity section of the balance sheet.
(c) in either the statement of retained earnings or the statement of changes in shareholders' equity as an adjustment to the beginning balance of retained earnings.
(d) in either the statement of retained earnings or the statement of changes in shareholders' equity as an adjustment to the ending balance of retained earnings.

(SO 5) AP 8. Which of the following is not included in a statement of changes in shareholders' equity?
(a) A reacquisition of share capital
(b) Accumulated other comprehensive income
(c) Stock dividends
(d) Fair value of common shares

(SO 6) AP 9. For the year ended May 31, 2014, Sonic Corporation reported profit of $42,000. At the beginning of the year, it had 10,000 common shares issued. On February 28, 2014, it had issued 8,000 common shares for cash. The market price per share was $66.50 on May 31, 2014. It had no preferred shares. What were its earnings per share and price-earnings ratios?
(a) $2.33 and 28 times
(b) $3.00 and 22 times
(c) $3.50 and 19 times
(d) $4.20 and 16 times

(SO 6) C 10. Bernard Dupuis is nearing retirement and would like to invest in shares that will give him a steady income. Bernard should choose shares with a high:
(a) earnings per share.
(b) price-earnings ratio.
(c) payout ratio.
(d) return on equity.

THE NAVIGATOR

▶ Questions

(SO 1) K   1. What entries are made for stock dividends on common shares on (a) the declaration date, (b) the record date, and (c) the distribution date?

(SO 1) C   2. Freddy Investor says, "The shares I recently bought just declared a 2-for-1 stock split. Now I've doubled my investment!" Is Freddy correct—is he any better off after the stock split?

(SO 1) C   3. Contrast the effects of a cash dividend, stock dividend, and stock split on a company's (a) assets, (b) liabilities, (c) share capital, (d) retained earnings, and (e) number of shares.

(SO 2) C   4. Why would a company repurchase some of its shares? Give some reasons.

(SO 2) C   5. Wilmor, Inc. repurchases 1,000 of its own common shares. What effect does this transaction have on (a) total assets, (b) total liabilities, and (c) total shareholders' equity?

(SO 2) C   6. Explain how the accounting for the reacquisition of shares changes depending on whether the reacquisition price is greater or lower than average cost.

(SO 2) C   7. Ciana Chiasson is confused. She says, "I don't understand why sometimes, when the price paid to reacquire shares is greater than their average cost, the 'loss on reacquisition' is debited to a contributed surplus account. But at other times, it is debited to the Retained Earnings account. And sometimes it is even debited to both!" Help Ciana understand.

(SO 3) C   8. Explain intraperiod income tax allocation and why it is important.

(SO 3) C   9. What are discontinued operations? Why is it important to report discontinued operations separately from profit or loss from continuing operations?

(SO 3) C   10. Explain the terms "comprehensive income," "other comprehensive income," and "accumulated other comprehensive income." Include in your explanation how and where they are reported in the financial statements.

(SO 3) C   11. Explain the two methods of preparing a statement of comprehensive income.

(SO 4) C   12. When is a company allowed to change an accounting policy? How should it be accounted for in the financial statements?

(SO 4) C   13. Under what circumstances will a company change an accounting estimate? How is it accounted for, and why is it not considered an error?

(SO 4) C   14. If there was an error in a revenue or expense in a prior period, why isn't that account adjusted when the error is corrected? Instead, how is that error corrected

in the accounting records and how is it reported in the financial statements?

(SO 5) K   15. Provide examples of transactions that increase shareholders' equity and transactions that decrease shareholders' equity. Identify which shareholders' equity account is changed and how.

(SO 5) K   16. How is comprehensive income reported in the statement of changes in shareholders' equity?

(SO 6) C   17. Distinguish between basic earnings per share and fully diluted earnings per share.

(SO 6) C   18. When calculating EPS: (a) Why is profit available to the common shareholders not always the same as profit? (b) Why is the weighted average number of shares used instead of the number of shares issued at the end of the year?

(SO 6) AP 19. Company A has a price-earnings ratio of 9 times and a payout ratio of 40%. Company B has a price-earnings ratio of 22 times and a payout ratio of 5%. Which company's shares would be better for an investor interested in large capital gains versus steady income? Why?

(SO 6) C   20. If all other factors stay the same, indicate whether each of the following is generally considered favourable or unfavourable by a potential investor: (a) a decrease in return on equity, (b) an increase in earnings per share, (c) a decrease in the price-earnings ratio, and (d) an increase in the payout ratio.

▶ Brief Exercises

Record stock dividend and determine percentage ownership. (SO 1) AP

BE14–1   On March 1, Houseboat Ltd. had 400,000 common shares issued and the balance in its Common Share account was $600,000. The company declared a 5% stock dividend to shareholders of record on March 14, to be distributed on March 31. The fair value per share was $5 on March 1, $4.85 on March 14, and $5.35 on March 31. (a) Prepare the entries on the appropriate dates to record the stock dividend. (b) Assume that Wei Tse owned 2,000 shares prior to the stock dividend. Determine Wei's percentage ownership of the company before and after the stock dividend.

Analyze impact of stock dividend. (SO 1) AP

BE14–2   The shareholders' equity section of Ferndale Corporation's balance sheet consists of 225,000 common shares for $2 million, and retained earnings of $600,000. A 10% stock dividend is declared when the fair value per share is $12. Show the before-and-after effects of the dividend on (a) share capital, (b) retained earnings, (c) total shareholders' equity, and (d) the number of shares.

Compare cash dividend, stock dividend, and stock split. (SO 1) AP

BE14–3   Indicate whether each of the following transactions would increase (+), decrease (−), or have no effect (NE) on total assets, total liabilities, total shareholders' equity, and the number of shares:

Transaction	Assets	Liabilities	Shareholders' Equity	Number of Shares
(a) Declared a cash dividend.				
(b) Paid the cash dividend declared in (a).				
(c) Declared a stock dividend.				
(d) Distributed the stock dividend declared in (c).				
(e) Split stock 2 for 1.				

Record reacquisition of shares. (SO 2) AP

BE14–4   On December 31, 2013, Liquorice Treats Limited reported 40,000 common shares issued for a total cost of $250,000. On April 5, 2014, it reacquired 8,000 of these shares. This is the first time Liquorice Treats has reacquired any of its shares. Record the reacquisition of the shares assuming the company paid (a) $45,000 and (b) $60,000 to reacquire the shares.

Calculate average cost per share; record reacquisition. (SO 2) AP

BE14–5   On February 7, 2014, Flathead Corp. had a balance of $315,000 in its common share account. These shares had been issued as follows:

Date	# of Shares Issued	Cost
March 1, 2012	10,000	$ 50,000
November 8, 2013	15,000	265,000

On February 8, 2014, Flathead paid $10,000 to reacquire 1,000 shares. On December 22, 2014, it paid $28,000 to reacquire 2,000 shares. (a) Determine the average cost per share on February 7, 2014. (b) Record the two transactions in which Flathead reacquired its shares.

BE14–6 Olivier Corporation reported the following pre-tax amounts for the year ended August 31, 2014: profit before income tax (on the company's continuing operations), $320,000; loss from operations of discontinued operations, $85,000; and gain on disposal of assets of discontinued operations, $60,000. Olivier is subject to a 20% income tax rate. Calculate (a) the income tax expense on continuing operations, (b) any income tax expense or savings on each item of discontinued operations, and (c) profit.

Calculate income tax on continuing and discontinued operations. (SO 3) AP

BE14–7 Refer to the data given for Olivier Corporation in BE14–6. Assume that the profit before income tax of $320,000 is from $500,000 of revenue and $180,000 of operating expenses. Prepare an income statement.

Prepare an income statement with discontinued operations. (SO 3) AP

BE14–8 For the year ended December 31, 2014, Jet Set Airlines reported profit of $920,000 and a gain on an equity investment of $66,000, before income tax. This gain is other comprehensive income. Jet Set has a tax rate of 30%. (a) Prepare a statement of comprehensive income. (b) Jet Set had an accumulated other comprehensive loss of $31,550 at January 1, 2014. What amount would it report in the shareholders' equity section of its balance sheet on December 31, 2014?

Prepare statement of comprehensive income. (SO 3) AP

BE14–9 On March 1, 2014, Broadfoot Bakeries, Inc. discovered an error in its inventory count on December 31, 2013. The error had caused the prior year's cost of goods sold to be overstated by $110,000. The income tax rate is 25%. Prepare the journal entry to correct this error.

Record correction of prior period error. (SO 4) AP

BE14–10 Broadfoot Bakeries, Inc. reported retained earnings of $394,000 on December 31, 2013. For the year ended December 31, 2014, the company had profit of $128,000, and it declared and paid dividends of $44,000. Assuming the company reports under ASPE, and referring to the data for Broadfoot Bakeries in BE14–9, prepare a statement of retained earnings.

Prepare a statement of retained earnings with correction of prior period error. (SO 4) AP

BE14–11 Peninsula Supply Corporation reported the following statement of changes in shareholders' equity for the years ended December 31, 2013 and 2014. Determine the missing amounts.

Complete a statement of changes in shareholders' equity. (SO 5) AP

PENINSULA SUPPLY CORPORATION
Statement of Changes in Shareholders' Equity
Year Ended December 31

	2014 Number of Shares	2014 Amount	2013 Number of Shares	2013 Amount
Common shares, unlimited authorized				
Balance, January 1	500,000	$ (b)	500,000	$600,000
Issued shares for cash	50,000	32,500		0
Reacquired shares	(25,000)	(c)		0
Balance, December 31	(a)	603,750	500,000	600,000
Contributed surplus—reacquired shares				
Balance, January 1		15,000		15,000
Reacquired common shares		8,000		0
Balance, December 31		(d)		15,000
Retained earnings				
Balance, January 1		179,500		190,000
Profit (loss)		22,500		(h)
Common dividends—Cash		(e)		(30,000)
Balance, December 31		181,000		179,500
Accumulated other comprehensive income				
Balance, January 1		51,000		(i)
Other comprehensive income (loss)		(f)		(3,000)
Balance, December 31		68,000		51,000
Shareholders' equity, December 31		$ (g)		$ (j)

Prepare a comprehensive income statement and shareholders' equity section of a balance sheet. (SO 3, 5) AP

BE14–12   Refer to the data for Peninsula Supply Corporation presented in BE14–11. (a) Prepare the comprehensive income statement for 2014. (b) Prepare the shareholders' equity section of the balance sheet at December 31, 2014.

Calculate weighted average number of shares. (SO 6) AP

BE14–13   Franklin Corporation had 20,000 common shares on January 1, 2014. On March 1, 5,000 shares were repurchased. On June 1 and September 30, 6,000 and 10,000 shares were issued, respectively. Calculate (a) the number of shares issued at December 31, 2014, and (b) the weighted average number of shares.

Calculate earnings per share. (SO 6) AP

BE14–14   Northlake Limited reports profit of $454,000 and its weighted average number of common shares is 220,000. Northlake also has 22,000, $2.50 preferred shares. Calculate earnings per share under each of the following independent assumptions:

(a) preferred shares are cumulative and the dividend was paid.
(b) preferred shares are cumulative and the dividend was not paid.
(c) preferred shares are noncumulative and the dividend was paid.
(d) preferred shares are noncumulative and the dividend was not paid.

Calculate price-earnings and payout ratios. (SO 6) AP

BE14–15   Highlink, Inc. reported earnings per share of $4. Its common shares were selling at $24 per share. During the same year, the company paid an $0.80 per share cash dividend. Calculate the price-earnings ratio and the payout ratio.

▶ Exercises

Compare cash dividend, stock dividend, and stock split. (SO 1) AP

E14–1   Smart Mart Inc. is considering one of three options: (1) paying a $0.40 cash dividend, (2) distributing a 5% stock dividend, or (3) effecting a 2-for-1 stock split. The current fair value is $14 per share.

Instructions

Help Smart Mart decide what to do by completing the following chart (treat each possibility independently):

	Before Action	After Cash Dividend	After Stock Dividend	After Stock Split
Total assets	$1,875,000			
Total liabilities	$ 75,000			
Common shares	1,200,000			
Retained earnings	600,000			
Total shareholders' equity	1,800,000			
Total liabilities and shareholders' equity	$1,875,000			
Number of common shares	60,000			

Prepare correcting entries for dividends and stock split. (SO 1) AP

E14–2   Before preparing financial statements for the current year, the chief accountant for Patel Ltd. discovered the following errors in the accounts:

1. Patel has 20,000, $4 noncumulative preferred shares issued. It paid the preferred shareholders the quarterly dividend, and recorded it as a debit to Dividends Expense and a credit to Cash.
2. A 5% stock dividend (1,000 shares) was declared on the common shares when the fair value per share was $12. To record the declaration, Retained Earnings was debited and Dividends Payable was credited. The shares have not been issued yet.
3. The company declared a 2-for-1 stock split on its 20,000, $4 noncumulative preferred shares. The average cost of the preferred shares before the split was $70. The split was recorded as a debit to Retained Earnings of $1.4 million and a credit to Preferred Shares of $1.4 million.
4. After the stock split described in (3) above, the declaration of the quarterly dividend was recorded as a debit to Cash Dividends—Preferred for $40,000 and a credit to Dividends Payable for $40,000.

Instructions

Prepare any correcting entries that are needed.

Record issue and reacquisition of shares. (SO 2) AP

E14–3   Moosonee Co. Ltd. had the following share transactions during its first year of operations:

Jan.   6   Issued 200,000 common shares for $1.50 per share.
       12   Issued 50,000 common shares for $1.75 per share.

Mar. 17   Issued 1,000 preferred shares for $105 per share.
July 18   Issued 1 million common shares for $2 per share.
Nov. 17   Reacquired 200,000 common shares for $1.95 per share.
Dec. 30   Reacquired 150,000 common shares for $1.80 per share.

Instructions

(a) Journalize the transactions.
(b) How many common shares remain at the end of the year and what is their average cost?

E14–4   Top Brands Limited reported the following selected information for the year ended March 31, 2014:

Advertising expense	$ 7,000	Interest expense	$ 5,500
Cash dividends	5,000	Loss on discontinued operations	18,000
Depreciation expense	3,000	Loss on equity investments	3,000
Fees earned	62,000	Rent revenue	34,000
Gain on disposal of equipment	1,500	Retained earnings, April 1, 2013	19,000
Income tax payable	6,600	Training programs expense	8,000

Prepare income statement with discontinued items and statement of comprehensive income. (SO 3) AP

The company's income tax rate is 30%. The company reports gains and losses on its equity investments as other comprehensive income.

Instructions

Prepare income statement and a separate statement of comprehensive income for Top Brands Limited.

E14–5   Shrink Ltd. has profit from continuing operations of $320,000 for the year ended December 31, 2014. It also has the following items (before considering income tax):

Prepare statement of comprehensive income, all-inclusive format, with discontinued operations. (SO 3) AP

1. A net gain of $60,000 from the discontinuance of a component of the entity, which includes a $90,000 profit from the operation of the segment and a $30,000 loss on its disposal
2. Other comprehensive income of a gain on equity investments of $20,000

   Assume that the income tax rate on all items is 30%.

Instructions

Prepare a partial statement of comprehensive income, beginning with profit from continuing operations, using the all-inclusive format.

E14–6   On July 9, 2014, Silver Fox Enterprises Inc. discovered it had recorded the $75,000 purchase of land as legal expense on November 8, 2013. The company had reported retained earnings of $573,500 at its previous year end, December 31, 2013.

   During 2014, Silver Fox had profit of $193,000 and it declared and paid cash dividends of $216,000. Silver Fox has a 25% income tax rate.

Record correction of prior period error and prepare statement of retained earnings. (SO 4) AP

Instructions

(a) Prepare the journal entry to correct the error.
(b) Assuming the company reports under ASPE, prepare a statement of retained earnings.
(c) If Silver Fox uses IFRS, what are the differences in how it would present this information?

E14–7   On January 1, 2014, Fyre Lite Corporation had retained earnings of $650,000. During the year, Fyre Lite had the following selected transactions:

Prepare a statement of retained earnings with correction of prior period error. (SO 1, 2, 3, 4) AP

1. Declared and paid cash dividends, $245,000.
2. Earned profit before income tax, $750,000.
3. Corrected a prior period error of $85,000, before income tax, which resulted in an understatement of profit in 2013.
4. Reacquired 25,000 common shares for $50,000 more than the original issue price. This was the first time the company had ever reacquired its own shares.
5. Completed a 3-for-1 stock split of the common shares.

   Fyre Lite has a 25% income tax rate and reports under ASPE.

Instructions

(a) Prepare a statement of retained earnings for the year ended December 31, 2014.
(b) If any of the above items are not included in this statement, indicate their presentation.

E14–8   Kettle Creek Corporation had the following transactions and events:

Indicate effects of transactions on shareholders' equity. (SO 1, 4, 5) AP

1. Declared a cash dividend.
2. Paid the cash dividend declared in (1).

3. Issued common shares for cash.
4. Completed a 2-for-1 stock split of the common shares.
5. Declared a stock dividend on the common shares.
6. Distributed the stock dividend declared in (5).
7. Made a correction of a prior period error for an understatement of profit.
8. Adopted a new accounting policy that resulted in the recording of a gain on a long-lived asset revaluation.
9. Repurchased common shares for less than their initial issue price.
10. Comprehensive income included profit and a gain on equity investments reported as other comprehensive income.

Instructions

Indicate the effect(s) of each of the above items on the subdivisions of shareholders' equity. Present your answer in tabular form with the following columns. Use "I" for increase, "D" for decrease, and "NE" for no effect. Item 1 is given as an example.

| Item | Contributed Capital | | Retained Earnings | Accumulated Other Comprehensive Income | Total Shareholders' Equity |
	Share Capital	Additional			
1.	NE	NE	D	NE	D

Prepare statement of comprehensive income and statement of changes in shareholders' equity.
(SO 1, 3, 5) AP

E14–9 On January 1, 2014, Hopkins Corporation had an unlimited number of common shares authorized, and 120,000 of them issued for $1.2 million. It also had retained earnings of $750,000 and accumulated other comprehensive income of $17,000. During the year, the following occurred:

1. Issued 60,000 common shares at $15 per share on July 1.
2. Declared a 3-for-2 stock split on September 30 when the fair value was $19 per share.
3. Declared a 5% stock dividend on December 9 to common shareholders of record at December 30, distributable on January 16, 2015. At the declaration date, the fair value of the common shares was $22 per share.
4. Earned profit of $390,000 for the year.
5. Loss on equity investments reported as other comprehensive income was $48,000 before income tax. The company's income tax rate is 35%.

Instructions

(a) Prepare a statement of comprehensive income starting with profit.
(b) Prepare a statement of changes in shareholders' equity.

Prepare statement of changes in shareholders' equity.
(SO 2, 3, 5) AP

E14–10 Ruby Red Rental Corporation had the following balances in its shareholders' equity accounts at January 1, 2014:

Accumulated other comprehensive income (loss)	$ (25,000)
Contributed Surplus—Reacquisition of Common Shares	540,000
Retained earnings	1,500,000
Common shares (32,000 shares)	800,000

Ruby Red had the following transactions and events during 2014:

Feb. 2	Repurchased 1,000 shares for $44,500.
Apr. 17	Declared and paid cash dividends of $70,000.
Oct. 29	Issued 2,000 shares for $104,000.
Dec. 31	Reported comprehensive income of $425,000, which included other comprehensive income of $40,000.

Instructions

Prepare a statement of changes in shareholders' equity at December 31, 2014.

Calculate earnings per share.
(SO 6) AP

E14–11 Salmon Limited reported profit of $465,325 for its November 30, 2014, year end. Cash dividends of $90,000 on the common shares and of $65,000 on the noncumulative preferred shares were declared and paid during the year. The following information is available regarding Salmon's common shares:

Dec. 1, 2013	The opening number of common shares was 60,000.
Feb. 28, 2014	Sold 10,000 common shares for $200,000 cash.
May 31, 2014	Reacquired 5,000 common shares for $90,000 cash.
Nov. 1, 2014	Issued 15,000 common shares in exchange for land with a fair value of $310,000.

Instructions

(a) Calculate the profit available for the common shareholders.
(b) Calculate the weighted average number of common shares for the year.
(c) Calculate earnings per share for the year.
(d) Calculate earnings per share if no dividends had been declared and paid during the year.

E14–12 On December 31 2013, Lewis Corporation has 3,000, $4 preferred shares and 100,000 common shares. During the year, the company had the following share transactions:

Calculate earnings per share. (SO 6) AP

Jan. 1	Sold 1,000 preferred shares for cash.
Mar. 31	Sold 12,000 common shares for cash.
June 1	Reacquired 14,000 common shares for cash.
Dec. 1	Sold 24,000 common shares for cash.

Lewis's profit in 2014 is $478,000.

Instructions

(a) Calculate the weighted average number of common shares for the year.
(b) Calculate earnings per share under each of the following four independent assumptions:
  1. Assume that the preferred shares are cumulative and that the dividend to the preferred shareholders was (i) declared, and (ii) not declared.
  2. Assume that the preferred shares are noncumulative and that the dividend to the preferred shareholders was (i) declared, and (ii) not declared.

E14–13 The following financial information is available for First Interprovincial Bank as at October 31 (in thousands, except for per share amounts):

Calculate ratios and comment. (SO 6) AP

	2014	2013	2012
Profit	$1,978	$2,131	$2,663
Preferred share dividends (total)	$73	$43	$30
Weighted average number of common shares	502	500	501
Dividends per common share	$2.50	$2.25	$2.10
Market price per common share	$43.00	$49.75	$56.25

Instructions

(a) Calculate the earnings per share, price-earnings ratio, and payout ratio for the common shareholders for each of the three years.
(b) Using the information in (a), comment on First Interprovincial Bank's earnings performance and dividend record.

▶ Problems: Set A

P14–1A The condensed balance sheet of Laporte Corporation reports the following:

Compare impact of cash dividend, stock dividend, and stock split. (SO 1) AP

LAPORTE CORPORATION
Balance Sheet (partial)
June 30, 2014

Total assets	$12,000,000
Liabilities and shareholders' equity	
Total liabilities	$ 4,000,000
Shareholders' equity	
Common shares, unlimited number authorized, 400,000 issued	2,000,000
Retained earnings	6,000,000
Total shareholders' equity	8,000,000
Total liabilities and shareholders' equity	$12,000,000

The market price of the common shares is currently $30 per share. Laporte wants to assess the impact of three possible alternatives on the corporation and its shareholders. The alternatives are:

1. Payment of a $1.50 per share cash dividend
2. Distribution of a 5% stock dividend
3. A 3-for-2 stock split

Instructions

(a) For each alternative, determine the impact on (1) assets, (2) liabilities, (3) common shares, (4) retained earnings, (5) total shareholders' equity, and (6) the number of shares.

(b) Assume a Laporte shareholder currently owns 1,000 common shares at a cost of $28,000. What is the impact of each alternative for the shareholder, assuming that the shares' market price changes proportionately with the alternative?

TAKING IT FURTHER   What are the advantages and disadvantages to the company of a stock split?

Record and post transactions; prepare shareholders' equity section. (SO 1, 2) AP

P14–2A   On December 31, 2013, LeBlanc Corporation had the following shareholders' equity accounts:

LEBLANC CORPORATION	
Balance Sheet (partial)	
December 31, 2013	
Shareholders' equity	
Common shares (unlimited number of shares authorized,	
90,000 issued)	$1,100,000
Retained earnings	540,000
Total shareholders' equity	$1,640,000

During the year, the following transactions occurred:

Jan.   15   Declared a $1 per share cash dividend to shareholders of record on January 31, payable February 15.
July   1   Announced a 3-for-2 stock split. The market price per share on the date of the announcement was $15.
Dec. 15   Declared a 10% stock dividend to shareholders of record on December 30, distributable on January 15. On December 15, the market price of each share was $10; on December 30, $12; and on January 15, $11.
        31   Determined that profit before income tax for the year was $450,000. The company has a 30% income tax rate.

Instructions

(a) Journalize the transactions and closing entries.
(b) Enter the beginning balances and post the entries in part (a) to the shareholders' equity accounts. (*Note:* Open additional shareholders' equity accounts as needed.)
(c) Prepare the shareholders' equity section of the balance sheet at December 31, 2014.

TAKING IT FURTHER   Stock splits and stock dividends do not change the company's total assets. Given that, why does share price change after a stock split or stock dividend?

Determine impact of reacquired shares. (SO 2) AP

P14–3A   Advanced Technologies Inc. reported the following information related to its shareholders' equity on January 1:

Common shares, 1,000,000 authorized, 500,000 shares issued	$1,500,000
Contributed surplus—reacquisition of common shares	15,000
Retained earnings	720,000

During the year, the following transactions related to common shares occurred in the order listed:

1. Issued 35,000 shares at $4.20 per share.
2. Reacquired 10,000 shares at $3.00 per share.
3. Issued 5,000 shares at $4.50 per share.
4. Reacquired 18,000 shares at $4 per share.
5. Reacquired 75,000 shares at $3 per share.

Instructions

(a) Calculate the number of shares authorized and issued at the end of the year.
(b) Determine the ending balances in each of the following accounts: Common Shares; Contributed Surplus—Reacquisition of Common Shares; and Retained Earnings.

TAKING IT FURTHER   Why is it important to report the number of shares issued? The number authorized?

Record stock dividends, splits, and reacquisition of shares. Show impact of transactions on accounts. (SO 1, 2) AP

P14–4A   The following shareholders' equity accounts are reported by Branch Inc. on January 1:

Common shares (unlimited authorized, 150,000 issued)	$2,400,000
Preferred shares ($4 cumulative, convertible, 100,000 authorized, 5,000 issued)	375,000
Contributed surplus—reacquisition of common shares	30,000
Retained earnings	1,275,000

The following selected transactions occurred during the year:

Feb. 11   Issued 50,000 common shares at $20 per share.

Mar. 2   Reacquired 20,000 common shares at $22 per share.

May 3   Shareholders converted 1,000 preferred shares into 4,000 common shares. The fair value per preferred share was $80; per common share, $24.

June 14   Split the common shares 2-for-1 when the common shares were trading at $30 per share.

July 25   Reacquired 500 preferred shares at $70 per share.

Sept. 16   Reacquired 50,000 common shares for $17 per share.

Oct. 27   Declared a 5% common stock dividend distributable on December 13 to shareholders of record on November 24. The fair value of the common shares on October 27 was $19 per share.

Dec. 13   Distributed the stock dividend declared on October 27. The fair value of the common shares on December 13 was $21 per share.

Instructions

(a) Prepare a chart that shows for each class of shares (1) number of shares issued, (2) total cost, and (3) average cost per share. Enter the January 1 data into the chart.

(b) Prepare journal entries for the transactions. Update the chart in (a) as required for the transactions. After each transaction, determine the number issued, total cost, and average cost per share.

(c) Show how each class of shares will be presented in the shareholders' equity section of the balance sheet at December 31.

TAKING IT FURTHER   Provide possible reasons why Branch Inc. split the common shares and issued a stock dividend.

P14–5A   The ledger of Port Hope Corporation at November 30, 2014, contains the following summary data:

Cash dividends—common	$ 65,000
Cash dividends—preferred	25,000
Common shares	325,000
Cost of goods sold	7,280,000
Depreciation expense	355,000
Net sales	9,124,000
Operating expenses	1,120,000
Other comprehensive loss (before income tax)	83,000
Other revenues	48,000
Preferred shares ($5 noncumulative)	400,000
Retained earnings, December 1, 2013	755,000

Prepare income statement with EPS and statement of comprehensive income. (SO 3, 6) AP

Your analysis reveals the following additional information:

1. The company has a 25% income tax rate.
2. The communications devices division was discontinued on August 31. The profit from operations for the division up to that day was $20,000 before income tax. The division was sold at a loss of $75,000 before income tax.
3. There were 200,000 common and 5,000 preferred shares issued on December 1, 2013, with no changes during the year.

Instructions

(a) Prepare a multiple-step income statement for the year including EPS.

(b) Prepare a statement of comprehensive income as a separate statement.

TAKING IT FURTHER   Why are gains and losses from discontinued operations reported separately from continuing operations?

P14–6A   The ledger of Zug Limited at October 31, 2014, contains the following summary data:

Cash dividends—common	$ 120,000
Common shares	650,000
Depreciation expense	87,000
Fees earned	1,476,000
Operating expenses	929,000
Other comprehensive gain (before income tax)	48,000
Interest expense	54,000
Retained earnings, November 1, 2013	575,000

Correct error from prior period; prepare statement of comprehensive income—all-inclusive format; show presentation of retained earnings. (SO 2, 3, 4) AP

Your analysis reveals the following additional information:

1. The company has a 25% income tax rate.
2. On March 19, 2014, Zug discovered an error made in the previous fiscal year. A $57,000 payment of a note payable had been recorded as interest expense.

3. On April 10, 2014, common shares costing $75,000 were reacquired for $97,500. This is the first time the company has reacquired common shares.

Instructions

(a) Prepare a journal entry to correct the prior period error.
(b) Prepare a comprehensive income statement on an all-inclusive basis.
(c) Illustrate how the changes in retained earnings will be shown in the financial statements.

TAKING IT FURTHER   If an error from a previous period is found and corrected, why is it also important to restate the prior years' data shown for comparative purposes?

Record and post transactions; prepare a statement of changes in shareholders' equity. (SO 2, 4, 5) AP

P14–7A   The post-closing trial balance of Jajoo Corporation at December 31, 2014, contains the following shareholders' equity accounts:

$5 noncumulative preferred shares (10,000 issued)	$1,100,000
Common shares (400,000 issued)	2,000,000
Retained earnings	3,146,000

A review of the accounting records reveals the following:

1. The January 1, 2014, balance in Common Shares was $1,280,000 (320,000 shares), the balance in Contributed Surplus—Reacquisition of Shares was $30,000, and the balance in Retained Earnings was $2,443,500.
2. One of the company's shareholders needed cash for a personal expenditure. On January 15, the company agreed to reacquire 20,000 shares from this shareholder for $7 per share.
3. On July 1, the company corrected a prior period error that resulted in an increase to the Long-Term Investments account, as well as to the prior year's profit of $250,000 before income tax.
4. On October 1, 100,000 common shares were sold for $8 per share.
5. The preferred shareholders' dividend was declared and paid in 2014 for two quarters. Due to a cash shortage, the last two quarters' dividends were not paid.
6. Profit for the year before income tax was $760,000. The company has a 25% income tax rate.

Instructions

(a) Open general ledger accounts for the shareholders' equity accounts listed in (1) above and enter opening balances.
(b) Prepare journal entries to record transactions (2) to (5) and post to general ledger accounts.
(c) Prepare entries to close dividends and the Income Summary account and post.
(d) Prepare a statement of changes in shareholders' equity for the year.
(e) Compare the balances in the general ledger accounts with the closing balances on the statement of changes in shareholders' equity.

TAKING IT FURTHER   Why is the prior period adjustment for the error in a prior year's profit recorded in the Retained Earnings account instead of being a correction to profit in the 2014 financial statements?

Record and post transactions; prepare financial statements. (SO 1, 2, 3, 4, 5) AP

P14–8A   The shareholders' equity accounts of Cedeno Inc. at December 31, 2013, are as follows:

Common shares (unlimited number of shares authorized, 1,000,000 issued)	$3,000,000
Stock dividends distributable	400,000
Contributed surplus—reacquired common shares	5,000
Retained earnings	1,200,000

Cedeno has a 30% income tax rate. During 2014, the following transactions and events occurred:

Jan.	20	Issued 100,000 common shares as a result of a 10% stock dividend declared on December 15, 2013. The shares' fair value was $4 on December 15 and $5 on January 20.
Feb.	12	Issued 50,000 common shares for $5 per share.
Mar.	31	Corrected an error in the December 31, 2013 inventory that had overstated the cost of goods sold for 2013 by $60,000.
Nov.	2	Reacquired 25,000 shares for $2.50 each.
Dec.	31	Declared a cash dividend to the common shareholders of $0.50 per share to shareholders of record at January 15, payable January 31.
	31	Determined that profit was $280,000.
	31	Determined that other comprehensive loss was $28,000 before income tax.

Instructions

(a) Journalize the transactions and summary closing entries.
(b) Enter the beginning balances and post the entries in (a) to the shareholders' equity accounts. (*Note*: Open additional shareholders' equity accounts as needed.)

(c) Prepare a statement of comprehensive income beginning with profit.
(d) Prepare a statement of changes in shareholders' equity.
(e) Prepare the shareholders' equity section of the balance sheet at December 31, 2014.

TAKING IT FURTHER   Explain the two methods of preparing a statement of comprehensive income. Is one method better than the other?

P14–9A   The shareholders' equity accounts of Tmao, Inc. at December 31, 2013, are as follows:

Preferred shares, $3 noncumulative, unlimited number authorized, 4,000 issued	$400,000
Common shares, unlimited number authorized, 160,000 issued	800,000
Retained earnings	450,000
Accumulated other comprehensive loss	(50,000)

Prepare a statement of changes in shareholders' equity. (SO 5) AP

Tmao has a 35% income tax rate. During the following fiscal year, ended December 31, 2014, the company had the following transactions and events:

Feb. 1   Discovered a $70,000 understatement of 2013 cost of goods sold.
July 12   Announced a 2-for-1 preferred stock split. The market price of the preferred shares at the date of announcement was $150.
Oct. 1   Adopted a new accounting policy that resulted in a cumulative decrease to prior years' profit of $30,000 before income tax.
Dec. 1   Declared a 10% stock dividend to common shareholders of record at December 20, distributable on January 12. The fair value of the common shares was $12 per share.
     18   Declared the annual cash dividend ($1.50 post-split) to the preferred shareholders of record on January 10, 2015, payable on January 31, 2015.
     31   Determined that for 2014, profit before income tax was $350,000 and other comprehensive income, net of income tax expense of $35,000, was $65,000.

Instructions
Prepare a statement of changes in shareholders' equity for the year ended December 31, 2014.

TAKING IT FURTHER   How does comprehensive income impact the shareholders' equity in the balance sheet? Is this the same for companies following ASPE?

P14–10A   The shareholders' equity accounts of Blue Bay Logistics Ltd. on April 1, 2013, the beginning of the fiscal year, are as follows:

Calculate earnings per share. (SO 6) AP

$6 preferred shares (20,000 issued)	$1,800,000
Common shares (500,000 issued)	3,750,000
Retained earnings	1,550,000
Total shareholders' equity	$7,100,000

During the year, the following transactions occurred:

2013

June 1   Reacquired 12,000 common shares for $9 per share.
July 1   Issued 50,000 common shares for $10 per share.
Sept. 30   Reacquired 8,000 common shares for $9.50 per share.

2014

Jan. 31   Issued 60,000 common shares in exchange for land. The land's fair value was $600,000.
Mar. 31   Profit for the year ended March 31, 2014, was $973,600.

Instructions
(a) Calculate the weighted average number of common shares for the year.
(b) Assuming the preferred shares are cumulative and one year in arrears:
  1. Calculate the earnings per share if no preferred dividends are declared during the year.
  2. Calculate the earnings per share if the preferred share dividends for the current and prior year are declared during the year.
(c) Assuming the preferred shares are noncumulative:
  1. Calculate the earnings per share if no preferred share dividends are declared during the year.
  2. Calculate the earnings per share if the company declares a preferred share dividend of $80,000.

TAKING IT FURTHER   Why is earnings per share an important measure for common shareholders but not for preferred shareholders?

Calculate ratios and comment. (SO 6) AN

P14–11A The following financial information (in millions except for market price per share) is for two major corporations for the three fiscal years ended December 31 as follows:

Canadian Pacific Railway Limited	2011	2010	2009
Weighted average number of common shares	169.5	168.8	166.3
Profit	$ 570	$ 651	$ 550
Dividends	$ 198	$ 179	$ 166
Market price per share (December 31)	$67.67	$64.81	$54.00

Canadian National Railway Company	2011	2010	2009
Weighted average number of common shares	451.1	466.3	469.2
Profit	$2,457	$2,104	$1,854
Dividends	$ 585	$ 503	$474
Market price per share (December 31)	$78.56	$66.47	$54.36

Neither company has preferred shares issued.

Instructions

(a) Calculate earnings per share and the price-earnings and dividend payout ratios for each company for 2011, 2010, and 2009. Comment on whether their ratios have improved or deteriorated.
(b) Compare Canadian Pacific's ratios with Canadian National's.

TAKING IT FURTHER Why is the presentation of fully diluted earnings per share required under IFRS, given that it is a *hypothetical* number?

Calculate and evaluate ratios with discontinued operations. (SO 4, 6) AP

P14–12A Highlander Inc. reported the following selected information for the last three years (in millions, except for per share amounts):

	2014	2013	2012
Net sales	$4,000	$3,100	$2,600
Average shareholders' equity	3,400	2,400	1,800
Preferred dividends	20	20	15
Profit from continuing operations	$1,160	$ 810	$ 570
Loss on disposal of discontinued operations	340		
Loss from discontinued operations	110	80	70
Profit	$ 710	$ 730	$ 500
Weighted average number of common shares	300	290	280
Market price per share	$45.50	$33.65	$44.80

Instructions

(a) Calculate Highlander's return on equity, earnings per share, and price-earnings ratios before and after discontinued operations for 2014, 2013, and 2012.
(b) Evaluate Highlander's performance over the last three years before and after discontinued operations.
(c) Explain how reporting discontinued operations separately would affect your analysis of Highlander's performance.

TAKING IT FURTHER Why is it important that discontinued operations be reported separately only if the operations qualify as a *component of an entity*?

▶ Problems: Set B

Compare impact of cash dividend, stock dividend, and stock split. (SO 1) AP

P14–1B The condensed balance sheet of Erickson Corporation reports the following:

ERICKSON CORPORATION Balance Sheet (partial) January 31, 2014		
Total assets		$9,000,000
Liabilities and shareholders' equity		
Liabilities		$2,500,000
Shareholders' equity		
Common shares, unlimited number authorized, 500,000 issued	$3,000,000	
Retained earnings	3,500,000	6,500,000
Total liabilities and shareholders' equity		$9,000,000

The market price of the common shares is currently $30 per share. Erickson wants to assess the impact of three possible alternatives on the corporation and its shareholders. The alternatives are:

1. Payment of a $1.50 per share cash dividend
2. Distribution of a 5% stock dividend
3. A 2-for-1 stock split

Instructions

(a) For each alternative, determine the impact on (1) assets, (2) liabilities, (3) common shares, (4) retained earnings, (5) total shareholders' equity, and (6) the number of shares.
(b) Assume an Erickson shareholder currently owns 2,000 common shares at a cost of $50,000. What is the impact of each alternative for the shareholder, assuming that the market price of the shares changes proportionately with the alternative?

TAKING IT FURTHER   What are the advantages and disadvantages to the company of a stock split?

P14–2B   On December 31, 2013, Asaad Corporation had the following shareholders' equity accounts:

Record and post transactions; prepare shareholders' equity section. (SO 1) AP

ASAAD CORPORATION	
Balance Sheet (partial)	
December 31, 2013	
Shareholders' equity	
Common shares (unlimited number of shares authorized,	
75,000 shares issued)	$1,700,000
Retained earnings	600,000
Total shareholders' equity	$2,300,000

During the year, the following transactions occurred:

Feb. 1   Declared a $1 cash dividend to shareholders of record on February 15 and payable on March 1.

Apr. 1   Announced a 2-for-1 stock split. The market price per share was $36 on the date of the announcement.

Dec. 1   Declared a 5% stock dividend to shareholders of record on December 20, distributable on January 5. On December 1, the shares' market price was $16 per share; on December 20, it was $18 per share; and on January 5, it was $15 per share.

31   Determined that profit before income tax for the year was $400,000. The company has a 25% income tax rate.

Instructions

(a) Journalize the transactions and closing entries.
(b) Enter the beginning balances and post the entries in (a) to the shareholders' equity accounts. (*Note:* Open additional shareholders' equity accounts as needed.)
(c) Prepare the shareholders' equity section of the balance sheet at December 31, 2014.

TAKING IT FURTHER   Stock splits and stock dividends do not change the company's total assets. Given that, why does the share price change after a stock split or stock dividend?

P14–3B   The following is related to the shareholders' equity of Adanac Limited on January 1:

Determine impact of reacquired shares. (SO 2) AP

Common shares, 150,000 authorized, 14,000 shares issued	$490,000
Contributed surplus—reacquisition of common shares	12,000
Retained earnings	220,000

During the year, the following transactions related to common shares occurred in the order listed:

1. Reacquired 600 shares at $44 per share.
2. Issued 3,600 shares at $47 per share.
3. Issued 1,000 shares at $64.50 per share.
4. Reacquired 1,200 shares at $58 per share.
5. Reacquired 1,500 shares at $36 per share.

Instructions

(a) Calculate the number of shares authorized and issued at the end of the year.

(b) Determine the ending balances in each of the following accounts: Common Shares; Contributed Surplus— Reacquisition of Common Shares; and Retained Earnings.

TAKING IT FURTHER Why do companies report the number of shares issued? The number of shares authorized?

Record stock dividends, splits, and reacquisition of shares. Show impact of transactions on accounts. (SO 1, 2) AP

P14–4B The following shareholders' equity accounts are reported by Talty Inc. on January 1:

Common shares (unlimited authorized, 500,000 issued)	$4,000,000
Preferred shares ($9 noncumulative, convertible, 100,000 authorized, 4,000 issued)	600,000
Contributed surplus—reacquisition of common shares	2,000
Retained earnings	1,958,000

The following selected transactions occurred during the year:

Jan. 17   Issued 50,000 common shares at $10 per share.

Feb. 27   Reacquired 20,000 common shares at $12 per share.

Mar. 31   Shareholders converted 2,000 preferred shares into 20,000 common shares. The fair value per preferred share was $160; per common share, $16.50.

Apr. 14   Split the common shares 2 for 1 when the common shares were trading at $20 per share.

June 25   Reacquired 500 preferred shares at $145 per share.

Aug. 16   Reacquired 100,000 common shares for $11 per share.

Oct. 17   Declared a 5% common stock dividend distributable on December 3 to shareholders of record on November 14. On October 17 the fair value of the common shares was $10.

Dec. 3   Distributed the stock dividend declared on October 17. On December 3 the fair value of the common shares was $12.50.

Instructions

(a) Prepare a chart that shows for each class of shares (1) number of shares, (2) cost of shares, and (3) average cost per share. Enter the January 1 data into the chart.

(b) Prepare journal entries for the transactions. Update the chart in (a) as required for the transactions. After each transaction, determine the number issued, total cost, and average cost per share.

(c) Show how each class of shares will be presented in the shareholders' equity section of the balance sheet at December 31.

TAKING IT FURTHER Provide possible reasons why Talty split the common shares and issued a stock dividend.

Prepare income statement with EPS and comprehensive income statement. (SO 3, 6) AP

P14–5B The ledger of Coquitlam Corporation at December 31, 2014, contains the following summary data:

Cash dividends—common	$ 125,000
Cash dividends—preferred	55,000
Cost of goods sold	888,000
Net sales	1,750,000
Operating expenses	451,000
Other comprehensive gain (before income tax)	47,000
Other expenses	18,000
Retained earnings, January 1, 2014	642,000

Your analysis reveals the following additional information:

1. The company has a 25% income tax rate.

2. The ceramics division was discontinued on July 31. The loss from operations for the division up to that day was $150,000 before income tax. The division was sold at a pre-tax gain of $70,000 before income tax.

3. There were 200,000 common and 100,000 preferred shares issued on December 31, 2013, with no changes during the year.

Instructions

(a) Prepare a multiple-step income statement for the year including EPS.

(b) Prepare a statement of comprehensive income as a separate statement.

TAKING IT FURTHER   Why are gains and losses from discontinued operations reported separately from continuing operations?

P14–6B   The ledger of Weather Vane Limited at September 30, 2014, contains the following summary data:

Cash dividends—common	$ 150,000
Common shares	750,000
Depreciation expense	74,000
Fees earned	1,647,000
Operating expenses	971,000
Other comprehensive loss (before income tax)	38,000
Other revenue	65,000
Retained earnings, October 1, 2013	845,000

Correct error from prior period; prepare statement of comprehensive income—all-inclusive format; show presentation of retained earnings. (SO 2, 3, 4) AP

Your analysis reveals the following additional information:

1. The company has a 25% income tax rate.
2. On July 9, 2014, Weather Vane discovered an error made in the previous fiscal year. A $61,500 payment of a note payable had been recorded as interest expense.
3. On August 18, 2014, common shares costing $57,500 were reacquired for $90,000. This is the first time the company has reacquired common shares.

Instructions

(a) Prepare a journal entry to correct the prior period error.
(b) Prepare a comprehensive income statement on an all-inclusive basis.
(c) Illustrate how the changes in retained earnings will be shown in the financial statements.

TAKING IT FURTHER   If an error from a previous period is found and corrected, why is it also important to restate the prior year's data shown for comparative purposes?

P14–7B   The post-closing trial balance of Michaud Corporation at December 31, 2014, contains the following shareholders' equity accounts:

$4 cumulative preferred shares (15,000 shares issued)	$ 850,000
Common shares (250,000 shares issued)	3,200,000
Contributed surplus—reacquisition of common shares	20,000
Retained earnings	1,418,000

Record and post transactions; prepare a statement of changes in shareholders' equity. (SO 2, 4, 5) AP

A review of the accounting records reveals the following:

1. The January 1 opening balance in Common Shares was $3,210,000 (255,000 shares) and the balance in Retained Earnings was $980,000.
2. On March 1, 20,000 common shares were sold for $15.50 per share.
3. One of the company's shareholders needed cash for personal reasons. On July 1, the company agreed to reacquire 25,000 shares from this shareholder for $12 per share.
4. On September 1, the company discovered a $60,000 error that overstated sales in 2013. All sales were made on account. The net-of-tax effect was properly debited to Retained Earnings. The company has a 30% income tax rate.
5. The preferred shareholders' dividend was declared and paid in 2014 for three quarters. Due to a cash shortage, the last quarter's dividend was not paid.
6. Profit for the year before income tax was $750,000.

Instructions

(a) Open general ledger accounts for the shareholders' equity accounts listed in (1) above and enter opening balances.
(b) Prepare journal entries to record transactions (2) to (5) and post to general ledger accounts.
(c) Prepare entries to close dividends and the Income Summary accounts and post.
(d) Prepare a statement of changes in shareholders' equity for the year.
(e) Compare the balances in the general ledger accounts with the closing balances on the statement of changes in shareholders' equity.

TAKING IT FURTHER   Why is the prior period adjustment for the error in 2013 sales recorded in the Retained Earnings account instead of being a correction to sales in the 2014 financial statements?

Record and post transactions; prepare financial statements. (SO 1, 2, 3, 4, 5) AP

P14–8B The shareholders' equity accounts of Fryman Ltd. at December 31, 2013, are as follows:

Preferred shares, $4 noncumulative, unlimited number authorized,	
12,000 issued	$800,000
Common shares, unlimited number authorized, 250,000 issued	500,000
Contributed surplus—reacquired common shares	100,000
Retained earnings	900,000
Accumulated other comprehensive loss	(50,000)

During 2014, the company had the following transactions and events:

Aug. 1   Discovered a $45,000 understatement of 2013 cost of goods sold due to an error in ending inventory. The company has a 30% income tax rate.

Oct. 15   Declared a 10% stock dividend to common shareholders of record on October 31, distributable on November 10. The fair value of the common shares was $18 per share on October 15, $19 per share on October 31, and $20 per share on November 10.

Dec. 15   Declared the annual cash dividend to the preferred shareholders of record on December 31, payable on January 15, 2015.

31   Determined that other comprehensive income for the year was $12,000 (before income tax) and profit was $395,000.

Instructions

(a) Journalize the transactions and summary closing entries.

(b) Enter the beginning balances in the accounts and post to the shareholders' equity accounts. (*Note*: Open additional shareholders' equity accounts as needed.)

(c) Prepare a statement of comprehensive income on an all-inclusive basis.

(d) Prepare a statement of changes in shareholders' equity for the year.

(e) Prepare the shareholders' equity section of the balance sheet at December 31, 2014.

TAKING IT FURTHER   Explain the two methods of preparing a statement of comprehensive income. Is one method better than the other?

Prepare a statement of changes in shareholders' equity. (SO 5) AP

P14–9B The shareholders' equity accounts of Kanada Inc. at September 30, 2013, are as follows:

Preferred shares, $5 noncumulative, unlimited number authorized,	
6,000 issued	$465,000
Common shares, unlimited number authorized, 25,000 issued	900,000
Retained earnings	540,000
Accumulated other comprehensive income	95,000

Kanada has a 30% income tax rate. During the following fiscal year, ended September 30, 2014, Kanada had the following transactions and events:

Mar. 14   Declared a 4% common stock dividend to shareholders of record at March 31, distributable on April 5. The fair value of the common shares was $10 per share on March 14, $11 on March 31, and $12 on April 5.

July 7   It was discovered that the computer system was incorrectly aging accounts receivable and therefore overestimating bad debts. The total effect of the error on prior years' profit was an increase of $33,000 before income tax.

Aug. 1   Discovered a $54,000 overstatement of cost of goods sold in the prior year's income statement.

Sept. 20   Declared the annual dividend payable to the preferred shareholders of record on October 5, payable on October 31.

25   Announced a 2-for-1 common stock split. The market price of the common shares at the date of announcement was $15 per share.

30   Determined that other comprehensive income for the year was $27,000 and profit was $325,000, both before income tax.

Instructions

Prepare a statement of changes in shareholders' equity for the year ended September 30, 2014.

TAKING IT FURTHER   How does comprehensive income impact the shareholders' equity in the balance sheet? Is this the same for companies following ASPE?

P14–10B   The shareholders' equity accounts of Gualtieri Inc. on August 1, 2013, the beginning of its fiscal year, are as follows:

Calculate earnings per share. (SO 6) AP

$4 preferred shares (25,000 issued)	$1,250,000
Common shares (350,000 issued)	3,750,000
Retained earnings	2,250,000
Total shareholders' equity	$7,250,000

During the year, the following transactions occurred:

Nov. 30   Issued 37,500 common shares for $12 per share.
Feb. 1   Reacquired 6,000 common shares for $10 per share.
Mar. 1   Issued 30,000 common shares in exchange for equipment. The equipment's fair value was $40,000.
July 31   Profit for the year ended July 31, 2014, was $1,022,800.

Instructions

(a) Calculate the weighted average number of common shares for the year.
(b) Assuming the preferred shares are cumulative and one year in arrears:
   1. Calculate the earnings per share if no preferred dividends are declared during the year.
   2. Calculate the earnings per share if the preferred share dividends for the current and prior year are declared during the year.
(c) Assuming the preferred shares are noncumulative:
   1. Calculate the earnings per share if no preferred share dividends are declared during the year.
   2. Calculate the earnings per share if the company declares a preferred share dividend of $60,000.

TAKING IT FURTHER   Why is it important to use a weighted average number of shares in the earnings per share calculations? Why not just use the average number of shares during the year?

P14–11B   The following financial information (in millions except for market price per share) is for two major corporations for the three fiscal years ended December 31 as follows:

Calculate ratios and comment. (SO 6) AN

Husky Energy Inc.	2011	2010
Weighted average number of common shares	923.8	852.7
Profit	$2,224	$947
Dividends—Common shareholders	$1,109	$1,020
Dividends—Preferred shareholders	$10	$0
Market price per share (December 31)	$24.55	$26.55

Suncor Energy Inc.	2011	2010
Weighted average number of common shares	1,571	1,562
Profit	$4,304	$3,829
Dividend—Common shareholders	$664	$611
Market price per share (December 31)	$29.38	$38.28

Suncor does not have preferred shares issued. Husky issued preferred shares in 2011.

Instructions

(a) Calculate earnings per share and the price-earnings and dividend payout ratios for each company for 2011 and 2010. Comment on whether their ratios have improved or deteriorated.
(b) Compare Husky's ratios with Suncor's.

TAKING IT FURTHER   Why is the presentation of fully diluted earnings per share required under IFRS, given that it is a *hypothetical* number?

Calculate and evaluate ratios with discontinued operations. (SO 4, 6) AP

P14–12B All Care Inc. reported the following selected information for the last three years (in millions, except for per share amounts):

	2014	2013	2012
Sales and operating revenues	$20,300	$24,900	$23,800
Average shareholders' equity	3,400	2,400	1,900
Preferred dividends	80	80	60
Profit from continuing operations	$ 1,250	$ 1,130	$ 990
Loss on disposal of discontinued operations	620		
Loss from discontinued operations	200	150	180
Profit	$ 430	$ 980	$ 810
Weighted average number of common shares	450	470	460
Market price per share	$ 24.40	$ 19.88	$ 21.60

Instructions

(a) Calculate All Care's return on equity, earnings per share, and price-earnings ratios before and after discontinued operations for 2014, 2013, and 2012.
(b) Evaluate All Care's performance over the last three years before and after discontinued operations.
(c) How would reporting discontinued operations affect your analysis of All Care's performance?

TAKING IT FURTHER Why is it important that discontinued operations be reported separately only if the operations qualify as a *component of an entity*?

◉ Continuing Cookie Chronicle

(**Note:** This is a continuation of the Cookie Chronicle from Chapters 1 through 13.)

Natalie is planning on completing college in April 2015. In the meantime, she tries to spend approximately 20 hours a week at Koebel's Family Bakery. She is developing an understanding of all of the business operations so she can step into her new position as administrator on May 1, 2015. There are challenges every day when operating a business and she is thrilled to be a part of the process. Janet and Brian are also thrilled to have Natalie on board and believe that Natalie's input has been instrumental in helping make some of their critical business decisions.

To ensure that Natalie does not consider other business opportunities and leave the bakery, Janet and Brian would like to provide Natalie with a greater ownership interest in Koebel's Family Bakery Ltd. An alternative that is being discussed is the buyback of shares by Koebel's Family Bakery from Janet and Brian to enable Natalie to hold a one-third ownership interest in the bakery without having to purchase additional shares.

Recall that on August 1, 2014, Natalie purchased 10 shares of Koebel's Family Bakery Ltd. for $1,200 per share and that Brian and Janet each own 100 of the remaining 200 shares.

The shareholders' equity accounts of Koebel's Family Bakery Ltd. are as follows:

Common shares	$ 12,200
Retained earnings	241,026

Janet and Brian are thinking that it might be best for all three of them to each own 10 shares of Koebel's Family Bakery Ltd. They are confused, however, about the process of shares being reacquired and have come to you with the following questions:

1. If Koebel's Family Bakery Ltd. reacquires the common shares we hold how will a fair value for each common share reacquired be determined?
2. Natalie has recently purchased shares in Koebel's Family Bakery Ltd. for $1,200 per share. Is this amount a fair value to use as a purchase price for reacquisition of the shares? Why or why not?
3. How much cash will Koebel's Family Bakery Ltd. need to reacquire the shares that we hold if we assume a price of $1,200 per share?
4. Last year the bakery paid total dividends of $85,000. If our shares are reacquired, will Koebel's Family Bakery Ltd. be able to pay a dividend next year? Do you think there will be enough in retained earnings to pay a dividend? Will the amount of the dividend we each receive change once Natalie owns a one-third interest in the company?
5. If we choose not to have the company reacquire our shares, then how can we ensure that Natalie stays on with us?

Instructions

(a) Answer Janet and Brian's questions.

(b) Prepare the journal entry to record the reacquisition of shares by Koebel's Family Bakery Ltd. from Janet and Brian assuming that $1,200 per share is a fair value.

(c) Calculate the amount of share capital after the shares have been reacquired from Janet and Brian and the average cost per share.

BROADENING YOUR PERSPECTIVE | CHAPTER 14

▶ Financial Reporting and Analysis

Financial Reporting Problem

BYP14–1 Refer to the consolidated financial statements and accompanying notes for **Reitmans (Canada) Limited** reproduced in Appendix A.

Instructions

(a) Did Reitmans report any of the following in fiscal 2012: (1) stock dividends or stock splits, (2) other comprehensive income, or (3) corrections of prior period errors?

(b) Did Reitmans repurchase any shares in fiscal 2012? If so, how much cash did it spend to reacquire the shares?

(c) Basic EPS of $0.72 for 2012 was reported in the chapter in Illustration 14-8. How much was basic EPS for 2011? Did EPS improve or weaken in 2012?

(d) Did Reitmans report any fully diluted EPS in fiscal 2012 and 2011? If yes, what was the difference between these amounts and the basic EPS in each year?

(e) Reitmans' price-earnings ratio for 2012 was reported in the chapter in Illustration 14-9. Its price-earnings ratio for 2011 was 13.4 times (based on a market value per share of $17.81 on January 29, 2011). Did the price-earnings ratio improve or weaken in 2012? Is your answer consistent with your findings in part (c)? Explain.

(f) Reitmans' payout ratio for 2012 was reported in the chapter in Illustration 14-10. Calculate its payout ratio for 2011. Explain what caused the difference between the two years.

Interpreting Financial Statements

BYP14–2 **Potash Corporation of Saskatchewan Inc.**, known as PotashCorp, is the world's largest fertilizer enterprise by capacity and a leading supplier to three distinct market categories: agriculture, animal nutrition, and industrial chemicals. On January 26, 2011, the company declared a 3-for-1 stock split on its common shares, for shareholders of record on February 14, 2011, with the share certificates to be distributed February 24, 2011. Financial information for PotashCorp for the years ended December 31, 2011 and 2010, follows (in millions of US dollars, except per share data):

	2011	2010
Profit (loss) for the year	$3,081	$1,775
Shareholders' equity at December 31	7,847	6,685
Cash dividends declared during the year	240	118
Number of shares outstanding (at year end)	858.7	887.9
Weighted average number of shares outstanding	855.7	886.4

Instructions

(a) Explain the different effects that a cash dividend, stock dividend, and stock split would have on PotashCorp's assets, liabilities, shareholders' equity, and the number of shares outstanding.

(b) What is the likely reason that PotashCorp has split its shares?

(c) The market price for the common shares on January 25, 2011, the day before the stock split was announced, was $161. What do you think the market price for a share would be immediately after the stock split? On February 14, 2011, after the stock split had taken effect, the stock price was $62.36. Does it appear that the stock market reacted favourably or unfavourably to the stock split?

(d) The cash dividend per share declared on common shares (before the stock split) in 2010 was $0.40. After the stock split in 2011, the cash dividend per share declared was $0.28. Is this better or worse than what you would have expected after the stock split and by how much?

(e) Calculate the return on shareholders' equity, earnings per share, and payout ratio for the shareholders for 2011 and 2010. Comment on the company's profitability. Shareholders' equity at December 31, 2009, was $6,305.

▶ Critical Thinking

Collaborative Learning Activity

Note to instructor: Additional instructions and material for this group activity can be found on the Instructor Resource Site and in *WileyPLUS*.

BYP14–3   In this group activity, you will complete a statement of changes in shareholders' equity and recreate the journal entries underlying those changes through your analysis of the incomplete information given.

Communication Activity

BYP14–4   Earnings per share is the most commonly cited financial ratio. Indeed, share prices rise and fall in reaction to a company's earnings per share. The price-earnings ratio is also published in many newspapers' stock market listings.

Instructions

Write a memo explaining why earnings per share and the price-earnings ratio are so important to investors. Explain how both ratios are calculated and how they relate to each other. Include in your memo an explanation of how to interpret a high or low price-earnings ratio. Also comment on why you think earnings per share is not required to be reported under ASPE.

Ethics Case

BYP14–5   Flambeau Corporation has paid 40 consecutive quarterly cash dividends (10 years' worth). Increasing competition over the last six months has greatly squeezed profit margins. With only enough cash to meet day-to-day operating needs, the president, Vince Ramsey, has decided that a stock dividend instead of a cash dividend should be declared. He tells Flambeau's financial vice-president, Janice Rahn, to issue a press release stating that the company is extending its consecutive dividend record with the issue of a 5% stock dividend. "Write the press release to convince the shareholders that the stock dividend is just as good as a cash dividend," Ramsey orders. "Just watch our share price rise when we announce the stock dividend. It must be a good thing if that happens."

Instructions

(a) Who are the stakeholders in this situation?

(b) Is there anything unethical about Ramsey's intentions or actions?

(c) As a shareholder, would you rather receive a cash dividend or a stock dividend? Why?

"All About You" Activity

BYP14–6   In the "All About You" feature, we learned about investing in shares of a company. You have recently inherited $10,000 and you are considering investing in **Canadian Tire Corporation, Limited**'s common shares and you want to learn more about the company.

Instructions

Go to Canadian Tire's website at http://corp.canadiantire.ca, click on "Investors," and then click on "Annual Reports." (*Note:* If you are not able to find the annual report on the Canadian Tire site—if, for example, Canadian Tire's shares are no longer publicly traded, then it may remove previously published annual reports and financial statements from its website—it is always available on SEDAR. See part [g] of this problem for instructions on how to use SEDAR.)

(a) Go to page 11 of the 2011 annual report, "Business at a Glance." What are Canadian Tire's four main business lines? How might this information help you with your investment decision?

(b) Go to page 37 of the 2011 annual report, which shows the table of contents of the "Management's Discussion and Analysis" (MD&A). According to the table of contents, what information is included in Canadian Tire's MD&A? How might the MD&A help you with your investment decision?

(c) Go to page 43 of the 2011 annual report, "4.0 Historical Performance Highlights." What were the cash dividends per share declared in 2011 and 2010? How might this information be helpful with your investment decision?

(d) Go to page 84 of the 2011 annual report, "Consolidated Statements of Income." What was Canadian Tire's basic earnings per share at December 31, 2011?

(e) On the "Investors" page of Canadian Tire's website, click on "Shareholders." What information is provided in this section of Canadian Tire's website? Go to "Stock Info" and click on "Historical Price Lookup" for the security "CTC.A." What was Canadian Tire's share price at December 30, 2011?

(f) Calculate Canadian Tire's price-earnings ratio at December 31, 2011.

(g) Go to www.sedar.com and click on "English." Click on "Company Profiles." Under "Public Companies," click on "C" and then scroll down and click on "Canadian Tire Corporation, Limited." Which stock exchange is Canadian Tire listed on? What is Canadian Tire's stock symbol? Who are Canadian Tire's auditors?

(h) On the Canadian Tire page you found in part (g), click on "View This Public Company's Documents." What types of documents are provided on this site?

(i) Go to www.google.ca/finance and search for Canadian Tire by inputting Canadian Tire's stock symbol into the search field. Scroll down and click on "More ratios from Thomson Reuters." What is Canadian Tire's most recent price-earnings ratio? What is the most recent industry average price-earnings ratio? Comment on Canadian Tire's price-earnings ratio compared with the industry average.

ANSWERS TO CHAPTER QUESTIONS

ANSWERS TO ACCOUNTING IN ACTION INSIGHT QUESTIONS

Across the Organization, p. 721

Q: If a company announces a reverse stock split, is this considered a positive or negative sign about the future of the company?

A: Although a company declares a reverse stock split because its share price is unacceptably low—and that happens when a company is not doing well—the reverse split doesn't change whether or not the company can improve its performance in the future. A reverse stock split, similar to a normal stock split, doesn't change anything about the company, because the total value of the company remains the same. Therefore, it can be argued that a reverse split shouldn't be considered either positive or negative.

All About You, p. 737

Q: If you were thinking of investing in a company, where might you find information about the company's dividend policy, its profitability, and its share price?

A: The company website will usually provide the company's annual report, which includes information about the company's performance and future plans in the Management Discussion and Analysis. As well, the annual report will include the financial statements, which provide information about the company's profitability and dividend policy. Some company websites also provide information on the share price. Another source is www.sedar.com, an official website that publishes public company annual reports that are filed with the Canadian Securities Administrators. As well, there are independent financial websites that provide share price information and comparable financial ratio information. Investors can also subscribe to services to obtain financial research reports on companies.

ANSWERS TO SELF-STUDY QUESTIONS

1. d   2. a   3. c   4. b   5. d   6. c   7. c   8. d   9. c   10. c

Remember to go back to the beginning of the chapter to check off your completed work!

CHAPTER FIFTEEN

NON-CURRENT LIABILITIES

 THE **NAVIGATOR**

- ☐ Understand *Concepts for Review*
- ☐ Read *Feature Story*
- ☐ Scan *Study Objectives*
- ☐ Read *Chapter Preview*
- ☐ Read text and answer *Before You Go On*
- ☐ Compare *IFRS and ASPE*
- ☐ Work *Demonstration Problems*
- ☐ Review *Summary of Study Objectives*
- ☐ Answer *Self-Study Questions*
- ☐ Complete assignments
- ☐ Go to *WileyPLUS* for practice and tutorials

CONCEPTS FOR **REVIEW**

Before studying this chapter, you should understand or, if necessary, review:

a. How to record adjusting entries for interest expense. (Ch. 3, pp. 125–126)

b. What a current liability is, and what a non-current liability is. (Ch. 4, pp. 188–189 and Ch. 10, pp. 526–530)

c. How to record entries for the issue of notes payable and related interest expense. (Ch. 10, pp. 527–528)

d. The fundamental qualitative characteristic of faithful representation. (Ch. 11, pp. 580–581)

e. How to calculate return on equity and earnings per share. (Ch. 13, p. 691 and Ch. 14, pp. 735–736)

DEBT ISSUE INJECTS POWER INTO ELECTRIC COMPANY

MONTREAL, Que.—Hydro-Québec generates, transmits, and distributes electricity for residents and businesses throughout the province of Quebec. This requires developing hydroelectric power to meet growing demand. The company conducts energy-related research and develops new generation, transmission, and distribution technologies. Its projects may include building hydroelectric facilities, refurbishing generating stations, adding transmission capacity, connecting communities to the grid, expanding energy interchanges with Ontario, the Atlantic Provinces, and the U.S. Northeast, or purchasing wind power from independent producers.

This type of development obviously requires a significant amount of capital. As Hydro-Québec's sole shareholder, the Quebec government guarantees most of its borrowings, which can be quite substantial.

The company raises funds by issuing bonds. For example, one issue was launched in July 2012 for $500 million. This debenture, which will mature on February 15, 2050, was issued at a premium price; that is, a price that is above its face value. The coupon rate was 5%, but the yield rate was 3.444%. Having a yield rate that is less than the coupon rate reduces the cost of borrowing for the company since the net proceeds will be slightly more than $500 million for each issue.

Hydro-Québec's decision to take on this long-term debt is simply "a question of cost," says Jean-Hugues Lafleur, Vice President, Financing, Treasury and Pension Fund. "[To have a rate] below 4% is a good opportunity to finance the company . . . Considering that inflation on a long-term basis is around 2% and being able to finance the company at below 4%, the real cost of the interest rate is something like 2%."

The funds will be used for Hydro-Québec's investment program and the refinancing of debt. "Our company has very long-term assets, so it just makes sense in terms of asset-liability management to issue long-term paper," Mr. Lafleur continues. "Most of our investment program is to build long-term facilities such as dams or generating stations. The depreciation periods for these assets can go up to 100 years."

For the last 10 years, Hydro-Québec's annual financing needs have been approximately $2.5 billion on average and have been met mainly on the Canadian market. Part of the company's financing and debt management strategy is to stagger debt maturities to maintain the stability of the annual financing program. Recent bond issues are added to others issued in previous years, all maturing on different dates. They are reported on the financial statements as liabilities and will be amortized over the duration of the debt at the yield to maturity rate, not the coupon rate.

The electricity company's investment and financing strategy has been effective. Credit rating agencies such as Moody's and Standard & Poor's all give Hydro-Québec an A rating or better.

The lead manager for Hydro-Québec's bond issue was National Bank Financial Inc., with RBC Dominion Securities Inc. and Scotia Capital Inc. acting as co-lead managers, and BMO Nesbitt Burns Inc., Casgrain & Company Limited, CIBC World Markets Inc., Desjardins Securities Inc., Laurentian Bank Securities Inc., and the Toronto Dominion Bank acting as other managers. With that type of backing, coupled with its success in debt management and research and investment, the Quebec utility will no doubt be able to continue to finance itself easily on the bond markets.

THE **NAVIGATOR**

>> STUDY **OBJECTIVES**

After studying this chapter, you should be able to:

1. Compare the impact of issuing debt instead of equity.

2. Account for bonds payable.

3. Account for instalment notes payable.

4. Account for leases.

5. Explain and illustrate the methods for the presentation and analysis of non-current liabilities.

THE **NAVIGATOR**

As you can see from the feature story, Hydro-Québec borrowed $500 million in July 2012 by issuing bonds. The bonds will mature on February 15, 2050, and the funds borrowed will be used to finance non-current assets such as dams or generating stations. The bonds are classified as non-current liabilities because they are obligations that are not due within the next year. In this chapter, we will explain the accounting for the major types of non-current liabilities reported on the balance sheet. These liabilities include bonds, instalment notes, and lease obligations.

The chapter is organized as follows:

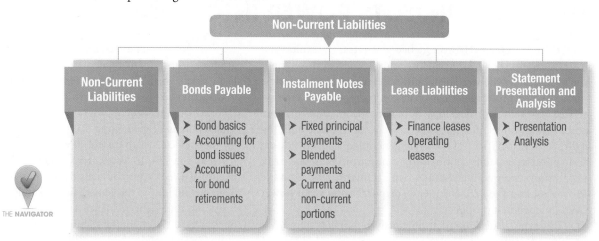

THE NAVIGATOR

Non-Current Liabilities

» STUDY OBJECTIVE 1

Compare the impact of issuing debt instead of equity.

Alternative terminology Non-current liabilities are also referred to as *long-term liabilities*.

You will recall from Chapter 10 that a current liability is an obligation (debt) that is expected to be settled within one year from the balance sheet date or during the company's normal operating cycle, whichever is longer. Debt that is not current is a **non-current liability**. Common examples of non-current liabilities include bonds payable, instalment notes payable, and finance leases. More specifically, non-current liabilities such as these are examples of financial instruments and are referred to as *financial liabilities* because there is a contract between two or more parties to pay cash in the future.

Just as people need money for long periods of time, so do companies. Sometimes, large corporations need much more money than the average bank can lend for certain types of projects, such as purchasing another company or constructing dams and generating stations as Hydro-Québec does. The solution is to raise money by issuing debt securities (such as bonds payable) or equity securities (such as common shares) to the investing public. In this way, thousands of investors each lend part of the capital that is needed. By issuing bonds, Hydro-Québec was able to raise $500 million in July 2012.

Whenever a company decides that it needs long-term financing, it must first decide if it should issue debt or equity. For a corporation that wants long-term financing, debt offers some advantages over equity, as shown in Illustration 15-1.

▶ **ILLUSTRATION** 15-1
Advantages of debt over equity financing

	1. Shareholder control is not affected. Debt holders (lenders) do not have voting rights, so the existing shareholders keep full control of the company.
	2. Income tax savings result. Interest expense is deductible for income tax purposes. Dividends are not.
	3. Earnings per share may be higher. Although interest expense reduces profit, earnings per share is often higher under debt financing because no additional common shares are issued.
	4. Return on equity may be higher. Although profit is lower, return on equity is often higher under debt financing because shareholders' equity is proportionately lower than profit.

To show the potential effect on earnings per share and return on equity, assume that Microsystems Inc. has 100,000 common shares and shareholders' equity of $2.5 million and is considering two plans for financing the construction of a new $5-million plant. Plan A is to use equity by issuing 200,000 common shares for $25 per share. Plan B is to use debt by issuing $5 million of 4% bonds payable. Once the new plant is built, Microsystems expects to earn an additional $1.5 million of profit before interest and income tax. The income tax rate is expected to be 30%.

The effects on earnings per share and return on equity for each plan are shown in Illustration 15-2.

▶ **ILLUSTRATION 15-2**
Comparison of effects
of issuing equity versus debt

	Plan A: Issue Equity	Plan B: Issue Debt
Profit before interest and income tax	$1,500,000	$1,500,000
Interest expense	0	200,000[6]
Profit before income tax	1,500,000	1,300,000
Income tax expense	450,000[1]	390,000[7]
Profit	$1,050,000	$ 910,000
Number of shares	300,000[2]	100,000
Earnings per share	$3.50[3]	$9.10[8]
Shareholders' equity	$8,550,000[4]	$ 3,410,000[9]
Return on equity	12%[5]	27%[10]

Calculations:
[1] 30% × $1,500,000 = $450,000
[2] 100,000 + 200,000 = 300,000
[3] $1,050,000 ÷ 300,000 = $3.50
[4] $2,500,000 + ($25 × 200,000) + $1,050,000 = $8,550,000
[5] $1,050,000 ÷ $8,550,000 = 12%
[6] $5,000,000 × 4% = $200,000
[7] 30% × $1,300,000 = $390,000
[8] $910,000 ÷ 100,000 = $9.10
[9] $2,500,000 + $910,000 = $3,410,000
[10] $910,000 ÷ $3,410,000 = 27%

Profit is $140,000 ($1,050,000 − $910,000) lower with long-term debt financing. However, when this profit is spread over 200,000 fewer shares, earnings per share jumps from $3.50 per share to $9.10 per share. We learned about earnings per share in Chapter 14. Earnings per share is calculated by dividing the profit available for the common shareholders by the weighted average number of shares. For this illustration, we have assumed that the shares were issued for the entire period.

After seeing the effect of debt on earnings per share, one might ask why companies do not rely exclusively on debt financing rather than equity financing. The answer is that debt is riskier than equity because interest must be paid regularly each period and the principal of the debt must be paid at maturity. If a company is unable to pay its interest or principal, creditors could force the company to sell its assets to repay its liabilities. In contrast, if equity is issued, a company is not required to pay dividends or repay the shareholders' investment.

Even if it is riskier, most companies still choose to issue debt. They do this because money that is borrowed increases earnings per share and it also produces a higher return on equity for the shareholders. You may have heard the saying about "using other people's money to make money." In general, debt can increase the return on equity if the company can borrow at one rate and invest the borrowed money in company operations that earn a higher rate. Borrowing at one rate and investing at a different rate is known as **financial leverage**. Financial leverage is said to be "positive" if the rate of return is higher than the rate of borrowing. It is said to be "negative" if the rate of return is lower than the rate of borrowing.

As we can see in Illustration 15-2, Microsystems' return on equity increases from 12% in Plan A, where equity financing is used, to 27% in Plan B, where debt financing is used. Even though profit is lower under debt financing, there is much less equity to spread the profit across. If equity financing is used, shareholders' equity is $8,550,000. If debt financing is used, shareholders' equity is only $3,410,000. In Chapter 13, we learned that the return on equity ratio is calculated by dividing profit by average shareholders' equity. For this illustration, we have assumed that the shareholders' equity is the average amount.

Each company must decide what the right mix of debt and equity is for its particular circumstances. There is a risk with debt financing, and the risk increases with the amount of debt a company has. The risk that goes with debt must be compared with the return that can be generated by using debt. As we have just seen, earnings per share and return on equity can improve with the use of debt. Later in this chapter, we will introduce some ratios that will help us evaluate whether a company has too much debt or if the debt is reasonable.

ACCOUNTING IN ACTION
ALL ABOUT YOU INSIGHT

Having enough cash to pay for education and living expenses while going to college or university is often a problem for students. One option is to use student loans. The federal, provincial, and territorial governments as well as private financial institutions all offer student loan programs.

Just like a business, a student can benefit from financial leverage, by borrowing for an education that will result in higher future earnings. Research shows that post-secondary graduates are more likely to be employed, and they earn more than those who do not continue their studies past high school. Over their working

life, a college graduate will earn $394,000 more than a high school graduate, while a bachelor's degree holder will earn $745,800 more, according to the former Canada Millennium Scholarship Foundation. Meanwhile, the Association of Universities and Colleges of Canada estimates that university graduates earn an average of $1.3 million more than high school graduates over their career.

While student loan programs offer interest-free financing while the student is in school, eventually they have to be paid. Just as with businesses, too much leverage can result in graduates struggling to make their loan payments.

Sources: Joseph Berger and Andrew Parkin, "The Value of a Degree: Education and Earnings in Canada," *The Price of Knowledge: Access and Student Finance in Canada,* vol. 4, chapter 1, 2009; Association of Universities and Colleges of Canada, "The Value of a University Degree," September 2010, available at www.aucc.ca/wp-content/uploads/2011/05/value-of-a-degree.pdf.

What should you consider in your decision about how much is appropriate to borrow for your education?

Action Plan

Alternative (a): Issue 100,000 common shares at a market price of $20 per share.

- Apply the tax rate to the increase in profit to determine the income tax expense.
- Deduct the income tax expense calculated from the increase in profit before interest and tax to determine the profit.
- Add the additional shares issued to the shares outstanding to determine the weighted average number of shares.
- Divide profit by the weighted average number of shares.

Alternative (b): Issue $2 million of 3% bonds at face value.

- Apply the interest rate on the bonds to the amount of bonds issued to determine the interest expense.
- Deduct the interest expense from the increase in profit before interest and tax to determine the profit before tax.
- Apply the tax rate to the profit before tax to determine income tax expense.
- Deduct the income tax expense calculated from the increase in profit before tax to determine the profit.
- Divide the profit by the number of shares outstanding.

 BEFORE YOU GO ON...

Do It

Nuens Ltd. is considering two alternatives to finance the purchase of new manufacturing equipment at the beginning of the year. The new equipment will increase profit before interest and tax by $3 million annually. The alternatives are:

(a) issue 100,000 shares at a market price of $20 per share, or

(b) issue $2 million of 3% bonds at face value.

Nuens has 400,000 common shares outstanding and $4 million of shareholders' equity. The tax rate is 30%.

Calculate the effects of each of the alternatives on earnings per share.

Solution

	Alternative (a) Issue shares	Alternative (b) Issue bonds
Profit before interest and tax	$3,000,000	$3,000,000
Interest expense ($2,000,000 × 3%)	0	60,000
Profit before income tax	3,000,000	2,940,000
Income tax expense	900,000	882,000
Profit	$2,100,000	$2,058,000
Number of shares	500,000	400,000
Earnings per share	$ 4.20	$ 5.15

Related exercise material: BE15–1 and E15–1.

THE **NAVIGATOR**

Bonds Payable

Like other kinds of non-current debt, **bonds** represent a promise to repay a principal amount at a specific maturity date. In addition, periodic interest is paid (normally semi-annually) at a specified rate on the principal amount. Bonds are also similar to shares: they are sold to, and purchased by, investors on organized securities exchanges. Bonds are usually sold in small denominations ($1,000 or multiples of $1,000). As a result, bonds attract many investors.

» **STUDY OBJECTIVE 2**

Account for bonds payable.

Bond credit-rating agencies help investors assess the risk level or creditworthiness of bonds. The highest-quality bonds are graded as AAA bonds, superior quality as AA, and good quality as A. Credit rating agencies all give Hydro-Québec an A rating or higher. The credit-rating scale goes down to C, and finally to the D or default category. Generally, bonds rated below BBB (or its equivalent) are called *junk bonds*. Junk bonds are considered speculative and have a higher risk of default (of not being repaid).

The Standard & Poor's credit rating agency also adds a plus or a minus to each grade category from A to C to distinguish credit risk even more. Hydro-Québec's bonds were rated A+ by Standard & Poor's, which indicates that the bonds are of good quality and have a low credit risk.

Interest rates are linked to credit ratings. Normally, the higher the credit rating, the lower the interest rate. For example, banks might pay 1% or 2% on a term deposit, because there is almost no risk. On the other hand, a corporate bond rated AAA might pay 3% or 4%. A corporate bond rated BBB will likely have to pay a higher rate because the risk is higher. Interest rates vary with risk, but they also vary with duration, the type of bond, the general state of the economy, and many other factors. So, although some interest rates have been given here as examples, they may be quite different right now in practice. Hydro-Québec took advantage of low interest rates in July 2012 and issued bonds at interest rates below 4%.

There are many different kinds of bonds. Most bonds are **term bonds**, which mature at a single specified future date. Large corporations like Hydro Quebec issue **debentures**, which are unsecured bonds that are issued against the company's general credit. Some companies issue **redeemable bonds** that can be retired (redeemed) at a stated dollar amount at the option of the company before they mature.

BOND BASICS

In the next few sections, we will look at some basic questions about bonds, including how they are issued and traded. We will also show you how to calculate the price the bonds will trade at. This is referred to as the **market value of the bonds**.

Issuing Procedures

In a corporation, approval by the board of directors is required before bonds can be issued. In authorizing the bond issue, the board of directors must state the number of bonds to be authorized (the total number of bonds the company is allowed to sell), the total face value, the contractual interest rate, and the maturity date. As happens with issues of share capital, the total number of bonds authorized is often more than the number of bonds the company plans to issue immediately. This is done intentionally to help ensure that the company will have the flexibility it needs to meet future cash requirements by selling more bonds.

The **face value** of the bonds is the amount that the company (known as the *issuer*) must pay at the maturity date. The **contractual interest rate** is the rate that is used to determine the amount of interest the borrower pays and the investor receives. Usually, the contractual rate is stated as an annual rate and interest is paid semi-annually. For example, the contractual interest rate on Hydro-Québec's bonds is 5% a year, but interest is paid semi-annually at a rate of 2.5% (5% $\times$ $^6/_{12}$). The **maturity date** is the date when the final payment is due to the investor from the company. The maturity date for Hydro-Québec's bonds is February 15, 2050. All of these details are included in a **bond certificate**, which is issued to investors to provide evidence of an investor's credit claim against the company.

Alternative terminology Face value is also called *par value* and *maturity value*. The contractual interest rate is commonly known as the *coupon interest rate* or *stated interest rate*.

Bond Trading

Corporate bonds, like share capital, are traded on organized securities exchanges. Thus, bondholders have the opportunity to convert their bonds into cash at any time by selling the bonds at the current market price. Illustration 15-3 shows one example of bond prices and yields, which are published daily in the financial press:

▶ **ILLUSTRATION 15-3**
Bond price and yield

Issuer	Coupon	Coupon Frequency	Maturity Date	Price	Yield
Bell CDA	6.100	S	2035-Mar-16	115.44	4.95

This bond listing for Bell Canada (Bell CDA) bonds indicates that these bonds have a contractual (coupon) interest rate of 6.1% per year and a semi-annual (S) interest payment (coupon frequency). This means Bell will pay each $1,000 bondholder interest of $30.50 ($1,000 × 6.1% × $^{6}/_{12}$) twice a year. The bonds mature on March 16, 2035.

Bond prices are quoted as a percentage of the bonds' face value, which is usually $1,000. In this particular case, the price of 115.44 means $1,154.40 ($1,000 × 115.44%) was the selling price, or market value, of each $1,000 bond on the date of the above listing. The yield, or market interest rate, on the bonds is 4.95% on the date of the above listing. The **market interest rate** is the rate that investors demand for lending their money. Note that the reason these bonds are currently selling at a premium is because the market interest rate is lower than the contractual interest rate. We will learn more about market interest rates and bond premiums in the next section.

Alternative terminology **Market interest rate or yield is also referred to as the *effective rate*.**

As is the case with share transactions, transactions between a bondholder and other investors are not journalized by the issuing corporation. For example, if Vinod Thakkar sells his Bell Canada bonds to Julie Tarrel, the transaction is between Vinod and Julie. There is no impact on the issuer's—Bell Canada's—financial position. Bell Canada (or its trustee) will change the name of the bondholder in its records. But the issuer—Bell Canada—only makes journal entries when it issues or buys back bonds and pays interest.

Determining the Market Value of Bonds

If you were an investor wanting to purchase a bond, how would you determine how much to pay? To be more specific, assume that Candlestick Inc. issues a zero-interest bond (pays no interest) with a face value of $1 million due in five years. For this bond, the only cash you receive is $1 million at the end of five years. Would you pay $1 million for this bond? We hope not! One million dollars received five years from now is not the same as $1 million received today.

The reason you should not pay $1 million relates to the time value of money. If you had $1 million today, you could invest it. From that investment, you would earn interest. At the end of five years, your investment would be worth much more than $1 million. If someone were to pay you $1 million five years from now, you would want to find out its equivalent today. In other words, you would want to determine how much must be invested today at current interest rates to have $1 million in five years. That amount—what must be invested today at a specific rate of interest over a specific amount of time—is called the **present value**.

The present value of a bond is the price or market value at which it should sell in the marketplace. Market value (present value), therefore, depends on the three factors: (1) the dollar amounts to be received in the future, (2) the length of time until the amounts are received, and (3) the market interest rate. The process of finding the present value is called *discounting the future amounts*.

To illustrate, assume that on January 1, 2014, Candlestick issues $1 million of 5% bonds due in five years, with interest payable semi-annually. The purchaser of the bonds would receive two cash inflows: (1) the principal of $1 million to be paid at maturity, and (2) 10 interest payments of $25,000 ($1,000,000 × 5% × $^{6}/_{12}$) received semi-annually over the term of the bonds. Illustration 15-4 shows the time diagram for both cash flows.

▶ **ILLUSTRATION 15-4**
Time diagram of bond cash flows

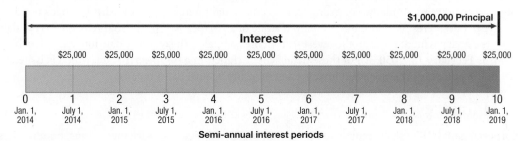

Note that there is no interest payment on January 1, 2014—time period 0—because the bonds have not been outstanding for any period of time, so no interest has been incurred.

The current market value of a bond is equal to the present value of all the future cash flows promised by the bond. A bond's future cash flows are the face value to be repaid at maturity and the periodic interest payments. The present value calculation of Candlestick's bonds is shown below. We will identify the variables and go through the procedures used to calculate the present value. As you read through these procedures, you should refer to this calculation.

Present value of $1 million (face value) received in 10 periods	
$1,000,000 × 0.78120 ($n = 10$, $i = 2.5\%$)[1]	$ 781,200
Present value of $25,000 (interest payments) received for each of 10 periods	
$25,000 × 8.75206 ($n = 10$, $i = 2.5\%$)	218,800
Present value (current market price) of bonds	**$1,000,000**

[1] When n = number of interest periods and i = interest rate.

There are standard tables available to determine the present value factors that are used (e.g., 0.78120 and 8.75206). We have reproduced these tables in Appendix PV—Present Value Concepts at the end of this book and you should look at them as you read the following procedures for calculating the present value of a bond.

1. **Calculating the present value of the face value of the bond:** Use Table PV-1 (the present value of 1) to determine the correct factor to use to calculate the present value of the face value, which is a single payment, paid at maturity. The appropriate factor is found at the intersection of the number of periods (n) and the interest rate (i).

   When interest is paid semi-annually, the number of periods, (n), will be double the number of years to maturity and the interest rate, (i), will be half of the annual market interest rate. In the Candlestick example, the five years to maturity means that there are 10 semi-annual interest periods [$n = 10$ or (5×2)]. The 5% annual market interest rate means that there is a 2.5% semi-annual market rate [$i = 2.5\%$ or $(5\% \times \frac{1}{12})$]. In the Candlestick example, the present value factor to be used for $n = 10$ and $i = 2.5\%$ is 0.78120.

2. **Calculating the present value of the interest payments:** Use Table PV-2 (the present value of an annuity of 1) to calculate the present value of the interest, which is paid every six months. In Candlestick's case, interest of $25,000 ($1,000,000 × 5% × $\frac{6}{12}$) is paid every six months. The present value factor is found using the same number of periods (n) and interest rate (i) as is used to calculate the present value of the principal. In Candlestick's case, the present value factor to be used to calculate the present value of the interest payments for $n = 10$ and $i = 2.5\%$ is 8.75206.

Note that the bonds' face value and contractual interest rate are always used to calculate the interest payment. While the contractual interest rate is used to determine the interest payment, the market interest rate is always used to determine the present value. In the Candlestick example, the contractual rate and the market rate are the same. When these two rates are the same, the present value (market value) of the bonds equals the face value.

The present value can also be determined mathematically using a financial calculator or spreadsheet program. The same variables as described above are used. The present value of the bond can be calculated in one calculation, rather than calculating the present value of the face value and the interest separately. The inputs (variables) required to calculate present value are the **future value** (FV), which is the face amount to be paid at maturity; the market rate of interest per interest period (i); the number of interest periods (n); and the interest payment (PMT). In the Candlestick example, the future value (FV) is $1 million, the interest rate (i) is 2.5%, the number of interest periods (n) is 10, and the payment (PMT) is $25,000.

The specific methodology and required settings differ for different financial calculators, so it is important to read the manual before using it to calculate present values. However, the inputs and the concepts are the same for all calculators. You should be aware that the present value amounts will most likely differ by a few dollars from those calculated using present value tables. This is because the factors in the present value tables are rounded to five decimal places.

There is further discussion of present value concepts in Appendix PV at the end of this book.

Discount or Premium on Bonds

The present value illustration above assumed that the market interest rate and the contractual interest rate paid on the bonds were the same. However, this is rarely the case because market interest rates change daily. They are influenced by the type of bond issued, the state of the economy, current industry conditions, and the company's performance. The market and contractual interest rates are often quite different. As a result, bonds sell below or above face value.

To illustrate, suppose that investors have one of two options: (1) purchase bonds that have just been issued with a contractual interest rate of 6%, or (2) purchase bonds issued at an earlier date with a lower contractual interest rate of 5%. If the bonds are of equal risk, investors will choose the 6% investment. To make the investments equal, investors will therefore demand a rate of interest higher than the 5% contractual interest rate provided in option 2. But investors cannot change the contractual interest rate. What they can do, instead, is pay less than the face value for the bonds. By paying less for the bonds, investors can effectively get the market interest rate of 6%. In these cases, bonds sell at a **discount**.

On the other hand, the market interest rate may be lower than the contractual interest rate. In that case, investors will have to pay more than face value for the bonds. That is, if the market interest rate is 4% and the contractual interest rate is 5%, the issuer will require more funds from the investors. In these cases, bonds sell at a **premium**. You will recall from the feature story that Hydro-Québec issued bonds with a contractual interest rate of 5% at a market rate of interest of 3.444%. Hydro-Québec sold these bonds at a premium because the market interest rate was lower than the contractual interest rate. The relationship between bond contractual interest rates and market interest rates, and the resultant selling price, is shown in Illustration 15-5.

▸ **ILLUSTRATION 15-5**
Interest rates and bond prices

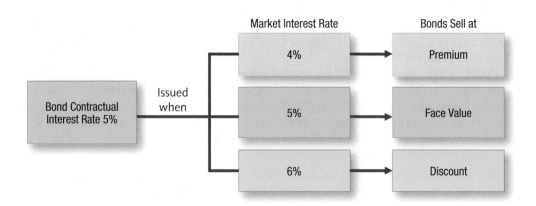

As was the case with Hydro-Québec's bond issue described in the feature story, issuing bonds at an amount different from face value is quite common. You recall that the board of directors is required to authorize a bond issue and that this authorization includes establishing the contractual interest rate. As mentioned earlier, the board may authorize more than they intend to issue immediately so that the company has flexibility to issue more bonds at later date. The board will establish a contractual interest rate based on the market rate when the bonds are authorized. However, by the time a company decides to issue the bonds, prints the bond certificates, and markets the bonds, it will be a coincidence if the market rate and the contractual rate are the same. Thus, the sale of bonds at a discount does not mean that the issuer's financial strength is questionable. Nor does the sale of bonds at a premium indicate superior financial strength. After the bonds are issued, the difference between the contractual rate and the market interest rate will change as the market interest rate fluctuates. However, the fluctuations in the market interest rate after the bonds are issued do not have an impact on the accounting for the bond issue.

ACCOUNTING FOR BOND ISSUES

Bonds can be issued at face value, below face value (at a discount), or above face value (at a premium).

Issuing Bonds at Face Value

To illustrate the accounting for bonds, let's continue the example discussed in the last section, where Candlestick Inc. issues five-year, 5%, $1-million bonds on January 1, 2014, to yield a market interest rate of 5%. These bonds are issued at 100 (100% of face value). The bonds' market value is equal to the face value.

The entry to record the sale is as follows:

Jan.	1	Cash	1,000,000	
		Bonds Payable		1,000,000
		To record sale of bonds at face value.		

A = L + SE
+1,000,000 +1,000,000
↑ Cash flows: +1,000,000

These bonds payable are reported at **amortized cost** in the non-current liabilities section of the balance sheet because the maturity date (January 1, 2019) is more than one year away. Amortized cost is the face value of the bonds minus any unamortized discount or plus any unamortized premium. In this example, because the bonds were issued at face value, the amortized cost is $1 million, the face value of the bonds.

Over the term (life) of the bonds, entries are required for bond interest. Interest is payable semi-annually on January 1 and July 1 on the bonds described above. As shown earlier, the semi-annual **interest payment** is determined using the face value of the bonds and the contractual interest rate. In the Candlestick bond example, the interest payment is $25,000 ($1,000,000 [face value] × 5% [contractual rate] × $^{6}/_{12}$).

The **effective-interest method** is used to calculate **interest expense** so that the expense reflects the actual cost of borrowing. The effective-interest method uses the market interest rate, at the date the bonds were issued, applied to the amortized cost of the bonds payable to determine interest expense. On July 1, 2014, the first interest payment date, Candlestick will record interest expense of $25,000 ($1,000,000 [amortized cost] × 5% [market rate] × $^{6}/_{12}$). In this example, the contractual interest rate is equal to the market rate, so the interest expense is equal to the interest payment. The entry for the interest payment, assuming no previous accrual of interest, is:

July	1	Interest Expense	25,000	
		Cash		25,000
		To record payment of bond interest.		

A = L + SE
−25,000 −25,000
↓ Cash flows: −25,000

At December 31, Candlestick's year end, an adjusting entry is needed to recognize the $25,000 of interest expense incurred since July 1. The entry is as follows:

Dec.	31	Interest Expense	25,000	
		Interest Payable		25,000
		To accrue bond interest.		

A = L + SE
+25,000 −25,000
Cash flows: no effect

Interest payable is classified as a current liability because it is scheduled for payment within the next year (in fact, it is due the next day in this case). When the interest is paid on January 1, 2015, Interest Payable is debited and Cash is credited for $25,000.

Issuing Bonds at a Discount

To illustrate the issue of bonds at a discount (below face value), assume that on January 1, 2014, the Candlestick bonds are issued to yield a market interest rate of 6% rather than 5%, as we assumed in the previous section.

Whether using the present value tables, a financial calculator, or a spreadsheet program, the following variables are used to determine the selling price of the bonds:

Future value (FV) = $1,000,000
Number of semi-annual interest periods (n) = 10 (5 years × 2)
Semi-annual market interest rate (i) = 3% (6% annual market rate × ½)
Interest payments (PMT) = $25,000 ($1,000,000 × 5% [contractual rate] × ½)

Remember to always use the market interest rate to determine the present value factor (i) and the contractual interest rate to determine the interest payment. Using the present value tables in Appendix PV, we can determine that the bonds will sell for $957,345 (95.7345% of face value):

Present value of $1 million received in 10 periods $1,000,000 × 0.74409 ($n$ = 10, i = 3%)	$744,090
Present value of $25,000 received for each of 10 periods $25,000 × 8.53020 ($n$ = 10, i = 3%)	213,255
Present value (market price) of bonds	$957,345

The issue price of $957,345 results in a bond discount of $42,655 ($1,000,000 − $957,345). The entry to record the bond issue is as follows:

A	=	L	+	SE
+957,345		+957,345		

↑ Cash flows: +957,345

Jan.	1	Cash	957,345	
		Bonds Payable		957,345
		To record sale of bonds at a discount.		

You will recall that bonds payable are reported at amortized cost. At the date the bonds are issued, the issue price is equal to amortized cost. In this example, the issue cost of $957,345 is equal to the face value of $1 million less the unamortized discount of $42,655, which, by definition, is the amortized cost.

The issue of bonds at a discount (below face value) will result in a total cost of borrowing that is higher than the bond interest paid. That is, the issuing corporation must pay not only the contractual interest rate over the term of the bonds, but it must also repay the face value (rather than the issue price) at maturity. Candlestick must repay $1 million at maturity even though it only received $957,345 from the sale of the bonds. Therefore, the difference between the issue price ($957,345) and the face value ($1,000,000) of the bonds—the discount ($42,655)—is an additional cost of borrowing.

Amortizing the Discount. The total cost of borrowing—the interest payments and bond discount—must be allocated to interest expense over the life of the bonds. The allocation of the bond discount over the life of the bonds is called **amortizing the discount**. The amortization of the discount increases the amount of interest expense that is reported each period. The higher interest expense reflects the actual cost of borrowing. Amortizing the discount over the life of the bonds is an example of ensuring that accounting information faithfully represents the economic reality of the events—an accounting concept we learned about in Chapter 11.

Recall that the effective-interest method is used to calculate the interest expense on all financial liabilities, such as bonds payable. This method is also used to calculate the amortization of the bond discount (and premiums, which will be discussed in the next section) each period. There are three steps required to calculate the amortization amount using the effective-interest method:

1. **Interest expense:** Calculate interest expense by multiplying the amortized cost of the bonds at the beginning of the interest period by the market (effective) interest rate.
2. **Interest paid (or accrued):** Calculate the bond interest paid by multiplying the face value of the bonds by the contractual interest rate.
3. **Amortization amount:** The amortization amount is the difference between the amounts calculated in steps (1) and (2).

These steps are shown in Illustration 15-6.

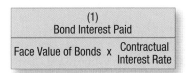

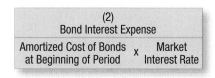

▶ **ILLUSTRATION 15-6**
Calculation of
amortization using the
effective-interest method

For Candlestick, interest expense for the first period is $28,720, calculated by multiplying the amortized cost of the bonds at the beginning of the period by the market interest rate ($957,345 × 6% × 6/12). The interest payment, $25,000, is calculated by multiplying the bonds' face value by the contractual interest rate ($1,000,000 × 5% × 6/12). The discount amortization is $3,720, the difference between the interest expense and the interest paid ($28,720 − $25,000).

We record the interest expense, amortization of the discount, and payment of interest on the first interest payment date as follows:

July 1	Interest Expense ($957,345 × 6% × 6/12)	28,720	
	Cash ($1,000,000 × 5% × 6/12)		25,000
	Bonds Payable ($28,720 − $25,000)		3,720
	To record payment of bond interest and amortization of bond discount.		

A = L + SE
−25,000 +3,720 −28,720

↓ Cash flows: −25,000

Note that the amortization of the bond discount is recorded as an increase (credit) in the Bonds Payable account, which reduces the bond discount. Also note that, as previously explained, the interest expense includes both the interest payment ($25,000) and the bond discount amortization ($3,720). Remember that issuing a bond at a discount increases the cost of borrowing above the contractual interest rate.

At the second interest period, the bond's amortized cost is now $961,065 ($957,345 + 3,720). The amortized cost will continue to increase by the amount of the discount amortization until at the maturity date the bonds' amortized cost equals their face value—the amount the company is required to pay the bondholders.

To calculate the interest expense for the second interest period, we multiply the amortized cost of the bonds by the market interest rate to arrive at $28,832 ($961,065 × 6% × 6/12). The interest payment is unchanged at $25,000. The amortization is $3,832, the difference between the interest expense and the interest paid ($28,832 − $25,000).

At Candlestick's year end, the following adjusting entry is made for the second interest period:

Dec. 31	Interest Expense ($961,065 × 6% × 6/12)	28,832	
	Interest Payable ($1,000,000 × 5% × 6/12)		25,000
	Bonds Payable ($28,832 − $25,000)		3,832
	To record accrual of bond interest and amortization of bond discount.		

A = L + SE
+3,832 −28,832
+25,000

Cash flows: no effect

Note that Interest Payable is credited rather than Cash because the next interest payment date is January 1. On January 1, the Interest Payable account will be debited and the Cash account credited.

To make it easier to calculate the interest expense and the discount amortization, a bond discount amortization schedule can be prepared first. Then the journal entries to record interest expense can be recorded using the information in the schedule. The bond discount amortization schedule for Candlestick is shown in Illustration 15-7. For simplicity, amounts have been rounded to the nearest dollar in this schedule.

Semi-Annual Interest Period	(A) Interest Payment ($1,000,000 × 5% × $^{6}/_{12}$)	(B) Interest Expense (D × 6% × $^{6}/_{12}$)	(C) Discount Amortization (B − A)	(D) Bond Amortized Cost (D + C)
Issue date (Jan. 1, 2014)				$ 957,345
1 (July 1)	$ 25,000	$ 28,720	$ 3,720	961,065
2 (Jan. 1, 2015)	25,000	28,832	3,832	964,897
3 (July 1)	25,000	28,947	3,947	968,844
4 (Jan. 1, 2016)	25,000	29,065	4,065	972,909
5 (July 1)	25,000	29,187	4,187	977,096
6 (Jan. 1, 2017)	25,000	29,313	4,313	981,409
7 (July 1)	25,000	29,442	4,442	985,851
8 (Jan. 1, 2018)	25,000	29,576	4,576	990,427
9 (July 1)	25,000	29,713	4,713	995,140
10 (Jan. 1, 2019)	25,000	29,860[1]	4,860	1,000,000
	$250,000	$292,655	$42,655	

[1] $6 difference due to rounding.

We have highlighted periods 1 and 2 in columns A, B, and C in the amortization schedule shown in Illustration 15-7 because these three columns give the numbers for each period's journal entries. You should compare the information in the schedule for periods 1 and 2, highlighted in red, with the July 1 and December 31, 2014, journal entries previously recorded.

- Column A gives the amount of the credit to Cash (or Interest Payable). Note that the amounts in this column stay the same because the face value of the bonds ($1,000,000) and the semi-annual contractual interest rate (2.5%) are the same each period.
- Column B shows the debit to Interest Expense. It is calculated by multiplying the bond's amortized cost at the beginning of the period by the semi-annual market interest rate. Note that while the semi-annual market interest rate (3%) stays constant each interest period, the interest expense increases because the bond's amortized cost increases.
- Column C is the credit to Bonds Payable. It is the amortization of the bond discount, which is the difference between the interest expense and the interest payment. The amounts in this column increase throughout the amortization period because the interest expense increases. Notice that the total of this column—$42,655—is equal to the discount when the bond was issued on January 1, 2014.
- Column D is the bond's amortized cost. Note that the amortized cost of the bonds increases by the discount amortization amount each period until it reaches the face value of $1 million at the end of period 10 (January 1, 2019), when the discount is fully amortized. This is because Candlestick must repay $1 million at maturity even though it received only $957,345 from the sale of the bonds on January 1, 2014.

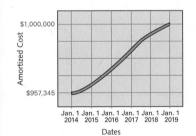

Issuing Bonds at a Premium

To illustrate the issue of bonds at a premium (above face value), assume instead that on January 1, 2014, Candlestick's five-year, 5% bonds are issued to yield a market interest rate of 4%. When the market interest rate is lower than the contractual interest rate, investors will pay a premium for the bonds. Receiving a premium will result in a cost of borrowing of 4%.

The variables used to determine the issue price of the bonds are:

Future value (FV) = $1,000,000
Number of semi-annual interest periods (n) = 10 (5 years × 2)
Semi-annual market interest rate (i) = 2% (4% annual market interest rate × $^{1}/_{12}$)
Semi-annual interest payments (PMT) = $25,000 ($1,000,000 × 5% [contractual rate] × $^{1}/_{12}$)

Note that the only variable that has changed from the previous example is the market interest rate. Using the present value tables in Appendix PV, we determine that the bonds will sell for $1,044,915 as follows:

Present value of $1 million received in 10 periods	
$1,000,000 \times 0.82035$ ($n = 10$, $i = 2$)	\$ 820,350
Present value of $25,000 received for each of 10 periods	
$25,000 \times 8.98259$ ($n = 10$, $i = 2$)	224,565
Present value (market price) of bonds (104.4915% of face value)	\$1,044,915

This issue price results in a premium of $44,915 ($1,044,915 − $1,000,000). The entry to record the sale would be as follows:

Jan. 1	Cash		1,044,915	
	Bonds Payable			1,044,915
	To record sale of bonds at a premium.			

A = L + SE
+1,044,915 +1,044,915

↑ Cash flows: +1,044,915

As previously stated, bonds are reported at amortized cost, which is equal to the issue price at the date the bonds are issued. In this example, the bonds' amortized cost is $1,044,915: the face value of the bonds of $1 million plus the unamortized premium of $44,915.

The issue of bonds above face value causes the total cost of borrowing to be less than the bond interest paid. The bond premium is considered a reduction in the cost of borrowing. Candlestick will repay only $1 million at maturity, even though it received $1,044,915 from the sale of the bonds.

Amortizing the Premium. The total cost of borrowing—the interest payments less the bond premium—must be allocated to interest expense over the life of the bonds. The allocation of the bond premium over the life of the bonds is called **amortizing the premium**. The amortization of the premium reduces the amount of interest expense that is recorded each period.

The same method—the effective-interest method—used to allocate bond discounts is also used to allocate bond premiums to interest expense. For the first interest period, the interest expense is $20,898, calculated by multiplying the bonds' carrying amount by the market interest rate ($1,044,915 \times 4\% \times {}^{6}/_{12}$). The interest payment, $25,000, is the same as for the bonds issued at discount as it is calculated by multiplying the bonds' face value by the contractual interest rate ($1,000,000 \times 5\% \times {}^{6}/_{12}$). The premium amortization is then calculated as the difference between the interest paid and the interest expense ($25,000 − $20,898 = $4,102).

The entry on the first interest payment date is as follows:

July 1	Interest Expense ($1,044,915 \times 4\% \times {}^{6}/_{12}$)		20,898	
	Bonds Payable ($25,000 − $20,898)		4,102	
	Cash ($1,000,000 \times 5\% \times {}^{6}/_{12}$)			25,000
	To record payment of bond interest and amortization			
	of bond premium.			

A = L + SE
−25,000 −4,102 −20,898

↓ Cash flows: −25,000

Note that the amortization of the bond premium is recorded as a decrease (debit) in the Bonds Payable account, which reduces the bond premium, and that the interest expense is less than the interest payment. This reflects the reduced cost of borrowing.

For the second interest period, the bonds' amortized cost is now $1,040,813 ($1,044,915 − 4,102). The amortized cost will continue to decrease by the amount of the premium amortization until at the maturity date, the bonds' amortized cost equals their face value—the amount the company is required to pay the bondholders.

To calculate the interest expense for the second interest period, we multiply the amortized cost of the bonds by the market interest rate to arrive at $20,816 ($1,040,813 \times 4\% \times {}^{6}/_{12}$). The interest payment is unchanged at $25,000. As before, the amortization is the difference between the interest paid and the interest expense ($25,000 − 20,816 = $4,184).

For the second interest period, at Candlestick's year end, the following adjusting entry is made:

Dec. 31	Interest Expense ($1,040,813 \times 4\% \times {}^{6}/_{12}$)		20,816	
	Bonds Payable ($25,000 − 20,816)		4,184	
	Interest Payable ($1,000,000 \times 5\% \times {}^{6}/_{12}$)			25,000
	To record accrual of bond interest and amortization			
	of bond premium.			

A = L + SE
−4,184 −20,816
+25,000

Cash flows: no effect

As in the case where bonds are issued at a discount, a bond premium amortization schedule can be prepared to make it easier to calculate interest expense and amortization of the premium. The bond premium amortization schedule is shown in Illustration 15-8. Figures have been rounded to the nearest dollar for simplicity.

▶ **ILLUSTRATION 15-8**
Bond premium amortization schedule—effective-interest method

Semi-Annual Interest Period	(A) Interest Payment ($1,000,000 × 5% × $^{6}/_{12}$)	(B) Interest Expense (D × 4% × $^{6}/_{12}$)	(C) Premium Amortization (A − B)	(D) Bond Amortized Cost (D − C)
Issue date (Jan. 1, 2014)				$1,044,915
1 (July 1)	$ 25,000	$ 20,898	$4,102	1,040,813
2 (Jan. 1, 2015)	25,000	20,816	4,184	1,036,629
3 (July 1)	25,000	20,733	4,267	1,032,362
4 (Jan. 1, 2016)	25,000	20,647	4,353	1,028,009
5 (July 1)	25,000	20,560	4,440	1,023,569
6 (Jan. 1, 2017)	25,000	20,471	4,529	1,019,040
7 (July 1)	25,000	20,381	4,619	1,014,421
8 (Jan. 1, 2018)	25,000	20,288	4,712	1,009,709
9 (July 1)	25,000	20,194	4,806	1,004,903
10 (Jan. 1, 2019)	25,000	20,097[1]	4,903	1,000,000
	$250,000	$205,085	$44,915	

[1]$1 difference due to rounding.

Recall from Illustration 15-7 that columns A, B, and C in the amortization schedule give the numbers for each period's journal entries. You should compare the information, highlighted in red, in the schedule for periods 1 and 2 with the July 1 and December 31, 2014, journal entries previously recorded.

- Column A gives the amount of the credit to Cash (or Interest Payable). The amounts in this column stay the same because the face value of the bonds and the semi-annual contractual interest rate are the same each period.
- Column B shows the debit to Interest Expense. It is calculated by multiplying the bonds' amortized cost at the beginning of the period by the semi-annual market interest rate. Note that while the semi-annual market interest rate (2%) stays constant each interest period, the interest expense decreases because the bond's amortized cost decreases.
- Column C is the debit to Bonds Payable. It is the difference between the interest payment and the interest expense. The amounts in this column increase throughout the amortization period because the interest expense decreases as the amortized cost of the bonds decreases. Notice that the total of this column—$44,915—is equal to the premium when the bond was issued on January 1, 2014.
- Column D is the bond's amortized cost. Note that the amortized cost of the bonds decreases by the premium amortization amount each period until it reaches the face value of $1 million at the end of period 10 (January 1, 2019). Note that even though Candlestick received $1,044,915 from the sale of the bonds on January 1, 2014, it is only required to pay $1 million at maturity.

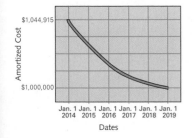

Comparison of Issuing Bonds at a Discount Versus at a Premium

Illustration 15-9 summarizes some of the differences between issuing a bond at a discount and a premium under the effective-interest method of amortization.

	Bond Issued at a Discount	Bond Issued at a Premium
Market interest rate	Greater than the contractual interest rate	Less than the contractual interest rate
Periodic interest payment	Same each period	Same each period
Periodic interest expense	Greater than the interest payment	Less than the interest payment
	Increases each period	Decreases each period
Bond's amortized cost	Increases to face value at maturity	Decreases to face value at maturity

▶ ILLUSTRATION 15-9
Comparison of the effects of issuing bonds at a discount or a premium

The effective-interest method is required for companies reporting under IFRS. Private companies reporting under ASPE can choose to use either the effective-interest method or other methods if they do not materially differ from the effective-interest method. Because the use of the effective-interest method is prevalent, we focus on this method in this text.

ACCOUNTING FOR BOND RETIREMENTS

Bonds may be retired either (1) when they mature, or (2) when the issuing corporation purchases them from the bondholders on the open market before they mature. Some bonds have special redemption provisions that allow them to be retired before they mature. As we learned earlier in this chapter, redeemable bonds can be retired at a stated dollar amount at the option of the company.

The retirement of bonds at and before maturity are explained in the following sections.

Redeeming Bonds at Maturity

Regardless of the issue price of bonds, the amortized cost of the bonds at maturity will equal their face value. By the time the bonds mature, any discount or premium will be fully amortized.

Assuming that the interest for the last interest period has been paid and recorded, the entry to record the redemption of the Candlestick bonds at maturity, January 1, 2019, is as follows:

Jan. 1	Bonds Payable	1,000,000	
	Cash		1,000,000
	To record redemption of bonds at maturity.		

A = L + SE
−1,000,000 −1,000,000

↓ Cash flows: −1,000,000

Because the amortized cost of the bonds equals the face value at maturity, there is no gain or loss.

Redeeming Bonds before Maturity

Why would a company want to have the option to retire its bonds early? If interest rates drop, it can be a good idea financially to retire the bond issue and replace it with a new bond issue at a lower interest rate. Or, a company may become financially able to repay its debt earlier than expected. When a company purchases non-redeemable bonds on the open market, it pays the going market price. If the bonds are redeemable, the company will pay the bondholders an amount that was specified at the time of issue, known as the **redemption price**. To make the bonds more attractive to investors, the redemption price is usually a few percentage points above the face value.

Alternative terminology Redemption price is also referred to as the *call price.*

If the bonds are redeemed between semi-annual interest payment dates, it will be necessary to pay the required interest and record the related amortization of any premiums or discounts. To record the redemption of bonds, it is necessary to (1) eliminate the amortized cost of the bonds (balance in Bonds Payable account), (2) record the cash paid, and (3) recognize the gain or loss on redemption.

A loss on redemption is recorded if the cash paid is more than the amortized cost of the bonds. There is a gain on redemption when the cash paid is less than the amortized cost of the bonds. This is shown in Illustration 15-10.

▶**ILLUSTRATION 15-10**
Loss and gain on
redemption of bonds

To illustrate, assume that Candlestick sells its bonds that were issued at a premium as described in the last section. It retires its bonds at 101 at the end of the fourth year (eighth period) after paying the semi-annual interest. The premium amortization schedule in Illustration 15-8 shows that the bonds' amortized cost at the redemption date (January 1, 2018) is $1,009,709. The entry to record the redemption on January 1, 2018 (end of the eighth interest period) is:

A	=	L	+	SE
−1,010,000		−1,009,709		−291

↓ Cash flows: −1,010,000

Jan.	1	Bonds Payable	1,009,709	
		Loss on Bond Redemption	291	
		Cash ($1,000,000 × 101%)		1,010,000
		To record redemption of bonds at 101.		

There is a loss on the bond redemption because Candlestick paid $1,010,000—$291 more to redeem the bonds than the amortized cost of the bonds of $1,009,709.

Losses and gains on bond redemption are reported separately in the income statement as other expenses or other revenues similar to interest expense.

BEFORE YOU GO ON...

Do It

Action Plan
- Identify the key inputs required to determine present value, whether using tables or a financial calculator. Remember to double the number of periods and halve the annual interest rate when the interest is paid semi-annually.
- To calculate the present value (issue price), use the semi-annual market interest rate for (*i*). Use the face value of the bonds and the contractual interest rate to calculate the semi-annual interest payments (*PMT*). The interest payments, which recur periodically, are an annuity. The face value of the bonds is the (*FV*), which is a single sum.
- Debit cash and credit bonds payable for the amount the bonds were issued at.

On January 1, 2013, R & B Inc. issues $500,000 of 10-year, 4% bonds to yield a market interest rate of 5%, which resulted in an issue price of 92.21. Interest is paid semi-annually on January 1 and July 1. On January 1, 2015, the company redeems the bonds at 97 after making and recording the semi-annual interest payment.

(a) Use present value factors to prove the issue price of the bonds of 92.21. Round all calculations to the nearest dollar.
(b) Prepare the entry to record the issue of the bonds on January 1, 2013.
(c) Prepare an amortization schedule for the first four interest periods. Round all calculations to the nearest dollar.
(d) Prepare the entries to record the accrual of interest and amortization of any bond discount or premium on December 31, 2014.
(e) Prepare the entry to record the payment of interest on January 1, 2015.
(f) Prepare the entry to record the redemption of the bonds on January 1, 2015.

Solution
(a) Key inputs: Future value (*FV*) = $500,000
   Semi-annual market interest rate (*i*) = 2.5% (5% × 6/12)
   Interest payment (*PMT*) = $10,000 ($500,000 × 4% × 6/12)
   Number of semi-annual periods (*n*) = 20 (10 × 2)

Present value of $500,000 received in 20 periods
500,000 × 0.61027 (*n* = 20, *i* = 2.5) $305,135
Present value of $10,000 received for each of 20 periods
$10,000 × 15.58916 (*n* = 20, *i* = 2.5) 155,892
Present value (issue price) $461,027

Proof: Issue price = $461,027 ÷ 500,000 = 92.21%

(b)

(1) Jan. 1, 2013	Cash	461,050	
	Bonds Payable		461,050
	To record issue of bonds at 92.21.		

(c)

R & B INC. Bond Discount Amortization Schedule Effective-Interest Method				
Semi-Annual Interest Period	(A) Interest Payment ($500,000 × 4% × $^6/_{12}$)	(B) Interest Expense (D × 5% × $^6/_{12}$)	(C) Discount Amortization (B − A)	(D) Bond Amortized Cost (D + C)
Issue date (Jan. 1, 2013)				$461,050
1 (July 1)	$10,000	$11,526	$1,526	462,576
2 (Jan. 1, 2014)	10,000	11,564	1,564	464,140
3 (July 1)	10,000	11,603	1,603	465,743
4 (Jan. 1, 2015)	10,000	11,643	1,643	467,386

(d) Dec. 31, 2014	Interest Expense	11,643	
	Bonds Payable		1,643
	Interest Payable		10,000
	To record accrual of interest and amortization of discount.		
(e) Jan. 1, 2015	Interest Payable	10,000	
	Cash		10,000
	To record payment of bond interest.		
(f) Jan. 1, 2015	Bonds Payable	467,386	
	Loss on Bond Redemption ($485,000 − $467,386)	17,614	
	Cash ($500,000 × 97%)		485,000
	To record redemption of bonds at 97.		

Related exercise material: BE15–2, BE15–3, BE15–4, BE15–5, BE15–6, BE15–7, BE15–8, BE15–9, E15–2, E15–3, E15–4, E15–5, E15–6, E15–7, and E15–8.

THE NAVIGATOR

- Calculate the interest expense by multiplying the semi-annual market rate (half of the market or yield rate) by the amortized cost of the bonds payable.
- The amount of the discount (premium) amortization is the difference between the interest payment and the interest expense.
- The amortized cost of the bonds issued at a discount increases by the amount of the discount amortization each interest period. The amortized cost of the bonds issued at a premium decreases by the amount of the premium amortization each interest period.
- To record the redemption, eliminate the amortized cost of the bonds, record the cash paid, and calculate and record the gain or loss (the difference between the cash paid and the amortized cost).

Instalment Notes Payable

» STUDY OBJECTIVE 3

Account for instalment notes payable.

You will recall that we first learned about notes payable in Chapter 10, where they were included as an example of a current liability. Non-current notes payable are similar to short-term notes payable except that the terms of the notes are normally for more than one year. While short-term notes are normally repayable in full at maturity, most non-current notes are repayable in a series of periodic payments and are referred to as **instalment notes**. These payments are known as **instalments** and are paid monthly, quarterly, semi-annually, or at another defined period.

Notes and bonds are also quite similar. Both have a fixed maturity date and pay interest. However, whereas bonds have a contractual or fixed interest rate, notes may have either a fixed interest rate or a floating interest rate. A **fixed interest rate** is constant for the entire term of the note. A **floating** (or **variable**) **interest rate** changes as market rates change. A floating interest rate is often based on the prime borrowing rate. Prime is the interest rate that banks charge their most creditworthy customers. This rate is usually increased by a specified percentage that matches the company's risk profile—in other words, it depends on how risky the company is judged to be.

Similar to bonds, a non-current note may be unsecured or secured. A secured note pledges title to specific assets as security for the loan, often known as **collateral**. Secured notes are commonly known as *mortgages*. A **mortgage note payable** is widely used by individuals to purchase homes. It is also used by many companies to acquire property, plant, and equipment. Unsecured notes are issued against the general credit of the borrower. There are no assets used as collateral.

As explained earlier, most non-current notes payable are paid in instalments. Each instalment payment consists of (1) interest on the unpaid balance of the loan, and (2) a reduction of loan principal. Payments generally take one of two forms: (1) fixed principal payments plus interest, or (2) blended principal and interest payments. Let's look at each of these payment patterns in more detail.

FIXED PRINCIPAL PAYMENTS

Instalment notes with fixed principal payments are repayable in **equal periodic amounts, plus interest**. To illustrate, assume that on January 1, 2014, Bélanger Ltée issues a $120,000, five-year, 7% note payable to finance a new research laboratory. The entry to record the issue of the note payable is as follows:

A = L + SE
+120,000 +120,000

↑ Cash flows: +120,000

Jan. 1	Cash	120,000	
	Notes Payable		120,000
	To record five-year, 7% note payable.		

The terms of the note provide for equal monthly instalment payments of $2,000 ($120,000 ÷ 60 monthly periods) on the first of each month, plus interest, based on an annual rate of 7%, on the outstanding principal balance. Monthly interest expense is calculated by multiplying the outstanding principal balance by the interest rate. The calculation of interest expense for notes payable is similar to that of bonds payable—both use the effective-interest method.

For the first payment date—February 1—interest expense is $700 ($120,000 × 7% × $\frac{1}{12}$). Since 7% is an annual interest rate, it must be adjusted for the monthly time period. The cash payment of $2,700 for the month of February is the sum of the instalment payment, $2,000, which is applied against the principal, plus the interest, $700.

The entry to record the first instalment payment on February 1 is as follows:

A = L + SE
−2,700 −2,000 −700

↓ Cash flows: −2,700

Feb. 1	Interest Expense ($120,000 × 7% × $\frac{1}{12}$)	700	
	Notes Payable	2,000	
	Cash ($2,000 + $700)		2,700
	To record monthly payment on note.		

An instalment payment schedule is a useful tool to help organize this information and prepare journal entries. The instalment payment schedule for the first few months for Bélanger Ltée, rounded to the nearest dollar, is shown in Illustration 15-11.

▶ ILLUSTRATION 15-11
Instalment payment schedule—fixed principal payments

		BÉLANGER LTÉE		
		Instalment Payment Schedule—Fixed Principal Payments		
Interest Period	(A) Cash Payment (B + C)	(B) Interest Expense (D × 7% × $\frac{1}{12}$)	(C) Reduction of Principal ($120,000 ÷ 60)	(D) Principal Balance (D − C)
Jan. 1				$120,000
Feb. 1	$2,700	$700	$2,000	118,000
Mar. 1	2,688	688	2,000	116,000
Apr. 1	2,677	677	2,000	114,000

Column A, the cash payment, is the total of the instalment payment, $2,000 (Column C), plus the interest (Column B). The cash payment changes each period because the interest amount changes. Column B determines the interest expense, which decreases each period because the principal balance, on which interest is calculated, decreases. Column C is the portion of the payment that is applied against the principal. The monthly reduction of principal of $2,000 per month is constant each period in a "fixed principal payment" pattern. Column D is the principal balance, which decreases each period by the amount of the instalment payment (Column C).

In summary, with fixed principal payments, the interest decreases each period (as the principal decreases). The portion applied to the reduction of loan principal stays constant, but because of the decreasing interest, the total cash payment decreases.

BLENDED PAYMENTS

Instalment notes with blended payments are repayable in **equal periodic amounts that include the principal and the interest**. With blended payments, the amounts of interest and principal that are applied to the loan change with each payment. Specifically, as happens with fixed principal payments, the interest decreases each period (as the principal decreases). In contrast to fixed principal payments, however, the portion that is applied to the loan principal increases each period.

To illustrate, assume that instead of fixed principal payments, Bélanger Ltée repays its $120,000 note payable in blended payments of $2,376 each month. The blended payment is calculated using present value calculations as shown in Appendix PV. As with the fixed principal payments illustrated in the previous section, monthly interest expense is calculated by multiplying the outstanding principal balance by the interest rate. For the first payment date—February 1—interest expense is $700 ($120,000 $\times$ 7% $\times$ $^1/_{12}$ months). The payment of $2,376 is fixed for each month, and includes interest and principal amounts, which will vary. In February, the principal balance will be reduced by $1,676, which is the difference between the payment of $2,376 and the interest amount of $700.

The entry to record the issue of the note payable is the same as in the previous section. The amounts in the journal entry to record the payment on February 1 change as follows:

Feb. 1	Interest Expense ($120,000 $\times$ 7% $\times$ $^1/_{12}$)	700	
	Notes Payable ($2,376 − $700)	1,676	
	Cash		2,376
	To record monthly payment on note.		

A = L + SE
−2,376   −1,676   −700
↓ Cash flows: −2,376

An instalment payment schedule can also be prepared for blended principal and interest payments. Illustration 15-12 shows the instalment payment schedule for the first few months for Bélanger Ltée, rounded to the nearest dollar.

BÉLANGER LTÉE Instalment Payment Schedule—Blended Payments				
	(A)	(B) Interest Expense (D × 7% × $^1/_{12}$)	(C) Reduction of Principal (A − B)	(D) Principal Balance (D − C)
Interest Period	Cash Payment			
Jan. 1				$120,000
Feb. 1	$2,376	$700	$1,676	118,324
Mar. 1	2,376	690	1,686	116,638
Apr. 1	2,376	680	1,696	114,942

▶ ILLUSTRATION 15-12
Instalment payment schedule—blended payments

Column A, the cash payment, is specified and is the same for each period. The amount of this cash payment can be calculated using present value techniques discussed earlier in the chapter and in Appendix PV to this textbook. Column B determines the interest expense, which decreases each period because the principal balance on which interest is calculated also decreases. Column C is the amount by which the principal is reduced. This is the difference between the cash payment of $2,376 (Column A) and the interest for the period (Column B). Consequently, this amount will increase each period. Column D is the principal balance, which decreases each period by an increasing amount; that is, by the reduction of the principal amount from Column C.

In summary, with blended payments, the interest decreases each period as the principal decreases. The cash payment stays constant, but because of the decreasing interest, the reduction of principal increases.

Illustration 15-13 summarizes the differences between instalment notes payable with fixed principal payments and blended principal payments.

▶ **ILLUSTRATION 15-13**
Difference between instalment notes with fixed principal payments and blended principal payments

Instalment Payment Pattern	Principal	Interest	Total Cash Payments
Fixed principal plus interest	Constant: Reduction of principal equal each period	Decreases: Interest expense decreases each period	Decreases: Total cash payment decreases each period
Blended principal and interest	Increases: Reduction of principal increases each period	Decreases: Interest expense decreases each period	Constant: Total cash payment equal each period

CURRENT AND NON-CURRENT PORTIONS

With both types of instalment notes payable, the reduction in principal for the next year must be reported as a current liability, and is normally called "Current portion of note payable." The remaining unpaid principal is classified as a non-current liability. No journal entry is necessary; it is simply a reclassification of amounts for the balance sheet. For example, consider the following fixed principal annual instalment payment schedule shown in Illustration 15-14.

▶ **ILLUSTRATION 15-14**
Current and non-current portion of note payable

Interest Period	Cash Payment	Interest Expense	Reduction of Principal	Principal Balance
Issue Date				$50,000
2013	$13,500	$3,500	$10,000	40,000
2014	12,800	2,800	10,000	30,000
2015	12,100	2,100	10,000	20,000
2016	11,400	1,400	10,000	10,000
2017	10,700	700	10,000	0

If financial statements were being prepared at the end of 2014, the company would report $30,000 as its total liability for the bank loan, shown in red in the principal balance column. Of this, $10,000 ($30,000 − $20,000)—the amount to be repaid within the next year (2015), which is also highlighted above in red—would be reported as a current liability. The company would report $20,000—the amount to be repaid beyond next year (2016 and 2017)—as a non-current liability. This amount is high-lighted in blue in the above table. Note that when the current portion ($10,000) and the non-current portion ($20,000) are added together, the amount should agree with the total amount owing at the end of 2014 ($30,000).

ACCOUNTING IN ACTION
BUSINESS INSIGHT

Canadians are racking up record levels of debt. Statistics Canada reported in 2012 that Canadian households owed an average amount equivalent to 152% of their incomes. The federal finance minister and governor of the Bank of Canada repeatedly warned Canadians to tighten their spending and save more for retirement. Many blamed record-low interest rates for enticing Canadians to borrow beyond their means, which is one reason why housing prices and mortgage debt were increasing. While banks were criticized for slashing mortgage rates in wars to lure customers, they were asking the federal government to reduce the maximum period for government-insured mortgages instead of hiking interest rates. The government did so in mid-2012, lowering the amortization period from 30 years to 25 years and limiting homeowners with government-insured mortgages to spending no more than 44% of income on housing and other debt. The government hoped the moves would curb mortgage debt, since it would be harder to get a mortgage in the first place, and the mortgages would have to be paid off faster.

Sources: Grant Robertson, "BMO Kicks Off New Mortgage Fight," *Globe and Mail*, March 7, 2012; Jason Fekete, "Ottawa Tightens Mortgage Rules to Avert Household Debt Crisis," *Financial Post*, June 21, 2012; Andy Johnson, "Canadian Consumer Debt Level Hits Record High," CTVNews.ca, August 23, 2012.

What impact will the decrease in the amortization period from 30 to 25 years have on homebuyers?

BEFORE YOU GO ON...

Do It

On December 31, 2013, Tian Inc. issued a $500,000, 15-year, 8% mortgage note payable. The terms provide for semi-annual blended payments of $28,915 on June 30 and December 31. (a) Prepare an instalment payment schedule for the first two years of the note (through to December 31, 2015). (b) Prepare the journal entries required to record the issue of the note on December 31, 2013, and the first two instalment payments. (c) Show the presentation of the liability on the balance sheet at December 31, 2014.

Solution

(a)

Interest Period	Cash Payment	Interest Expense	Reduction of Principal	Principal Balance
Dec. 31, 2013				$500,000
June 30, 2014	$28,915	$20,000	$ 8,915	491,085
Dec. 31, 2014	28,915	19,643	9,272	481,813
June 30, 2015	28,915	19,273	9,642	472,171
Dec. 31, 2015	28,915	18,887	10,028	462,143

(b)

Dec. 31, 2013	Cash	500,000	
	Mortgage Note Payable		500,000
	To record issue of 15-year, 8% mortgage note payable.		
June 30, 2014	Interest Expense ($500,000 × 8% × $^6/_{12}$)	20,000	
	Mortgage Note Payable ($28,915 − $20,000)	8,915	
	Cash		28,915
	To record semi-annual payment on note.		
Dec. 31, 2014	Interest Expense ($491,085 × 8% × $^6/_{12}$)	19,643	
	Mortgage Note Payable ($28,915 − $19,643)	9,272	
	Cash		28,915
	To record semi-annual payment on note.		

(c)

TIAN INC. December 31, 2014 Balance Sheet (Partial)	
Current liabilities	
Current portion of mortgage note payable ($9,642 + $10,028)	$ 19,670
Non-current liabilities	
Mortgage note payable	462,143
Total liabilities	$481,813

Related exercise material: BE15–10, BE15–11, BE15–12, BE15–13, E15–9, E15–10, E15–11, E15–12, and E15–13.

THE NAVIGATOR

Action Plan

- For the instalment payment schedule, multiply the interest rate by the principal balance at the beginning of the period to determine the interest expense. Remember to adjust the interest rate to the semi-annual rate. The reduction of principal is the difference between the cash payment and the interest expense.
- Use the amortization table to record the semi-annual mortgage payments.
- Remember to separate the current and non-current portions of the note in the balance sheet. The current portion is the amount of principal that will be repaid in the next year (2015). The total of the current and non-current portions should equal the outstanding principal balance in the amortization table at December 31, 2014.

Lease Liabilities

A **lease** is a contractual arrangement between two parties. A party that owns an asset (the **lessor**) agrees to allow another party (the **lessee**) to use the specified property for a series of cash payments over an agreed period of time. Why would anyone want to lease property rather than buy it? There are many advantages to leasing an asset instead of purchasing it.

» STUDY OBJECTIVE 4

Account for leases.

1. **Reduced risk of obsolescence:** Obsolescence is the process by which an asset becomes out of date before it physically wears out. Frequently, lease terms allow the party using the asset (the lessee) to

exchange the asset for a more modern or technologically capable asset if it becomes outdated. This is much easier than trying to sell an obsolete asset.

2. **100% financing:** To purchase an asset, most companies must borrow money, which usually requires a down payment of at least 20%. Leasing an asset does not usually require any money down, which helps to conserve cash. In addition, interest payments are often fixed for the term of the lease, unlike other financing, which often has a floating interest rate.

3. **Income tax advantages:** When a company owns a depreciable asset, it can only deduct the depreciation expense (called *capital cost allowance* for income tax purposes) on its income tax return. However, when a company leases an asset, it can deduct 100% of the lease payment on its income tax return.

For financial reporting purposes, leases are classified as either finance leases or operating leases. Whether a lease is a finance lease or an operating lease depends on the economic reality of the transaction rather than the legal form of the lease agreement. We will discuss these two types of leases in the next sections.

Illustration 15-15 summarizes the major difference between an operating and a finance lease.

▶**ILLUSTRATION 15-15**
Types of leases

Finance Lease	Operating Lease

Lessee has substantially all of the benefits and risks of ownership.	Lessor has substantially all of the benefits and risks of ownership.

FINANCE LEASES

In a **finance lease** contract, substantially all of the benefits and risks of ownership of the property leased are transferred to the lessee, giving the lessee control of the property. Remember that the definition of an asset is based on control and not legal ownership, so essentially a company acquires an asset and finances the acquisition through periodic payments. Therefore, under a finance lease, both an asset and a liability are shown on the balance sheet. Under ASPE, a finance lease is called a **capital lease**.

Finance leases are a good example of the application of the "faithful representation" characteristic of accounting information from Chapter 11. In order for accounting information to be a faithful representation of the transaction, it must show the economic reality, and not just the legal form, of the transaction. If the economic reality of a lease agreement results in substantially all of the benefits and risks of ownership being transferred to the lessee and the obligation to make periodic payments, the faithful representation characteristic requires the accounting information to show the asset and a liability.

Accountants must use professional judgement in deciding if a lease should be classified as a finance lease. Under IFRS, the lessee must classify the lease as a finance lease and record an asset and a lease liability if any of the following qualitative conditions exists.

1. **Transfer of ownership:** If the lease transfers ownership of the asset to the lessee during or at the end of the lease term, the leased asset and lease liability should be recorded on the lessee's books.

2. **Option to buy:** If the lessee has an option to purchase the asset during the lease term at a price that is much below its fair value (called a *bargain purchase option*), we can assume that the lessee will choose to use this option. Thus, the leased asset and lease liability should be recorded on the lessee's books.

3. **Lease term:** If the lease term is for the major part of the economic life of the leased property, the asset has effectively been purchased and should be recorded as an asset along with the lease liability by the lessee. Under IFRS, professional judgement is used to assess if the lease term is for the major part of the economic life. In comparison, under ASPE, a lease is classified as a capital lease if the lease term is equal to 75% or more of the economic life of the leased property.

4. **Purchase price:** If the present value of the lease payments amounts to substantially all of the fair value of the leased property, the lessee has essentially paid for the asset. As a result, the leased asset and lease liability should be recorded on the books of the lessee. Similar to condition 3, under IFRS, professional judgement is used and under ASPE, a specific benchmark is used to assess if this condition is met. Under ASPE, if the present value of the lease payments is equal to or greater than 90% of the fair value of the leased property, then the lease is a capital lease.

5. **Specialized asset:** If the leased asset is of such a specialized nature that only the lessee can use it, the leased asset and lease liability should be recorded on the lessee's books. ASPE does not include this condition.

To illustrate, assume that Fortune Ltd., a public company using IFRS, decides to lease new equipment. The lease period is 10 years and the economic life of the leased equipment is estimated to be 14 years. The present value of the lease payments is $170,000 and the fair market value of the equipment is $200,000. There is no transfer of ownership during the lease term.

In this example, Fortune has essentially acquired the equipment. Conditions (3) and (4) listed above have both been met. First, the lease term is for the major part of the economic life of the asset (10 years ÷ 14 years = 71.43%). Second, the present value of cash payments amounts to substantially all of the equipment's fair market value ($170,000 ÷ $200,000 = 85%). The present value of the cash payments in a finance lease is calculated in the same way that was explained earlier in the chapter for bond interest payments.

Note that, while two conditions were met in this case, only one condition has to be met for the lease to be treated as a finance lease. The entry to record the transaction is as follows:

Nov. 27	Leased Asset—Equipment	170,000	
	Lease Liability		170,000
	To record leased asset and lease liability.		

A = L + SE
+170,000 +170,000
Cash flows: no effect

The leased asset is reported on the balance sheet under property, plant, and equipment. The portion of the lease liability that is expected to be paid in the next year is reported as a current liability. The remainder is classified as a non-current liability.

After it is acquired, the leased asset is depreciated just as any other long-lived asset is. In addition, the lease payment is allocated between interest expense and the reduction of the principal balance of the lease liability, similar to what was shown earlier in the chapter for blended principal and interest payments on notes payable.

OPERATING LEASES

If the benefits and risks of ownership are not transferred to the lessee, and from an economic point of view the lease is a rental agreement, the lease is classified as an operating lease. Rental of an apartment and rental of a car are examples of **operating leases**. Under an operating lease, the lease (or rental) payments are recorded as an expense by the lessee and as revenue by the lessor. For example, assume that a sales representative for Western Inc. leases a car from Hertz car rental at the airport on July 17. Hertz charges a total of $275. The entry by the lessee, Western Inc., would be as follows:

July 17	Car Rental Expense	275	
	Cash		275
	To record payment of lease rental charge.		

A = L + SE
−275   −275
↓ Cash flows: −275

Many operating leases are short-term, such as the rental of an apartment or car as described above. Others are for an extended period of time. Operating leases that cover a long period of time are sometimes seen as a form of off–balance sheet financing. **Off–balance sheet financing** occurs when liabilities are kept off of a company's balance sheet. Many people argue that, if an operating lease results in the long-term use of an asset and an unavoidable obligation, it should be recorded as an asset and a liability. To reduce these concerns, companies are required to report their operating lease obligations in detail in a note to the financial statements. This allows analysts and other financial statement users to adjust ratios such as debt to total assets (which we will learn about in the next section of this chapter) by adding leased assets and lease liabilities if this treatment is considered more appropriate.

To address the concern about off–balance sheet financing, the International Accounting Standards Board and the Financial Accounting Standards Board in the United States are currently working on a joint project on leases that recognizes that, under any lease agreement, the right to use property by the lessee meets the definition of an asset and the related obligation to make periodic rental payments meets the definition of a liability. The boards are therefore proposing that all leases be accounted for by recording an asset and liability.

To summarize, for a finance lease, both an asset and a liability are reported in the balance sheet. Two expenses—depreciation expense related to the leased asset and interest expense related to the lease liability—are reported in the income statement. For an operating lease, no asset or liability is reported in the balance sheet. The only expense that is reported in the income statement is rental expense.

Action Plan

- Know the five qualitative conditions to distinguish between an operating and a finance lease under IFRS. A lease is considered to be a finance lease if any one of the following conditions is met: (1) there will be a transfer of ownership, (2) there is a bargain purchase option, (3) the lease term is for the major part of the economic life, (4) the present value of the lease payments amounts to substantially all of the fair value of the leased property, and (5) the asset is a specialized asset.

- Understand the impact of an operating and a finance lease on the income statement and balance sheet. With an operating lease, no asset or liability is recorded; with a finance lease, both an asset and a liability are recorded.

BEFORE YOU GO ON...

Do It

The Alert Company has the following two leasing options to acquire a new machine:

	Lease Option 1	Lease Option 2
Transfer of ownership	No	No
Bargain purchase option	No	No
Lease term	8 years	2 years
Estimated useful life	11 years	5 years
Fair market value	$20,000	$20,000
Present value of lease payments	$17,000	$9,000

Discuss how each lease option would affect Alert's financial statements assuming the company uses IFRS.

Solution

Lease option 1 would be recorded as a finance lease because the lease term is a major part of the economic life of the machinery (8 years ÷ 11 years = 72.7%). Because of this, an asset and a liability would be reported on the balance sheet. Depreciation expense and interest expense would be reported on the income statement.

Lease option 2 would be recorded as an operating lease as none of the five conditions of a finance lease have been met. There would be no impact on the balance sheet, but the lease payments would be reported as rental expense on the income statement.

Related exercise material: BE15–14, BE15–15, BE15–16, and E15–14.

THE NAVIGATOR

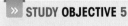

» STUDY OBJECTIVE 5

Explain and illustrate the methods for the presentation and analysis of non-current liabilities.

Statement Presentation and Analysis

Liabilities are a significant amount on the financial statements and they have to be disclosed in detail so they can be properly understood by investors and creditors. These and other users are very interested in assessing a company's solvency (its ability to pay) with regard to its non-current liabilities. We will look at the presentation and analysis of liabilities in the next sections.

PRESENTATION

The liabilities section of the balance sheet for Wick Company Ltd. is presented below:

WICK COMPANY LTD. **Balance Sheet (partial)** **December 31, 2014**		
Current Liabilities		
Accounts payable		$ 70,000
Interest payable		18,400
Current portion of mortgage note payable		55,520
Current portion of lease liability		113,220
Total current liabilities		257,140
Non-current liabilities		
Bonds payable, 4%, due in 2018		920,000
Mortgage notes payable, 8%, due in 2021		444,480
Lease liability		526,780
Total non-current liabilities		1,891,260
Total liabilities		$2,148,400

You will recall that the principal payments for the next year on notes payable and lease liabilities are reported in current liabilities and the remaining unpaid principal is classified in non-current liabilities. In the Wick example, the company has a mortgage note payable of $500,000 ($55,520 + $444,480); $55,520 will be paid in 2015 and the remaining amount of $444,480 classified in non-current liabilities will be paid off in instalments from 2016 to 2021. Similarly, the current portion of the lease liability ($113,220) is the principal payments on the leases that will be made in 2015 and the non-current lease liability ($526,780) is the principal amount that will be paid in 2016 and future years.

Note that Wick is reporting bond interest payable of $18,400 in current liabilities as the interest will be paid in 2015 and bonds payable of $920,000 in non-current liabilities because the bonds mature in 2018. Note that there is no current portion of bonds payable as the bonds are paid off in one lump sum at maturity.

Full disclosure of debt is very important. Summary data are usually presented in the balance sheet, and detailed data (interest rate, maturity date, redemption price, convertibility, and any assets pledged as collateral) are shown in a supporting schedule or in the notes to the financial statements. The amount of debt maturing within 12 months of the balance sheet date should be reported under current liabilities.

ANALYSIS

A company's investors and creditors are interested in analyzing its liquidity and solvency. Short-term creditors are interested in liquidity ratios, which measure a company's ability to repay its short-term debt and to meet unexpected needs for cash. We learned about liquidity ratios such as the current ratio, inventory turnover, and receivables turnover in earlier chapters.

Long-term creditors and investors are more interested in solvency ratios, which measure a company's ability to repay its non-current liabilities and survive over a long period of time. They are particularly interested in a company's ability to pay interest when it is due and to repay its debt at maturity. Two examples of solvency ratios are debt to total assets and the interest coverage ratio. They are explained next.

Debt to Total Assets

Debt to total assets measures the percentage of the total assets that is financed by creditors rather than by shareholders. Financing provided by creditors is riskier than financing provided by shareholders, because debt must be repaid at specific points in time whether the company is doing well or not.

Helpful hint Some users measure the percentage of the total assets that is financed by shareholders. This ratio is called the *debt to equity ratio.*

Illustration 15-16 shows how the debt to total assets ratio is calculated. Using data from Reitmans' financial statements (in thousands), the ratio is calculated by dividing total liabilities (both current and long-term) by total assets ($ in thousands).

▶ **ILLUSTRATION 15-16**
Debt to total assets

Total Liabilities	÷	Total Assets	=	Debt to Total Assets
$141,009	÷	$633,861	=	22%

This means that 22% of Reitmans' assets are financed by creditors. The remainder, 78% (100% − 22%), has been financed by shareholders. In general, the higher the percentage of debt to total assets, the greater the risk that the company may be unable to meet its maturing obligations.

While you may assume that having no, or a low, debt to total assets ratio is ideal, recall that we learned at the beginning of this chapter that some debt may be good for a company. As previously shown, in some circumstances, a company can increase its earnings per share and return on equity by increasing how much debt financing it relies on.

Interest Coverage

The debt to total assets ratio must be interpreted in light of the company's ability to handle its debt. That is, a company might have a high debt to total assets ratio but still be able to easily pay its interest payments. Alternatively, a company may have a low debt to total assets ratio and struggle to cover its interest payments.

Alternative terminology The interest coverage ratio is also commonly known as the times interest earned ratio.

The **interest coverage ratio** indicates the company's ability to meet interest payments as they come due. It is calculated by dividing profit before interest expense and income tax expense by interest expense. The numerator is often abbreviated and called **EBIT**, which stands for "earnings before interest and tax." EBIT can be calculated by adding back interest expense and income tax expense to profit. Because these amounts were originally deducted to determine profit, adding them back has the effect of cancelling them.

Illustration 15-17 calculates interest coverage for Reitmans ($ in thousands).

▶ **ILLUSTRATION 15-17**
Interest coverage

Profit + Interest Expense + Income Tax Expense (EBIT)	÷	Interest Expense	=	Interest Coverage
$47,539 + $1,509 + $18,333	÷	$1,509	=	45 times

With an interest coverage ratio (EBIT) of 45 times Reitmans appears well equipped to handle its interest payments.

Action Plan
- Divide the total liabilities by the total assets to calculate the debt to total assets ratio.
- Add the interest expense and income tax expense to profit to calculate earnings before interest and income tax.
- Divide the earnings before interest and income tax expense by the interest expense to calculate the interest coverage ratio.

 **BEFORE YOU GO ON...**

Do It

Gleason Ltd. reported the following selected data at December 31 2013 and 2012.

	2013	2012
Total assets	$515,000	$529,000
Total liabilities	309,000	302,000
Interest expense	13,000	12,000
Income tax expense	25,500	22,500
Profit	85,000	75,000

Calculate Gleason Ltd.'s (a) debt to total assets, and (b) interest coverage ratios for each of the years 2013 and 2012 and comment on any trends.

Solution

	2013	2012
(a) Debt to total assets	$309,000 ÷ 515,000 = 60%	$302,000 ÷ 529,000 = 57%
(b) Interest coverage	($85,000 + 25,500 + 13,000) ÷ 13,000 = 9.5 times	($75,000 + 22,500 + 12,000) ÷ 12,000 = 9.1 times

Gleason's debt to total assets increased in 2013 over 2012. In general, the higher the debt to total assets, the greater the risk that the company may be unable to meet its maturing obligations. The company's interest coverage ratio increased to 9.5 times. In general it is better to have a higher interest coverage ratio. Even though Gleason's debt to total assets increased, given the increase in interest coverage, the company seems well equipped to meet its interest payments.

Related exercise material: BE15–17, BE15–18, BE15–19, E15–15, E15–16, and E15–17.

THE **NAVIGATOR**

Comparing IFRS and ASPE

Key Differences	International Financial Reporting Standards (IFRS)	Accounting Standards for Private Enterprises (ASPE)
Bond discount and premium amortization	Must use the effective-interest method to amortize any bond discount or premium.	Normally will use the effective-interest method to amortize any bond discount or premium but permitted to use alternative methods if the results do not differ materially from the effective-interest method.
Leases: terminology	Non-operating leases are called "finance leases."	Non-operating leases are called "capital leases."
Leases: classification as finance/capital lease	• Professional judgement is used to assess whether the lease term is the major part of economic life or if the present value of the lease payments amount to substantially the fair value of the leased property. • Lease of a specialized asset is a finance lease.	• Specific benchmarks are used when assessing lease term (75%) and the present value of the lease payments (90%). • Does not include the specialized asset condition.

THE **NAVIGATOR**

Demonstration Problem 1

Demonstration Problems

On January 1, 2011, Feng Inc. issued $500,000 of 10-year, 7% bonds at 93.205 because the market interest rate was 8%. Interest is payable semi-annually on January 1 and July 1. Feng's year end is June 30. On January 1, 2014, Feng redeemed all of these bonds at 90 after making the semi-annual interest payment.

Instructions

(a) Using present value factors, prove the issue price of the bonds of 93.205. Round all calculations to the nearest dollar.

(b) Prepare the journal entry to record the issue of the bonds on January 1, 2011.

ACTION PLAN

- Calculate the proceeds using the stated percentage rate; multiply the face value by the issue price expressed as a percentage (e.g., 93.205%).

- Identify the key inputs required to determine present value, whether using tables or a financial calculator.

- Calculate the present value (issue price) using the semi-annual market interest rate for (i). Use the face value of the bonds and the contractual interest rate to calculate the semi-annual interest payments. The face value of the bonds is the (FV), which is a single sum. The interest payments, which recur periodically, are an annuity. Don't forget to double the number of interest periods and halve the interest rate for semi-annual interest.

- If the proceeds are greater than the face value, the difference is a premium. If the proceeds are less than the face value, the difference is a discount.

- Debit cash and credit bonds payable for the amount the bonds were issued at.

- Calculate the interest expense by multiplying the semi-annual market rate by the amortized cost of the bonds payable.

- The amount of the discount (premium) amortization is the difference between the interest payment and the interest expense.

- Amortization of a bond discount increases interest expense; amortization of a bond premium decreases interest expense.

- To record the redemption: update any partial period interest and amortization if required, (2) eliminate the amortized cost of the bonds by removing the balance from the Bonds Payable account, (3) record the cash paid, and (4) calculate and record the gain or loss (the difference between the cash paid and the amortized cost).

(c) Prepare a bond discount amortization schedule for the first six interest periods.

(d) Prepare the journal entry to accrue the first interest payment on June 30.

(e) Show the presentation of the interest payable and the bonds payable on Feng's balance sheet on June 30, 2011.

(f) Prepare the journal entry to record the payment of the interest on January 1, 2014, and the redemption of the bonds on January 1, 2014.

Solution to Demonstration Problem 1

(a)

(1)	$500,000 × 93.205%	$466,025
(2)	Key inputs:	
	Future value (FV) = $500,000	
	Market interest rate (i) = 4% (8% × $^6/_{12}$)	
	Interest payment (PMT) = $17,500 ($500,000 × 7% × $^6/_{12}$)	
	Number of semi-annual periods (n) = 20 (10 × 2)	
	Present value of $500,000 received in 20 periods	
	$500,000 × 0.45639 ($n$ = 20, i = 4%)	$228,195
	Present value of $17,500 received for each of 20 periods	
	$17,500 × 13.59033 ($n$ = 20, i = 4%)	237,830
	Present value (market price) of bonds	$466,025

(b)

Jan. 1, 2011	Cash	466,025	
	Bonds Payable		466,025
	To record issue of 10-year, 7% bonds.		

(c)

FENG INC.
Bond Discount Amortization Schedule
Effective-Interest Method

Semi-Annual Interest Period	(A) Interest Payment ($500,000 × 7% × $^6/_{12}$)	(B) Interest Expense (D × 8% × $^6/_{12}$)	(C) Discount Amortization (B − A)	(D) Bond Amortized Cost (D + C)
Issue date (Jan. 1, 2011)				$466,025
1 (July 1)	$17,500	$18,641	$1,141	467,166
2 (Jan. 1, 2012)	17,500	18,687	1,187	468,353
3 (July 1)	17,500	18,734	1,234	469,587
4 (Jan. 1, 2013)	17,500	18,783	1,283	470,870
5 (July 1)	17,500	18,835	1,335	472,205
6 (Jan. 1, 2014)	17,500	18,888	1,388	473,593

(d)

June 30, 2011	Bond Interest Expense	18,641	
	Bonds Payable		1,141
	Interest Payable		17,500
	To record accrual of semi-annual interest.		

(e)

FENG INC.	
Balance sheet (partial)	
June 30, 2011	
Current liabilities	
Interest payable	17,500
Non-current liabilities	
Bonds payable	$467,166

(f)

Jan. 1, 2014	Interest Expense	18,888	
	Bonds Payable		1,388
	Cash		17,500
	To record accrual of semi-annual interest.		
Jan. 1, 2014	Bonds Payable	473, 593	
	Cash ($500,000 × 90%)		450,000
	Gain on Redemption of Bonds		
	($473,593 − 450,000)		23,593
	To record redemption of bonds.		

THE NAVIGATOR

Demonstration Problem 2

Note: This demonstration problem uses the same facts as those shown in the "Do It" problem at the end of the Instalment Notes Payable section, but the nature and amount of the payment are changed.

On December 31, 2013, Tian Inc. issued a $500,000, 15-year, 8% mortgage note payable. The terms provide for semi-annual fixed principal payments of $16,667 on June 30 and December 31. Tian's year end is December 31.

Instructions

Round your answers to the nearest dollar.

(a) Prepare an instalment payment schedule for the first two years of the note (through to December 31, 2015).

(b) Prepare the journal entries to record the issue of the note on December 31, 2013, and the first two instalment payments.

(c) Indicate the current and non-current amounts for the mortgage note payable at December 31, 2014.

(d) What is the difference between your results here using a fixed principal payment and the results shown using a blended payment for the same situation illustrated in the "Do It" problem at the end of the Instalment Notes Payable section?

ACTION PLAN

- Determine the amount of the fixed principal payment by dividing the principal borrowed ($500,000) by the number of periods (15 years × 2).

- Determine the interest expense for the mortgage by multiplying the semi-annual interest rate by the principal balance at the beginning of the period. The cash payment is the total of the principal payment and interest expense.

- Use the payment schedule to record the reduction of principal, the interest expense, and the cash payment.

- The current portion of the mortgage note payable is the amount of principal that will be repaid in the next year. The non-current portion is the remaining balance.

Solution to Demonstration Problem 2

(a)

Semi-Annual Interest Period	Cash Payment	Interest Expense	Reduction of Principal	Principal Balance
Issue Date (Dec. 31, 2013)				$500,000
1 (June 30, 2014)	$36,667[1]	$20,000[2]	$16,667[3]	483,333[4]
2 (Dec. 31)	36,000	19,333	16,667	466,666
3 (June 30, 2015)	35,334	18,667	16,667	449,999
4 (Dec. 31)	34,667	18,000	16,667	433,332

[1] $20,000 + $16,667 = $36,667
[2] $500,000 × 8% × 6/12 = $20,000
[3] $500,000 ÷ 30 periods = $16,667
[4] $500,000 − $16,667 = $483,333

(b)

Dec. 31, 2013	Cash	500,000	
	Mortgage Note Payable		500,000
	To record issue of 15-year, 8% mortgage note payable.		
June 30, 2014	Interest Expense	20,000	
	Mortgage Note Payable	16,667	
	Cash		36,667
	To record semi-annual payment on note.		
Dec. 31, 2014	Interest Expense	19,333	
	Mortgage Note Payable	16,667	
	Cash		36,000
	To record semi-annual payment on note.		

(c) The current liability is $33,334 ($16,667 + $16,667).
The non-current liability is $433,332.

The total liability is $466,666, the balance at the end of the second period, December 31, 2014.

(d) In a blended payment situation, the cash payment stays constant. In a fixed principal payment situation, the reduction of the principal stays constant. In both situations, the same amount of principal is repaid over the same period of time—just in a different payment pattern.

THE NAVIGATOR

▶ Summary of Study Objectives

1. ***Compare the impact of issuing debt instead of equity.*** Debt offers the following advantages over equity: (1) shareholder control is not affected, (2) income tax savings result, (3) earnings per share may be higher, and (4) return on equity may be higher.

2. ***Account for bonds payable.*** The market value of bonds is determined using present value factors to determine the present value of the interest and principal cash flows generated by the bond relative to the current market interest rate. When bonds are issued, the Bonds Payable account is credited for the bonds' market value (present value). Bonds are issued at a discount if the market interest rate is higher than the contractual interest rate. Bonds are issued at a premium if the market interest rate is lower than the contractual interest rate.

Bond discounts and bond premiums are amortized to interest expense over the life of the bond using the effective-interest method of amortization. Amortization of the bond discount or premium is the difference between the interest paid and the interest expense. Interest paid is calculated by multiplying the face value of the bonds by the contractual interest rate. Interest expense is calculated by multiplying the amortized cost of the bonds at the beginning of the interest period by the market interest rate. The amortization of a bond discount increases interest expense.

The amortization of a bond premium decreases interest expense.

When bonds are retired at maturity, Bonds Payable is debited and Cash is credited. There is no gain or loss at retirement. When bonds are redeemed before maturity, it is necessary to (1) pay and record any unrecorded interest, (2) eliminate the amortized cost of the bonds at the redemption date, (3) record the cash paid, and (4) recognize any gain or loss on redemption.

3. ***Account for instalment notes payable.*** Instalment notes payable are repayable in a series of instalments. Each payment consists of (1) interest on the unpaid balance of the note, and (2) a reduction of the principal balance. These payments can be either (1) fixed principal plus interest payments or (2) blended principal and interest payments. With fixed principal payments, the reduction in principal is constant but the cash payment and interest decrease each period (as the principal decreases). With blended payments, the cash payment is constant but the interest decreases and the principal reduction increases each period.

4. ***Account for leases.*** For a finance or capital lease, the transaction is considered to be equivalent to a purchase of an asset. The lessee records the asset and the related

obligation at the present value of the future lease payments. The income statement reflects both the interest expense and depreciation expense. For an operating lease, lease (or rental) payments are recorded as an expense by the lessee (renter).

5. **_Explain and illustrate the methods for the presentation and analysis of non-current liabilities._** The current portion of debt is the amount of the principal that must be paid within one year of the balance sheet date. This amount is reported as a current liability in the balance sheet, and the remaining portion of the principal is reported as a non-current liability. The nature of each liability should be described in the notes accompanying the financial statements. A company's long-term solvency may be analyzed by calculating two ratios. Debt to total assets indicates the proportion of company assets that is financed by debt. Interest coverage measures a company's ability to meet its interest payments as they come due.

Flash cards

THE NAVIGATOR

▶ Glossary

Amortized cost   The face value (principal amount) of the bonds less any unamortized discount or plus any unamortized premium. (p. 773)

Amortizing the discount   The allocation of the bond discount to interest expense over the life of the bonds. (p. 774)

Amortizing the premium   The allocation of the bond premium to interest expense over the life of the bonds. (p. 777)

Bond   A debt security that is traded on an organized securities exchange, is issued to investors, and has these properties: the principal amount will be repaid at a designated maturity date and periodic interest is paid (normally semi-annually) at a specified rate on the principal amount. (p. 769)

Bond certificate   A legal document indicating the name of the issuer, the face value of the bond, and other data such as the contractual interest rate and maturity date of the bond. (p. 769)

Capital lease   A lease that transfers substantially all the benefits and risks of ownership to the lessee, so that the lease effectively results in a purchase of the asset under ASPE. Referred to a _finance lease_ under IFRS. (p. 786)

Collateral   Assets pledged as security on a loan. (p. 781)

Contractual interest rate   The rate that determines the amount of interest the borrower pays and the investor receives. (p. 769)

Debentures   Bonds issued against the general credit of the borrower. Also called _unsecured bonds._ (p. 769)

Debt to total assets   The ratio of total liabilities to total assets. Indicates the proportion of assets that is financed by debt. (p. 789)

Discount (on bonds payable)   The difference that results when bonds' selling price is less than their face value. This occurs when the market interest rate is greater than the contractual interest rate. (p. 772)

EBIT   Earnings before interest and tax, calculated as profit + interest expense + income tax expense. (p. 790)

Effective-interest method of amortization   A method of calculating interest expense and of amortizing a bond discount or bond premium that results in periodic interest expense equal to a constant percentage of the amortized cost of the bonds. (p. 773)

Face value   The amount of principal that the issuer must pay at the bond's maturity date. (p. 769)

Finance lease   A lease that transfers all the benefits and risks of ownership to the lessee, so that the lease effectively results in a purchase of the asset under IFRS. Also called _capital lease_ under ASPE. (p. 786)

Financial leverage   Borrowing at one rate and investing at a different rate. (p. 767)

Fixed interest rate   An interest rate that is constant (unchanged) over the term of the debt. (p. 781)

Floating (or variable) interest rate   An interest rate that changes over the term of the debt with fluctuating market rates. (p. 781)

Future value   An amount that will be paid in the future. In the case of bonds payable, it is the face amount of the bonds. (p. 771)

Instalment note   Normally a long-term note that is payable in series of periodic payments. (p. 781)

Instalments   A series of periodic payments made to repay a note payable. (p. 781)

Interest coverage ratio   A measure of a company's ability to meet its interest obligations. It is calculated by dividing profit (earnings) before interest expense and income tax expense (EBIT) by interest expense. (p. 790)

Lease   A contractual arrangement between two parties where the party that owns an asset agrees to allow another party to use the specified property for a series of cash payments over an agreed period of time. (p. 785)

Lessee   The renter of a property. (p. 785)

Lessor   The owner of an asset for rent. (p. 785)

Market (effective) interest rate The rate that investors require for lending money to a company. (p. 770)

Market value of the bond The price that the bond trades at. (p. 769)

Maturity date The date on which the final payment on a debt security is due to be repaid by the issuer to the investor. (p. 769)

Mortgage note payable An instalment note payable that pledges title to specific assets as security for a loan. (p. 781)

Non-current liability Obligations that are expected to be paid after one year or longer. (p. 766)

Off–balance sheet financing The intentional effort by a company to structure its financing arrangements to avoid showing liabilities on its books. (p. 788)

Operating lease A lease where the benefits and risks of ownership are not transferred to the lessee. (p. 787)

Premium (on bonds payable) The difference that results when bonds' selling price is greater than their face value. This occurs when the market interest rate is less than the contractual interest rate. (p. 772)

Present value The amount that must be invested today at a specified interest rate to have a certain amount in the future. (p. 770)

Redeemable bonds Bonds that the issuer can retire at a stated dollar amount before maturity. Also known as *callable bonds*. (p. 769)

Redemption price An amount that a company pays to buy back bonds that is specified at the time the bonds are issued. (p. 779)

Term bonds Bonds that mature at a single specified future date. (p. 769)

▶ Self-Study Questions

Answers are at the end of the chapter.

(SO 1) K 1. The best description of positive financial leverage is:
   (a) a company borrows at a rate that is lower than the return it earns on its investment.
   (b) a company does not have to pay dividends.
   (c) a company borrows at a rate that is higher than the return it earns on its investment.
   (d) a company's income tax is reduced because of the interest paid on its debt.

(SO 2) K 2. If bonds are issued at a discount, it indicates that:
   (a) the contractual interest rate is higher than the market interest rate.
   (b) the market interest rate is higher than the contractual interest rate.
   (c) the contractual interest rate and the market interest rate are the same.
   (d) the bonds are junk bonds.

(SO 2) K 3. Communications Inc. issues $1 million of 10-year, 4% bonds when the market rate of interest is 5%. Interest is paid semi-annually. Investors will:
   (a) not buy the bonds because the market rate of interest is higher than the contractual rate of interest.
   (b) buy the bonds for $1 million.
   (c) buy the bonds for more than $1 million.
   (d) buy the bonds for less than $1 million.

(SO 2) AP 4. On January 1, Shears Corp. issues $400,000 of five-year, 4% bonds at 101. The entry to record the issue of the bonds is:
   (a) debit to Cash for $400,000 and credit to Bonds Payable for $400,000.
   (b) credit to Cash for $400,000 and debit to Bonds Payable for $400,000.
   (c) credit to Cash for $404,000 and debit to Bonds Payable for $404,000.

   (d) debit to Cash for $404,000 and credit to Bonds Payable for $404,000.

(SO 2) K 5. When bonds are issued at a discount, the discount is amortized over the life of the bonds. The best reason for amortizing the bond discount is to:
   (a) reflect that the bond discount is considered an increase in the cost of borrowing.
   (b) decrease the carrying value of the bond to its face value at maturity.
   (c) reflect that the bond discount is considered a reduction in the cost of borrowing.
   (d) ensure the bond payable is recorded at its fair value over the life of the bond.

(SO 2) AP 6. On January 1, Dias Corporation issued $2 million of five-year, 7% bonds with interest payable on July 1 and January 1. The bonds sold for $1,918,880. The market rate of interest for these bonds was 8%. On the first interest date, the entry to record the payment of semi-annual interest would be:
   (a) a debit to Interest Expense of $67,161, a credit to Cash of $70,000, and a debit to Bonds Payable of $2,839.
   (b) a debit to Interest Expense of $70,000 and a credit to Cash of $70,000.
   (c) a debit to Interest Expense of $80,000, a credit to Cash of $70,000, and a credit to Bonds Payable of $10,000.
   (d) a debit to Interest Expense of $76,755, a credit to Cash of $70,000, and a credit to Bonds Payable of $6,755.

(SO 2) AP 7. Gester Corporation redeems its $100,000 face value bonds at 105 on January 1, after the payment of semi-annual interest. The amortized cost of the

bonds at the redemption date is $103,745. The entry to record the redemption will be:
(a) a debit to Bonds Payable of $103,745 and a credit to Cash of $103,745.
(b) a debit to Bonds Payable of $100,000, a debit to Loss on Bond Redemption of $3,745, and a credit to Cash of $103,745.
(c) a debit to Bonds Payable of $103,745, a debit to Loss on Bond Redemption of $1,255, and a credit to Cash of $105,000.
(d) a debit to Bonds Payable of $105,000 and a credit to Cash of $105,000.

(SO 3) AP 8. Zhang Inc. issues a $497,000, three-year, 7% instalment note payable on January 1. The note will be paid in three annual blended payments of $189,383 each. What is the amount of interest expense that should be recognized by Zhang in the second year?
(a) $21,533
(b) $23,193
(c) $23,968
(d) $34,790

(SO 3) AP 9. Assume that the note issued by Zhang Inc. in question 8 above will be paid with fixed principal payments of $165,667 each. What is the amount of interest expense that should be recognized by Zhang in the second year?
(a) $25,628
(b) $23,193
(c) $11,596
(d) $34,790

(SO 3) AP 10. Manufacturing Inc. issued a $100,000, five-year, 5% note payable on January 1, 2014. The terms provide for annual blended payments of $23,098. The entry to record the first payment on December 31, 2014, is:

(a) a debit to Interest Expense of $5,000, a debit to Notes Payable of $18,098, and a credit to Cash of $23,098.
(b) a debit to Notes Payable of $23,098 and a credit to Cash of $23,098.
(c) a debit to Interest Expense of $5,000, a debit to Notes Payable of $23,098, and a credit to Cash of $28,098.
(d) a debit to Notes Payable of $20,000, a debit to Interest Expense of $3,098, and a credit to Cash of $23,098.

(SO 4) C 11. The lease term for Lease A is equal to 74% of the estimated economic life of the leased property. The lease term for Lease B is equal to 45% of the estimated economic life of the leased property. Assuming the lessee reports under IFRS and no other conditions are met, how should the lessee classify these leases?

	Lease A	Lease B
(a)	Operating lease	Finance lease
(b)	Operating lease	Operating lease
(c)	Finance lease	Operating lease
(d)	Finance lease	Finance lease

(SO 5) AN 12. Which of the following situations would most likely indicate that a company's solvency has deteriorated?
(a) Increasing debt to total assets and increasing interest coverage ratios
(b) Decreasing debt to total assets and decreasing interest coverage ratios
(c) Increasing debt to total assets and decreasing interest coverage ratios
(d) Decreasing debt to total assets and increasing interest coverage ratios

THE NAVIGATOR

▶ Questions

(SO 1) C 1. What is the difference between a current liability and a non-current liability? Give two examples of each type of liability.

(SO 1) C 2. As a source of long-term financing, what are the major advantages of using debt over equity? What are the disadvantages?

(SO 1) C 3. Amanda knows that interest expense reduces profit. So she doesn't understand how earnings per share and return on equity can be higher when a company finances with debt than if the company issues equity. Explain this to Amanda.

(SO 2) C 4. (a) Explain the difference between a contractual interest rate and market interest rate. (b) Explain why one rate changes over the term of the bonds and the other stays the same.

(SO 2) C 5. Eduardo wants to know why a board of directors doesn't set the contractual interest rate at the market interest rate on the date of issue when it authorizes a

bond issue. He argues that if the contractual interest rate was set at the market rate, then companies would not have to issue bonds at a premium or discount. Explain this to Eduardo.

(SO 2) C 6. Assume that Stoney Inc. sold bonds with a face value of $100,000 for $102,000. Was the market interest rate equal to, less than, or greater than the bonds' contractual interest rate? Explain.

(SO 2) C 7. How will the total cost of borrowing be affected if a bond is sold (a) at a discount and (b) at a premium?

(SO 2) C 8. Geoff doesn't understand why the interest expense recorded is higher than the cash paid for interest when bonds are issued at a discount and why the interest expense is lower than the cash paid when bonds are issued at premium. Explain this to Geoff.

(SO 2) K 9. Explain how the bond discount amortization is calculated using the effective-interest method when bonds are issued at a discount.

(SO 2) C   10. Why is there no gain or loss when bonds are redeemed at maturity, but there usually is a gain or loss when bonds are redeemed before maturity?

(SO 3) C   11. The Canada Student Loans Program charges interest at prime plus an added percentage, such as 2.5%, on its loans to students. Is this a fixed or floating rate? Explain.

(SO 3) C   12. What is the difference between instalment notes payable with fixed principal payments and those with blended payments?

(SO 3) AP 13. Pavlina borrowed $15,000 from the bank and signed a three-year, 6% instalment note payable with fixed principal payments. She wants to know how to calculate what the annual fixed principal payment will be. Explain.

(SO 3) AP 14. Bob Holowachuk, a friend of yours, recently purchased a home for $300,000. He paid $30,000 as a cash down payment and financed the remainder with a 20-year, 6% mortgage, payable in blended payments of $1,934 per month. At the end of the first month, Bob received a statement from the bank indicating that only $584 of the principal was paid during the month. At this rate, he calculated that it will take over 38 years to pay off the mortgage. Do you agree? Explain.

(SO 4) C   15. (a) What is a lease? (b) Distinguish between a finance lease and an operating lease.

(SO 4) C   16. Why might a company choose to lease equipment instead of purchasing equipment?

(SO 4) C   17. What is off–balance sheet financing? Why are long-term operating leases considered to be a form of off–balance sheet financing?

(SO 4) AP 18. What is the impact on a company's balance sheet and income statement if it accounts for a lease as an operating lease instead of as a finance lease?

(SO 4) C   19. Josh doesn't understand why leased property can be recorded as an asset when a company does not own the property. Explain this to Josh.

(SO 5) K   20. In addition to what is reported in the balance sheet for non-current liabilities, what information is provided in the notes to the financial statements?

(SO 5) K   21. How are the current and non-current portions of a mortgage note payable determined for presenting them in the liabilities section of the balance sheet?

(SO 5) K   22. Distinguish between liquidity and solvency. Mention two ratios that are used to measure each.

(SO 5) C   23. Huan Yue is wondering why the debt to total assets and interest coverage ratios are calculated. Answer her question and explain why the debt to total assets ratio should never be interpreted without also referring to the interest coverage ratio.

(SO 5) C   24. Ling Wei doesn't understand how the interest coverage ratio can decrease when the debt to total assets increased. Explain this to Ling.

▶ Brief Exercises

Compare debt and equity financing alternatives.
(SO 1) AP

BE15–1   Olga Inc. is considering two alternatives to finance its construction of a new $4-million plant at the beginning of the year: (a) issue 200,000 common shares at a market price of $20 per share, or (b) issue $4 million of 6% bonds at face value. Once the new plant is built, Olga expects to earn an additional $1 million of profit before interest and income tax. It has 500,000 common shares and $10 million of shareholders' equity before the new financing. Complete the following table for the year.

	(a) Issue Equity	(b) Issue Debt
Profit before interest and income tax	$1,000,000	$1,000,000
Interest expense		
Profit before income tax		
Income tax expense (25%)		
Profit		
Number of shares		
Earnings per share		

Calculate present value of bond. (SO 2) AP

BE15–2   Carvel Corp. issued $500,000 of 10-year, 5% bonds with interest payable semi-annually. How much did Carvel receive from the sale of these bonds if the market interest rate was (a) 4%, (b) 5%, and (c) 6%?

Record bond transactions. (SO 2) AP

BE15–3   Rockwell Corporation issued $2 million of five-year, 3% bonds dated January 1, 2014, at 100. Interest is payable semi-annually on January 1 and July 1. Rockwell has a December 31 year end.

(a) Prepare the journal entry to record the sale of these bonds on January 1, 2014.
(b) Prepare the journal entry to record the first interest payment on July 1, 2014.
(c) Prepare the adjusting journal entry on December 31, 2014, to accrue the interest expense.

BE15–4   The Town of Moosawaw issued $1 million of five-year, 5% bonds dated January 1, 2014. Interest is payable semi-annually on July 1 and January 1.

Record issue of bonds; show balance sheet presentation. (SO 2) AP

(a) Record the sale of these bonds on January 1, 2014, and the first interest payment on July 1, 2014, assuming that the bonds were issued at 98 and that the semi-annual amortization amount for the first interest period is $1,766.

(b) Record the sale of these bonds on January 1, 2014, and the first interest payment on July 1, 2014, assuming that the bonds were issued at 100.

(c) Record the sale of these bonds on January 1, 2014, and the first interest payment on July 1, 2014, assuming that the bonds were issued at 102 and that the semi-annual amortization amount for the first interest period is $1,804.

(d) What will be the amortized cost at maturity, January 1, 2019, under each of the three different issue prices?

BE15–5   On May 1, 2014, Jianhua Corporation issued $120,000 of 10-year, 6% bonds, with interest payable semi-annually on November 1 and May 1. The bonds were issued to yield a market interest rate of 5%.

Record bond transactions using effective-interest amortization. (SO 2) AP

(a) Calculate the proceeds from the bonds' issue.
(b) Record the issue of the bonds on May 1, 2014.
(c) Record the payment of interest on November 1, 2014.

BE15–6   A partial bond amortization schedule for $2-million, 5-year bonds is presented below:

Complete amortization schedule and answer questions. (SO 2) AP

Semi-Annual Interest Period	Interest [2]	Interest [3]	[1] Amortization	Bond Amortized Cost
Issue Date				$1,912,479
1 (Apr. 30)	$40,000	[4]	$7,812	1,920,291
2 (Oct. 31)	40,000	$48,007	[5]	[6]

(a) Fill in the missing words or amounts for items [1] through [6].
(b) What is the bonds' face value?
(c) What is the bonds' contractual interest rate? The market interest rate?
(d) Explain why interest expense differs from the amount of interest paid.

BE15–7   Elsworth Ltd. issued $1 million of five-year, 4% bonds dated May 1, 2014, for $1,046,110 when the market interest rate was 3%. Interest is paid semi-annually on May 1 and November 1. Prepare an amortization schedule for the first three interest payments.

Prepare amortization schedule. (SO 2) AP

BE15–8   A partial bond amortization schedule for Chiasson Corp. is provided below. Chiasson has a December 31 year end.

Record bond interest using amortization schedule. (SO 2) AP

Semi-Annual Interest Period	Interest Payment	Interest Expense	Amortization	Bond Amortized Cost
Jan. 1, 2014				$286,872
July 1, 2014	$6,000	$7,172	$1,172	288,044
Jan. 1, 2015	6,000	7,201	1,201	289,245
July 1, 2015	6,000	7,231	1,231	290,476

(a) Was the bond issued at a premium or discount?
(b) Record the interest payment on July 1, 2014.
(c) Record the adjusting entry on December 31, 2014.
(d) Record the interest payment on January 1, 2015.

BE15–9   Refer to the amortization schedule presented in BE15–8 for Chiasson Corp.

Record redemption of bonds using amortization schedule. (SO 2) AP

(a) Assuming Chiasson redeems these bonds at 100 on January 1, 2015, after the interest has been paid, prepare the journal entry to record the redemption.

(b) Assuming Chiasson redeems these bonds at 101 on January 1, 2015, after the interest has been paid, prepare the journal entry to record the redemption.

(c) Assuming Chiasson redeems these bonds at 95 on January 1, 2015, after the interest has been paid, prepare the journal entry to record the redemption.

BE15–10   You qualify for a $10,000 loan from the Canada Student Loans Program to help finance your education. Once you graduate, you start repaying this note payable at an interest rate of 4.8%. The monthly cash payment is $105.09, principal and interest, for 120 payments (10 years). Prepare an instalment payment schedule for the first four payments.

Prepare instalment payment schedule. (SO 3) AP

Record note transactions.
(SO 3) AP

BE15–11 Eyre Inc. issues a $360,000, 10-year, 6% mortgage note payable on November 30, 2013, to obtain financing for a new building. The terms provide for monthly instalment payments. Prepare the journal entries to record the mortgage loan on November 30, 2013, and the first two payments on December 31, 2013, and January 31, 2014, assuming the payment is:

(a) a fixed principal payment of $3,000.
(b) a blended payment of $3,997.

Calculate current and non-current portion of notes payable. (SO 3) AP

BE15–12 The following instalment payment schedule is for an instalment note payable:

Interest Period	Cash Payment	Interest Expense	Reduction of Principal	Principal Balance
Jan. 1, 2013				$40,000
Jan. 1, 2014	12,000	2,000	10,000	30,000
Jan. 1, 2015	11,500	1,500	10,000	20,000
Jan. 1, 2016	11,000	1,000	10,000	10,000
Jan. 1, 2017	10,500	500	10,000	0

(a) What are the non-current and current portions of the note at December 31, 2013?
(b) What are the non-current and current portions of the note at December 31, 2016?

Record note transaction; show balance sheet presentation.
(SO 3) AP

BE15–13 Elbow Lake Corp. issues a $600,000, four-year, 4% note payable on March 31, 2013. The terms provide for fixed principal payments annually of $150,000.

(a) Prepare the journal entries to record the note on March 31, 2013, and the first payment on March 31, 2014.
(b) Show the balance sheet presentation of the current and non-current liability related to the note as at March 31, 2014.

Analyze lease. (SO 4) AP

BE15–14 Paget Ltd., a public company, signed a five-year lease agreement with Equipco Ltd. for manufacturing equipment that had been specifically designed for a specialized patented manufacturing process. Paget holds the exclusive rights to the manufacturing process. The equipment's estimated economic life is seven years. The equipment will be returned to Equipco at the end of the lease term. Indicate if the lease is a finance lease or operating lease. Explain.

Record lease. (SO 4) AP

BE15–15 Pierre Paquin leases office space for $2,500 per month from Privateer Commercial Realty Ltd. The lease agreement is for five years. Prepare the journal entry to record the monthly lease payment by the lessee.

Record lease. (SO 4) AP

BE15–16 Chang Corp. leases new manufacturing equipment from Bracer Construction, Inc. The present value of the lease payments is $300,000 and the fair value is $320,000.

(a) Which company is the lessor and which company is the lessee?
(b) Prepare the journal entry to record the lease for the lessee.

Show balance sheet presentation. (SO 5) AP

BE15–17 Cooke Inc. issued a $240,000, 10-year, 8% note payable on October 1, 2013. The terms provide for blended payments of $8,773 payable in quarterly instalments on January 1, April 1, July 1, and October 1. Below is a partial instalment schedule for the note payable.

Interest Period	Cash Payment	Interest Expense	Reduction of Principal	Principal Balance
Oct. 1, 2013				$240,000
Jan. 1, 2014	$8,773	$4,800	$3,973	236,027
Apr. 1, 2014	8,773	4,721	4,052	231,975
July 1, 2014	8,773	4,639	4,134	227,841
Oct. 1, 2014	8,773	4,557	4,216	223,625
Jan. 1, 2015	8,773	4,472	4,301	219,324

Show the balance sheet presentation of the current and non-current liability related to the note as at December 31, 2013.

Prepare liabilities section of balance sheet. (SO 5) AP

BE15–18 Selected liability items for Waugh Corporation at December 31, 2014, follow. Prepare the liabilities section of Waugh's balance sheet.

Accounts payable	$ 48,000	Income tax payable	$ 8,000
Bonds payable, due 2028	1,035,000	Notes payable, (net of current portion)	145,000
Current portion of notes payable	25,000	Interest payable	26,000
Current portion of lease liability	25,000	Total lease liability	75,000

BE15–19   Molson Coors Brewing Company reported the following selected data at December 31, 2011 (in US$ millions):

Calculate solvency ratios.
(SO 5) AP

Total assets	$12,423.8
Total liabilities	4,733.6
Interest expense	118.7
Income tax expense	99.4
Profit	677.1

Calculate the company's (a) debt to total assets, and (b) interest coverage ratios.

▶ Exercises

E15–1   East-West Airlines is considering two alternatives to finance the purchase of a fleet of airplanes. These alternatives are (1) to issue 120,000 common shares at $45 per share, and (2) to issue 10-year, 5% bonds for $5.4 million. It is estimated that the company will earn an additional $1.2 million before interest and income tax as a result of this purchase. The company has an income tax rate of 30%. It has 200,000 common shares issued and average shareholders' equity of $12 million before the new financing.

Compare debt and equity financing alternatives.
(SO 1) AP

Instructions

(a) Calculate the profit for each financing alternative.
(b) Calculate the earnings per share and return on equity for each alternative.
(c) Which financing alternative would you recommend for East-West Airlines? Why?

E15–2   Central College is about to issue $1 million of 10-year bonds that pay a 6% annual interest rate, with interest payable semi-annually.

Calculate present value of bonds. (SO 2) AP

Instructions

(a) Calculate the issue price of these bonds if the market interest rate is (1) 5%, (2) 6%, and (3) 7%.
(b) Calculate the interest expense for the first interest period if the market interest rate is (1) 5%, (2) 6%, and (3) 7%.
(c) Calculate the interest payment if the market interest rate is (1) 5%, (2) 6%, and (3) 7%.

E15–3   On September 1, 2013, Priora Corporation issued $600,000 of 10-year, 3% bonds at 96. Interest is payable semi-annually on September 1 and March 1. Priora's fiscal year end is February 28.

Record bond transactions; show balance sheet presentation. (SO 2) AP

Instructions

(a) Is the market rate of interest higher or lower than 3%? Explain.
(b) Record the issue of the bonds on September 1, 2013.
(c) Record the accrual of interest on February 28, 2014, assuming the semi-annual amortization amount for this interest period is $1,014.
(d) Identify what amounts, if any, would be reported as a current liability and non-current liability with respect to the bonds and bond interest accounts on February 28, 2014.
(e) Record the payment of interest on March 1, 2014.

E15–4   On July 31, 2013, Mooney Inc. issued $500,000 of five-year, 4% bonds at 102. Interest is payable semi-annually on July 31 and January 31. Mooney's fiscal year end is January 31.

Record bond transactions; show balance sheet presentation. (SO 2) AP

Instructions

(a) Is the market rate of interest higher or lower than 4%? Explain.
(b) Record the issue of the bonds on July 31, 2013.
(c) Record the payment of interest on January 31, 2014, assuming the semi-annual amortization amount for this interest period is $923.
(d) Identify what amounts, if any, would be reported as a current liability and non-current liability with respect to the bonds and bond interest accounts on January 31, 2014.

E15–5   Bight Corporation issued $400,000 five-year bonds on April 1, 2011. Interest is paid semi-annually on April 1 and October 1 and the company's year end is March 31. Below is a partial amortization schedule for the first few years of the bond issue.

Answer questions about amortization schedule.
(SO 2) AP

Semi-Annual Interest Period	Interest Payment	Interest Expense	Amortization	Bond Amortized Cost
April 1, 2011				$418,444
October 1, 2011	$8,000	$6,277	$1,723	416,721
April 1, 2012	8,000	6,251	1,749	414,972
October 1, 2012	8,000	6,225	1,775	413,197
April 1, 2013	8,000	6,198	1,802	411,395
October 1, 2013	8,000	6,171	1,829	409,566
April 1, 2014	8,000	6,143	1,857	407,709

Instructions

(a) Were the bonds issued at a discount or at a premium?

(b) What is the bonds' face value?

(c) What will the bonds' amortized cost be at the maturity date?

(d) What is the bonds' contractual interest rate? The market interest rate?

(e) Identify what amounts, if any, would be reported as a current liability and non-current liability with respect to the bonds and bond interest accounts on March 31, 2013.

(f) What will be the total interest payment over the five-year life of the bonds? Total interest expense?

(g) Would your answers in part (f) change if the bonds had been issued at a discount instead of a premium or at a premium instead of a discount? Explain.

Record interest and redemption of bonds.
(SO 2) AP

E15–6 On January 1, 2012, Chilton Ltd. issued $500,000, 5%, five-year bonds. The bonds were issued to yield a market interest rate of 6%. Chilton's year end is December 31. On January 1, 2014 immediately after making and recording the semi-annual interest payment, Chilton redeemed the bonds. A partial bond amortization schedule is presented below.

Semi-Annual Interest Period	Interest Payment	Interest Expense	Amortization	Bond Amortized Cost
January 1, 2012				$478,674
July 1, 2012	$12,500	$14,360	$1,860	480,534
January 1, 2013	12,500	14,416	1,916	482,450
July 1, 2013	12,500	14,474	1,974	484,424
January 1, 2014	12,500	14,533	2,033	486,457
July 1, 2014	12,500	14,594	2,094	488,551
January 1, 2015	12,500	14,657	2,157	490,708

Instructions

(a) Prepare the journal entry to record the payment of interest on July 1, 2013.

(b) Prepare the journal entry to accrue the interest expense on December 31, 2013.

(c) Prepare the journal entry to record the payment of interest on January 1, 2014.

(d) Prepare the journal entry to record the redemption of the bonds assuming they were redeemed at 100.

(e) Prepare the journal entry to record the redemption of the bonds assuming they were redeemed at 96.

Record interest and redemption of bonds.
(SO 2) AP

E15–7 Ontario Inc. issued $800,000 of 10-year, 4% bonds on January 1, 2013, when the market interest rate was 5%. Interest is payable semi-annually on July 1 and January 1. Ontario has a December 31 year end.

Instructions

(a) Calculate the bonds' issue price.

(b) Record the issue of the bonds.

(c) Prepare an amortization schedule through to December 31, 2014 (four interest periods).

(d) Record the accrual of the interest on December 31, 2014.

(e) Identify what amounts, if any, would be reported as a current liability and a non-current liability with respect to the bonds and bond interest accounts on December 31, 2014.

(f) Record the payment of interest on January 1, 2015.

Record bond transactions.
(SO 2, 6) AP

E15–8 Tagawa Corporation issued $600,000 of 10-year, 8% bonds on January 1, 2014, for $642,637. This price resulted in a market interest rate of 7% on the bonds. Interest is payable semi-annually on July 1 and January 1. Tagawa has a December 31 year end. On January 1, 2015 immediately after making and recording the semi-annual interest payment, the bonds were redeemed at 104.

Instructions

(a) Record the issue of the bonds on January 1, 2014.

(b) Prepare an amortization schedule through to December 31, 2015 (four interest periods).

(c) Record the payment of interest on July 1, 2014.
(d) Record the accrual of interest on December 31, 2014.
(e) Record the redemption of the bonds on January 1, 2015.

E15–9   Cove Resort Corp. issued a 20-year, 5%, $300,000 mortgage note payable to finance the construction of a new building on December 31, 2014. The terms provide for semi-annual instalment payments on June 30 and December 31.

Record mortgage note payable. (SO 3) AP

Instructions

Prepare the journal entries to record the mortgage note payable and the first two instalment payments assuming the payment is:

(a) a fixed principal payment of $7,500.
(b) a blended payment of $11,951.

E15–10   The following instalment payment schedule is for an instalment note payable:

Analyze instalment payment schedule and identify current and non-current portions. (SO 3) AP

Interest Period	Cash Payment	Interest Expense	Reduction of Principal	Principal Balance
Jan. 1, 2013				100,000
Jan. 1, 2014	23,097	5,000	18,097	81,903
Jan. 1, 2015	23,097	4,095	19,002	62,901
Jan. 1, 2016	23,097	3,145	19,952	42,949
Jan. 1, 2017	23,097	2,147	20,950	21,999
Jan. 1, 2018	23,097	1,100	21,999	0

Instructions

(a) Is this a fixed principal or blended payment schedule?
(b) What is the interest rate on the note?
(c) Prepare the journal entry to record the first instalment payment.
(d) What are the non-current and current portions of the note at the end of period 2?

E15–11   The following instalment payment schedule is for an instalment note payable:

Analyze instalment payment schedule and identify current and non-current portions. (SO 3) AP

Interest Period	Cash Payment	Interest Expense	Reduction of Principal	Principal Balance
Jan. 1, 2013				$150,000
July 1, 2013	24,750	6,000	18,750	131,250
Jan. 1, 2014	24,000	5,250	18,750	112,500
July 1, 2014	23,250	4,500	18,750	93,750
Jan. 1, 2015	22,500	3,750	18,750	75,000

Instructions

(a) Is this a fixed principal or blended payment schedule?
(b) What is the interest rate on the note?
(c) What is the maturity date on the note?
(d) Prepare the journal entry to record the first instalment payment.
(e) What are the non-current and current portions of the note at the end of period 2?

E15–12   On January 1, 2014, Wolstenholme Corp. borrows $15,000 by signing a three-year, 6% note payable. The note is repayable in three annual blended payments of $5,612 on December 31 of each year.

Prepare instalment payment schedule and record note payable. Identify balance sheet presentation. (SO 3) AP

Instructions

(a) Prepare an instalment payment schedule for the note.
(b) Prepare journal entries to record the note and the first instalment payment.
(c) What amounts would be reported as current and non-current in the liabilities section of Wolstenholme's balance sheet on December 31, 2014?

E15–13   Referring to the data presented in E15–12 for Wolstenholme Corp., assume the payments are annual fixed principal payments instead of blended payments.

Prepare instalment payment schedule and record note payable. Identify balance sheet presentation. (SO 3) AP

Instructions

(a) Calculate the annual principal payment.
(b) Prepare an instalment payment schedule for the note.
(c) Prepare journal entries to record the note and the first instalment payment.
(d) What amounts would be reported as current and non-current in the liabilities section of Wolstenholme's balance sheet on December 31, 2014?

Analyze and record leases.
(SO 4) AP

E15–14 Two independent situations follow:

1. Ready Car Rental leased a car to Dumfries Company for one year. Terms of the lease agreement call for monthly payments of $750, beginning on May 21, 2014.
2. On January 1, 2014, InSynch Ltd. entered into an agreement to lease 60 computers from HiTech Electronics. The terms of the lease agreement require three annual payments of $43,737 (including 5.5% interest), beginning on December 31, 2014. The present value of the three payments is $118,000 and the market value of the computers is $120,000.

Instructions

(a) What kind of lease—operating or finance—should be recorded in each of the above situations? Explain your rationale.
(b) Prepare the journal entry, if any, that each company must make to record the lease agreement.

Analyze solvency.
(SO 4, 5) AP

E15–15 **Shoppers Drug Mart Corporation** reported the following selected data (in millions):

	2011	2010
Total assets	$7,300.3	$7,044.2
Total liabilities	3,032.5	2,941.6
Profit	613.9	591.9
Income tax expense	232.9	244.8
Interest expense	64.0	60.6

Instructions

(a) Calculate the debt to total assets and interest coverage ratios for 2011 and 2010. Did Shoppers' solvency improve, worsen, or remain unchanged in 2011?
(b) The notes to Shoppers Drug Mart's financial statements show that the company has future operating lease commitments totalling $4.3 billion. What is the significance of these unrecorded obligations when analyzing Shoppers Drug Mart's solvency?

Calculate ratios under financing alternatives.
(SO 1, 5) AP

E15–16 The Utopia Paper Company requires $5 million of financing to upgrade its production facilities. It has a choice to finance the upgrade with a 6% non-current loan or to issue additional shares. The company currently has total assets of $12 million, total liabilities of $8 million, shareholders' equity of $4 million, and profit of $2 million. It projects that profit will be $315,000 higher if debt is issued and $525,000 higher if shares are issued. Assume the project is invested in at the beginning of the year.

Instructions

(a) Calculate the debt to total assets and return on equity ratios under each financing alternative.
(b) Which financing alternative would you recommend for Utopia Paper? Why?

Prepare non-current liabilities section of balance sheet.
(SO 5) AP

E15–17 The adjusted trial balance for Ray Corporation at July 31, 2014 the corporation's fiscal year-end, contained the following:

Accounts payable	$ 96,000	Note payable	$140,000
Accounts receivable	112,000	Lease liability	65,000
Bonds payable, due 2018	205,000	Note receivable, due December 2014	35,000
Interest payable	5,000	Unearned revenue	10,000

Of the lease liability amount, $16,250 is due within the next year. Total payments on the note payable in the fiscal year 2015 will be $27,000: $7,000 is for interest and $20,000 for principal repayments.

Instructions

(a) Prepare the non-current liabilities section of the balance sheet as at July 31, 2014.
(b) Some of the accounts above belong in the balance sheet but not in its non-current liabilities section. What is the correct classification for them?

▶ Problems: Set A

Record bond transactions.
(SO 2) AP

P15–1A The following is from Deshwar Corp.'s balance sheet:

DESHWAR CORP Balance Sheet (partial) December 31, 2013	
Current liabilities	
Interest payable	$ 50,000
Non-current liabilities	
Bonds payable, due January 1, 2017	2,500,000

Interest is payable semi-annually on January 1 and July 1. The bonds were issued at par.

Instructions

(a) What is the contractual rate of interest on the bonds?
(b) Record the payment of the bond interest on January 1, 2014.
(c) Assume that on January 1, 2014, after paying interest, Deshwar redeems $625,000 of the bonds at 102. Record the redemption of the bonds.
(d) Record the payment of the bond interest on July 1, 2014, on the remaining bonds.
(e) Prepare the adjusting entry on December 31, 2014, to accrue the interest on the remaining bonds.
(f) Prepare the entry to record the repayment of the remaining bonds on January 1, 2017.

TAKING IT FURTHER   Was the market rate of interest higher or lower than the contractual rate of interest on January 1, 2014, when the bonds were redeemed? Explain.

P15–2A   On May 1, 2013, MEM Corp. issued $900,000 of five-year, 7% bonds at 103. The bonds pay interest annually on May 1. MEM's year end is April 30.

Record bond transactions; show balance sheet presentation. (SO 2) AP

Instructions

(a) Record the issue of the bonds on May 1, 2013.
(b) Record the accrual of interest on April 30, 2014, assuming the amortization amount is $4,763.
(c) What amounts related to the bonds would be reported as current and non-current in the liabilities section of MEM's April 30, 2014, balance sheet?
(d) Record the payment of interest on May 1, 2014.
(e) Assume that on May 1, 2014, after payment of the interest, MEM redeems all of the bonds at 104. Record the redemption of the bonds.

TAKING IT FURTHER   What was the market rate of interest on May 1, 2013, when MEM issued the bonds?

P15–3A   On July 1, 2013, Webhancer Corp. issued $4 million of 10-year, 5% bonds at $4,327,029. This price resulted in a 4% market interest rate on the bonds. The bonds pay semi-annual interest on July 1 and January 1, and Webhancer has a December 31 year end.

Record bond transactions and answer questions. (SO 2) AP

Instructions

(a) Record the following transactions:
  1. The issue of the bonds on July 1, 2013
  2. The accrual of interest on December 31, 2013
  3. The payment of interest on January 1, 2014
  4. The payment of interest on July 1, 2014
(b) Answer the following questions:
  1. What amount of interest expense is reported for 2013?
  2. Would the bond interest expense reported in 2013 be the same as, greater than, or less than the amount that would be reported if the bonds had been issued at a discount rather than at a premium? Explain.
  3. Determine the total cost of borrowing over the life of the bonds.
  4. Would the total bond interest expense be greater than, the same as, or less than the total interest expense that would be reported if the bonds had been issued at a discount rather than at a premium? Explain.
  5. Assuming that the bonds were issued at a market interest rate of 6%, calculate the issue price of the bonds. Determine the total cost of borrowing over the life of the bonds.

TAKING IT FURTHER   Explain what the impact would be on interest expense if the market rate of interest changed to 4.5% in December 2013 after the bonds were issued.

P15–4A   On January 1, 2013, Global Satellites issued $1.4-million, 10-year bonds. The bonds pay semi-annual interest on July 1 and January 1, and Global has a December 31 year end. A partial bond amortization schedule is presented below:

Fill in missing amounts in amortization schedule, record bond transactions, and show balance sheet presentation. (SO 2, 5) AP

Semi-Annual Interest Period	Interest Payment	Interest Expense	Amortization	Bond Amortized Cost
January 1, 2013				$1,300,514
July 1, 2013	$[1]	$[2]	$3,518	1,304,032
January 1, 2014	42,000	45,641	3,641	1,307,673
July 1, 2014	42,000	45,769	[3]	1,311,442
January 1, 2015	42,000	45,900	[4]	[5]
July 1, 2015	42,000	46,037	4,037	1,319,379
January 1, 2016	42,000	46,178	4,178	1,323,557

Instructions

(a) Were the bonds issued at a premium or a discount?

(b) Fill in the missing amounts for [1] through [5].

(c) What is the face value of the bonds?

(d) What is the contractual rate of interest?

(e) What was the market interest rate when the bonds were issued?

(f) Record the issue of the bonds on January 1, 2013.

(g) Record the interest payment on July 1, 2014.

(h) Record the accrual of interest on December 31, 2014.

(i) What amounts would be reported as current and non-current in the liabilities section of Global's December 31, 2014, balance sheet?

(j) Record the interest payment on January 1, 2015.

(k) Assuming, immediately after the interest payment the bonds were redeemed on January 1, 2015, when the market interest rate was 5%, calculate the amount Global paid to redeem the bonds. (*Hint*: Use the number of interest periods remaining to calculate the amount paid to redeem the bonds.)

(l) Record the redemption of the bonds on January 1, 2015.

TAKING IT FURTHER Why would Global's board of directors not have set the contractual interest rate at the market interest rate on the date of issue when it authorized the bond issue?

Record bond transactions; show balance sheet presentation. (SO 2, 5) AP

P15–5A On January 1, 2013, Alberta Hydro Ltd. issued bonds with a maturity value of $8 million when the market rate of interest was 4%. The bonds have a coupon (contractual) interest rate of 5% and mature on January 1, 2023. Interest on the bonds is payable semi-annually on July 1 and January 1 of each year. The company's year end is December 31.

Instructions

(a) Calculate the issue price of the bonds.

(b) Prepare a bond amortization schedule from date of issue up to and including January 1, 2015.

(c) Prepare all of the required journal entries related to the bonds that Alberta Hydro will record during 2013, including any adjusting journal entries at December 31, 2013.

(d) What amounts would be reported as current and non-current in the liabilities section of Alberta Hydro's December 31, 2013, balance sheet?

(e) Record the payment of interest on January 1, 2014.

(f) The bonds were redeemed on January 1, 2015 (after the interest had been paid and recorded) at 102. Prepare the journal entry for the redemption of the bonds.

(g) Assume instead the bonds were not redeemed on January 1, 2015. Record the entry for the repayment of the bonds on January 1, 2023.

(h) What will be the total interest payment over the 10-year life of the bonds? What will be the total interest expense over the 10-year life of the bonds?

TAKING IT FURTHER Explain why the total interest payment over the 10-year life of the bonds is equal to or different than the total interest expense over the 10-year life of the bonds.

Prepare instalment payment schedule, record note transactions, and show balance sheet presentation. (SO 3, 5) AP

P15–6A A local company has just approached a venture capitalist for financing to develop a ski hill. On April 1, 2013, the venture capitalist loaned the company $1 million at an interest rate of 5%. The loan is repayable over four years in fixed principal payments. The first payment is due March 31, 2014. The ski hill operator's year end will be December 31.

Instructions

(a) Record the issue of the note payable on April 1, 2013.

(b) Calculate the amount of the fixed principal payment.

(c) Prepare an instalment payment schedule.

(d) Record the accrual of interest on December 31, 2013, and the instalment payment on March 31, 2014.

(e) What amounts would be reported as current and non-current in the liabilities section of the company's December 31, 2013, balance sheet?

(f) Record the accrual of interest on December 31, 2014, and the instalment payment on March 31, 2015.

TAKING IT FURTHER Explain how the interest expense and reduction of the note payable would change in (b) and (c) if the note had been repayable in blended payments of $282,012, rather than in fixed principal payments.

Record note transactions. (SO 3) AP

P15–7A Olsen Well Services Ltd. purchased equipment for $900,000 on September 30, 2013. The equipment was purchased with a $150,000 cash down payment and through the issue of a $750,000, five-year, 3.6% mortgage note payable for the balance. The terms provide for the mortgage to be repaid in monthly blended payments of $13,677 starting on October 31.

Instructions

(a) Record the issue of the note payable on September 30.

(b) Record the first two instalment payments on October 31 and November 30.

(c) Repeat part (b) assuming that the terms provided for monthly fixed principal payments of $12,500, rather than blended payments of $13,677.

TAKING IT FURTHER   If the instalments are fixed principal payments of $12,500, will the interest expense over the life of the note be greater than, the same as, or less than if the instalments are a blended payment of $13,677? Explain.

P15–8A   Kinyae Electronics issues a $700,000, 10-year, 7% mortgage note payable on December 31, 2013, to help finance a plant expansion. The terms of the note provide for semi-annual blended payments of $49,253. Payments are due on June 30 and December 31.

Prepare instalment payment schedule and record note transactions. Show balance sheet presentation. (SO 3) AP

Instructions

(a) Prepare an instalment payment schedule for the first two years. Round all calculations to the nearest dollar.

(b) Record the issue of the mortgage note payable on December 31, 2013.

(c) Show how the mortgage liability should be reported on the balance sheet at December 31, 2013. (*Hint*: Remember to report any current portion separately from the non-current liability.)

(d) Record the first two instalment payments on June 30, 2014, and December 31, 2014.

(e) If Kinyae made instalments of fixed principal payments on a semi-annual basis, what would the fixed principal payment be?

(f) Assuming Kinyae made fixed principal payments, record the first two instalments.

TAKING IT FURTHER   Indicate the advantages and disadvantages of making fixed principal payments versus blended payments.

P15–9A   Three different lease transactions are presented below for Manitoba Enterprises, a public company. Assume that all lease transactions start on January 1, 2014. Manitoba does not receive title to the properties, either during the lease term or at the end of it. The yearly rental for each of the leases is paid on January 1 starting on January 1, 2014.

Analyze lease situations. Discuss financial statement presentation. (SO 4) AP

	Manufacturing Equipment	Vehicles	Office Equipment
Lease term	5 years	6 years	3 years
Estimated economic life	15 years	7 years	6 years
Yearly rental payment	$14,000	$14,981	$ 3,900
Fair market value of leased asset	$98,000	$85,000	$17,500
Present value of lease rental payments	$55,000	$74,800	$ 9,500

Instructions

(a) Which of the above leases are operating leases and which are finance leases? Explain.

(b) How should the lease transaction for each of the above assets be recorded on January 1, 2014?

(c) Describe how the lease transaction would be reported on the 2014 income statement and balance sheet for each of the above assets.

TAKING IT FURTHER   For each of the leases, prepare any required adjusting journal entries on December 31, 2014. Assume that Manitoba Enterprises would pay 8% interest if it borrowed cash and purchased the equipment instead of leasing it.

P15–10A   **Loblaw Companies Limited** reported the following selected information (in millions):

Calculate and analyze solvency ratios. (SO 4, 5) AN

	2011	2010
Total assets	$17,428	$16,841
Total liabilities	11,421	11,238
Interest expense	327	353
Income tax expense	288	319
Profit	769	675

Instructions

(a) Calculate Loblaw's debt to total assets and interest coverage ratios for each year.

(b) Based on the ratios calculated in part (a), what conclusions can you make about Loblaw's solvency?

TAKING IT FURTHER   Loblaw had total operating lease commitments of $1,179 million in 2011 and $1,101 million in 2010. Explain the impact that an operating lease has on a company's solvency ratios. Does this information change any of your conclusions in part (b)?

Prepare liabilities section of balance sheet and analyze leverage. (SO 5) AP

P15–11A The adjusted trial balance for Sykes Ltd. at October 31, 2014, contained the following:

Accounts payable	$ 57,000	Income tax payable	$ 5,900
Accounts receivable	98,000	Note payable	230,211
Allowance for doubtful accounts	4,900	Interest expense	53,330
Bonds payable, due 2020	500,000	Lease liability	40,243
Interest payable	15,000	Note receivable, due 2015	35,000
Common shares	350,000	Retained earnings, November 1, 2013	824,793
Dividends	25,000	Unearned revenue	10,000
Income tax expense	11,800		

Of the lease liability amount, $26,430 is due within the next year. Total payments on the note payable in the next 12 months will be $20,800, of which $11,125 is for interest. Sykes reported profit for the year ended October 31, 2014, of $36,000. No common shares were issued during the year.

Instructions

(a) Prepare the liabilities and shareholders' equity section of the balance sheet.
(b) Calculate Sykes's debt to assets and interest coverage ratios for the year ended October 31, 2014.
(c) Based on the ratios calculated in part (b), what conclusions can you make about Sykes's solvency?

TAKING IT FURTHER What other information would help in the analysis of the company's solvency?

▶ Problems: Set B

Record bond transactions. (SO 2) AP

P15–1B The following selected information is from Universal Corporation's balance sheet:

UNIVERSAL CORPORATION
Balance Sheet (partial)
December 31, 2013

Current liabilities	
Interest payable	$ 18,000
Non-current liabilities	
Bonds payable, due January 1, 2015	1,200,000

Interest is payable semi-annually on January 1 and July 1. The bonds were issued at par.

Instructions

(a) What is the contractual rate of interest on the bonds?
(b) Record the payment of the bond interest on January 1, 2014.
(c) Assume that on January 1, 2014, after paying interest, Universal Corporation redeems $400,000 of the bonds at 98. Record the redemption of the bonds.
(d) Record the payment of the bond interest on July 1, 2014, on the remaining bonds.
(e) Prepare the adjusting entry on December 31, 2014, to accrue the interest on the remaining bonds.
(f) Prepare the entry to record the repayment of the remaining bonds on January 1, 2015.

TAKING IT FURTHER Was the market rate of interest higher or lower than the contractual rate of interest on January 1, 2014, when the bonds were redeemed? Explain.

Record bond transactions; show balance sheet presentation. (SO 2) AP

P15–2B On October 1, 2013, PFQ Corp. issued $800,000 of 10-year, 5% bonds at 98. The bonds pay interest annually on October 1. PFQ's year end is September 30.

Instructions

(a) Record the issue of the bonds on October 1, 2013.
(b) Record the accrual of interest on September 30, 2014, assuming the amortization amount is $1,257.
(c) What amounts related to the bonds would be reported as current and non-current in the liabilities section of PFQ's September 30, 2014, balance sheet?
(d) Record the payment of interest on October 1, 2014.
(e) Assume that on October 1, 2014, after payment of the interest, PFQ redeems all of the bonds at 97. Record the redemption of the bonds.

TAKING IT FURTHER What was the market rate of interest on October 1, 2013, when PFQ issued the bonds?

P15–3B   On July 1, 2013, Waubonsee Ltd. issued $3.2 million of 10-year, 6% bonds at $3,449,423. This price resulted in a market interest rate of 5%. The bonds pay semi-annual interest on July 1 and January 1, and Waubonsee has a December 31 year end.

Record bond transactions and answer questions. (SO 2) AP

Instructions

(a) Record the following transactions:
1. The issue of the bonds on July 1, 2013
2. The accrual of interest on December 31, 2013
3. The payment of interest on January 1, 2014
4. The payment of interest on July 1, 2014

(b) Answer the following questions:
1. What amount of interest expense is reported for 2013?
2. Would the interest expense reported in 2013 be the same as, greater than, or less than the amount that would be reported if the bonds had been issued at a discount rather than at a premium? Explain.
3. Determine the total cost of borrowing over the life of the bonds.
4. Would the total interest expense be greater than, the same as, or less than the total interest expense that would be reported if the bonds had been issued at a discount rather than at a premium? Explain.
5. Assuming that the bonds were issued at a market interest rate of 7%, calculate the issue price of the bonds. Determine the total cost of borrowing over the life of the bonds.

TAKING IT FURTHER   Explain what the impact would be on interest expense if the market rate of interest changed to 5.5% in December 2013 after the bonds were issued.

P15–4B   On January 1, 2013, Ponasis Corporation issued $2.5-million, 10-year bonds. The bonds pay semi-annual interest on July 1 and January 1, and Ponasis has a December 31 year end. Presented below is a partial amortization schedule.

Fill in missing amounts in amortization schedule, record bond transactions, and show balance sheet presentation. (SO 2, 5) AP

Semi-Annual Interest Period	Interest Payment	Interest Expense	Amortization	Bond Amortized Cost
January 1, 2013				$[1]
July 1, 2013	$62,500	$[2]	$8,412	2,695,981
January 1, 2014	[3]	53,920	8,580	2,687,401
July 1, 2014	62,500	53,748	8,752	2,678,649
January 1, 2015	62,500	53,573	[4]	[5]
July 1, 2015	62,500	53,394	9,106	2,660,616
January 1, 2016	62,500	53,212	9,288	2,651,328

Instructions

(a) Were the bonds issued at a discount or a premium?
(b) Fill in the missing amounts for [1] through [5].
(c) What is the face value of the bonds?
(d) What is the contractual rate of interest?
(e) What was the market interest rate when the bonds were issued?
(f) Record the issue of the bonds on July 1, 2013.
(g) Record the interest payment on July 1, 2014.
(h) Record the accrual of interest on December 31, 2014.
(i) What amounts would be reported as current and non-current in the liabilities section of Ponasis's December 31, 2014, balance sheet?
(j) Record the interest payment on January 1, 2015.
(k) Assuming that immediately after the interest payment the bonds were redeemed on January 1, 2015, when the market interest rate was 5%, calculate the amount Ponasis paid to redeem the bonds.
(l) Record the redemption of the bonds on January 1, 2015.

TAKING IT FURTHER   Why would Ponasis's board of directors not have set the contractual interest rate at the market interest rate on the date of issue when it authorized the bond issue?

P15–5B   On January 1, 2013, Vision Inc. issued bonds with a maturity value of $5 million when the market rate of interest was 5%. The bonds have a coupon (contractual) interest rate of 4% and mature on January 1, 2018. Interest on the bonds is payable semi-annually on July 1 and January 1 of each year. The company's year end is December 31.

Record bond transactions; . show balance sheet presentation. (SO 2) AP

Instructions

(a) Calculate the bonds' issue price.
(b) Prepare a bond amortization schedule from date of issue up to and including January 1, 2015.

(c) Prepare all of the required journal entries related to the bonds that Vision will record during 2013, including any adjusting journal entries at December 31, 2013.

(d) What amounts would be reported as current and non-current in the liabilities section of Vision's December 31, 2013, balance sheet?

(e) Record the payment of interest on January 1, 2014.

(f) The bonds were redeemed on January 1, 2015 (after the interest had been paid and recorded) at 98. Prepare the journal entry for the redemption of the bonds.

(g) Assume instead the bonds were not redeemed on January 1, 2015. Record the entry for the repayment of the bonds on January 1, 2018.

(h) What will be the total interest payment over the five-year life of the bonds? What will be the total interest expense over the five-year life of the bonds?

TAKING IT FURTHER Explain why the total interest payment over the five-year life of the bonds is equal to or different than the total interest expense over the five-year life of the bonds.

Prepare instalment payment schedule, record note transactions, and show balance sheet presentation. (SO 3, 5) AP

P15–6B Peter Furlong has just approached a venture capitalist for financing for his sailing school. The lenders are willing to lend Peter $120,000 in exchange for a note payable at a high-risk interest rate of 7%. The note is payable over three years in blended payments of $22,520. Payments are made semi-annually on October 31 and April 30. Peter receives the $120,000 on May 1, 2014, the first day of his fiscal year.

Instructions

(a) Record the issue of the note payable on May 1.

(b) Prepare an instalment payment schedule.

(c) Record the first two instalment payments on October 31 and April 30.

(d) What amounts would be reported as current and non-current in the liabilities section of the company's April 30, 2015, balance sheet?

(e) If the note had been repayable in fixed principal payments, rather than in blended payments, calculate how much the cash payments would have been on October 31 and April 30.

TAKING IT FURTHER Indicate which instalment payment method (blended or fixed) results in the largest principal repayment on April 30, 2017 (the date of the last payment). Explain.

Record note transactions. (SO 3) AP

P15–7B Solar Power Corporation purchased equipment for $800,000 on September 30, 2013. The equipment was purchased with a $50,000 down payment and the issue of a $750,000, three-year, 4% mortgage note payable for the balance. The terms provide for quarterly blended payments of $66,637 starting on December 31. Solar Power's year end is December 31.

Instructions

(a) Record the purchase of equipment on September 30, 2013.

(b) Record the first two instalment payments on December 31, 2013, and March 31, 2014.

(c) Repeat part (b) assuming that the terms provided for quarterly fixed principal payments of $62,500, rather than blended payments of $66,637.

TAKING IT FURTHER What will be the total interest expense over the life of the note if blended payments of $66,637 are made on a quarterly basis over three years?

Prepare instalment payment schedule and record note transactions. Show balance sheet presentation. (SO 3, 5) AP

P15–8B Elite Electronics issues a $450,000, 10-year, 7.5% mortgage note payable on December 31, 2013. The terms of the note provide for semi-annual fixed principal payments of $22,500, plus interest, on June 30 and December 31. Elite Electronics' year end is December 31.

Instructions

(a) Prepare an instalment payment schedule for the first two years. Round all calculations to the nearest dollar.

(b) Record the issue of the mortgage note payable on December 31, 2013.

(c) Show how the mortgage liability should be reported on the balance sheet at December 31, 2013. (*Hint*: Remember to report any current portion separately from the non-current liability.)

(d) Record the first two instalment payments on June 30, 2014, and December 31, 2014.

TAKING IT FURTHER If the semi-annual payments were blended, would the amount of cash paid on a semi-annual basis be greater than, equal to, or less than the fixed principal payments made for the first two instalments? For the last instalment?

Analyze lease situations. Discuss financial statement presentation. (SO 4) AP

P15–9B Presented below are three different lease transactions that occurred for Klippert Inc., a public company. Assume that all lease contracts start on January 1, 2014. Klippert does not receive title to any of the properties, either during the lease term or at the end of it. Annual lease payments are made on January 1 of each year starting on January 1, 2014.

	Manufacturing Equipment	Equipment	Vehicles
Annual lease rental payment	$8,823	$4,800	$7,000
Lease term	6 years	3 years	3 years
Estimated economic life	7 years	7 years	7 years
Fair market value of lease asset	$51,000	$19,000	$21,000
Present value of lease rental payments	$45,000	$11,000	$11,000

Instructions

(a) Which of the leases above are operating leases and which are finance leases? Explain.

(b) How should the lease transaction for each of the above assets be recorded on January 1, 2014?

(c) Describe how the lease transaction would be reported on the income statement and balance sheet for each of the above assets for 2014.

TAKING IT FURTHER   For each of the leases, prepare any required adjusting journal entries on December 31, 2014. Assume that Klippert Inc. would pay 7% interest if it borrowed cash and purchased the equipment instead of leasing the equipment.

P15–10B   Maple Leaf Foods Inc. reported the following selected information (in thousands):

Calculate and analyze solvency ratios. (SO 4, 5) AN

	2011	2010
Total assets	$2,940,459	$2,834,910
Total liabilities	2,010,346	1,848,138
Interest expense	70,747	64,874
Income tax expense	24,469	19,077
Profit	87,331	35,613

Instructions

(a) Calculate Maple Leaf Foods' debt to total assets and interest coverage ratios for each year.

(b) Based on the ratios calculated in (a), what conclusions can you make about Maple Leaf Foods Inc.'s solvency?

TAKING IT FURTHER   Maple Leaf Foods Inc. had total operating lease, rent and other commitments that required annual payments of $334,837 thousand at the end of 2011. Explain the impact that an operating lease has on a company's solvency ratios. Does this information change any of your conclusions in (b)?

P15–11B   The adjusted trial balance for Carey Corporation at December 31, 2014, contained the following:

Prepare liabilities section of balance sheet and analyze leverage. (SO 5) AP

Accounts payable	$ 76,000	Income tax payable	$ 37,176
Accounts receivable	89,000	Note payable	158,666
Allowance for doubtful accounts	4,450	Interest expense	49,568
Bonds payable, due 2019	1,000,000	Lease liability	99,869
Interest payable	30,000	Note receivable, due 2016	65,000
Common shares	425,000	Retained earnings, January 1, 2014	608,820
Dividends	40,000	Unearned revenue	25,000
Income tax expense	74,353		

Of the lease liability amount, $22,800 is due within the next year. Total payments on the instalment note payable in 2015 will be $24,400, of which $7,480 is for interest. Carey reported profit for the year ended December 31, 2014, of $173,500. No common shares were issued during the year.

Instructions

(a) Prepare the liabilities and shareholders' equity section of the balance sheet.

(b) Calculate Carey's debt to assets and interest coverage ratios for the year ended December 31, 2014.

(c) Based on the ratios calculated in part (b), what conclusions can you make about Carey's solvency?

TAKING IT FURTHER   Are long-term creditors more concerned with solvency or liquidity? Explain.

▶ Continuing Cookie Chronicle

(*Note:* This is a continuation of the Cookie Chronicle from Chapters 1 through 14.)

Janet, Brian, and Natalie have recently negotiated a contract to provide cupcakes on a weekly basis to a number of coffee shops in their area. As a result of the anticipated demand for cupcakes, they are making plans to purchase an additional commercial oven. The cost of this oven is estimated at $25,000, and the company already has $4,000 set aside for the purchase. Janet, Brian, and Natalie have met with their bank manager. She is willing to lend Koebel's Family Bakery Ltd. $21,000 on September 1, 2014, for a period of three years at a 4% interest rate.

The bank manager has set out the following two payment alternatives:

Alternative 1: The terms provide for fixed principal payments of $3,500 on September 1 and March 1 of each year.
Alternative 2: The terms provide for blended payments of $3,749 on September 1 and March 1 of each year.

Janet, Brian, and Natalie ask you to help them decide which alternative is better for them.

Instructions

(a) Prepare instalment payment schedules for each of the alternatives for the full term of the loan.
(b) Prepare the journal entry for the purchase of the oven and the issue of the note payable on September 1, 2014.
(c) Prepare the journal entries for the first two instalment payments under each alternative.
(d) Determine the current portion of the note payable and the non-current portion of the note payable as at July 31, 2015, the company's year end, under each alternative.
(e) Prepare the adjusting journal entries required at July 31, 2015, the company's year end, under each alternative.
(f) Which payment alternative do you recommend? Why?

CHAPTER 15 | BROADENING YOUR PERSPECTIVE

▶ Financial Reporting and Analysis

Financial Reporting Problem

BYP15–1 Refer to the consolidated financial statements and notes of **Reitmans (Canada) Limited** in Appendix A.

Instructions

(a) Referring to Note 14, what was the long-term total debt (mortgage payable) reported by Reitmans in the schedule at January 28, 2012, and January 29, 2011? By how much has Reitmans' total debt increased (decreased) since January 29, 2011?
(b) Does Reitmans separate the current portion of its debt from its non-current debt? If so, how much of its debt is currently due? Where is the current portion of its long-term debt reported in Reitmans' balance sheet?
(c) What kind of long-term debt does Reitmans have? What is the long-term debt secured by?
(d) What is the interest rate on Reitmans' long-term debt? When will the long-term debt be fully paid?
(e) What amount of the debt will be reported as a current liability in Reitmans' January 2013 balance sheet assuming that Reitmans does not borrow any additional debt?
(f) Does Reitmans have any off–balance sheet financing? (*Hint:* Consider the information in Note 18.)
(g) Reitmans' debt to total assets and interest coverage ratios for fiscal 2012 were calculated in Illustrations 15-16 and 15-17, respectively, in the chapter. Calculate these ratios for fiscal 2011. Comment on whether Reitmans' solvency improved or worsened in 2012.

Interpreting Financial Statements

BYP15–2 **Gap Inc.** and **Le Château Inc.** are specialty clothing merchandisers. Here are recent financial data for the companies:

	Gap Inc. (in millions of U.S. dollars)	**Le Château** (in thousands of Canadian dollars)
Balance sheet data	January 28, 2012	January 28, 2012
Total assets	$7,422	$233,794
Total liabilities	4,667	90,689
	Year ended	Year ended
Income statement data	January 28, 2012	January 28, 2012
Interest expense	74	1,974
Income tax expense (recovery)	536	(596)
Profit (loss)	833	(2,386)

Instructions

(a) Note that Gap Inc.'s financial information is reported in millions of U.S. dollars and Le Château's is reported in thousands of Canadian dollars. Explain why calculating and comparing ratios, for each of the companies, will make it possible to compare Gap Inc. and Le Château, given this difference in financial reporting.
(b) Calculate the debt to total assets and interest coverage ratios for Gap and Le Château.

(c) Discuss the solvency of each company compared with the other.

(d) The notes to the financial statements for Gap and Le Château indicate that the companies have significant operating lease commitments. Discuss the implications of these operating leases for each company's solvency.

(e) During January 2012, Le Château borrowed $10 million from a company owned by one of the company's directors. The loan is a four-year unsecured loan that bears a 7.5% interest rate. It is repayable in monthly instalments starting February 2013. What was the impact of this loan on Le Château's solvency ratios for 2012?

(f) In January 2012, the banks' prime lending rate was 3%. In your opinion, why might Le Château have borrowed the $10 million described in part (e) at 7.5% from a company owned by one of the directors?

▶ Critical Thinking

Collaborative Learning Activity

Note to instructor: Additional instructions and material for this group activity can be found on the Instructor Resource Site and in *WileyPLUS*.

BYP15–3   In this group activity, you will analyze and compare three financing alternatives for the purchase of a new vehicle. Your instructor will evaluate your group on your analysis as well as your rationale for selecting one of the alternatives.

Communication Activity

BYP15–4   Financial statement users are interested in the obligations that a company has from past transactions. It is important to determine which liabilities are current and which are non-current. Some company obligations are not recorded on the balance sheet itself, however; instead they are disclosed in the notes to the financial statements.

Instructions

Write a memorandum to a friend of yours who has inherited some money and would like to invest in some companies. Your friend plans to get professional advice before investing but would like you to review some basics with her. For instance, she is trying to determine the amount of cash that a company will have to pay within the next five years. She knows she should start with the liabilities that are on the balance sheet, but she is wondering if any of those can be settled without the company having to write a cheque. She would also like to know what kinds of liabilities could be buried somewhere in the notes to the financial statements. (*Hint:* A review of Reitmans' financial statements and notes to the financial statements in Appendix A will help you.)

Ethics Case

BYP15–5   Lehman Brothers, a giant investment company in the United States, announced in September 2008 that it would file for bankruptcy protection after suffering huge losses in the mortgage market. In 2010, the bankruptcy examiner's report stated that Lehman's accounting had misled investors. One of the tricks that Lehman used was to temporarily transfer investment assets to a related company in exchange for cash. The company then used the cash to temporarily reduce its liabilities by paying off debt, thus making its balance sheet look better than it was. After the company's financial statements were published, it borrowed the cash again and took back the assets.

Instructions

(a) Who are the stakeholders in this situation?

(b) Explain what the impact of paying debt off will be on the debt to total assets ratio.

(c) Explain how paying debt off and then immediately borrowing again, right after the financial statements are published, could mislead investors. (*Hint*: Consider the fundamental qualitative characteristics, discussed in Chapter 11, that accounting information should have to be useful to investors and creditors.)

"All About You" Activity

BYP15–6   As indicated in the "All About You" feature in this chapter, a student can benefit from financial leverage by borrowing to pay for an education. However, too much leverage can result in graduates struggling to make their loan payments. With most government student loan programs, you have at least six months' grace after your post-secondary education before you have to start paying back your loan. If you take advantage of the grace period, the maximum number of monthly payments is 114; however, you may request an extended amortization period of up to 174 months by revising the terms of your loan agreement.

Go to the Loan Repayment Estimator found at www.canlearn.ca to answer the following questions regarding monthly payments and the total interest payable on student loans. To find the Loan Repayment Calculator on the website, click on "Online Tools" and click on the link "Loan Repayment Estimator."

(a) Interest on loans may be at a fixed interest rate or a floating interest rate. What is the difference between the two interest rates? Are there any advantages of having one over the other if interest rates rise over your payment period?

(b) What is the prime rate of interest indicated in the Loan Repayment Estimator? How is the fixed rate of interest calculated in the Loan Repayment Estimator? Assuming the prime rate of interest indicated in the calculator, what will be the fixed rate of interest?

(c) Under Option 1 in the Loan Repayment Estimator, enter the loan amount of $20,000 and assume that you take advantage of the grace period and the grace period interest is included in your loan balance. Also assume a fixed interest rate and 114 months of repayment.
  1. What is the amount of each monthly payment?
  2. How much interest is payable over the 114 months?

(d) Under Option 2 in the Loan Repayment Estimator, enter the amount of $30,000, and assume that you take advantage of the grace period and that the grace period interest is included in your loan balance. Also assume a fixed interest rate and 114 months of repayment.
  1. What is the amount of each monthly payment?
  2. How much interest is payable over the 114 months?

(e) Under Option 1 in the Loan Repayment Estimator, enter the amount of $30,000 and assume that you take advantage of the grace period and the grace period interest is included in your loan balance. Also assume a fixed interest rate and 174 months of repayment.
  1. What is the amount of each monthly payment?
  2. How much interest is payable over the 174 months?

(f) Assume that you accept a position when you graduate that pays you an annual salary of $48,000. After the required deductions for income tax, CPP, EI, and health benefits, your monthly paycheque is $2,800. You rent an apartment for $750 a month, have monthly payments on a car loan of $300, and your other costs for groceries, cable, Internet, insurance, gas, and phone total $1,100. How much will you have left at the end of the month to make payments on your student loan and other expenditures, such as clothes and entertainment? Can you afford to repay a $20,000 student loan? A $30,000 student loan?

ANSWERS TO CHAPTER QUESTIONS

ANSWERS TO ACCOUNTING IN ACTION INSIGHT QUESTIONS

All About You p. 768

Q: What should you consider in your decision about how much is appropriate to borrow for your education?

A: You should consider the cost of tuition and books; living expenses; other sources of cash, such as parents, part-time job, and scholarships and grants; expected income upon graduation; living expenses and other financial commitments after graduation; and expected interest rates and payment schedule on the student loan.

Business Insight, p. 784

Q: What impact will the decrease in the amortization period from 30 to 25 years have on homebuyers?

A: The amortization period is the period over which the principal will be paid. Reducing the amortization period will result in homebuyers making higher monthly payments. With the government also limiting homeowners with government-insured mortgages to spending no more than 44% of their incomes on housing and other debt, many homebuyers will be forced to purchase less expensive homes.

ANSWERS TO SELF-STUDY QUESTIONS

1. a   2. b   3. d   4. d   5. a   6. d   7. c   8. c   9. b   10. a   11. c   12. c

Remember to go back to the beginning of the chapter to check off your completed work!

 THE **NAVIGATOR**

☐ Understand *Concepts for Review*

☐ Read *Feature Story*

☐ Scan *Study Objectives*

☐ Read *Chapter Preview*

☐ Read text and answer *Before You Go On*

☐ Review *Comparing IFRS and ASPE*

☐ Work *Demonstration Problem*

☐ Review *Summary of Study Objectives*

☐ Answer *Self-Study Questions*

☐ Complete assignments

☐ Go to *WileyPLUS* for practice and tutorials

CONCEPTS FOR **REVIEW**

Before studying this chapter, you should understand or, if necessary, review:

a. How to calculate and record interest. (Ch. 3, pp. 125–126, Ch. 8, pp. 428–429, and Ch. 15, pp. 782–784)

b. Where short- and long-term investments are classified on a balance sheet. (Ch. 4, pp. 184–187)

c. What comprehensive income is. (Ch. 14, p. 726)

d. The statement of comprehensive income. (Ch. 14, p. 727)

e. How to record bond transactions using the effective-interest method. (Ch. 15, pp. 773–780)

MANAGING MONEY FOR CLIENTS AND THE COMPANY

TORONTO, Ont.—Like all large organizations, Scotiabank manages its money through a number of investment vehicles. It has two main areas of investments: its regular banking operations and strategic acquisitions.

"In banks, we're always changing the mix of financial assets, looking for different opportunities," says Sean McGuckin, Senior Vice President and Head, Risk Policy & Capital Markets, "whereas for non-financial institutions, financial assets may not be their primary assets. It could be property, plant, and equipment, oil in the ground, what have you. So they may take a longer-term view on some of their investments." Scotiabank is like an individual investor who reviews and rebalances his or her portfolio regularly, rather than one who buys stocks and holds them over time with little adjustment.

In its regular banking operations, Scotiabank holds investments in trading portfolios and treasury portfolios. In its trading environment, Scotiabank buys and sells securities primarily to facilitate customer requests and invests in certain securities to adjust its trading risk profile. These may be debt instruments such as bonds, or equity instruments such as common and preferred shares. Scotiabank's treasury investments strengthen the organization's liquidity profile by having some assets on hand that it could quickly convert into cash if needed. The bank also uses various investments in fixed-term securities or variable-rate securities to help adjust its interest rate exposure. These investments can be held for a few days or longer. As well, the bank may also invest in long-term instruments, for example, five-year government bonds.

Scotiabank also invests strategically by acquiring all or a portion of other companies. "Our strategy, like most companies, is to grow," Mr. McGuckin explains. "You can grow either organically over time by continuing to build out your business, or you can acquire growth, i.e., buy a company." If a business fits within Scotiabank's overall strategy, it may buy shares in that company.

In 2012, Scotiabank announced its intention, subject to regulatory approvals, to purchase ING Bank of Canada (ING DIRECT) from Netherlands-based parent ING Group for $3.126 billion in cash, which was expected to result in a net investment by Scotiabank of approximately $1.9 billion after deducting the excess capital currently at ING DIRECT. "ING DIRECT will benefit from the backing of a strong, stable Canadian shareholder with the additional resources to enable it to expand and grow. This in turn will provide our shareholders with a new source of incremental earnings beginning in year one, and a new deposit base to further diversify our funding," said Scotiabank President and CEO Rick Waugh, at the time the agreement was announced.

These strategic investments have the additional benefits of allowing Scotiabank to diversify into different revenue streams and leverage its existing business since the acquired companies may have products that would be of interest to existing customers.

In fact, there are many reasons and ways in which organizations make investments, whether they are non-strategic investments to earn a higher return on extra cash than from a bank account, or strategic investments to influence or control another company, such as a competitor, supplier, or complementary business that their customers may benefit from.

SOURCES: "Scotiabank Reaches Agreement to Acquire ING Bank of Canada and Announces Common Share Offering," Scotiabank news release, August 29, 2012; Sunny Freeman, The Canadian Press, "Scotiabank to Buy ING Bank of Canada for $3.13 Billion in Cash," Canada.com, August 29, 2012. Kimmel et al. (2011), *Financial Accounting*, Fifth Canadian Edition, Toronto, ON: John Wiley & Sons Canada, Ltd.

THE NAVIGATOR

STUDY **OBJECTIVES**

After studying this chapter, you should be able to:

1. Identify reasons to invest, and classify investments.

2. Account for debt investments that are reported at amortized cost.

3. Account for trading investments.

4. Account for strategic investments.

5. Indicate how investments are reported in the financial statements.

THE NAVIGATOR

Investments can include debt and equity, and can be made by individuals or corporations. As indicated in our feature story on Scotiabank, investments are made to generate investment income or for strategic purposes. They can be held for a short or long period of time. The way in which a company accounts for its investments is determined by the nature and purpose of the investment.

The chapter is organized as follows:

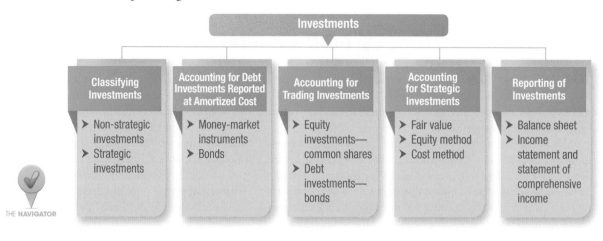

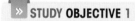

THE **NAVIGATOR**

» **STUDY OBJECTIVE 1**

Identify reasons to invest, and classify investments.

Helpful hint Debt and equity instruments are also referred to as *debt and equity securities* and these terms will be used interchangeably throughout the chapter.

▶ **ILLUSTRATION** 16-1
Why businesses invest

Classifying Investments

Corporations generally purchase **debt instruments** (term deposits, treasury bills, bonds, or similar items that can be bought and sold) and **equity instruments** (preferred and common shares of another company) for one of two reasons. They either purchase an instrument as (1) a **non-strategic investment** to generate investment income, or (2) a **strategic investment** with the intention of establishing and maintaining a long-term operating relationship with another company. These reasons are shown in Illustration 16-1.

Reason	Purpose	Type of Investment
 Non-strategic investment	To generate investment income	• Debt instruments (money-market instruments, bonds) • Equity instruments (preferred and common shares)
Strategic investment	To maintain an operating relationship, or influence or control another company	Equity instruments (common shares)

NON-STRATEGIC INVESTMENTS

There are several reasons for a company to purchase debt or equity **securities** of another company as a non-strategic investment. A corporation may have cash that it does not immediately need. Until the cash is needed, the corporation may decide to invest it to earn a higher return than it would get if it just kept the excess cash in the bank. As indicated in our feature story, Scotiabank's treasury investments are investments that can be quickly converted to cash when needed.

When investing excess cash for short periods of time, corporations invest in debt securities—usually money-market instruments, which are low-risk and highly liquid. **Money-market instruments** include money-market funds, term deposits, and treasury bills. It is not wise to invest short-term excess cash in equity securities, because share prices can drop suddenly and dramatically. If a company does invest in shares and the price of the shares falls, when the company needs cash again, it will be forced to sell the shares at a loss. Money-market instruments do not change in fair value. Their value comes from the interest they generate.

Excess cash may also be invested for the longer term in debt securities (such as bonds) to generate a steady source of interest income. Or it may be invested in equity securities to generate dividend income. Preferred shares are usually purchased for dividend purposes, but both common and preferred shares can and do pay dividends.

Companies also invest in debt and equity securities hoping that they can sell them at a higher price than they originally paid for them. They speculate that the investment will increase in value and result in a gain when it is sold. Some companies, such as financial institutions like Scotiabank, are in the business of actively buying and selling securities in the hope of generating investment income from price fluctuations. Debt and equity securities that are purchased for the purpose of selling in the short term at a gain are referred to as **trading investments**.

Alternative terminology Trading investments are also referred to as *trading securities* or *held-for-trading investments*.

Classifying Non-Strategic Investments

Investments should be classified and reported in the financial statements in such a way as to provide users of financial statements with relevant information for decisions. This includes information that allows financial statement users to predict a company's future cash flows.

Generally a non-strategic investment is classified and reported based on the purpose of the investment and on whether it is debt or equity. Illustration 16-2 shows how companies reporting under IFRS classify and value non-strategic investments.

Type of Instrument	Purpose	Balance Sheet Classification and Valuation	
Short-term debt instruments	Held to earn interest income	Current assets	Amortized cost
Long-term debt instruments	Held to earn interest income	Non-current assets	Amortized cost
Short- or long-term debt instruments	Trading	Current assets	Fair value
Equity instruments	Trading	Current assets	Fair value

▶ **ILLUSTRATION 16-2**
Classification and reporting of non-strategic investments under IFRS

Note that the purpose of the investment is the more important factor in determining the balance sheet classification and valuation. The type of instrument does have an impact, as shown above, but the main consideration is why management purchases the investment. For the most part, IFRS and ASPE follow similar accounting for investments; however, for some investments under ASPE, the accounting is different than under IFRS. We will point out the differences as we look at the accounting for the different types of investments. If you understand the different accounting methods, then you can apply the concepts to either IFRS or ASPE in the appropriate situation. We will look at the accounting for non-strategic investments in the following sections.

STRATEGIC INVESTMENTS

While either debt or equity securities can be purchased as a non-strategic investment, only equity securities (normally common shares) can be purchased as a strategic investment. Only equity securities give the investor the right to vote at shareholders' meetings. Thus only investments in equity securities can result in influence or control over another company.

Companies make strategic investments for different reasons. A company may make a strategic investment to become part of a different industry when it buys some or all of the common shares of another company in a related or new industry or it may invest in a company in the same industry to expand its operations or eliminate some of the competition. As indicated in our feature story, Scotiabank invests strategically by acquiring all or a portion of other companies. In 2012, Scotiabank announced its intention to purchase ING Bank of Canada (ING Direct).

The percentage of ownership or the degree of influence determines how a strategic investment is reported. The reporting of strategic investments will be discussed later in the chapter. Note also that, while non-strategic investments can be either short- or long-term, strategic investments can only be long-term.

ACCOUNTING IN ACTION
BUSINESS INSIGHT

In 2011, retail giant Canadian Tire Corporation became even larger with the acquisition of all of the outstanding common shares of The Forzani Group Ltd. Forzani was Canada's leading sporting goods retailer, with more than 500 retail outlets nationwide, under banners such as Sport Chek and Sports Experts, in big box stores and malls. Forzani's annual revenues were approximately $1.4 billion. The acquisition means that Canadian Tire has more than 1,000 combined sports outlets across the country, which will strengthen the company's competitive position against foreign competitors. The sale to Canadian Tire had the unanimous approval of Forzani's board of directors. Canadian Tire expected to finance the $771-million acquisition with cash on hand and short-term financing.

Sources: "Canadian Tire Corporation Announces Friendly, All-Cash Offer to Acquire the Forzani Group Ltd.," company news release, May 9, 2011; Marina Strauss, "Canadian Tire Acquires 'A New Set of Customers,'" *Globe and Mail*, May 9, 2011; "Canadian Tire to Buy Forzani Group," CBC News, May 9, 2011.

Was the acquisition of Forzani by Canadian Tire a non-strategic or strategic investment?

BEFORE YOU GO ON...

Do It

ABC Corp., a public company reporting under IFRS, made the following investments during the year.

1. Purchased 20% of the common shares of one of its suppliers to ensure that there is a reliable source of raw materials.
2. Purchased bonds to earn interest income.
3. Purchased common shares of a company, to be sold if the share price increases.
4. Purchased bonds with the intent to trade at a gain.
5. Purchased 100% of the common shares of ABC's major competitor.

(a) For each investment, indicate if it is a strategic investment or a non-strategic investment.
(b) For each non-strategic investment, indicate if it should be reported at amortized cost or fair value.

Action Plan

- Non-strategic investments are purchased to earn investment income.
- Strategic investments are purchased with the intention of establishing a long-term relationship with the company.

Solution

(a)	(b)
1. Strategic	
2. Non-strategic	amortized cost
3. Non-strategic	fair value
4. Non-strategic	fair value
5. Strategic	

Related exercise material: BE16–1, BE16–2, E16–1, and E16–2.

THE NAVIGATOR

Accounting for Debt Investments Reported at Amortized Cost

As mentioned in the previous section, under IFRS, debt instruments purchased to earn interest income are reported at amortized cost. Under ASPE, all investments in debt instruments are reported at amortized cost, whether they are purchased to trade or to earn interest. You will recall from Chapter 15 that amortized cost is the maturity value or principal less any unamortized discount, or plus any unamortized premium, and that the effective-interest method is used to amortize any discount or premium and record interest expense on long-term debt. This method is also used to record interest revenue and amortize any premiums or discounts on debt investments reported at amortized cost. By using the effective-interest method, interest revenue reflects the actual interest earned on the investment.

Debt instruments that are valued at amortized cost can include both short-term and long-term debt instruments. **Short-term debt instruments** are instruments that will mature within 12 months of the balance sheet date. **Long-term debt instruments** are instruments with a maturity of longer than 12 months after the balance sheet date. Regardless of the term of the debt, the accounting for all debt instruments reported at amortized cost has some basic similarities. Entries are required to record the following.

1. **The acquisition:** Debt instruments are recorded at the purchase price paid for the investment.
2. **Interest revenue and amortization of any discount or premium:** Interest revenue is recognized as it accrues and any discount or premium is amortized using the effective-interest method. The investment is reported at amortized cost on the balance sheet.
3. **The sale or disposition at maturity:** When the instrument matures or is sold, the cash received is recorded, and its carrying amount (amortized cost) is eliminated. If the instrument is sold before maturity, a gain is recorded if the cash received is greater than the amortized cost of the investment and a loss is recorded if the cash received is less than the amortized cost. This is shown in illustration 16-3.

» **STUDY OBJECTIVE 2**

Account for debt investments that are reported at amortized cost.

ASPE

▶ **ILLUSTRATION 16-3**
Gain and loss on sale of investment in debt instrument valued at amortized cost

You will recall that debt instruments include money-market instruments as well as bonds, and a large variety of other debt securities. The following sections illustrate accounting for debt investments at amortized cost for both money-market instruments and bonds.

MONEY-MARKET INSTRUMENTS

As we have learned, money-market instruments are reasonably safe investments that allow a company to earn a higher interest rate than can normally be earned on a regular bank account balance. Examples of money-market instruments are term deposits, treasury bills, and money-market funds. The following looks at the accounting for treasury bills.

Government of Canada treasury bills are short-term debt instruments issued by the federal government. These instruments are a safe investment with a wide variety of maturity dates up to a maximum of one year. Treasury bills are purchased at a discount to the face value (maturity value), and the difference between purchase price and value at maturity, or date sold, is the interest earned on the investment. Treasury bills may be quickly converted to cash before their maturity date because there is a well-established resale market.

Recording Acquisitions of Treasury Bills

Treasury bills are recorded at their purchase price. For example, assume that on October 1, 2014, Sulphur Research Limited purchases a $10,000, 150-day treasury bill for $9,756. The treasury bills are trading at a market interest rate of 6% annually. The entry to record the investment is as follows:

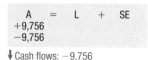

A = L + SE
+9,756
−9,756

↓ Cash flows: −9,756

Oct. 1	Short-Term Investment—Treasury Bill	9,756	
	Cash		9,756
	To record purchase of 150-day treasury bill at 6%.		

Note that the treasury bill is recorded at the purchase price on October 1. The treasury bill was purchased at a discount of $244, the difference between face value ($10,000) and the purchase price ($9,756). Investments in treasury bills are reported as current assets on the balance sheet. As we learned in Chapter 7, investments in treasury bills of less than 90 days are usually classified as cash equivalents.

Recording Interest Revenue and Amortizing the Discount

Interest revenue is calculated by multiplying the market interest rate by the instrument's carrying value. The discount is amortized over the term of the treasury bill using the effective-interest method. As interest revenue is not received during the term of the treasury bill, the discount amortization is equal to interest revenue.

Sulphur Research Limited's year end is December 31, so interest revenue of $146 is accrued for the months of October, November, and December ($9,756 × 6% × ³⁄₁₂ rounded to the nearest dollar). The adjusting journal entry at December 31 follows:

A = L + SE
+146   +146

Cash flows: no effect

Dec. 31	Short-Term Investment—Treasury Bill	146	
	Interest Revenue		146
	To accrue interest revenue and amortize discount.		

Note that the debit to the treasury bill investment account reduces the discount by the amount of the interest revenue. The treasury bill is reported on the December 31 balance sheet at its amortized cost of $9,902 ($9,756 + $146). Interest revenue is reported under other revenues in the income statement.

Recording the Maturity of Treasury Bills

On February 28, 2015, when the treasury bill matures, it is necessary to (1) update the interest and amortize the discount for the latest period, and (2) record the receipt of cash and remove the treasury bill investment account. The interest revenue of $98 is for the months of January and February and is equal to the difference between the face value ($10,000) and the amortized cost ($9,902), the balance in the Short-Term Investment account at December 31. The entry to record the interest revenue and amortize the discount is as follows:

A = L + SE
+98   +98

Cash flows: no effect

Feb. 28	Short-Term Investment—Treasury Bill	98	
	Interest Revenue		98
	To accrue interest revenue and amortize discount.		

Note that the amortized cost of the treasury bill is now $10,000 ($9,902 + $98), equal to its face value. The entry to record the receipt of cash and eliminate the treasury bill is as follows:

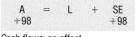

A = L + SE
+10,000
−10,000

↑ Cash flows: +10,000

Feb. 28	Cash	10,000	
	Short-Term Investment—Treasury Bill		10,000
	To record the receipt of cash and eliminate the treasury bill.		

BONDS

Bonds were discussed in Chapter 15 from the liability side; that is, from the issuer's perspective. Corporations, governments, and universities issue bonds that are then purchased by investors. The issuer of the bonds is known as the **investee**. The purchaser of the bonds, or the bondholder, is known as the **investor**. The investor's accounting for bonds reported at amortized cost is illustrated below. To illustrate the investor's accounting, we will use the Candlestick Inc. bond example in Chapter 15. Recall that Candlestick, the investee, issued $1 million of five-year, 5% bonds on January 1, 2014, and that interest is paid semi-annually on January 1 and July 1.

Recording Acquisition of Bonds

At acquisition, the investment in bonds is recorded at the purchase price. Recall from Chapter 15 that bonds will sell at a premium (purchase price is above face value) if the market interest rate is lower than the contract rate of 5%. Bonds are sold at a discount (purchase price is below face value) if the market interest rate is higher than the contract rate of 5%.

Assume that Candlestick issues the bonds, at a premium, to yield a market interest rate of 4% and that Kadir Inc., the investor, purchases $100,000 (10%) of these bonds. The market price of the bonds is 104.4915. Kadir will pay $104,491 ($100,000 × 1.044915) and records the purchase as follows:

Jan. 1	Long-Term Investment—Candlestick Bonds	104,491	
	Cash		104,491
	To record purchase of Candlestick bonds.		

A = L + SE
+104,491
−104,491

↓ Cash flows: −104,491

Given that the bonds are being held to earn interest revenue and not to trade, and the term of the bonds is five years, the bonds will be reported in non-current assets on the balance sheet.

As you go through this illustration of accounting for bonds at amortized cost from the investor's perspective, you may want to refer to the section on "Issuing Bonds at a Premium" in Chapter 15 to see the similarities and differences in the accounting for bonds between the investor and investee. Note that the amount Kadir Inc. paid for the Candlestick bonds is 10% ($1,044,915 × 10%) of the amount that Candlestick recorded in Bonds Payable when it issued the bonds.

Recording Interest Revenue and Amortizing the Discount or Premium

When bonds are reported at amortized cost, any premium or discount recorded in the investment account is amortized to interest revenue over the remaining term of the bonds. If there is a bond premium, interest revenue is reduced by the amortization amount. If there is a bond discount, interest revenue is increased by the amortization amount. Recall from earlier in the chapter that, like the issuer of the bonds, the investor uses the effective-interest method of amortization.

To continue the Kadir example, recall that Candlestick makes semi-annual interest payments on July 1 and January 1. The interest received, $2,500, is calculated by multiplying the bonds' face value by the contractual interest rate ($100,000 × 5% × $^6/_{12}$). Interest revenue is calculated by multiplying the amortized cost (carrying value) of the long-term investment by the market interest rate. On July 1, 2014, Kadir will record $2,090 interest revenue ($104,491 × 4% × $^6/_{12}$). The amortization of the premium or discount is the difference between the interest received and the interest revenue or $410 ($2,500 − $2,090). The premium amortization is credited to the investment account, which reduces the amortized cost (carrying amount) of the investment.

The entry to record the receipt of the interest and amortization of the premium on July 1, 2014, is as follows:

July 1	Cash	2,500	
	Long-Term Investment—Candlestick Bonds		410
	Interest Revenue		2,090
	To record receipt of interest on Candlestick bonds.		

A = L + SE
+2,500   +2,090
−410

↑ Cash flows: +2,500

The interest revenue is less than the cash received. The purchase of the bonds at a premium causes the total interest earned to be less than the total interest received. If Kadir holds the bonds until maturity, the long-term investment's amortized cost (carrying value) will be $100,000, the face value of the bonds.

Normally, investors prepare an amortization schedule to make it easier to calculate the interest revenue and the premium or discount amortization. The amortization schedule is very similar to the one shown in Chapter 15's Illustration 15-8 for the investee, Candlestick Inc. For Kadir, the investor, the amortization schedule shows interest received instead of interest paid in column A and interest revenue instead of interest expense in column B.

▶ **ILLUSTRATION 16-4**
Comparison of bond investment and liability

Illustration 16-4 compares the recording of the bonds as an investment for Kadir Inc. (the investor) and as a liability for Candlestick (the investee) for the bond issue and first interest payment date.

KADIR INC. (INVESTOR)			
Jan. 1	Long-Term Investment— Candlestick Bonds	104,491	
	Cash		104,491
July 1	Cash	2,500	
	Long-Term Investment— Candlestick Bonds		410
	Interest Revenue		2,090

CANDLESTICK INC. (INVESTEE)			
Jan. 1	Cash	1,044,915	
	Bonds Payable		1,044,915
July 1	Interest Expense	20,898	
	Bonds Payable	4,102	
	Cash		25,000

Note that on January 1, 2014, Kadir recorded a non-current asset, and Candlestick recorded a non-current liability. On July 1, 2014, Kadir recorded interest revenue and Candlestick recorded interest expense.

In this example, because Kadir (the investor) purchased 10% of the Candlestick bonds, the interest that Kadir receives semi-annually ($2,500) is 10% of the interest paid ($25,000) by Candlestick. Also note that, because Kadir purchased the bonds directly from Candlestick, the interest revenue ($2,090) and premium amortization ($410) are 10% of the interest expense ($20,898) and premium amortization ($4,102) that are recorded by Candlestick.

Recording the Maturity of Bonds

Regardless of the bonds' purchase price, their amortized cost at maturity will equal their face value. By the time the bonds mature, any discount or premium will be fully amortized. Assuming that the interest for the last interest period has been received and recorded, the entry to record the receipt of cash for the Candlestick Bonds at maturity, January 1, 2019, is as follows:

A = L + SE
+100,000
−100,000

↑ Cash flows: +100,000

Jan. 1	Cash	100,000	
	Long-Term Investment—Candlestick Bonds		100,000
	To record maturity of Candlestick bonds.		

Because the amortized cost of the bonds equals the face value at maturity, there is no gain or loss.

Sale of Bonds Before Maturity

Although a company may purchase bonds to earn interest revenue, it may be necessary to sell the bonds before maturity if the company needs the cash, or the company may choose to sell the bonds because interest rates have increased and it can earn a higher return.

To record the sale of bonds, it is necessary to first update any unrecorded interest and the amortization of the discount or premium. Then an entry is prepared to (1) record the cash received, (2) remove the amortized cost of the bonds, and (3) recognize the gain or loss on sale. Interest must be updated if the bonds are sold between semi-annual interest payment dates.

To illustrate, assume Kadir sells its investment in Candlestick Bonds on January 1, 2017, for $99,500. The amortized cost of the bonds on January 1, 2017, is $101,904. Assuming that the interest for the interest date of January 1, 2017, has been received and recorded, the entry to record the sale of the bonds is as follows:

Jan. 1	Cash	99,500	
	Loss on Sale of Candlestick Bonds	2,404	
	Long-Term Investment—Candlestick Bonds		101,904
	To record sale of Candlestick bonds.		

A = L + SE
+99,500   −2,404
−101,904

↑ Cash flows: +99,500

As shown in Illustration 16-3, a loss is recognized on the sale of the bonds as the bonds were sold at a price ($99,500) that was less than the amortized cost ($101,904). Conversely, a gain on sale is recognized if the bonds are sold at a price that is greater than the amortized cost of the bonds. Losses and gains on sale are reported in other expenses or other revenues, respectively.

BEFORE YOU GO ON...

Do It

During 2014, Wang Corporation had the following transactions for debt investments purchased to earn interest:

Jan.	1	Purchased 10-year, 5% Hillary Corp. bonds with a face value of $30,000 for $27,768. The market interest rate is 6%. Interest is payable semi-annually on July 1 and January 1.
Apr.	1	Purchased a $20,000, 120-day treasury bill for $19,600.
July	1	Received semi-annual interest on investment in Hilary bonds.
July	31	Received cash for the maturity of the treasury bill.

(a) Prepare a bond amortization schedule for the first three interest periods for Wang's investment in the Hillary bonds.
(b) Record the above transactions for Wang Corporation.
(c) Prepare the adjusting entry for the accrual of interest on December 31, Wang's year end.

Solution

(a)

		Bond Discount Amortization Schedule—Investee			
		Effective-Interest Method			
		(A)	(B)	(C)	(D)
Interest Period		Interest Received ($30,000 × 5% × 6/12)	Interest Revenue (D × 6% × 6/12)	Discount Amortization (A − B)	Bond Amortized Cost (D + C)
Purchase Jan. 1, 2014					$27,768
(1) July 1, 2014		$750	$833	$83	27,851
(2) Jan. 1, 2015		750	836	86	27,937
(3) July 1, 2015		750	838	88	28,025
(4) Jan. 1, 2016		750	841	91	28,116

(b)

Jan.	1	Long-Term Investment—Hillary Bonds	27,768	
		Cash		27,768
		To record purchase of Hillary bonds.		
Apr.	1	Short-Term Investment—Treasury Bill	19,600	
		Cash		19,600
		To record purchase of treasury bill.		

Action Plan

- To create the amortization table, calculate the cash interest received by multiplying the face value of the bonds by the semi-annual contractual interest rate. Calculate the interest revenue by multiplying the amortized cost of the bonds by the semi-annual market interest rate.
- In the amortization table, the amount of the discount (premium) amortization is the difference between the interest received and the interest revenue. The amortized cost of the bonds purchased increases by the amount of the discount amortization and decreases by the amount of the premium amortization.
- When investments are purchased, they are recorded at their purchase price.
- Interest revenue is recorded as it accrues.
- The investments are reported at amortized cost on the balance sheet; therefore, premiums and discounts on these investments are amortized when interest revenue is recognized. Use the amortization schedule to record the interest revenue on the bonds.
- When the investments mature, the cash received is recorded and the investment account is eliminated.

BEFORE YOU GO ON continued...

July	1	Cash	750	
		Long-Term Investment—Hillary Bonds	83	
		Interest Revenue		833
		To record interest received on bonds.		
July	31	Short-Term Investment—Treasury Bill	400	
		Interest Revenue		400
		To record interest revenue on treasury bill.		
		Cash	20,000	
		Short-Term Investment—Treasury Bill		20,000
		To record maturity of treasury bill.		
(c)				
Dec.	31	Interest Receivable	750	
		Long-Term Investment—Hillary Bonds	86	
		Interest Revenue		836
		To accrue semi-annual interest on Hillary bonds.		

THE **NAVIGATOR**

Related exercise material: BE16–3, BE16–4, BE16–5, E16–3, E16–4, and E16–6.

Accounting for Trading Investments

> **» STUDY OBJECTIVE 3**
>
> Account for trading investments.

Illustration 16-2 showed that debt and equity instruments purchased principally for trading are reported at fair value on the balance sheet. Under IFRS, trading investments reported at fair value may include investments in common or preferred shares and debt instruments such as bonds that are purchased with the intent of selling the instrument at a gain. Under ASPE, only trading investments in equity securities will be reported at fair value.

Alternative terminology Another common term for fair value is *market value.*

You will recall from Chapter 1 that **fair value** is generally the amount an asset could be sold for in the market. Debt and equity instruments purchased for trading are typically traded on public markets, so the fair value of the instrument is typically the quoted market price. The advantage of using fair value is that it allows users to better predict the future cash flows and assess the company's liquidity and solvency.

In accounting for trading investments reported at fair value, entries are required to record the following.

1. **The acquisition:** Trading investments are recorded at their fair value on the date of purchase.
2. **Interest and dividend revenue:** Interest revenue is recognized as it accrues and dividend revenue is recognized when the company receives the cash dividend or becomes entitled to the cash dividend. You will recall from Chapter 13 that an investor will be entitled to receive a dividend from the company paying dividends (investee) if the investor holds the shares on the date of record.
3. **Fair value adjustments:** Because trading investments are reported at fair value on the balance sheet, accounting entries are required to adjust the investment's carrying value for any increases or decreases in its fair value. This is referred to as a **fair value adjustment**. A gain is recorded if the fair value is higher than the carrying value and a loss is recorded if the fair value is less than the carrying value. This is shown in Illustration 16-5.

> ▸**ILLUSTRATION 16-5**
> Gains and losses on fair value adjustments

Fair Value versus Carrying Value	Change to Carrying Value of Asset	Income Statement Account
Fair value higher than carrying value	Increase carrying value of investment to fair value	Record a gain on fair value adjustment
Fair value less than carrying value	Decrease carrying value of investment to fair value	Record a loss on fair value adjustment

Gains and losses on fair value adjustments for trading investments are reported in the income statement.

4. **The sale of the investment:** When the investment is sold, the cash received is recorded, the investment account is eliminated, and a gain or loss is recorded. Like investments reported at amortized cost, the gain or loss is equal to the difference between the cash received and the carrying value of the investment.

EQUITY INVESTMENTS—COMMON SHARES

Recording Acquisitions of Shares

When an equity instrument is purchased for trading, the investment is recorded at fair value, which is equal to the price the shares are trading at on the date of purchase. Assume, for example, that on July 1, 2014, Leonard Corporation purchases 500 common shares of Gleason Ltd. at $30 per share. Leonard Corporation purchased the shares to trade.

The entry to record the equity investment is as follows:

Helpful hint The entries for investments in common shares are also used for investments in preferred shares.

July 1	Trading Investments—Gleason Common Shares	15,000	
	Cash (500 × $30)		15,000
	To record purchase of 500 Gleason common shares.		

A = L + SE
+15,000
−15,000

⬇ Cash flows: −15,000

Since this investment was made with the intent of selling it at a profit, the investment is reported as a current asset on the balance sheet.

Recording Dividend Revenue

During the time the shares are held, entries are required for any cash dividends that are received. If a $2 per share dividend is received by Leonard on December 1, the entry is as follows:

Dec. 1	Cash (500 × $2)	1,000	
	Dividend Revenue		1,000
	To record receipt of cash dividend.		

A = L + SE
+1,000 +1,000

⬆ Cash flows: +1,000

Dividend revenue is reported under other revenues in the income statement.

Recording Fair Value Adjustments at the Balance Sheet Date

On December 31, 2014, Leonard's fiscal year end, Gleason Ltd.'s shares are trading on the stock exchange at $33. This is an increase of $3 ($33 − $30) per share and, as explained earlier, results in a gain. The entry to record the adjustment to fair value is as follows:

Dec. 31	Trading Investments—Gleason Common Shares (500 × $3)	1,500	
	Gain on Fair Value Adjustment of Trading Investments		1,500
	To record adjustment of Gleason shares to fair value.		

A = L + SE
+1,500 +1,500

Cash flows: no effect

The investment in Gleason shares will be reported on the balance sheet at its fair value of $16,500 ($15,000 + $1,500), which is the new carrying value of the investment. The gain on fair value adjustment is reported under other revenues in the income statement.

Recording Sales of Shares

When shares are sold, the difference between the proceeds from the sale and the carrying value of the shares is recognized as a gain or loss. Assume that Leonard receives proceeds of $17,000 on the sale of its Gleason common shares on October 10, 2015. Because the shares' carrying value is $16,500, there is a gain of $500 ($17,000 − $16,500). The entry to record the sale is as follows:

Oct. 10	Cash	17,000	
	Trading Investments—Gleason Common Shares		16,500
	Gain on Sale of Trading Investments ($17,000 − $16,500)		500
	To record sale of Gleason common shares.		

A = L + SE
+17,000 +500
−16,500

⬆ Cash flows: +17,000

This gain is reported under other revenue in the income statement.

DEBT INVESTMENTS—BONDS

Recording Acquisitions of Bonds

The following example illustrates the accounting for bonds purchased to trade. Remember that the reporting of bonds at fair value will only apply to companies following IFRS, as companies reporting under ASPE report all debt investments at amortized cost. At acquisition, an investment in bonds for trading purposes is recorded at its fair value, which is equal to the price the bonds are trading at on the date of purchase. Assume Kuhl Corporation acquires $50,000 face value of Doan Inc. 10-year, 6% bonds on January 1, 2014, at a discount for $49,000. Kuhl Corporation purchased the bonds to trade. The entry to record the investment is as follows:

A = L + SE				
+49,000	Jan. 1	Trading Investments—Doan Bonds	49,000	
−49,000		Cash		49,000
↓Cash flows: −49,000		To record purchase of Doan bonds.		

Recording Interest Revenue

The bonds pay interest of $1,500 ($50,000 × 6% × $^{6}/_{12}$) semi-annually on July 1 and January 1. The following entry records the receipt of interest on July 1, 2014.

A = L + SE				
+1,500 +1,500	July 1	Cash	1,500	
		Interest Revenue		1,500
↑Cash flows: +1,500		To record receipt of interest on Doan bonds.		

Note that interest revenue is equal to the cash received. The $1,000 discount, the difference between the face value ($50,000) and the purchase price ($49,000) on the bonds, is not amortized to interest revenue. The bonds are purchased to trade and are held for a short period of time; therefore, any misstatement of interest revenue from not amortizing the premium or discount is considered insignificant.

Assuming Kuhl's financial year end is December 31, an entry is required to accrue interest revenue for the interest earned. The following entry records the accrual of interest on December 31:

A = L + SE				
+1,500 +1,500	Dec. 31	Interest Receivable	1,500	
		Interest Revenue		1,500
Cash flows: no effect		To record accrual of interest on Doan bonds.		

Note that on January 1, 2015, when the interest payment is received from Doan, interest receivable will be credited.

Recording Fair Value Adjustments at the Balance Sheet Date

You will recall from Chapter 15 that bonds trade on the public market at prices that reflect the current market interest rate. If the market interest rate changes after a company purchases bonds, the bonds' fair value will be different from their purchase price. If the market interest rate increases, the bonds' fair value will decrease, and if the market interest rate decreases, the bonds' fair value will increase. Assume that on December 31, 2014, Kuhl's financial year end, the market interest rate increased and the bonds are trading at $48,000. The entry to record the adjustment to fair value is as follows:

A = L + SE				
−1,000 −1,000	Dec. 31	Loss on Fair Value Adjustment of Trading Investments	1,000	
		($49,000 − $48,000)		
Cash flows: no effect		Trading Investments—Doan Bonds		1,000
		To record adjustment to fair value.		

The investment in Doan bonds will be reported on the balance sheet in current assets at its fair value of $48,000, which is the new carrying value of the bonds. The loss on fair value adjustment is reported under other expenses in the income statement.

Recording Sales of Bonds

When the bonds are sold, it is necessary to first update any unrecorded interest up to the date of sale. Then (1) debit Cash for the proceeds received, (2) credit the investment account for the bonds' carrying value, and (3) record any gain or loss on sale. Any difference between the proceeds from the sale of the bonds and the carrying value is recorded as a gain or loss.

Assume, for example, that Kuhl receives $47,500 on the sale of the Doan bonds on July 1, 2015, after receiving (and recording) the interest due. Since the bonds' carrying value is $48,000, a loss of $500 is recorded. The entry to record the sale is as follows:

July 1	Cash	47,500	
	Loss on Sale of Trading Investments ($48,000 − $47,500)	500	
	Trading Investments—Doan Bonds		48,000
	To record sale of Doan bonds.		

A = L + SE
+47,500   −500
−48,000

↑ Cash flows: +47,500

The loss on the sale of the bonds is reported as other expenses in the income statement.

Recording Bonds for Investor and Investee

Using the Kuhl Corporation example, Illustration 16-6 compares the recording of the bonds as a trading investment reported at fair value for Kuhl (the investor) and the recording of the bonds as a long-term liability for Doan (the investee). For the purpose of this illustration, we have assumed that the discount amortization is $150 for the first interest period, $140 for the second interest period, and $130 for the third interest period.

▶ ILLUSTRATION 16-6
Comparison of debt trading investment and long-term liability

KUHL CORPORATION (INVESTOR)			
Jan. 1	Trading Investments—Doan Bonds	49,000	
	Cash		49,000
July 1	Cash	1,500	
	Interest Revenue		1,500
Dec. 31	Interest Receivable	1,500	
	Interest Revenue		1,500
31	Loss on Fair Value Adjustment of Trading Investments	1,000	
	Trading Investments—Doan Bonds		1,000
Jan. 1	Cash	1,500	
	Interest Receivable		1,500
July 1	Cash	1,500	
	Interest Revenue		1,500
1	Cash	47,500	
	Loss on Sale of Trading Investments	500	
	Trading Investments—Doan Bonds		48,000

DOAN INC. (INVESTEE)			
Jan. 1	Cash	49,000	
	Bonds Payable		49,000
July 1	Interest Expense	1,650	
	Bonds Payable		150
	Cash		1,500
Dec. 31	Interest Expense	1,640	
	Bonds Payable		140
	Interest Payable		1,500
Jan. 1	Interest Payable	1,500	
	Cash		1,500
July 1	Interest Expense	1,630	
	Bonds Payable		130
	Cash		1,500

Note that accounting for a trading investment in bonds (an asset) for an investor differs from the accounting for bonds payable (a liability) for an investee in several ways. First, the investor does not amortize any premium or discount. Second, the investee does not record a fair value adjustment. Last, assuming that Kuhl, the investor, sold its bonds on the open market, the investee or issuer, Doan Inc., is not affected by this transaction. It would only be affected if the bonds were redeemed before maturity or repaid at maturity.

BEFORE YOU GO ON...

Do It

During 2014, Lang Corporation had the following transactions:

Jan.	2	Purchased an investment in Utility Corp. $20,000, five-year, 4% bonds for $20,455 to trade. The market interest rate is 3.5%.
July	1	Received semi-annual interest on the Utility Corp. bonds.
	2	Sold half of the Utility Corp. bonds for $10,500.
Sept.	1	Purchased 1,000 common shares of Electric Ltd. for $15 per share to trade.
Nov.	1	Received a $2 dividend on the Electric Ltd. shares.
Dec.	31	The Utility Corp. bonds' fair value was $9,750. The Electric Ltd. shares were trading at $14 per share.

(a) Record the above transactions.
(b) Prepare the required adjusting journal entries at December 31, Lang's financial year end.
(c) Identify where the investments would be reported in the balance sheet.
(d) Identify where the interest revenue, dividend revenue, and gains and losses will be reported.
(e) Assume that on January 15, 2015, Lang sells the Electric Ltd. shares for $13.50 per share. Record the sale of the shares.

Solution

(a)

Jan.	2	Trading Investments—Utility Corp. Bonds	20,455	
		Cash		20,455
		To record purchase of Utility Corp. bonds.		
July	1	Cash	400	
		Interest Revenue		400
		To record receipt of interest.		
	2	Cash	10,500	
		Trading Investments—Utility Corp. Bonds		10,228
		Gain on Sale of Trading Investments		272
		To record sale of half of Utility Corp. bonds.		
Sept.	1	Trading Investments—Electric Ltd. Common Shares	15,000	
		Cash		15,000
		To record purchase of Electric Ltd. common shares.		
Nov.	1	Cash	2,000	
		Dividend Revenue		2,000
		To record dividends received (1,000 × $2).		

(b)

Dec.	31	Interest Receivable ($10,000 × 4% × $^{6}/_{12}$)	200	
		Interest Revenue		200
		To accrue semi-annual interest on Utility Corp. bonds.		
	31	Loss on Fair Value Adjustment on Trading Investments	477	
		Trading Investments—Utility Corp. Bonds		477
		To record fair value adjustment on bonds ($10,227 − $9,750).		
	31	Loss on Fair Value Adjustment on Trading Investments	1,000	
		Trading Investments—Electric Ltd. Common Shares		1,000
		To record fair value adjustment on Electric Ltd. common shares [1,000 × ($15 − $14)].		

Action Plan
- Record the interest received as the amount of interest revenue.
- When the bonds are sold, the difference between the bonds' carrying value and the proceeds is reported as a gain or loss.
- Record the interest accrued on the bonds held for the period July 2 to December 31.
- Fair value adjustments are the difference between the investments' carrying value and fair value.
- When the shares are sold, the difference between the shares' carrying value and the proceeds is reported as a gain or loss.

(c) The investments will be reported in current assets on the balance sheet.
(d) Interest revenue, dividend revenue, and gain on sale will be reported in other revenues in the income statement. The losses from the fair value adjustments will be reported in other expenses in the income statement.

(e)

Jan.	15	Cash (1,000 × $13.50)	13,500	
		Loss on Sale of Trading Investments ($14,000 − $13,500)	500	
		Trading Investments—Electric Ltd. Common Shares		14,000
		To record sale of Electric Ltd. common shares.		

THE **NAVIGATOR**

Related exercise material: BE16–6, BE16–7, BE16–8, BE16–9, BE16–10, E16–5, E16–7, E16–8, E16–9, and E16–10.

Accounting for Strategic Investments

Recall from the start of the chapter that strategic investments are always long-term investments in equity securities. The accounting for strategic investments is based on how much influence the investor has over the operating and financial affairs of the issuing corporation (the investee). The degree of influence depends primarily on the percentage of common shares owned by the investor. Illustration 16-7 shows the general accounting guidelines for the levels of influence.

» STUDY **OBJECTIVE 4**

Account for strategic investments.

▶ **ILLUSTRATION 16-7**
Financial reporting guidelines for strategic investments

Investor's Ownership Interest in Investee's Common Shares	Presumed Influence on Investee	Financial Reporting Guidelines
Less than 20%	Insignificant	Fair value
20% to 50%	Significant	Equity method
Greater than 50%	Control	Consolidation

A company may invest in equity securities to maintain a long-term operating relationship. An investor company that owns less than 20% of the common shares of another company is generally presumed not to have significant influence over the decisions of the investee company. Under IFRS, a long-term equity investment where there is no significant influence is reported at fair value. Under ASPE, the investment would be reported at fair value if there is a quoted market price for the shares, and would be reported at cost if there is no quoted market price.

When an investor owns 20% to 50% of the common shares of another company, the investor is generally presumed to have a significant influence over the investee's decisions and the investor uses the equity method to account for and report the investment. Significant influence is the ability to participate in the investee's operating and financial policy decisions. When an investee can be significantly influenced, it is known as an **associate**.

The influence that an investor is assumed to have may be weakened by other factors. For example, an investor that acquires a 25% interest as the result of a "hostile" takeover may not have significant influence over the investee. Among the questions that should be answered to determine an investor's influence are:

1. Does the investor have representation on the investee's board of directors?
2. Does the investor participate in the investee's policy-making process?
3. Are there material transactions between the investor and investee?
4. Are the common shares that are held by other shareholders concentrated among a few investors or dispersed among many?

In other words, companies are required to use judgement when determining if significant influence exists instead of blindly following the guidelines. If circumstances exist that indicate the investor does not have significant influence, regardless of the amount owned, the investment is reported at fair value. The exception, as noted above, is that when the company is reporting under ASPE, the investment would be reported at cost if there is no quoted market price for the shares.

Typically, when an investor owns more than 50% of a corporation's common shares, it has more than significant influence—it has control. Control is the power to direct the operating and financial activities of the investee. Like significant influence, professional judgement is required to determine if there is control. There may be situations where an investor owns more than 50% of the common shares but it is not able to exert control over the investee. Conversely, there may be situations where the investor has less than 50% of the common shares and is able to exert control over the investee. If the investor has control over an investee, it is known as the **parent company** and the investee is known as the **subsidiary company**. Even though the investee is a separate legal entity, it is part of a group of corporations controlled by the parent. In order to show the users of the parents' financial statements the full extent of the group's operations, the financial statements of all the companies within the group are combined, resulting in **consolidated financial statements**. The process of preparing consolidated financial statements is complex and is addressed in advanced accounting courses.

FAIR VALUE

Similar to the accounting for trading investments reported at fair value, a fair value adjustment is recorded for strategic investments reported at fair value if the fair value of the investment increases or decreases.

However, if the investment is going to be held and not sold, then it may be inappropriate to affect a company's profit with the gains and losses on fair value adjustments caused by market fluctuations. Instead, companies reporting under IFRS can elect to report these gains and losses in other comprehensive income. You will recall from Chapter 14 that companies reporting under ASPE do not report comprehensive income; therefore, any gains and losses on fair value adjustment are reported in profit.

If a company reporting under IFRS decides to report the gains and losses on fair value adjustments in other comprehensive income, then the cumulative net gain or loss on that investment is transferred to retained earnings when the investment is sold. Dividends earned on the investment are reported in other revenues in the income statement as they are earned.

For companies reporting under ASPE or reporting under IFRS that elect to report gains or losses on fair value adjustments in profit, the accounting for the fair value adjustment is identical to the accounting for trading investments.

Similar to trading investments, dividends earned on strategic investments reported at fair value are reported in other revenue in the income statement as they are earned. Note that, unlike trading investments, strategic investments are classified as non-current.

The entries for an investment in common shares where gains and losses on fair value adjustments are reported in other comprehensive income are illustrated with the following example.

Recording Acquisitions of Shares

Assume that Cooke Ltd. purchases 5,000 common shares of Depres Company for $20 per share on October 1, 2014. Cooke Ltd. intends to hold the investment for strategic reasons, but does not have significant influence over Depres. Cooke Ltd. has elected to report the gains and losses resulting from the fair value adjustments in other comprehensive income. The entry to record the acquisition is as follows:

A = L + SE			
+100,000 −100,000			

↓ Cash flows: −100,000

Oct. 1	Long-Term Investment—Depres Common Shares	100,000	
	Cash (5,000 × $20)		100,000
	To record purchase of 5,000 Depres common shares.		

Recording Dividend Revenue

Assume that on November 1, 2014, Depres pays a dividend of $3 per share. The entry to record the dividend revenue is as follows:

A = L + SE			
+15,000 +15,000			

↑ Cash flows: +15,000

Nov. 1	Cash (5,000 × $3)	15,000	
	Dividend Revenue		15,000
	To record receipt of cash dividend.		

The dividend revenue is reported under other revenues in the income statement.

Recording the Fair Value Adjustment at Balance Sheet Date

Assume that on December 31, 2014, Cooke Ltd.'s financial year end, Depres common shares are trading at $22, an increase of $2 per share since the shares were purchased on October 1. The entry to record the change in fair value is as follows:

Dec. 31	Long-Term Investment—Depres Common Shares (5,000 × $2)	10,000	
	Other Comprehensive Income—Gain on Fair Value Adjustment		10,000
	To record adjustment to fair value.		

A = L + SE
+10,000   +10,000
Cash flows: no effect

Recall from Chapter 14 that gains and losses included in other comprehensive income are reported in the statement of comprehensive income net of tax. Assuming a 30% tax rate, $7,000 ($10,000 − [$10,000 × 30%]) will be reported as other comprehensive income in the statement. As a result, Accumulated Other Comprehensive Income will be increased by the fair value adjustment of $7,000. You will recall from Chapter 14 that Accumulated Other Comprehensive Income is reported in shareholders' equity.

Investments for which fair value adjustments are reported in other comprehensive income may also be called **available-for-sale investments**. However, this term is expected to be discontinued under the adoption of the most recent IFRS standards and therefore has not been used in this textbook.

EQUITY METHOD

As noted earlier, when an investor company has significant influence over the investee (which is known as an associate), the equity method is generally used to account for the investment. However, note that ASPE does permit companies to report investments with significant influence at fair value if there is a quoted market price for the shares or at cost if there is no quoted market price.

Under the **equity method**, the investment in common shares is initially recorded at cost in a non-current asset account called Investment in Associates. Cost includes the purchase price of the shares and any transaction costs paid to purchase them. After that, the investment account is adjusted annually to show the investor's equity in the associate. When the associate reports a profit, the investor will increase the investment account for its share of the associate's profit. It would be wrong to delay recognizing the investor's share of profit until a cash dividend is declared, as that approach would ignore the fact that the investor and associate are, in some sense, one company, and that the investor benefits from and can influence the timing of the distribution of the associate's profit.

Helpful hint Under the equity method, revenue is recognized on the accrual basis; that is, when it is earned by the associate.

Each year, the investor adjusts the investment account to do the following.

1. **Record its share of the associate's profit (loss):** Increase (debit) the investment account and increase (credit) revenue for the investor's share of the associate's profit. Conversely, when the associate has a loss, the investor increases (debits) a loss account and decreases (credits) the investment account for its share of the associate's loss.
2. **Record the dividends received:** Decrease (credit) the investment account when dividends are received. The investment account is reduced for dividends received because the associate's net assets are decreased when a dividend is paid.

Recording Acquisitions of Shares

Assume that Milar Corporation (the investor) acquires 30% of the common shares of Beck Corporation (the associate) for $120,000 on January 1, 2014, and that Milar has significant influence over Beck. The entry to record the investment is:

Jan. 1	Investment in Associate—Beck Corporation	120,000	
	Cash		120,000
	To record purchase of Beck common shares.		

A = L + SE
+120,000
−120,000
↓ Cash flows: −120,000

Recording Investment Revenue

For the year ended December 31, 2014, Beck reports profit of $100,000. It declares and pays a $40,000 cash dividend. Milar is required to record (1) its share of Beck's profit, $30,000 (30% × $100,000), and (2) a reduction in the investment account for the dividends received, $12,000 ($40,000 × 30%). The entries are as follows:

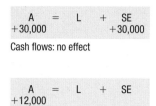

A = L + SE
+30,000   +30,000
Cash flows: no effect

A = L + SE
+12,000
−12,000
↕ Cash flows: +12,000

		(1)		
Dec. 31	Investment in Associate—Beck Corporation		30,000	
	Revenue from Investment in Associate			30,000
	To record 30% equity in Beck's profit.			
		(2)		
31	Cash		12,000	
	Investment in Associate—Beck Corporation			12,000
	To record dividends received.			

After the transactions for the year have been posted, the investment and revenue accounts will show the following:

Investment in Associate—Beck Corporation				Revenue from Investment in Associate		
Jan. 1	120,000				Dec. 31	30,000
Dec. 31	30,000	Dec. 31	12,000			
Dec. 31	Bal. 138,000					

During the year, the investment account has increased by $18,000 ($138,000 − $120,000). This $18,000 is Milar's 30% equity in the $60,000 increase in Beck's retained earnings ($100,000 − $40,000). In addition, Milar will report $30,000 of revenue from its investment, which is 30% of Beck's profit of $100,000.

The difference between profits reported when an investment is reported at fair value and when the equity method is used can be significant. If Milar were assumed not to have significant influence, it would report $12,000 of dividend revenue (30% × $40,000) as part of profit. It would also have to report a gain or loss from the fair value adjustment in either profit or other comprehensive income.

COST METHOD

You will recall that companies reporting under ASPE use the cost method to report strategic investments when there is no quoted market price for investments, if (1) there is not significant influence, or (2) the company chooses to use the cost method for significant influence investments. Under the cost method, the investment is initially recorded at cost and is not subsequently adjusted until sold. Dividend revenue is reported in profit. The investment is reported at cost on the balance sheet in non-current assets.

Recording Acquisitions of Shares

Assume that Passera Corporation (the investor) reports under ASPE and on July 1, 2014, acquires 1,000 common shares of Beale Corporation (the investee) at $40 per share. Beale Corporation is also a private company and there is no quoted market price for its shares. The cost method will be used to account for the investment. The entry to record the investment is:

A = L + SE
+40,000
−40,000
↓ Cash flows: −40,000

July 1	Long-Term Investment—Beale Common Shares		40,000	
	Cash			40,000
	To record purchase of Beale common shares.			

The investment will be reported in the balance sheet in non-current assets.

Recording Dividend Revenue

Like investments in equity securities reported at fair value, dividend revenue is recorded when the investee declares cash dividends. On October 1, Beale declares and pays a $2 per share dividend. The entry to record the dividend is:

Oct. 1	Cash (1,000 × $2)	2,000	
	Dividend Revenue		2,000
	To record receipt of cash dividend.		

A = L + SE
+2,000   +2,000

↑ Cash flows: +2,000

Dividend revenue is reported as other revenue in the income statement.

Recording Sale of Shares

If the shares are sold, it is necessary to (1) debit Cash for the proceeds received, (2) credit the investment account for the cost of the shares, and (3) record any gain or loss on sale. Any difference between the proceeds from the sale of the shares and the cost of the shares is recorded as a gain or a loss. Assume that Passera Corporation sells the Beale shares for $39,000 on December 10. Because the shares cost $40,000, a loss of $1,000 is realized on the sale. The entry to record the sale is:

Dec. 10	Cash	39,000	
	Loss on Sale of Long-term Investment— Beale		
	Common Shares ($40,000 − 39,000)	1,000	
	Long-Term Investment—Beale Common Shares		40,000
	To record sale of Beale common shares.		

A = L + SE
+39,000   −1,000
−40,000

↑ Cash flows: +39,000

The loss on sale is reported in other expenses in the income statement.

BEFORE YOU GO ON...

Do It

CJW Inc., a public company, made the following two investments during 2014:

1. Acquired 20% of the 400,000 common shares of Stillwater Corp. for $6 per share on January 2, 2014. On August 30, 2014, Stillwater paid a $0.10 per share dividend. On December 31, 2014, Stillwater reported profit of $244,000 for the year. Assume CJW has significant influence over Stillwater.
2. Acquired 10% of the 200,000 common shares of Roughwater Ltd. for $5 per share on September 15, 2014. CJW intends to hold the investment for strategic reasons but does not have significant influence, and reports gains or losses on fair value adjustments as other comprehensive income. On December 31, the shares were trading at $4 per share.

Prepare all necessary journal entries for CJW Inc. for 2014.

Action Plan

- Use the equity method for ownership when there is significant influence (normally ownership of 20% or more of the common shares of another corporation).
- Under the equity method, recognize investment revenue when the associate declares a profit. The distribution of dividends is not income; rather, it reduces the equity investment.
- Use the fair value method for a strategic long-term investment where there is not significant influence and record the gain or loss in other comprehensive income.

Solution

Jan. 2	Investment in Associate—Stillwater	480,000	
	Cash (80,000 × $6)		480,000
	To record purchase of 80,000 Stillwater common shares		
	(400,000 × 20% = 80,000 shares).		
Aug. 30	Cash	8,000	
	Investment in Associate—Stillwater		8,000
	To record receipt of cash dividend ($0.10 × 80,000).		
Sept. 15	Long-Term Investment—Roughwater Common Shares	100,000	
	Cash (20,000 × $5)		100,000
	To record purchase of 20,000 Roughwater common		
	shares (200,000 × 10%).		
Dec. 31	Investment in Associate—Stillwater	48,800	
	Revenue from Investment in Associate		48,800
	To record 20% equity in Stillwater's profit ($244,000 × 20%).		
31	Other Comprehensive Income—Loss on Fair Value Adjustment	20,000	
	Long-Term Investment—Roughwater Common Shares		20,000
	To record adjustment to fair value [20,000 × ($5 − $4)].		

Related exercise material: BE16–11, BE16–12, BE16-13, E16–11, and E16–12.

THE **NAVIGATOR**

Reporting of Investments

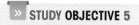

» STUDY OBJECTIVE 5

Indicate how investments are reported in the financial statements.

This section reviews the presentation of investments in the balance sheet, income statement, and statement of comprehensive income.

BALANCE SHEET

Under IFRS, debt and equity investments are classified as one of the following: (1) trading investments, (2) debt investments reported at amortized cost, (3) long-term equity investments reported at fair value, or (4) equity investments accounted for using the equity method. In addition to these classifications, under ASPE, some equity investments may be valued at cost if there is no quoted market price. These different types of investments will be reported on the balance sheet in either current assets or non-current assets.

Investments Classified as Current Assets

Trading investments are always classified as current assets, because management purchased the investment for the purpose of selling it in the near future at a gain. Recall that trading investments may include short-term and long-term debt instruments and equity securities.

Short-term debt instruments, such as term deposits and government treasury bills with maturities of less than 12 months purchased to earn interest, are included in current assets and reported at amortized cost. If the company has more than one such investment, they are either grouped together or presented in current assets in order of their liquidity. IFRS requires that trading investments and investments reported at amortized cost be separately disclosed.

You will recall from Chapter 7 that short-term debt investments that are held to earn interest and that have maturities of three months or less from the date they are purchased are generally combined with cash and reported as a single line item called "cash and cash equivalents."

Illustration 16-8 shows one possible presentation of short-term investments on the balance sheet for Skaweniio Corporation.

▶ **ILLUSTRATION 16-8**
Presentation of short-term investments

SKAWENIIO CORPORATION Balance Sheet (partial) December 31, 2014	
Assets	
Current assets	
Cash and cash equivalents	$ 28,000
Treasury bills—at amortized cost	15,000
Trading investments—at fair value	143,000

Investments Classified as Non-Current Assets

Long-term debt instruments, such as bonds, that are held to earn interest income are classified as non-current assets until they are about to mature. Any portion that is expected to mature within the year is classified as a current asset. In addition, all equity securities that are purchased for strategic purposes are also classified as non-current assets.

Separate disclosure is required for long-term investments reported at fair value, at cost, and at amortized cost, and for investments accounted for using the equity method. In addition, for equity investments reported at fair value, those investments where gains and losses are reported in other comprehensive income and those where gains and losses are reported in the income statement should be separately disclosed.

Illustration 16-9 summarizes the reporting and valuation requirements of both short- and long-term investments on the balance sheet.

▸ **ILLUSTRATION 16-9**
Reporting and valuation
of investments

Classification	Investment Category	Valuation	
		IFRS	**ASPE**
Current assets	Trading investments—equity	Fair value	Fair value
	Trading investments—debt	Fair value	Amortized cost
	Short-term debt investments to earn interest	Amortized cost	Amortized cost
Non-current assets	Long-term debt investments to earn interest	Amortized cost	Amortized cost
	Strategic investments— without significant influence	Fair value	Fair value if there is a quoted market price Cost if there is no quoted market price
	Strategic investments—with significant influence	Equity method (cost plus share of associate's profit less dividends)	Equity method (cost plus share of associate's profit less dividends) or Fair value if there is a quoted market price Cost if there is no quoted market price

INCOME STATEMENT AND STATEMENT OF COMPREHENSIVE INCOME

This chapter has shown that companies can earn different types of income on investments, including (1) interest revenue, (2) dividend revenue, (3) gains or losses on fair value adjustments, (4) gains or losses on sale of the investment, and (5) equity income from a strategic investment with significant influence. Most of these items are included in profit in the non-operating section of the income statement. But you will recall that a company reporting under IFRS may choose to include gains and losses on fair value adjustments of strategic investments without significant influence in other comprehensive income. This is summarized in Illustration 16-10.

ACCOUNTING IN ACTION
ALL ABOUT YOU INSIGHT

Canadians need to save for many different things over their lifetimes. To reduce taxes on savings and help individuals achieve their goals, the Canadian government introduced a new investment vehicle, the tax-free savings account (TFSA), starting in 2009. Canadians aged 18 and older can contribute up to $5,000 every year to a TFSA. Investment income on the TFSA is not taxable. If an individual is not able to contribute the allowed $5,000 per year, they are able to carry forward any unused contribution to future years. Funds can be withdrawn from the TFSA at any time and for any purpose. The amount withdrawn can be put back in the TFSA at a later date. Canadians from all income levels can participate.

Source: www.tfsa.gc.ca

Is it beneficial for you, while you are a student, to invest in a TFSA even though you may not have taxable income? Would you classify your investment in a TFSA as a long-term or short-term investment?

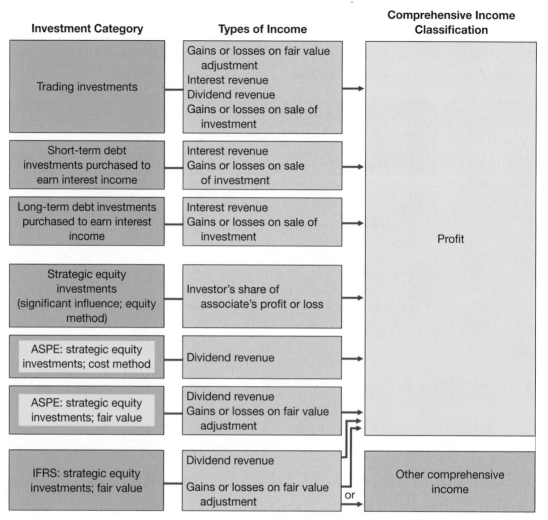

Investment Category	Types of Income	Comprehensive Income Classification
Trading investments	Gains or losses on fair value adjustment · Interest revenue · Dividend revenue · Gains or losses on sale of investment	
Short-term debt investments purchased to earn interest income	Interest revenue · Gains or losses on sale of investment	
Long-term debt investments purchased to earn interest income	Interest revenue · Gains or losses on sale of investment	Profit
Strategic equity investments (significant influence; equity method)	Investor's share of associate's profit or loss	
ASPE: strategic equity investments; cost method	Dividend revenue	
ASPE: strategic equity investments; fair value	Dividend revenue · Gains or losses on fair value adjustment	
IFRS: strategic equity investments; fair value	Dividend revenue · Gains or losses on fair value adjustment	or · Other comprehensive income

---

BEFORE YOU GO ON...

Do It

Zaboschuk Corporation, a public company, has the following asset account balances at December 31, 2014. Prepare the assets section of Zaboschuk's balance sheet at December 31.

Accounts receivable	$ 84,000
Accumulated depreciation—buildings	200,000
Accumulated depreciation—equipment	54,000
Allowance for doubtful accounts	4,000
Buildings	800,000
Cash	21,000
Equipment	180,000
Investment in associates	150,000
Goodwill	170,000
Inventory	130,000
Land	200,000
Long-term bond investment—amortized cost	50,000
Long-term equity investment—fair value	90,000
Money-market instruments (maturity 120 days—amortized cost)	15,000
Prepaid insurance	23,000
Trading investments	65,000

Action Plan

- Organize each asset account into its proper classification: current assets; long-term investments; property, plant, and equipment; and intangible assets.
- Remember that contra asset accounts reduce the related account balance and asset accounts increase the related account balance.

Solution

ZABOSCHUK CORPORATION
Balance Sheet (partial)
December 31, 2014

Assets

Current assets			
Cash			$ 21,000
Money-market instruments—amortized cost			15,000
Trading investments—fair value			65,000
Accounts receivable		$ 84,000	
Less: Allowance for doubtful accounts		4,000	80,000
Inventory			130,000
Prepaid insurance			23,000
Total current assets			334,000
Non-current assets			
Long-term investments			
Equity investment—fair value			90,000
Bond investment—amortized cost			50,000
Investment in associates			150,000
Total long-term investments			290,000
Property, plant, and equipment			
Land		$200,000	
Buildings	$800,000		
Less: Accumulated depreciation	200,000	600,000	
Equipment	$180,000		
Less: Accumulated depreciation	54,000	126,000	
Total property, plant, and equipment			926,000
Goodwill			170,000
Total assets			$1,720,000

THE **NAVIGATOR**

Related exercise material: BE16–14, BE16–15, BE16–16, E16-13 and E16–14.

▊Comparing IFRS and ASPE▊

Key Differences	International Financial Reporting Standards (IFRS)	Accounting Standards for Private Enterprises (ASPE)
Debt investments	Debt instruments purchased to trade: fair value. Debt instruments purchased to earn interest: amortized cost.	All debt instruments: amortized cost.
Strategic equity investment, no significant influence	Must use fair value.	Use fair value if quoted market price available. Use cost if quoted market price not available.
Strategic investment– significant influence	Must use equity method.	May use equity method, or fair value if quoted market price available, or cost if quoted market price not available.
Fair value adjustments on non-trading investments	May elect to report in other comprehensive income.	Report in profit.

THE **NAVIGATOR**

Demonstration Problem

ACTION PLAN

• Keep a running balance of the number of shares purchased and sold.

• Calculate the gain or loss on sale by subtracting the securities' carrying value from the proceeds.

• Determine the adjustment to fair value based on the difference between the securities' total cost and total fair value.

• Calculate the interest revenue on the bonds by multiplying the amortized cost of the bonds by the semi-annual market interest rate. Calculate the interest receivable by multiplying the face value of the bonds by the semi-annual contractual rate. Increase the investment in bonds by the difference between the interest receivable and the interest revenue.

• Determine the equity method investment income by multiplying the associate's profit by the percent of the common shares the investor company owns.

• Determine the profit before income tax by adding the other revenues and expenses to profit from operations.

• Calculate income tax expense by multiplying profit before income tax by the tax rate.

• Calculate the other comprehensive income reported in the comprehensive income statement by deducting the income tax on the fair value adjustment from the fair value adjustment.

• Calculate the accumulated other comprehensive income by adding the opening balance (zero in the first year of operations) and the fair value adjustment net of tax.

In its first year of operations, which ended December 31, 2014, Northstar Finance Corporation had the following selected transactions.

Jan.	1	Purchased 25% of the common shares of Southview Finance Ltd. for $125,000. Northstar purchased the investment for strategic purposes.
Mar.	14	Purchased a $10,000 treasury bill for $9,950.
May	5	Purchased 15% of the common shares of Eastgate Financial Co. for $28,000. Northstar purchased the investment for strategic purposes.
June	1	Purchased 600 Sanburg common shares for trading at $24.50 per share.
	29	Treasury bill matured and the company received $10,000.
July	1	Purchased $100,000 of Lower Corporation 10-year, 5% bonds for 95.7 to earn interest. The market interest rate is 6%. Interest is paid semi-annually, on July 1 and January 1.
	1	Purchased 800 Cey Corporation common shares for trading at $33.75 per share.
Sept.	1	Received a $1 per share cash dividend from Cey Corporation.
Oct.	8	Received dividends of $5,000 from Southview Finance Ltd.
Nov.	1	Sold 200 Sanburg common shares for $26.25 per share.
Dec.	15	Received a $0.50 per share cash dividend on Sanburg common shares.
	31	The fair values per share were $25 for Sanburg and $30 for Cey.
	31	Accrued interest revenue on the Lower Corporation bonds.
	31	The fair value of the Eastgate common shares was $26,000. Northstar has chosen to record the gains and losses on the fair value adjustment in other comprehensive income.
	31	Southview reported profit of $90,000 for the year ended December 31, 2014.
	31	Northstar reported profit from operations of $250,000 for the year ended December 31, 2014. Northstar's income tax rate is 30%.

Instructions

(a) Record the transactions.

(b) Prepare the adjusting entries at December 31 to report the securities at their fair value.

(c) Prepare a statement of comprehensive income starting with profit from operations.

(d) Show the presentation of the investment accounts and accumulated other comprehensive income in the balance sheet.

Solution to Demonstration Problem

(a)

Jan. 1	Investment in Associate—Southview Finance	125,000	
	Cash		125,000
	To record purchase of strategic investment in Southview.		
Mar. 14	Short-Term Investment—Treasury Bills	9,950	
	Cash		9,950
	To record purchase of treasury bill.		
May 5	Long-Term Investment—Eastgate Financial Co.		
	Common Shares	28,000	
	Cash		28,000
	To record purchase of strategic investment in common shares of Eastgate Financial.		
June 1	Trading Investments—Sanburg Common Shares	14,700	
	Cash (600 × $24.50)		14,700
	To record purchase of 600 Sanburg common shares.		
29	Short-Term Investment—Treasury Bills	50	
	Interest revenue		50
	Cash	10,000	
	Short-Term Investment—Treasury Bills		10,000
	To record maturity of treasury bill.		

July 1	Long-Term Investment—Lower Corporation Bonds	95,700	
	Cash		95,700
	To record purchase of long-term investment— Lower Corporation bonds.		
1	Trading Investments—Cey Common Shares	27,000	
	Cash (800 × $33.75)		27,000
	To record purchase of 800 Cey common shares.		
Sept. 1	Cash (800 × $1)	800	
	Dividend Revenue		800
	To record receipt of $1 per share dividend from Cey.		
Oct. 8	Cash	5,000	
	Investment in Associate—Southview Finance		5,000
	To record receipt of $5,000 dividends from Southview Finance Co.		
Nov. 1	Cash (200 × $26.25)	5,250	
	Trading Investments—Sanburg Common Shares [(200 ÷ 600) × $14,700)]		4,900
	Gain on Sale of Trading Investments		350
	To record sale of 200 Sanburg common shares.		
Dec. 15	Cash [(600 − 200) × $0.50]	200	
	Dividend Revenue		200
	To record receipt of $0.50 per share dividend from Sanburg.		

(b)

Trading Investments	Cost	Fair Value	Gain (Loss) on Fair Value Adjustment
Sanburg common shares (400)	$ 9,800	$10,000	$ 200
Cey common shares (800)	27,000	24,000	(3,000)
Total	$36,800	$34,000	$(2,800)

Dec. 31	Loss on Fair Value Adjustment of Trading Investments	2,800	
	Trading Investments—Sanburg Common Shares	200	
	Trading Investments—Cey Common Shares		3,000
	To record fair value adjustment on trading investments.		
31	Interest Receivable ($100,000 × 5% × $^6/_{12}$)	2,500	
	Long-Term Investment—Lower Corporation Bonds	371	
	Interest Revenue ($95,700 × 6% × $^6/_{12}$)		2,871
	To record the accrual of interest on the Lower Corporation bonds.		
31	Other Comprehensive Income—Loss on Fair Value Adjustment ($28,000 − $26,000)	2,000	
	Long-Term Investment—Eastgate Financial Co. Common Shares		2,000
	To record loss on fair value adjustment on long-term investment.		
31	Investment in Associate—Southview Finance ($90,000 × 25%)	22,500	
	Revenue from Investment in Associate		22,500
	To record 25% equity in Southview Finance Co.'s profit.		

(c)

NORTHSTAR FINANCE CORPORATION
Statement of Comprehensive Income
Year Ended December 31, 2014

Profit from operations	$250,000
Other revenues and expenses	
Other revenue	
Revenue from investment in associate	22,500
Interest revenue ($2,871 + $50)	2,921
Dividend revenue ($800 + $200)	1,000
Gain on sale of trading investments	350
	26,771
Other expenses	
Loss on fair value adjustment of trading investments	2,800
Total other revenues and expenses	23,971
Profit before income tax	273,971
Income tax ($273,971 × 30%)	82,191
Profit	191,780
Other comprehensive income (loss)	
Loss on fair value adjustment, net of $600 income tax	1,400
($2,000 − [$2,000 × 30%])	
Comprehensive income	$190,380

(d)

NORTHSTAR FINANCE CORPORATION
Balance Sheet (partial)
December 31, 2014

Assets	
Current assets	
Trading investments—at fair value	$ 34,000
Long-term investments	
Bond investment—amortized cost ($95,700 + $371)	96,071
Equity investment—fair value ($28,000 − $2,000)	26,000
Investment in associate ($125,000 + $22,500 − $5,000)	142,500
Total long-term investments	264,571
Liabilities and Shareholders' Equity	
Shareholders' equity	
Accumulated other comprehensive income (loss)	(1,400)

THE NAVIGATOR

Summary of Study Objectives

1. ***Identify reasons to invest, and classify investments.*** Companies purchase debt and equity securities of other companies for two main reasons: (1) for non-strategic reasons as a source of investment income, and (2) for strategic reasons, such as gaining control of a competitor, influencing strategic alliances, or moving into a new line of business.

   Non-strategic investments are debt and equity securities that are purchased for purposes of earning interest or dividend revenue or for the purpose of selling them in the short term at a gain. Investments purchased for selling in the short term are referred to as trading investments and are reported at fair value. Debt investments reported at amortized cost may be short-term or long-term. Strategic investments are always investments in equity securities and are classified as long-term investments.

2. ***Account for debt investments that are reported at amortized cost.*** Companies reporting under IFRS report debt investments purchased for the purposes of earning interest income at amortized cost. Companies reporting under ASPE report all investments in debt instruments at amortized cost. Debt investments include money-market instruments, bonds, and similar items. Entries are required to record the (1) acquisition, (2) interest revenue, and (3) maturity or sale. Interest revenue is recognized as it accrues and any discount or premium is amortized using the effective-interest method.

3. ***Account for trading investments.*** Trading investments are reported at fair value. Under IFRS, these investments can be either debt or equity securities that are purchased for the purpose of selling in the short term at a gain. Under ASPE, only investments in equity securities will be reported at fair value. An equity investment may be in either preferred or common shares of another corporation. Entries are required to record the (1) acquisition, (2) investment revenue, (3) fair value adjustments, and (4) sale. The gains and losses resulting from fair value adjustments are reported in profit.

4. ***Account for strategic investments.*** Strategic investments are long-term investments in common shares of another company. The accounting for strategic investments is based on how much influence the investor has over the operating and financial affairs of the issuing corporation (the investee). When the investor company does not have significant influence (ownership is usually less than 20%) over the investee company, the investment is reported at fair value. Under IFRS, gains and losses resulting from fair value adjustments can be reported in other comprehensive income. Under ASPE, if there is not a quoted market price, the investment is reported at cost. Under the cost method, the investment is initially recorded at cost and is not subsequently adjusted until sold.

When there is significant influence (ownership is usually 20% or more), the investee is called an associate. The equity method is used to account for investments with significant influence. The equity method records investment revenue when profit is reported by the associate and increases the investor's investment account accordingly. Dividends that are received reduce the value of the investment account. Under ASPE, companies can elect to report investments with significant influence at fair value if there is a quoted market price. In the absence of a quoted market price, the investment may be reported at cost.

5. ***Indicate how investments are reported in the financial statements.*** Trading investments are presented in the current assets section of the balance sheet. This includes equity investments and short- and long-term debt investments as long as they have been purchased for trading. Debt investments reported at amortized cost, maturing within 12 months of the balance sheet date, are also reported in current assets. Debt instruments reported at amortized cost with maturity dates of longer than 12 months from the date of the balance sheet and equity investments that are purchased for strategic purposes are reported in long-term investments. Gains and losses resulting from fair value adjustments that are reported in the income statement are presented in other revenues or other expenses. If any gains and losses resulting from fair value adjustments on strategic equity investments are reported in other comprehensive income, then this is added to accumulated other comprehensive income in the shareholders' equity section of the balance sheet.

When a company controls the common shares of another company (that is, its ownership is usually greater than 50%), consolidated financial statements are prepared. THE NAVIGATOR

Flash cards

▶ Glossary

Associate   The investee when the investor has significant influence. (p. 831)

Available-for-sale investments   Debt or equity investments for which the gains or losses on fair value adjustment are reported in other comprehensive income. (p. 833)

Consolidated financial statements   Financial statements that combine the parent company's financial statements with the financial statements of the companies that are controlled by the parent. (p. 832)

Debt instruments   Debt obligations such as money-market instruments, bonds, or similar items that can be bought and sold. Also called *debt securities*. (p. 818)

Equity instruments   An ownership interest in a corporation such as preferred and common shares. Also called *equity securities*. (p. 818)

Equity method   An accounting method in which the investment in common shares is initially recorded at cost. The investment account is then adjusted annually to show the investor's equity in the associate (investee). (p. 833)

Fair value   The amount the investment can be sold for in the market. Typically this will be the quoted market price in a public market. (p. 826)

Fair value adjustment   An accounting entry to adjust the carrying value of the investment for any increases or decreases in its fair value. (p. 826)

Investee   The corporation that issues (sells) the debt or equity securities that investors purchase. (p. 823)

Investor   The corporation that buys (owns) the debt or equity securities issued by another company. (p. 823)

Long-term debt instruments Debt instruments with a maturity of longer than 12 months after the balance sheet date. (p. 821)

Money-market instruments Short-term debt instruments that are low-risk and highly liquid, such as money-market funds, term deposits, and treasury bills. (p. 819)

Non-strategic investment An investment that is purchased mainly to generate investment income. (p. 818)

Parent company A company that controls, or owns more than 50% of the common shares of, another company. (p. 832)

Securities Debt or equity instruments that a company may invest in. (p. 818)

Short-term debt instruments Debt instruments that mature within 12 months of the balance sheet date. (p. 821)

Strategic investment An investment in equity securities that is purchased to maintain a long-term operating relationship with another company. (p. 818)

Subsidiary company A company whose common shares are controlled by another company (usually more than 50% of its common shares are owned by the other company). (p. 832)

Trading investments Debt or equity securities that are bought and held for sale in the near term, mainly to generate earnings from short-term price differences. Also referred to as *trading securities* and *held-for-trading investments*. (p. 819)

▶ Self-Study Questions

Answers are at the end of the chapter.

(SO 1) K **1.** Under IFRS, the most important factor for determining the classification and valuation of a non-strategic investment is:
  (a) whether the investment is in a debt instrument or an equity instrument.
  (b) whether the investment is in a private or public corporation.
  (c) whether the investment is a long-term or current investment.
  (d) the purpose of the investment.

(SO 1) K **2.** The most significant difference between a trading investment and a strategic investment is:
  (a) trading investments may earn dividend income, whereas strategic investments may not.
  (b) equity instruments purchased for trading are more likely to be listed on a public stock exchange.
  (c) strategic investments are usually investments in private corporations, whereas trading investments are not.
  (d) a trading investment is purchased for resale in the near future at a gain and a strategic investment is purchased to have a long-term operating relationship between the companies.

(SO 2) K **3.** Which of the following statements is false?
  (a) Debt instruments purchased to earn interest are reported at amortized cost.
  (b) Debt instruments purchased by a company reporting under IFRS must be reported at fair value.
  (c) Debt instruments include term deposits, treasury bills, money-market funds, and bonds.
  (d) The discount or premium on bonds reported at amortized cost is amortized using the effective-interest method.

(SO 2) AP **4.** The accounting entry to record the accrual of interest on a treasury bill is:
  (a) debit interest revenue and credit short-term investment in treasury bill.

  (b) debit interest revenue and credit cash.
  (c) debit short-term investment in treasury bill and credit interest revenue.
  (d) debit cash and credit short-term investment in treasury bill.

(SO 3, 4) K **5.** Which securities are valued at fair value in public companies?
  (a) Short-term investment in debt instrument held to earn interest
  (b) Long-term investment in 25% of the common shares of an associate
  (c) Long-term investment in bonds held to earn interest
  (d) Trading investments in debt or equity securities

(SO 3) AP **6.** During 2014, Boscha Ltd. purchased common shares in International Inc. for $240,000 for purposes of trading. At December 31, the fair value of the shares is $225,000. The journal entry to adjust the trading investment at year end is:

(a) Loss on Fair Value Adjustment of Trading Investments	15,000	
Trading Investments—International Inc.		15,000
(b) Trading Investments—International Inc.	15,000	
Gain on Fair Value Adjustment of Trading Investments		15,000
(c) Other Comprehensive Income—Loss on Fair Value Adjustment	15,000	
Trading Investments—International Inc.		15,000

  (d) No journal entry is required because losses are not recorded until the investment is sold.

(SO 4) K **7.** The equity method of accounting for an investment in common shares is normally used when the investor owns:
  (a) less than 20% of the investee's common shares.
  (b) 20% or more of the investee's common shares.

(c) 20% or more of the investee's preferred shares.

(d) more than 50% of the investee's common shares.

(SO 4) AP 8. The Big K Ranch owns 20% of the Little L Ranch's common shares. The Little L Ranch reported profit of $150,000 and paid dividends of $40,000 this year. How much investment revenue would the Big K Ranch report if it used the equity method?

(a) $22,000

(b) $30,000

(c) $110,000

(d) $8,000

(SO 5) K 9. Which of the following is *false*? ASPE requires that:

(a) debt investments be reported at amortized cost.

(b) equity investments of 20% of the investee's common shares must be reported using the equity method.

(c) gains and losses on fair value adjustments must be reported in profit.

(d) equity investments of less than 20% for which there is not a quoted market price must be reported at cost.

(SO 3, 5) 10. During 2014, Voser Ltd. purchased 100,000 common shares of Canadian Corp. for $325,000 when the shares were trading at $3.25 per share. The shares were purchased for purposes of trading.
AP

On September 30, Voser received $15,000 of dividends from Canadian Corp. At December 31, the shares were trading at $3.50 per share. Voser Ltd. would report the following in its December 31 financial statements:

(a) Trading investments—Canadian Corp. in the amount of $325,000 in current assets on the balance sheet, dividend revenues of $15,000 in other revenues in the income statement, and a $25,000 gain on fair value adjustment in other revenues in the income statement.

(b) Trading investments—Canadian Corp. in the amount of $350,000 in current assets on the balance sheet, dividends of $15,000 as a deduction from retained earnings, and a $25,000 gain on fair value adjustment in other revenues in the income statement.

(c) Trading investments—Canadian Corp. in the amount of $350,000 in current assets on the balance sheet, dividend revenues of $15,000 in other revenues in the income statement, and a $25,000 gain on fair value adjustment in other revenues in the income statement.

(d) Trading investments—Canadian Corp. in the amount of $325,000 in current assets on the balance sheet and dividend revenues of $15,000 in other revenues in the income statement.

THE NAVIGATOR

⦿ Questions

(SO 1) C 1. Why might a corporation purchase debt or equity securities of another company?

(SO 2) C 2. What are the differences between non-strategic and strategic investments?

(SO 1) C 3. On December 9, 2011, **Bell Canada** and **Rogers Communications** announced the two companies were jointly acquiring a 79.53% interest in **Maple Leaf Sports and Entertainment** (MLSE). MLSE owns several professional sports teams including the Toronto Maple Leafs and the Toronto Raptors. Is this a non-strategic investment or a strategic investment by Bell Canada and Rogers Communications? Explain.

(SO 2, 3) C 4. In what ways does reporting investments held to earn interest at amortized cost provide users of financial statements with relevant information? What relevant information does reporting trading investments at fair value provide users of financial statements?

(SO 2, 3) C 5. When is it appropriate to report an investment in bonds at amortized cost? At fair value?

(SO 2, 3) C 6. For public companies, what are the differences between the accounting for bonds purchased for trading and bonds held to earn interest revenue?

(SO 2, 3) C 7. Larson Inc., a public company, purchased bonds on the public market at a discount. If Larson considers this to be a long-term investment made to earn interest income instead of an investment purchased for

trading, will this have an impact on Larson's recognition of interest revenue from the investment? Why or why not?

(SO 4) K 8. When is it appropriate for a public company to report gains and losses on fair value adjustments in other comprehensive income?

(SO 4) K 9. When is it appropriate for companies reporting under ASPE to use the cost method to report investments?

(SO 4) K 10. When should a strategic investment be (a) reported at fair value and (b) accounted for using the equity method?

(SO 4) C 11. Explain why the equity method is not used for strategic investments without significant influence.

(SO 4) C 12. Identify what is included in the carrying value of a strategic investment using the (a) fair value model, (b) cost model, and (c) equity method.

(SO 4) K 13. When is an investee referred to as an associate? When is an investee referred to as a subsidiary?

(SO 4) C 14. Opal Limited owns 80% of the common shares of Fashion Runway Inc. What is the presumed level of influence for this investment? What kind of financial statements should Opal prepare to properly present this investment?

(SO 5) K 15. Explain why trading investments are always reported as current assets and yet investments to earn interest may be reported as current or non-current assets.

(SO 5) K 16. Identify the proper statement presentation of the following investments: (a) trading investments, (b) short-term debt investments purchased to earn interest, (c) debt investments purchased to earn interest with maturities longer than 12 months, (d) strategic investments reported at fair value, and (e) strategic investments accounted for using the equity method.

(SO 5) C 17. When may a company report gains or losses on fair value adjustments through other comprehensive income? Why might a company choose to report these gains and losses in other comprehensive income?

▶ Brief Exercises

Identify terminology.
(SO 1) K

BE16–1   The following terms were introduced in this chapter:

1. Strategic investments
2. Non-strategic investments
3. Trading investments
4. Debt investments reported at amortized cost

Match each term with the following definitions:

(a) _____ Debt securities that are held to earn interest income
(b) _____ Investments purchased to influence or control another company
(c) _____ Debt or equity securities that are bought and held for sale in the near term at a profit
(d) _____ Investments purchased mainly to generate investment income

Classify investments.
(SO 1) C

BE16–2   For each of the following investments, identify the (a) reason for the investment (non-strategic or strategic), (b) balance sheet classification (current or non-current asset), and (c) the valuation reported on the balance sheet. Assume that the investor is a public company. The first one has been done for you as an example.

Investment	(a) Reason	(b) Classification	(c) Valuation
1. 120-day treasury bill	Non-strategic	Current asset	Amortized cost
2. Common shares purchased by a bank for resale in the near future at a gain			
3. 15% of the common shares of a public company purchased to hold with the intent of acquiring control of the company			
4. 5-year bonds purchased by a company reporting under ASPE, to hold and earn interest			
5. 10-year bonds purchased, by a public company, to sell in the near future at a gain			
6. 5-year bonds purchased, by a public company, to hold and earn interest			

Account for debt investment reported at amortized cost.
(SO 2) AP

BE16–3   On December 2, 2014, Nudesign Furniture Ltd. purchased a $150,000, Canadian government 120-day treasury bill for $148,900. On December 31, $275 of interest had accrued on the treasury bill. On April 1, 2015, the treasury bill matured. Prepare the journal entries to record the (a) purchase of the treasury bill; (b) accrual of interest on December 31, 2014; and (c) receipt of cash on April 1, 2015.

Account for debt investment reported at amortized cost.
(SO 2) AP

BE16–4   On January 1, 2014, Chan Ltd. purchased $600,000 of five-year, 4% bonds at par from Pullen Corporation. Interest is received semi-annually on July 1 and January 1. Chan purchased the bonds to earn interest. At December 31, 2014, the bonds were trading at 101. Prepare the journal entries to record (a) the purchase of the bonds on January 1, (b) the receipt of interest on July 1, and (c) any adjusting entries required at December 31.

Account for debt investment reported at amortized cost.
(SO 2) AP

BE16–5   Strand Corp. purchased $300,000 of five-year, 4% Hydrocor bonds at 99 on June 30, 2014. Strand Corp. purchased the bonds to earn interest. Interest is paid semi-annually each June 30 and December 31. The semi-annual amortization amount for the first interest period is $273. At December 31, 2014, the bonds were trading at 98. Prepare the required journal entries on June 30 and December 31, 2014.

Account for trading investment. (SO 3) AP

BE16–6   Using the data presented in BE16–5, assume Strand Corp. is a public company and that it purchased Hydrocor's bonds to trade. Prepare the journal entries to record (a) the purchase of the bonds on June 30, 2014; (b) the receipt of the first interest payment on December 31, 2014; and (c) any required adjusting journal entries on December 31, 2014.

BE16–7   Using the data presented in BE16–5 and BE16–6, assume Strand Corp. sells the bonds on January 1, 2015, at 98. Prepare the journal entry to record the sale of the bonds under each set of assumptions.

Account for sale of trading investment. (SO 3) AP

BE16–8   On August 1, McLain Finance Inc. buys 3,000 Datawave common shares as a trading investment for $114,000 cash. On October 15, McLain receives a cash dividend of $2.75 per share from Datawave. On December 1, McLain sells the shares for $120,000 cash. Prepare the journal entries to record the (a) purchase of the shares, (b) receipt of the dividend, and (c) sale of the shares.

Account for trading investment. (SO 3) AP

BE16–9   Nakagama Limited owns 10,000 common shares of Deal Inc. purchased for selling in the near term. The carrying value of Deal Inc.'s common shares at November 30, 2014, is $46,000. The fair value of the investment at November 30 and December 31, 2014, is $44,000 and $47,000, respectively. The company prepares adjusting journal entries monthly. Prepare the required adjusting entries to record the securities at fair value at November 30 and December 31.

Account for trading investment. (SO 3) AP

BE16–10   Using the data presented in BE16–9, assume that the investment in Deal Inc.'s common shares is sold on January 15, 2015, for $49,000. Prepare the journal entry to record the sale of the investment.

Account for trading investment. (SO 3) AP

BE16–11   On January 1, Poitras Ltée, a public company, purchases 20% of Hook Corporation's common shares for $250,000 for strategic purposes. For the year ended December 31, Hook reports profit of $220,000 and pays a $15,000 cash dividend. The fair value of Poitras' investment in Hook at December 31 is $270,000. Prepare journal entries required assuming Poitras (a) does not have significant influence over Hook, and (b) does have significant influence over Hook.

Account for strategic investment. (SO 4) AP

BE16–12   Wren Inc., a public company, owns 20% of Dong Ltd.'s common shares for strategic purposes. The investment's carrying value at January 1, 2014, is $300,000. During the year, Dong reported profit of $250,000 and paid a dividend of $20,000. The investment's fair value on December 31, 2014, Wren's year end, is $315,000. Where appropriate, Wren reports fair value adjustments in other comprehensive income.

Compare impact of reporting at fair value and using the equity method. (SO 4) AP

(a) Assuming Wren does not have significant influence over Dong, indicate the amount reported for the long-term investment at December 31, the amount of investment income reported in the income statement, and the amount of investment income reported in other comprehensive income.
(b) Assuming Wren does have significant influence over Dong, indicate the amount reported for the long-term investment at December 31, the amount of investment income reported in the income statement, and the amount of investment income reported in other comprehensive income.

BE16–13   On January 1, 2014, McAdam Ltd., a private company reporting under ASPE, purchased 25% of the common shares of Tomecek Corporation for $175,000. Tomecek reported profit of $85,000 for 2014 and paid dividends of $12,000 on December 31, 2014. McAdam's year end is December 31. Assuming that there is not a quoted market price for Tomecek's shares, and that McAdam elects to report investments with significant influence using the cost method, prepare the required journal entries.

Account for strategic investment at cost. (SO 4) AP

BE16–14   Atwater Corporation, a public corporation, reported a gain on fair value adjustment of $46,000 net of tax on its strategic investment reported at fair value, and a loss on fair value adjustment of $50,000 before tax on its trading investments for the year ended April 30, 2014. The company's profit was $650,000 and it has a 35% income tax rate. Where Atwater has the choice, it reports gains and losses in other comprehensive income. Prepare a statement of comprehensive income.

Prepare statement of comprehensive income. (SO 5) AP

BE16–15   Indicate on which financial statement (that is, balance sheet, income statement, or statement of comprehensive income) each of the following accounts would be reported if the investor is a public company. Where the company has the choice, it reports gains and losses in other comprehensive income and the company presents the statement of comprehensive income separately from the income statement. Also give the appropriate financial statement classification (e.g., current assets, non-current assets, or other revenue).

Classify accounts. (SO 5) AP

Account	Financial Statement	Classification
Trading investments		
Dividend revenue		
Investment in associate		
Long-term investment—bonds		
Gain on sale of trading investments		
Gain on fair value adjustment for trading investments		
Loss on fair value adjustment for strategic investments		
Interest revenue on bonds purchased for trading		

Report investments on balance sheet. (SO 5) AP

BE16–16   Sabre Corporation, a public company, has the following investments at November 30, 2014:

1. Trading investments: common shares of National Bank, carrying value $25,000, fair value $26,000, and five-year, 5% bonds of Turbo Corp., carrying value $50,000, fair value $48,000
2. Strategic investment: 15% of the common shares of Sword Corp., carrying value $108,000, fair value $105,000
3. Strategic investment: common shares of Epee Inc. (30% ownership), cost $210,000, equity method balance $250,000
4. Debt investment purchased to earn interest: bonds of Ghoti Ltd. maturing in four years, amortized cost $150,000, fair value $175,000
5. Debt investment purchased to earn interest: Canadian government 120-day treasury bill, purchased at $25,000, $125 interest accrued to November 30, 2014

Show how the investments would be reported in the assets section of the balance sheet.

▶ Exercises

Distinguish between non-strategic and strategic investments. (SO 1) C

E16–1   Awisse Telecommunications Ltd. has several investments in debt and equity securities of other companies.

1. 15% of the common shares of Lewis Telecommunications Inc., with the intent of purchasing at least 10% more of the common shares and requesting a seat on Lewis's board of directors.
2. 100% of the 15-year bonds issued by Li Internet Ltd., intended to be held for 15 years to earn interest.
3. 95% of the common shares of Barlow Internet Services Inc.
4. 120-day treasury bill.
5. 10% of the common shares of Talk to Us Ltd., to be sold if the share price increases.

Instructions

Indicate whether each of the above investments is a non-strategic or strategic investment and explain why.

Classify investments. (SO 1) C

E16–2   Kroshka Holdings Corporation has several investments in the debt and equity securities of other companies:

1. 10-year BCE bonds, purchased to earn interest.
2. 10-year GE bonds, intended to be sold if interest rates go down.
3. 1-year Government of Canada bonds, purchased to earn interest.
4. 180-day treasury bill, intended to be held to earn interest.
5. Bank of Montreal preferred shares, purchased to sell in the near term at a profit.
6. Tim Hortons common shares, purchased to sell in the near term at a profit.
7. 60% of the common shares of Pizzutto Holdings Corporation, a major competitor of Kroshka Holdings.
8. 22% of the common shares of Kesha Inc., one of Kroshka Holdings' suppliers.

Instructions

(a) Indicate whether each of the above investments is a non-strategic or strategic investment.
(b) Indicate whether each of the above investments would be classified as a current asset or non-current asset on Kroshka Holdings' balance sheet.
(c) For each investment that you classified as non-strategic, indicate the value the investment will be reported at on the balance sheet assuming that Kroshka is a public company.
(d) How would your response to part (c) change if Kroshka were a private company reporting under ASPE?

Record debt investments reported at amortized cost. (SO 2) AP

E16–3   Stevens Corporation, during the year ended October 31, 2015, had the following transactions for money-market instruments purchased to earn interest:

Jan. 2   Purchased a 120-day, $40,000 treasury bill maturing on May 1 for $39,760.
May 1   The treasury bill matured.
Aug. 1   Invested $65,000 in a money-market fund.
     31   Received notification that $163 of interest had been earned and added to the fund.
Sept. 30   Received notification that $163 of interest had been earned and added to the fund.
Oct. 1   Purchased a 90-day, 2.4%, $30,000 treasury bill for $29,821.
     15   Cashed the money-market fund and received $65,408.

Instructions

(a) Prepare the journal entries to record the above transactions.
(b) Prepare any required adjusting journal entries at October 31.

E16–4   On July 1, 2014, Imperial Inc., a public company, purchased $500,000 of Acme Corp. 10-year, 4% bonds for $461,000 to earn interest. The bonds had a market interest rate of 5%. The bonds pay interest semi-annually on January 1 and July 1. Imperial Inc. has a December 31 year end. At December 31, 2014, the bonds are trading at 96.

Record debt investment reported at amortized cost and bond liability. (SO 2) AP

Instructions

(a) Assuming Imperial Inc. purchased the bonds from Acme Corp., record the purchase of the bonds on July 1 for (1) Imperial Inc., and (2) Acme Corp.

(b) Record any adjusting journal entries that are required at December 31 for (1) Imperial Inc., and (2) Acme Corp.

(c) Record the receipt of the first interest payment on January 1, 2015, for (1) Imperial Inc., and (2) Acme Corp.

(d) Compare the accounting for the bond investment with that of the bond liability.

E16–5   Using the data presented in E16–4, assume that Imperial Inc. purchased the bonds to trade.

Record debt investment for trading purposes. (SO 3) AP

Instructions

(a) Record the purchase of the bonds on July 1, 2014.

(b) Record any adjusting journal entries that are required at December 31, 2014.

(c) Indicate how the investment is presented on Imperial Inc.'s December 31, 2014, balance sheet.

(d) Record the receipt of the first interest payment on January 1, 2015.

(e) Assume the bonds are sold on the market at 97 on July 1, 2015, after the semi-annual interest payment has been received and recorded. Record the sale of the bonds.

(f) Explain why Acme Corp. will not record an entry for the bonds sold by Imperial on July 1, 2015.

E16–6   On April 1, 2013, Bight Corporation issued $400,000, five-year bonds. On this date, Shoreline Corporation purchased the bonds from Bight to earn interest. Interest is received semi-annually on April 1 and October 1 and Shoreline's year end is March 31. Below is a partial amortization schedule for the first few years of the bond issue.

Use a bond amortization schedule to record debt investment transactions at amortized cost. (SO 2) AP

Semi-Annual Interest Period	Interest Received	Interest Revenue	Amortization	Bond Amortized Cost
April 1, 2013				$418,444
October 1, 2013	$8,000	$6,277	$1,723	416,721
April 1, 2014	8,000	6,251	1,749	414,972
October 1, 2014	8,000	6,225	1,775	413,197

Instructions

(a) Were the bonds purchased at a discount or at a premium?

(b) What is the face value of the bonds?

(c) What will the bonds' amortized cost be at the maturity date?

(d) What is the bonds' contractual interest rate? The market interest rate?

(e) Prepare the journal entries to record the purchase of the bonds, the receipt of interest on October 1, 2013, the accrual of interest on March 31, 2014, and the receipt of interest on April 1, 2014.

(f) If Shoreline holds the investment until maturity, what will be the total interest received over the 10-year life of the bonds? Total interest revenue?

E16–7   Piper Corporation, a public company, had the following transactions with trading investments:

Record debt trading investment transactions. (SO 3) AP

Jan.	1	Purchased $120,000 of Harris Corp. 6% bonds at 101, to yield a market interest rate of 5.8%. Interest is payable semi-annually on July 1 and January 1.
July	1	Received semi-annual interest on Harris bonds.
	1	Sold half of the Harris bonds for $64,000.
Dec.	31	Accrued interest at Piper's year end.
	31	Piper's bonds were trading at 100.

Instructions

(a) Record the above transactions.

(b) How would your entry on July 1 change if the bonds were purchased to earn interest?

E16–8   Following is information for Marcel Lteé's trading investments. Marcel is a public company and has a December 31 year end.

Record debt and equity trading investments. (SO 3) AP

2014

Sept. 28	Purchased 3,500 shares of Cygman Limited for $40 per share.
Oct. 1	Purchased $300,000 of Rauk Inc. 4% bonds at face value. The bonds pay interest semi-annually on April 1 and October 1.
Nov. 12	Sold 1,900 Cygman shares for $42 per share.
Dec. 1	Received $1.50 per share dividend from Cygman.
31	Cygman shares were trading at $38 per share and the Rauk bonds were trading at 101.

2015

Mar. 31	Sold the remaining Cygman shares for $40 per share.
Apr. 1	Received interest on the Rauk bonds.
Oct. 1	Received interest on the Rauk bonds.
Dec. 31	Rauk bonds were trading at 100.

Instructions

Record the above transactions, including any required adjusting entries, for 2014 and 2015.

Record adjusting entry for trading investments, show statement presentation, and record sale. (SO 3) AP

E16–9 At December 31, 2014, the trading investments for Yanik, Inc., are as follows:

Security	Carrying Value	Fair Value
Co. A common shares	$18,500	$16,000
Co. B preferred shares	12,500	14,000
Co. C five-year, 4% bonds	23,000	19,000
Totals	$54,000	$49,000

Instructions

(a) Prepare the adjusting entries required at December 31 to report the investment portfolio at fair value.

(b) Show the financial statement presentation of the trading investments and the gains and losses on fair value adjustments at December 31, 2014.

(c) Assuming that on March 20, 2015, Yanik sold Co. B preferred shares for $13,500, prepare the journal entry to record this transaction.

Determine equity trading investment transactions. (SO 3) AP

E16–10 The following was reported by Church Financial in its December 31, 2014, financial statements:

Trading investments, December 31, 2013	$11,000
Trading investments, December 31, 2014	15,000
Gain on fair value adjustment	2,500
Loss on sale of trading investment	3,000

The carrying value of the investments sold was $4,000.

Instructions

(a) What is the cash amount received on the sale of the investment?

(b) Prepare the journal entries that were recorded by Church to record the sale of the investment and the gain on fair value adjustment at December 31, 2014.

(c) Post the journal entries to the Trading Investments T account.

(d) Calculate the amount of trading investments purchased in 2014. Prepare the entry to record the purchase.

Record strategic equity investments. (SO 4) AP

E16–11 Visage Cosmetics is a public company and, where it has the choice, reports gains and losses on investments in other comprehensive income. Visage had the following transactions in 2014:

1. Visage Cosmetics acquires 40% of Diner Limited's 30,000 common shares for $18 per share on January 2, 2014. On June 15, Diner pays a cash dividend of $30,000. On December 31, Diner reports profit of $380,000 for the year. At December 31, Diner shares are trading at $22 per share.

2. Visage Cosmetics acquires 10% of Image Fashion Inc.'s 400,000 common shares for $12 per share on March 18, 2014. On June 30, Image Fashion pays a cash dividend of $44,000. On December 31, Image Fashion reports profit of $252,000 for the year. At December 31, Image Fashion shares are trading at $11 per share.

Instructions

Record the above transactions and any required adjusting journal entries for the year ended December 31, 2014, assuming Visage Cosmetics intends to hold both investments for strategic purposes.

Record strategic equity investment; determine balance sheet presentation. (SO 4, 5) AP

E16–12 On January 1, 2014, Unique Limited, a private company, buys 25% of Walla Walla Corporation's 200,000 common shares for $480,000. On December 31, 2014, Walla Walla pays a $35,000 cash dividend and reports profit of $280,000. At December 31, 2014, Walla Walla's shares are trading at $12.50 per share. Both companies have a December 31 year end. Unique has significant influence over Walla Walla.

Instructions

(a) Record the above transactions assuming Unique uses the equity method to report its investment in Walla Walla.

(b) Determine the amounts to be reported on Unique's balance sheet and income statement for its investment in Walla Walla shares at December 31.

(c) Repeat parts (a) and (b) assuming Unique has elected not to use the equity method for significant influence investments.

(d) Repeat parts (a) and (b) assuming Unique has elected not to use the equity method for significant influence investments. Assume that Walla Walla shares are not publicly traded and that no quoted market price is available.

E16–13   You are provided with the following balance sheet accounts of New Bay Inc., a public company, as at December 31, 2014:

Prepare balance sheet.
(SO 5) AP

Accounts payable	$ 35,000
Accounts receivable	60,000
Accumulated depreciation—equipment	40,000
Accumulated other comprehensive income	2,000
Allowance for doubtful accounts	10,000
Bonds payable, 8%, due 2016	268,000
Cash	22,000
Common shares, 10,000, no par value unlimited	
authorized, 10,000 issued	100,000
Equipment	66,000
Investment in associates	55,000
Interest payable	18,000
Interest receivable	1,500
Long-term equity investment, fair value	25,000
Long-term investment—Aliant Inc. bonds	180,000
Note receivable, 5%, due April 21, 2018	60,000
Retained earnings	45,000
Trading investments, at fair value	48,500

Instructions

Prepare New Bay's classified balance sheet at December 31, 2014.

E16–14   You are provided with the following income accounts of Oakridge Ltd. for the year ended December 31, 2014. Oakridge reported profit from operations of $125,000 for the year ended December 31, 2014. Oakridge's income tax rate is 30%.

Prepare statement of comprehensive income.
(SO 5) AP

Interest revenue	$5,000
Gain on sale—trading investments	1,500
Other comprehensive income—gain on fair value adjustment	3,000
Loss on fair value adjustment—trading investments	7,500
Interest expense	8,000

Instructions

(a) Does Oakridge use ASPE or IFRS? Explain.

(b) Prepare a statement of comprehensive income starting with profit from operations.

▶ Problems: Set A

P16–1A   On January 1, 2014, Morrison Inc., a public company, purchased $600,000 of Pearl Corporation's five-year, 4% bonds for $627,660, when the market interest rate was 3%. Interest is received semi-annually on July 1 and January 1. Morrison's year end is December 31. Morrison intends to hold Pearl's bonds until January 1, 2019, the date the bonds mature. The bonds' fair value on December 31, 2014, was $620,000.

Record debt investment; show statement presentation.
(SO 2, 3, 5) AP

Instructions

(a) Record the purchase of the bonds on January 1, 2014.

(b) Prepare the entry to record the receipt of interest on July 1, 2014.

(c) Prepare the adjusting entries required at December 31, 2014.

(d) Show the financial presentation of the bonds for Morrison on December 31, 2014.

(e) Prepare the entry to record the receipt of interest on January 1, 2015.

(f) Prepare the entry to record the repayment of the bonds on January 1, 2019. Assume the entry to record the last interest payment has been recorded.

(g) How would your answers to parts (b) through (e) change if the bonds were purchased for the purpose of trading?

TAKING IT FURTHER   What was the market interest rate on December 31, 2014, when the bonds' fair value was $631,500? (*Hint:* How many interest periods are left after January 1, 2015?)

Record debt investments at amortized cost; show statement presentation.
(SO 2, 5) AP

P16–2A   Liu Corporation had the following transactions in debt instruments purchased to earn interest during the year ended December 31, 2014:

Jan.   1   Purchased a 180-day (six-month) Canadian government treasury bill for $98,039.
June 30   Treasury bill matured. Received $100,000 cash.
July   5   Purchased a money-market fund for $25,000.
Oct.   1   Cashed in the money-market fund, receiving $25,185.
       1   Purchased a six-month, 3%, term deposit for $75,000.
Dec. 31   Accrued semi-annual interest on the term deposit.

Instructions

(a) Record the transactions.

(b) Show the financial statement presentation of the investment at December 31 and any related accounts.

TAKING IT FURTHER   What was the annual rate of interest earned on the treasury bill?

Record debt investment at amortized cost and fair value, prepare bond amortization schedule, and record liability; show statement presentation.
(SO 2, 3, 5) AP

P16–3A   On January 1, 2014, Power Ltd. issued bonds with a maturity value of $5 million for $4,797,000, when the market rate of interest was 8%. The bonds have a coupon (contractual) interest rate of 7% and mature on January 1, 2019. Interest on the bonds is payable semi-annually on July 1 and January 1 of each year. On January 1, 2014, Finance Company purchased Power Ltd. bonds with a maturity value of $1 million to earn interest. On December 31, 2014, the bonds were trading at 98. Both companies' year end is December 31.

Instructions

(a) What amount did Finance Company pay for Power Ltd.'s bonds?

(b) Prepare the journal entry for Finance Company (investor) on January 1, 2014.

(c) Prepare a bond amortization schedule for Finance Company for the first four interest periods.

(d) Prepare the journal entries for Finance Company to record (1) the receipt of interest on July 1, 2014; (2) the accrual of interest on December 31, 2014; and (3) the receipt of interest on January 1, 2015.

(e) Show how the bonds and related income statement accounts would be presented in Finance Company's financial statements for the year ended December 31, 2014.

(f) Prepare the journal entry for Power Ltd. (investee) on January 1, 2014.

(g) Using the bond amortization schedule prepared in part (c) to calculate the interest expense and interest payments, prepare the journal entries for Power Ltd. to record (1) the payment of interest on July 1, 2014; (2) the accrual of interest on December 31, 2014; and (3) the payment of interest on January 1, 2015.

(h) Show how the bonds and related income statement accounts would be presented in Power Ltd.'s financial statements for the year ended December 31, 2014.

(i) Assume that Finance Company reports under IFRS and that it purchased the bonds to trade. Prepare any required journal entries or adjusting journal entries on July 1, 2014, and December 31, 2014.

(j) Assuming Finance Company purchased the bonds for purposes of trading, show how the bonds and related income statement accounts would be presented in Finance Company's financial statements for the year ended December 31, 2014.

TAKING IT FURTHER   Assume that Finance Company needed cash and sold the bonds on the open market on January 1, 2015, for 99.5 after receiving and recording the semi-annual interest payment. Indicate the amount of gain or loss that Finance Company would record if the bonds were purchased to (1) earn interest, and (2) trade.

Record equity and debt trading investments; show statement presentation.
(SO 3, 5) AP

P16–4A   During the year ended December 31, 2014, Rakai Corporation, a public company, had the following transactions in trading investments:

Feb.   1   Purchased 575 IBF common shares for $25,300.
Mar.   1   Purchased 1,500 Raimundo common shares for $48,000.
Apr.   1   Purchased $200,000 of CRT 3% bonds for $210,000. Interest is payable semi-annually on April 1 and October 1.
July   1   Received a cash dividend of $1.50 per share on the IBF common shares.
Aug.   1   Sold 250 IBF common shares at $48 per share.

Oct. 1   Received the semi-annual interest on the CRT bonds.
      1   Sold the CRT bonds for $215,000.
Dec. 31   The fair values of the IBF and Raimundo common shares were $50 and $28 per share, respectively.

Instructions

(a) Record the transactions and any required year-end adjusting entries.

(b) Show the financial statement presentation of the trading investments and any related accounts in the financial statements for the year ended December 31, 2014.

TAKING IT FURTHER   If Rakai Corporation anticipated that it would need the cash that was used to invest in the trading investments in the near future, should the company have invested in equity securities? What would you recommend to the company?

P16–5A   During 2013, Financial Holdings purchased equity securities for trading. At December 31, 2013, the securities for Financial Holdings were as follows:

Record equity trading investments; show statement presentation. (SO 3, 5) AP

Security	Quantity	Cost	Market Value
Sabo common shares	1,000	$15,000	$13,500
PYK $1.50 preferred shares	2,000	24,000	24,500
Total		$39,000	$38,000

The following transactions with respect to Financial Holdings' investments occurred during 2014:

Jan. 15   Purchased 1,500 common shares of Hazmi for $15.00 per share. The shares were purchased to trade.
Mar. 20   Received dividends on the PYK preferred shares of $1.50 per share.
June 15   Sold 750 of the Sabo common shares for $15.75 per share.
Aug. 5   Received dividends on the Sabo common shares of $2.50 per share.
Oct. 15   Received an additional 1,500 common shares of Hazmi as a result of a 2-for-1 stock split.

At December 31, 2014, the securities held by Financial Holdings were trading on the TSX at the following prices:

Security	Price
Sabo common shares	$16.00
PYK $1.50 preferred shares	13.75
Hazmi common shares	7.00

Instructions

(a) Show how the securities would be reported on Financial Holdings' December 31, 2013, balance sheet.

(b) Assuming that the purchases of Sabo common shares and PYK preferred shares were Financial Holdings' only investment transactions in 2013, show what would be reported in the company's December 31, 2013, income statement.

(c) Record Financial Holdings' 2014 transactions and any required adjusting journal entries at December 31, 2014.

TAKING IT FURTHER   Calculate the total profit/loss (over the life of the investment) that Financial Holdings made on the 750 Sabo common shares sold on June 15. Explain how and when it was recognized on the income statement.

P16–6A   Olsztyn Inc., a public company, had the following investment transactions:

Identify impact of investments on financial statements. (SO 2, 3, 4, 5) AP

1. Purchased Arichat Corporation common shares as a trading investment.
2. Purchased Bombardier bonds to earn interest.
3. Received interest on Bombardier bonds.
4. Purchased 10% of Havenot's common shares. The company intends to bid on Havenot's remaining common shares.
5. Purchased 40% of LaHave Ltd.'s common shares, which was enough to achieve significant influence.
6. LaHave paid a cash dividend.
7. Havenot paid a cash dividend.
8. Received LaHave's financial statements, which reported profit for the year.
9. Received Havenot's financial statements, which reported a loss for the year.
10. The fair value of Arichat's common shares was higher than carrying value at year end.
11. The fair value of Bombardier's bonds was lower than carrying value at year end.
12. The fair value of Havenot's common shares was lower than carrying value at year end.
13. The fair value of LaHave Ltd.'s common shares was higher than carrying value at year end.

Instructions

Using the following table format, indicate whether each of the above transactions would result in an increase (+), a decrease (−), or no effect (NE) in each category. The first one has been done for you as an example. Where Olsztyn has the choice, it reports gains and losses in other comprehensive income.

	Balance Sheet			Income Statement			Statement of Comprehensive Income
Assets	Liabilities	Shareholders' Equity		Revenues	Expenses	Profit	Other Comprehensive Income
1. NE (+/–)	NE	NE		NE	NE	NE	NE

TAKING IT FURTHER   Assume instead that Olsztyn Inc. is a private company. How would your response to the question differ if the company reported under ASPE?

Record strategic equity investments, using fair value and equity methods. Show statement presentation. (SO 4, 5) AP

P16–7A   Sub Corporation has 1 million common shares issued. On January 10, 2015, Par Inc. purchased a block of these shares on the open market at $10 per share to hold as a strategic investment. Sub reported profit of $260,000 for the year ended December 31, 2015, and paid a $0.35 per share dividend on December 15, 2015. Sub's common shares were trading at $12 per share on December 31, 2015.

This problem assumes three independent situations that relate to how Par, a public company, would report its investment:

Situation 1: Par purchased 100,000 Sub common shares.
Situation 2: Par purchased 300,000 Sub common shares.
Situation 3: Par purchased 1 million Sub common shares.

Instructions

(a) For each situation, identify what method Par should use to account for its investment in Sub common shares.
(b) For situations 1 and 2, record all transactions for Par related to the investment for the year ended December 31, 2015. Assume that, where Par has a choice, it reports gains and losses in other comprehensive income.
(c) For situation 2, what other method could Par use if it was reporting under ASPE instead of IFRS and: (1) Sub's shares traded on an active market? (2) Sub's shares did not trade on an active market? Record Par's transactions for 2015 assuming it uses the alternative method allowed when Sub's shares do not trade on an active market.
(d) For situation 2, compare Par's balance sheet and comprehensive income statement accounts that relate to this investment at December 31 if (1) the investment is reported at fair value, (2) the cost method is used, and (3) the equity method is used to account for the investment.

TAKING IT FURTHER   Why do you think the options in part (c) are allowed for companies reporting under ASPE?

Analyze strategic investment and compare fair value, equity method, and cost method. (SO 4) AN

P16–8A   Sandhu Ltd. has 400,000 common shares authorized and 120,000 shares issued on December 31, 2013. On January 2, 2014, Kang Inc., which reports under IFRS, purchased shares of Sandhu for $40 per share on the stock market from another investor. Kang intends to hold these shares as a long-term investment.

Kang's accountant prepared a trial balance as at December 31, 2014, under the assumption that Kang could not exercise significant influence over Sandhu. Under this assumption, the trial balance included the following accounts and amounts related to the Sandhu investment:

Long-term investment	$1,320,000
Dividend revenue	90,000
Unrealized gain on long-term investment OCI	120,000

Instructions

(a) How many shares of Sandhu did Kang purchase on January 2? (*Hint:* Subtract the unrealized gain from the investment account.)
(b) What percentage of Sandhu does Kang own?
(c) What was the amount of the cash dividend per share that Kang received from Sandhu in 2014?
(d) What was the fair value per share of Sandhu shares at December 31, 2014?
(e) Assume that after closely examining the situation, Kang's auditors determine that Kang does have significant influence over Sandhu. Accordingly, the investment account is adjusted to $1.4 million at December 31, 2014. What was the profit reported by Sandhu for the year ended December 31, 2014?
(f) Assuming that Kang does have significant influence over Sandhu, what amount will Kang report on its income statement for 2014 with regard to this investment?

(g) How would your answer to part (f) change if Kang reported under ASPE and chose to use the cost method to account for its investment in Sandhu because the shares did not trade in an active market?

<u>TAKING IT FURTHER</u>   What are the potential advantages to a company of having significant influence over another company? Explain.

P16–9A   Silver Lining Corporation, a public company, is a large silver producer. Where appropriate, the company has chosen to report fair value adjustments in other comprehensive income. Selected condensed information (in millions) for Silver Lining Corporation follows for the year ended December 31, 2015:

Prepare income statement and statement of comprehensive income. (SO 5) AP

Cost of sales	$2,214
Loss from investment in associate	6
Silver sales	3,350
Income tax expense	60
Interest expense	7
Interest revenue	38
Operating expenses	639
Dividend revenue	6
Loss on fair value adjustments—trading investments	27
Gains on fair value adjustments—strategic investment (net of taxes of $5)	12

Instructions

(a) Prepare an income statement and a separate statement of comprehensive income for the year ended December 31, 2015.

(b) Silver Lining Corporation had an opening balance in its Accumulated Other Comprehensive Income account of $49 million. What is the ending balance it would report in the shareholders' equity section of its balance sheet at December 31, 2015?

<u>TAKING IT FURTHER</u>   If a company has purchased common shares of another company as a trading investment, IFRS generally does not allow the investor to reclassify the trading investment as a long-term investment. Why do standard setters want to prevent companies from reclassifying investments?

P16–10A   Presented in alphabetical order, the following data are from the accounting records of Stinson Corporation, a public company, at April 30, 2015:

Prepare statement of comprehensive income and balance sheet. (SO 5) AP

Accounts payable	$ 65,000
Accounts receivable	48,000
Accumulated depreciation—equipment	72,000
Accumulated other comprehensive income	18,000
Bonds payable, due 2019	150,000
Cash	100,480
Common shares (no par value, unlimited authorized, 200,000 issued)	300,000
Depreciation expense	27,500
Dividend revenue	11,000
Equipment	275,000
Gain on fair value adjustment of trading investments	1,500
Gain on sale of trading investments	3,000
Income tax expense	82,860
Income tax payable	25,000
Interest expense	7,500
Interest receivable—bonds	1,680
Interest revenue	3,360
Investment in associate	170,000
Long-term investment—bonds due 2016	24,000
Long-term investment—Verma common shares	220,000
Loss on fair value adjustment of trading investment—bonds	1,500
Other comprehensive income—loss on fair value adjustment, net of $3,600 tax	12,000
Rent expense	79,000
Retained earnings	161,660
Salary expense	235,000
Service revenues	550,000
Trading investments—Anderson common shares	15,000
Trading investments—bonds	61,000

Instructions

Prepare a statement of comprehensive income and balance sheet at April 30, 2015.

TAKING IT FURTHER   How would the balance sheet and income statement differ with respect to Stinson's investments if it were a private company and it reported under ASPE?

⊙ Problems: Set B

Record debt investments; show statement presentation. (SO 2, 3, 5) AP

P16–1B   On July 1, 2014, Givarz Corporation, a public company, purchased $300,000 of Schuett Corp. 10-year, 3% bonds at 91.8 when the market rate of interest was 4%. Interest is received semi-annually on July 1 and January 1. Givarz's year end is December 31. Givarz intends to hold the bonds until July 1, 2024, the date the bonds mature. The bonds were trading at 96 on December 31, 2014.

Instructions

(a) Record the purchase of the bonds on July 1, 2014.
(b) Prepare the adjusting entries required at December 31, 2014.
(c) Show the financial presentation of the investment in Schuett Corp.'s bonds on December 31, 2014.
(d) Prepare the entry to record the receipt of interest on January 1, 2015.
(e) Prepare the entry to record the receipt of interest on July 1, 2015.
(f) Prepare the entry to record the repayment of the bonds on July 1, 2024. Assume the entry to record the last interest payment has been recorded.
(g) How would your answers to parts (b) through (e) change if the bonds were purchased for the purpose of trading?

TAKING IT FURTHER   What was the market interest rate on December 31, 2014, when the bonds were trading at 96? (*Hint*: How many interest periods are left after December 31, 2014?)

Record debt investments; show statement presentation. (SO 2, 5) AP

P16–2B   Lannan Corp. had the following debt instrument transactions during the year ended December 31, 2014. The debt instruments were purchased to earn interest.

Feb.	1	Purchased six-month term deposit for $50,000.
Aug.	1	Term deposit matured and $51,250 cash was received.
	1	Purchased a money-market fund for $55,000.
Dec.	1	Cashed in money-market fund and received $55,735 cash.
	1	Purchased a 90-day (three-month) treasury bill for $99,260.
	31	The treasury bill's value with accrued interest was $99,508.

Instructions

(a) Record the transactions.
(b) Show the financial statement presentation of the debt investments and any related accounts at December 31.

TAKING IT FURTHER   What was the annual rate of interest on the term deposit that Lannan Corp. purchased on February 1, 2014?

Record debt investment at amortized cost and fair value, prepare bond amortization schedule, and record liability; show statement presentation. (SO 2, 3, 5) AP

P16–3B   On January 1, 2014, Surge Ltd. issued bonds with a maturity value of $6 million at 104 when the market rate of interest was 4.5%. The bonds have a coupon (contractual) interest rate of 5% and mature on January 1, 2024. Interest on the bonds is payable semi-annually on July 1 and January 1 of each year. On January 1, 2014, Treasury Ltd. purchased Surge Ltd. bonds with a maturity value of $2 million to earn interest. On December 31, 2014, the bonds were trading at 103. Both companies' year end is December 31.

Instructions

(a) What amount did Treasury Ltd. pay for Surge Ltd.'s bonds?
(b) Prepare the journal entry for Treasury Ltd. (investor) on January 1, 2014.
(c) Prepare a bond amortization schedule for Treasury Ltd. for the first four interest periods.
(d) Prepare the journal entries for Treasury Ltd. to record the receipt of interest on July 1, 2014, the accrual of interest on December 31, 2014, and the receipt of interest on January 1, 2015. Show how the bonds and related income statement accounts would be presented in Treasury Ltd.'s financial statements for the year ended December 31, 2014.
(e) Prepare the journal entry for Surge Ltd. (investee) on January 1, 2014.

(f) Using the bond amortization schedule prepared in part (c) to calculate the interest expense and interest payments, prepare the journal entries for Surge Ltd. to record the payment of interest on July 1, 2014, the accrual of interest on December 31, 2014, and the payment of interest on January 1, 2015.

(g) Show how the bonds and related income statement accounts would be presented in Surge Ltd.'s financial statements for the year ended December 31, 2014.

(h) Assume that Treasury Ltd. reports under IFRS and that it purchased the bonds to trade. Prepare any required journal entries or adjusting journal entries on July 1, 2014, and December 31, 2014.

(i) Assuming Treasury Ltd. purchased the bonds for purposes of trading, show how the bonds and related income statement accounts would be presented in Treasury Ltd.'s financial statements for the year ended December 31, 2014.

TAKING IT FURTHER   Did the market interest rate on the bonds increase or decrease between January 1, 2014, and December 31, 2014? Will Treasury Ltd. want the market interest rate on the bonds to increase or decrease if it holds the bonds to earn interest? Explain.

P16–4B   During the year ended December 31, 2014, Mead Investment Corporation, a public company, had the following transactions in trading investments:

Record debt and equity trading investments; show statement presentation. (SO 3, 5) AP

Feb.	1	Purchased 2,400 Lemelin common shares for $63,600.
Mar.	1	Purchased 600 RSD common shares for $7,500.
Apr.	1	Purchased $100,000 of MRT 4% bonds at 98. Interest is payable semi-annually on April 1 and October 1.
July	1	Received a cash dividend of $2 per share on the Lemelin common shares.
Aug.	1	Sold 1,600 Lemelin common shares at $25 per share.
Oct.	1	Received the semi-annual interest on the MRT bonds.
	2	Sold the MRT bonds for 100.
Dec.	31	The fair values of the Lemelin and RSD common shares were $28 and $14 per share, respectively.

Instructions

(a) Record the transactions and any required year-end adjusting entries.

(b) Show the financial statement presentation of the trading investments and any related accounts in Mead's financial statements for the year ended December 31, 2014.

TAKING IT FURTHER   When Mead invested in the MRT bonds, was it anticipating that the market interest rate would go up or down? Explain.

P16–5B   During 2013, Commercial Inc. purchased equity securities for trading. At December 31, 2013, the securities for Commercial Inc. were as follows:

Record equity trading investments; show statement presentation. (SO 3, 5) AP

Security	Quantity	Cost	Market Value
Fahim common shares	1,500	$36,000	$39,000
PLJ common shares	2,000	14,000	16,000
Total		$50,000	$55,000

The following transactions with respect to Commercial Inc.'s investments occurred during 2014:

Feb.	10	Purchased 2,500 common shares of Almira for $12.00 per share. The shares were purchased for trading.
Apr.	15	Sold 1,250 of the Fahim common shares for $27.00 per share.
June	15	Purchased an additional 1,000 of Fahim common shares for $27.50 per share.
Aug.	5	Received dividends on the PLJ common shares of $2.50 per share.
Oct.	15	Received an additional 250 common shares of Almira as a result of a 10% stock dividend.

At December 31, 2014, the securities held by Commercial Inc. were trading on the TSX at the following prices:

Security	Price
Fahim common shares	$30.00
PLJ common shares	6.00
Almira common shares	12.50

Instructions

(a) Show how the securities would be reported on Commercial Inc.'s December 31, 2013, balance sheet.

(b) Assuming that the purchases of Fahim and PLJ common shares were Commercial Inc.'s only investment transactions in 2013, show what would be reported in the company's December 31, 2013, income statement.

(c) Record Commercial Inc.'s 2014 transactions and any required adjusting journal entries at December 31, 2014.

TAKING IT FURTHER   Calculate the total profit/loss (over the life of the investment) that Commercial Inc. made on the 1,250 Fahim common shares sold on April 15. Explain how and when it was recognized on the income statement.

Identify impact of investments on financial statements. (SO 2, 3, 4, 5) AP

P16–6B   Abioye Inc., a public company, had the following investment transactions:

1. Purchased Chang Corporation preferred shares as trading investment.
2. Received a stock dividend on the Chang preferred shares.
3. Purchased Government of Canada bonds for cash as a trading investment.
4. Accrued interest on the Government of Canada bonds.
5. Purchased Micmac Inc.'s bonds to earn interest.
6. Sold half of the Chang preferred shares at a price less than originally paid.
7. Purchased 25% of Xing Ltd.'s common shares, which was enough to achieve significant influence.
8. Accrued interest on Micmac Inc. bonds.
9. Xing paid a cash dividend.
10. Purchased 12% of the common shares of Sarolta Ltd. Abioye has made a hostile bid to acquire Sarolta's remaining common shares.
11. Received a dividend on the Sarolta Ltd. shares.
12. Received Sarolta's financial statements, which reported a profit for the year.
13. Received Xing's financial statements, which reported a loss for the year.
14. The fair value of Chang's preferred shares was lower than carrying value at year end.
15. The fair value of the Government of Canada bonds was higher than carrying value at year end.
16. The fair value of Sarolta's common shares was higher than carrying value at year end.
17. The fair value of Micmac Inc.'s bonds was lower than carrying value at year end.

Instructions

Using the following table format, indicate whether each of the above transactions would result in an increase (+), a decrease (−), or no effect (NE) in each category. The first one has been done for you as an example. Where Abioye has a choice, it reports gains and losses in other comprehensive income.

Balance Sheet			Income Statement			Statement of Comprehensive Income
Assets	Liabilities	Shareholders' Equity	Revenues	Expenses	Profit	Other Comprehensive Income
NE (+/−)	NE	NE	NE	NE	NE	NE

TAKING IT FURTHER   Assume instead that Abioye Inc. is a Canadian private company. How would your response to the question differ if the company reported under ASPE?

Record strategic equity investments, using fair value, cost, and equity methods. Show statement presentation. (SO 4, 5) AP

P16–7B   Hat Limited has 300,000 common shares issued. On October 1, 2014, Pankaj Inc. purchased a block of these shares on the open market at $40 per share to hold as a strategic equity investment. Hat reported profit of $675,000 for the year ended September 30, 2015, and paid a $0.40 per share dividend. Hat's shares were trading at $43 per share on September 30, 2015.

This problem assumes three independent situations that relate to how Pankaj, a public company, would report its investment:

Situation 1: Pankaj purchased 30,000 Hat common shares.
Situation 2: Pankaj purchased 90,000 Hat common shares.
Situation 3: Pankaj purchased 300,000 Hat common shares.

Instructions

(a) For each situation, identify what method Pankaj Inc. should use to account for its investment in Hat Limited.
(b) For situations 1 and 2, record all transactions for Pankaj related to the investment for the year ended September 30, 2015. Assume that, where Pankaj has a choice, it reports gains and losses in other comprehensive income.
(c) For situation 2, what other method could Pankaj use if it was reporting under ASPE instead of IFRS and: (1) Hat's shares traded on an active market? (2) Hat's shares did not trade on an active market? Record all

transactions for Pankaj for 2015 assuming Pankaj uses the alternative method allowed when Hat's shares do not trade on an active market.

(d) For situation 2, compare Pankaj's balance sheet and comprehensive income statement accounts that relate to this investment at September 30 if (1) the investment is reported at fair value, (2) the cost method is used, and (3) the equity method is used to account for the investment.

TAKING IT FURTHER   Assuming that Hat's shares were trading on a public market at $45 on September 30, 2016, and Pankaj owned 30,000 common shares of Hat, what amount would be reported in accumulated other comprehensive income at September 30, 2016, relating to this investment? Assume that Pankaj has a 30% tax rate.

P16–8B   On January 2, 2014, Hadley Inc., which reports under IFRS, purchased shares of Letourneau Corp. for $10 a share. Hadley intends to hold these shares as a long-term investment. During 2014, Letourneau reported profit of $1 million and paid cash dividends of $200,000. The investment's fair value at December 31, 2014, was $970,000.

Hadley's accountant prepared a trial balance as at December 31, 2014, under the assumption that Hadley could exercise significant influence over Letourneau. The trial balance included the following:

Investment in associate	$960,000
Revenue from investment in associate	200,000

Analyze strategic investment and compare fair value, equity method, and cost method. (SO 4) AN

(a) What percentage of Letourneau's shares does Hadley own? (*Hint*: The ownership percentage can be determined using the investment revenue.)
(b) What was the amount of cash dividend that Hadley received from Letourneau?
(c) How many Letourneau shares did Hadley purchase on January 2?
(d) Assume that after closely examining the situation, Hadley's auditors determine that Hadley does not have significant influence over Letourneau. What amount should be reported on Hadley's balance sheet at December 31, 2014? What will be reported in Hadley's income statement for the year ended December 31, 2014?
(e) How would your answer to part (d) change if Hadley reported under ASPE and Letourneau's shares were not traded on an active market?

TAKING IT FURTHER   What factors should be considered when determining whether a company has significant influence over another company? Could a company have significant influence over another company if it owned 19% of the common shares of the investee? Explain.

P16–9B   Selected condensed information (in millions) for Investments R Us Company, a public company, follows for the year ended December 31, 2015. Where appropriate, the company has chosen to report fair value adjustments in other comprehensive income.

Prepare income statement and statement of comprehensive income. (SO 5) AP

Revenue from investment in associate	$ 4
Gain on fair value adjustment of trading investments	2
Gain on disposal of land	26
Income tax expense	781
Interest expense	299
Interest revenue	6
Dividend revenue	3
Operating expenses	4,616
Loss on sale of trading investments	194
Loss on fair value adjustment—strategic equity investment (net of tax)	68
Other expenses	21
Revenues	7,240

Instructions

(a) Prepare an income statement and separate statement of comprehensive income for the year ended December 31, 2015.
(b) Investments R Us Company had an opening balance in its Accumulated Other Comprehensive Loss account of $150 million. What is the ending balance it would report in the shareholders' equity section of its balance sheet at December 31, 2015?

TAKING IT FURTHER   Explain why a company may want to report gains and losses on fair value adjustments for its investments in other comprehensive income instead of including them in profit.

Prepare statement of comprehensive income and balance sheet. (SO 5) AP

P16–10B Presented in alphabetical order, the following data are from the accounting records of Vladimir Corporation, at December 31, 2014:

Accounts payable	$ 85,000
Accounts receivable	68,000
Accumulated depreciation—equipment	92,000
Accumulated other comprehensive income	28,000
Allowance for doubtful accounts	4,000
Bonds payable	250,000
Cash	150,000
Common shares (no par value, unlimited authorized, 200,000 issued)	250,000
Depreciation expense	28,000
Dividend revenue	9,000
Equipment	288,000
Gain on fair value adjustment of trading investments—bonds	2,600
Gain on sale of trading investments—common shares	2,500
Income tax expense	79,290
Income tax payable	16,000
Interest expense	12,500
Interest payable	5,000
Interest revenue	3,300
Investment in associate	215,000
Long-term investment—bonds due 2016	36,000
Long-term investment—Burma common shares	185,000
Loss on fair value adjustment of trading investments—common shares	1,500
Notes receivable—due 2017	75,000
Other comprehensive income—gain on fair value adjustment, net of $3,600 tax	12,000
Rent expense	45,000
Retained earnings	?
Revenue from investment in associate	31,000
Salary expense	335,000
Service revenues	651,000
Trading investments—common shares	37,000
Trading investments—bonds	82,500

Instructions

Prepare a statement of comprehensive income and balance sheet at December 31, 2014.

TAKING IT FURTHER   Indicate if there would be any differences in reporting Vladimir's investments if it were a private company and it reported under ASPE. Explain.

Continuing Cookie Chronicle

(*Note*: This is a continuation of the Cookie Chronicle from Chapters 1 through 15.)

Janet, Brian, and Natalie have been approached by Ken Thornton, a shareholder of La Madeleine Ltd., a private company. Ken wants to retire and would like to sell his 1,000 shares in La Madeleine, which represent 20% of all shares issued. La Madeleine is currently operated by Ken's twin daughters, who each own 40% of the common shares. La Madeleine operates a bakery that specializes in making fancy French cookies.

The business has been operating for approximately five years, and in the last two years, Ken has lost interest and left the day-to-day operations to his daughters. Both daughters at times find the work at the bakery over-whelming. They would like to have a third shareholder involved to take over some of the responsibilities of running a small business. Both feel that Janet, Brian, and Natalie are entrepreneurial in spirit and that their expertise would be a welcome addition to the business operation.

Ken has met with Janet, Brian, and Natalie to discuss the business operation. All have concluded that there would be many advantages for Koebel's Family Bakery Ltd. to acquire an interest in La Madeleine Ltd. One of the major advantages would be the sale of fancy French cookies and Koebel's cupcakes at both bakeries.

Despite the apparent advantages, Janet, Brian, and Natalie are still not convinced that they should participate in this business venture. They come to you with the following questions:

1. We are a little concerned about how much influence we would have in the decision-making process for La Madeleine Ltd. Would the amount of influence we have affect how we account for this investment? (Recall that Koebel's Family Bakery Ltd. reports using ASPE.)

2. Can you think of other advantages of going ahead with this investment?
3. Can you think of any disadvantages of going ahead with this investment?

Instructions

(a) Answer Janet, Brian, and Natalie's questions.
(b) What other information would you likely obtain before you recommend whether this investment should be accounted for using the equity method?
(c) Explain to Janet, Brian, and Natalie some of the differences in accounting for this investment on Koebel's Family Bakery Ltd.'s balance sheet if the cost method was chosen instead of the equity method.

Cumulative Coverage—Chapters 13 to 16

Plankton Corporation's trial balance at December 31, 2015, is presented below:

PLANKTON CORPORATION Trial Balance December 31, 2015		
	Debit	Credit
Cash	$ 48,000	
Accounts receivable	51,000	
Allowance for doubtful accounts		$ 2,500
Merchandise inventory	22,700	
Investment in associate—RES	85,000	
Long-term equity investment—BCB common shares	30,000	
Land	90,000	
Building	200,000	
Accumulated depreciation—building		40,000
Equipment	40,000	
Accumulated depreciation—equipment		15,000
Accounts payable		18,775
Income tax payable		4,500
Bonds payable (6%, due January 1, 2019)		126,025
Common shares, unlimited number of no par value shares authorized, 100,000 issued		100,000
Retained earnings		110,775
Accumulated other comprehensive income		5,000
Sales		750,000
Cost of goods sold	370,000	
Operating expenses	180,000	
Interest revenue		375
Interest expense	6,250	
Income tax expense	50,000	
Total	$1,172,950	$1,172,950

All transactions and adjustments for 2015 have been recorded and reported in the trial balance except for the items described below.

Jan. 7   Issued 1,000 preferred shares for $25,000. In total, 100,000, $2, non-cumulative, convertible, preferred shares are authorized. Each preferred share is convertible into five common shares.

Mar. 16   Purchased 800 common shares of Osborne Inc., to trade, for $24 per share.

July 1   Purchased $100,000, Solar Inc. 10-year, 5% bonds at 108.2, when the market interest rate was 4%. Interest is received semi-annually on July 1 and January 1. Plankton purchased the bonds to earn interest.

Aug. 2   Sold the Osborne common shares for $25 per share.

5   Invested $20,000 in a money-market fund.

Sept. 25   Five hundred of the preferred shares issued on January 7 were converted into common shares.

Oct. 24   Cashed in the money-market fund, receiving $20,000 plus $200 interest.

Nov. 30   Obtained a $50,000 bank loan by issuing a three-year, 6% note payable. Plankton is required to make equal blended payments of $1,521 at the end of each month. The first payment was made on December 31. Note that at December 31, $15,757 of the note payable is due within the next year.

Dec.	1	Declared the annual dividend on the preferred shares on December 1 to shareholders of record on December 23, payable on January 15.
	31	Plankton owns 40% of RES. RES earned $20,000 and paid dividends of $1,200 in 2015. The fair value of the company's investment in RES was $98,000.
	31	Semi-annual interest is receivable on the Solar Inc. bonds on January 1, 2016. The bonds were trading at 106 on December 31, 2015.
	31	The annual interest is due on the bonds payable on January 1, 2016. The par value of the bonds is $130,000 and the bonds were issued when the market interest rate was 7%.
	31	The fair value of the company's investment in BCB common shares was $28,000.

Instructions

(a) Record the transactions.

(b) Prepare an updated trial balance at December 31, 2015, that includes these transactions.

(c) Using the income statement accounts in the trial balance, calculate income before income tax. Assuming Plankton has a 27% income tax rate, prepare the journal entry to adjust income taxes for the year. Note that Plankton has recorded $50,000 of income tax expense for the year to date. Update the trial balance for this additional entry. For the purposes of this question, ignore the income tax relating to other comprehensive income.

(d) Prepare the following financial statements for Plankton: (1) income statement, (2) statement of comprehensive income, (3) statement of changes in shareholders' equity, and (4) balance sheet. For the purposes of this question, ignore the income tax on other comprehensive income and accumulated other comprehensive Income.

(e) Assuming instead that Plankton purchased the Solar Inc. bonds to trade, describe how the investment and related income should be valued and reported in Plankton's financial statements.

(f) For each of Plankton's investments, explain how the valuation and reporting of the investment and related income accounts might differ if Plankton were a private company reporting under ASPE.

CHAPTER 16   BROADENING YOUR PERSPECTIVE

Financial Reporting and Analysis

Financial Reporting Problem

BYP16–1   Refer to the financial statements and accompanying notes for **Reitmans (Canada) Limited** presented in Appendix A. In its comprehensive income statement for the year ended January 28, 2012, Reitmans reported $530,000 of fair value gains on investments in other comprehensive income.

Instructions

Would these fair value gains relate to trading investments or other investments? Explain.

Interpreting Financial Statements

BYP16–2   **Royal Bank of Canada** is one of the largest banks in Canada. According to its 2011 annual report, it had approximately 74,000 employees serving 15 million customers throughout the world. The bank's business largely involves borrowing money and lending it to others, but at any given time it will have a large amount of money invested in securities when it is not out on loan. It also acts as an investment dealer, buying investments from one client and selling them to another. The company reported the following information in its 2011 financial statements (in millions of dollars):

	2011	2010
Trading investments		
Debt instruments	$106,766	$106,396
Equity instruments	38,508	38,529
	$145,274	$144,925

Instructions

(a) In your opinion, why does the Royal Bank have a higher percentage of its trading investments in debt instruments than in equity instruments?

(b) How will the trading investments in debt instruments be valued on the Royal Bank's balance sheet?

(c) At November 1, 2011, 34.5% of the Royal Bank's trading investments in debt instruments were Canadian government debt instruments and 18.3% were U.S. government debt instruments. In your opinion, why does the Royal Bank have a higher percentage of its trading investments in debt instruments in government instruments as opposed to other debt instruments?

(d) The Royal Bank also reported other investments for which the gains and losses on fair value adjustments are reported in other comprehensive income. What are the advantages of reporting gains and losses in other comprehensive income instead of profit? What are the disadvantages?

▶ Critical Thinking

Collaborative Learning Activity

Note to instructor: Additional instructions and material for this group activity can be found on the Instructor Resource Site and in *WileyPLUS.*

BYP16–3   In this group activity, you will compare the accounting for bonds payable with the accounting for a long-term investment in bonds. Time permitting, your instructor may also ask you to compare this with the accounting for an investment in bonds held for trading purposes.

Communication Activity

BYP16–4   Under International Financial Reporting Standards, investments in debt instruments are reported at either amortized cost or fair value. The president of Lunn Financial Enterprises does not understand why there are two methods and wonders why all debt investments are not reported at amortized cost.

Instructions

Write a memo to the president of Lunn Financial Enterprises, explaining when it is appropriate to report debt investments at amortized cost and when it is appropriate to report debt investments at fair value. Discuss in your memo why reporting different debt investments using different methods gives better information for investors and creditors to evaluate the performance of the company's investment portfolio.

Ethics Case

BYP16–5   Kreiter Financial Services Limited, public company, purchased a large portfolio of debt and equity investments during 2015. The portfolio's total fair value at December 31, 2015, is greater than its total cost. Some securities have increased in value and others have decreased. Vicki Lemke, the financial vice-president, and Ula Greenwood, the controller, are busy classifying the securities in the portfolio for the first time.

Lemke suggests classifying the securities as follows:

1. Securities that have increased in value as trading investments.
2. Equity securities that have decreased in value as strategic investments and record the fair value adjustments on these securities in other comprehensive income.
3. Debt securities that have decreased in value as debt investments purchased to earn interest.

Greenwood disagrees. She says that they should follow the GAAP recommendations on how investments should be classified.

Instructions

(a) What will be the effect on profit if the investments are reported as Lemke suggests? Be specific.
(b) Is there anything unethical in what Lemke proposes?
(c) Who are the stakeholders affected by their proposals?
(d) Which qualitative characteristics of financial reporting are not met if the investments are classified based on performance?
(e) How should the investments be classified?

"All About You" Activity

BYP16–6   As indicated in the "All About You" feature in this chapter, any Canadian aged 18 or older can save up to $5,000 every year in a tax-free savings account (TFSA). TFSA savings can be used for any purpose, including for a vacation, to buy a car, or to start a small business. The goal of TFSAs is to allow Canadians to save more and achieve their goals quicker.

Instructions

Go to www.tfsa.gc.ca.

(a) Click on "TFSA vs. RRSP." What is the purpose of an RRSP? Is an investment in an RRSP a strategic or non-strategic investment? Is an investment in a TFSA a strategic or non-strategic investment?

(b) Click on the link "TFSA calculator." Note that the government allows a variety of investment options, including equity securities listed on a stock exchange and bonds. What types of investment income will you earn on equity securities? Bonds? What might be the benefits of investing in equity securities? The risks?

(c) Click on the link "TFSA calculator." Scroll down to the heading "TFSA Calculator" and click on the on-line "TFSA Calculator." Assume the following:

    1. Your income range for income tax purposes: $10,000 − $39,999
    2. Monthly investment in a TFSA: $200
    3. Rate of return: 6%
    4. Term of investment: 20 years

How much more will you save in a TFSA than in a taxable savings account?

(d) Assume the same as in part (c) except assume that your income range for income tax purposes is $40,000 to $79,999. How much more will you save in a TFSA than in a taxable savings account?

(e) What assumptions are used in the TFSA calculator with respect to:

    1. when the annual investment is made?
    2. provincial tax rates?
    3. the investment portfolio?

ANSWERS TO CHAPTER QUESTIONS

ANSWERS TO ACCOUNTING IN ACTION INSIGHT QUESTIONS

Business Insight, p. 820

Q: Was the acquisition of Forzani by Canadian Tire a non-strategic or strategic investment?

A: The acquisition of Forzani by Canadian Tire is a strategic investment. The acquisition provides Canadian Tire with over 1,000 sporting good outlets, which will strengthen the company's competitive position against foreign companies.

All About You, p. 837

Q: Is it beneficial for you, while you are a student, to invest in a TFSA even though you may not have taxable income? Would you classify your investment in a TFSA as a long-term or short-term investment?

A: Yes, provided you have cash that you do not need in the short term, it is beneficial for you to contribute to a TFSA. Investments earn investment income. By contributing to a TFSA sooner rather than later, you will be able to protect more investment income from being taxed. The investment in a TFSA will be a long-term investment.

ANSWERS TO SELF-STUDY QUESTIONS

1. d   2. d   3. b   4. c   5. d   6. a   7. b   8. b   9. b   10. c

Remember to go back to the beginning of the chapter to check off your completed work!

←

CHAPTER SEVENTEEN

THE CASH FLOW STATEMENT

 THE **NAVIGATOR**

- ☐ Understand *Concepts for Review*
- ☐ Read *Feature Story*
- ☐ Scan *Study Objectives*
- ☐ Read *Chapter Preview*
- ☐ Read text and answer *Before You Go On*
- ☐ Review *Comparing IFRS and ASPE*
- ☐ Work *Demonstration Problem*
- ☐ Review *Summary of Study Objectives*
- ☐ Answer *Self-Study Questions*
- ☐ Complete assignments
- ☐ Go to *WileyPLUS* for practice and tutorials

CONCEPTS FOR **REVIEW**

Before studying this chapter, you should understand or, if necessary, review:

a. The difference between the accrual basis and the cash basis of accounting. (Ch. 3, p. 113)

b. The definition of cash and cash equivalents. (Ch. 7 p. 382)

c. The major items included in a corporation's balance sheet. (Ch. 4, pp. 184–192 and Ch. 13, pp. 689–691)

d. The major items included in a corporation's income statement. (Ch. 13, pp. 682–684)

e. The declaration and payment of dividends. (Ch. 13, pp. 684–686)

f. The accounting for reacquisition of shares. (Ch. 14, pp. 722–724)

g. The amortization of premiums and discounts on bonds payable and long-term investment in bonds. (Ch. 15, pp. 773–779 and Ch.16, pp. 823–824)

h. The accounting for trading investments. (Ch. 16, pp. 826–830)

CASH MANAGEMENT KEEPS CLEARWATER SAILING

BEDFORD, N.S.—Clearwater Seafoods is a leader in the global seafood industry, recognized for its consistent quality, wide diversity, and commitment to preserving the environment. Operating for more than 30 years, Clearwater manages a large fleet of vessels in Canada and Argentina, as well as several processing plants throughout Eastern Canada, and exports its products throughout the world, with a focus on the United States, Asia, and Western Europe.

After experiencing challenging conditions in 2008 and 2009, due in part to the global liquidity crisis, Clearwater had strong operating results in 2010 and 2011. "On the back of these strong results, we refinanced our debt facilities several times during this period, each time increasing our flexibility and reducing our cost," says Tyrone Cotie, Treasurer at Clearwater.

Over the past several years Clearwater has formalized a number of its policies and goals to promote strong liquidity and continued access to capital to fund its growth plan.

To maintain adequate liquidity, Clearwater uses cash balances, together with available credit, when funding seasonal working capital demands, capital expenditures, and other commitments. Due to the seasonality of Clearwater's business, sales and gross profit are typically higher in the second half of the calendar year and capital expenditures are typically higher in the first half of the year. This usually results in Clearwater using up some of its liquidity in the first half of the year.

Clearwater's short-term goal is to generate cash flows from operations to fund interest, scheduled loan payments, and capital expenditures and to use free cash flow to reduce debt and invest in growth securities. Clearwater's goal is to grow free cash flows such that it can reduce debt and pay a sustainable dividend to its shareholders.

Clearwater is focused on managing its free cash flows by managing working capital and capital spending. It manages its investment in trade receivables through having tight collection terms and manages its investment in inventories through regular forecasting and close review of any slow-moving items.

To manage its capital spending, Clearwater grades investments in property, plant, equipment and harvesting licences as either return on investment (ROI) or maintenance capital. Significant expenditures that are expected to have a return in excess of the cost of capital are classified as ROI, while expenditures that have less than the average cost of capital are classified as maintenance, as are all refits of its vessels. In addition, Clearwater regularly reviews and liquidates underperforming and non-core assets.

Cash flows generated from operations are a key indicator of the company's health. "The sustainability of a business is ultimately linked to its ability to generate cash," Mr. Cotie says.

THE NAVIGATOR

STUDY **OBJECTIVES**

After studying this chapter, you should be able to:

1. Describe the purpose and content of the cash flow statement.

2. Prepare a cash flow statement using either the indirect or the direct method.

3. Analyze the cash flow statement.

THE NAVIGATOR

As Tyrone Cotie in our feature story states, the sustainability of a business is ultimately linked to its ability to generate cash. So how do companies generate cash? How do they use cash? How is this information presented in the financial statements so users can assess a company's ability to generate cash? This chapter, which presents the cash flow statement, will answer these and similar questions.

The chapter is organized as follows:

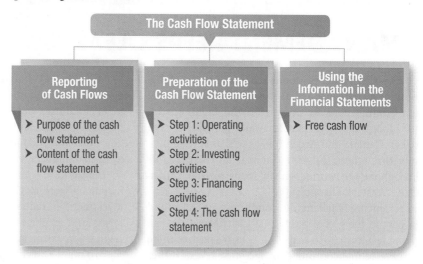

Reporting of Cash Flows

» **STUDY OBJECTIVE 1**

Describe the purpose and content of the cash flow statement.

The financial statements we have studied so far present only partial information about a company's cash flows (cash receipts and cash payments). For example, comparative balance sheets show the increase in property, plant, and equipment during the year, but they do not show how the additions were financed or paid for. The income statement shows profit, but it does not indicate the amount of cash that was generated by operations. The statement of comprehensive income reports changes in fair values of certain equity investments, but not the cash generated from the sale of these investments. Similarly, the statement of retained earnings or the statement of changes in shareholders' equity shows the amount of cash dividends that was declared, but not the amount of cash dividends that was actually paid during the year.

PURPOSE OF THE CASH FLOW STATEMENT

Alternative terminology Under IFRS, the cash flow statement is commonly referred to as the *statement of cash flows*.

The **cash flow statement** gives information about the cash receipts, cash payments, and net change in cash that result from operating, investing, and financing activities during a period. In other words, the statement provides information about where the cash came from, what the cash was used for, and how much it changed. Reporting the causes of changes in cash helps investors, creditors, and other interested parties understand what is happening to a company's most liquid resource—its cash.

The information in a cash flow statement should help investors, creditors, and others evaluate the following aspects of the company's financial position.

1. **Ability to generate future cash flows:** Investors, creditors, and others are interested in how much cash the company will generate in the future. By examining the cash flow statement, and seeing where cash came from and what it was used for, users can predict the amounts, timing, and uncertainty of future cash flows better than they can from examining just the balance sheet and income statement.
2. **Ability to pay dividends and meet obligations:** If a company does not have enough cash, employees cannot be paid, debts settled, or dividends paid. Employees, creditors, and shareholders are particularly interested in this statement because it is the only one that shows the flow of cash in a company.
3. **Investing and financing transactions during the period:** By examining where the cash came from and what it was used for, users can better understand why non-current assets and liabilities changed during the period.

4. **Difference between profit and cash provided (used) by operating activities:** Profit gives information about the success or failure of a business. However, some people are critical of accrual-based profit because it requires many estimates, allocations, and assumptions. As a result, the reliability of the profit amount is often challenged. This is not true of cash. If readers of the cash flow statement understand the reasons for the difference between profit and net cash provided by operating activities, they can then decide for themselves how reliable the profit amount is.

CONTENT OF THE CASH FLOW STATEMENT

Before we can start preparing the cash flow statement, we must first understand what it includes and why. We will begin by reviewing the definition of cash used in the cash flow statement and then we will discuss how cash receipts and payments are classified within the statement.

Definition of Cash

The cash flow statement is often prepared using "cash and cash equivalents" as its basis. You will recall from Chapter 7 that cash consists of cash on hand (coins, paper currency, cheques) and money on deposit at a bank less any bank overdrafts, and that cash equivalents are short-term, highly liquid debt investments that are readily convertible to known amounts of cash. Generally, only debt investments that are due within three months can be considered cash equivalents. Because of the varying definitions of "cash" that can be used in this statement, companies must clearly define cash as it is used in their particular statement.

Classification of Cash Flows

The cash flow statement classifies cash receipts and cash payments into three types of activities: (1) operating, (2) investing, and (3) financing activities. The transactions and other events for each kind of activity are as follows:

1. **Operating activities** include the cash effects of transactions that create revenues and expenses. They affect profit and generally relate to changes in noncash current assets and liabilities.
2. **Investing activities** include (a) purchasing and disposing of non-trading investments (including non-trading short-term investments) and long-lived assets, and (b) lending money and collecting the loans. They generally affect non-current asset accounts. Note that generally accepted accounting principles require the purchase and sale of trading investments to be included in operating activities and not investing activities.
3. **Financing activities** include (a) obtaining cash from issuing debt and repaying the amounts borrowed, and (b) obtaining cash from shareholders and paying them dividends. Financing activities generally affect non-current liability and shareholders' equity accounts.

Illustration 17-1 lists typical cash receipts (inflows) and cash payments (outflows) in each of the three classifications.

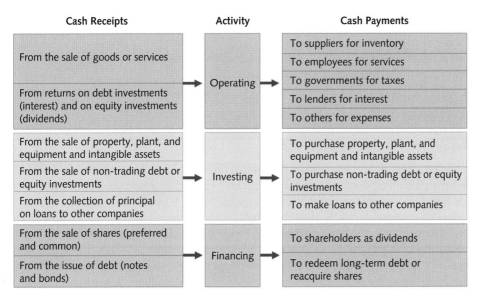

▶ **ILLUSTRATION 17-1**
Cash receipts and payments classified by activity

As you can see, some cash flows that are related to investing or financing activities are classified as operating activities. For example, receipts of investment revenue (interest and dividends) earned from debt or equity securities are classified as operating activities. So are payments of interest to lenders of debt. Why are these considered operating activities? It is because these items are reported in the income statement where results of operations are shown.

Illustration 17-2 shows general guidelines that can be followed in the classification of cash flows.

▶**ILLUSTRATION 17-2**
Operating, investing,
and financing activities

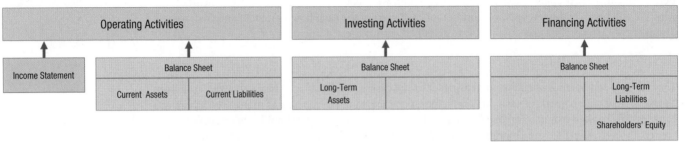

Note that these are general guidelines and that there are some exceptions to these guidelines. There are situations when current asset and current liability accounts do not result from operating activities. One such example is notes receivable that have been issued for lending purposes rather than for trade. The issue and repayment of notes receivable such as these are reported in the investing section. Similarly, short-term notes payable that do not relate to purchase transactions are an example of a current liability that does not relate to operating activities. These are shown in the financing activities section of the cash flow statement. Another example is short-term investments purchased to earn interest. These investments are reported in the investing activities section.

Companies reporting under IFRS have a choice as to where to classify interest and dividends. Interest and dividends received may be classified as either an operating or investing activity; interest and dividends paid may be classified as either an operating or financing activity. Once the choice is made, it must be applied consistently.

Private companies reporting under ASPE must classify interest (received and paid) and dividends received as operating activities. Under ASPE, dividends paid are classified as financing activities. Although public companies have a choice under IFRS as to how to classify interest and dividends, most public companies follow the classification required under ASPE. Because the classification required under ASPE is the most common practice, we have illustrated this classification in Illustration 17-2 and follow it in this textbook.

Significant Noncash Activities

Not all of a company's significant investing and financing activities involve cash. The following are examples of significant noncash activities:

1. Issue of debt to purchase assets
2. Issue of common shares to purchase assets
3. Conversion of debt or preferred shares to common shares
4. Exchange of property, plant, and equipment

Significant investing and financing activities that do not affect cash are not reported in the body of the cash flow statement. These noncash activities are reported in a note to the financial statements. Note that this disclosure requirement also includes the noncash portion of a partial cash transaction, as the following example shows. Assume that a building is purchased for $10 million with a $1-million cash down payment, and the remainder financed with a mortgage note payable. The cash flow statement would disclose only the $1 million cash paid (as an investing activity). The acquisition of the building (a $10-million investing activity) by a mortgage note payable (a $9-million financing activity) would be disclosed in the notes and cross-referenced to the $1-million cash outflow reported in the investing activities section of the cash flow statement.

ACCOUNTING IN ACTION
ALL ABOUT YOU INSIGHT

Similar to a business, you need to consider your cash situation. How much can you afford to spend, and what are your sources of cash? For many Canadians, using a credit card to easily access cash means they spend more than they can afford. In 2011, the average Canadian's debt load, excluding mortgages, reached a record high of $25,960, although the amount of credit card debt declined by 3.4% as Canadians moved more of their credit card balances to lines of credit, which charge lower interest rates. Observers say that while consumers are getting smarter about credit, they're still spending too much. "It's about attacking lifestyle issues—fundamental buying and spending," said Keith Emery, operations director of Credit Canada, a non-profit credit counselling agency that helps consumers get out of debt.

Sources: Tracy Sherlock, "Canadians Trimming Credit Card Debts: Study," *Vancouver Sun*, July 20, 2012; Roma Luciw, "Average Canadian's Consumer Debt Hits $25,960," *Globe and Mail*, February 23, 2012; "Credit Card Debt Falls in 2011," The Canadian Press, January 10, 2012; Marlene Habib, "Credit Card Debt Eases but Still Dogs Canadians," CBC News, October 26, 2011.

Is it appropriate to use your credit card to pay for your operating activities such as your groceries, clothes, and entertainment? Is it appropriate to use your credit card to finance your investment activities such as tuition or, if you have a large enough limit, a car?

 BEFORE YOU GO ON...

Do It

Carrier Moulding Ltd. had the following transactions:

1. Issued common shares for cash.
2. Sold a long-term equity investment.
3. Purchased a tractor-trailer truck. Made a cash down payment and financed the remainder with a mortgage note payable.
4. Paid for inventory purchases.
5. Collected cash for services provided.
6. Paid the blended monthly mortgage payment (interest and principal) on the note payable.

Classify each of these transactions by type of cash flow activity. Indicate whether the transaction would be reported as a cash inflow or cash outflow.

Solution

1. Financing activity; cash inflow
2. Investing activity; cash inflow
3. Investing activity; cash outflow for down payment. The remainder is a noncash investing (tractor-trailer truck) and financing (mortgage note payable) activity.
4. Operating activity; cash outflow
5. Operating activity; cash inflow
6. Operating activity; cash outflow for the interest portion of the payment. Financing activity; cash outflow for the principal portion of the payment.

THE NAVIGATOR

Related exercise material: BE17–1, BE17–2, and E17–1.

Action Plan

- Identify the three types of activities that are used to report all cash inflows and outflows.
- Report as operating activities the cash effects of transactions that create revenues and expenses, and that are included when profit is determined.
- Report as investing activities transactions to (a) acquire and dispose of non-trading investments and long-lived assets, and (b) lend money and collect loans.
- Report as financing activities transactions to (a) obtain cash by issuing debt and repaying the amounts borrowed, and (b) obtain cash from shareholders and pay them dividends.

» **STUDY OBJECTIVE 2**

Prepare a cash flow statement using either the indirect or the direct method.

Preparation of the Cash Flow Statement

In Chapter 1, we showed the cash flow statement for Softbyte in Illustration 1-11, which has been reproduced here in Illustration 17-3.

SOFTBYTE Cash Flow Statement Month Ended September 30, 2014		
Operating activities		
Cash receipts from customers	$ 3,300	
Cash payments for operating expenses	(1,950)	
Net cash provided by operating activities		$ 1,350
Investing activities		
Purchase of equipment	$(7,000)	
Net cash used by investing activities		(7,000)
Financing activities		
Investments by owner	$15,000	
Drawings by owner	(1,300)	
Net cash provided by financing activities		13,700
Net increase in cash		8,050
Cash, September 1, 2011		0
Cash, September 30, 2011		$ 8,050

The cash flow statement covers the same period of time as the income statement and statements of comprehensive income, retained earnings, and changes in shareholders' equity (e.g., for the year ended). As explained earlier in the chapter, note that the cash inflows and outflows are classified into the three types of activities (operating, investing, and financing) that we discussed in the preceding section. The operating activities section is always presented first. We will learn there are two methods to prepare the operating activities section: the indirect method and the direct method. In Illustration 17-3, Softbyte's operating activities section has been prepared using the direct method.

The operating activities section is followed by the investing activities and financing activities sections. Any significant noncash investing and financing activities are reported in a note to the financial statements.

A subtotal is calculated for each of the sections (operating, investing, and financing) to determine the net increase or decrease in cash from each activity. If there is a net increase in cash, we say that cash was "provided by" that activity. If there is a net decrease in cash, we say that cash was "used by" that activity. Illustration 17-3 shows that Softbyte's operating and financing activities provided cash and its investing activities used cash.

The subtotals for the three activities are totalled to determine the net increase or decrease in cash for the period. This amount is then added to (if a net increase) or subtracted from (if a net decrease) the beginning-of-period cash balance to obtain the end-of-period cash balance. The end-of-period cash balance must agree with the cash balance reported on the balance sheet. Illustration 17-3 shows a net increase in Softbyte's cash of $8,050. As the company was started on September 1, 2014, with a zero cash balance, this increase resulted in a $8,050 cash balance at September 30, 2014, the amount reported on both the cash flow statement in Illustration 17-3 and on the balance sheet in Illustration 1-11.

Now that we understand the content and format of a cash flow statement, where do we find the information to prepare it? We could examine the cash account in the general ledger and sort each cash receipt and payment into the different types of operating activities, investing activities, or financing activities shown in Illustration 17-1. But this is not practical or necessary. Instead, we prepare the cash flow by examining the changes in all of the other accounts.

The information to prepare this statement usually comes from three sources:

1. The **comparative balance sheet** shows the balances at the beginning and end of the period for each asset, liability, and shareholders' equity item. This information is used to determine the changes in each asset, liability, and shareholders' equity item during that period.
2. The **income statement** helps us determine the amount of cash provided or used by operating activities during the period.
3. **Additional information** includes transaction data that are needed to determine how cash was provided or used during the period. The statement of comprehensive income and the statements of retained earnings or changes in shareholders' equity (or the statement of owner's equity in a proprietorship) also provide information about cash receipts and payments.

The four steps to prepare the cash flow statement from these data sources are shown in Illustration 17-4.

Step 1: Prepare operating activities section.
Determine the net cash provided (used) by operating activities by converting net income from an accrual basis to a cash basis. To do this, analyze the current year's income statement, relevant current asset and current liability accounts from the comparative balance sheets, and selected information.

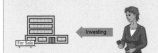

Step 2: Prepare investing activities section.
Determine the net cash provided (used) by investing activities by analyzing changes in non-current asset accounts from the comparative balance sheets, and selected information.

Step 3: Prepare financing activities section.
Determine the net cash provided (used) by financing activities by analyzing changes in non-current liability and equity accounts from the comparative balance sheets, and selected information.

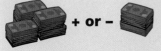

Step 4: Complete the cash flow statement.
Determine the net increase (decrease) in cash. Compare the net change in cash reported on the statement of cash flows with the change in cash reported on the statement of financial position to make sure the amounts agree.

▸ ILLUSTRATION 17-4
Steps in preparing the cash flow statement

To explain and illustrate the preparation of a cash flow statement, we will use financial information from Computer Services Corporation. Illustration 17-5 presents Computer Services' current- and prior-year balance sheets, its current-year income statement, and related financial information.

▸ ILLUSTRATION 17-5
Computer Services' financial information

COMPUTER SERVICES CORPORATION **Balance Sheets** **December 31**			
Assets	**2014**	**2013**	**Increase (Decrease)**
Current assets			
Cash	$ 55,000	$ 33,000	$ 22,000
Accounts receivable	20,000	30,000	(10,000)
Inventory	15,000	10,000	5,000
Prepaid expenses	5,000	1,000	4,000
Property, plant, and equipment			
Land	130,000	20,000	110,000
Building	160,000	40,000	120,000
Accumulated depreciation—building	(11,000)	(5,000)	6,000
Equipment	27,000	10,000	17,000
Accumulated depreciation—equipment	(3,000)	(1,000)	2,000
Total assets	$398,000	$138,000	
Liabilities and Shareholders' Equity			
Current liabilities			
Accounts payable	$ 28,000	$ 12,000	$ 16,000
Income tax payable	6,000	8,000	(2,000)
Non-current liabilities			
Bonds payable	130,000	20,000	110,000
Shareholders' equity			
Common shares	70,000	50,000	20,000
Retained earnings	164,000	48,000	116,000
Total liabilities and shareholders' equity	$398,000	$138,000	

COMPUTER SERVICES CORPORATION Income Statement Year Ended December 31, 2014		
Sales revenue		$507,000
Cost of goods sold		150,000
Gross profit		357,000
Operating expenses	$111,000	
Depreciation expense	9,000	
Loss on sale of equipment	3,000	123,000
Profit from operations		234,000
Other expenses		
Interest expense		42,000
Profit before income tax		192,000
Income tax expense		47,000
Profit		$145,000

Additional information for 2014:

1. A $29,000 cash dividend was paid.
2. Land was acquired by issuing $110,000 of long-term bonds.
3. Equipment costing $25,000 was purchased for cash.
4. Equipment with a carrying amount of $7,000 (cost of $8,000, less accumulated depreciation of $1,000) was sold for $4,000 cash.
5. Depreciation expense consists of $6,000 for the building and $3,000 for equipment.

We will now apply the four steps using the above information for Computer Services Corporation. In the following sections, we will review the journal entries to record transactions and analyze T accounts for balance sheet accounts in order to help you understand the preparation of the cash flow statement.

STEP 1: OPERATING ACTIVITIES

Determine the Net Cash Provided (Used) by Operating Activities by Converting Profit from an Accrual Basis to a Cash Basis

In order to perform this step and determine the cash provided (used) by operating activities, profit must be converted from an accrual basis to a cash basis. Why is this necessary? Under generally accepted accounting principles, companies use the accrual basis of accounting. For example, sales revenues are recorded for both cash sales and sales on account. Similarly, many expenses are recorded that have not yet been paid in cash and some expenses incurred, such as depreciation, are never paid in cash. Thus, under the accrual basis of accounting, profit is not the same as net cash provided by operating activities.

Profit can be converted to net cash provided (used) by operating activities by one of two methods: (1) the indirect method or (2) the direct method. Illustration 17-6 shows an example, using assumed data for a service company, of cash flow from operating activities prepared under both methods.

Note that both methods arrive at the same total amount for "Net cash provided (used) by operating activities" of $101,000. The difference is which items they disclose. The **indirect method** converts total profit from an accrual basis to a cash basis by starting with profit of $100,000 and adjusting it for items that do not affect cash. The **direct method** converts each individual revenue and expense account from an accrual basis to a cash basis, to report cash receipts and payments for major classes of operating activities.

The two methods are explained in two independent sections. Section 1 explains the indirect method and section 2 explains the direct method. Your instructor may ask you to learn only one of

▶ILLUSTRATION 17-6
Cash flow from operating activities under the indirect method and direct method

SAMPLE
Cash Flow Statement (partial)
Year ended December 31, XXXX

Indirect Method			Direct Method		
Operating activities			Operating activities		
Profit		$100,000	Cash receipts from		
Adjustments to reconcile			customers		$185,000
profit to net cash			Cash payments		
provided (used) by			For operating		
operating activities:			expenses	$(54,000)	
Depreciation expense	$ 6,000		For interest	(5,000)	
Gain on sale of equipment	(4,000)		For income tax	(25,000)	(84,00)
Decrease in accounts					
receivable	2,000				
Decrease in accounts					
payable	(3,000)	1,000			
Net cash provided by			Net cash provided by		
operating activities		101,000	operating activities		101,000

the methods. If so, when you have finished the section assigned by your instructor, turn to "Step 2: Investing Activities."

SECTION 1: INDIRECT METHOD

While the direct method is preferred by standard setters, most companies use the indirect method. They prefer this method for three reasons: (1) it is easier to prepare, (2) it focuses on the differences between profit and net cash flow from operating activities, and (3) it reveals less detail to competitors.

Illustration 17-7 shows three types of adjustments that are made to adjust profit for items that affect accrual-based profit but do not affect cash. The first two types of adjustments are found on the income statement. The last type of adjustment—changes to current asset and current liability accounts—is found on the balance sheet.

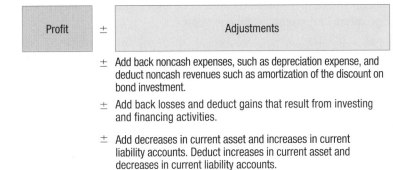

▶ILLUSTRATION 17-7
Adjustments to convert profit to net cash provided (used) by operating activities

The next three subsections explain each type of adjustment.

Noncash Expenses and Revenues

Depreciation Expense. The income statement includes expenses that do not use cash, such as depreciation expense. For example, Computer Services' income statement reports a depreciation expense of $9,000, which was recorded as follows:

Depreciation Expense	9,000	
Accumulated Depreciation—Building		6,000
Accumulated Depreciation—Equipment		3,000

Helpful hint Expenses with no cash outflows are added back to profit in the indirect method. Revenues with no cash inflows are deducted from profit in the indirect method.

A	=	L	+	SE
−6,000				−9,000
−3,000				

Cash flows: no effect

As shown in the journal entry, depreciation does not use cash, so depreciation expense is added back to profit in order to arrive at net cash provided (used) by operating activities. It is important to understand that depreciation expense is not added to operating activities as if it were a source of cash. **It is added to cancel the deduction that was created by the depreciation expense when profit was determined.**

A partial operating activities section of the cash flow statement for Computer Services is shown below, with the addition of the noncash expense to profit highlighted in red.

Operating activities	
Profit	$145,000
Adjustments to reconcile profit to net cash provided (used) by operating activities:	
Depreciation expense	9,000

Amortization of Bonds Payable Premiums and Discounts. Another example of a noncash expense is the amortization of the discounts and premiums on bonds payable when bonds are not issued at par. Recall from Chapter 15 that the journal entries to record interest expense and amortize bonds payable discounts and premiums, using assumed data, are as follows.

A = L + SE
−25,000 +1,000 −26,000

↓ Cash flows: −25,000

A = L + SE
−25,000 −1,500 −23,500

↓ Cash flows: −25,000

Bonds Payable Issued at a Discount			Bonds Payable Issued at a Premium		
Interest Expense	26,000		Interest Expense	23,500	
Bonds Payable		1,000	Bonds Payable	1,500	
Cash		25,000	Cash		25,000

The amortization of a bond discount results in interest expense being higher than the cash paid to the bond investors. So the amortization of a bond discount, the amount credited to bonds payable, must be added back to profit to determine the net cash provided (used) by operating activities.

The amortization of a bond premium for the issuer results in interest expense being lower than the cash payment to the bond investors. So the amortization of a bond premium, the amount debited to bonds payable, must be deducted from profit to determine the net cash provided (used) by operating activities.

Note that the Computer Services bonds payable were issued at par and thus there was no discount or premium to amortize. The amounts shown in the previous journal entries were included only to help you understand the impact of a premium or discount, when one exists.

Amortization of Premiums and Discounts on Long-Term Investments in Bonds. Profit must also be adjusted for the effects of the amortization of discounts and premiums for investments in bonds. Recall from Chapter 16 that the journal entries to amortize discounts and premiums on long-term investments in bonds using assumed data are as follows:

A = L + SE
+25,000   +26,000
+1,000

↑ Cash flows: +25,000

A = L + SE
+25,000   +23,500
−1,500

↑ Cash flows: +25,000

Long-Term Bond Investment at a Discount			Long-Term Bond Investment at a Premium		
Cash	25,000		Cash	25,000	
Long-Term Investment—			Long-Term Investment—		
Bonds	1,000		Bonds		1,500
Interest Revenue		26,000	Interest Revenue		23,500

The amortization of a bond discount for an investor results in interest revenue being greater than the cash receipts. Thus the amortization of the discount must be deducted from profit. Conversely, the amortization of a bond premium for an investor results in interest revenue being less than the cash receipts, so the amortization of the premium must be added to profit.

Gains and Losses

Cash received from the sale of long-lived assets should be reported in the investing activities section of the cash flow statement. Consequently, all gains and losses from investing activities must be eliminated from profit to arrive at net cash from operating activities.

Why is this necessary? Perhaps it will help if we review the accounting for the sale of a long-lived asset. The sale of a long-lived asset is recorded by (1) recognizing the cash that is received, (2) removing the asset and accumulated depreciation account, and (3) recognizing any gain or loss on the sale.

Helpful hint Gains are deducted from, and losses are added to, profit in the indirect method.

To illustrate, recall that Computer Services' income statement reported a $3,000 loss on the sale of equipment. With the additional information provided in Illustration 17-5, we can reconstruct the journal entry to record the sale of equipment:

Cash	4,000	
Accumulated Depreciation—Equipment	1,000	
Loss on Sale of Equipment	3,000	
Equipment		8,000

A	=	L	+	SE
+4,000				−3,000
+1,000				
−8,000				

↑ Cash flows: +4,000

The $4,000 of cash that is received is not considered part of operating activities; rather it is part of investing activities. Selling long-lived assets is not part of a company's primary activities. **There is therefore no cash inflow (or outflow) from operating activities**. Logically, then, to calculate the net cash provided (used) by operating activities, we have to eliminate the gain or loss on the sale of an asset from profit.

To eliminate the $3,000 loss on the sale of equipment, we have to add it back to profit to arrive at net cash provided (used) by operating activities. Adding back the loss cancels the original deduction. This is illustrated in the following partial cash flow statement for Computer Services:

Operating activities	
Profit	$145,000
Adjustments to reconcile profit to net cash provided (used) by operating activities:	
Depreciation expense	9,000
Loss on sale of equipment	3,000

If a gain on sale occurs, the gain is deducted from profit in order to determine net cash provided (used) by operating activities. For both a gain and a loss, the actual amount of cash received from the sale of the asset is reported as a source of cash in the investing activities section of the cash flow statement.

Gains and losses are also possible in other circumstances, such as when debt is retired. The same adjustment guidelines apply to debt as described for gains and losses on the sale of assets, except that the cash paid to retire the debt is reported in financing activities, rather than investing activities.

Changes in Noncash Current Asset and Current Liability Accounts

In addition to the noncash expenses and revenues and gains and losses discussed in the previous two sections, there are other reasons why profit is not the same amount as cash from operations. We know that revenues and expenses are recorded using accrual basis accounting, not cash basis accounting. When revenues and expenses are recorded using accrual basis accounting, it is necessary to adjust profit for the changes in the related noncash current assets and current liabilities to determine the amount of cash provided from operations. In this section, we will illustrate why these adjustments are necessary and how the adjustments are determined.

Changes in Noncash Current Assets. The adjustments to profit that are required for changes in noncash current asset accounts to arrive at net cash provided (used) by operating activities are shown in Illustration 17-8.

Increase in noncash current assets	Deduct
Decrease in noncash current assets	Add

▶ **ILLUSTRATION 17-8**
Adjustments to profit for changes in noncash current asset accounts

We will illustrate these adjustments by analyzing the changes in Computer Services' current asset accounts and related journal entries.

Changes in Accounts Receivable. Illustration 17-5 indicated that Computer Services had $507,000 in sales revenue reported on its income statement. Assuming all sales are on account, the entry to record sales is (in summary for the year):

A = L + SE
+507,000   +507,000
Cash flows: no effect

Accounts Receivable	507,000	
Sales Revenue		507,000

Sales increased profit by $507,000, but did cash also increase by the same amount? To answer this question, we need to analyze Computer Services' accounts receivable because accounts receivable is increased when a sale is made and decreased when cash is collected. Illustration 17-5 indicates that Computer Services started the year with a balance of $30,000 in accounts receivable and ended with $20,000. Using these amounts and the sales recorded in the above journal entry, we analyze the Accounts Receivable account to determine the amount of cash collected from customers as follows:

$10,000 net decrease

Accounts Receivable				
Jan. 1	Balance	30,000		
	Sales revenue	507,000	Receipts from customers	517,000
Dec. 31	Balance	20,000		

Note that cash receipts from customers are $517,000, which is $10,000 ($517,000 − $507,000) larger than sales revenue. Also note that Computer Services' accounts receivable decreased by $10,000 (from $30,000 to $20,000) during the year. When accounts receivable decrease during the year, revenues on an accrual basis are lower than revenues on a cash basis. In other words, more cash was collected during the period than was recorded as revenue.

Thus, in order to adjust profit to cash provided (used) by operating activities, we have to add $10,000 for the decrease in accounts receivable. This is illustrated in the following partial cash flow statement for Computer Services:

Operating activities	
Profit	$145,000
Adjustments to reconcile profit to net cash provided (used) by operating activities:	
Depreciation expense	9,000
Loss on sale of equipment	3,000
Decrease in accounts receivable	10,000

Using the same logic, this means that when the accounts receivable balance increases during the year, revenues on an accrual basis are higher than cash receipts. Therefore, the amount of the increase in accounts receivable is deducted from profit to arrive at net cash provided (used) by operating activities.

You should also note that the adjustment to profit, for the decrease in accounts receivable, is the same regardless of the actual amount of sales on account during the year. For example, we could have assumed all of the $507,000 sales were for cash. Since accounts receivable still decreased by $10,000, it means that $10,000 of cash was collected from customers, over and above the cash sales during the year.

Changes in Inventory. Computer Services reported $150,000 of cost of goods sold expense in its income statement. Assuming a perpetual inventory system is being used, the summary journal entry to record Computer Services' cost of goods sold is as follows:

A = L + SE
−150,000   −150,000
Cash flows: no effect

Cost of Goods Sold	150,000	
Inventory		150,000

Cost of goods sold decreased profit by $150,000, but how much cash was used to pay for inventory during the period? To answer this question, we need to first determine the cost of goods purchased for the period by analyzing the Inventory account. Recall that the Inventory account decreases when inventory is sold and increases when inventory is purchased. Illustration 17-5 indicates that Computer Services started the year with a balance of $10,000 in inventory and ended with $15,000. Using these amounts and the cost of goods sold recorded in the above journal entry, we analyze the Inventory account to determine the cost of goods purchased as follows:

Inventory				
Jan. 1 Balance	10,000			
Purchases	155,000	Cost of goods sold	150,000	$5,000 net increase
Dec. 31 Balance	15,000			

The cost of goods purchased during the period is $155,000, which is $5,000 ($155,000 − $150,000) greater than the cost of goods sold expense reported in the income statement. Note that this difference is equal to the increase in inventory during the period ($15,000 − $10,000). When the inventory account increases, more inventory was purchased during the period than was recorded as cost of goods sold. Since the cost of goods sold of $150,000 has already been deducted on the income statement, we simply deduct the $5,000 increase in inventory on the cash flow statement. This deduction is illustrated in the partial cash flow statement for Computer Services (Illustration 17-10) presented at the end of this section.

Following the same logic, if inventory had decreased, this would mean that the cost of goods purchased was less than the cost of goods sold and we would add the decrease back to profit.

This adjustment does not completely convert cost of goods sold to cash paid for inventory. It just converts the cost of goods sold to the cost of goods purchased during the year. The analysis of accounts payable—shown later—completes the calculation of payments made to suppliers by converting the cost of goods purchased from an accrual basis to a cash basis.

Changes in Prepaid Expenses. Computer Services reported $111,000 of operating expenses in its income statement. This means that profit decreased by $111,000, but what was the amount of cash paid for operating expenses? To answer this question, we analyze the Prepaid Expenses account because the account is increased when a prepayment is made and decreased when an expense is recorded in the income statement. To help us determine the cash paid for operating expenses, we can assume the following summary journal entry was made to record the operating expenses:

Operating Expenses	111,000	
Prepaid Expenses		111,000

$$A = L + SE$$
$$-111,000 \qquad -111,000$$
Cash flows: no effect

Computer Services started the year with a balance of $1,000 in the Prepaid Expense account and ended with $5,000. Using these amounts and the operating expenses recorded in the above journal entry, we analyze the Prepaid Expenses account to determine the cash paid for operating expenses as follows:

Prepaid Expenses				
Jan. 1 Balance	1,000			
Payments for expenses	115,000	Operating expenses	111,000	$4,000 net increase
Dec. 31 Balance	5,000			

The cash paid for operating expenses is $115,000, which is $4,000 ($115,000 − $111,000) greater than the operating expenses reported in the income statement. Note that this difference is equal to the increase in prepaid expenses during the period ($5,000 − $1,000). When prepaid expenses increase, cash paid for expenses is higher than the expenses reported in the income statement on an accrual basis. In other words, cash payments were made in the current period, but the expenses will not be recorded in the income statement until future periods. Since operating expenses of $111,000 have already been deducted on the income statement, we simply deduct the $4,000 increase in prepaid expenses on the cash flow statement to convert profit to net cash provided (used) by operating activities. This deduction is illustrated in the partial cash flow statement for Computer Services (Illustration 17-10) presented at the end of this section.

If prepaid expenses decreased during the period, this would mean that the cash paid for expenses was less than the operating expenses recorded in the income statement and we would add the decrease back to profit when calculating cash provided (used) by operating activities.

If Computer Services had any accrued expenses payable, such as Salaries Payable, these would also have to be considered before we could completely determine the amount of cash paid for operating expenses. We will look at changes in current liability accounts in the next section.

Changes in Trading Investments. You will recall that trading investments are classified as an operating activity. Like changes in other noncash current assets, increases in trading investments will be deducted from profit and decreases in trading investments will be added to profit when calculating cash provided (used) by operating activities.

Changes in Current Liabilities. The adjustments to profit that are required for changes in noncash current liability accounts to arrive at net cash provided (used) by operating activities are shown in Illustration 17-9.

▶ **ILLUSTRATION 17-9**
Adjustments to profit for changes in noncash current liability accounts

Increase in noncash current liabilities	Add
Decrease in noncash current liabilities	Deduct

We will illustrate these adjustments by analyzing the changes in Computer Services' current liability accounts: Accounts Payable and Income Tax Payable.

Changes in Accounts Payable. In some companies, the Accounts Payable account is used to record only purchases of inventory on account and an accrued expense payable account is used to record other credit purchases. For simplicity, in this chapter we have made this assumption.

You will recall that we determined, in the analysis of Computer Services' Inventory account earlier, that the cost of goods purchased was $155,000. Assuming all of the purchases were on account, the entry to record the purchases is (in summary):

A = L + SE
+155,000   +155,000

Cash flows: no effect

Inventory	155,000	
Accounts Payable		155,000

The amount of inventory purchased was $155,000, but what amount of cash was paid to suppliers for goods purchased? We can answer this question by analyzing the Accounts Payable account, because it is increased by the cost of goods purchased and decreased by cash paid to suppliers. Illustration 17-5 indicates that Computer Services started the year with a balance of $12,000 in accounts payable and ended with $28,000. Using these amounts and the accounts payable recorded in the above journal entry, we analyze the Accounts Payable account to determine the cash paid for inventory as follows:

$16,000 net increase

Accounts Payable			
Payments to suppliers	139,000	Jan. 1 Balance	12,000
		Purchases	155,000
		Dec. 31 Balance	28,000

The cash paid to suppliers for inventory is $139,000, which is $16,000 ($155,000 − $139,000) less than the cost of goods purchased. Note that this difference is equal to the increase in accounts payable during the period ($28,000 − $12,000). When the balance in the Accounts Payable account increases, it means that the cash paid to suppliers was less than the purchases made during the period. Since cost of goods sold of $150,000 has already been deducted on the income statement and we have also deducted the $5,000 increase in inventory to adjust for the cost of goods purchased, we simply add the $16,000 increase in accounts payable on the cash flow statement to convert profit to net cash provided (used) by operating activities. This deduction is illustrated in the partial cash flow statement for Computer Services (Illustration 17-10) presented at the end of this section.

Note that if the Accounts Payable account decreased, it would mean that the cash paid to suppliers was more than the cost of goods purchased. Therefore the decrease is deducted from profit.

In summary, the conversion of the cost of goods sold on the income statement to the cash paid for goods purchased involves two steps: (1) The change in the Inventory account adjusts the cost of goods sold to the cost of goods purchased. (2) The change in the Accounts Payable account adjusts the cost of goods purchased to the payments to suppliers. These changes for Computer Services are summarized as follows:

Cost of goods sold	$150,000
Add: Increase in inventory	5,000
Cost of goods purchased	155,000
Less: Increase in accounts payable	16,000
Cash payments to suppliers	$139,000

Changes in Income Tax Payable. Computer Services reported $47,000 in income tax expense on the income statement. The journal entry to record the income tax expense is as follows:

Income Tax Expense	47,000	
Income Tax Payable		47,000

A = L + SE
    +47,000   −47,000
Cash flows: no effect

This means that profit decreased by $47,000, but how much cash was paid for income tax? To answer this question, we need to analyze Computer Services' Income Tax Payable account because it increases when income tax expense is recorded and decreases when income tax is paid. Computer Services started the year with a balance of $8,000 in Income Tax Payable and ended with $6,000. Using these amounts and the income tax payable recorded in the above journal entry, we analyze the Income Tax Payable account to determine the cash paid for income tax as follows:

Income Tax Payable				
Payments for income tax	49,000	Jan. 1	Balance	8,000
			Income tax expense	47,000
		Dec. 31	Balance	6,000

$2,000 net decrease

The cash paid for income tax is $49,000, which is $2,000 ($49,000 − $47,000) more than the income tax expense. Note that this difference is equal to the decrease in income tax payable during the period ($8,000 − $6,000). When the Income Tax Payable account decreases, it means that more income tax was paid than recorded as expense in the income statement. Since income tax expense of $47,000 has already been deducted on the income statement, we simply deduct the $2,000 decrease in income tax payable on the cash flow statement to convert profit to net cash provided (used) by operating activities. This deduction is illustrated in the partial cash flow statement for Computer Services (Illustration 17-10) presented at the end of this section.

If Computer Services had other accrued expenses payable, they would be analyzed similarly to the Income Tax Payable account.

The partial cash flow statement that follows in Illustration 17-10 shows the impact on operating activities of the changes in current asset and current liability accounts (the changes are highlighted in red). It also shows the adjustments that were described earlier for noncash expenses and gains and losses. The operating activities section of the cash flow statement is now complete.

Helpful hint Whether the indirect or direct method (described in Section 2 below) is used, net cash provided (used) by operating activities will be the same.

COMPUTER SERVICES CORPORATION		
Cash Flow Statement (partial)		
Year Ended December 31, 2014		
Operating activities		
Profit		$145,000
Adjustments to reconcile profit to net cash		
provided (used) by operating activities:		
Depreciation expense	$ 9,000	
Loss on sale of equipment	3,000	
Decrease in accounts receivable	10,000	
Increase in inventory	(5,000)	
Increase in prepaid expenses	(4,000)	
Increase in accounts payable	16,000	
Decrease in income tax payable	(2,000)	27,000
Net cash provided by operating activities		172,000

Note that the increase or decrease for each noncash current asset and current liability has been either added or deducted as originally shown in Illustrations 17-8 and 17-9. In summary, Computer Services earned a profit of $145,000 and the profit-generating activities generated cash of $172,000 during the year.

Summary of Conversion to Net Cash Provided (Used) by Operating Activities—Indirect Method

As shown in Illustration 17-10, the cash flow statement prepared by the indirect method starts with profit. Profit is then adjusted to arrive at net cash provided (used) by operating activities. Adjustments to profit that are typically required are summarized as follows:

Noncash expenses	Depreciation expense	Add
	Amortization expense (intangible assets)	Add
	Amortization of discount on bond payable	Add
	Amortization of premium on bond payable	Deduct
Noncash revenues	Amortization of discount on bond investment	Deduct
	Amortization of premium on bond investment	Add
Gains and losses	Gain on sale of asset	Deduct
	Loss on sale of asset	Add
Changes in noncash current asset and current liability accounts	Increase in current asset account	Deduct
	Decrease in current asset account	Add
	Increase in current liability account	Add
	Decrease in current liability account	Deduct

 BEFORE YOU GO ON...

Do It

Selected financial information follows for Reynolds Ltd. at December 31. Prepare the operating activities section of the cash flow statement using the indirect method.

	2014	2013	Increase (Decrease)
Current assets			
Cash	$54,000	$37,000	$17,000
Accounts receivable	68,000	26,000	42,000
Inventories	54,000	10,000	44,000
Prepaid expenses	4,000	6,000	(2,000)
Current liabilities			
Accounts payable	23,000	50,000	(27,000)
Accrued expenses payable	10,000	0	10,000

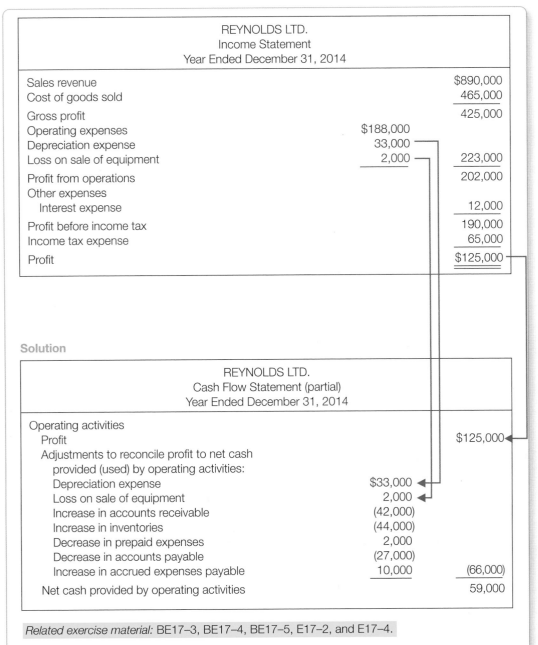

REYNOLDS LTD.
Income Statement
Year Ended December 31, 2014

Sales revenue		$890,000
Cost of goods sold		465,000
Gross profit		425,000
Operating expenses	$188,000	
Depreciation expense	33,000	
Loss on sale of equipment	2,000	223,000
Profit from operations		202,000
Other expenses		
Interest expense		12,000
Profit before income tax		190,000
Income tax expense		65,000
Profit		$125,000

Action Plan

- Start with profit reported on the income statement to determine the net cash provided (used) by operating activities.
- Examine the income statement: Add noncash expenses and deduct noncash revenues. Add losses and deduct gains.
- Analyze the current assets and current liabilities in the balance sheet. Add decreases in related noncash current asset accounts and increases in related noncash liability accounts. Deduct increases in related noncash current asset and decreases in related noncash liability accounts.

Solution

REYNOLDS LTD.
Cash Flow Statement (partial)
Year Ended December 31, 2014

Operating activities		
Profit		$125,000
Adjustments to reconcile profit to net cash provided (used) by operating activities:		
Depreciation expense	$33,000	
Loss on sale of equipment	2,000	
Increase in accounts receivable	(42,000)	
Increase in inventories	(44,000)	
Decrease in prepaid expenses	2,000	
Decrease in accounts payable	(27,000)	
Increase in accrued expenses payable	10,000	(66,000)
Net cash provided by operating activities		59,000

Related exercise material: BE17–3, BE17–4, BE17–5, E17–2, and E17–4.

THE NAVIGATOR

SECTION 2: DIRECT METHOD

As mentioned earlier in the chapter, although both the indirect and direct methods of determining cash provided (used) by operating activities are acceptable choices under IFRS and ASPE, the direct method is preferred by the standard setters. As presented in Illustration 17-6, a cash flow statement prepared under the direct method reports cash receipts and cash payments for major classes of operating activities. By reporting cash receipts and payments, the direct method provides information that is useful to investors and creditors in predicting future cash flows that is not available under the indirect method. The difference between the cash receipts and cash payments is the net cash provided (used) by operating activities. These relationships are shown in Illustration 17-11.

▶ ILLUSTRATION 17-11
Major classes of
operating cash receipts
and payments

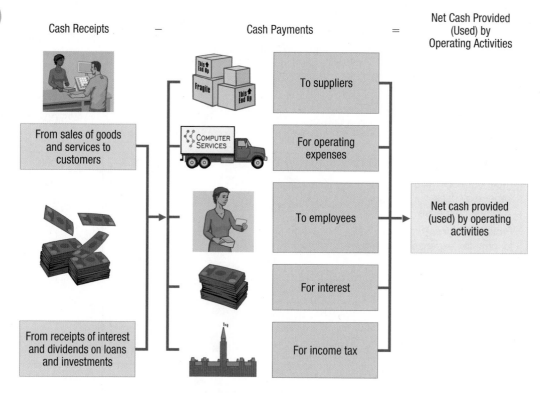

Cash Receipts − Cash Payments = Net Cash Provided (Used) by Operating Activities

Helpful hint In the indirect method, profit is adjusted to determine cash provided (used) in operating activities. In the direct method, each revenue and expense is adjusted to determine cash receipts and cash payments for operating activities.

Under the direct method, net cash provided (used) by operating activities is calculated by adjusting each individual revenue and expense item in the income statement from the accrual basis to the cash basis. The adjustments that are required to convert the related revenues and expenses from an accrual system to a cash system are summarized in Illustration 17-12.

▶ ILLUSTRATION 17-12
Summary of
adjustments required to
convert revenues and
expenses from accrual to cash

	Revenues	Expenses
Current assets		
Increase in account balance	Deduct	Add
Decrease in account balance	Add	Deduct
Current liabilities		
Increase in account balance	Add	Deduct
Decrease in account balance	Deduct	Add

We will explain the reasoning behind these adjustments for Computer Services Corporation, first for cash receipts and then for cash payments, in the following subsections.

Cash Receipts

Computer Services has only one source of cash receipts: its customers.

Cash Receipts from Customers. The income statement for Computer Services reported sales revenue from customers of $507,000. But how much was received in cash from customers? To answer this question, we need to analyze Computer Services' accounts receivable because Accounts Receivable is increased when a sale is made and decreased when cash is collected.

Assuming all the sales are on account, Computer Services' journal entry to record sales is (in summary for the year):

A	=	L	+	SE
+507,000				+507,000

Cash flows: no effect

| Accounts Receivable | 507,000 | |
| Sales Revenue | | 507,000 |

Illustration 17-5 indicates that Computer Services started the year with a balance of $30,000 in Accounts Receivable and ended with $20,000. Using these amounts and the sales recorded in the above journal entry, we analyze the Accounts Receivable account to determine the amount of cash collected from customers as follows:

Accounts Receivable				
Jan. 1	Balance	30,000		
	Sales revenue	507,000	Receipts from customers	517,000
Dec. 31	Balance	20,000		

} $10,000 net decrease

The analysis of the accounts receivable shows that cash receipts from customers that are reported in the cash flow statement are $517,000. Note that cash receipts from customers are $10,000 ($517,000 − $507,000) greater than sales revenue. Note also that this is equal to the $10,000 decrease in accounts receivable during the year ($30,000 − $20,000). When the Accounts Receivable account decreases during the year, revenues on an accrual basis are lower than revenues on a cash basis. In other words, more cash was collected during the period than was recorded as revenue.

Note that this is basically the same analysis that we illustrated in the previous section on the indirect method. The difference between the two methods is in the presentation of the information on the cash flow statement.

To summarize, cash receipts from customers ($517,000) can be calculated by adding the decrease in accounts receivable ($10,000) to sales revenues ($507,000). This calculation is shown in Illustration 17-13.

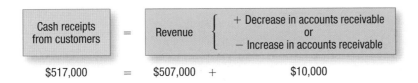

▶ILLUSTRATION 17-13
Formula to calculate cash receipts from customers—direct method

When the Accounts Receivable account balance increases during the year, revenues on an accrual basis are higher than cash receipts. In other words, revenues have increased, but not all of these revenues resulted in cash receipts. Therefore, the amount of the increase in accounts receivable is deducted from sales revenues to arrive at cash receipts from customers.

Cash Receipts from Interest and Dividends. Computer Services does not have cash receipts from any source other than customers. If an income statement reports other revenues, such as interest and/or dividend revenue, these amounts must be adjusted for any accrued amounts receivable to determine the actual cash receipts. As in Illustration 17-13, increases in accrued receivables would be deducted from accrual-based revenues. Decreases in accrued receivable accounts would be added to accrual-based revenues.

In addition, interest revenue from a long-term investment in bonds must be adjusted for the amortization of any discount or premium on the investment. Recall from Chapter 16 that the journal entries to amortize bond discounts and premiums on investments using assumed data are as follows:

Long-Term Bond Investment at a Discount			Long-Term Bond Investment at a Premium		
Cash	25,000		Cash	25,000	
Long-Term Investment—			Long-Term Investment—		
Bonds	1,000		Bonds		1,500
Interest Revenue		26,000	Interest Revenue		23,500

A   =   L   +   SE
+25,000   +26,000
+1,000

↑ Cash flows: +25,000

A   =   L   +   SE
+25,000   +23,500
−1,500

↑ Cash flows: +25,000

The amortization of a bond discount for an investor results in interest revenue being greater than the cash receipts. Thus the amortization of the discount must be deducted from interest revenue to calculate cash receipts from interest. Conversely, the amortization of a bond premium for an investor results in interest revenue being less than the cash receipts and so the amortization of the premium must be added to interest revenue to calculate cash receipts from interest.

Cash Payments

Computer Services has many sources of cash payments: to suppliers and for operating expenses, interest, and income taxes. We will analyze each of these in the next sections.

Cash Payments to Suppliers. Computer Services reported cost of goods sold of $150,000 on its income statement. But how much cash was paid to suppliers? To answer that, two steps are required:

1. Determine the cost of goods purchased for the year.
2. Then determine cash payments to suppliers.

The two steps in adjusting cost of goods sold to cash payments to suppliers can be performed by an analysis of the Inventory and Accounts Payable accounts.

Step 1: Cost of Goods Purchased. Computer Services reported $150,000 in cost of goods sold expense in its income statement. Assuming a perpetual inventory system is being used, the summary journal entry to record the cost of goods sold is as follows:

A = L + SE
−150,000   −150,000
Cash flows: no effect

| Cost of Goods Sold | 150,000 | |
| Inventory | | 150,000 |

By analyzing the inventory account, we can determine the cost of goods purchased. The Inventory account increases when inventory purchases are made and decreases when inventory is sold. Computer Services started the year with a balance of $10,000 in inventory and ended with $15,000. Using these amounts and the cost of goods sold recorded in the above journal entry, we analyze the Inventory account to determine the cost of goods purchased as follows:

$5,000 net increase

Inventory				
Jan. 1	Balance	10,000		
	Purchases	155,000	Cost of goods sold	150,000
Dec. 31	Balance	15,000		

The cost of goods purchased during the period is $155,000, which is $5,000 ($155,000 − $150,000) greater than the cost of goods sold expense reported in the income statement. Note that this difference is equal to the $5,000 increase in the Inventory account during the period ($15,000 − $10,000). When the Inventory account increases, more goods were purchased during the period than was recorded in cost of goods sold. Thus, cost of goods purchased ($155,000) can be calculated by simply adding the increase in inventory ($5,000) to cost of goods sold ($150,000).

Following the same logic, if the Inventory account decreased, this would mean that the cost of goods purchased was less than the cost of goods sold and the decrease in inventory can be deducted from cost of goods sold to arrive at cost of goods purchased.

Step 2: Cash Payments to Suppliers. Assuming all of the purchases were on account, the journal entry to record the purchases is (in summary):

A = L + SE
+155,000   +155,000
Cash flows: no effect

| Inventory | 155,000 | |
| Accounts Payable | | 155,000 |

By analyzing the Accounts Payable account, we can determine the cash payments to suppliers because the account is increased by the cost of goods purchased and decreased by cash paid to suppliers. Computer Services started the year with a balance of $12,000 in accounts payable and ended with $28,000. Using these amounts and the purchases of inventory in the previous journal entry, we analyze the Accounts Payable account to determine the cash paid to suppliers as follows:

$16,000 net increase

Accounts Payable				
Payments to suppliers	139,000	Jan. 1	Balance	12,000
			Purchases	155,000
		Dec. 31	Balance	28,000

The cash payments to suppliers are $139,000, which is $16,000 ($155,000 − $139,000) less than the cost of goods purchased. Note that this difference is equal to the $16,000 increase in the Accounts Payable account during the period ($28,000 − $12,000). When the Accounts Payable account increases, it means that the cash paid to suppliers was less than the purchases made during the period. Thus cash payments to suppliers ($139,000) can be calculated by deducting the increase in accounts payable ($16,000) from cost of goods purchased ($155,000).

Note that, if accounts payable decreased, it would mean that the cash paid to suppliers was more than the cost of goods purchased. Thus the decrease in accounts payable is added to the cost of goods purchased to arrive at cash payments to suppliers.

To summarize, the calculation of cash payments to suppliers is calculated as shown in Illustration 17-14.

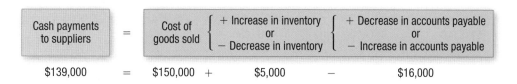

▶ **ILLUSTRATION 17-14**
Formula to calculate cash payments to suppliers— direct method

In this analysis, we have assumed that the Accounts Payable account is used only to record purchases of inventory on account. An accrued expenses payable account is used to record other credit purchases.

Cash Payments for Operating Expenses. Computer Services reported $111,000 of operating expenses in its income statement. This means that profit decreased by $111,000, but what was the amount of cash paid for operating expenses? To answer this question, we need to analyze the Prepaid Expenses account because it is increased when a prepayment is made and decreased when an expense is recorded in the income statement. Assume the following summary journal entry was made to record the operating expenses:

| Operating Expenses | 111,000 | |
| Prepaid Expenses | | 111,000 |

A = L + SE
−111,000   −111,000
Cash flows: no effect

Computer Services started the year with a balance of $1,000 in the Prepaid Expenses account and ended with $5,000. Using these amounts and the operating expenses recorded in the previous journal entry, we analyze the Prepaid Expenses account to determine the cash paid for operating expenses as follows:

	Prepaid Expenses			
Jan. 1	Balance	1,000		
	Payments for expenses	115,000	Operating expenses	111,000
Dec. 31	Balance	5,000		

} $4,000 net increase

The cash paid for operating expenses is $115,000, which is $4,000 ($115,000 − $111,000) greater than the operating expenses reported in the income statement. Note that this difference is equal to the $4,000 increase in the Prepaid Expenses account during the period ($5,000 − $1,000). When the balance in the Prepaid Expenses account increases, this means cash paid for expenses is higher than the expenses reported in the income statement. In other words, cash payments were made in the current period, but the expenses will not be recorded in the income statement until future periods. Thus cash payments for operating expenses ($115,000) is calculated by adding the increase ($4,000) in prepaid expenses to the operating expenses ($111,000) reported in the income statement. If prepaid expenses decrease, the decrease is deducted from operating expenses.

Operating expenses must also be adjusted for changes in accrued liability accounts (also called accrued expenses payable). Computer Services does not have any accrued expenses payable related to its operating expenses. If it did, any changes in the Accrued Expenses Payable account would affect operating expenses as follows: When accrued expenses payable increase during the year, operating expenses reported are higher than they are on a cash basis. To determine cash payments for operating expenses, an increase in accrued expenses payable is deducted from operating expenses. On the other hand, a decrease in accrued expenses payable is added to operating expenses because the cash payments are greater than the operating expenses.

To summarize, Computer Services' cash payments for operating expenses were $115,000, calculated as in Illustration 17-15.

▶ILLUSTRATION **17-15**
Formula to calculate cash payments for operating expenses—direct method

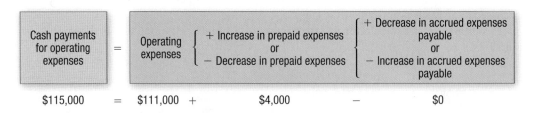

$115,000 = $111,000 + $4,000 − $0

Cash Payments to Employees. Companies may report payments to employees separately from operating expenses. To determine payments to employees, you would have to know the salary expense amount on the income statement and any salaries payable on the comparative balance sheets. Cash payments to employees, reported on the cash flow statement, would equal the salary expense, plus any decrease (or less any increase) during the period in salaries payable.

Cash Payments for Interest. Computer Services reports $42,000 of interest expense on its income statement in Illustration 17-5. This amount equals the cash paid, since the comparative balance sheets indicated no interest payable at the beginning or end of the year. If the comparative balance sheets reported interest payable, cash payments for interest would be calculated by adding a decrease in interest payable to interest expense and deducting an increase in interest payable to interest expense.

If a company has bonds payable sold at a premium or discount, interest expense will include the amortization of bond discounts and premiums. That means interest expense will not equal the cash payments for interest. Recall from Chapter 15 that the journal entries, using assumed data, to record interest expense and amortize bond discounts and premiums are recorded as follows:

A = L + SE
−25,000 +1,000 −26,000

↓ Cash flows: −25,000

A = L + SE
−25,000 −1,500 −23,500

↓ Cash flows: −25,000

Bonds Payable Issued at a Discount			Bonds Payable Issued at a Premium		
Interest Expense	26,000		Interest Expense	23,500	
Bonds Payable		1,000	Bonds Payable	1,500	
Cash		25,000	Cash		25,000

The amortization of a bonds payable discount results in interest expense being higher than the cash payment to the bond investors. So the amortization of a bond discount, the amount credited to bonds payable, must be deducted from interest expense to determine cash payments for interest.

The amortization of a bonds payable premium results in interest expense being lower than the cash payment to the bond investors. So the amortization of a bond premium, the amount debited to bonds payable, must be added to interest expense to determine cash payments for interest.

To summarize, the relationship among cash payments for interest, interest expense, changes in interest payable (if any), and amortization of premiums or discounts (if any) is shown in Illustration 17-16.

▶ILLUSTRATION **17-16**
Formula to calculate cash payments for interest—direct method

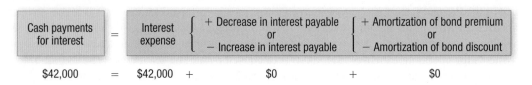

$42,000 = $42,000 + $0 + $0

Note that the Computer Services bonds payable were issued at par and thus there was no discount or premium to amortize. The amounts shown in the previous journal entries were included only to help you understand the impact of a premium or discount, when one exists.

Cash Payments for Income Tax. Computer Services reported $47,000 in income tax expense on the income statement. The journal entry to record the income tax expense is as follows:

Income Tax Expense	47,000	
Income Tax Payable		47,000

A	=	L	+	SE
		+47,000		−47,000

Cash flows: no effect

This means that profit decreased by $47,000, but how much cash was paid for income tax? To answer this question, we need to analyze Computer Services' Income Tax Payable account because it increases when income tax expense is recorded and decreases when income tax is paid. Computer Services started the year with a balance of $8,000 in income tax payable and ended with $6,000. Using these amounts and the income tax payable recorded in the above journal entry, we analyze the Income Tax Payable account to determine the cash paid for income tax as follows:

Income Tax Payable

Payments for income tax	49,000	Jan. 1	Balance	8,000	} $2,000 net decrease
			Income tax expense	47,000	
		Dec. 31	Balance	6,000	

The cash paid for income tax is $49,000, which is $2,000 ($49,000 − $47,000) more than the income tax expense. Note that this difference is equal to the $2,000 decrease in income tax payable during the period ($8,000 − $6,000). When income tax payable decreases, it means that more income tax was paid than recorded as expense in the income statement. Thus the payments for income tax ($49,000) are calculated by adding the decrease in income tax payable ($2,000) to income tax expense ($47,000). An increase in income tax payable is deducted from income tax expense.

The relationship among cash payments for income tax, income tax expense, and changes in income tax payable is shown in Illustration 17-17.

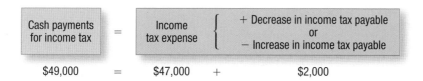

$49,000	=	$47,000	+ $2,000

▶ **ILLUSTRATION 17-17**
Formula to calculate cash payments for income tax—direct method

Cash Payments (Receipts) for Trading Investments. You will recall that trading investments are classified as an operating activity. Thus any cash payments made to purchase trading investments and any cash receipts for the sale of trading investments will be reported in the operating activities section of the cash flow statement. Typically, the payments and receipts for trading investments are reported as a net amount. For example, if cash paid to purchase trading investments is greater than cash received for the sale of trading investments, a net cash payment is reported.

All of the revenues and expenses in the Computer Services income statement have now been adjusted to a cash basis. This information is put together in Illustration 17-18, which shows the operating activities section of the cash flow statement using the direct method.

Helpful hint **Note that in the operating activities section, positive numbers indicate cash inflows (receipts) and negative numbers indicate cash outflows (payments). As well, whether the direct or indirect method is used, net cash provided (used) by operating activities will be the same.**

▶ **ILLUSTRATION 17-18**
Net cash provided by operating activities—direct method

COMPUTER SERVICES CORPORATION
Cash Flow Statement (partial)
Year Ended December 31, 2014

Operating activities		
Cash receipts from customers		$517,000
Cash payments		
To suppliers	$(139,000)	
For operating expenses	(115,000)	
For interest	(42,000)	
For income tax	(49,000)	(345,000)
Net cash provided by operating activities		172,000

Action Plan

- Determine the net cash provided (used) by operating activities by adjusting each revenue and expense item for changes in the related current asset and current liability account.
- To adjust revenues for changes in related current asset and current liability accounts, add decreases in current asset accounts and increases in current liability accounts. Deduct increases in current asset accounts and decreases in current liability accounts.
- To adjust expenses for changes in related current asset and current liability accounts, add increases in current asset accounts and decreases in current liability accounts. Deduct decreases in current asset accounts and increases in current liability accounts.
- Assume that the accounts payable relate to suppliers and that the accrued expenses payable relate to operating expenses.
- Report cash receipts and cash payments by major sources and uses: cash receipts from customers and cash payments to suppliers, for operating expenses, to employees, for interest, and for income taxes.

BEFORE YOU GO ON...

Do It

Selected financial information follows for Reynolds Ltd. at December 31. Prepare the operating activities section of the cash flow statement using the direct method.

	2014	2013	Increase (Decrease)
Current assets			
Cash	$54,000	$37,000	$17,000
Accounts receivable	68,000	26,000	42,000
Inventories	54,000	10,000	44,000
Prepaid expenses	4,000	6,000	(2,000)
Current liabilities			
Accounts payable	23,000	50,000	(27,000)
Accrued expenses payable	10,000	0	10,000

REYNOLDS LTD.
Income Statement
Year Ended December 31, 2014

Sales revenue		$890,000
Cost of goods sold		465,000
Gross profit		425,000
Operating expenses	$188,000	
Depreciation expense	33,000	
Loss on sale of equipment	2,000	223,000
Profit from operations		202,000
Other expenses		
Interest expense		12,000
Profit before income tax		190,000
Income tax expense		65,000
Profit		$125,000

Solution

REYNOLDS LTD.
Cash Flow Statement (partial)
Year Ended December 31, 2014

Operating activities		
Cash receipts from customers		$848,000[1]
Cash payments		
To suppliers	$(536,000)[2]	
For operating expenses	(176,000)[3]	
For interest	(12,000)	
For income tax	(65,000)	(789,000)
Net cash provided by operating activities		59,000

Calculations:

[1] Cash receipts from customers: $890,000 − $42,000 = $848,000
[2] Payments to suppliers: $465,000 + $44,000 + $27,000 = $536,000
[3] Payments for operating expenses: $188,000 − $2,000 − $10,000 = $176,000

Related exercise material: BE17–6, BE17–7, BE17–8, BE17–9, BE17–10, BE17–11, BE17–12, BE17–13, E17–3, E17–5, E17–6, and E17–7.

THE **NAVIGATOR**

STEP 2: INVESTING ACTIVITIES

Determine the Net Cash Provided (Used) by Investing Activities by Analyzing Changes in Long-Term Asset Accounts

Regardless of whether the indirect or direct method is used to calculate operating activities, investing and financing activities are measured and reported in the same way. Investing activities affect long-term asset accounts, such as long-term investments; property, plant, and equipment; and intangible assets. There are exceptions. For example, short-term debt instruments purchased to earn interest and short-term notes receivable issued for loans rather than for trade transactions are reported as investing activities.

To determine the investing activities, the balance sheet and additional information in Illustration 17-5 must be examined. The change in each long-term asset account is analyzed to determine what effect, if any, it had on cash. Computer Services has no short-term investments or notes receivable but does have three long-term asset accounts that must be analyzed: Land, Building, and Equipment.

LAND

Land increased by $110,000 during the year, as reported in Computer Services' balance sheet. The additional information in Illustration 17-5 states that this land was purchased by issuing long-term bonds. The journal entry to record the purchase of the land is as follows:

Land	110,000	
Bonds Payable		110,000

A = L + SE
+110,000 +110,000
Cash flows: no effect

As shown in the journal entry, issuing bonds for land has no effect on cash and is not reported in the cash flow statement. It is, however, a significant noncash investing and financing activity that must be disclosed in a note to the statement.

BUILDING

The Building account increased by $120,000 during the year. What caused this increase? No additional information has been given for this change. Whenever unexplained differences in accounts occur, we assume the transaction was for cash. That is, we would assume the entry to record the acquisition or expansion of the building is as follows:

Building	120,000	
Cash		120,000

A = L + SE
+120,000
−120,000
↓ Cash flows: −120,000

The cash outflow for the purchase of the building is reported as an investing activity in the cash flow statement.

Accumulated Depreciation—Building

The Accumulated Depreciation—Building account increased by $6,000 during the year:

Accumulated Depreciation—Building		
	Jan. 1 Balance	5,000
	Depreciation expense	6,000
	Dec. 31 Balance	11,000

$6,000 net increase

As explained in the additional information in Illustration 17-5, this increase resulted from the depreciation expense reported on the income statement for the building. The journal entry to record the depreciation expense is as follows:

Depreciation Expense	6,000	
Accumulated Depreciation—Building		6,000

A = L + SE
−6,000 −6,000
Cash flows: no effect

As the journal entry shows, depreciation expense is a noncash charge and does not affect the cash flow statement.

EQUIPMENT

Computer Services' Equipment account increased by $17,000. The additional information in Illustration 17-5 explains that this was a net increase resulting from two different transactions: (1) a purchase of equipment for $25,000 cash, and (2) a sale of equipment with a carrying amount of $7,000 (cost of $8,000, less accumulated depreciation of $1,000) for $4,000 cash. The journal entry to record the purchase of equipment is as follows:

A = L + SE
+25,000
−25,000

↓ Cash flows: −25,000

Equipment	25,000	
Cash		25,000

The purchase of the equipment is reported as a $25,000 cash outflow in the investing section of the cash flow statement.

The journal entry to record the sale of the equipment is as follows:

A = L + SE
+4,000   −3,000
+1,000
−8,000

↑ Cash flows: +4,000

Cash	4,000	
Accumulated Depreciation—Equipment	1,000	
Loss on Sale of Equipment	3,000	
Equipment		8,000

The $4,000 cash proceeds from the sale of the equipment is reported as a cash inflow in the investing section of the cash flow statement.

The T account below summarizes the changes in the Equipment account during the year:

$17,000 net increase {

Equipment				
Jan. 1	Balance	10,000		
	Purchases of equipment	25,000	Cost of equipment sold	8,000
Dec. 31	Balance	27,000		

Note that, for the sale of the equipment, it is the cash proceeds that are reported on the cash flow statement, not the cost of the equipment sold, that is credited to the Equipment account.

Also note that each transaction, both the purchase and the sale, must be reported separately on the cash flow statement. It is not correct to report the net change in a long-term balance sheet account as simply an increase or decrease in that account.

In the above example, you were given additional information about both the purchase and the sale of equipment. Often, in analyzing accounts, you will be given just one piece of information and are expected to deduce the information that is missing. For example, if you knew the beginning and ending balances of the Equipment account as well as the fact that the cost of the equipment sold was $8,000, you could determine that the cost of the equipment purchased must have been $25,000.

Accumulated Depreciation—Equipment

The accumulated depreciation for equipment increased by $2,000. This change does not represent the depreciation expense for the year. In fact, the additional information in Illustration 17-5 told us that there was $3,000 of depreciation expense for the equipment and that the equipment sold had $1,000 of accumulated depreciation.

The journal entry to record the depreciation expense is as follows:

A = L + SE
−3,000   −3,000

Cash flows: no effect

Depreciation Expense	3,000	
Accumulated Depreciation—Equipment		3,000

This journal entry, combined with the journal entry shown earlier for the sale of the equipment, helps us understand the changes to the accumulated depreciation account. The T account below for Accumulated Depreciation—Equipment shows that these two items explain the overall net increase of $2,000.

Accumulated Depreciation—Equipment				
		Jan. 1 Balance	1,000	
Sale of equipment	1,000	Depreciation expense	3,000	} $2,000 net increase
		Dec. 31 Balance	3,000	

As we have seen, the sale of the equipment affects one account on Computer Services' income statement (Loss on Sale of Equipment) and three accounts on its balance sheet (Cash, Equipment, and Accumulated Depreciation). In the cash flow statement, it is important to report the effects of this sale in one place: the investing activities section. The overall result is that the sale of the equipment ends up having no impact on the operating activities section of the cash flow statement. Instead, the cash proceeds received from the sale of the equipment are shown fully in the investing activities section.

The investing activities section of Computer Services' cash flow statement is shown in Illustration 17-19 and reports the changes in the three accounts: Land, Building, and Equipment.

Helpful hint Note that in the investing activities section, positive numbers indicate cash inflows (receipts) and negative numbers indicate cash outflows (payments).

▶ ILLUSTRATION 17-19
Net cash used by investing activities

COMPUTER SERVICES CORPORATION
Cash Flow Statement (partial)
Year Ended December 31, 2014

Investing activities		
Purchase of building	$(120,000)	
Purchase of equipment	(25,000)	
Sale of equipment	4,000	
Net cash used by investing activities		$(141,000)
Note x: Significant noncash investing and financing activities		
Issue of bonds to purchase land		$110,000

Action Plan
- Prepare a T account for Accumulated Depreciation—Equipment and record the beginning and ending balances and the depreciation expense. Recall that depreciation expense increases accumulated depreciation. Use this information to calculate the accumulated depreciation of the equipment sold during the year.
- Prepare a T account for Equipment and record the beginning and ending balances and the cost of the equipment sold. Use this information to calculate the cost of the equipment purchased.

BEFORE YOU GO ON...

Do It

Umiujaq Corporation reported an opening balance of $146,000 and an ending balance of $135,000 in its Equipment account and an opening balance of $47,000 and an ending balance of $62,000 in its Accumulated Depreciation—Equipment account. During the year, it sold equipment with a cost of $21,000 for cash at a gain on the sale of $1,000. It also purchased equipment for cash. It recorded depreciation expense of $31,000. Calculate (a) the cash received from the sale of the equipment, and (b) the cash paid for equipment.

Solution

(a) Cash received from sale of equipment = $6,000

Accumulated Depreciation—Equipment			
		Opening balance	47,000
Sale of equipment	16,000*	Depreciation expense	31,000
		Ending balance	62,000

* $16,000 = $47,000 + $31,000 − $62,000

Carrying amount of equipment sold: $21,000 − $16,000 = $5,000
Carrying amount of the equipment sold plus the gain on sale = $5,000 + $1,000 = $6,000

- Prepare journal entries to help you determine the impact of the transactions on cash.
- Calculate the carrying amount of the equipment sold. Remember that the carrying amount is equal to the cost of the equipment sold less the accumulated depreciation on the equipment sold.
- Calculate the cash proceeds on the sale of the equipment. Since there is a gain on sale, the equipment sold for more than its carrying amount. Therefore, add the gain on sale to the carrying amount to determine the cash proceeds.

BEFORE YOU GO ON continued...

The journal entries to record the depreciation expense and the sale of the equipment are as follows:

Depreciation Expense	31,000	
Accumulated Depreciation—Equipment		31,000
Cash	6,000	
Accumulated Depreciation—Equipment	16,000	
Gain on Sale of Equipment		1,000
Equipment		21,000

(b) Cash paid for equipment = $10,000

Equipment

Opening bal.	146,000		
Purchase of Equipment	10,000**	Sale of Equipment	21,000
Ending bal.	135,000		

** $10,000 = $135,000 + $21,000 − $146,000

The journal entry to record the purchase of equipment is as follows:

Equipment	10,000	
Cash		10,000

Related exercise material: BE17–14 and BE17–15.

THE NAVIGATOR

STEP 3: FINANCING ACTIVITIES

Determine the Net Cash Provided (Used) by Financing Activities by Analyzing Changes in Long-Term Liability and Equity Accounts

The third step in preparing a cash flow statement is to analyze the changes in long-term liability and equity accounts. If short-term notes payable are issued for lending purposes rather than for trade, they should also be reported in the financing activities section. Computer Services has no notes payable but has one long-term liability account, Bonds Payable, and two shareholders' equity accounts, Common Shares and Retained Earnings.

BONDS PAYABLE

Bonds Payable increased by $110,000. As indicated earlier, land was acquired from the issue of these bonds. This noncash transaction is reported as a note to the cash flow statement because it is a significant financing activity.

COMMON SHARES

Computer Services' Common Shares account increased by $20,000. Since there is no additional information about any reacquisition of shares, we assume that this change is due entirely to the issue of additional common shares for cash. The entry to record the issue of common shares is as follows:

Cash		20,000	
Common Shares			20,000

A	=	L	+	SE
+20,000				+20,000

↑ Cash flows: +20,000

This cash inflow is reported in the financing activities section of the cash flow statement. If the company had also reacquired shares, the amount of cash paid to reacquire the common shares would be reported as a cash outflow in the financing section.

RETAINED EARNINGS

Retained earnings increased by $116,000 during the year, but what caused this increase? Were there any non-operating cash transactions that changed retained earnings? We know that profit increases retained earnings and that Computer Services reported profit of $145,000 for the year. The journal entry to record profit in the Retained Earnings account is as follows:

Income Summary		145,000	
Retained Earnings			145,000

A	=	L	+	SE
				−145,000
				+145,000

Cash flows: no effect

Computer Services started the year with $48,000 in its Retained Earnings account and ended the year with $164,000. Using these amounts and the profit recorded in the above journal entry, we analyze the Retained Earnings account to determine the dividends declared as follows:

	Retained Earnings			
Cash dividend 29,000	Jan. 1	Balance	48,000	
		Profit	145,000	} $116,000 net increase
	Dec. 31	Balance	164,000	

Note that the Retained Earnings account above only reports the dividend declared. This amount must be adjusted to determine the dividend paid, if there is any change in the balance of the Dividends Payable account reported in the current liabilities section of the balance sheet. The relationship among cash payments for dividends, dividends declared, and changes in dividends payable is shown in Illustration 17-20.

▶ **ILLUSTRATION 17-20**
Formula to calculate dividends paid in cash

The additional information in Illustration 17-5 indicates that Computer Services paid a cash dividend of $29,000. In this example, the dividends declared are equal to the dividends paid. The cash dividend paid is reported as a cash outflow in the financing activities section of the cash flow statement.

The financing activities section of Computer Services' cash flow statement is shown in Illustration 17-21 and reports the issue of common shares and payment of a dividend. The information on the significant noncash financing activity of bonds being issued to purchase land has already been illustrated and is not included here.

Helpful hint Note that in the financing activities section, positive numbers indicate cash inflows (receipts) and negative numbers indicate cash outflows (payments).

▶ILLUSTRATION **17-21**
Net cash used by
financing activities

COMPUTER SERVICES CORPORATION Cash Flow Statement (partial) Year Ended December 31, 2014		
Financing activities		
Issue of common shares	$20,000	
Payment of cash dividend	(29,000)	
Net cash used by financing activities		$(9,000)

BEFORE YOU GO ON...

Do It

La Tuque Corporation reported an opening balance of $80,000 and an ending balance of $95,000 in its Common Shares account and an opening balance of $15,000 and an ending balance of $20,000 in its Contributed Surplus—Reacquisition of Common Shares account. During the year, it issued $50,000 of common shares for cash and reacquired common shares for cash. Calculate the cash paid to reacquire the shares.

Action Plan

- Prepare a T account for Common Shares and record the beginning and ending balances and the cost of the new shares issued. Use this information to determine the cost of the shares reacquired.
- Prepare a T account for Contributed Surplus— Reacquisition of Common Shares and record the beginning and ending balances. Use this information to determine the change in the account as a result of the reacquisition of the shares.
- Prepare journal entries to help you record the transactions in the Common Shares and Contributed Surplus— Reacquisition of Common Shares accounts, and to determine the impact on cash.
- An increase in contributed surplus indicates that the company paid less than the cost of the common shares to reacquire them. Deduct this increase from the cost of the shares to determine the cash paid.

Solution

Cash paid to reacquire shares = $30,000

The journal entry to record the issue of shares is as follows:

Cash	50,000	
Common Shares		50,000

Common Shares			
		Opening balance	80,000
Reacquisition of shares	35,000*	Issue of shares	50,000
		Ending balance	95,000

* $35,000 = $80,000 + $50,000 − $95,000

Contributed Surplus—Reacquisition of Common Shares		
	Opening balance	15,000
	Reacquisition of shares	5,000**
	Ending balance	20,000

** $5,000 = $20,000 − $15,000

The journal entry to record the reacquisition of common shares is as follows:

Common Shares	35,000	
Contributed Surplus—Reacquisition of Common Shares		5,000
Cash***		30,000

***Cash paid for reacquisition of shares: $35,000 − $5,000 = $30,000

Related exercise material: BE17–16, BE17–17, and E17–9.

THE **NAVIGATOR**

STEP 4: THE CASH FLOW STATEMENT

Prepare the Cash Flow Statement and Determine the Net Increase (Decrease) in Cash

The final step is to calculate the overall net increase or decrease in cash for the year by adding cash provided or used in each of the three sections of the cash flow statement. Computer Services' net increase in cash of $22,000 is calculated as follows:

Net cash provided by operating activities	$172,000
Net cash used by investing activities	(141,000)
Net cash used by financing activities	(9,000)
Net increase in cash	$ 22,000

The $22,000 net increase in cash is then added to cash at the beginning of the year of $33,000 to equal $55,000 of cash at the end of the year. This number is compared with the cash account balance in the end-of-the-year balance sheet, which also shows that cash is $55,000 at the end of the year. This is known as proving the cash balance. If cash at the end of the year on the cash flow statement is not equal to cash on the balance sheet, there is an error in the cash flow statement, which will need to be found and corrected.

Using this information and the partial cash flow statements shown in Illustrations 17-10, 17-18, 17-19, and 17-21, we can now present a complete cash flow statement for Computer Services Corporation. Illustration 17-22 presents the statement using the indirect method of preparing the operating activities section from Illustration 17-10. Illustration 17-23 presents the statement using the direct method of preparing the operating activities section from Illustration 17-18. Notice that, while the operating activities sections differ in the indirect and direct methods, the investing and financing activities sections are exactly the same in the two statements.

▸ ILLUSTRATION 17-22
Cash flow statement—
indirect method

COMPUTER SERVICES CORPORATION
Cash Flow Statement
Year Ended December 31, 2014

Operating activities			
Profit			$145,000
Adjustments to reconcile profit to net cash			
provided (used) by operating activities:			
Depreciation expense		$ 9,000	
Loss on sale of equipment		3,000	
Decrease in accounts receivable		10,000	
Increase in inventory		(5,000)	
Increase in prepaid expenses		(4,000)	
Increase in accounts payable		16,000	
Decrease in income tax payable		(2,000)	27,000
Net cash provided by operating activities			172,000
Investing activities			
Purchase of building		$(120,000)	
Purchase of equipment		(25,000)	
Sale of equipment		4,000	
Net cash used by investing activities			(141,000)
Financing activities			
Issue of common shares		$ 20,000	
Payment of cash dividend		(29,000)	
Net cash used by financing activities			(9,000)
Net increase in cash			22,000
Cash, January 1			33,000
Cash, December 31			$ 55,000

Note x: Significant noncash investing and financing activities;	
Issue of bonds to purchase land	$110,000

▶ILLUSTRATION 17-23
Cash flow statement—
direct method

COMPUTER SERVICES CORPORATION
Cash Flow Statement
Year Ended December 31, 2014

Operating activities		
Cash receipts from customers		$517,000
Cash payments		
To suppliers	$(139,000)	
For operating expenses	(115,000)	
For interest	(42,000)	
For income tax	(49,000)	(345,000)
Net cash provided by operating activities		172,000
Investing activities		
Purchase of building	$(120,000)	
Purchase of equipment	(25,000)	
Sale of equipment	4,000	
Net cash used by investing activities		(141,000)
Financing activities		
Issue of common shares	20,000	
Payment of cash dividend	(29,000)	
Net cash used by financing activities		(9,000)
Net increase in cash		22,000
Cash, January 1		33,000
Cash, December 31		$ 55,000

Note x: Significant noncash investing and financing activities;
      Issue of bonds to purchase land $110,000

 BEFORE YOU GO ON...

Do It

Selected information follows for Reynolds Ltd. at December 31. Prepare a cash flow statement.

	2014	2013	Increase (Decrease)
Cash	$ 54,000	$ 37,000	$ 17,000
Property, plant, and equipment			
Land	45,000	70,000	(25,000)
Buildings	200,000	200,000	0
Accumulated depreciation—buildings	(21,000)	(11,000)	10,000
Equipment	193,000	68,000	125,000
Accumulated depreciation—equipment	(28,000)	(10,000)	18,000
Long-term liabilities and shareholders' equity			
Bonds payable	110,000	150,000	(40,000)
Common shares	220,000	60,000	160,000
Retained earnings	206,000	136,000	70,000

Additional information:
1. Cash provided from operating activities was $59,000 as shown in the Before You Go On at the end of the section "Step 1: Operating Activities."
2. Equipment was bought for cash. Equipment with a cost of $41,000 and a carrying amount of $36,000 was sold at a loss of $2,000.
3. Bonds of $40,000 were redeemed at their face value for cash.
4. Profit was $125,000 and a cash dividend was paid.

Solution

Action Plan
- Determine the net cash provided (used) by investing activities. Investing activities generally relate to changes in long-term asset accounts.
- Determine the net cash provided (used) by financing activities. Financing activities generally relate to changes in long-term liability and shareholders' equity accounts.
- Determine the net increase (decrease) in cash and add it to the beginning-of-period cash. Verify that this amount agrees with the end-of-period cash balance reported on the balance sheet.

REYNOLDS LTD.
Cash Flow Statement
Year Ended December 31, 2014

Operating activities		
Net cash provided by operating activities		$ 59,000
Investing activities		
Sale of land	$ 25,000	
Sale of equipment	34,000[1]	
Purchase of equipment	(166,000)[2]	
Net cash used by investing activities		(107,000)
Financing activities		
Redemption of bonds	$ (40,000)	
Issue of common shares	160,000	
Payment of dividends	(55,000)[3]	
Net cash provided by financing activities		65,000
Net increase in cash		17,000
Cash, January 1		37,000
Cash, December 31		$ 54,000

[1]Sale of equipment: $36,000 (carrying amount) − $2,000 (loss) = $34,000
[2]Purchase of equipment: $68,000 (opening Equipment balance) − $41,000 (cost of equipment sold) − $193,000 (ending Equipment balance) = $166,000 (purchase of equipment)
[3]Payment of dividends: $136,000 (opening Retained Earnings) + $125,000 (profit) − $206,000 (ending Retained Earnings) = $55,000 (Dividends)

Related exercise material: BE17–18, E17-10, E17–11, and E17–12.

THE NAVIGATOR

Using the Information in the Financial Statements

The cash flow statement gives information about a company's financial health that cannot be found in the other financial statements. None of the other financial statements give enough information for decision-making by themselves. The income statement; statements of comprehensive income, retained earnings, and changes in shareholders' equity; and the balance sheet must be read along with the cash flow statement in order to fully understand a company's financial situation.

» STUDY **OBJECTIVE 3**

Analyze the cash flow statement.

For example, the income statement might show a profitable company. However, a rapidly growing company might also find it difficult to pay its current liabilities because its cash is being used to finance its growth. Both successful and unsuccessful companies can have problems with cash flow. According to Clearwater Seafoods in our feature story, the sustainability of a business is linked to its ability to generate cash. Clearwater considers cash flows generated from operations as a key indicator of the company's health.

Consider the condensed income and cash flow data shown below for three different companies, each operating in the same industry.

	Company A	Company B	Company C
Profit (loss)	$ 75,000	$ 25,000	$(50,000)
Cash provided (used) by operating activities	$100,000	$(25,000)	$(25,000)
Cash provided (used) by investing activities	(50,000)	(25,000)	35,000
Cash provided (used) by financing activities	(25,000)	75,000	15,000
Net increase in cash	$ 25,000	$ 25,000	$ 25,000

In this example, we have assumed that each company has the same change in cash, an increase of $25,000. However, this increase in cash is generated quite differently by each company. Company A reports profit of $75,000 and a positive cash flow from operating activities of $100,000. How can Company A's cash provided by operating activities be higher than its profit? This could occur in any of these three situations: if it has (1) noncash expenses such as depreciation, (2) reduced current assets such as receivables or inventory, or (3) increased current liabilities such as accounts payable. Depending on which of the situations created Company A's higher cash flow from operating activities, there could be different implications. For example, if receivables are lower, this could be because the company is collecting them faster. If so, this is a good thing. Alternatively, receivables could have decreased because sales decreased. This is not good, and has implications for future profitability.

For now, we know that Company A's operating activities produced a positive cash flow of $100,000, which allowed it to invest $50,000 in its long-lived assets and repay $25,000 of its debt and/or pay dividends. Based only on this information, Company A appears to be in a strong financial position. As explained in the feature story about Clearwater, cash flows generated from operations are a key indicator of a company's health.

Company B, which also produced a positive profit, used $25,000 in its operating activities. How could Company B's profit result in a negative operating cash flow? Company B may be in the early start-up stages of its development. It may have quickly increasing receivables and inventories, with lower amounts of noncash expenses. It was able to end up with the same cash balance as Company A only because it borrowed money. If Company B is indeed a new and rapidly growing company, this is fine. If not, this type of cash flow pattern would not be sustainable in the long run.

Assuming Company B is a start-up company, its cash flow figures appear to be reasonable. For example, early in its operations, during its growth stage, one would expect a company to generate a small amount of profit (or a loss) and negative cash from its operating activities. It will likely also be spending large amounts to purchase productive assets, and will finance these purchases by issuing debt or equity securities. Thus, during its early years, cash from operating and investing activities will likely be negative, while cash from financing activities will be positive.

Company C, which reported both a loss and a negative cash flow from operating activities, is able to produce a positive change in cash only by selling long-lived assets and borrowing additional debt. A company that generates cash mainly from investing activities is usually in a downsizing or restructuring situation. This is fine if the assets being disposed of are unnecessary or unprofitable. However, if the company is in a position where it must sell off income-producing assets to generate cash, then this will affect future revenue and profitability.

As you can see from the above example, analyzing cash flows from different activities along with the information in the other financial statements can provide significant information about a company's overall financial health and activities.

FREE CASH FLOW

Another way of evaluating cash flows is to determine how much discretionary cash flow a company has—in other words, how much cash it has available to expand, repay debt, pay dividends, or do whatever it best determines. This discretionary cash flow is a measure of solvency known as "free cash flow." As indicated in the feature story, Clearwater's goal is to grow free cash flows so it can reduce debt and pay a sustainable dividend to its shareholders.

Free cash flow describes the cash remaining from operating activities after making cash outlays for capital expenditures. Using net cash provided by operating activities as a proxy for free cash flow is not enough as it does not take into account the fact that a company must invest in productive assets, such as property, plant, and equipment, just to maintain its current level of operations. However, the cash flow statement rarely separates investing activities into those required for maintenance and those used for expansion. So we are often forced to use the net cash used by investing activities rather than capital expenditures incurred to maintain productive capacity when calculating free cash flow.

To calculate free cash flow, the net cash used for investing activities is deducted from the net cash provided by operating activities. Illustration 17-24 uses data from Reitmans' cash flow statement (in thousands) to illustrate the calculation of free cash flow.

▶ ILLUSTRATION
Free cash flow

Cash Provided (Used) by Operating Activities	−	Cash Used (Provided) by Investing Activities	=	Free Cash Flow
$96,937	−	$59,574	=	$37,363

Reitmans had a positive free cash flow of $37,363 thousand. The cash Reitmans produced from operating activities was more than sufficient to cover its current year's investing activities. We are not able to determine whether these investing activities were incurred by Reitmans to maintain its existing productive capacity, to expand, or for both purposes. However, we do know from the cash flow statement that Reitmans used all of its free cash flow, as well as cash and cash equivalents on hand from the previous year, to repurchase shares and pay long-term debt and dividends. This resulted in an overall reduction in cash and cash equivalents.

ACCOUNTING IN ACTION
ETHICS INSIGHT

While investors tend to view the cash flow statement as a true picture of a company's financial situation, some advisors say it can be manipulated to make things look better. Among other things, management can misclassify cash into operating, investing, and financing activities. That is what allegedly happened with Sino-Forest Corp., a Chinese-based forestry company with an office in Canada. When the company

acquired timber in China, it recorded the purchases on the cash flow statement as cash used in investing activities. After selling the timber, Sino-Forest treated the sales revenue as cash provided by operating activities. As a result, the cash flow statement showed cash inflow from the sale of timber in its operating activities and cash outflow for the purchase of the timber in its investing activities—allegedly overstating cash from operations by excluding the cost of timber sold. Most companies record such purchases as an outflow of cash from operating activities. In 2012, Sino-Forest sought bankruptcy protection and put itself up for sale. Investors who lost billions of dollars after allegations that the company exaggerated its assets were considering launching a class action lawsuit. At the time of writing, Sino-Forest was being investigated by Canadian authorities for fraud, which the company denied.

Sources: Jeff Gray and Andy Hoffman, "Report Alleges Possibility Sino-Forest 'An Accounting Fiction,'" *Globe and Mail*, July 18, 2012; Charmaine Noronha, "Timber Company Sino-Forest Files for Bankruptcy in Ontario Court," Associated Press, *The China Post*, April 1, 2012; Al Rosen and Mark Rosen, "Don't Be Suckered by Cash Flow Statements," Advisor.ca, August 1, 2011.

Why would management of a company want to overstate cash flow from operating activities?

 BEFORE YOU GO ON...

Do It

Speyside Inc. reported the following information:

	2015	2014
Profit (loss)	$50,000	$(5,000)
Cash provided (used) by operating activities	25,000	(10,000)
Cash provided (used) by investing activities	(10,000)	(70,000)
Cash provided (used) by financing activities	(8,000)	100,000

Calculate free cash flow for each of the years and comment on Speyside's stage of development in 2014 and 2015.

Solution

	2015	2014
Free cash flow	$15,000 = 25,000 − 10,000	$(80,000) = (10,000) + (70,000)

Speyside had negative free cash flow in 2014 and its cash was provided through its financing activities, indicating the company may have been in the start-up phase of its development. In 2015, the company had positive free cash flow and was profitable, indicating that the company was able to start generating profit and cash from its operations, continue to invest, and have cash available to reduce financing or pay dividends.

Related exercise material: BE17–19, E17–13, and E17–14.

Action Plan
- Calculate the free cash flow by deducting cash provided (used) by investing activities from cash provided (used) by operating activities.

THE **NAVIGATOR**

▌Comparing IFRS and ASPE ▌

Key Differences	International Financial Reporting Standards (IFRS)	Accounting Standards for Private Enterprises (ASPE)
Classification of interest and dividends	Interest and dividends received may be classified as operating or investing activities.	Interest and dividends received are classified as operating activities.
	Interest and dividends paid may be classified as operating or financing activities.	Interest paid is classified as an operating activity. Dividends paid are classified as a financing activity.
	Once the choice is made, it must be applied consistently.	

THE NAVIGATOR

Demonstration Problem

The income statement for the year ended December 31, 2014, for Kosinski Manufacturing Ltd. contains the following condensed information:

KOSINSKI MANUFACTURING LTD.
Income Statement
Year Ended December 31, 2014

Sales		$6,583,000
Cost of goods sold		3,572,000
Gross profit		3,011,000
Operating expenses	$2,289,000	
Gain on sale of equipment	(24,000)	2,265,000
Profit from operations		746,000
Other expenses		
Interest expense		85,000
Profit before income tax		661,000
Income tax expense		298,000
Profit		$ 363,000

Kosinski's comparative balance sheet at December 31 contained the following account balances:

	2014	2013
Cash	$ 204,500	$ 180,000
Accounts receivable	775,000	610,000
Inventories	834,000	917,000
Prepaid expenses	29,000	25,000
Equipment	6,906,000	7,065,000
Accumulated depreciation—equipment	(2,497,000)	(2,355,000)
Total assets	$6,251,500	$6,442,000
Accounts payable	$ 517,000	$ 601,000
Interest payable	6,000	0
Income taxes payable	24,500	20,000
Dividends payable	5,000	10,000
Long-term notes payable	1,500,000	2,000,000
Common shares	3,075,000	3,000,000
Retained earnings	1,124,000	811,000
Total liabilities and shareholders' equity	$6,251,500	$6,442,000

Additional information:

1. Operating expenses include depreciation expense of $880,000.
2. Accounts payable relate to the purchase of inventory.
3. Equipment that cost $984,000 was sold at a gain of $24,000.
4. New equipment was purchased during the year for $825,000.
5. Dividends declared in 2014 totalled $50,000.
6. Common shares were sold for $75,000 cash.

Instructions

Prepare the cash flow statement using (a) the indirect method or (b) the direct method, as assigned by your instructor.

Solution to Demonstration Problem

(a) Indirect method

KOSINSKI MANUFACTURING LTD.
Cash Flow Statement
Year Ended December 31, 2014

Operating activities		
Profit		$363,000
Adjustments to reconcile profit to net cash		
provided by operating activities:		
Depreciation expense	$ 880,000	
Gain on sale of equipment	(24,000)	
Increase in accounts receivable	(165,000)	
Decrease in inventories	83,000	
Increase in prepaid expenses	(4,000)	
Decrease in accounts payable	(84,000)	
Increase in interest payable	6,000	
Increase in income taxes payable	4,500	696,500
Net cash provided by operating activities		1,059,500
Investing activities		
Sale of equipment	$ 270,000	
Purchase of equipment	(825,000)	
Net cash used by investing activities		(555,000)
Financing activities		
Repayment of notes payable ($2,000,000 − $1,500,000)	$(500,000)	
Issue of common shares	75,000	
Payment of cash dividends ($50,000 + $10,000 − $5,000)	(55,000)	
Net cash used by financing activities		(480,000)
Net increase in cash		24,500
Cash, January 1		180,000
Cash, December 31		$ 204,500

Calculations:
    Accumulated depreciation on machinery sold: $2,355,000 (accumulated depreciation
        beginning) + $880,000 (depreciation expense) − $2,497,000 (accumulated
        depreciation ending) = $738,000
    Carrying amount of machinery sold: $984,000 (cost of equipment sold) − $738,000
        (accumulated depreciation) = $246,000
    Proceeds on sale: $246,000 (carrying amount) + $24,000 (gain) = $270,000

(b) Direct method

KOSINSKI MANUFACTURING LTD.
Cash Flow Statement
Year Ended December 31, 2014

Operating activities		
Cash receipts from customers		$6,418,000[1]
Cash payments		
To suppliers	$(3,573,000)[2]	
For operating expenses	(1,413,000)[3]	
For interest	(79,000)[4]	
For income tax	(293,500)[5]	(5,358,500)
Net cash provided by operating activities		1,059,500
Investing activities		
Sale of machinery	$ 270,000	
Purchase of machinery	(825,000)	
Net cash used by investing activities		(555,000)
Financing activities		
Repayment of note payable	$ (500,000)	
Issue of common shares	75,000	
Payment of cash dividends	(55,000)	
Net cash used by financing activities		(480,000)
Net increase in cash		24,500
Cash, January		180,000
Cash, December 31		$ 204,500

Calculations:
[1]Cash receipts from customers: $6,583,000 (sales) − $165,000 = $6,418,000
[2]$3,572,000 − $83,000 + $84,000 = $3,573,000
[3]$2,289,000 − $880,000 + $4,000 = $1,413,000
[4]$85,000 − $6,000 = $79,000
[5]$298,000 − $4,500 = $293,500

THE **NAVIGATOR**

Summary of Study Objectives

1. ***Describe the purpose and content of the cash flow statement.*** The cash flow statement gives information about the cash receipts and cash payments resulting from a company's operating, investing, and financing activities during the period.

   In general, operating activities include the cash effects of transactions that affect profit. Investing activities generally include cash flows resulting from changes in long-term asset items. Financing activities generally include cash flows resulting from changes in long-term liability and shareholders' equity items.

2. ***Prepare a cash flow statement using either the indirect or the direct method.*** There are four steps to prepare a cash flow statement: (1) Determine the net cash provided (used) by operating activities. In the indirect method, this is done by converting profit from an accrual basis to a cash basis. In the direct method, this is done by converting each revenue and expense from an accrual basis to a cash basis. (2) Analyze the changes in long-term asset accounts and record them as investing activities, or as significant non-cash transactions. (3) Analyze the changes in long-term liability and equity accounts and record them as financing activities, or as significant noncash transactions. (4) Prepare the cash flow statement and determine the net increase or decrease in cash.

3. ***Analyze the cash flow statement.*** The cash flow statement must be read along with the other financial statements in order to adequately assess a company's financial position. In addition, it is important to understand how the net change in cash is affected by each type of activity—operating, investing, and financing—especially when different companies are being compared. Free cash flow is a measure of solvency: it indicates how much of the cash that was generated from operating activities during the current year is available after making necessary payments for capital expenditures. It is calculated by subtracting the cash used by investing activities from the cash provided by operating activities.

THE **NAVIGATOR**

Glossary

Cash flow statement A financial statement that gives information about a company's cash receipts and cash payments during a period and classifies them as operating, investing, and financing activities. (p. 868)

Direct method A method of determining the net cash provided (used) by operating activities by adjusting each item in the income statement from the accrual basis to the cash basis. (p. 874)

Financing activities Cash flow activities from long-term liability and equity accounts. These include (a) obtaining cash by issuing debt and repaying the amounts borrowed, and (b) obtaining cash from shareholders and providing them with a return on their investment. (p. 869)

Free cash flow Cash provided by operating activities less cash used by investing activities. (p. 900)

Indirect method A method of preparing a cash flow statement in which profit is adjusted for items that did not affect cash, to determine net cash provided (used) by operating activities. (p. 874)

Investing activities Cash flow activities from long-term asset accounts. These include (a) acquiring and disposing of investments and long-lived assets, and (b) lending money and collecting on those loans. (p. 869)

Operating activities Cash flow activities that include the cash effects of transactions that create revenues and expenses, and thus affect profit. (p. 869)

Flash cards

Self-Study Questions

Answers are at the end of the chapter.

(SO 1) C 1. Which of the following is an example of a cash flow from an operating activity?
(a) A payment of cash for income tax
(b) A receipt of cash from the sale of common shares
(c) A payment of cash for the purchase of equipment used in operations
(d) A receipt of cash from the issue of a mortgage payable

(SO 1) C 2. Which of the following is an example of a cash flow from an investing activity?
(a) A receipt of cash from the issue of bonds
(b) A payment of cash to purchase common shares
(c) A receipt of cash from the sale of equipment
(d) The acquisition of land by issuing bonds

(SO 1) C 3. For a company reporting under ASPE, which of the following is an example of a cash flow from a financing activity?
(a) A receipt of cash from the sale of land
(b) An issue of debt for land
(c) A payment of dividends
(d) A cash purchase of inventory

(SO 2) AP 4. A company had profit of $215,000. Depreciation expense is $27,000. During the year, Accounts Receivable and Inventory increased by $25,000 and $18,000, respectively. Prepaid Expenses and Accounts Payable decreased by $2,000 and $8,000, respectively. There was also a loss on the sale of equipment of $3,000. Net cash provided by operating activities is:
(a) $196,000.
(b) $245,000.
(c) $193,000.
(d) $234,000.

(SO 2) C 5. It is necessary to make an adjustment for the gain or loss on a sale of a long-lived asset to determine cash provided (used) by operating activities under the indirect method because
(a) the sale of a long-lived asset is a financing activity, not an operating activity.
(b) the gain or loss is generally not recorded in the same period that cash is received from the sale of the long-lived asset.
(c) the gain or loss on the sale of a long-lived asset is the result of incorrectly recording depreciation expense over the life of the asset.
(d) the gain or loss is not equal to the cash proceeds received on the sale.

(SO 2) AP 6. The beginning balance in Accounts Receivable is $44,000. The ending balance is $42,000. Sales during the period are $149,000. Cash receipts from customers are:
(a) $151,000.
(b) $149,000.
(c) $147,000.
(d) $107,000.

(SO 2) AP 7. Retained earnings were $197,000 at the beginning of the year and $386,500 at the end of the year. Profit was $200,000. Dividends payable were $2,000 at the beginning of the year and $2,500 at the end of the year. What amount should be reported in the financing activities section of the cash flow statement for dividend payments?
(a) $500
(b) $10,000
(c) $10,500
(d) $11,000

(SO 2) AP 8. The acquisition of land by issuing common shares is
   (a) reported in the cash flow statement as both an investing and a financing transaction.
   (b) a noncash transaction and would be reported in the cash flow statement only if using the indirect method.
   (c) reported in the cash flow statement only if the statement is prepared using the direct method.
   (d) an investing and financing transaction that is not reported in the cash flow statement because it is a noncash transaction.

THE NAVIGATOR

(SO 3) C 9. If a company is in its first year of business and is rapidly growing, it would be normal to see:
   (a) negative cash from operating and investing activities, and positive cash from financing activities.
   (b) negative cash from operating activities, and positive cash from investing and financing activities.
   (c) positive cash from operating activities, and negative cash from investing and financing activities.
   (d) positive cash from operating and financing activities, and negative cash from investing activities.

(SO 3) K 10. Free cash flow gives an indication of a company's ability to generate:
   (a) sales.
   (b) profit.
   (c) cash for discretionary uses.
   (d) cash for investments.

▶ Questions

(SO 1) C 1. What is a cash flow statement and how is it useful to investors and creditors?

(SO 1) K 2. How is cash generally defined for purposes of the cash flow statement?

(SO 1) C 3. What are "cash equivalents"? Why might a company include cash equivalents with cash when preparing its cash flow statement?

(SO 1) C 4. Identify, and describe the differences among, the three types of activities reported in the cash flow statement. Give an example of each.

(SO 1) K 5. What are the general guidelines in terms of the classification of income statement and balance sheet items to operating, investing, and financing activities? Give an example of an exception to these guidelines.

(SO 1) C 6. Mandeep, the president of Cool Air Inc., a public company, asked the controller to reclassify $1 million of cash payments for interest from the operating activities section to the financing section of the cash flow statement. "We can change it back next year and report it in operating activities next year if we want to." Explain why Mandeep may want to reclassify the interest payments. Is Mandeep correct about changing the classification the following year? Why or why not?

(SO 1) K 7. During the year, Wind and Solar Power Ltd. issued $1 million of common shares in exchange for windmill equipment. Geoff, the chief financial officer, argues that the acquisition of equipment is an investing activity and the issue of common shares is a financing activity and therefore should be reported in the cash flow statement. Is Geoff correct? Explain why or why not.

(SO 2) C 8. What information is used in preparing the cash flow statement?

(SO 2) C 9. Explain why the increase or decrease in cash is not equal to the profit or loss reported in the income statement. How can a company's cash balance decrease when the company has earned profit? Conversely, how can cash increase when a company has incurred a loss?

(SO 2) C 10. Explain why increases in noncash current asset account balances are deducted from profit and increases in noncash current liability account balances are added to profit when determining cash provided (used) by operating activities using the indirect method.

(SO 2) C 11. Fresh Foods Inc. uses the indirect method to report cash provided from operating activities. Vijaya, the company president, argues, "Depreciation should not be reported as a cash inflow in the operating section of the cash flow statement, because it is not a cash flow." Is Vijaya correct? Explain why or why not.

(SO 2) C 12. Gail doesn't understand why losses are added and gains are deducted from profit when calculating cash provided (used) by operating activities in the indirect method. She argues that losses must be deducted and gains added as they are on the income statement. Explain to Gail why she is wrong.

(SO 2) C 13. For bonds payable, explain why the amortization of a bond discount is added and the amortization of a bond premium is deducted when calculating cash provided (used) by operating activities in the indirect method.

(SO 2) C 14. Environmental Equipment Ltd. reported $500,000 of sales on its income statement and $475,000 of cash collected from customers on its cash flow statement. Provide reasons why cash collected from customers is not equal to the sales reported in the income statement.

(SO 2) C 15. Under the direct method, why is depreciation expense not reported in the operating activities section?

(SO 2) A 16. During the year, Financial Services Inc. purchased $1 million of 10-year bonds for $980,000 to earn interest. Financial Services reported interest revenue of $27,300 on its investment in the bonds in its income statement and cash receipts for interest of $25,000 in its cash flow statement. Terry, the VP finance, argued, "The cash receipts for interest must be understated; the company has received all the interest owed to it. Therefore, the cash collected should equal the interest revenue reported." Is Terry correct? Explain why or why not.

(SO 2) C   17. Contrast the advantages and disadvantages of the direct and indirect methods of preparing the cash flow statement. Are both methods acceptable? Which method is preferred by standard setters? Which method is more popular? Why?

(SO 2) C   18. Goh Corporation changed its method of reporting operating activities from the indirect method to the direct method in order to make its cash flow statement more informative to its readers. Will this change increase, decrease, or not affect the net cash provided (used) by operating activities? Explain.

(SO 2) C   19. Explain how the sale of equipment at a gain is reported on a cash flow statement. Do the same for the sale of equipment at a loss.

(SO 2) C   20. If a company reported cash dividends of $80,000 in its statement of changes in shareholders' equity, would this amount also be reported as a cash outflow in the cash flow statement? Explain why or why not.

(SO 2) C   21. When should short-term notes receivable be reported in the operating activities section and when should they be reported in the investing activities section of the cash flow statement?

(SO 3) C   22. In general, should a financially healthy, growing company be providing or using cash in each of the three activities in the cash flow statement? Explain why this would normally be expected.

(SO 3) C   23. A company reported a small profit on the income statement and negative cash flow from operating and investing activities on the cash flow statement. The company reported positive cash flow from its financing activities. What might this indicate about the company's stage of development? Explain.

(SO 3) C   24. How is it possible for a company to report positive net cash from operating activities but have a negative free cash flow?

▶ Brief Exercises

BE17–1   For each of the following transactions, indicate whether it will increase (+), decrease (−), or have no effect (NE) on a company's cash flows:

(a) _____ Repayment of a mortgage payable
(b) _____ Sale of land for cash at a loss
(c) _____ Reacquisition of common shares
(d) _____ Purchase of a trading investment
(e) _____ Acquisition of equipment by an issue of common shares
(f) _____ Issuing preferred shares for cash
(g) _____ Collection of accounts receivable
(h) _____ Recording depreciation expense
(i) _____ Declaring cash dividends

Indicate impact of transactions on cash. (SO 1) AP

BE17–2   Assuming the company is reporting under ASPE, classify each of the transactions listed in BE17–1 as an operating (O), investing (I), financing (F), or significant noncash investing and financing activity (NC). If a transaction does not belong in any of these classifications, explain why.

Classify transactions by activity. (SO 1) C

BE17–3   Indicate whether each of the following transactions would be added to (+) or subtracted from (−) profit in determining the cash provided (used) by operating activities using the indirect method:

(a) _____ Depreciation expense
(b) _____ Decrease in accounts receivable
(c) _____ Increase in inventory
(d) _____ Decrease in accounts payable
(e) _____ Increase in income tax payable
(f) _____ Loss on sale of equipment
(g) _____ Gain on the sale of a long-term equity investment
(h) _____ Impairment loss for goodwill
(i) _____ Decrease in prepaid insurance

Indicate impact on cash from operating activities—indirect method. (SO 2) AP

BE17–4   Diamond Ltd. reported profit of $850,000 for the year ended November 30, 2014. Depreciation expense for the year was $175,000, accounts receivable decreased by $80,000, prepaid expenses increased by $35,000, accounts payable decreased by $170,000, and the company incurred a loss on sale of equipment of $25,000. Calculate the net cash provided (used) by operating activities using the indirect method.

Calculate cash from operating activities—indirect method. (SO 2) AP

Calculate cash from operating activities—indirect method. (SO 2) AP

BE17–5 Mirzaei Ltd. reported the following information in its balance sheet and income statement for the year ended March 31, 2014:

	2014	2013
Trading investments	$ 15,000	$10,000
Accounts receivable	60,000	40,000
Inventory	63,000	70,000
Prepaid expenses	4,000	6,000
Accounts payable	35,000	40,000
Income tax payable	16,000	10,000
Depreciation expense	50,000	
Gain on sale of equipment	45,200	
Profit	330,000	

Calculate the net cash provided (used) by operating activities using the indirect method.

Calculate cash receipts from customers—direct method. (SO 2) AP

BE17–6 Westcoast Corporation reported the following in its December 31, 2014, financial statements.

	2014	2013
Accounts receivable balance, December 31	$123,850	$137,500
Sales revenue	640,000	

Calculate the cash receipts from customers.

Calculate cash payments to suppliers—direct method. (SO 2) AP

BE17–7 Winter Sportswear Inc. reported the following in its December 31, 2014, financial statements.

	2014	2013
Inventory	$55,600	$50,000
Accounts payable	62,200	55,000
Cost of goods sold	89,500	

Calculate (a) the cost of goods purchased, and (b) cash payments to suppliers.

Calculate cash payments for operating expenses—direct method. (SO 2) AP

BE17–8 Linus Corporation reported the following in its March 31, 2014, financial statements.

	2014	2013
Prepaid expenses	$ 23,400	$12,500
Accrued expenses payable	14,900	8,500
Operating expenses	100,000	

Calculate the cash payments for operating expenses.

Calculate cash payments to employees—direct method. (SO 2) AP

BE17–9 ICE Inc. reported the following in its December 31, 2014, financial statements.

	2014	2013
Salaries payable	$ 2,500	$4,000
Salaries expense	188,000	

Calculate the cash payments to employees.

Calculate cash payments for interest—direct method. (SO 2) AP

BE17–10 RES Inc. reported the following with respect to its bonds payable in the 2014 financial statements.

	2014	2013
Interest payable	$ 10,000	$ 10,000
Bonds payable	455,000	460,000
Interest expense	25,000	

(a) Were the bonds sold at a premium or a discount?
(b) Calculate the cash payments for interest.

Calculate cash payments for trading investments—direct method. (SO 2) AP

BE17–11 Financial Traders Inc. reported the following with respect to its trading investments in the 2014 financial statements.

	2014	2013
Trading investments	$45,000	$30,000
Loss on fair value adjustment	5,500	

Calculate cash payments for the purchase of trading investments. The company did not sell any trading investments during 2014. (*Hint*: Prepare a T account for the Trading Investments account and record the beginning and closing balance and the entry to record the loss on fair value adjustment.)

BE17–12 Home Grocery Corporation reported the following in its 2014 financial statements.

Calculate cash payments for income tax—direct method. (SO 2) AP

	2014	2013
Income tax payable	$17,000	$8,000
Income tax expense	90,000	

Calculate the cash payments for income tax.

BE17–13 Angus Meat Corporation reported the following information for the year ended December 31:

Calculate cash from operating activities—direct method. (SO 2) AP

Balance sheet accounts:	2014	2013	Income statement accounts:	2014
Accounts receivable	$85,000	$60,000	Sales	$375,000
Inventory	62,000	55,000	Gain on sale of land	15,000
Prepaid expenses	5,000	9,000	Cost of goods sold	150,000
Accounts payable	35,000	42,000	Operating expenses	75,000
Income tax payable	14,000	9,000	Depreciation expense	20,000
			Income tax expense	50,000

Calculate the net cash provided (used) by operating activities using the direct method.

BE17–14 The T accounts for equipment and the related accumulated depreciation for Trevis Corporation are as follows:

Calculate cash received from sale of equipment. (SO 2) AP

Equipment				Accumulated Depreciation—Equipment				
Beg. Bal.	80,000						Beg. bal.	44,500
Purchases	41,600	Disposals	24,000	Disposals	5,500		Depreciation	12,000
End. Bal.	97,600						End. bal.	51,000

In addition, Trevis's income statement reported a loss on the sale of equipment of $1,500. (a) What will be reported on the cash flow statement with regard to the sale of equipment if Trevis uses the indirect method? (b) If Trevis uses the direct method?

BE17–15 Selected information follows for Cathrea Select Corporation at December 31:

Prepare the investing activities section of the cash flow statement. (SO 2) AP

	2014	2013
Land	$ 95,000	$ 180,000
Buildings	250,000	250,000
Accumulated depreciation—buildings	(55,000)	(45,000)
Equipment	237,000	148,000
Accumulated depreciation—equipment	(86,000)	(78,000)

Additional information:

1. Land was sold for cash at a gain of $35,000.
2. Equipment was bought for cash.
3. Equipment with a cost of $58,000 and a carrying amount of $18,000 was sold at a gain of $5,000.

Prepare the investing activities section of the cash flow statement.

BE17–16 The following was reported in Sanaz Ltd.'s 2014 financial statements.

Calculate cash paid for dividends. (SO 2) AP

	2014	2013
Dividends payable	$ 24,000	$ 20,000
Retained earnings	261,000	114,000
Profit	197,000	

Calculate cash payments for dividends.

BE17–17 Selected information follows for Cathrea Select Corporation at December 31:

Prepare the financing activities section of the cash flow statement. (SO 2) AP

	2014	2013
Dividends payable	$ 20,000	$ 15,000
Bonds payable	995,000	990,000
Mortgage notes payable	475,000	200,000
Common shares	55,000	45,000
Retained earnings	165,000	85,000

Additional information:

1. Interest expense on the bonds payable was $55,000, which included $5,000 of amortization of the bond discount.
2. Principal payments on the mortgage payable were $25,000.
3. A building was purchased for $500,000 by paying $200,000 cash and signing a mortgage note payable for the balance.
4. Profit for the year was $145,000.

Assuming the company reports under ASPE, prepare the financing activities section of the cash flow statement.

Prepare cash flow statement.
(SO 2) AP

BE17–18   The following information is available for Baker Corporation for the year ended April 30, 2014:

Cash, May 1, 2013	$ 8,500
Cash provided by operating activities	49,000
Other cash receipts	
Sale of equipment at a loss of $1,200	6,000
Issue of non-trade note payable	20,000
Other cash payments	
Dividends	25,000
Reacquisition of common shares	19,000
Purchase of land for $100,000, partially financed by issuing a	
$75,000 mortgage note payable	25,000
Additional information	
Issued a $75,000 mortgage note payable to partially finance	
purchase of land for $100,000.	

Prepare a cash flow statement for the year, including any required note disclosure.

Use cash flows to identify new company. (SO 3) AN

BE17–19   Two companies reported the following information.

	Company A	Company B
Profit (loss)	$ (5,000)	$100,000
Cash provided (used) by operating activities	(10,000)	50,000
Cash provided (used) by investing activities	(70,000)	30,000
Cash provided (used) by financing activities	120,000	(100,000)

(a) Calculate free cash flow for each company.
(b) Which company is more likely to be in the early stages of its development? Explain.

▶ Exercises

Classify transactions.
(SO 1) AP

E17–1   Eng Corporation, a private corporation reporting under ASPE, had the following transactions:

Transaction	(a) Classification	(b) Cash Inflow or Outflow
1. Sold inventory for $1,000 cash.	O	+$1,000
2. Purchased a machine for $30,000. Made a $5,000 down payment and issued a long-term note for the remainder.	_____	_____
3. Issued common shares for $50,000.	_____	_____
4. Collected $16,000 of accounts receivable.	_____	_____
5. Paid a $25,000 cash dividend.	_____	_____
6. Sold a long-term equity investment with a carrying value of $15,000 for $10,000.	_____	_____
7. Redeemed bonds having an amortized cost of $200,000 for $175,000.	_____	_____
8. Paid $18,000 on accounts payable.	_____	_____
9. Purchased inventory for $28,000 on account.	_____	_____
10. Purchased a long-term investment in bonds for $100,000.	_____	_____
11. Sold equipment with a carrying amount of $16,000 for $13,000.	_____	_____
12. Paid $12,000 interest expense on long-term notes payable.	_____	_____

Instructions

Complete the above table for each of the following requirements. The first one has been done for you as an example.

(a) Classify each transaction as an operating activity (O), investing activity (I), financing activity (F), or noncash transaction (NC).
(b) Specify whether the transaction represents a cash inflow (+), cash outflow (−), or has no effect (NE) on cash, and in what amount.

E17–2   Pesci Ltd. is a private company reporting under ASPE. Its income statement and changes in current assets and current liabilities for the year are reported below:

Prepare operating activities section—indirect method.
(SO 2) AP

PESCI LTD.		
Income Statement		
Year Ended November 30, 2014		
Sales		$948,000
Cost of goods sold		490,000
Gross profit		458,000
Operating expenses	$310,000	
Depreciation expense	50,000	
Gain on sale of equipment	(10,000)	350,000
Profit before income tax		108,000
Income tax expense		30,000
Profit		$ 78,000
Changes in current assets and current liabilities were as follows:		
Accounts receivable	$36,000	decrease
Inventory	19,000	increase
Prepaid expenses	2,000	increase
Accounts payable	12,000	decrease
Dividends payable	5,000	decrease
Income taxes payable	4,000	decrease

Instructions

Prepare the operating activities section of the cash flow statement using the indirect method.

E17–3   Using the data presented for Pesci Ltd. in E17–2, prepare the operating activities section of the cash flow statement using the direct method.

Prepare operating activities section—direct method.
(SO 2) AP

E17–4   The current assets and liabilities sections of the comparative balance sheets of Charron Inc., a private company reporting under ASPE, at October 31 are presented below:

Prepare operating activities section—indirect method.
(SO 2) AP

CHARRON INC.		
Comparative Balance Sheet Accounts		
	2014	2013
Cash	$99,000	$105,000
Trading investments	12,000	0
Accounts receivable	52,000	41,000
Inventory	32,500	46,000
Prepaid expenses	7,500	5,800
Accounts payable	43,000	36,000
Accrued expenses payable	5,000	8,000
Dividends payable	24,000	17,000
Income taxes payable	6,800	11,800

CHARRON INC.
Income Statement
Year Ended October 31, 2014

Sales		$625,000
Cost of goods sold		390,000
Gross profit		235,000
Operating expenses	$88,000	
Depreciation expense	23,000	
Gain on fair value adjustment—trading investments	(2,000)	
Loss on sale of equipment	10,000	119,000
Profit before income taxes		116,000
Income taxes		29,000
Profit		$ 87,000

Instructions

Prepare the operating activities section of the cash flow statement using the indirect method.

Calculate operating cash flows—direct method.
(SO 2) AP

E17–5 The following information is taken from the general ledger of Robinson Limited:

1. Sales revenue	$275,000
Accounts receivable, January 1	22,900
Accounts receivable, December 31	37,000
2. Cost of goods sold	$110,000
Inventory, January 1	9,200
Inventory, December 31	5,900
Accounts payable, January 1	8,600
Accounts payable, December 31	6,900
3. Operating expenses	$ 70,000
Depreciation expense (included in operating expenses)	20,000
Prepaid expenses, January 1	3,000
Prepaid expenses, December 31	5,500
Accrued expenses payable, January 1	6,500
Accrued expenses payable, December 31	4,500
4. Interest expense	$ 18,000
Interest payable, January 1	4,000
Interest payable, December 31	4,000
Bonds payable, January 1	395,000
Bonds payable, December 31	397,000
5. Gain on fair value adjustment	$ 6,000
Trading investments, January 1	8,000
Trading investments, December 31	17,000

Instructions

Using the direct method, calculate:
(a) cash receipts from customers
(b) cash payments to suppliers
(c) cash payments for operating expenses
(d) cash payments for interest expense
(e) cash payments for trading investments

Prepare operating activities section—direct method.
(SO 2) AP

E17–6 McTavish Ltd. completed its first year of operations on September 30, 2014. McTavish reported the following information at September 30, 2014:

McTAVISH LTD.
Selected balance sheet account balances at September 30, 2014

Accounts receivable	$23,000
Prepaid expenses	3,100
Accrued expenses payable	10,500
Interest payable	500
Dividends payable	3,800
Income taxes payable	9,800

McTAVISH LTD.
Income Statement
Year Ended September 30, 2014

Service revenue		$285,000
Operating expenses	$122,000	
Depreciation expense	12,300	
Gain on sale of equipment	(5,750)	128,550
Profit from operations		156,450
Interest expense		4,000
Profit before income tax		152,450
Income tax expense		38,500
Profit		$113,950

Instructions

Assuming that McTavish reports under ASPE, prepare the operating section of a cash flow statement using the direct method.

E17–7   The income statement and account balances for Charron Inc. are presented in E17–4.

Instructions

Prepare the operating section of a cash flow statement using the direct method.

Prepare operating activities section—direct method. (SO 2) AP

E17–8   Dupré Corp. is a private company reporting under ASPE. The following selected accounts are from the general ledger for the year ended December 31, 2014:

Determine investing and financing activities. (SO 2) AP

Equipment					Accumulated Depreciation—Equipment			
Jan. 1	260,000						Jan. 1	117,000
July 31	65,000	Nov. 10	46,000	Nov. 10	38,000			
Sept. 2	53,000						Dec. 31	33,000
Dec. 31	332,000						Dec. 31	112,000

Notes Payable					Retained Earnings			
		Jan. 1	0				Jan. 1	130,000
Dec. 2	10,000	Sept. 2	50,000	Aug. 23	8,000		Dec. 31	84,000
		Dec. 31	40,000				Dec. 31	206,000

Additional information:

July 31	Equipment was purchased for cash.
Sept. 2	Equipment was purchased and partially financed through the issue of a note.
Aug. 23	A cash dividend was paid.
Nov. 10	A loss of $3,000 was incurred on the sale of equipment.
Dec. 2	A partial payment on the note payable was made plus $375 of interest.
Dec. 31	Depreciation expense was recorded for the year.
Dec. 31	Closing entries were recorded.

Instructions

From the postings in the above accounts and additional information provided, indicate what information would be reported in the investing and/or financing activities sections of the cash flow statement, including any required note disclosure.

Determine investing and financing activities. (SO 2) AP

E17–9 Preferred Homes Ltd., a private company reporting under ASPE, reported the following for the year ended September 30, 2014:

	2014	2013
Land	$300,000	$200,000
Building	350,000	350,000
Equipment	139,000	125,000
Accumulated depreciation	65,000	55,000
Dividends payable	10,000	20,000
Mortgage note payable	110,000	50,000
Common shares	225,000	150,000
Contributed surplus-reacquisition of common shares	10,000	0
Retained earnings	220,000	80,000
Depreciation expense	15,000	
Gain on equipment sold	2,000	
Profit	210,000	

Additional information:

1. Equipment was purchased for $20,000.
2. Land was purchased for $35,000 cash and a mortgage note payable was issued.
3. Common shares were issued for $100,000 cash.
4. During the year Preferred Homes Ltd. redeemed some common shares.

Instructions

Prepare the investing and financing activities sections of the cash flow statement and any required note disclosure. (*Hint:* Use "T" accounts to help you calculate the cash flows.)

Prepare cash flow statement— indirect method. (SO 2) AP

E17–10 Savary Limited is a private company reporting under ASPE. Its comparative balance sheet at December 31 is as follows:

SAVARY LIMITED
Balance Sheet
December 31

Assets	2014	2013
Cash	$ 114,000	$ 85,000
Accounts receivable	750,000	600,000
Inventory	500,000	330,000
Prepaid insurance	18,000	25,000
Equipment and vehicles	1,250,000	1,000,000
Accumulated depreciation	(350,000)	(280,000)
Total assets	$2,282,000	$1,760,000
Liabilities and Shareholders' Equity		
Accounts payable	$ 226,000	$ 200,000
Salaries payable	30,000	40,000
Interest payable	26,000	20,000
Notes payable (non-trade)	500,000	350,000
Preferred shares	200,000	0
Common shares	400,000	400,000
Retained earnings	900,000	750,000
Total liabilities and shareholders' equity	$2,282,000	$1,760,000

Additional information:

1. Profit for 2014 was $200,000.

2. Equipment was purchased during the year. No equipment was sold.
3. Cash dividends were paid to the preferred shareholders during the year.

Instructions

Prepare the cash flow statement using the indirect method.

E17–11 The accounting records of Flypaper Airlines Inc. reveal the following transactions and events for the year ended March 31, 2014:

Prepare cash flow statement—direct method. (SO 2) AP

Payment of interest	$ 8,000	Payment of salaries	$ 51,000
Cash sales	53,000	Depreciation expense	16,000
Receipt of dividend revenue	14,000	Proceeds from sale of aircraft	212,000
Payment of income tax	7,500	Purchase of equipment for cash	22,000
Profit	38,000	Loss on sale of aircraft	3,000
Payment of accounts payable	110,000	Payment of dividends	14,000
Payment for land	174,000	Payment of operating expenses	28,000
Collection of accounts receivable	201,000	Net receipts for trading investments	5,600
Common shares issued in exchange for land	35,000		

Additional information:

Flypaper Airlines' cash on April 1, 2013, was $35,000.

Instructions

Assuming Flypaper reports under ASPE, prepare a cash flow statement using the direct method.

E17–12 The comparative balance sheet for Storm Adventures Ltd., a private company reporting under ASPE, follows:

Prepare cash flow statement—indirect and direct methods. (SO 2) AP

STORM ADVENTURES LTD. Balance Sheet December 31		
Assets	**2014**	**2013**
Cash	$ 43,000	$ 12,600
Accounts receivable	76,000	85,000
Inventories	160,000	172,000
Prepaid expenses	12,000	5,000
Land	50,000	75,000
Equipment	270,000	190,000
Accumulated depreciation	(90,000)	(40,000)
Total assets	$ 521,000	$499,600
Liabilities and Shareholders' Equity		
Accounts payable	$ 43,000	$ 38,000
Dividends payable	7,500	5,000
Income taxes payable	2,500	6,000
Bonds payable	120,000	180,000
Common shares	207,000	167,000
Retained earnings	141,000	103,600
Total liabilities and shareholders' equity	$ 521,000	$499,600

Additional information:

1. Profit for 2014 was $69,900.
2. Bonds payable of $60,000 were retired at maturity.
3. Common shares were issued for $40,000.
4. Land was sold at a loss of $10,000.
5. No equipment was sold during 2014.
6. Net sales for the year were $678,000.
7. Cost of goods sold for the year was $439,800.
8. Operating expenses (not including depreciation expense) were $80,000.
9. Interest expense was $5,000.
10. Income tax expense was $23,300.

Instructions

Prepare a cash flow statement using (a) the indirect method or (b) the direct method, as assigned by your instructor.

Compare cash flows for two companies. (SO 3) AN

E17–13 Condensed cash flow statements are as follows for two companies operating in the same industry:

	Company A	Company B
Cash provided (used) by operating activities	$200,000	$(180,000)
Cash provided (used) by investing activities	(20,000)	(20,000)
Cash provided (used) by financing activities	(60,000)	320,000
Increase in cash	120,000	120,000
Cash, beginning of period	30,000	30,000
Cash, end of period	$150,000	$ 150,000

Instructions

Which company is in a better financial position? Explain why.

Calculate and discuss free cash flow. (SO 3) AN

E17–14 Selected information for a recent year follows for **Bank of Montreal** and **Scotiabank** (in millions):

	Bank of Montreal	Scotiabank
Profit	$ 3,266	$ 5,268
Cash provided (used) by operating activities	572	1,063
Cash provided (used) by investing activities	(12,768)	(33,778)
Cash provided (used) by financing activities	13,757	33,338

Instructions

(a) Calculate the increase or decrease in cash for each company.
(b) Calculate the free cash flow for each company.
(c) Which company appears to be in a stronger financial position? Explain.
(d) In what way might a bank's free cash flow be different from the free cash flow of a manufacturing company?

▶ Problems: Set A

Classify transactions by activity. Indicate impact on cash and profit. (SO 1) AP

P17–1A You are provided with the following transactions that took place during a recent fiscal year:

Transaction	(a) Classification	(b) Cash	(c) Profit
1. Paid telephone bill for the month.	O	—	—
2. Sold equipment for cash, at a loss.			
3. Sold a trading investment, at a gain.			
4. Acquired a building by paying 10% in cash and signing a mortgage payable for the balance.			
5. Made principal repayments on the mortgage.			
6. Paid interest on the mortgage.			
7. Sold inventory on account, at a price greater than cost.			
8. Paid wages owing (previously accrued) to employees.			
9. Declared and distributed a stock dividend to common shareholders.			
10. Paid rent in advance.			
11. Sold inventory for cash, at a price greater than cost.			
12. Wrote down the value of inventory to net realizable value, which was lower than cost.			
13. Received semi-annual bond interest.			
14. Received dividends on an investment in associate.			
15. Issued common shares.			
16. Paid a cash dividend to common shareholders.			
17. Collected cash from customers on account.			
18. Collected service revenue in advance.			

Instructions

Assuming the company is reporting under IFRS, complete the above table for each of the following requirements. The first one has been done for you as an example.

(a) Classify each transaction as an operating activity (O), an investing activity (I), a financing activity (F), or a noncash transaction (NC) on the cash flow statement. If there is a choice of how a transaction is classified, indicate the alternative classifications.

(b) Specify whether the transaction will increase (+), decrease (−), or have no effect (NE) on cash reported on the balance sheet.

(c) Specify whether the transaction will increase (+), decrease (−), or have no effect (NE) on profit reported on the income statement.

TAKING IT FURTHER   Explain how an operating activity can increase cash but not increase profit.

P17–2A   Molloy Ltd. reported the following for the fiscal year 2014:

Prepare operating activities section—indirect and direct methods. (SO 2) AP

MOLLOY LTD. Income Statement Year Ended September 30, 2014		
Sales		$580,000
Cost of goods sold		340,000
Gross profit		240,000
Operating expenses	$ 96,000	
Depreciation expense	25,000	
Gain on sale of land	(35,000)	86,000
Profit before income tax		154,000
Income tax expense		38,000
Profit		$116,000

Additional information:

1. Accounts receivable decreased by $15,000 during the year.
2. Inventory increased by $7,000 during the year.
3. Prepaid expenses decreased by $5,000 during the year.
4. Accounts payable to suppliers increased by $10,000 during the year.
5. Accrued expenses payable increased by $4,000 during the year.
6. Income tax payable decreased by $6,000 during the year.

Instructions

Prepare the operating activities section of the cash flow statement using (a) the indirect method or (b) the direct method, as assigned by your instructor.

TAKING IT FURTHER   In what circumstances will the direct method result in a different amount of cash provided (used) by operations than the indirect method.

P17–3A   The income statement of Hanalei International Inc. contained the following condensed information:

Prepare operating activities section—indirect and direct methods. (SO 2) AP

HANALEI INTERNATIONAL INC. Income Statement Year Ended December 31, 2014		
Service revenue		$480,000
Operating expenses	$245,000	
Depreciation expense	35,000	
Loss on sale of equipment	25,000	305,000
Profit from operations		175,000
Other revenues and expenses		
Interest expense		10,000
Profit before income taxes		165,000
Income tax expense		41,250
Profit		$123,750

Hanalei's balance sheet contained the following comparative data at December 31:

	2014	2013
Accounts receivable	$52,000	$40,000
Prepaid insurance	5,000	8,000
Accounts payable	30,000	41,000
Interest payable	2,000	1,250
Income tax payable	3,000	4,500
Unearned revenue	12,000	8,000

Additional information: Accounts payable relate to operating expenses.

Instructions

Assuming Hanalei reports under ASPE, prepare the operating activities section of the cash flow statement using (a) the indirect method or (b) the direct method, as assigned by your instructor.

TAKING IT FURTHER What are the advantages and disadvantages of the direct method of determining cash provided (used) by operating activities?

Calculate cash flows for investing and financing activities. (SO 2) AP

P17–4A The following selected account balances were reported in Trudeau Inc's financial statements. Trudeau Inc., a private company reporting under ASPE, at year end:

	2014	2013
Cash	$ 22,125	$ 10,000
Buildings	850,000	750,000
Equipment	393,000	340,000
Land	100,000	60,000
Accumulated depreciation—buildings	307,500	300,000
Accumulated depreciation—equipment	124,000	94,000
Dividends payable	6,250	2,500
Bonds payable	590,000	585,000
Mortgage notes payable	340,000	310,000
Preferred shares: 2,250 shares in 2014; 2,750 in 2013	225,000	275,000
Common shares: 54,000 shares in 2014; 40,000 in 2013	540,000	410,000
Contributed surplus—reacquisition of common shares	2,000	0
Retained earnings	200,000	100,000
Cash dividends declared	25,000	10,000
Depreciation expense—buildings	25,000	42,500
Depreciation expense—equipment	49,125	27,000
Gain on sale of equipment	1,000	0
Loss on sale of building	10,000	0
Interest expense	48,250	44,750

Additional information:

1. Purchased $75,000 of equipment for $10,000 cash and a mortgage note payable for the remainder.
2. Equipment was also sold during the year.
3. Sold a building that originally cost $50,000.
4. Used cash to purchase land and a building.
5. Included in interest expense is amortization of the bond payable discount, $5,000.
6. Mortgage payments included interest and principal amounts.
7. Converted 500 preferred shares to 5,000 common shares.
8. Common shares were issued for cash.
9. Reacquired 1,000 common shares with an average cost of $10/share for cash during the year.

Instructions

(a) Determine the amount of any cash inflows or outflows related to investing activities in 2014. (*Hint:* Use "T" accounts to calculate the cash flows.)

(b) What was the amount of profit reported by Trudeau Inc. in 2014?

(c) Determine the amount of any cash inflows or outflows related to financing activities in 2014. (*Hint:* Use "T" accounts to calculate the cash flows.)

(d) Identify and determine the amount of any noncash financing activities in 2014.

(e) Calculate the cash from net cash provided (used) by operating activities. (*Hint*: Using the cash balances provided, calculate increase or decrease in cash first.)

TAKING IT FURTHER   Is it unfavourable for a company to have a net cash outflow from investing activities?

P17–5A   Coyote Ltd., a private company reporting under ASPE, reported the following for the years ended May 31, 2014 and 2013.

Prepare a cash flow statement—indirect method. (SO 2) AP

COYOTE LTD. Balance Sheet May 31		
Assets	2014	2013
Cash	$ 12,600	$ 43,000
Accounts receivable	85,000	76,000
Inventories	172,000	160,000
Prepaid expenses	5,000	7,500
Land	125,000	75,000
Equipment	325,000	190,000
Accumulated depreciation	(68,250)	(40,000)
Total assets	$656,350	$511,500
Liabilities and Shareholders' Equity		
Accounts payable	$ 43,000	$ 38,000
Dividends payable	7,500	5,000
Income taxes payable	2,500	6,000
Mortgage note payable	125,000	80,000
Common shares	217,000	167,000
Retained earnings	261,350	215,500
Total liabilities and shareholders' equity	$656,350	$511,500

Additional information:

1. Profit for 2014 was $108,000.
2. Common shares were issued for $50,000.
3. Land with a cost of $50,000 was sold at a loss of $20,000.
4. Purchased land with a cost of $100,000 with a $55,000 down payment and financed the remainder with a mortgage note payable.
5. No equipment was sold during 2014.

Instructions

Prepare a cash flow statement for the year using the indirect method.

TAKING IT FURTHER   Is it unfavourable for a company to have a net cash outflow from financing activities?

P17–6A   Refer to the information presented for Coyote Ltd. in P17–5A.

Prepare cash flow statement—direct method. (SO 2) AP

Additional information:

1. Net sales for the year were $673,250.
2. Cost of goods sold for the year was $403,950.
3. Operating expenses, including depreciation expense, were $100,300.
4. Interest expense was $5,000.
5. Income tax expense was $36,000.
6. Accounts payable is used for merchandise purchases.

Instructions

Prepare a cash flow statement for the year using the direct method.

TAKING IT FURTHER   Indicate what transactions might be classified differently if the company was reporting under IFRS instead of ASPE.

Prepare cash flow statement—
indirect method. (SO 2) AP

P17–7A Condensed financial data follow for E-Perform Ltd.

E-PERFORM LTD.
Balance Sheet
December 31

Assets	2014	2013
Cash	$ 97,800	$ 48,400
Accounts receivable	75,800	43,000
Inventory	122,500	92,850
Prepaid expenses	38,400	26,000
Long-term equity investments	128,000	114,000
Property, plant, and equipment	270,000	242,500
Accumulated depreciation	(50,000)	(52,000)
Total assets	$682,500	$514,750

Liabilities and Shareholders' Equity	2014	2013
Accounts payable	$ 93,000	$ 77,300
Accrued expenses payable	11,500	7,000
Notes payable (non-trade)	110,000	150,000
Common shares	220,000	175,000
Retained earnings	234,000	105,450
Accumulated other comprehensive income	14,000	0
Total liabilities and shareholders' equity	$682,500	$514,750

E-PERFORM LTD.
Income Statement
Year Ended December 31, 2014

Sales		$492,780
Cost of goods sold		185,460
Gross profit		307,320
Operating expenses	$62,410	
Depreciation expense	46,500	
Loss on sale of equipment	7,500	116,410
Profit from operations		190,910
Other expenses		
Interest expense		4,730
Profit before income tax		186,180
Income tax expense		45,000
Profit		$141,180

Additional information:

1. New equipment costing $85,000 was purchased for $25,000 cash and a $60,000 note payable.
2. Equipment with an original cost of $57,500 was sold at a loss of $7,500.
3. Notes payable matured during the year and were repaid.
4. E-Perform records any gains and losses on its long-term equity investment as other comprehensive income. There were no purchases or sales of long-term equity investments during the year.

Instructions

Prepare a cash flow statement for the year using the indirect method.

TAKING IT FURTHER If a company has a loss, does that also mean that there has been a net reduction in cash from operating activities? Explain.

Prepare cash flow statement—
direct method. (SO 2) AP

P17–8A Refer to the information presented for E-Perform Ltd. in P17–7A.

Additional information:

1. Accounts payable relate only to merchandise creditors.
2. Accrued expenses payable and prepaid expenses relate to operating expenses.

Instructions

Prepare a cash flow statement for the year using the direct method.

TAKING IT FURTHER   E-Perform Ltd.'s cash balance more than doubled in 2014. Briefly explain what caused this, using the cash flow statement.

P17–9A   The financial statements of Wetaskiwin Ltd., private company reporting under ASPE, follow:

Prepare cash flow statement—indirect method. (SO 2) AP

WETASKIWIN LTD.
Balance Sheet
December 31

Assets	2014	2013
Cash	$ 9,000	$ 10,000
Short-term notes receivable	14,000	23,000
Accounts receivable	28,000	14,000
Inventory	29,000	25,000
Property, plant, and equipment	73,000	78,000
Accumulated depreciation	(30,000)	(24,000)
Total assets	$123,000	$126,000

Liabilities and Shareholders' Equity		
Accounts payable	$ 25,000	$ 43,000
Income tax payable	3,000	20,000
Notes payable	15,000	10,000
Common shares	25,000	25,000
Retained earnings	55,000	28,000
Total liabilities and shareholders' equity	$123,000	$126,000

WETASKIWIN LTD.
Income Statement
Year Ended December 31, 2014

Sales		$286,000
Cost of goods sold		194,000
Gross profit		92,000
Operating expenses	$38,000	
Loss on sale of equipment	2,000	40,000
Profit from operations		52,000
Other revenues and expenses		
Interest revenue	$(1,000)	
Interest expense	2,000	1,000
Profit before income tax		51,000
Income tax expense		15,000
Profit		$ 36,000

Additional information:

1. Short-term notes receivable are from loans to other companies. During the year, the company collected the outstanding balance at December 31, 2013, and made new loans in the amount of $14,000.
2. Equipment was sold during the year. This equipment cost $15,000 originally and had a carrying amount of $10,000 at the time of sale.
3. Equipment costing $10,000 was purchased in exchange for a $10,000 note payable.
4. Depreciation expense is included in operating expenses.

Instructions

Prepare a cash flow statement for the year using the indirect method.

TAKING IT FURTHER   Wetaskiwin Ltd. had a relatively small change in its cash balance in 2014; cash decreased by only $1,000. Is it still necessary or important to prepare a cash flow statement? Explain.

Prepare cash flow statement—
direct method. (SO 2) AP

P17–10A Refer to the information presented Wetaskiwin Ltd. in P17–9A.

Additional information:

1. Accounts receivable are from the sale of merchandise on credit.
2. Accounts payable relate to the purchase of merchandise on credit.

Instructions

Prepare a cash flow statement for the year using the direct method.

TAKING IT FURTHER Wetaskiwin Ltd. had a positive cash balance at the beginning and end of 2014. Given that, is it possible that the company could have had a negative cash balance at one or more points during the year? Explain.

Prepare cash flow statement—
indirect method. (SO 2) AP

P17–11A Presented below is the comparative balance sheet for Diatessaron Inc., a private company reporting under ASPE, at December 31, 2014 and 2013:

DIATESSARON INC.
Balance Sheet
December 31

Assets	2014	2013
Cash	$ 67,000	$ 98,000
Accounts receivable	101,000	75,000
Inventory	205,000	155,500
Long-term debt investment	101,500	0
Property, plant, and equipment	535,000	460,000
Less: Accumulated depreciation	(162,500)	(140,000)
	$847,000	$648,500

Liabilities and Shareholders' Equity		
Accounts payable	$ 57,500	$ 47,000
Dividends payable	6,000	0
Income tax payable	14,000	15,000
Long-term notes payable	25,000	0
Common shares	630,000	525,000
Retained earnings	114,500	61,500
	$847,000	$648,500

DIATESSARON INC.
Income Statement
Year Ended December 31, 2014

Sales		$663,000
Cost of goods sold		432,000
Gross profit		231,000
Operating expenses	$147,500	
Loss on sale of equipment	3,000	150,500
Profit from operations		80,500
Interest expense	3,000	
Interest revenue	(4,500)	(1,500)
Profit before income tax		82,000
Income tax expense		14,000
Profit		$ 68,000

Additional information:

1. Cash dividends of $15,000 were declared.
2. A long-term debt investment was acquired for cash at a cost of $102,000.
3. Depreciation expense is included in the operating expenses.
4. The company issued 10,500 common shares for cash on March 2, 2014. The fair value of the shares was $10 per share. The proceeds were used to purchase additional equipment.

5. Equipment that originally cost $30,000 was sold during the year for cash. The equipment had a carrying value of $9,000 at the time of sale.
6. The company issued a note payable for $28,000 and repaid $3,000 by year end.

Instructions

Prepare a cash flow statement for the year using the indirect method.

TAKING IT FURTHER   Is it necessary to show both the proceeds from issuing a new note payable and the partial repayment of notes payable? Or is it sufficient to simply show the net increase or decrease in notes payable, as is done with accounts payable? Explain.

P17–12A   Refer to the information presented for Diatessaron Inc. in P17–11A.

Prepare cash flow statement— direct method. (SO 2) AP

Additional information:

1. All purchases of inventory are on credit.
2. Accounts payable is used only to record purchases of inventory.

Instructions

Prepare a cash flow statement for the year using the direct method.

TAKING IT FURTHER   Why is it necessary to know that Accounts Payable is used for purchases of inventory when using the direct method, but not the indirect method?

P17–13A   Selected information (in US$ millions) for two close competitors, **Potash Corporation of Saskatchewan Inc.** and **Agrium Inc.**, follows for the year ended December 31, 2011:

Calculate free cash flow and evaluate cash. (SO 3) AN

	Potash	Agrium
Profit	$3,081	$1,508
Cash provided by operating activities	3,485	1,350
Cash used by investing activities	(2,251)	(151)
Cash used by financing activities	(1,216)	(423)
Cash and cash equivalents, end of period	430	635
Dividends paid	(208)	(18)

Instructions

(a) Calculate the free cash flow for each company.
(b) Which company appears to be in the stronger financial position?

TAKING IT FURTHER   By comparing the companies' cash flows, can you tell which company is likely in a growth stage? Explain.

▶ Problems: Set B

P17–1B   You are provided with the following transactions that took place during a recent fiscal year:

Classify transactions by activity. Indicate impact on cash and profit. (SO 1) AP

Transaction	(a) Classification	(b) Cash	(c) Profit
1. Paid wages to employees.	O	—	—
2. Sold land for cash, at a gain.			
3. Acquired land by issuing common shares.			
4. Paid a cash dividend to preferred shareholders.			
5. Performed services for cash.			
6. Performed services on account.			
7. Purchased inventory for cash.			
8. Purchased inventory on account.			
9. Paid income tax.			
10. Made principal repayment on a trade note payable.			
11. Paid semi-annual bond interest.			
12. Received rent from a tenant in advance.			

13. Recorded depreciation expense.	____	____	____
14. Reacquired common shares at a price greater than the average cost of the shares.	____	____	____
15. Issued preferred shares for cash.	____	____	____
16. Collected cash from customers on account.	____	____	____
17. Issued a non-trade note payable.	____	____	____
18. Paid insurance for the month.	____	____	____

Instructions

Assuming the company is reporting under IFRS, complete the above table for each of the following requirements, assuming none of the transactions were previously accrued. The first one has been done for you as an example.

(a) Classify each transaction as an operating activity (O), an investing activity (I), a financing activity (F), or a noncash transaction (NC) on the cash flow statement. If there is choice on how a transaction is classified, indicate the alternative classifications.

(b) Specify whether the transaction will increase (+), decrease (−), or have no effect (NE) on cash reported on the balance sheet.

(c) Specify whether the transaction will increase (+), decrease (−), or have no effect (NE) on profit reported on the income statement.

TAKING IT FURTHER   Explain how an operating activity can decrease cash but not decrease profit.

Prepare operating activities section—indirect and direct methods. (SO 2) AP

P17–2B   Lui Inc. reported the following for the fiscal year 2014:

LUI INC.
Income Statement
Year Ended May 31, 2014

Sales		$820,000
Cost of goods sold		492,000
Gross profit		328,000
Operating expenses	$162,000	
Depreciation expense	28,500	
Loss on sale of equipment	9,500	200,000
Profit from operations		128,000
Other expenses		
Interest expense		7,500
Profit before income taxes		120,500
Income tax expense		30,000
Profit		$ 90,500

Additional information:

1. Accounts receivable decreased by $21,000 during the year.
2. Inventory increased by $32,000 during the year.
3. Prepaid expenses decreased by $7,000 during the year.
4. Accounts payable to suppliers decreased by $5,000 during the year.
5. Accrued expenses payable increased by $8,500 during the year.
6. Interest payable increased by $3,500 during the year.
7. Income tax payable decreased by $6,500 during the year.

Instructions

Assuming the company reports under ASPE, prepare the operating activities section of the cash flow statement using (a) the indirect method or (b) the direct method, as assigned by your instructor.

TAKING IT FURTHER   Will the amount of cash provided (used) by operations always be the same amount if it is determined by using the direct method or the indirect method? Explain.

P17–3B   Sable Island Ltd. is a private company reporting under ASPE. Its income statement contained the following condensed information: *Prepare operating activities section—indirect and direct methods. (SO 2) AP*

<table>
<tr><td colspan="3" align="center">SABLE ISLAND LTD.
Income Statement
Year Ended December 31, 2014</td></tr>
<tr><td>Fees earned</td><td></td><td>$900,000</td></tr>
<tr><td>Operating expenses</td><td>$642,000</td><td></td></tr>
<tr><td>Depreciation expense</td><td>50,000</td><td></td></tr>
<tr><td>Gain on sale of equipment</td><td>(23,000)</td><td>669,000</td></tr>
<tr><td>Profit from operations</td><td></td><td>231,000</td></tr>
<tr><td>Other expenses</td><td></td><td></td></tr>
<tr><td>   Interest expense</td><td></td><td>5,000</td></tr>
<tr><td>Profit before income tax</td><td></td><td>226,000</td></tr>
<tr><td>Income tax expense</td><td></td><td>56,500</td></tr>
<tr><td>Profit</td><td></td><td>$169,500</td></tr>
</table>

Sable Island's balance sheet contained the following comparative data at December 31:

	2014	2013
Accounts receivable	$48,000	$56,000
Prepaid expenses	14,000	11,500
Accounts payable	41,000	36,000
Income tax payable	4,000	9,250
Interest payable	1,000	550
Unearned revenue	13,750	10,000

Additional information: Accounts payable relate to operating expenses.

Instructions

Prepare the operating activities section of the cash flow statement using (a) the indirect method or (b) the direct method, as assigned by your instructor.

TAKING IT FURTHER   What are the advantages and disadvantages of the indirect method of determining cash provided (used) by operating activities?

P17–4B   Bird Corp., a private company reporting under ASPE, reported the following in its financial statements: *Calculate cash flows for investing and financing activities. (SO 2) AP*

	2014	2013
Cash	$ 21,000	$ 5,000
Accumulated depreciation—buildings	578,750	600,000
Accumulated depreciation—equipment	218,000	192,000
Depreciation expense—buildings	31,250	30,000
Depreciation expense—equipment	48,000	45,000
Buildings	1,310,000	1,250,000
Equipment	492,000	480,000
Land	250,000	200,000
Bonds payable	214,000	216,000
Long-term notes payable	240,000	350,000
Mortgage note payable	155,000	0
Preferred shares: 7,000 shares in 2014; 5,000 in 2013	175,000	125,000
Common shares: 8,000 shares in 2014; 10,000 in 2013	123,200	154,000
Contributed surplus—reacquisition of common shares	1,500	0
Cash dividends—preferred	6,250	6,250
Retained earnings	300,000	240,000
Interest expense	23,000	28,000
Loss on sale of equipment	5,000	0
Gain on sale of building	18,000	0

Additional information:

1. Purchased land for $50,000 and buildings for $130,000 by making a $25,000 down payment and financing the remainder with a mortgage note payable.
2. A building was sold during the year.
3. Cash was used to purchase equipment.
4. Equipment with an original cost of $28,000 was sold during the year.
5. Interest expense includes amortization of the bond premium.
6. The company paid $170,000 of notes payable that matured during the year.
7. The company reacquired 2,000 common shares in 2014, with an average cost of $30,800.
8. Preferred shares were sold for cash.

Instructions

(a) Determine the amount of any cash inflows or outflows related to investing activities in 2014. (*Hint:* Use "T" accounts to calculate the cash flows.)
(b) What was the amount of profit reported by Bird Corp. in 2014?
(c) Determine the amount of any cash inflows or outflows related to financing activities in 2014. (*Hint:* Use "T" accounts to calculate the cash flows.)
(d) Identify and determine the amount of any noncash financing activities in 2014.
(e) Calculate the cash from net cash provided (used) by operating activities. (*Hint:* Using the cash balances provided, calculate increase or decrease in cash first.)

TAKING IT FURTHER Is it favourable for a company to have a net cash inflow from investing activities?

Prepare a cash flow statement —indirect method.
(SO 2) AP

P17–5B King Corp., a private company reporting under ASPE, reported the following for the years ended July 31, 2014 and 2013.

KING CORP. Balance Sheet July 31		
Assets	2014	2013
Cash	$ 24,200	$ 11,000
Accounts receivable	106,000	92,000
Inventories	202,000	190,000
Prepaid expenses	7,500	6,000
Note receivable	40,000	5,000
Land	145,000	105,000
Equipment	225,000	170,000
Accumulated depreciation	(81,000)	(35,000)
Total assets	$668,700	$544,000
Liabilities and Shareholders' Equity		
Accounts payable	$ 33,000	$ 42,000
Accrued expenses payable	6,500	3,800
Income taxes payable	6,000	1,500
Mortgage note payable	65,000	80,000
Common shares	185,000	150,000
Retained earnings	373,200	266,700
Total liabilities and shareholders' equity	$668,700	$544,000

Additional information:

1. Profit for 2014 was $106,500.
2. Common shares were issued for $35,000.
3. Land with a cost of $60,000 was sold at a gain of $30,000; $55,000 cash was received and a note receivable was issued for the remainder.
4. Purchased land with a cost of $100,000 with cash.
5. Equipment with a cost of $25,000 and carrying value of $20,000 was sold for $14,000 cash.
6. Equipment was purchased with cash.

Instructions

Prepare a cash flow statement for the year using the indirect method.

TAKING IT FURTHER Is it favourable for a company to have a net cash inflow from financing activities?

P17–6B   Refer to the information presented for King Corp. in P17–5B.

Additional information:

1. Net sales for the year were $927,250.
2. Cost of goods sold for the year was $552,750.
3. Operating expenses, including depreciation expense, were $241,000.
4. Interest revenue was $3,500.
5. Interest expense was $6,500.
6. Income tax expense was $48,000.
7. Accounts payable relate to merchandise purchases and accrued expenses payable relate to operating expenses.

Instructions

Prepare a cash flow statement for the year using the direct method.

TAKING IT FURTHER   Indicate what transactions might be classified differently if the company was reporting under IFRS instead of ASPE.

Prepare cash flow statement—direct method. (SO 2) AP

P17–7B   Presented below are the comparative balance sheets and income statement for Wayfarer Inc., a private company reporting under ASPE.

Prepare cash flow statement—indirect method. (SO 2) AP

WAYFARER INC. Balance Sheet December 31		
Assets	2014	2013
Cash	$ 120,600	$ 176,400
Accounts receivable	181,800	135,000
Inventory	369,000	257,400
Long-term debt investment	176,400	0
Property, plant, and equipment	1,008,000	828,000
Less: Accumulated depreciation	(292,500)	(252,000)
	$1,563,300	$1,144,800
Liabilities and Shareholders' Equity		
Accounts payable	$ 157,500	$ 117,000
Dividends payable	10,800	0
Income tax payable	25,200	28,800
Long-term notes payable	81,000	0
Common shares	1,170,000	945,000
Retained earnings	118,800	54,000
	$1,563,300	$1,144,800

WAYFARER INC. Income Statement Year Ended December 31, 2014		
Sales		$1,137,600
Cost of goods sold		772,200
Gross profit		365,400
Operating expenses	$265,500	
Loss on sale of equipment	3,600	269,100
Profit from operations		96,300
Interest expense	$ 5,400	
Interest revenue	(9,900)	(4,500)
Profit before income tax		100,800
Income tax expense		25,200
Profit		$ 75,600

Additional information:

1. Cash dividends of $10,800 were declared on December 30, 2014, payable on January 15, 2012.
2. A long-term debt investment was acquired for cash at a cost of $175,500.
3. Depreciation expense is included in the operating expenses.

4. The company issued 22,500 common shares for cash on March 2, 2014. The fair value of the shares was $10 per share. The proceeds were used to purchase additional equipment.
5. Equipment that originally cost $45,000 was sold during the year for cash. The equipment had a net book value of $16,200 at the time of sale.
6. The company issued a note payable for $90,000 and repaid $9,000 of it by year end.

Instructions

Prepare a cash flow statement for the year using the indirect method.

TAKING IT FURTHER   If a company earns a profit during the year, does that always mean that there has been a net increase in cash from operating activities? Explain.

Prepare cash flow statement— direct method. (SO 2) AP

P17–8B   Refer to the information presented for Wayfarer Inc. in P17–7B.

Additional information:

1. Accounts Payable is used for merchandise purchases.
2. Accounts receivable relate to merchandise sales.

Instructions

Prepare a cash flow statement for the year using the direct method.

TAKING IT FURTHER   Wayfarer Inc.'s cash balance decreased by $55,800 in 2014. Briefly explain what caused this, using the cash flow statement. Should management be concerned about this decrease?

Prepare cash flow statement— indirect method. (SO 2) AP

P17–9B   Condensed financial data follow for Galenti, Inc. Galenti is a private company reporting under ASPE.

GALENTI, INC.
Balance Sheet
December 31

Assets	2014	2013
Cash	$ 102,700	$ 47,250
Trading investments	94,500	107,000
Accounts receivable	80,800	37,000
Inventory	111,900	102,650
Prepaid expenses	10,000	16,000
Property, plant, and equipment	290,000	205,000
Accumulated depreciation	(49,500)	(40,000)
Total assets	$640,400	$474,900
Liabilities and Shareholders' Equity		
Accounts payable	$ 62,700	$ 54,280
Accrued expenses payable	12,100	18,830
Notes payable	140,000	80,000
Common shares	250,000	200,000
Retained earnings	175,600	121,790
Total liabilities and shareholders' equity	$640,400	$474,900

GALENTI, INC.
Income Statement
Year Ended December 31, 2014

Revenues		
Sales		$307,500
Gain on sale of equipment		8,750
		316,250
Expenses		
Cost of goods sold	$99,460	
Operating expenses	24,670	
Depreciation expense	58,700	
Interest expense	2,940	
Loss on sale of trading investments	7,500	193,270
Profit before income tax		122,980
Income tax expense		32,670
Profit		$ 90,310

Additional information:

1. Trading investments were sold for $15,000, resulting in a loss of $7,500. There were no fair value adjustments in 2014.
2. New equipment costing $141,000 was purchased for $71,000 cash and a $70,000 note payable.
3. Equipment with an original cost of $56,000 was sold, resulting in a gain of $8,750.
4. Notes payable that matured during the year were paid in cash.

Instructions

Prepare a cash flow statement for the year using the indirect method.

TAKING IT FURTHER   Galenti had a large cash balance ($102,700) at December 31, 2014. What recommendations with respect to cash management might you make to Galenti's management? Explain.

P17–10B   Refer to the information presented for Galenti, Inc. in P17–9B.

Prepare cash flow statement—direct method. (SO 2) AP

Additional information:

1. Accounts Payable is used for merchandise purchases.
2. Prepaid expenses and accrued expenses payable relate to operating expenses.
3. Accounts receivable relate to merchandise sales.

Instructions

Prepare a cash flow statement for the year using the direct method.

TAKING IT FURTHER   Inventory and accounts payable both increased during 2014. Explain how these changes are reported on the cash flow statement when using the direct method.

P17–11B   The financial statements of Milk River Ltd. follow:

Prepare cash flow statement—indirect method. (SO 2) AP

MILK RIVER LTD.
Balance Sheet
December 31

Assets	2014	2013
Cash	$ 13,000	$ 5,000
Accounts receivable	32,000	24,000
Inventory	33,000	20,000
Property, plant, and equipment	90,000	78,000
Accumulated depreciation	(30,000)	(24,000)
Goodwill	5,000	16,000
Total assets	$143,000	$119,000
Liabilities and Shareholders' Equity		
Accounts payable	$ 18,000	$ 15,000
Income taxes payable	2,000	4,000
Notes payable	42,000	52,750
Common shares	18,000	14,000
Retained earnings	63,000	33,250
Total liabilities and shareholders' equity	$143,000	$119,000

MILK RIVER LTD.
Income Statement
Year Ended December 31, 2014

Sales		$256,000
Cost of goods sold		140,000
Gross profit		116,000
Operating expenses	$64,000	
Gain on sale of equipment	(2,000)	
Impairment loss on goodwill	11,000	73,000
Profit from operations		43,000
Other revenues and expenses		
Interest expense		4,000
Profit before income tax		39,000
Income tax expense		9,250
Profit		$ 29,750

Additional information:

1. Equipment costing $24,000 was purchased with an $8,000 down payment and the remainder was financed with a note payable.
2. During the year, equipment was sold for $10,500 cash. This equipment had cost $12,000 originally and had a carrying amount of $8,500 at the time of sale.
3. All depreciation expenses are in the operating expenses category.
4. Notes payable were also repaid during the year.

Instructions

Prepare a cash flow statement for the year using the indirect method.

TAKING IT FURTHER If equipment was both purchased and sold during the year, is it important to show both of these transactions? Or is it sufficient to show only the net increase or decrease in equipment, similar to how increases and decreases in inventory are shown?

Prepare cash flow statement—direct method. (SO 2) AP

P17–12B Refer to the information presented for Milk River Ltd. in P17–11B. Further analysis reveals that accounts payable relate to purchases of merchandise inventory.

Instructions

Prepare a cash flow statement for the year using the direct method.

TAKING IT FURTHER Explain why it is important to know if the company paid cash or financed the purchase of equipment and how this is shown on the cash flow statement.

Calculate free cash flow and evaluate cash. (SO 3) AN

P17–13B Selected information for two competitors, The Gap Inc. and Le Château Inc., follows for year ended January 28, 2012:

	The Gap (in millions of U.S. dollars)	Le Château (in thousands of Canadian dollars)
Profit	$ 833	$ (2,386)
Cash provided (used) by operating activities	1,363	(11,304)
Cash provided (used) by investing activities	(454)	6,545
Cash used by financing activities	(602)	(5,709)
Cash and cash equivalents, end of period	1,885	7,193

Instructions

(a) Calculate the free cash flow for each company.
(b) Which company appears to be in the stronger financial position?

TAKING IT FURTHER By comparing the companies' cash flows, can you tell which company might be downsizing? Explain.

▶ Continuing Cookie Chronicle

(*Note*: This is a continuation of the Cookie Chronicle from Chapters 1 through 16.)

Koebel's Family Bakery Ltd. has been providing cupcakes to Coffee Beans Ltd., a private company, on a weekly basis over the last two years. Coffee Beans, thrilled with the quality of goods and service it is receiving from Koebel's, has approached the Koebels to join its team. Coffee Beans is expanding and hopes that the Koebels would consider the sale of Koebel's Family Bakery Ltd. shares to Coffee Beans. In exchange, Janet, Brian, and Natalie would then become both shareholders and employees of Coffee Beans Ltd.

Janet, Brian, and Natalie have worked hard to achieve the success that Koebel's Family Bakery has achieved. They are reluctant to join another team unless they can be reasonably assured that there will be future growth in the business they are investing in.

Selected information for Koebel's Family Bakery and Coffee Beans follows:

	Koebel's Family Bakery Ltd. Year Ended July 31, 2015	Coffee Beans Ltd. Year Ended November 30, 2014	Coffee Beans Ltd. Year Ended November 30, 2013
Profit	$ 199,629	$ 1,465,466	$ 1,259,966
Net cash provided by operating activities	$235,279	$1,137,650	$ 2,324,547
Net cash used by investing activities	(157,833)	(4,545,728)	(3,036,676)
Net cash (used) provided by financing activities	(37,071)	7,406,647	955,201
Cash, end of year	199,443	4,469,552	470,983
Current liabilities	31,121	5,190,005	5,046,240
Total liabilities	81,551	10,398,638	7,076,968
Dividends paid	120,000	0	0

Instructions

(a) Calculate the net increase in cash and the amount of cash at the beginning of the year that would have been included on the of cash flow statement for each company.
(b) Calculate free cash flow for each company.
(c) Compare the provision and use of cash in each of the three activities—operating, investing, and financing—by each company.
(d) Based on information provided in parts (a) and (b), identify why Coffee Beans is pursuing an investment in Koebel's Family Bakery Ltd.
(e) Based on information provided in parts (a) and (b), identify for the Koebels some of the issues they should consider and additional information they would require before making the decision to sell their shares and/or be employed by Coffee Beans Ltd.

BROADENING YOUR PERSPECTIVE   CHAPTER 17

 Financial Reporting and Analysis

Financial Reporting Problem

BYP17–1   Refer to the consolidated financial statements for **Reitmans (Canada) Limited**, which are reproduced in Appendix A at the end of the textbook.

Instructions

(a) How does Reitmans define "cash" for the purpose of its cash flow statement?
(b) What was the increase or decrease in cash for the year ended January 28, 2012?
(c) What were the significant investing activities reported in Reitmans' 2012 cash flow statement?
(d) What were the significant financing activities reported in Reitmans' 2012 cash flow statement?
(e) Did Reitmans report any significant noncash investing and financing activities in 2012?

Interpreting Financial Statements

BYP17–2 **Andrew Peller Limited** is a leading producer and marketer of quality wines in Canada, with wineries in British Columbia, Ontario, and Nova Scotia. The company's March 31, 2012, balance sheet reported current assets of $137.4 million and current liabilities of $102.5 million, including bank indebtedness (negative cash balance) of $57.5 million. Andrew Peller Limited reported a profit for fiscal 2012 of $13 million. The company reported on its cash flow statement for 2013 that it generated $7.0 million of cash from operating activities. The company used $9.2 million in investing activities, primarily for the purchase of property and equipment. The company's financing activities provided $2.2 million cash. The company paid dividends in the amount of $4.9 million during 2012.

Instructions

(a) What was Andrew Peller Limited's increase or decrease in cash during the year?
(b) Do you believe that Andrew Peller Limited's creditors should be worried about its lack of cash? Explain why or why not.
(c) How is it possible for a company to report a profit of $13 million and generate $7 million of cash from its operating activities?
(d) Calculate Andrew Peller Limited's free cash flow for fiscal 2012. Explain what this free cash flow means.

▶ Critical Thinking

Collaborative Learning Activity

Note to instructor: Additional instructions and handout material for this group activity can be found on the Instructor Resource Site and in *WileyPLUS*.

BYP17–3 In this group activity, you will be given a balance sheet at the beginning of the year, the income statement and cash flow statement for the year, and additional data. Using that information, you will prepare the year-end balance sheet.

Communication Activity

BYP17–4 Many investors today prefer the cash flow statement over the income statement. They believe that cash-based data are a better measure of performance than accrual-based data because the estimates and judgements that are required for accrual accounting allow management too much discretion to manipulate the results.

Instructions

Write a brief memo explaining whether or not it is harder for management to manipulate income using cash-based data than accrual-based data. In your answer, say which financial statement, in your opinion, is the best measure of a company's performance, and explain why.

Ethics Case

BYP17–5 Paradis Corporation has paid cash dividends for eight years in a row. The board of directors' policy requires that, in order to declare a dividend, cash provided by operating activities as reported in Paradis' cash flow statement must exceed $1 million. President and CEO Phil Monat's job is secure as long as he produces annual operating cash flows to support the usual dividend.

At the end of the current year, controller Rick Kwan informs president Monat of some disappointing news. The net cash provided by operating activities is only $970,000. The president says to Rick, "We must get that amount above $1 million. Isn't there some way to increase this amount?" Rick answers, "These figures were prepared by my assistant. I'll go back to my office and see what I can do." The president replies, "I know you won't let me down, Rick."

After examining the cash flow statement carefully, Rick concludes that he can get the operating cash flows above $1 million by reclassifying interest paid from the operating activities section, where it has been classified in the past, to the financing activities section. The company is a publicly traded company reporting under IFRS. He returns to the president, saying, "You can tell the board to declare its usual dividend. Our net cash flow provided by operating activities is $1.03 million." "Good man, Rick! I knew I could count on you," exclaims the president.

Instructions

(a) Should any other factors, besides cash provided by operating activities, be considered by the board in setting the dividend policy?
(b) Who are the stakeholders in this situation?

(c) Was there anything unethical about the president's actions? Was there anything unethical about the controller's actions?

(d) Are the board members or anyone else likely to discover the reclassification?

(e) Would your answers to parts (b) and (c) change if Paradis were a private company reporting under ASPE?

"All About You" Activity

BYP17–6   In the "All About You" feature, you read that many Canadians have big debt loads and negative cash flows. Assume you are a student enrolled in your second year of university and have just learned about the importance of managing cash flows and how to prepare a cash flow statement. You want to use your knowledge to prepare a cash budget for the upcoming year, September 1, 2013, to August 31, 2014. To help you prepare next year's cash budget, you have prepared a cash flow statement for the past year, September 1, 2012, to August 31, 2013.

MY CASH FLOW STATEMENT
Year Ended August 31, 2013

Operating Activities	
Cash received from summer job	$ 8,000
Cash contribution from parents	3,600
Cash paid for rent, utilities, cable, Internet	(4,000)
Cash paid for groceries	(3,200)
Cash paid for clothes	(3,000)
Cash paid for gas, insurance, parking	(4,420)
Cash paid for miscellaneous	(500)
Cash paid for interest on credit card	(180)
Cash used in operating activities	(3,700)
Investing Activities	
Tuition and books	(7,000)
Laptop and printer	(1,200)
Cash used in investing activities	(8,200)
Financing Activities	
Student loan	7,500
Loan from parents	1,500
Purchases on credit card	1,000
Cash provided from financing activities	10,000
Decrease in cash	(1,900)
Cash, September 1, 2012	4,000
Cash, August 31, 2013	$ 2,100

Instructions

(a) Comment on your cash position on August 31, 2013, compared with September 1, 2012.

(b) Prepare a cash flow forecast for September 1, 2013, to August 31, 2014, based on the following estimates and assumptions:

1. Tuition and books $7,500

2. Student loan $7,500

3. Your parents will contribute $4,000 toward your rent, utilities, cable, and Internet. You will not have to pay your parents back for this contribution.

4. Rent, utilities, cable, and Internet $4,000

5. Groceries $3,600

6. Gas, insurance, and parking $4,600

7. Clothes $3,000

8. Miscellaneous $500

9. You plan to pay off the amount owed on your credit card right away.

10. Your parents will lend you an additional $1,500 if you need it.

11. You are pretty sure that you will be rehired by the same company next summer; however, you do not think you will get a raise in pay.

(c) What is the amount of cash you forecast you will have at August 31, 2014?

(d) Will you need to borrow the additional $1,500 from your parents?

(e) Will you be able to pay off the $1,000 owed on your credit card? Should you try to do so?

(f) What actions may you be able to take to improve your cash flow?

ANSWERS TO CHAPTER QUESTIONS

ANSWERS TO ACCOUNTING IN ACTION INSIGHT QUESTIONS

All About You, p. 871

Q: Is it appropriate to use your credit card to pay for your operating activities such as your groceries, clothes, and entertainment? Is it appropriate to use your credit card to finance your investment activities such as tuition or, if you have a large enough limit, a car?

A: Credit cards should never be used for a long-term financing activity because of the high interest rates charged by credit card companies. They can be effectively used for short-term operating activities such as paying for your groceries, clothes, and entertainment, provided that you are able to pay off the full amount of your credit card balance when the payment is due and avoid any interest charges. And credit cards should only be used for long-term investing activities if you will have enough cash to pay off the credit card bill before its due date and avoid interest charges. Long-term investment activities should be financed with long-term financing, if you do not have the cash to pay off the credit card bill before its due date. If you are buying a car or financing your education, you need either a long-term bank loan or a student loan where your payment schedule will match your long-term use of that car or education.

Ethics, p. 901

Q: Why would management of a company want to overstate cash flow from operating activities?

A: The ability to generate cash flows from operating activities is critical to a company's ability to survive and expand. A company must generate cash flows from its operations to pay off debt, pay dividends, and invest in new assets that will allow the company grow. Generally, investors and creditors will be more willing to invest or lend to companies that report higher cash flows from operating activities.

ANSWERS TO SELF-STUDY QUESTIONS

1. a   2. c   3. c   4. a   5. d   6. a   7. b   8. d   9. a   10. c

THE **NAVIGATOR**

- ☐ Understand *Concepts for Review*
- ☐ Read *Feature Story*
- ☐ Scan *Study Objectives*
- ☐ Read *Chapter Preview*
- ☐ Read text and answer *Before You Go On*
- ☐ Review *Comparing IFRS and ASPE*
- ☐ Work *Demonstration Problem*
- ☐ Review *Summary of Study Objectives*
- ☐ Answer *Self-Study Questions*
- ☐ Complete assignments
- ☐ Go to *WileyPLUS* for practice and tutorials

CONCEPTS FOR **REVIEW**

Before studying this chapter, you should understand or, if necessary, review:

a. The content and classification of a balance sheet. (Ch. 4, pp. 184–192, and Ch. 13, pp. 689–690)

b. The content and classification of a multiple-step income statement. (Ch. 5, pp. 184–193)

c. The content of a statement of comprehensive income. (Ch. 14, pp. 726–727)

d. The ratios introduced in previous chapters: current ratio, acid-test (Ch. 4, pp. 193–195); gross profit margin, profit margin (Ch. 5, pp. 257–258); inventory turnover, days sales in inventory (Ch. 6, pp. 320–321); receivables turnover, collection period, operating cycle (Ch. 8, pp. 431–433); asset turnover, return on assets (Ch. 9, pp. 494–495); return on equity (Ch. 13, p. 691); earnings per share, price-earnings, payout (Ch. 14, pp. 735–736); debt to total assets, interest coverage (Ch. 15, pp. 789–791); and free cash flow (Ch. 17, pp. 900–901).

PRESENTING THE WHOLE PICTURE

TORONTO, Ont.—In the high-stakes world of investing and lending, it's not who you know that counts, but what you know. Effective communication enables investors, creditors, and others to know whether a company is doing well, what its past performance has been, and what its future prospects are. The annual report plays a significant role in keeping a company's stakeholders informed.

While most annual reports follow the same basic format, they can vary in their presentation, content, and most importantly, the quality of the information they provide. That's where the annual Corporate Reporting Awards from the Canadian Institute of Chartered Accountants (CICA) come in. "Successful companies understand it is good business to get their story out in a useful, understandable, relevant, and reliable way," said CICA's president and CEO, Kevin Dancey. "The awards program goes beyond identifying and honouring the best reporting practices; it aims to spread the best to the rest."

Canadian Tire Corporation, Limited has been one of the winners of the CICA's Corporate Reporting Awards for five of the past seven years, including the current year, in its category: consumer products. Its annual report starts by identifying reasons to invest in Canadian Tire, including its positive financial highlights and key financial measures. It clearly identifies who and what Canadian Tire is, and has been, over its 90-year history in Canada.

Canadian Tire's annual report, similar to other corporate annual reports, features messages from its chairperson and its CEO, information about the company's products and services, financial statements accompanied by a management discussion and analysis (MD&A), and information about its leadership team and board of directors. Its MD&A includes an in-depth presentation of its strategic goals, including what has been accomplished as well as what has not, and its plans for the future. This year's corporate reporting awards judges said it was noteworthy that "the messaging to shareholders emphasizes the organization's strategies to manage the economy and competitiveness of the industry."

The company's annual report clearly communicates meaningful and transparent information to its stakeholders. "Canadian Tire strives to maintain a high standard of disclosure and investor communication" and is committed to "full and transparent disclosure," the company's 2011 annual report states.

THE **NAVIGATOR**

STUDY **OBJECTIVES**

After studying this chapter, you should be able to:

1. Identify the need for, and tools of, financial statement analysis.
2. Explain and apply horizontal analysis.
3. Explain and apply vertical analysis.
4. Identify and use ratios to analyze liquidity.
5. Identify and use ratios to analyze solvency.
6. Identify and use ratios to analyze profitability.
7. Recognize the limitations of financial statement analysis.

THE **NAVIGATOR**

An important lesson can be learned from Canadian Tire's annual report described in our feature story. Effective communication is the key to decision-making. The purpose of this chapter is to introduce the tools used in financial statement analysis to help users evaluate, and make decisions about, a company's financial performance and position.

We will use three common tools of analysis—horizontal, vertical, and ratio—to analyze the financial statements of a hypothetical publicly traded, regional chain of stores called Hometown Tires and More. We will then compare this analysis with Canadian Tire, a publicly traded national chain of stores and one of Hometown Tires and More's competitors. We will conclude our discussion with some of the limiting factors users should be aware of in their analysis of financial information.

The chapter is organized as follows:

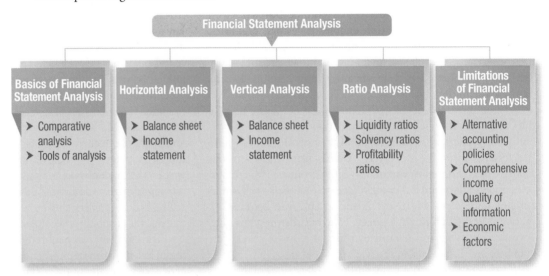

Financial Statement Analysis

Basics of Financial Statement Analysis	Horizontal Analysis	Vertical Analysis	Ratio Analysis	Limitations of Financial Statement Analysis
➤ Comparative analysis ➤ Tools of analysis	➤ Balance sheet ➤ Income statement	➤ Balance sheet ➤ Income statement	➤ Liquidity ratios ➤ Solvency ratios ➤ Profitability ratios	➤ Alternative accounting policies ➤ Comprehensive income ➤ Quality of information ➤ Economic factors

Basics of Financial Statement Analysis

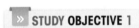

» STUDY OBJECTIVE 1

Identify the need for, and tools of, financial statement analysis.

Financial statement analysis involves evaluating three characteristics of a company: its liquidity, solvency, and profitability. We learned in Chapters 1 and 11 that the objective of financial reporting is to give capital providers (i.e., investors and creditors) information useful for decision-making. Each of these primary users—investors and creditors—is interested in a company's liquidity, solvency, and/or profitability depending on its decision needs.

For example, short-term creditors, such as a suppliers or bankers, are primarily interested in liquidity—the ability of a borrower to pay its obligations when they come due. The borrower's liquidity is extremely important in evaluating the safety of a short-term loan. A long-term creditor, such as a bondholder, is most interested in solvency measures to determine the company's ability to survive over a long period of time. Long-term creditors consider such measures as the amount of debt in the company's capital structure and its ability to meet interest payments. Investors (both current and potential shareholders) are interested in a company's profitability. They want to assess the probability of receiving dividend income and the growth potential of the share price. Creditors are also often interested in profitability, because a company's profit, or lack of it, can affect its ability to obtain financing.

COMPARATIVE ANALYSIS

In analyzing financial statements, the users of financial information must make comparisons in order to evaluate a company's past and current performance and position, and to use this information to help determine future expectations. Comparisons are needed because, although every item reported in a financial statement has significance, it has limited value on its own. When Canadian Tire reported trade and other receivables of $829.3 million on its balance sheet dated December 31, 2011, we know that the company had that amount of receivables on that date. However, we do not know if that amount is an increase or decrease compared with past years, or if Canadian Tire is collecting its receivables on a timely basis. To get this information, the amount of receivables must be compared with other financial statement data.

When you compare any one financial statement item with a related financial statement item or items, the value and usefulness of the information increases for analysis purposes. Comparisons can be made on several different bases, including the following:

1. **Intracompany basis.** This basis compares an item or financial relationship inside or within a company in the current year with one or more prior years. Intracompany comparisons are useful for identifying changes in financial relationships and discovering trends.
2. **Intercompany basis.** This basis compares an item or financial relationship of one company with the same item or relationship in one or more competing companies. Intercompany comparisons are useful for understanding a company's competitive position.

In some circumstances, a third basis of comparison, an industry basis, is also performed. This basis compares an item or financial relationship of a company with industry averages. However, for a company like Canadian Tire, determining which industry it is actually in can be problematic as it sells much more than tires. Canadian Tire sells a wide range of home, tools, leisure, and automotive products in its retail stores, in addition to apparel, sporting goods, gasoline, and financial services in some of its other businesses. Consequently, comparison with industry averages for diversified companies such as Canadian Tire has less relevance than intra- and intercompany comparisons.

TOOLS OF ANALYSIS

We use various tools to evaluate the significance of financial statement data for decision-making. Three commonly used tools are:

1. **Horizontal analysis.** This tool compares data, such as line items in a company's financial statements, by expressing them as percentage increases and decreases over two or more years (periods).
2. **Vertical analysis.** This tool compares data by expressing line items in a company's financial statement as a percentage of a total amount within the same financial statement and year (period).
3. **Ratio analysis.** This tool expresses the relationship between selected items of financial statement data within the same year (period).

Horizontal analysis helps identify changes and trends over time. For example, Canadian Tire could compare its trade and other receivables balance over the last five years to determine whether it has increased or decreased over that period of time. Horizontal analysis is used mainly in intracompany comparisons. As we learned above, an intracompany analysis involves financial data *within* a company.

Vertical analysis focuses on the relationships between items on the same financial statement. For example, Canadian Tire could compare its trade and other receivables with its total assets to determine the relative proportion of its receivables in an intracompany comparison. Or it could compare this percentage relationship with that of one of its competitors in an intercompany comparison. Vertical analysis is used in both intracompany and intercompany comparisons. It is helpful to compare the relative contribution made by each financial statement item both *within* a company (intracompany) and *between* two or more companies (intercompany).

Vertical percentages can also be compared across time. Canadian Tire can compare its trade and other receivables as a percentage of its total assets for the current year with that of prior years (intracompany), and can compare this percentage with that of its competitors (intercompany).

Ratio analysis helps us understand the relationship among selected items presented in one or more financial statements. For example, horizontal analysis can determine whether Canadian Tire's receivables have increased or decreased over time and vertical analysis can determine the proportion that Canadian Tire's receivables constitute of its total assets. However, only ratio analysis can relate receivables to revenues by calculating the receivables turnover ratio to determine how effectively the company is collecting its receivables. Ratio analysis is also used in both intracompany and intercompany comparisons. Canadian Tire can compare its receivables turnover ratio for the current year with that of prior years (intracompany), and can compare this ratio with that of its competitors (intercompany).

While horizontal and vertical analysis are being introduced in this chapter, you should already have some familiarity with ratio analysis, which was introduced in past chapters. In the following sections, we will explain and illustrate each of the three types of analysis: horizontal, vertical, and ratio.

BEFORE YOU GO ON...

Do It

Identify the appropriate basis of comparison and tool of analysis for each of the following financial situations.

	Basis of Comparison	Tool of Analysis
1. Analysis of a company's operating expenses over a 10-year period		
2. Comparison of a company's cost of goods sold with its net sales for the current period		
3. Comparison of a company's profit versus its net sales (profit margin) for the current period with that of a competitor		

Action Plan

- Recall that the two bases of comparison are intracompany and intercompany. "Intra" means within and "inter" means between.
- Recall that there are three tools of analysis: horizontal, vertical, and ratio.

THE NAVIGATOR

Solution

	Basis of Comparison	Tool of Analysis
1.	Intracompany	Horizontal
2.	Intracompany	Vertical
3.	Intercompany	Ratio

Related exercise material: BE18–1 and BE18–2.

Horizontal Analysis

» **STUDY OBJECTIVE 2**

Explain and apply horizontal analysis.

Horizontal analysis, also called **trend analysis**, is a technique for comparing a series of data, such as line items in a company's financial statements, over a period of time. The term "horizontal analysis" means that we view financial statement data from left to right (or right to left) across time.

The purpose of horizontal analysis is to determine the percentage increase or decrease that has taken place over time. This change may be expressed as a percentage of a base period or as a percentage change between periods. For example, total revenue figures and horizontal analysis percentages for Canadian Tire for the most recent five-year period are shown in Illustration 18-1.

▶ **ILLUSTRATION 18-1**
Horizontal analysis for Canadian Tire's revenue

CANADIAN TIRE CORPORATION, LIMITED Year Ended December 31 (in millions)					
	2011	**2010**	**2009**	**2008**	**2007**
Revenue	$10,387.1	$9,213.1	$8,686.5	$9,121.3	$8,606.1
% of base-year (2007) amount	120.7%	107.1%	100.9%	106.0%	100.0%
% change between years	12.7%	6.1%	(4.8)%	6.0%	—

If we assume that 2007 is the base year, we can express revenue as a percentage of the base-year amount. We call this a **horizontal percentage of base-period amount**. It is calculated by dividing the amount for the specific year (or period) we are analyzing by the base-year (or period) amount, as shown in Illustration 18-2.

▶ **ILLUSTRATION 18-2**
Horizontal percentage of base-period amount formula

$$\text{Horizontal Percentage of Base-Period Amount} = \text{Analysis-Period Amount} \div \text{Base-Period Amount}$$

$$120.7\% = \$10,387.1 \div \$8,606.1$$

We can determine that Canadian Tire's total revenue in 2011 is 120.7% of the total revenue in 2007 by dividing $10,387.1 million by $8,606.1 million. In other words, revenue in 2011 is 20.7%

greater than revenue four years earlier, in 2007. From this horizontal analysis of a base-year amount, shown in the second row of Illustration 18-1, we can easily see Canadian Tire's revenue trend. Revenue has increased each year except in 2009.

We can also use horizontal analysis to measure the percentage change between any two periods of time. This is known as a **horizontal percentage change for period**. It is calculated by dividing the dollar amount of the change between the specific year (or period) under analysis and the prior year (or period) by the prior-year (or period) amount, as shown in Illustration 18-3.

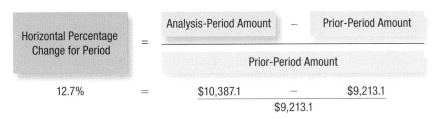

$$\text{Horizontal Percentage Change for Period} = \frac{\text{Analysis-Period Amount} - \text{Prior-Period Amount}}{\text{Prior-Period Amount}}$$

$$12.7\% = \frac{\$10,387.1 - \$9,213.1}{\$9,213.1}$$

▶ILLUSTRATION 18-3
Horizontal percentage change for period formula

For example, we can determine that Canadian Tire's revenue increased by $1,174 million ($10,387.1 million – $9,213.1 million) between 2010 and 2011. This increase can then be expressed as a percentage, 12.7%, by dividing the amount of the change between the two years, $1,174 million, by the amount in the prior year, $9,213.1 million. That is, in 2011, revenue increased by 12.7% compared with 2010. The horizontal percentage change for the period in Canadian Tire's revenue between each of the last five years (i.e., between 2011 and 2010, 2010 and 2009, 2009 and 2008, and 2008 and 2007) is presented in the last row of Illustration 18-1. No percentage change can be calculated for 2007 since 2006 data are not included.

BALANCE SHEET

To further illustrate horizontal analysis, we will use the hypothetical financial statements of Hometown Tires and More Inc. Its two-year condensed balance sheet, which shows dollar amount and percentage changes, is presented in Illustration 18-4.

▶ILLUSTRATION 18-4
Horizontal analysis of balance sheet—percentage change for period

HOMETOWN TIRES AND MORE INC. Balance Sheet December 31				
			Increase (Decrease)	
Assets	2011	2010	Amount	Percentage
Current assets				
Cash	$ 50,000	$ 55,000	$ (5,000)	(9.1)%
Trading investments	20,000	35,000	(15,000)	(42.9)%
Accounts receivable	72,500	50,000	22,500	45.0%
Inventory	372,500	340,000	32,500	9.6%
Prepaid expenses	30,000	20,000	10,000	50.0%
Total current assets	545,000	500,000	45,000	9.0%
Property, plant, and equipment	400,000	450,000	(50,000)	(11.1)%
Intangible assets	55,000	65,000	(10,000)	(15.4)%
Total assets	$1,000,000	$1,015,000	$(15,000)	(1.5)%
Liabilities and Shareholders' Equity				
Liabilities				
Current liabilities	$ 337,700	$ 333,500	$ 4,200	1.3%
Non-current liabilities	400,000	475,000	(75,000)	(15.8)%
Total liabilities	737,700	808,500	(70,800)	(8.8)%
Shareholders' equity				
Common shares (300,000 shares issued)	90,000	90,000	0	0.0%
Retained earnings	152,300	96,500	55,800	57.8%
Accumulated other comprehensive income	20,000	20,000	0	0.0%
Total shareholders' equity	262,300	206,500	55,800	27.0%
Total liabilities and shareholders' equity	$1,000,000	$1,015,000	$(15,000)	(1.5)%

The horizontal percentages in Illustration 18-4 are an example of a percentage change for a period, and not a percentage of a base-period amount. It makes sense to calculate the percentage change for a period in this illustration since only two periods are under analysis. Note that, in a horizontal analysis, while the amount column of the increase or decrease is additive (e.g., the decrease in total liabilities of $70,800 is equal to +$4,200 − $75,000), the percentage column is not additive (8.8% is not equal to +1.3% − 15.8%).

The horizontal analysis of Hometown Tires and More's comparative balance sheet shows that several changes have occurred between 2010 and 2011. In the current assets section, trading investments decreased by $15,000, or 42.9%. We will learn when we look at the income statement later that this change was due to a decline in the fair value of the investments and not to the sale of any of these investments. Recall from Chapter 16 that losses on fair value adjustments of trading investments are reported in the income statement and not in the statement of comprehensive income. This is why accumulated other comprehensive income, shown in the shareholders' equity section of the balance sheet, did not change between 2010 and 2011.

Accounts receivable increased by $22,500, or 45%. We will look at the income statement in the next section to determine whether sales increased by the same proportion as receivables. If not, this may indicate that the receivables are slow-moving.

Inventory increased by a larger dollar amount, $32,500, than did accounts receivable but not by as large a percentage: 9.6% for inventory compared with 45% for accounts receivable. Inventory may have changed because of increased sales; we will investigate this further when we analyze the income statement. Prepaid expenses also increased by 50% in 2011. One has to be careful in interpreting percentage changes like this. Because it is a proportionately large change ($10,000) on a small amount ($20,000), the percentage change is not as meaningful as it first appears.

The carrying amounts of both property, plant, and equipment and intangible assets decreased in 2011. This means that the company is disposing of more long-lived assets than it is acquiring (or that its depreciation and amortization exceeds the acquisition of new assets). Overall, total assets decreased by $15,000, or 1.5%, from 2010 to 2011.

Current liabilities increased by 1.3%. Changes in current assets and current liabilities usually move in the same direction; that is, normally both will increase or both will decrease. In this case, both have risen, although current assets have increased more than current liabilities. This is better than the inverse: current liabilities increasing more than current assets.

Non-current liabilities decreased by $75,000, or 15.8%, in 2011. Retained earnings in the shareholders' equity section of the balance sheet increased significantly in 2011, by 57.8%. This suggests that Hometown Tires and More is financing its business by retaining profit, rather than by adding to its debt.

INCOME STATEMENT

Illustration 18-5 presents a horizontal analysis of Hometown Tires and More's condensed income statement for the years 2010 and 2011.

▶ ILLUSTRATION 18-5
Horizontal analysis of income statement—percentage change for period

HOMETOWN TIRES AND MORE INC. Income Statement Years Ended December 31			Increase (Decrease)	
	2011	2010	Amount	Percentage
Sales	$2,095,000	$1,960,000	$135,000	6.9%
Sales returns and allowances	98,000	123,000	(25,000)	(20.3)%
Net sales	1,997,000	1,837,000	160,000	8.7%
Cost of goods sold	1,381,000	1,240,000	141,000	11.4%
Gross profit	616,000	597,000	19,000	3.2%
Operating expenses	457,000	440,000	17,000	3.9%
Profit from operations	159,000	157,000	2,000	1.3%
Other expenses				
Interest expense	27,000	29,500	(2,500)	(8.5)%
Loss on fair value adjustment of trading investments	15,000	0	15,000	n/a
Profit before income tax	117,000	127,500	(10,500)	(8.2)%
Income tax expense	23,400	25,500	(2,100)	(8.2)%
Profit	$ 93,600	$ 102,000	$ (8,400)	(8.2)%

Horizontal analysis of the income statement, illustrating dollar amounts and percentage changes for the period, shows that net sales increased by 8.7%. Sales do not appear to have increased at the same rate as receivables. Recall from Illustration 18-4 that receivables increased by 45%. Later in the chapter, we will look at the receivables turnover ratio in the ratio analysis section to determine whether receivables are being collected more slowly or not. However, we must be cautious in over-interpreting this increase. This type of business relies a lot on cash sales, not credit sales.

To continue with our horizontal analysis of the income statement, we can observe that similar to net sales, cost of goods sold also increased. However, it is interesting to note that while cost of goods sold increased by 11.4%, net sales only increased by 8.7%. This is not a sustainable situation over the long run and the relationship between pricing and costs will need to be carefully monitored. Recall also that in Illustration 18-4 we observed that inventory increased by 9.6%. The cost of goods sold increased not only at a faster rate than sales, but also at a faster rate than inventory. We will look at the inventory turnover ratio later in the chapter to determine whether these increases are reasonable.

The net result of the changes in net sales and cost of goods sold is an increase in gross profit of 3.2%. Operating expenses outpaced this percentage increase at 3.9%. Normally, management tries to control operating expenses wherever possible, so we would hope to see operating expenses decrease or at least increase at a lower rate than gross profit.

Other expenses increased, primarily because of the loss on fair value adjustment related to the trading investments that was mentioned in the last section. Note that profit declined by the same amount as profit before income tax, 8.2%. This indicates that although income tax expense declined in 2011, its decline was proportionate to profit before income tax in each year (that is, income tax expense is unchanged at 20% of profit before income tax in each year).

A horizontal analysis of the changes between periods is pretty straightforward and is quite useful. But complications can occur in making the calculations. If an item has a small value in a base or prior year and a large value in the next year, the percentage change may not be meaningful. In addition, if a negative amount appears in the base or prior year and there is a positive amount the following year, or vice versa, no percentage change can be calculated. Or, if an item has no value in a base or prior year and a value in the next year, no percentage change can be calculated. That was the case with the loss on fair value adjustment of trading investments reported in 2011. Because there was no loss reported in 2010, no percentage change could be calculated.

We have not included a horizontal analysis of Hometown Tires and More's statement of changes in shareholders' equity or cash flow statement. An analysis of these statements is not as useful as the horizontal analyses performed on the balance sheet and income statement. The amounts presented in the statement of changes in shareholders' equity and cash flow statement give details about the changes between two periods. The value of these statements comes from the analysis of the changes during the year, and not from percentage comparisons of these changes against a base amount.

Hometown Tires and More did not have any other comprehensive income in 2011, so it did not present a separate statement of comprehensive income. However, if it had, it might have been useful to analyze the changes in its sources of other comprehensive income. You should note, however, that these changes can vary widely from year to year, which can result in a horizontal analysis of other comprehensive income having limited value.

BEFORE YOU GO ON...

Do It

Selected, condensed information (in thousands) from Bonora Ltd.'s income statements follows:

	2014	2013	2012	2011
Net sales	$8,646	$9,468	$6,294	$5,035
Cost of goods sold	6,746	7,322	5,217	4,099
Gross profit	1,900	2,146	1,077	936
Operating expenses	1,396	1,504	948	641
Profit from operations	504	642	129	295
Income tax expense	76	96	19	44
Profit	$ 428	$ 546	$ 110	$ 251

Action Plan

- Horizontal percentage of base-year amount: Set the base-year (2011) dollar amounts at 100%. Express each subsequent year's amount as a percentage of the base-year amount by dividing the dollar amount for the year under analysis by the base-year amount.
- Horizontal percentage change for year: Find the percentage change between two years by dividing the dollar amount of the change between the current year and the prior year by the prior-year amount.

THE NAVIGATOR

⊙ **BEFORE YOU GO ON** continued...

(a) Using horizontal analysis, calculate the percentage of the base-year amount for 2011 to 2014, assuming that 2011 is the base year.

(b) Using horizontal analysis, calculate the percentage change between each of the following sets of years: 2014 and 2013; 2013 and 2012; and 2012 and 2011.

Solution

(a) Horizontal percentage of base-year amount

	2014	2013	2012	2011
Net sales	171.7%	188.0%	125.0%	100.0%
Cost of goods sold	164.6%	178.6%	127.3%	100.0%
Gross profit	203.0%	229.3%	115.1%	100.0%
Operating expenses	217.8%	234.6%	147.9%	100.0%
Profit from operations	170.8%	217.6%	43.7%	100.0%
Income tax expense	172.7%	218.2%	43.2%	100.0%
Profit	170.5%	217.5%	43.8%	100.0%

(b) Horizontal percentage change for year

	2013 to 2014	2012 to 2013	2011 to 2012
Net sales	(8.7)%	50.4%	25.0%
Cost of goods sold	(7.9)%	40.3%	27.3%
Gross profit	(11.5)%	99.3%	15.1%
Operating expenses	(7.2)%	58.6%	47.9%
Profit from operations	(21.5)%	397.7%	(56.3)%
Income tax expense	(20.8)%	405.3%	(56.8)%
Profit	(21.6)%	396.4%	(56.2)%

Related exercise material: BE18–3, BE18–4, E18–1, and E18–2.

Vertical Analysis

Vertical analysis, also called **common size analysis**, is a technique for comparing an amount in a company's financial statements with a total (base) amount within the same financial statement. The term "vertical analysis" means that we view financial statement data from up to down (or down to up) within the same period of time.

Note that while horizontal analysis compares data across more than one year, vertical analysis compares data within the same year. These data are expressed as a percentage, known as the **vertical percentage of base amount**. It is calculated by dividing the financial statement amount under analysis by the relevant total or base amount for that particular financial statement, as shown in Illustration 18-6.

▶ **ILLUSTRATION** 18-6
Vertical percentage of base amount formula

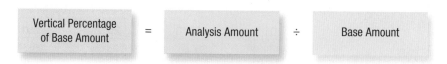

| Vertical Percentage of Base Amount | = | Analysis Amount | ÷ | Base Amount |

The base amount commonly used for the balance sheet is *total assets*. The base amount for the income statement is usually *revenues* for a service company and *net sales* for a merchandising company.

BALANCE SHEET

We will illustrate vertical analysis using Hometown Tires and More's balance sheet by first calculating a vertical percentage of a base amount for two years in an intracompany comparison. Then we will vertically compare Hometown Tires and More's balance sheet to a competitor's balance sheet in an intercompany comparison.

Intracompany Comparison

Illustration 18-7 shows a vertical analysis of Hometown Tires and More's comparative balance sheet. As was mentioned above, this analysis uses *total assets* as the base amount. Note that *total liabilities and shareholders' equity* equals total assets so the same base amount (e.g., total assets) can be used for both assets as well as liabilities and shareholders' equity items.

▶ ILLUSTRATION 18-7
Vertical analysis of balance sheet—percentage of base amount

HOMETOWN TIRES AND MORE INC.
Balance Sheet
December 31

	2011 Amount	2011 Percentage	2010 Amount	2010 Percentage
Assets				
Current assets				
Cash	$ 50,000	5.0%	$ 55,000	5.4%
Trading investments	20,000	2.0%	35,000	3.5%
Accounts receivable	72,500	7.2%	50,000	4.9%
Inventory	372,500	37.3%	340,000	33.5%
Prepaid expenses	30,000	3.0%	20,000	2.0%
Total current assets	545,000	54.5%	500,000	49.3%
Property, plant, and equipment	400,000	40.0%	450,000	44.3%
Intangible assets	55,000	5.5%	65,000	6.4%
Total assets	$1,000,000	100.0%	$1,015,000	100.0%
Liabilities and Shareholders' Equity				
Liabilities				
Current liabilities	$ 337,700	33.8%	$ 333,500	32.9%
Non-current liabilities	400,000	40.0%	475,000	46.8%
Total liabilities	737,700	73.8%	808,500	79.7%
Shareholders' equity				
Common shares (300,000 shares issued)	90,000	9.0%	90,000	8.8%
Retained earnings	152,300	15.2%	96,500	9.5%
Accumulated other comprehensive income	20,000	2.0%	20,000	2.0%
Total shareholders' equity	262,300	26.2%	206,500	20.3%
Total liabilities and shareholders' equity	$1,000,000	100.0%	$1,015,000	100.0%

Vertical analysis shows the size of each item in the balance sheet compared with a base amount for each of 2011 and 2010. In addition to reviewing the respective proportion of each item in the balance sheet within a specific year, vertical analysis can also be used to compare changes in the individual asset, liability, and shareholders' equity items between years.

For example, we can see that current assets increased from 49.3% of total assets in 2010 to 54.5% of total assets in 2011. We can also see that the biggest change was in inventory, which increased from 33.5% of total assets in 2010 to 37.3% in 2011. This is contrary to what we first observed in Illustration 18-4, where it appeared that prepaid expenses had the greatest percentage increase in the current assets category. In Illustration 18-7, prepaid expenses increased by only one percentage point of total assets, from 2% in 2010 to 3% in 2011. You will recall our earlier words of caution about interpreting such a large percentage change (the 50% horizontal percentage change for period) as was presented for prepaid expenses in Illustration 18-4.

The carrying amounts of property, plant, and equipment and intangible assets decreased in absolute dollar amounts, as we saw in Illustration 18-4, and also decreased as relative percentages of total assets, as shown in Illustration 18-7. Property, plant, and equipment decreased from 44.3% in 2010 to 40% in 2011 and intangible assets decreased from 6.4% in 2010 to 5.5% in 2011.

Non-current liabilities decreased from 46.8% to 40%, while retained earnings increased from 9.5% to 15.2% of total liabilities and shareholders' equity between 2010 and 2011. These results reinforce the earlier observation that Hometown Tires and More is financing its growth by retaining profit, rather than by issuing additional debt.

Note that Hometown Tires and More has only one class of share capital—common shares—issued. Its common shares didn't actually change between 2010 and 2011, yet common shares are a different percentage of total assets in each year (8.8% in 2010 and 9.0% in 2011). This is because the base (total assets) has changed in each year while the amount of common shares has not.

Intercompany Comparison

The above vertical analysis illustrated an intracompany comparison—we compared changes in Hometown Tires and More's balance sheet between 2010 and 2011. We can also use vertical analysis to compare companies in an intercompany comparison. This is a particularly helpful technique when companies are of different sizes.

For example, Hometown Tires and More's main competitor is Canadian Tire. Using vertical analysis, the condensed balance sheet (or the income statement) of the small retail company Hometown Tires and More can be more meaningfully compared with the balance sheet (or income statement) of the giant retailer Canadian Tire, as shown in Illustration 18-8.

▶ILLUSTRATION 18-8
Intercompany balance sheet comparison—vertical analysis

BALANCE SHEETS **December 31, 2011** **(in thousands)**				
	Hometown Tires and More		**Canadian Tire**	
Assets	Amount (in thousands)	Percentage	Amount (in millions)	Percentage
Current assets	$ 545.0	54.5%	$ 6,956.6	56.4%
Long-term receivables and other assets	0.0	0.0%	778.1	6.3%
Long-term investments	0.0	0.0%	128.2	1.0%
Property, plant, and equipment	400.0	40.0%	3,365.9	27.3%
Intangible assets	55.0	5.5%	1,110.0	9.0%
Total assets	$1,000.0	100.0%	$12,338.8	100.0%
Liabilities and Shareholders' Equity				
Liabilities				
Current liabilities	$ 337.7	33.8%	$ 4,153.0	33.7%
Non-current liabilities	400.0	40.0%	3,776.8	30.6%
Total liabilities	737.7	73.8%	7,929.8	64.3%
Shareholders' equity				
Share capital	90.0	9.0%	711.6	5.8%
Retained earnings	152.3	15.2%	3,686.4	29.9%
Accumulated other comprehensive income	20.0	2.0%	11.0	0.0%
Total shareholders' equity	262.3	26.2%	4,409.0	35.7%
Total liabilities and shareholders' equity	$1,000.0	100.0%	$12,338.8	100.0%

Canadian Tire's total assets are 12,339 times greater than the total assets of the much smaller Hometown Tires and More. Vertical analysis helps eliminate this difference in size. For example, although Hometown Tires and More has fewer dollars of property, plant, and equipment compared with Canadian Tire ($400,000 compared with $3,365.9 million), using percentages, its proportion of property, plant, and equipment is much larger (40% compared with 27.3%).

Although Hometown Tires and More has fewer dollars of debt than Canadian Tire ($737,700 compared with $7,929.8 million), it has a higher debt percentage than does Canadian Tire (73.8% compared with 64.3%). This is not surprising given that Hometown Tires and More, as a much smaller company, may not have the same access to equity financing as does Canadian Tire. Alternatively, it may have deliberately chosen to finance its operations with more debt than equity proportionately than Canadian Tire. Regardless of the rationale, the company does have a lower equity base than Canadian Tire (26.2% compared with 35.7%).

INCOME STATEMENT

We would like to now illustrate an intracompany comparison using vertical analysis of Hometown Tires and More's income statement. A vertical analysis of the percentage of the base amount for each of 2010 and 2011 is shown in Illustration 18-9, with *net sales* used as the base amount.

HOMETOWN TIRES AND MORE INC.
Income Statement
Year Ended December 31

	2011		2010	
	Amount	Percentage	Amount	Percentage
Sales	$2,095,000	104.9%	$1,960,000	106.7%
Sales returns and allowances	98,000	4.9%	123,000	6.7%
Net sales	1,997,000	100.0%	1,837,000	100.0%
Cost of goods sold	1,381,000	69.2%	1,240,000	67.5%
Gross profit	616,000	30.8%	597,000	32.5%
Operating expenses	457,000	22.9%	440,000	24.0%
Profit from operations	159,000	7.9%	157,000	8.5%
Other expenses				
Interest expense	27,000	1.3%	29,500	1.6%
Loss on fair value adjustment of trading investments	15,000	0.7%	0	0.0%
Profit before income tax	117,000	5.9%	127,500	6.9%
Income tax expense	23,400	1.2%	25,500	1.4%
Profit	$ 93,600	4.7%	$ 102,000	5.5%

▶ **ILLUSTRATION 18-9**
Vertical analysis of income statement—percentage of base amount

We can see that the cost of goods sold as a percentage of net sales increased by 1.7 percentage points (from 67.5% to 69.2%) between 2010 and 2011. Operating expenses declined as a percentage of net sales by 1.1 percentage points (from 24.0% to 22.9%). As a result, profit from operations did not change substantially between 2010 and 2011: it declined by 0.6 percentage points (from 8.5% to 7.9%). Profit before income tax declined between 2010 and 2011 from 6.9% to 5.9%. Profit declined as well as a percentage of net sales from 2010 to 2011: it decreased by 0.8 percentage points. Although we saw Hometown Tires and More's profit decrease by 8.2% between 2010 and 2011 in Illustration 18-5, its profitability is relatively unchanged (less than 1%) in comparison with net sales.

A vertical analysis can also be performed on the statement of comprehensive income, statement of changes in shareholders' equity, and cash flow statement. However, this is rarely done as there is no logical base amount.

Vertical analysis can also be applied to intercompany comparisons of the income statement, similar to our comparison of Hometown Tires and More and Canadian Tire in the balance sheet section above although we have not chosen to do so here.

BEFORE YOU GO ON...

Do It

Selected, condensed information (in thousands) from Bonora Ltd.'s income statements follows:

	2014	2013	2012	2011
Net sales	$8,646	$9,468	$6,294	$5,035
Cost of goods sold	6,746	7,322	5,217	4,099
Gross profit	1,900	2,146	1,077	936
Operating expenses	1,396	1,504	948	641
Profit from operations	504	642	129	295
Income tax expense	76	96	19	44
Profit	$ 428	$ 546	$ 110	$ 251

Action Plan

- Vertical percentage of base amount: Find the relative percentage by dividing the specific income statement amount by the base amount (net sales) for each year.

Using vertical analysis, calculate the percentage of the base amount for each year.

Solution

	2014	2013	2012	2011
Net sales	100%	100%	100%	100%
Cost of goods sold	78%	77%	83%	81%
Gross profit	22%	23%	17%	19%
Operating expenses	16%	16%	15%	13%
Profit from operations	6%	7%	2%	6%
Income tax expense	1%	1%	0%	1%
Profit	5%	6%	2%	5%

THE NAVIGATOR

Related exercise material: BE18–5, BE18–6, E18–3, E18–4, and E18–5.

Ratio Analysis

Ratio analysis expresses the relationships between selected financial statement items and is the most widely used tool of financial analysis. Ratios are generally classified into three types:

1. **Liquidity ratios.** These measure a company's short-term ability to pay its maturing obligations and to meet unexpected needs for cash.
2. **Solvency ratios.** These measure a company's ability to survive over a long period of time.
3. **Profitability ratios.** These measure a company's operating success for a specific period of time.

In earlier chapters, we presented liquidity, solvency, and profitability ratios for evaluating a company's financial condition. In this section, we provide an example of a comprehensive financial analysis using these ratios. This analysis uses two bases for comparisons: (1) intracompany, comparing two years of data (2010 and 2011) for Hometown Tires and More, and (2) intercompany, comparing Hometown Tires and More with Canadian Tire, its main competitor, for the year ended December 31, 2011.

You will recall that Hometown Tires and More's balance sheet was presented earlier in the chapter in Illustration 18-4 and its income statement in Illustration 18-5. We will use the information in these two financial statements, plus additional data that will be introduced as required, to calculate Hometown Tires and More's ratios in the next three sections. You can use these data to review the calculations for each 2011 ratio calculated for Hometown Tires and More to make sure you understand where the numbers came from. Detailed calculations are not shown for the ratios presented for Hometown Tires and More for 2010 or for Canadian Tire for 2011.

LIQUIDITY RATIOS

Liquidity ratios measure a company's short-term ability to pay its maturing obligations and to meet unexpected needs for cash. Short-term creditors, such as suppliers and bankers, are particularly interested in assessing liquidity. Liquidity ratios include the current ratio, the acid-test ratio, receivables turnover, collection period, inventory turnover, days sales in inventory, and the operating cycle.

STUDY OBJECTIVE 4

Identify and use ratios to analyze liquidity.

Current Ratio

The current ratio is a widely used measure of a company's liquidity and short-term debt-paying ability. The ratio is calculated by dividing current assets by current liabilities. The 2011 and 2010 current ratios for Hometown Tires and More (intracompany basis of comparison) and 2011 current ratio for Canadian Tire (intercompany basis of comparison) are shown below.

	$\text{Current ratio} = \dfrac{\text{Current assets}}{\text{Current liabilities}}$	
Hometown Tires and More **2011** $\dfrac{\$545,000}{\$337,700} = 1.6{:}1$	Hometown Tires and More **2010** = 1.5:1	Intracompany
	Canadian Tire **2011** = 1.7:1	Intercompany

What does the ratio actually mean? The 2011 ratio of 1.6:1 means that for every dollar of current liabilities, Hometown Tires and More has $1.60 of current assets. Hometown Tires and More's current ratio increased slightly between 2010 and 2011. Although its 2011 ratio is marginally lower than Canadian Tire's current ratio of 1.7:1, Hometown Tires and More appears to have more than enough current assets to pay its current liabilities.

Acid-Test Ratio

The current ratio is only one measure of liquidity. It does not consider what the current assets are composed of. For example, a satisfactory current ratio does not disclose the fact that a portion of the current assets may be tied up in inventory or prepayments. The acid-test ratio differs from the current ratio by excluding assets that are less liquid, such as inventory, which takes longer to be converted to cash. For merchandising companies, inventory must be sold before any accounts receivable or cash can be created.

The acid-test ratio is calculated by dividing the sum of cash, short-term investments, and receivables by current liabilities. You will recall from Chapter 16 that short-term investments include trading investments, such as reported by Hometown Tires and More, and short-term debt instruments purchased to earn interest.

The 2011 and 2010 acid-test ratios for Hometown Tires and More and 2011 acid-test ratio for Canadian Tire are shown below.

	$\text{Acid-test ratio} = \dfrac{\text{Cash} + \text{Short-term investments} + \text{Receivables}}{\text{Current liabilities}}$	
Hometown Tires and More **2011** $\dfrac{\$50,000 + \$20,000 + \$72,500}{\$337,700} = 0.4{:}1$	Hometown Tires and More **2010** = 0.4:1	Intracompany
	Canadian Tire **2011** = 0.3:1	Intercompany

What does the ratio actually mean? The 2011 ratio of 0.4:1 means that for every dollar of current liabilities, Hometown Tires and More has $0.40 of highly liquid current assets. The company's acid-test ratio is unchanged from 2010. However, it is much lower than its current ratio of 1.6:1. This likely means that Hometown Tires and More has a large balance in its inventory and/or prepaid accounts. In addition, given that the current ratio increased while the acid-test ratio did not change in 2011, inventory and/or prepaid expenses likely increased. We will investigate the liquidity of both companies' inventory shortly, as this is the more significant account of the two.

Hometown Tires and More's acid-test ratio is marginally higher than that of Canadian Tire. This is interesting given that its current ratio was lower. Hometown Tires and More has a higher proportion of liquid assets (cash, short-term investments, and receivables) compared with its current liabilities than does Canadian Tire.

Receivables Turnover

Helpful hint To calculate an average balance sheet amount such as accounts receivable, add together the balance at the beginning of the year (which is the same as the balance at the end of the prior year) and the balance at the end of the year and divide the sum by 2.

The acid-test ratio does not consider the impact of uncollectible receivables on liquidity. A dollar of cash is more available to pay bills than a dollar of an overdue account receivable. The receivables turnover ratio is used to assess the liquidity of the receivables. It measures the number of times, on average, that receivables are collected during the period. The receivables turnover is calculated by dividing net credit sales (net sales less cash sales) by the average gross accounts receivable.

You will recall from earlier chapters that when a figure from the income statement is compared with a figure from the balance sheet in a ratio, the balance sheet figure is averaged by adding together the beginning and ending balances and dividing them by 2. That is because income statement figures cover a period of time (i.e., a year) and balance sheet figures are at a point in time—in this case, the beginning and the end of the year. That is why average receivables are used in the calculation of the receivables turnover ratio shown below. Comparisons of end-of-period figures with end-of-period figures, or period figures with period figures, do not require averaging, as we saw in the current ratio and acid-test ratios calculated above.

Assuming that all sales are credit sales and that there is no allowance for doubtful accounts, the 2011 and 2010 receivables turnover figures for Hometown Tires and More and 2011 receivables turnover ratio for Canadian Tire are shown below.

Receivables turnover = $\dfrac{\text{Net credit sales}}{\text{Average gross accounts receivable}}$		
Hometown Tires and More **2011** $\dfrac{\$1,997,000}{(\$72,500 + \$50,000) \div 2} = 32.6 \text{ times}$	Hometown Tires and More **2010** = 38.7 times	Intracompany
	Canadian Tire **2011** = 13.8 times	Intercompany

Hometown Tires and More's receivables turn over (i.e., they are collected) 32.6 times a year. In general, the faster the receivables turnover, the better and more reliable the current ratio is for assessing liquidity.

Although Hometown Tires and More's receivables turnover declined (worsened) from 38.7 times in 2010 to 32.6 times in 2011, it is still much higher than Canadian Tire's receivables turnover of 13.8 times a year. Why is Hometown Tires and More's receivables turnover so much higher than that of Canadian Tire? Hometown Tires and More likely has fewer sales on account and therefore fewer receivables. More of its sales are for cash. Canadian Tire, on the other hand, has receivables from its franchise stores and company credit card, which may take longer to collect.

It is important to be careful in interpreting this ratio. We assumed that all sales were credit sales, when in fact, this is not a reasonable assumption. Companies do not disclose their credit and cash sales separately. However, intracompany and intercompany comparisons can still be made, since the same assumption—all sales were credit sales—was applied to Canadian Tire's data.

Collection Period. A popular variation of the receivables turnover is to convert it into a collection period stated in days. This is calculated by dividing the receivables turnover into the number of days in a year (365 days). Hometown Tires and More's collection period for 2011 and 2010 and Canadian Tire's collection period for 2011 are shown below.

Collection period = $\dfrac{\text{Days in year}}{\text{Receivables turnover}}$		
Hometown Tires and More **2011** $\dfrac{365 \text{ days}}{32.6} = 11 \text{ days}$	Hometown Tires and More **2010** = 9 days	Intracompany
	Canadian Tire **2011** = 26 days	Intercompany

The effectiveness of a company's credit and collection policies is much easier to interpret using the collection period, rather than the receivables turnover ratio. Hometown Tires and More's receivables were collected every 11 days in 2011. Although weaker than in 2010, they are still being collected faster than those of Canadian Tire. In addition, this collection period is well under the normal 30-day payment period. The general rule is that the collection period should not be more than the credit-term period (the time allowed for payment). Even Canadian Tire's higher collection period of 26 days is still a reasonable one. So, despite earlier concerns, receivables management appears to be in good shape for both companies.

ACCOUNTING IN ACTION
ACROSS THE ORGANIZATION

It is during economic downturns that a company's receivables turnover and average collection period ratios need to be closely watched. During difficult times, management may face pressure to loosen the company's credit policy in order to boost sales. If credit is extended to risky customers who pay late, or who do not pay at all, then the average collection period will increase and the receivables turnover will decrease. That's why it is important to interpret a company's ability to manage its receivables in the context of its current credit policy, economic conditions, and industry averages, as well as prior receivables ratios.

What other liquidity ratios should be monitored, and by what department(s), across the organization?

Inventory Turnover

Inventory turnover measures the average number of times that the inventory is sold during the period. Its purpose is to measure the liquidity of the inventory. The inventory turnover is calculated by dividing the cost of goods sold by the average inventory.

Hometown Tires and More's 2011 and 2010 inventory turnover figures and the 2011 inventory turnover ratio for Canadian Tire are shown below.

Inventory turnover = $\dfrac{\text{Cost of goods sold}}{\text{Average inventory}}$		
Hometown Tires and More 2011	Hometown Tires and More **2010** = 3.9 times	Intracompany
$\dfrac{\$1,381,000}{(\$372,500 + \$340,000) \div 2}$ = 3.9 times	Canadian Tire **2011** = 6.2 times	Intercompany

Hometown Tires and More turns over (sells) its entire inventory 3.9 times a year. Its inventory turnover was unchanged between 2010 and 2011. Hometown Tires and More's turnover ratio of 3.9 times is low compared with that of Canadian Tire's turnover of 6.2 times.

Generally, the faster inventory is sold, the less cash there is tied up in inventory and the less chance there is of inventory becoming obsolete. In addition, the higher the inventory turnover, the more reliable the current ratio is for assessing liquidity. We made this same statement earlier in this chapter with respect to the receivables turnover ratio. That is, if the receivables and inventory turnover ratios are declining, the current ratio may increase simply because of higher balances of receivables and inventory included in current assets. In such cases, the turnover ratios are more relevant than the current ratio as measures of liquidity.

Days Sales in Inventory. A variant of inventory turnover is the days sales in inventory. This is calculated by dividing the inventory turnover into the number of days in a year (365 days). Hometown

Tires and More's days sales in inventory for 2011 and 2010 and the 2011 days sales in inventory for Canadian Tire are shown below.

Days sales in inventory $= \dfrac{\text{Days in year}}{\text{Inventory turnover}}$		
Hometown Tires and More **2011** $\dfrac{365 \text{ days}}{3.9} = 94 \text{ days}$	Hometown Tires and More **2010** = 94 days	Intracompany
	Canadian Tire **2011** = 59 days	Intercompany

Hometown Tires and More's inventory turnover of 3.9 times divided into 365 days is approximately 94 days. In other words, Hometown Tires and More has 94 days' (more than three months') worth of inventory on hand. This is relatively slow compared with Canadian Tire's 59 days.

It is important to use judgement in interpreting both the inventory turnover and days sales in inventory ratios. Remember that Hometown Tires and More is composed of a few stores throughout the region, while Canadian Tire has more than 1,700 stores across the nation. Canadian Tire is large enough to take advantage of just-in-time and other computerized inventory management techniques, whereas Hometown Tires and More likely does not have such sophisticated inventory options.

Nonetheless, Hometown Tires and More must keep a close eye on its inventory. It runs the risk of being left with unsaleable inventory, not to mention the additional costs of financing and carrying this inventory over a longer period of time.

Operating Cycle

Alternative terminology   The *operating cycle* is also known as the *cash conversion cycle*.

The operating cycle measures the average time it takes to purchase inventory, sell it on account, and collect the cash from customers. It is calculated by adding the days sales in inventory and the collection period together. The 2011 and 2010 operating cycle figures for Hometown Tires and More and 2011 operating cycle for Canadian Tire are shown below.

Operating cycle = Days sales in inventory + Collection period		
Hometown Tires and More **2011** 94 days + 11 days = 105 days	Hometown Tires and More **2010** = 103 days	Intracompany
	Canadian Tire **2011** = 85 days	Intercompany

In 2011, it took Hometown Tires and More an average of 105 days (more than three months) from the time it purchased its inventory to sell it on account and collect the cash. This was two days slower than its operating cycle in 2010. Canadian Tire's operating cycle was much faster (shorter) than Hometown Tires and More's in 2011.

Liquidity Conclusion

In an intracompany comparison for the years 2011 and 2010, as shown in Illustration 18-10, Hometown Tires and More's current ratio increased slightly while its acid-test and inventory turnover ratios remained unchanged from 2010 to 2011. Although its receivables turnover ratio declined, it is

▶ILLUSTRATION **18-10**
Intracompany comparison of liquidity ratios

HOMETOWN TIRES AND MORE INC.			
Liquidity Ratio	**2011**	**2010**	**Comparison**
Current ratio	1.6:1	1.5:1	Better
Acid-test ratio	0.4:1	0.4:1	No change
Receivables turnover	32.6 times	38.7 times	Worse
Collection period	11 days	9 days	Worse
Inventory turnover	3.9 times	3.9 times	No change
Days sales in inventory	94 days	94 days	No change
Operating cycle	105 days	103 days	Worse

still a strong result, and well within the normal collection period. And while its inventory turnover ratio did not change between 2010 and 2011, it is taking a long time to sell its inventory, which could be problematic in future. Because Hometown Tires and More's receivables turnover ratio declined, its operating cycle—composed of both receivables and inventory—also declined in 2011.

In an intercompany comparison for 2011, as shown in Illustration 18-11, Hometown Tires and More's overall liquidity is worse than that of Canadian Tire. While its acid-test ratio, receivables turnover, and collection period are better than that of Canadian Tire, this is not as significant a factor in assessing its liquidity as is the management of its inventory. HomeTown Tires and More's inventory turnover, days sales in inventory, and resulting operating cycle are worse than that of Canadian Tire.

Liquidity Ratio	Hometown Tires and More	Canadian Tire	Comparison
Current ratio	1.6:1	1.7:1	Worse
Acid-test ratio	0.4:1	0.3:1	Better
Receivables turnover	32.6 times	13.8 times	Better
Collection period	11 days	26 days	Better
Inventory turnover	3.9 times	6.2 times	Worse
Days sales in inventory	94 days	59 days	Worse
Operating cycle	105 days	85 days	Worse

▶ **ILLUSTRATION 18-11**
Intercompany comparison of liquidity ratios

Summary of Liquidity Ratios

Illustration 18-12 summarizes the liquidity ratios we have used in this chapter, and throughout the textbook. In addition to the ratio formula and purpose, the desired direction (higher or lower) of the result is included.

▶ **ILLUSTRATION 18-12**
Liquidity ratios

Liquidity Ratio	Formula	Purpose	Desired Result
Current ratio	$\dfrac{\text{Current assets}}{\text{Current liabilities}}$	Measures short-term debt-paying ability.	Higher
Acid-test	$\dfrac{\text{Cash + Short-term investments + Accounts receivable}}{\text{Current liabilities}}$	Measures immediate short-term debt-paying ability.	Higher
Receivables turnover	$\dfrac{\text{Net credit sales}}{\text{Average gross accounts receivable}}$	Measures liquidity of receivables.	Higher
Collection period	$\dfrac{\text{Days in year}}{\text{Receivables turnover}}$	Measures number of days receivables are outstanding.	Lower
Inventory turnover	$\dfrac{\text{Cost of goods sold}}{\text{Average inventory}}$	Measures liquidity of inventory.	Higher
Days sales in inventory	$\dfrac{\text{Days in year}}{\text{Inventory turnover}}$	Measures number of days inventory is on hand.	Lower
Operating cycle	Days sales in inventory + Collection period	Measures number of days to purchase inventory, sell it on account, and collect the cash.	Lower

To summarize, a higher result is generally considered to be better for the current, acid-test, receivables turnover, and inventory turnover ratios. For those ratios that use turnover ratios in their denominators—the collection period and days sales in inventory—as well as the operating cycle, which is the combination of both of these, a lower result is better. That is, you want to take fewer days to collect receivables and have fewer days of inventory on hand—a lower operating cycle—than the opposite situation.

Of course, there are exceptions. A current ratio can be artificially high at times because of higher balances of receivables and inventory included in current assets that are the result of slow-moving inventory or uncollectible receivables. This is why it is important never to conclude an assessment of liquidity based only on one ratio. In the case of the current ratio, it should always be interpreted along with the acid-test, receivables turnover, and inventory turnover ratios. Likewise, the acid-test ratio should always be interpreted along with the receivables turnover ratio.

 BEFORE YOU GO ON...

Do It

The following liquidity ratios are available for two fast food companies:

	Henny Penny	Chicken Licken
Current ratio	1.3:1	1.5:1
Acid-test ratio	1.0:1	0.8:1
Receivables turnover	52 times	73 times
Inventory turnover	40 times	26 times

(a) Calculate the collection period, days sales in inventory, and operating cycle for each company.
(b) Indicate which company—Henny Penny or Chicken Licken—has the better result for each of the ratios provided above, in addition to the ratios you calculated in (a).
(c) Overall, which of the two companies is more liquid? Explain.

Solution

(a)

	Henny Penny	Chicken Licken
Collection period	365 ÷ 52 = 7 days	365 ÷ 73 = 5 days
Days sales in inventory	365 ÷ 40 times = 9 days	365 ÷ 26 = 14 days
Operating cycle	7 + 9 = 16 days	5 + 14 = 19 days

(b)

	Henny Penny	Chicken Licken	Comparison
Current ratio	1.3:1	1.5:1	Chicken Licken
Acid-test ratio	1.0:1	0.8:1	Henny Penny
Receivables turnover	52 times	73 times	Chicken Licken
Inventory turnover	40 times	26 times	Henny Penny
Collection period	7 days	5 days	Chicken Licken
Days sales in inventory	9 days	14 days	Henny Penny
Operating cycle	16 days	19 days	Henny Penny

(c) Henny Penny is the more liquid of the two companies. Although its receivables turnover is not as strong as that of Chicken Licken (52 times compared with 73 times), the collection period is still only 7 days, which is an excellent collection period by any standard. Of course, you wouldn't expect a fast food business to have many receivables anyway.

Henny Penny's inventory turnover, which is more important for a fast food business, is stronger than that of Chicken Licken. This slower inventory turnover may be artificially making Chicken Licken's current ratio look better than that of Henny Penny. This hunch is proven by the fact that although Chicken Licken has the (apparently) better current ratio, Henny Penny has the better acid-test ratio, which excludes the effect of inventory. In addition, Henny Penny has the better operating cycle of the two companies.

Related exercise material: BE18–7, BE18–8, BE18–9, E18–6, and E18–7.

Action Plan
- Review the formula for each ratio so you understand how it is calculated and how to interpret it.
- Remember that for liquidity ratios, a higher result is usually better except for the collection period, days sales in inventory, and operating cycle ratios.
- Review the impact of the receivables and inventory turnover ratios on the current ratio before concluding your analysis.
- Consider any industry factors that may affect your analysis.

THE NAVIGATOR

SOLVENCY RATIOS

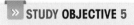 **STUDY OBJECTIVE 5**

Identify and use ratios to analyze solvency.

Solvency ratios measure a company's ability to survive over a long period of time. Long-term creditors are interested in a company's long-term solvency, particularly its ability to pay interest as it comes due and to repay the face value of debt at maturity. Solvency ratios include debt to total assets, interest coverage, and free cash flow.

Debt to Total Assets

Debt to total assets measures the percentage of the total assets that is provided by creditors. It is calculated by dividing total liabilities (both current and long-term) by total assets. The higher the percentage of total debt to total assets, the greater the risk that the company may be unable to meet its maturing obligations. The lower the debt to total assets ratio, the more net assets there are to repay creditors if the company becomes insolvent. So, from a lender's point of view, a low ratio of debt to total assets is desirable.

Hometown Tires and More's 2011 and 2010 debt to total assets ratios and the 2011 debt to total assets ratio for Canadian Tire are shown below.

Debt to total assets = $\dfrac{\text{Total liabilities}}{\text{Total assets}}$		
Hometown Tires and More **2011** $\dfrac{\$737,700}{\$1,000,000} = 73.8\%$	Hometown Tires and More **2010** = 79.7%	Intracompany
	Canadian Tire **2011** = 64.3%	Intercompany

A ratio of 73.8% means that creditors have provided 73.8% of Hometown Tires and More's total assets. Although its ratio declined (improved) in 2011, Hometown Tires and More's debt to total assets ratio is higher (worse) than Canadian Tire's ratio of 64.3%.

Although Hometown Tires and More has a high debt position, a more relevant calculation is whether or not it can afford this level of debt. The debt to total assets ratio should never be interpreted without also looking at the interest coverage ratio, discussed in the next section. A company may have a low debt to total assets ratio but be unable to cover its interest obligations. Alternatively, a company may have a high debt to total assets ratio but be easily able to cover its interest.

Interest Coverage

The interest coverage ratio gives an indication of the company's ability to make its interest payments as they come due. It is calculated by dividing profit before interest expense and income tax expense by interest expense. Note that the interest coverage ratio uses profit before interest expense and income tax expense. This is often abbreviated as EBIT, which stands for earnings before interest and tax. The term "earnings" is used instead of "profit" in this phrase—both are commonly used and mean the same thing. EBIT represents the amount that is considered to be available to cover interest.

The 2011 and 2010 interest coverage ratios for Hometown Tires and More and 2011 interest coverage ratio for Canadian Tire are shown below.

Interest coverage = $\dfrac{\text{Profit} + \text{Interest expense} + \text{Income tax expense}}{\text{Interest expense}}$		
Hometown Tires and More **2011** $\dfrac{\$93,600 + \$27,000 + \$23,400}{\$27,000} = 5.3$ times	Hometown Tires and More **2010** = 5.3 times	Intracompany
	Canadian Tire **2011** = 5.1 times	Intercompany

Despite Hometown Tires and More's high debt to total assets ratio, it is able to cover its interest payments. Its profit before interest and income tax was 5.3 times the amount needed for interest expense in 2011 and 2010. Hometown Tires and More's interest coverage remained unchanged in 2011, despite the improvement in its debt to total assets ratio. It is interesting to note that, although Hometown Tires and More's debt to total assets ratio was worse than that of Canadian Tire, its interest coverage ratio is slightly better than Canadian Tire's coverage ratio of 5.1 times. Nonetheless, both companies are well equipped to handle their interest payments, with coverage ratios in excess of 5 times.

Free Cash Flow

One indication of a company's solvency, as well as of its ability to expand operations, repay debt, or pay dividends, is the amount of excess cash it generates after paying to maintain its current productive capacity. This amount is referred to as free cash flow.

Hometown Tires and More's cash flow statement was not included in the illustrations shown earlier in the chapter. For your information and for the purpose of the calculation below, its cash provided by operating activities for the year ended December 31, 2011, was $122,800 and its cash used by investing activities was $40,000 for the same period.

The 2011 and 2010 free cash flow amounts for Hometown Tires and More and 2011 free cash flow for Canadian Tire are shown below.

Free cash flow = Cash provided (used) by operating activities − Cash used (provided) by investing activities		
Hometown Tires and More **2011** $122,800 − $40,000 = $82,800	Hometown Tires and More **2010** = $100,000	Intracompany
	Canadian Tire **2011** = $244.1 million	Intercompany

Hometown Tires and More has $82,800 of "free" cash to invest in additional property, plant, and equipment; repay debt; and/or pay dividends. This is less than the $100,000 it had available in 2010. Canadian Tire reported a larger amount of free cash in 2011. It generated $244.1 million more from its operating activities than it spent on investing activities. However, as noted earlier, it is hard to make a meaningful comparison of absolute dollar amounts for two companies of such different sizes.

Solvency Conclusion

In an intracompany comparison for the years 2011 and 2010, as shown in Illustration 18-13, Hometown Tires and More's solvency generally improved in 2011, as its debt to total assets ratio improved and its interest coverage ratio remained unchanged. Its free cash flow declined.

▶ILLUSTRATION 18-13
Intracompany comparison of solvency ratios

HOMETOWN TIRES AND MORE

Solvency Ratio	2011	2010	Comparison
Debt to total assets	73.8%	79.7%	Better
Interest coverage	5.3 times	5.3 times	No change
Free cash flow	$82,800	$100,000	Worse

Despite an improvement in solvency within Hometown Tires and More, in an intercompany comparison shown in Illustration 18-14, its solvency was found to be generally worse than that of Canadian Tire in 2011. Despite having a slightly higher interest coverage ratio, it has a much larger proportion of debt to assets and lower free cash flow.

▶ILLUSTRATION 18-14
Intercompany comparison of solvency ratios

Solvency Ratio	Hometown Tires and More	Canadian Tire	Comparison
Debt to total assets	73.8%	64.3%	Worse
Interest coverage	5.3 times	5.1 times	Better
Free cash flow	$82,800	$244,100,000	Worse

It is important to distinguish between Hometown Tires and More and Canadian Tire in this analysis, as they are very different types of companies. Hometown Tires and More, as a small regional company, relies mainly on debt for its financing and has to generate enough profit to cover its interest payments. In contrast, Canadian Tire, a large national company, relies more on equity for its financing needs.

Summary of Solvency Ratios

Illustration 18-15 summarizes the solvency ratios we have used in this chapter, and throughout the textbook.

Solvency Ratio	Formula	Purpose	Desired Result
Debt to total assets	$\dfrac{\text{Total liabilities}}{\text{Total assets}}$	Measures percentage of total assets provided by creditors.	Lower
Interest coverage	$\dfrac{\text{Profit} + \text{Interest expense} + \text{Income tax expense (EBIT)}}{\text{Income expense}}$	Measures ability to meet interest payments.	Higher
Free cash flow	Cash provided (used) by operating activities − Cash used (provided) by investing activities	Measures cash generated from operating activities that management can use after paying capital expenditures.	Higher

▶ **ILLUSTRATION 18-15**
Solvency ratios

For the debt to total assets ratio, a lower result is generally considered to be better. Having less debt reduces a company's dependence on debt financing and offers more flexibility for future financing alternatives. For the interest coverage ratio and free cash flow measure, a higher result is better.

It is important to interpret the debt to total assets and interest coverage ratios together. For example, a company may have a high debt to total assets ratio and a high interest coverage ratio, which indicates that it is able to handle a high level of debt. Or, it may have a low debt to total assets ratio and a low interest coverage ratio, indicating it has difficulty in paying its interest even for a low amount of debt. Consequently, you should always interpret a company's solvency after considering the interrelationship of these two ratios.

 BEFORE YOU GO ON...

Do It

Selected information from the financial statements of the Home Affairs Corporation follows:

	2014	2013
Total assets	$1,000,000	$1,015,000
Total liabilities	737,000	809,000
Interest expense	32,000	32,500
Income tax expense	48,400	50,500
Profit	193,600	202,000

(a) Calculate the debt to total assets and interest coverage ratios for each year.
(b) Indicate whether each of the ratios you calculated in (a) has improved or deteriorated in 2014, compared to 2013.
(c) Overall, has Home Affairs' solvency improved or deteriorated in 2014?

Solution
(a) and (b)

	(a)		(b)
	2014	**2013**	Comparison
Debt to total assets	$\dfrac{\$737,700}{\$1,000,000} = 73.7\%$	$\dfrac{\$809,000}{\$1,015,000} = 79.7\%$	Better
Interest coverage	$\dfrac{\$193,600 + \$32,000 + \$48,400}{\$32,000}$	$\dfrac{\$202,000 + \$32,500 + \$50,500}{\$32,500}$	
	= 8.6 times	= 8.8 times	Worse

(c) Overall, Home Affairs' solvency has improved in 2012. The debt to total assets ratio has declined (improved) in 2012. While the interest coverage ratio declined (deteriorated) marginally between 2011 and 2012, the company still has a strong coverage ratio at 8.6 times. Taken together, this leads us to conclude that overall solvency has improved.

Related exercise material: BE18–10, BE18–11, BE18–12, E18–8, and E18–9.

Action Plan
• Review the formula for each ratio so you understand how it is calculated and how to interpret it.
• The debt to total assets ratio should always be interpreted together with the interest coverage ratio.
• Remember that for debt to total assets, a lower result is better. For other solvency ratios, a higher result is better.

THE **NAVIGATOR**

PROFITABILITY RATIOS

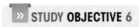

Profitability ratios measure a company's operating success for a specific period of time. A company's profit, or lack of it, affects its ability to obtain debt and equity financing, its liquidity position, and its growth. Investors and creditors are therefore interested in evaluating profitability. Profitability ratios include the gross profit margin, profit margin, asset turnover, return on assets, return on equity, earnings per share, price-earnings, and payout ratios.

Gross Profit Margin

The gross profit margin is determined by dividing gross profit (net sales less cost of goods sold) by net sales. This ratio indicates the relative relationship between net sales and cost of goods sold. Gross profit margins should be watched closely over time. If the gross profit margin is too high, the company may lose sales if its pricing is not competitive. If the gross profit margin is too low, the company may not have enough margin to cover its expenses.

Hometown Tires and More's gross profit margin figures for 2011 and 2010 and Canadian Tire's gross profit margin for 2011 are shown below.

$$\text{Gross profit margin} = \frac{\text{Gross profit}}{\text{Net sales}}$$

Hometown Tires and More **2011** $\dfrac{\$616,000}{\$1,997,000} = 30.8\%$	Hometown Tires and More **2010** = 32.5%	Intracompany
	Canadian Tire **2011** = 29.5%	Intercompany

Hometown Tires and More's gross profit margin for 2011 means that 30.8 cents of each dollar of its sales that year went to cover operating and other expenses and generate a profit. Hometown Tires and More's gross profit margin declined slightly, from 32.5% in 2010 to 30.8% in 2011.

Hometown Tires and More's gross profit margin is slightly higher than Canadian Tire's. This could be the result of several factors. It may be that Hometown Tires and More sells a different mix of merchandise than does Canadian Tire. In addition, Hometown Tires and More's prices may be higher in general not only because of increased costs, but also because the company offers a higher level of personal service.

Profit Margin

Profit margin is a measure of the percentage of each dollar of sales that results in profit. It is calculated by dividing profit by net sales. Hometown Tires and More's 2011 and 2010 profit margin figures and Canadian Tire's 2011 profit margin are shown below.

$$\text{Profit margin} = \frac{\text{Profit}}{\text{Net sales}}$$

Hometown Tires and More **2011** $\dfrac{\$93,600}{\$1,997,000} = 4.7\%$	Hometown Tires and More **2010** = 5.6%	Intracompany
	Canadian Tire **2011** = 4.5%	Intercompany

Hometown Tires and More's profit margin declined between 2010 and 2011, at 4.7% of net sales, primarily because of the loss due to the fair value adjustment of trading investments. The profit margin, although declining, is still above that of Canadian Tire.

Asset Turnover

Asset turnover measures how efficiently a company uses its assets to generate sales. It is determined by dividing net sales by average total assets. The resulting number shows the dollars of sales produced by each dollar of assets.

The 2011 and 2010 asset turnover ratios for Hometown Tires and More and 2011 asset turnover ratio for Canadian Tire are shown below.

Asset turnover $= \dfrac{\text{Net sales}}{\text{Average total assets}}$		
Hometown Tires and More **2011** $\dfrac{\$1,997,000}{(\$1,000,000 + \$1,015,000) \div 2} = 2.0 \text{ times}$	Hometown Tires and More **2010** = 1.7 times	Intracompany
	Canadian Tire **2011** = 0.9 times	Intercompany

In 2011, Hometown Tires and More generated $2 of sales for each dollar it had invested in assets. This ratio improved from 2010, when its asset turnover was 1.7 times, or $1.70 of sales for each dollar of assets. Its 2011 asset turnover is also much higher than that of Canadian Tire. Its assets may be newer and more efficient than Canadian Tire's.

Return on Assets

An overall measure of profitability is return on assets. This ratio is calculated by dividing profit by average total assets. Hometown Tires and More's return on assets figures for 2011 and 2010 and Canadian Tire's return on assets for 2011 are shown below.

Return on assets $= \dfrac{\text{Profit}}{\text{Average total assets}}$		
Hometown Tires and More **2011** $\dfrac{\$93,600}{(\$1,000,000 + \$1,015,000) \div 2} = 9.3\%$	Hometown Tires and More **2010** = 9.7%	Intracompany
	Canadian Tire **2011** = 4.0%	Intercompany

Hometown Tires and More's return on assets declined (worsened) from 2010 to 2011. Still, its 2011 return of 9.3% is more than double that of Canadian Tire. Although the percentage is high, it must be analyzed in perspective. Hometown Tires and More's assets have been decreasing and profit is being compared with a relatively small asset base. Consequently, it results in a higher percentage proportionately.

Return on Equity

A popular measure of profitability is the return on equity ratio. This ratio shows how many dollars of profit were earned for each dollar invested by the shareholders. It is calculated by dividing profit by average total shareholders' equity.

Alternative terminology *Return on equity* is also known as *return on investment*.

Although we calculate this ratio using total shareholders' equity below, it can also be calculated using only the common shareholders' equity if there is more than one class of shares. In such cases, the numerator, profit, is reduced by any preferred dividends to determine the profit available for common shareholders. The denominator, average total shareholders' equity, is reduced by any share capital belonging to the preferred shareholders to determine average common shareholders' equity. You will recall that Hometown Tires and More has only one class of share capital—common shares—so it has no preferred shares or preferred dividends.

The return on equity figures for Hometown Tires and More for 2011 and 2010 and return on equity for Canadian Tire for 2011 are shown below.

Return on equity $= \dfrac{\text{Profit}}{\text{Average shareholders' equity}}$		
Hometown Tires and More **2011** $\dfrac{\$93,600}{(\$262,300 + \$206,500) \div 2} = 39.9\%$	Hometown Tires and More **2010** = 50.9%	Intracompany
	Canadian Tire **2011** = 11.1%	Intercompany

Although it declined (worsened) in 2011, Hometown Tires and More's return on equity is unusually high at 39.9%. The return on equity figure for Canadian Tire is much lower at 11.1%.

Note that Hometown Tires and More's 2011 return on equity of 39.9% is much higher than its return on assets of 9.3%. The reason is that Hometown Tires and More has made effective use of financial leverage. You will recall that we first learned about financial leverage in Chapter 15. Financial leverage is said to be positive if a company is able to earn a higher return on equity by using borrowed money in its operations than it has to pay on the borrowed money. Use of financial leverage has enabled Hometown Tires and More to use money supplied by creditors to increase its return to the shareholders. Recall that Hometown Tires and More has proportionately more debt than Canadian Tire. Given that it is able to create positive financial leverage on its borrowings, it is not surprising that Hometown Tires and More's return on equity is higher than Canadian Tire's.

Earnings per Share (EPS)

Earnings per share is a measure of the profit earned on each common share. Shareholders usually think in terms of the number of shares they own or plan to buy or sell. Reducing profit to a per-share basis gives a useful measure of profitability. This measure is widely used and reported. Because of the importance of the earnings per share ratio, publicly traded companies are required to present it directly on the income statement. As we mentioned earlier in this textbook, private companies using ASPE are not required to report earnings per share.

Earnings per share is calculated by dividing the profit available to common shareholders (profit less preferred dividends) by the weighted average number of common shares. Hometown Tires and More's profit was reported in Illustration 18-5 and its number of common shares was reported in Illustration 18-4. You will recall that Hometown Tires and More does not have any preferred shares, so there are no preferred dividends to consider in this calculation. There has been no change in the number of common shares over the past three years; consequently, the weighted average number of shares is the same as the issued number—300,000.

The earnings per share figures for Hometown Tires and More for 2011 and 2010 and earnings per share for Canadian Tire for 2011 are shown below.

Earnings per share $= \dfrac{\text{Profit} - \text{Preferred dividends}}{\text{Weighted average number of common shares}}$		
Hometown Tires and More 2011 $\dfrac{\$93,600 - \$0}{300,000} = \$0.31$	**Hometown Tires and More 2010** $= \$0.34$	Intracompany
	Canadian Tire 2011 $= \$5.73$	Intercompany

Hometown Tires and More's earnings per share declined by $0.03 per share ($0.34 − $0.31) in 2011. Comparisons with Canadian Tire are not meaningful, because of the large differences in the number of shares issued by companies for different purposes. The only meaningful EPS comparison is an intracompany one.

Price-Earnings (PE) Ratio

The price-earnings (PE) ratio is an often-quoted measure of the ratio of the market price of each common share to the earnings per share. The price-earnings ratio reflects investors' assessments of a company's future profitability. It is calculated by dividing the market price per share by earnings per share. The current market price of Hometown Tires and More's shares is $1.40/share. Earnings per share were calculated above.

The price-earnings ratios for Hometown Tires and More for 2011 and 2010 and the price-earnings ratio for Canadian Tire for 2011 are shown below.

Price-earnings ratio = $\dfrac{\text{Market price per share}}{\text{Earnings per share}}$		
Hometown Tires and More **2011** $\dfrac{\$1.40}{\$0.31} = 4.5$ times	Hometown Tires and More **2010** = 3.5 times	Intracompany
	Canadian Tire **2011** = 12.7 times	Intercompany

In 2011, Hometown Tires and More's shares were valued at 4.5 times its earnings. The earnings per share, although declining, are still strong and the price of the shares has increased, indicating investors believe the company has expectations of future increases in profitability. Canadian Tire's 2011 price-earnings ratio is 12.7 times, which is much higher than Hometown Tires and More's ratio of 4.5 times.

In general, a higher price-earnings ratio means that investors favour the company. They are willing to pay more for the shares because they believe the company has good prospects for long-term growth and profit in the future.

Payout Ratio

The payout ratio measures the percentage of profit distributed as cash dividends. It is calculated by dividing cash dividends by profit. Hometown Tires and More paid $37,800 in dividends in 2011. Its profit was reported earlier in Illustration 18-5.

The 2011 and 2010 payout ratios for Hometown Tires and More and 2011 payout ratio for Canadian Tire are shown below.

Payout ratio = $\dfrac{\text{Cash dividends}}{\text{Profit}}$		
Hometown Tires and More **2011** $\dfrac{\$37,800}{\$93,600} = 40.4\%$	Hometown Tires and More **2010** = 35.3%	Intracompany
	Canadian Tire **2011** = 19.6%	Intercompany

Hometown Tires and More's 2011 payout ratio of 40.4% increased over its 2010 payout ratio and is more than double the payout ratio of Canadian Tire. Many companies with stable earnings have high payout ratios. For example, BCE Inc. recently had a payout ratio in excess of 70%. Companies that are expanding rapidly normally have low, or no, payout ratios. Research In Motion, for example, had a zero payout ratio.

Profitability Conclusion

In an intracompany comparison, as shown in Illustration 18-16, Hometown Tires and More's overall profitability declined between 2010 and 2011. All of its profitability measures declined except for its asset turnover, price-earnings, and payout ratios.

HOMETOWN TIRES AND MORE			
Profitability Ratio	**2011**	**2010**	**Comparison**
Gross profit margin	30.8%	32.5%	Worse
Profit margin	4.7%	5.6%	Worse
Asset turnover	2.0 times	1.7 times	Better
Return on assets	9.3%	9.7%	Worse
Return on equity	39.9%	50.9%	Worse
Earnings per share	$0.31	$0.34	Worse
Price-earnings ratio	4.5 times	3.5 times	Better
Payout ratio	40.4%	35.3%	Better

▸ ILLUSTRATION 18-16
Intracompany comparison of profitability ratios

In an intercompany comparison, as shown in Illustration 18-17, Hometown Tires and More's overall profitability is better than that of Canadian Tire on all but one measure. Despite its lower profitability performance, investors are favouring Canadian Tire rather than Hometown Tires and More, as evidenced by the price-earnings ratio.

▶**ILLUSTRATION 18-17**
Intercompany comparison of profitability ratios

Profitability Ratio	Hometown Tires and More	Canadian Tire	Comparison
Gross profit margin	30.8%	29.5%	Better
Profit margin	4.7%	4.5%	Better
Asset turnover	2.0 times	0.9 times	Better
Return on assets	9.3%	4.0%	Better
Return on equity	39.9%	11.1%	Better
Earnings per share	$0.31	$5.73	n/a
Price-earnings ratio	4.5 times	12.7 times	Worse
Payout ratio	40.4%	19.6%	Better

Summary of Profitability Ratios

▶**ILLUSTRATION 18-18**
Profitability ratios

Illustration 18-18 summarizes the profitability ratios we have used in this chapter, and throughout the textbook.

Profitability Ratio	Formula	Purpose	Desired Result
Gross profit margin	$\dfrac{\text{Gross profit}}{\text{Net sales}}$	Measures margin between selling price and cost of goods sold.	Higher
Profit margin	$\dfrac{\text{Profit}}{\text{Net sales}}$	Measures amount of profit generated by each dollar of sales.	Higher
Asset turnover	$\dfrac{\text{Net sales}}{\text{Average total assets}}$	Measures how efficiently assets are used to generate sales.	Higher
Return on assets	$\dfrac{\text{Profit}}{\text{Average total assets}}$	Measures overall profitability of assets.	Higher
Return on equity	$\dfrac{\text{Profit}}{\text{Average shareholders' equity}}$	Measures profitability of shareholders' investment.	Higher
Earnings per share	$\dfrac{\text{Profit} - \text{Preferred dividends}}{\text{Weighted average number of common shares}}$	Measures amount of profit earned on each common share.	Higher
Price-earnings ratio	$\dfrac{\text{Market price per share}}{\text{Earnings per share}}$	Measures relationship between market price per share and earnings per share.	Higher
Payout ratio	$\dfrac{\text{Cash dividends}}{\text{Profit}}$	Measures percentage of profit distributed as cash dividends.	Higher

For the profitability ratios shown in Illustration 18-18, a higher result is generally considered to be better. However, there are some user-related considerations with respect to the price-earnings and payout ratios that must be understood. A higher price-earnings ratio generally means that investors favour that company and have high expectations of future profitability. However, some investors avoid shares with high PE ratios in the belief that they are overpriced, so not everyone prefers a high PE ratio.

Investors interested in purchasing a company's shares for income purposes (in the form of a dividend) are interested in companies with a high payout ratio. Investors more interested in purchasing a company's shares for growth purposes (for the share price's appreciation) are interested in a low payout ratio. They would prefer to see the company retain its profit rather than pay it out.

We have shown liquidity, solvency, and profitability ratios in separate sections in this chapter. However, it is important to recognize that financial statement analysis should not focus on one section in isolation from the others. Liquidity, solvency, and profitability are closely interrelated in most companies.

For example, a company's profitability is affected by the availability of financing and short-term liquidity. Similarly, a company's solvency not only requires satisfactory liquidity but is also affected by its profitability.

It is also important to recognize that the ratios shown in Illustrations 18-12, 18-15, and 18-18 are only examples of commonly used ratios. You will find more examples as you learn more about financial analysis.

ACCOUNTING IN ACTION
ALL ABOUT YOU INSIGHT

More Canadians are investing in the stock market largely because of the ease of trading stocks on-line. Traders range from students like you tracking their investments to seniors making adjustments to their retirement savings. Everybody wants to buy and sell stocks just at the right time. How do investors predict what stock prices will do and when to buy and sell stock?

Two early pioneers in providing investment advice to the masses were Tom and David Gardner, brothers who created an on-line investor service called The Motley Fool. Tom and David view themselves as twenty-first-century "fools," revealing the "truths" of the stock markets to small investors. Its website offers Fool followers stock quotes, company research reports, personal finance information, news, on-line seminars, and message boards. The Motley Fool has grown substantially since its inception in 1993, offering even the most inexperienced investor the basic advice needed to master his or her own financial affairs.

Critics of on-line investor services, and in particular message boards, contend that they can exacerbate the rumour mill. They suggest that, because of the excitement created by some message board postings, share prices can get bid up to unreasonable levels. One potentially troubling aspect of message boards is that participants on a board rarely give their real identities—instead using aliases. Consequently, there is little to stop people from putting misinformation on the board to influence a share's price in the direction they desire.

Sources: Motley Fool website, http://www.fool.com; Don E. Giacomino and Michael D. Akers, "Examining an Online Investment Research Service: The Motley Fool," *Journal of Business and Economics Research*, volume 9, number 1, January 2011; Stacy Forster, "Motley Fool to 'Educate, Amuse, Enrich'...and Advise Investors," *The Wall Street Journal Online*, September 6, 2001.

Suppose you are thinking about investing in shares of Tim Hortons. You scanned a variety of investor websites and found messages posted by two different investors. One says it's time to buy Tim Hortons shares; the other says it isn't. How should you decide whether to buy the shares or not?

 BEFORE YOU GO ON...

Do It

Selected information from the financial statements of two competitor companies follows:

	Papat Corporation	Bearton Limited
Total assets, beginning of year	$388,000	$372,000
Total assets, end of year	434,000	536,000
Total shareholders' equity, beginning of year	269,000	296,000
Total shareholders' equity, end of year	294,000	344,000
Net sales	660,000	780,000
Gross profit	175,000	248,000
Profit	68,000	105,000

(a) For each company, calculate the following ratios: gross profit margin, profit margin, asset turnover, return on assets, and return on equity.

(b) Indicate which company—Papat or Bearton—has the better result for each of the ratios you calculated in (a).

(c) Overall, which of the two companies is more profitable? Explain.

Action Plan

- Review the formula for each ratio so you understand how it is calculated and how to interpret it.
- Don't forget to average the balance sheet figures [(beginning of period + end of period) ÷ 2] when comparing them with a period figure (e.g., net sales and profit).
- Remember that for profitability ratios, a higher result is usually better.

BEFORE YOU GO ON continued...

Solution

(a)

	Papat	Bearton
Gross profit margin	$\dfrac{\$175{,}000}{\$660{,}000} = 26.5\%$	$\dfrac{\$248{,}000}{\$780{,}000} = 31.8\%$
Profit margin	$\dfrac{\$68{,}000}{\$660{,}000} = 10.3\%$	$\dfrac{\$105{,}000}{\$780{,}000} = 13.5\%$
Asset turnover	$\dfrac{\$660{,}000}{(\$388{,}000 + \$434{,}000) \div 2} = 1.6 \text{ times}$	$\dfrac{\$780{,}000}{(\$372{,}000 + \$536{,}000) \div 2} = 1.7 \text{ times}$
Return on assets	$\dfrac{\$68{,}000}{(\$388{,}000 + \$434{,}000) \div 2} = 16.5\%$	$\dfrac{\$105{,}000}{(\$372{,}000 + \$536{,}000) \div 2} = 23.1\%$
Return on equity	$\dfrac{\$68{,}000}{(\$269{,}000 + \$294{,}000) \div 2} = 24.2\%$	$\dfrac{\$105{,}000}{(\$296{,}000 + \$344{,}000) \div 2} = 32.8\%$

(b)

	Papat	Bearton	Comparison
Gross profit margin	26.5%	31.8%	Bearton
Profit margin	10.3%	13.5%	Bearton
Asset turnover	1.6 times	1.7 times	Bearton
Return on assets	16.5%	23.1%	Bearton
Return on equity	24.2%	32.8%	Bearton

(c) Bearton Limited is more profitable than Papat Corporation on all profitability ratios.

Related exercise material: BE18–13, BE18–14, BE18–15, BE18–16, BE18–17, E18–10, E18–11, E18–12, E18–13, E18–14, and E18–15.

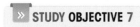

THE NAVIGATOR

Limitations of Financial Statement Analysis

» **STUDY OBJECTIVE 7**

Recognize the limitations of financial statement analysis.

Business decisions are frequently made by using one or more of the analytical tools illustrated in this chapter. But you should be aware of the limitations of these tools and of the financial statements they are based on.

ALTERNATIVE ACCOUNTING POLICIES

There are a wide variety of different accounting policies and practices that companies can use. For example, companies may use different inventory cost determination methods (specific identification, FIFO, or average) or different depreciation methods (straight-line, diminishing-balance, or units-of-production) depending on the pattern of the revenues (economic benefits) their assets produce. Different methods can result in differing financial positions and performance, which will reduce comparability.

For example, Canadian Tire uses the diminishing-balance method of depreciation for much of its property, plant, and equipment. Hometown Tires and More uses the straight-line method of depreciation. Consequently, profit and total assets could be different—depending on the amount of property, plant, and equipment and at what point in its useful life it is—simply because of the use of different depreciation methods. This would affect a number of solvency and profitability ratios.

Recall, however, that although depreciation expense and the carrying amount of property, plant, and equipment may be different in one or more periods because of the choice of depreciation methods, in total, over the life of the assets, there is no difference. We call differences created from alternative accounting policies "artificial" or timing differences. Although it is possible to detect differences in accounting policies by reading the notes to the financial statements, adjusting the financial data to compensate for the use of different policies can be difficult for the average user. In real life, analysts spend a great deal of time adjusting financial statement data for these types of differences in order to improve the comparability of the ratios.

Intercompany comparability may also be hindered by differing accounting policy options available for private companies. While Hometown Tires and More is a publicly traded company using IFRS, it may have competitors that are private companies. You will recall that private companies have the choice of adopting IFRS or Accounting Standards for Private Enterprises. If a private company has chosen not to adopt IFRS, which is the most likely scenario, further complications can arise in trying to compare a private company with a public company for certain accounting policies.

Intracompany comparability can be affected by the use of different accounting policies over different periods of time. As has been discussed throughout this text, publicly traded companies such as Canadian Tire adopted IFRS effective January 1, 2011. Although results for the 2010 fiscal year were required to be restated using IFRS for comparability purposes, prior years may not have been converted from Canadian generally accepted accounting principles into IFRS. In fact, Canadian Tire notes in the 10-year summary of financial information included in its annual report that results for the years 2002 through 2009 have *not* been converted to IFRS. Consequently, comparing ratios based on IFRS figures with those based on pre-changeover Canadian GAAP may result in misleading trends.

COMPREHENSIVE INCOME

Most financial analysis ratios exclude other comprehensive income. For example, profitability ratios generally use data from the income statement and not the statement of comprehensive income, which includes both profit and other comprehensive income. In fact, there are no standard ratio formulas incorporating comprehensive income.

Nonetheless, it is important to review the amount and source of other comprehensive income in any financial analysis. For example, Canadian Tire reported a profit of $467 million for the year ended December 31, 2011. During the same year, it reported other comprehensive income—primarily from derivatives—of $29.1 million, which resulted in total comprehensive income of $496.1 million ($467.0 + $29.1). Canadian Tire's profit margin, illustrated earlier in this chapter, was 4.5%. However, if a profit margin was calculated using total comprehensive income rather than just profit, it would have been 4.8% instead of 4.5%.

This difference is not significant enough to affect decision-making. However, in cases where other comprehensive income is significant, and depending on the source of the income, some analysts will adjust profitability ratios to incorporate the effect of total comprehensive income. Of course you will recall from past chapters that private companies following ASPE do not report comprehensive income, so this limitation would apply only to public and private companies following IFRS.

QUALITY OF INFORMATION

In evaluating a company's financial performance, the quality of the information provided is extremely important. A company that has a high quality index includes full and transparent information that will not confuse or mislead users of the financial statements. As we discussed in our feature story, financial statements for companies like Canadian Tire, with full and transparent disclosure practices, have a high quality of information value. Other companies may limit the information they disclose. In such cases, the quality of the information will decrease.

Fortunately, the chief executive officer and chief financial officer of a publicly traded company must ensure, and personally declare, that the reported financial information is accurate, relevant, and understandable. In addition, audit committees are held responsible for reviewing the quality of the underlying estimates, accounting policies, and judgements involved in the preparation of the financial statements.

A strong corporate governance process, including an active board of directors and audit committee, is essential to ensuring the quality of information. Canadian Tire has received commendations from the judges in this year's Corporate Reporting Awards program mentioned in our chapter-opening feature story for its corporate governance disclosure. According to the judges, "The expectations and responsibilities of directors are clearly outlined, well organized and easy-to-read in the corporate governance disclosures."

ECONOMIC FACTORS

You cannot properly interpret a financial analysis without also considering the economic circumstances in which a company operates. Economic measures such as the rate of interest, unemployment, and changes in demand and supply can have a significant impact on a company's performance.

For example, in 2011 we saw many companies restructure or downsize their operations. Others closed or were bought by other companies; and still others were evaluating their options to operate effectively during what has been termed an "economic slump." During times like these, horizontal analyses and ratios compared across years can lose much of their relevance. When losses result in negative numbers, it is difficult to calculate percentages and ratios, much less interpret them. Vertical analyses become more useful in such times. If a company has losses, they must be assessed based on the factors driving the loss in the current period. Less attention should be paid to comparing the losses with results from prior periods.

One must use this information, along with non-financial information, to try to assess what changes relate to the economic situation and what changes relate to factors that management can, or should be able to, control. For example, have operating expenses increased faster than revenues? Why? Are consumers not spending? Are prices too high? Have expenses not been adequately controlled or adjusted for the current marketplace? Particular attention must be paid to the company's results compared with those of its competitors.

Action Plan

- Recall the formula for profit margin: Profit ÷ Net sales (or Revenue). Substitute total comprehensive income instead of profit to determine the impact of other comprehensive income on profitability.
- To determine the significance of other comprehensive income, compare the ratios with and without other comprehensive income and assess whether the change in the ratio is significant enough to affect decision-making.

THE **NAVIGATOR**

◉ BEFORE YOU GO ON...

Do It

HSBC Bank Canada reported the following selected information (in millions) for the year ended December 31, 2011:

Total revenue	$3,250
Profit	704
Other comprehensive income	203
Total comprehensive income	907

(a) Calculate the profit margin using (1) profit as the numerator, and (2) total comprehensive income as the numerator.

(b) Should other comprehensive income be considered a significant factor in the analysis of HSBC Bank's profitability?

Solution

(a)

($ in millions)	(1)	(2)
Profit margin	$\dfrac{\$704}{\$3,250} = 21.7\%$	$\dfrac{\$907}{\$3,250} = 27.9\%$

(b) The two ratios differ by 28.6% [(27.9% − 21.7%) ÷ 21.7%]. The inclusion of other comprehensive income in the calculation of the profitability ratios is likely significant enough to make a difference in a user's decision-making.

Related exercise material: BE18–18 and E18–16.

▮Comparing IFRS and ASPE ▮

Key Differences	International Financial Reporting Standards (IFRS)	Accounting Standards for Private Enterprises (ASPE)
Earnings per share	Must be calculated and reported on the face of the income statement or statement of comprehensive income.	Earnings per share are not required to be reported.
Differences in accounting policy	Depending on the extent and significance of differences in accounting policies, comparisons may be difficult if a publicly traded company is compared with a private company using ASPE.	Depending on the extent and significance of differences in accounting policies, comparisons may be difficult if a private company using ASPE is compared with a public or private company using IFRS.
Comprehensive income	If other comprehensive income is significant, selected profitability ratios should be recalculated using total comprehensive income rather than profit.	Comprehensive income is not reported.

THE **NAVIGATOR**

Demonstration Problem

Selected liquidity, solvency, and profitability ratios follow for two companies for a recent year:

	Kicking Horse	La Biche
Liquidity		
Current ratio	2.2:1	1.8:1
Collection period	28 days	20 days
Days sales in inventory	66 days	58 days
Solvency		
Debt to total assets	44.2%	44.4%
Interest coverage	9.1 times	10.2 times
Profitability		
Gross profit margin	37.1%	39.5%
Profit margin	8.8%	16.3%
Asset turnover	0.1 times	0.1 times
Return on assets	0.9%	1.6%
Return on equity	1.6%	2.9%

Instructions

(a) For each of the above ratios, identify which company, Kicking Horse (KH) or La Biche (LB), has the stronger result.
(b) Which company is more liquid? Explain.
(c) Which company is more solvent? Explain.
(d) Which company is more profitable? Explain.

Solution to Demonstration Problem

(a)	Stronger Result		Stronger Result
Current ratio	KH	Gross profit margin	LB
Collection period	LB	Profit margin	LB
Days sales in inventory	LB	Asset turnover	No difference
Debt to total assets	KH	Return on assets	LB
Interest coverage	LB	Return on equity	LB

ACTION PLAN

• Remember that for liquidity ratios, a higher result is usually better unless a ratio is the inverse of an original ratio (e.g., collection period that uses the receivables turnover ratio in the denominator), in which case a lower result is better.

• The current ratio should always be interpreted together with the receivables turnover/ collection period and inventory turnover/days sales in inventory ratios to ensure that the current ratio has not been artificially inflated by slow-moving receivables or inventory.

• The debt to total assets ratio, for which a lower result is usually better, should always be interpreted together with the interest coverage ratio, for which a higher result is usually better.

• Remember that for profitability ratios, a higher result is usually better.

(b) La Biche is more liquid than Kicking Horse. Although Kicking Horse appears to have a stronger current ratio than La Biche, it is slower at collecting its receivables and selling its inventory. Regardless, it should be noted that both companies still have good collection periods (less than 30 days). Still, La Biche's operating cycle is only 78 days (20 + 58) compared with Kicking Horse's 94 days (28 + 66).

(c) La Biche is more solvent than Kicking Horse. Although its debt to total assets ratio is marginally higher (worse) than that of Kicking Horse, its interest coverage ratio is also higher (better), indicating its ability to handle its debt.

(d) La Biche is more profitable than Kicking Horse on all profitability measures except for asset turnover, which is the same for both companies.

THE NAVIGATOR

▶ Summary of Study Objectives

1. *Identify the need for, and tools of, financial statement analysis.* Users of financial statements make comparisons in order to evaluate a company's past, current, and future performance and position. There are two commonly used bases of comparison: intracompany (within a company) and intercompany (between companies). The tools of financial analysis include horizontal, vertical, and ratio analysis.

2. *Explain and apply horizontal analysis.* Horizontal analysis is a technique for evaluating a series of data, such as line items in a company's financial statements, by expressing them as percentage increases or decreases over two or more periods of time. The horizontal percentage of a base-period amount is calculated by dividing the amount for the specific period under analysis by a base-period amount. This percentage calculation normally covers multiple periods. The horizontal percentage change for a period is calculated by dividing the dollar amount of the change between the specific period under analysis and the prior period by the prior-period amount. This percentage calculation normally covers two periods only.

3. *Explain and apply vertical analysis.* Vertical analysis is a technique for evaluating data within one period by expressing each item in a financial statement as a percentage of a relevant total (base amount) in the same financial statement. The vertical percentage of a base-period amount is calculated by dividing the financial statement amount under analysis by the base amount for that particular financial statement, which is usually total assets for the balance sheet and revenues or net sales for the income statement.

4. *Identify and use ratios to analyze liquidity.* Liquidity ratios include the current ratio, acid-test ratio, receivables turnover, collection period, inventory turnover, days sales in inventory, and operating cycle. The formula, purpose, and desired result for each liquidity ratio are presented in Illustration 18-12.

5. *Identify and use ratios to analyze solvency.* Solvency ratios include debt to total assets, interest coverage, and free cash flow. The formula, purpose, and desired result for each solvency ratio are presented in Illustration 18-15.

6. *Identify and use ratios to analyze profitability.* Profitability ratios include the gross profit margin, profit margin, asset turnover, return on assets, return on equity, earnings per share, price-earnings, and payout ratios. The formula, purpose, and desired result for each profitability ratio are presented in Illustration 18-18.

7. *Recognize the limitations of financial statement analysis.* The usefulness of analytical tools can be limited by (1) the use of alternative accounting policies, (2) significant amounts of other comprehensive income, (3) the quality of the information provided, and (4) economic factors.

THE NAVIGATOR

▶ Glossary

Horizontal analysis A technique for evaluating a series of financial statement data over multiple periods of time to determine the percentage increase or decrease that has taken place. Also known as trend analysis. (p. 940)

Horizontal percentage change for period A percentage measuring the change from one period to the next period. It is calculated by dividing the dollar amount of the change between the specific period under analysis and the prior period by the prior-period amount. (p. 941)

Horizontal percentage of base-period amount A percentage measuring the change since a base period. It is calculated by dividing the amount for the specific period under analysis by the base-period amount. (p. 940)

Liquidity ratios Measures of a company's short-term ability to pay its maturing obligations and to meet unexpected needs for cash. (p. 949)

Profitability ratios Measures of a company's operating success for a specific period of time. (p. 958)

Ratio analysis A technique for evaluating financial statements that expresses the relationship between selected financial statement data. (p. 948)

Solvency ratios Measures of a company's ability to survive over a long period of time. (p. 954)

Vertical analysis A technique for evaluating financial statement data within a period. Each item in a financial statement is expressed as a percentage of a total or base amount. Total assets is usually the base amount used in the balance sheet; total revenues or net sales in the income statement. Also known as common size analysis. (p. 944)

Vertical percentage of base amount A percentage measuring the proportion of an amount in a financial statement within a period. It is calculated by dividing the financial statement amount under analysis by the base amount for that particular financial statement and period of time. (p. 944)

THE NAVIGATOR

Flash cards

● Self-Study Questions
Answers are at the end of the chapter.

(SO 1) K **1.** A comparison of operating expenses for a company over a five-year period is an example of which of the following comparative bases and analysis tools?
(a) Intracompany, horizontal analysis
(b) Intracompany, vertical analysis
(c) Intercompany, horizontal analysis
(d) Intercompany, vertical analysis

(SO 2) AP **2.** Rankin Corporation reported net sales of $300,000, $330,000, and $360,000 in the years 2012, 2013, and 2014, respectively. If 2012 is the base year, what is the horizontal percentage of the base-year amount for 2014?
(a) 83%
(c) 110%
(b) 92%
(d) 120%

(SO 2) AP **3.** As indicated in Question 2 above, Rankin Corporation reported net sales of $300,000, $330,000, and $360,000 in the years 2012, 2013, and 2014, respectively. What is the horizontal percentage change for each year?
(a) 110% from 2012 to 2013 and 109% from 2013 to 2014
(b) 110% from 2012 to 2013 and 120% from 2013 to 2014
(c) 10% from 2012 to 2013 and 9% from 2013 to 2014
(d) 10% from 2012 to 2013 and 20% from 2013 to 2014

(SO 3) C **4.** The following schedule shows what type of analysis?

	2014		2013	
	Amount	Percentage	Amount	Percentage
Current assets	$200,000	25%	$175,000	21%
Property, plant, and equipment	600,000	75%	650,000	79%
Total assets	$800,000	100%	$825,000	100%

(a) Horizontal analysis
(b) Ratio analysis
(c) Vertical analysis
(d) Intercompany comparison

(SO 3) K **5.** In a vertical analysis, the base amount for depreciation expense is generally:
(a) net sales.
(b) depreciation expense in a previous year.
(c) total assets.
(d) total property, plant, and equipment.

Use the following selected financial data to answer items 6 to 8. Round all ratios to one decimal spot. Calculations involving days should be rounded to the nearest day.

	2014	2013
Accounts receivable	$ 45,000	$ 41,000
Inventory	34,000	28,000
Total shareholders' equity	572,000	438,000
Net credit sales	684,000	597,000
Cost of goods sold	450,000	398,000
Interest expense	14,000	12,000
Income tax expense	22,000	18,000
Profit	134,000	90,000

(SO 4) AP **6.** What is the operating cycle for 2014?
(a) 20 days
(c) 101 days
(b) 48 days
(d) 124 days

(SO 5) AP **7.** What is the interest coverage ratio for 2014?
(a) 7.3 times
(c) 11.2 times
(b) 10.6 times
(d) 12.1 times

(SO 6) AP **8.** What is the return on equity for 2014?
(a) 22.2%
(c) 26.5%
(b) 23.4%
(d) 135.4%

(SO 4, 5, 6) AN **9.** Which of the following changes in ratios are *both* indicative of an improvement rather than a deterioration in a company's financial situation?
(a) Increasing debt to total assets and interest coverage ratios
(b) Increasing current ratio and increasing days sales in inventory
(c) Decreasing asset turnover and return on equity ratios
(d) Decreasing collection period and increasing gross profit margin

THE NAVIGATOR

(SO 7) C 10. Which of the following situations most likely indicates that a financial analysis should be interpreted with caution?
(a) Different inventory cost formulas are being used by competing companies with similar inventory.
(b) A company had no other comprehensive income.
(c) The economy is stable.
(d) The quality of information is high.

▶ Questions

(SO 1) C 1. What are the differences among the two bases of comparison: (a) intracompany and (b) intercompany?

(SO 1) C 2. (a) Identify the three commonly used tools of analysis. (b) Explain whether each is normally used in an intracompany and/or intercompany comparison.

(SO 2) K 3. Explain how the percentage of a base-period amount and the percentage change for a period are calculated in horizontal analysis.

(SO 2) C 4. Explain how a horizontal analysis is affected if an account (a) has no value in a base year and a value in the next year, or (b) has a negative value in the base year and a positive value in the next year.

(SO 2, 3) C 5. Horizontal analysis and vertical analysis are two different tools used in financial statement analysis. Explain how they are similar, and how they differ.

(SO 2, 3) C 6. **Facebook** became a public corporation in May 2012. Can a meaningful horizontal and vertical analysis be prepared for its first full year of operations as a public company, the year ended December 31, 2012? Explain.

(SO 3) K 7. What base amount is usually assigned a 100% value in a vertical analysis of (a) the balance sheet and (b) the income statement?

(SO 3) C 8. Can vertical analysis be used to compare two companies of different sizes, such as **Walmart**, the world's largest retailer, and **Costco**, the eighth-largest retailer in the world? Explain.

(SO 4) K 9. (a) What do liquidity ratios measure? (b) What types of users would be most interested in liquidity ratios?

(SO 4) AN 10. A high current ratio does not always indicate that a company has a strong liquidity position. Describe two situations that might result in the current ratio appearing to be "artificially" high.

(SO 4) AN 11. Aubut Corporation, a large national retail store, has an operating cycle of 30 days. Its nearest competitor has an operating cycle of 10 days. Does Aubut have a liquidity problem?

(SO 4) C 12. Identify for which liquidity ratios a lower result might be better, and explain why.

(SO 5) K 13. (a) What do solvency ratios measure? (b) What types of users would be most interested in solvency ratios?

(SO 5) C 14. Wong Ltd. reported a debt to total assets of 37% and an interest coverage ratio of 3 times in the current year. Its nearest competitor has a debt to total assets ratio of 39% and an interest coverage ratio of 2.5 times. Is Wong's solvency better or worse than that of its competitor?

(SO 5) C 15. Identify for which solvency ratios a lower result might be better, and explain why.

(SO 6) K 16. (a) What do profitability ratios measure? (b) What types of users would be most interested in profitability ratios?

(SO 6) AN 17. The return on assets for **McDonald's** is 16.9%. During the same period, it reported a return on equity of 37.9%. Has McDonald's made effective use of leverage? Explain.

(SO 6) AN 18. If you were an investor interested in buying the shares of a company with growth potential, would you look for a company that had high or low price-earnings and payout ratios? If you were interested in buying the shares of a company with income potential, would your answer change? Explain.

(SO 4, 5, 6) C 19. Name the ratio(s) that should be used to help answer each of the following questions.
(a) How efficient is a company at using its assets to produce sales?
(b) What is the company's ability to pay its obligations immediately without selling inventory?
(c) How long does it take to purchase inventory, sell it on account, and collect the cash?
(d) How many dollars of profit were earned for each dollar invested by the shareholders?
(e) How able is a company to pay interest charges as they come due?

(SO 7) C 20. Identify and briefly explain the limitations of financial statement analysis.

(SO 7) AN 21. **McCain Foods** and **Cavendish Farms** are both private companies in the food-processing industry. McCain Foods uses IFRS and Cavendish Farms uses ASPE. What impact might these differing standards have when comparing ratios of these two companies?

(SO 7) C 22. Explain what other comprehensive income is and when it should be considered in comparing ratios from one company to another.

Brief Exercises

BE18–1   Match each of the following terms with the most appropriate description.

Match terms with descriptions. (SO 1) K

Terms	Description
_____ 1. Intracompany	(a) An analysis tool that expresses relationships among selected items of financial statement data
_____ 2. Intercompany	(b) An analysis tool that evaluates data by expressing an item in a financial statement as a percentage of a total or base amount within the same financial statement
_____ 3. Horizontal analysis	(c) Comparisons made between companies
_____ 4. Vertical analysis	(d) An analysis tool that evaluates data by calculating and comparing the percentage increase or decrease of an item in a financial statement over multiple periods of time
_____ 5. Ratio analysis	(e) Comparisons made within a company

BE18–2   Identify the appropriate basis of comparison—intracompany or intercompany—and better tool of analysis—horizontal or vertical—to use for each of the following financial situations.

Identify comparisons and tools. (SO 1) C

	Basis of Comparison	Tool of Analysis
1. Analysis of a company's dividend history		
2. Comparison of different-sized companies		
3. Comparison of gross profit to net sales among competitors		
4. Calculation of a company's sales growth over time		

BE18–3   Comparative data (in thousands) from the balance sheet of Winisk Ltd. are shown below. Using horizontal analysis, calculate the percentage of the base-year amount, assuming 2012 is the base year.

Prepare horizontal analysis. (SO 2) AP

	2014	2013	2012
Cash	$ 24	$ 45	$ 30
Accounts receivable	268	227	197
Inventory	499	481	395
Prepaid expenses	22	0	10
Total current assets	$813	$753	$632

BE18–4   Refer to BE18–3. Using horizontal analysis, calculate the percentage change for each year.

Prepare horizontal analysis. (SO 2) AP

BE18–5   Comparative data from the balance sheet of Rioux Ltd. are shown below. (a) Using horizontal analysis, calculate the percentage of the base-year amount, using 2012 as the base year. (b) Using vertical analysis, calculate the percentage of the base amount for each year.

Prepare horizontal and vertical analyses. (SO 2, 3) AP

	2014	2013	2012
Current assets	$1,530,000	$1,175,000	$1,225,000
Property, plant, and equipment	3,130,000	2,800,000	2,850,000
Goodwill	90,000	100,000	0
Total assets	$4,750,000	$4,075,000	$4,075,000

BE18–6   Selected data (in thousands) from the income statement of JTI Inc. are shown below. Using vertical analysis, calculate the percentage of the base amount for the current year.

Prepare vertical analysis. (SO 3) AP

Net sales	$1,934
Cost of goods sold	1,612
Gross profit	322
Operating expenses	218
Profit before income tax	104
Income tax expense	31
Profit	$ 73

Compare liquidity ratios.
(SO 4) C

BE18–7   For each of the following liquidity ratios, indicate whether the change would be viewed as an improvement or deterioration:

(a) A decrease in the receivables turnover
(b) A decrease in the collection period
(c) An increase in the days sales in inventory
(d) An increase in the inventory turnover
(e) A decrease in the acid-test ratio
(f) An increase in the operating cycle

Calculate and evaluate
liquidity ratios. (SO 4) AN

BE18–8   Selected financial data for Shumway Ltd. are shown below. (a) Calculate for each of 2013 and 2014, the following ratios: (1) receivables turnover, (2) collection period, (3) inventory turnover. (4) days sales in inventory, and (5) operating cycle. (b) Based on the ratios calculated in (a), what conclusion(s) can be drawn about the management of the receivables and inventory?

	2014	2013	2012
Net sales	$6,420,000	$6,240,000	$5,430,000
Cost of goods sold	4,540,000	4,550,000	3,950,000
Accounts receivable (gross)	850,000	750,000	650,000
Inventory	1,020,000	980,000	840,000

Evaluate liquidity.
(SO 4) AN

BE18–9   Holysh Inc. reported a current ratio of 1.5:1 in the current year, which is higher than last year's current ratio of 1.3:1. It also reported an acid-test ratio of 1:1, which is higher than last year's acid-test ratio of 0.6:1; receivables turnover of 8 times, which is less than last year's receivables turnover of 9 times; and an inventory turnover of 6 times, which is less than last year's inventory turnover of 7 times. Is Holysh's liquidity improving or deteriorating? Explain.

Compare solvency ratios.
(SO 5) C

BE18–10   For each of the following solvency ratios, indicate whether the change would be viewed as an improvement or deterioration:

(a) A decrease in debt to total assets
(b) A decrease in interest coverage
(c) An increase in free cash flow
(d) A decrease in debt to total assets combined with an increase in interest coverage

Calculate solvency ratios.
(SO 5) AP

BE18–11   **Shoppers Drug Mart** reported the following selected financial data (in thousands) for a recent year:

Interest expense	$ 64,038
Income tax expense	232,933
Profit	613,934
Total assets	7,300,310
Total liabilities	3,032,480
Cash provided by operating activities	973,838
Cash used by investing activities	349,172

Calculate the following ratios: (a) debt to total assets, (b) interest coverage, and (c) free cash flow.

Evaluate solvency.
(SO 5) AN

BE18–12   The Culleye Corporation reported the following solvency ratios:

	2014	2013
Debt to total assets	56.0%	52.8%
Interest coverage	5.1 times	3.3 times

(a) Identify if each of the above solvency ratios is better or worse in 2014, compared with 2013.
(b) Has Culleye's overall solvency position improved or deteriorated in 2014? Explain.

Compare profitability ratios.
(SO 6) C

BE18–13   For each of the following profitability ratios, indicate whether the change would be viewed as an improvement or deterioration:

(a) An increase in the gross profit margin
(b) A decrease in asset turnover
(c) An increase in return on equity
(d) A decrease in earnings per share
(e) A decrease in the profit margin

Calculate profitability ratios.
(SO 6) AP

BE18–14   **Loblaw** reported sales of $31,250 million, cost of goods sold of $23,894 million, and profit of $769 million for a recent year. Its total assets were $16,841 million at the beginning of the year and $17,428 million at the end of the year. Calculate the (a) gross profit margin, (b) profit margin, (c) asset turnover, and (d) return on assets ratios.

BE18–15 Recently, the price-earnings ratio of **Apple** was 17 times and the price-earnings ratio of the **Bank of Montreal** was 11 times. The payout ratio of each company was 0% and 53%, respectively. Which company's shares would you purchase for growth? For income? Explain.

Evaluate investor ratios. (SO 6) AN

BE18–16 (a) Indicate whether each of the following ratios is a liquidity (L) ratio, a solvency (S) ratio, or a profitability (P) ratio. (b) Indicate whether a higher or lower result is normally desirable.

Classify ratios. (SO 4, 5, 6) K

(a)   (b)
_____   _____   Acid-test
_____   _____   Asset turnover
_____   _____   Collection period
_____   _____   Debt to total assets
_____   _____   Gross profit margin
_____   _____   Interest coverage
_____   _____   Inventory turnover
_____   _____   Operating cycle
_____   _____   Profit margin
_____   _____   Return on equity

BE18–17 Selected comparative information (in thousands) is available for the Halpenny Corporation.

Calculate averages. (SO 4, 6) AP

	2014	2013	2012
Accounts receivable	$ 1,090	$ 965	$ 880
Total assets	27,510	26,760	23,815
Total shareholders' equity	12,830	12,575	10,930

Halpenny wishes to calculate ratios for 2014 and 2013. (a) Calculate the average amounts to be used for accounts receivable, total assets, and total shareholders' equity in a ratio calculation in (1) 2014 and (2) 2013. (b) Identify for which ratio each of the above average amounts would be used. (c) Why are averages used in certain ratio calculations and not in others?

BE18–18 Stirling Corporation and Bute Inc. have similar types of inventory. At the end of the current year, Stirling reported an average inventory amount of $10,000, calculated using the FIFO cost formula. Bute reported an average inventory amount of $12,000, calculated using the average cost formula. Stirling reported cost of goods sold of $200,000, while Bute reported cost of goods sold of $180,000. Inventory prices have been falling during the current year. (a) Calculate the inventory turnover ratio for each company. (b) How might the fact that Stirling and Bute use different inventory cost formulas affect your comparison of the inventory turnover ratio between the two companies?

Evaluate impact of alternative cost formulas on inventory turnover. (SO 4, 7) AN

▶ Exercises

E18–1 Comparative data from the balance sheet of Dressaire Inc. are shown below.

Prepare horizontal analysis. (SO 2) AP

	2014	2013	2012
Current assets	$120,000	$ 80,000	$100,000
Non-current assets	400,000	350,000	300,000
Current liabilities	90,000	70,000	65,000
Non-current liabilities	145,000	125,000	150,000
Common shares	150,000	115,000	100,000
Retained earnings	135,000	120,000	85,000

Instructions

(a) Using horizontal analysis, calculate the percentage of the base-year amount, using 2012 as the base year.
(b) Using horizontal analysis, calculate the percentage change for each year.

E18–2 Selected horizontal percentages of the base-year amount from Coastal Ltd.'s horizontally analyzed income statement are shown below.

Determine change in profit. (SO 2) AN

	2014	2013	2012
Net sales	101%	110%	100%
Cost of goods sold	100%	111%	100%
Operating expenses	99%	112%	100%
Income tax expense	106%	105%	100%

Instructions

Based on the above horizontal percentages, did Coastal's profit increase, decrease, or remain unchanged over the three-year period? Explain.

Prepare vertical analysis.
(SO 3) AP

E18-3 Comparative data from the income statement of Fleetwood Corporation are shown below.

	2014	2013
Net sales	$800,000	$600,000
Cost of goods sold	550,000	375,000
Gross profit	250,000	225,000
Operating expenses	175,000	125,000
Profit before income tax	75,000	100,000
Income tax expense	18,750	25,000
Profit	$ 56,250	$ 75,000

Instructions

Using vertical analysis, calculate the percentage of the base amount for each year.

Prepare horizontal and vertical analyses and identify changes. (SO 2, 3) AN

E18-4 Comparative data from the balance sheet of **lululemon athletica** are shown below.

LULULEMON ATHLETICA INC. Balance Sheet January 29, 2012, and January 30, 2011 (in U.S. thousands)		
Assets	2012	2011
Current assets	$527,093	$389,279
Non-current assets	207,541	110,023
Total assets	$734,634	$499,302
Liabilities and Shareholders' Equity		
Current liabilities	$103,439	$ 85,364
Non-current liabilities	25,014	19,645
Total liabilities	128,453	105,009
Shareholders' equity	606,181	394,293
Total liabilities and shareholders' equity	$734,634	$499,302

Instructions

(a) Using horizontal analysis, calculate the percentage change for 2012.
(b) Using vertical analysis, calculate the percentage of the base amount for each year.
(c) Based on your calculations in (a) and (b), identify any significant changes from 2011 to 2012.

Determine change in profit.
(SO 3) AN

E18-5 Selected vertical percentages of the base amount from Waubon Corp.'s vertically analyzed income statement are shown below.

	2012	2011	2010
Net sales	100.0%	100.0%	100.0%
Cost of goods sold	59.4%	60.5%	60.0%
Operating expenses	19.6%	20.4%	20.0%
Income tax expense	4.2%	3.8%	4.0%

Instructions

Based on the above vertical percentages, did Waubon's profit as a percentage of sales increase, decrease, or remain unchanged over the three-year period? Explain.

Calculate and compare liquidity ratios. (SO 4) AP

E18-6 Nordstar, Inc. operates hardware stores in several provinces. Selected comparative financial statement data are shown below.

```
                    NORDSTAR, INC.
                  Balance Sheet (partial)
                 December 31 (in millions)

                            2014        2013        2012

Current assets
  Cash                     $    30     $    91     $    60
  Short-term investments        55          60          40
  Accounts receivable          676         586         496
  Inventory                    628         525         575
  Prepaid expenses              41          52          29

Total current assets        $1,430      $1,314      $1,200

Total current liabilities   $  890      $  825      $  750
```

Additional information:

(in millions)	2014	2013
Net credit sales	$4,190	$3,940
Cost of goods sold	2,900	2,650

Instructions

(a) Calculate all possible liquidity ratios for 2014 and 2013.

(b) Indicate whether each of the liquidity ratios calculated in (a) is better or worse in 2014.

E18–7 The following selected ratios are available for Pampered Pets Inc.:   *Evaluate liquidity. (SO 4) AN*

	2014	2013	2012
Current ratio	2.6:1	1.4:1	2.1:1
Acid-test	0.8:1	0.6:1	0.7:1
Receivables turnover	6.7 times	7.4 times	8.2 times
Inventory turnover	7.5 times	8.7 times	9.9 times
Operating cycle	103 days	91 days	81 days

Instructions

(a) Has the company's collection of its receivables improved or weakened over the last three years?

(b) Is the company selling its inventory faster or slower than in past years?

(c) Overall, has the company's liquidity improved or weakened over the last three years? Explain.

E18–8 The following selected information (in thousands) is available for Osborne Inc.:   *Calculate and compare solvency ratios. (SO 5) AP*

	2014	2013
Total assets	$3,886	$3,708
Total liabilities	2,177	1,959
Interest expense	14	27
Income tax expense	174	152
Profit	406	375
Cash provided by operating activities	850	580
Cash used by investing activities	400	300

Instructions

(a) Calculate all possible solvency ratios for 2014 and 2013.

(b) Indicate whether each of the solvency ratios calculated in (a) is better or worse in 2014.

E18–9 The following selected ratios are available for Ice Inc.:   *Evaluate solvency. (SO 5) AN*

	2014	2013	2012
Debt to total assets	50%	45%	40%
Interest coverage	2.0 times	1.5 times	1.0 times

Instructions

(a) Has the debt to total assets improved or weakened over the last three years?

(b) Has the interest coverage improved or weakened over the last three years?

(c) Overall, has the company's solvency improved or weakened over the last three years?

Calculate and compare profitability ratios. (SO 6) AP

E18–10 The following selected information is for Xtreme Corporation:

	2014	2013	2012
Total assets	$350,000	$275,000	$274,467
Total shareholders' equity	133,500	100,000	50,000
Net sales	500,000	400,000	300,000
Cost of goods sold	375,000	290,000	180,000
Profit	33,500	30,000	20,000

Instructions

(a) Calculate the gross profit margin, profit margin, asset turnover, return on assets, and return on equity ratios for 2014 and 2013.

(b) Indicate whether each of the profitability ratios calculated in (a) is better or worse in 2014.

Evaluate profitability. (SO 6) AN

E18–11 **Talisman Energy** and **Suncor Energy** reported the following investor-related information recently:

	Talisman Energy	Suncor Energy
Earnings per share	$1.35	$3.02
Payout ratio	19.9%	14.3%
Price-earnings ratio	11.6 times	9.6 times
Profit margin	16.6%	11.7%
Return on equity	14.6%	12.4%

Instructions

(a) Based on the above information, can you tell which company is more profitable?

(b) Which company do investors favour?

(c) Which company would investors most likely purchase shares in for growth purposes? For dividend income?

Classify and compare ratios. (SO 1, 4, 5, 6) C

E18–12 The following is a selected list of ratios comparing Long Inc. and Circular Corporation for a recent year:

	Long	Circular	(a)	(b)
Acid-test	1.1:1	0.8:1		
Asset turnover	1.7 times	1.6 times		
Current ratio	1.3:1	1.6:1		
Debt to total assets	30.1%	40.6%		
Gross profit margin	38.7%	38.6%		
Interest coverage	5.6 times	2.3 times		
Inventory turnover	5.8 times	5.1 times		
Operating cycle	119 days	134 days		
Profit margin	10.4%	8.5%		
Receivables turnover	6.5 times	5.9 times		
Return on assets	17.2%	13.7%		
Return on equity	24.8%	28.2%		

Instructions

(a) Classify each of the above ratios as a liquidity (L), solvency (S), or profitability (P) ratio.

(b) For each of the above ratios, indicate whether Long's ratio is better (B) or worse (W) than that reported by Circular.

(c) Identify whether the comparison done in (b) is an intracompany comparison or an intercompany comparison.

E18–13   Selected comparative financial data (in thousands, except for share price) for **Indigo Books & Music** are shown below.

Calculate and classify ratios. (SO 4, 5, 6) AP

	2011	2010
Revenue	$1,017,325	$968,927
Interest expense	212	214
Income tax expense	2,682	12,537
Profit	11,346	34,923
Total current assets	342,373	351,044
Total assets	516,180	519,842
Total current liabilities	238,434	244,665
Total liabilities	246,713	254,042
Total shareholders' equity	263,120	258,969
Cash provided by operating activities	18,441	62,245
Cash used by investing activities	43,201	48,947
Market price per share	12.29	16.73
Weighted average number of common shares	24,874	24,550

Instructions

(a) Calculate the following ratios for 2011:
1. Asset turnover
2. Current ratio
3. Debt to total assets
4. Earnings per share
5. Free cash flow
6. Interest coverage
7. Price-earnings ratio
8. Profit margin
9. Return on assets
10. Return on equity

(b) Indicate whether each of the above ratios is a measure of liquidity (L), solvency (S), or profitability (P).

E18–14   Presented below is an incomplete income statement for Riverdance Limited.

Calculate missing information. (SO 4, 5, 6) AN

RIVERDANCE LIMITED Income Statement Year Ended December 31, 2014	
Net sales	(a)
Cost of goods sold	(b)
Gross profit	(c)
Operating expenses	(d)
Profit before income taxes	(e)
Income tax expense	(f)
Profit	(g)

Additional information:
1. The asset turnover is 3 times and average total assets are $100,000.
2. The gross profit margin is 40%.
3. The income tax rate is 25%.
4. The profit margin is 15%.

Instructions

Calculate the missing information using the ratios. (*Hint:* Start with one ratio and get as much information as possible from it before trying another ratio. You may not be able to calculate the missing amounts in the same sequence as they are presented above.)

Calculate missing
information. (SO 4, 5, 6) AN

E18–15   Presented below is an incomplete balance sheet for the Main River Corp.

MAIN RIVER CORP.
Balance Sheet
December 31, 2014

Assets
Current assets
Cash	$20,000
Accounts receivable	(a)
Inventory	(b)
Total current assets	365,000
Non-current assets	435,000
Total assets	$ (c)

Liabilities and Shareholders' Equity
Current liabilities	$ (d)
Non-current liabilities	(e)
Total liabilities	(f)
Shareholders' equity	(g)
Total liabilities and shareholders' equity	$ (h)

Additional information:
1. Assume average balances equal ending balances for the purpose of this exercise.
2. The receivables turnover ratio is 13 times and net credit sales are $1,950,000.
3. The inventory turnover ratio is 6.5 times and cost of goods sold is $1,267,500.
4. The current ratio is 2:1.
5. The debt to total assets ratio is 70%.

Instructions

Calculate the missing information using the ratios. (*Hint*: Start with one ratio and get as much information as possible from it before trying another ratio. You may not be able to calculate the missing amounts in the same sequence as they are presented above.)

Determine impact of other
comprehensive income on
profitability. (SO 6, 7) AN

E18–16   A company reported the following selected information (in thousands):

	2014	2013	2012
Profit	$933	$ 867	$1,321
Other comprehensive income (loss)	(117)	793	(2,658)
Total comprehensive income (loss)	816	1,660	(1,337)

Instructions

Explain whether other comprehensive income would affect your analysis of this company's profitability, and if so how.

Problems: Set A

P18–1A   The following condensed financial information is available for **WestJet Airlines**:

Prepare horizontal analysis
and identify changes.
(SO 2, 7) AN

WESTJET AIRLINES LTD.
Income Statement
Year Ended December 31 (in millions)

	2011	2010	2009	2008
Revenue	$3,072	$2,607	$2,281	$2,550
Operating expenses	2,815	2,416	2,070	2,257
Profit from operations	257	191	211	293
Other expenses	49	58	74	38
Profit before income taxes	208	133	137	255
Income tax expense	59	43	39	77
Profit	$ 149	$ 90	$ 98	$ 178

WESTJET AIRLINES LTD.
Balance Sheet
December 31 (in thousands)

Assets	2011	2010	2009	2008
Current assets	$1,425	$1,285	$1,129	$ 926
Non-current assets	2,049	2,099	2,221	2,353
Total assets	$3,474	$3,384	$3,350	$3,279
Liabilities and Shareholders' Equity				
Current liabilities	$ 942	$ 840	$ 756	$ 740
Non-current liabilities	1,162	1,240	1,362	1,453
Total liabilities	2,104	2,080	2,118	2,193
Shareholders' equity	1,370	1,304	1,232	1,086
Total liabilities and shareholders' equity	$3,474	$3,384	$3,350	$3,279

Instructions
(a) Using horizontal analysis, calculate the percentage of the base-year amount for the income statement and balance sheet, assuming 2008 is the base year.
(b) Using the horizontal analyses you prepared in (a), identify any significant changes between 2008 and 2011.
(c) Which do you think would be more useful—calculating the percentage of the base-year amount or calculating the percentage change between periods—to analyze WestJet between 2008 and 2011? Explain.

TAKING IT FURTHER   WestJet's financial information for 2010 and 2011 was prepared using IFRS. The financial information for 2008 and 2009 was prepared using the pre-changeover Canadian GAAP. How might these differing standards affect your interpretation of the horizontal analysis?

P18–2A   A horizontal and vertical analysis of the income statement for a retail company selling a wide variety of general merchandise is shown below.

Interpret horizontal and
vertical analysis.
(SO 2, 3, 7) AN

RETAIL CORPORATION Horizontal Income Statement Year Ended January 31				
	2014	2013	2012	2011
Net sales	140.0%	111.0%	114.0%	100.0%
Cost of goods sold	148.3%	113.3%	116.7%	100.0%
Gross profit	127.5%	107.5%	110.0%	100.0%
Operating expenses	171.4%	133.1%	126.9%	100.0%
Profit from operations	93.3%	87.6%	96.9%	100.0%
Other revenues and expenses				
Interest expense	40.0%	60.0%	80.0%	100.0%
Other revenue	240.0%	140.0%	200.0%	100.0%
Profit before income tax	140.0%	110.8%	113.8%	100.0%
Income tax expense	160.0%	116.0%	124.0%	100.0%
Profit	135.2%	109.5%	111.4%	100.0%

RETAIL CORPORATION Vertical Income Statement Year Ended January 31				
	2014	2013	2012	2011
Net sales	100.0%	100.0%	100.0%	100.0%
Cost of goods sold	63.6%	61.2%	61.4%	60.0%
Gross profit	36.4%	38.8%	38.6%	40.0%
Operating expenses	21.4%	21.0%	19.5%	17.5%
Profit from operations	15.0%	17.8%	19.1%	22.5%
Other revenues and expenses				
Interest expense	(2.9)%	(5.4)%	(7.0)%	(10.0)%
Other revenue	0.9%	0.6%	0.9%	0.5%
Profit before income tax	13.0%	13.0%	13.0%	13.0%
Income tax expense	2.9%	2.6%	2.7%	2.5%
Profit	10.1%	10.4%	10.3%	10.5%

Instructions

(a) How effectively has the company controlled its cost of goods sold and operating expenses over the four-year period?

(b) Identify any other income statement components that have significantly changed over the four-year period for the company.

(c) Identify any additional information that might be helpful to you in your analysis of this company over the four-year period.

TAKING IT FURTHER In a vertical analysis, the company's profit before income tax has remained unchanged at 13% of revenue over the four-year period. Yet, in a horizontal analysis, profit before income tax has grown 40% over that period of time. Explain how this is possible.

P18–3A   Comparative income statement data for Chen Inc. and Chuan Ltd., two competitors, are shown below for the year ended December 31, 2014.

	Chen	Chuan
Net sales	$1,849,035	$539,038
Cost of goods sold	1,060,490	338,006
Gross profit	788,545	201,032
Operating expenses	502,275	89,000
Profit from operations	286,270	112,032
Interest expense	6,800	1,252
Profit before income tax	279,470	110,780
Income tax expense	83,841	27,695
Profit	$ 195,629	$ 83,085
Additional information:		
Average total assets	$ 894,750	$251,313
Average total shareholders' equity	724,430	186,238

Prepare vertical analysis, calculate profitability ratios, and compare. (SO 1, 3, 6) AN

Instructions

(a) Using vertical analysis, calculate the percentage of the base amount for each year of the income statement for each company.

(b) Calculate the gross profit margin, profit margin, asset turnover, return on assets, and return on equity ratios for 2014 for each company.

(c) Using the information calculated in (a) and (b), compare the profitability of each company.

(d) Is your comparison in (c) an intracompany comparison or an intercompany comparison? Explain.

TAKING IT FURTHER   How is your assessment of profitability affected by the differing sizes of the two companies, if at all? Explain.

P18–4A   Comparative financial statements for The Cable Company Ltd. are shown below.

Calculate ratios. (SO 4, 5, 6) AP

THE CABLE COMPANY LTD.
Income Statement
Year Ended December 31

	2014	2013
Net sales	$1,948,500	$1,700,500
Cost of goods sold	1,025,500	946,000
Gross profit	923,000	754,500
Operating expenses	516,000	449,000
Profit from operations	407,000	305,500
Interest expense	28,000	19,000
Profit before income tax	379,000	286,500
Income tax expense	113,700	86,000
Profit	$ 265,300	$ 200,500

THE CABLE COMPANY LTD.
Balance Sheet
December 31

Assets	2014	2013
Current assets		
Cash	$ 68,100	$ 64,200
Accounts receivable	107,800	102,800
Inventory	143,000	115,500
Total current assets	318,900	282,500
Equity investments	54,000	50,000
Property, plant, and equipment	625,300	520,300
Total assets	$998,200	$852,800
Liabilities and Shareholders' Equity		
Current liabilities		
Accounts payable	$155,000	$125,400
Income tax payable	43,500	42,000
Current portion of mortgage payable	10,000	20,000
Total current liabilities	208,500	187,400
Mortgage payable	104,000	200,000
Total liabilities	312,500	387,400
Shareholders' equity		
Common shares (56,000 issued in 2014; 60,000 in 2013)	168,000	180,000
Retained earnings	517,700	285,400
Total shareholders' equity	685,700	465,400
Total liabilities and shareholders' equity	$998,200	$852,800

Additional information:

1. All sales were on account.
2. The allowance for doubtful accounts was $5,400 in 2014 and $5,100 in 2013.
3. On July 1, 2014, 4,000 shares were reacquired for $10 per share and cancelled.
4. In 2014, $5,000 of dividends were paid to the common shareholders.
5. Cash provided by operating activities was $316,200.
6. Cash used by investing activities was $161,300.

Instructions

Calculate all possible liquidity, solvency, and profitability ratios for 2014.

TAKING IT FURTHER Based on the ratios you have calculated for 2014, can you determine whether The Cable Company's liquidity, solvency, and profitability are strong or weak? If not, what additional information would you require?

Calculate and evaluate ratios. (SO 1, 4, 5, 6) AN

P18–5A Comparative financial statements for Click and Clack Ltd. are shown below.

CLICK AND CLACK LTD.
Income Statement
Year Ended December 31

	2014	2013
Net sales	$900,000	$840,000
Cost of goods sold	620,000	575,000
Gross profit	280,000	265,000
Operating expenses	164,000	160,000
Profit from operations	116,000	105,000
Other revenues and expenses		
Interest expense	(35,000)	(20,000)
Gain on fair value adjustment of trading investments	5,000	0
Profit before income tax	86,000	85,000
Income tax expense	22,000	20,000
Profit	$ 64,000	$ 65,000

```
                        CLICK AND CLACK LTD.
                           Balance Sheet
                           December 31

  Assets                              2014         2013         2012

  Cash                             $ 70,000     $ 65,000     $ 10,000
  Trading investments                45,000       40,000       20,000
  Accounts receivable                94,000       90,000       88,000
  Inventories                       130,000      125,000       97,000
  Prepaid expenses                   25,000       23,000      115,000
  Land, buildings, and equipment    390,000      305,000      300,000

    Total assets                   $754,000     $648,000     $630,000

  Liabilities and Shareholders' Equity
  Liabilities
    Notes payable                  $110,000     $100,000     $100,000
    Accounts payable                 45,000       42,000       60,000
    Accrued liabilities              32,000       40,000       30,000
    Bonds payable, due 2018         190,000      150,000      181,000

      Total liabilities            377,000      332,000      371,000
  Shareholders' equity
    Common shares (20,000 issued)   200,000      200,000      200,000
    Retained earnings               177,000      116,000       59,000

    Total shareholders' equity      377,000      316,000      259,000

  Total liabilities and shareholders' equity  $754,000  $648,000  $630,000
```

Additional information:

1. Seventy-five percent of the sales were on account.
2. The allowance for doubtful accounts was $4,000 in 2014, $5,000 in 2013, and $3,000 in 2012.
3. In 2014 and 2013, dividends of $3,000 and $8,000, respectively, were paid to the common shareholders.
4. Cash provided by operating activities was $73,500 in 2014 and $129,000 in 2013.
5. Cash used by investing activities was $115,500 in 2014 and $35,000 in 2013.

Instructions

(a) Calculate all possible liquidity, solvency, and profitability ratios for 2014 and 2013.
(b) Identify whether the change in each ratio from 2013 to 2014 calculated in (a) was favourable (F), unfavourable (U), or no change (NC).
(c) Explain whether overall (1) liquidity, (2) solvency, and (3) profitability improved, deteriorated, or remained the same between 2013 and 2014.

TAKING IT FURTHER   Does this problem employ an intracompany comparison or an intercompany comparison? Which do you think is more useful?

P18–6A   Selected financial data for **Tim Hortons** and **Starbucks** are presented below for a recent year.

Calculate and evaluate ratios. (SO 4, 5, 6, 7) AN

	Tim Hortons (in CAD$ millions)	Starbucks (in US$ millions)
Statement of Comprehensive Income (Loss)		
Total revenue	$2,536.5	$11,700.4
Cost of sales	1,527.4	4,949.3
Gross profit	1,009.1	6,751.1
Operating expenses	136.9	5,022.6
Profit from operations	872.2	1,728.5
Interest expense	26.6	33.3
Other non-operating income	(2.4)	(115.9)
Profit before income tax	848.0	1,811.1
Income tax expense	200.9	563.1
Profit	647.1	1,248.0
Other comprehensive loss	(46.7)	(10.9)
Total comprehensive income	$ 600.4	$ 1,237.1

	Tim Hortons (in CAD$ millions)	Starbucks (in US$ millions)
Balance Sheet		
Current assets	$1,009.1	$ 3,794.9
Non-current assets	1,472.4	3,565.5
Total assets	$2,481.5	$ 7,360.4
Current liabilities	$ 491.5	$ 2,075.8
Non-current liabilities	547.6	897.3
Total liabilities	1,039.1	2,973.1
Shareholders' equity	1,442.4	4,387.3
Total liabilities and shareholders' equity	$2,481.5	$ 7,360.4
Additional information:		
Average accounts receivable	$ 181.0	$ 344.6
Average inventories	90.6	754.6
Average total assets	2,287.9	6,873.2
Average total shareholders' equity	1,349.1	4,034.8

Instructions

(a) For each company, calculate the following ratios:
1. Current ratio
2. Receivables turnover
3. Inventory turnover
4. Operating cycle
5. Debt to total assets
6. Interest coverage
7. Gross profit margin
8. Profit margin
9. Asset turnover
10. Return on assets
11. Return on equity

(b) Compare the liquidity, solvency, and profitability of the two companies.

TAKING IT FURTHER How should other comprehensive loss be factored into your analysis above?

Evaluate ratios.
(SO 4, 5, 6) AN

P18–7A Selected ratios for two companies operating in the office supply industry follow.

Ratio	Fournitures Ltée	Supplies Unlimited
Acid-test	1.0:1	0.8:1
Asset turnover	2.6 times	2.2 times
Current ratio	1.7:1	2.8:1
Debt to total assets	35.0%	30.3%
Gross profit margin	23.9%	35.4%
Interest coverage	4.2 times	6.6 times
Inventory turnover	6.0 times	3.1 times
Operating cycle	92 days	158 days
Price-earnings ratio	19.0 times	15.2 times
Profit margin	5.6%	4.1%
Receivables turnover	11.8 times	9.1 times
Return on assets	14.6%	9.0%
Return on equity	19.8%	12.5%

Instructions

(a) Both companies offer their customers credit terms of net 30 days. Indicate the ratio(s) that should be used to assess how well the accounts receivable are managed. Which company appears to be managing its accounts receivable better?

(b) Indicate the ratio(s) that should be used to assess inventory management. Which company appears to be managing its inventory better?

(c) Supplies Unlimited's current ratio is higher than Fourniture's. Identify two possible reasons for this.

(d) Which company is more solvent? Identify the ratio(s) that should be used to determine this and defend your choice.

(e) You notice that Fourniture's gross profit margin is significantly less than Supplies Unlimited's but its profit margin is higher. Identify two possible reasons for this.

(f) Which company do investors appear to believe has greater prospects for future profitability? Indicate the ratio(s) you used to reach this conclusion and explain your reasoning.

TAKING IT FURTHER   Which company is using leverage more effectively? Explain.

P18–8A   The following ratios are available for agricultural chemicals competitors **Potash Corporation of Sas katchewan (PotashCorp)** and **Agrium** for a recent year:

Evaluate ratios.
(SO 4, 5, 6) AN

	PotashCorp	Agrium
Liquidity		
Current ratio	1.1:1	2.1:1
Acid-test	0.8:1	1.2:1
Receivables turnover	10.7 times	8.3 times
Inventory turnover	6.8 times	4.1 times
Operating cycle	88 days	133 days
Solvency		
Debt to total assets	36.6%	26.9%
Interest coverage	18.3 times	63.1 times
Profitability		
Gross profit margin	49.2%	28.0%
Profit margin	35.4%	9.8%
Asset turnover	0.6 times	1.2 times
Return on assets	19.4%	11.6%
Return on equity	42.4%	25.9%

Instructions

(a) Which company is more liquid? Explain.

(b) Which company is more solvent? Explain.

(c) Which company is more profitable? Explain.

TAKING IT FURTHER   The price-earnings ratio for Potash Corp is 12.3 times, compared with Agrium's PE ratio of 9 times. Which company do investors favour? Is your answer consistent with your analysis of the two companies' profitability in (c)?

P18–9A   Presented here are an incomplete income statement and balance sheet for Schwenke Corporation.

Calculate missing information. (SO 4, 5, 6) AN

SCHWENKE CORPORATION
Income Statement
Year Ended December 31, 2014

Net sales	$ (a)
Cost of goods sold	(b)
Gross profit	(c)
Operating expenses	333,750
Profit from operations	(d)
Interest expense	10,500
Profit before income taxes	(e)
Income tax expense	(f)
Profit	$124,600

SCHWENKE CORPORATION
Balance Sheet
December 31, 2014

Assets		
Current assets		
Cash	$	7,500
Accounts receivable		(g)
Inventory		(h)
Total current assets		(i)
Property, plant, and equipment		(j)
Total assets	$	(k)
Liabilities		
Current liabilities	$	(l)
Non-current liabilities		120,000
Total liabilities		(m)
Shareholders' Equity		
Common shares		250,000
Retained earnings		400,000
Total shareholders' equity		650,000
Total liabilities and shareholders' equity	$	(n)

Additional information:

1. The gross profit margin is 40%.
2. The income tax rate is 20%.
3. The inventory turnover is 8 times.
4. The current ratio is 3:1.
5. The asset turnover is 1.5 times.

Instructions

Calculate the missing information using the ratios. Use ending balances instead of average balances, where averages are required for ratio calculations. Show your calculations.

TAKING IT FURTHER Why is it not possible to calculate the missing amounts in the same sequence (i.e., a, b, c, etc.) that they are presented above?

Problems: Set B

Prepare horizontal analysis and identify changes. (SO 2, 7) AN

P18–1B The following condensed financial information is available for the Micro Brewery Inc.

MICRO BREWERY INC.
Income Statement
Year Ended December 31

	2014	2013	2012	2011
Sales revenue	$551,830	$451,300	$462,320	$376,330
Cost of goods sold	263,850	207,350	202,160	149,050
Gross profit	287,980	243,950	260,160	227,280
Operating expenses	204,550	202,620	191,800	185,230
Profit from operations	83,430	41,330	68,360	42,050
Other income (expenses)	1,470	2,170	3,040	2,200
Profit before income taxes	84,900	43,500	71,400	44,250
Income tax expense	14,433	7,395	12,138	7,523
Profit	$ 70,467	$ 36,105	$ 59,262	$ 36,727

MICRO BREWERY INC.
Balance Sheet
December 31

Assets	2014	2013	2012	2011
Current assets	$ 90,890	$ 69,060	$ 79,830	$ 66,830
Non-current assets	416,870	438,810	277,552	292,160
Total assets	$507,760	$507,870	$357,382	$358,990
Liabilities and Shareholders' Equity				
Liabilities				
Current liabilities	$ 45,750	$ 43,220	$ 37,250	$ 46,750
Non-current liabilities	26,216	59,323	20,910	52,280
Total liabilities	71,966	102,543	58,160	99,030
Shareholders' equity				
Common shares	110,000	110,000	10,000	10,000
Retained earnings	325,794	295,328	289,222	249,960
Total shareholders' equity	435,794	405,327	299,222	259,960
Total liabilities and shareholders' equity	$507,760	$507,870	$357,382	$358,990

Instructions

(a) Using horizontal analysis, calculate the percentage of the base-year amount for the income statement and balance sheet, assuming 2011 is the base year.
(b) Using the horizontal analyses you prepared in (a), identify any significant changes between 2011 and 2014.
(c) Is it possible to prepare a meaningful horizontal analysis of the percentage change for each year for Micro Brewery? Explain.

TAKING IT FURTHER   Micro Brewery's financial information for 2014 and 2013 was prepared using IFRS, which the company converted to when it became a publicly-traded company on January 1, 2013. The financial information for 2012 and 2011 was prepared using ASPE, the accounting standards the company used prior to 2013. How might these differing standards affect your interpretation of the horizontal analysis?

P18–2B   A horizontal and vertical analysis of the income statement for a service company providing consulting services is shown below.

Interpret horizontal and vertical analysis.
(SO 2, 3, 7) AN

SERVICE CORPORATION
Horizontal Income Statement
Year Ended January 31

	2014	2013	2012	2011
Revenue	120.0%	110.0%	114.0%	100.0%
Operating expenses	118.6%	111.4%	114.3%	100.0%
Profit from operations	123.3%	106.7%	113.3%	100.0%
Other revenues and expenses				
Interest expense	40.0%	60.0%	80.0%	100.0%
Other revenue	240.0%	140.0%	200.0%	100.0%
Profit before income tax	166.8%	130.2%	131.7%	100.0%
Income tax expense	166.8%	130.2%	131.7%	100.0%
Profit	166.8%	130.2%	131.7%	100.0%

SERVICE CORPORATION
Vertical Income Statement
Year Ended January 31

	2014	2013	2012	2011
Revenue	100.0%	100.0%	100.0%	100.0%
Operating expenses	69.2%	70.9%	70.2%	70.0%
Profit from operations	30.8%	29.1%	29.8%	30.0%
Other revenues and expenses				
Interest expense	(3.3)%	(5.4)%	(7.0)%	(10.0)%
Other revenue	1.0%	0.6%	0.9%	0.5%
Profit before income tax	28.5%	24.3%	23.7%	20.5%
Income tax expense	5.7%	4.9%	4.8%	4.1%
Profit	22.8%	19.4%	18.9%	16.4%

Instructions

(a) How effectively has the company controlled its operating expenses over the four-year period?

(b) Identify any other income statement components that have significantly changed over the four-year period for the company.

(c) Identify any additional information that might be helpful to you in your analysis of this company over the four-year period.

TAKING IT FURTHER In a horizontal analysis, the company's income tax expense has changed exactly as much as profit (66.8%) over the four-year period. Yet, in a vertical analysis, the income tax percentage is different than the profit percentage in each period. Explain how this is possible.

Prepare vertical analysis, calculate profitability ratios, and compare.
(SO 1, 3, 6) AN

P18–3B Comparative income statement data for Manitou Ltd. and Muskoka Ltd., two competitors, are shown below for the year ended June 30, 2014.

	Manitou	Muskoka
Net sales	$360,000	$1,400,000
Cost of goods sold	200,000	720,000
Gross profit	160,000	680,000
Operating expenses	60,000	272,000
Profit from operations	100,000	408,000
Rental income	12,000	24,000
Profit before income tax	112,000	432,000
Income tax expense	22,400	95,040
Profit	$ 89,600	$ 336,960
Additional information:		
Average total assets	$457,500	$1,725,000
Average total shareholders' equity	204,800	743,480

Instructions

(a) Using vertical analysis, calculate the percentage of the base amount for each year of the income statement for each company.

(b) Calculate the gross profit margin, profit margin, asset turnover, return on assets, and return on equity ratios for 2014 for each company.

(c) Using the information calculated in (a) and (b), compare the profitability of each company.

(d) Is your comparison in (c) an intracompany comparison or an intercompany comparison? Explain.

TAKING IT FURTHER How is your assessment of profitability affected by the differing sizes of the two companies, if at all? Explain.

P18–4B   Comparative financial statements for The Rose Packing Corporation are shown below.

Calculate ratios.
(SO 4, 5, 6) AP

THE ROSE PACKING CORPORATION Income Statement Year Ended December 31		
	2014	2013
Net sales	$790,000	$624,000
Cost of goods sold	540,000	405,600
Gross profit	250,000	218,400
Operating expenses	153,880	149,760
Profit from operations	96,120	68,640
Interest expense	3,200	1,200
Loss on fair value adjustment of trading		
investments	6,720	6,000
Profit before income tax	86,200	61,440
Income tax expense	12,930	9,216
Profit	$ 73,270	$ 52,224

THE ROSE PACKING CORPORATION Balance Sheet December 31		
Assets	2014	2013
Current assets		
Cash	$ 23,100	$ 11,600
Trading investments	26,280	33,000
Accounts receivable	104,720	93,800
Inventory	96,400	74,000
Total current assets	250,500	212,400
Property, plant, and equipment	465,300	459,600
Total assets	$715,800	$672,000
Liabilities and Shareholders' Equity		
Current liabilities		
Accounts payable	$164,850	$130,000
Income tax payable	2,500	4,000
Other payables and accruals	12,800	22,000
Total current liabilities	180,150	156,000
Bonds payable	90,000	120,000
Total liabilities	270,150	276,000
Shareholders' equity		
Common shares (15,000 issued)	150,000	150,000
Retained earnings	295,650	246,000
Total shareholders' equity	445,650	396,000
Total liabilities and shareholders' equity	$715,800	$672,000

Additional information:

1. All sales were on account.
2. The allowance for doubtful accounts was $5,500 in 2014 and $4,500 in 2013.

3. In 2014, $23,620 of dividends were paid to the common shareholders.
4. Cash provided by operating activities was $116,780.
5. Cash used by investing activities was $51,660.

Instructions

Calculate all possible liquidity, solvency, and profitability ratios for 2014.

TAKING IT FURTHER Based on the ratios you have calculated for 2014, can you determine whether Rose Packing's liquidity, solvency, and profitability are strong or weak? If not, what additional information would you require?

Calculate and evaluate ratios. (SO 1, 4, 5, 6) AN

P18–5B Comparative financial statements for Track Ltd. are shown below.

TRACK LTD. Income Statement Year Ended December 31		
	2014	2013
Net sales	$1,000,000	$940,000
Cost of goods sold	650,000	635,000
Gross profit	350,000	305,000
Operating expenses	200,000	180,000
Profit from operations	150,000	125,000
Interest expense (net)	35,000	35,000
Profit before income taxes	115,000	90,000
Income tax expense	17,250	13,500
Profit	$ 97,750	$ 76,500

TRACK LTD. Balance Sheet December 31			
Assets	2014	2013	2012
Cash	$ 50,000	$ 42,000	$ 33,000
Accounts receivable	100,000	87,000	77,000
Inventories	240,000	200,000	150,000
Prepaid expenses	25,000	31,000	30,000
Long-term debt investments	180,000	100,000	50,000
Land	75,000	75,000	75,000
Building and equipment	570,000	600,000	660,000
Total assets	$1,240,000	$1,135,000	$1,075,000
Liabilities and Shareholders' Equity			
Liabilities			
Notes payable	$ 125,000	$ 125,000	$ 125,000
Accounts payable	160,750	140,000	71,000
Accrued liabilities	52,000	50,000	20,000
Bonds payable, due 2018	100,000	100,000	200,000
Total liabilities	437,750	415,000	416,000
Shareholders' equity			
Preferred shares	200,000	200,000	200,000
Common shares (100,000 issued)	300,000	300,000	300,000
Retained earnings	302,250	220,000	159,000
Total shareholders' equity	802,250	720,000	659,000
Total liabilities and shareholders' equity	$1,240,000	$1,135,000	$1,075,000

Additional information:

1. All sales were on account.
2. The allowance for doubtful accounts was $5,000 in 2014, $4,000 in 2013, and $3,000 in 2012.
3. In each of 2014 and 2013, $15,500 of dividends were paid to the preferred shareholders.
4. Cash provided by operating activities was $133,500 in 2014 and $180,500 in 2013.
5. Cash used by investing activities was $110,000 in 2014 and $56,000 in 2013.

Instructions

(a) Calculate all possible liquidity, solvency, and profitability ratios for 2014 and 2013.
(b) Identify whether the change in each ratio from 2013 to 2014 calculated in (a) was favourable (F), unfavourable (U), or no change (NC).
(c) Explain whether overall (1) liquidity, (2) solvency, and (3) profitability improved, deteriorated, or remained the same between 2013 and 2014.

TAKING IT FURTHER   Does this problem employ an intracompany comparison or an intercompany comparison? Which do you think is more useful?

P18–6B   Early in 2013, **Leon's Furniture** acquired its closest competitor, **The Brick**. Selected financial data (in thousands) for the two companies, prior to the acquisition, are presented below.

Calculate and evaluate ratios.
(SO 4, 5, 6, 7) AN

	The Brick	Leon's
Statement of Comprehensive Income (Loss)		
Net sales	$1,351,648	$682,836
Cost of goods sold	753,977	394,099
Gross profit	597,671	288,737
Operating expenses	489,532	213,416
Profit from operations	108,139	75,321
Interest expense	30,979	-
Other non-operating expenses (income)	26,844	(3,527)
Profit before income taxes	50,316	78,848
Income tax expense	14,443	22,182
Profit	35,873	56,666
Other comprehensive loss	(170)	(584)
Total comprehensive income	$ 35,703	$ 56,082
Statement of Financial Position		
Current assets	$ 388,087	$343,772
Non-current assets	378,395	251,567
Total assets	$ 766,482	$595,339
Current liabilities	$ 280,005	$139,123
Non-current liabilities	394,831	30,755
Total liabilities	674,836	169,878
Shareholders' equity	91,646	425,461
Total liabilities and shareholders' equity	$ 766,482	$595,339
Additional information:		
Average accounts receivable	$ 72,760	$ 28,753
Average inventories	167,264	86,627
Average total assets	750,182	581,007
Average total shareholders' equity	82,584	417,874

Instructions

(a) For each company, calculate the following ratios:
   1. Current ratio
   2. Receivables turnover
   3. Inventory turnover
   4. Operating cycle
   5. Debt to total assets
   6. Interest coverage
   7. Gross profit margin

8. Profit margin
9. Asset turnover
10. Return on assets
11. Return on equity

(b) Compare the liquidity, solvency, and profitability of the two companies.

TAKING IT FURTHER How should other comprehensive loss be factored into your analysis above?

Evaluate ratios.
(SO 4, 5, 6) AN

P18–7B Selected ratios for two companies operating in the beverage industry follow.

Ratio	Refresh Ltd.	Flavour Corp.
Acid-test	0:6:1	0:8:1
Asset turnover	1.0 times	1.0 times
Current ratio	2.2:1	1.6:1
Debt to total assets	56.0%	72.0%
Gross profit margin	73.8%	60.0%
Interest coverage	12.3 times	6.9 times
Inventory turnover	5.8 times	9.9 times
Operating cycle	98 days	74 days
Price-earnings ratio	20.3 times	14.3 times
Profit margin	9.3%	10.2%
Receivables turnover	10.4 times	9.8 times
Return on assets	11.2%	10.1%
Return on equity	25.7%	29.8%

Instructions

(a) Both companies offer their customers credit terms of net 30 days. Indicate the ratio(s) that should be used to assess how well the accounts receivable are managed. Which company appears to be managing its accounts receivable better?

(b) Indicate the ratio(s) that should be used to assess inventory management. Which company appears to be managing its inventory better?

(c) Refresh's current ratio is higher than Flavour's. Identify two possible reasons for this.

(d) Which company is more solvent? Identify the ratio(s) that should be used to determine this and defend your choice.

(e) You notice that Refresh's gross profit margin is significantly more than Flavour's but its profit margin is lower. Identify two possible reasons for this.

(f) Which company do investors appear to believe has greater prospects for future profitability? Indicate the ratio(s) you used to reach this conclusion and explain your reasoning.

TAKING IT FURTHER Which company is using leverage more effectively? Explain.

Evaluate ratios.
(SO 4, 5, 6) AN

P18–8B The following ratios are available for toolmakers **Stanley Black & Decker** and **Snap-On** for a recent year:

Liquidity	Stanley	Snap-On
Current ratio	1.3:1	2.7:1
Acid-test	0.9:1	2.0:1
Receivables turnover	6.5 times	5.7 times
Inventory turnover	4.5 times	4.0 times
Operating cycle	137 days	155 days
Solvency		
Debt to total assets	33.6%	37.9%
Interest coverage	5.7 times	6.4 times
Profitability		
Gross profit margin	36.6%	46.8%
Profit margin	6.1%	10.2%
Asset turnover	0.7 times	0.8 times
Return on assets	4.1%	7.8%
Return on equity	9.2%	18.8%

Instructions

(a) Which company is more liquid? Explain.

(b) Which company is more solvent? Explain.

(c) Which company is more profitable? Explain.

TAKING IT FURTHER   Stanley's price-earnings ratio is 19 times, compared with Snap-On's PE ratio of 12.4 times. Which company do investors favour? Is your answer consistent with your analysis of the two companies' profitability in (c)?

P18–9B   Presented here are an incomplete income statement and balance sheet for Vieux Corporation.

Calculate missing information.
(SO 4, 5, 6) AN

VIEUX CORPORATION Income Statement Year ended December 31, 2014	
Net sales	$11,000,000
Cost of goods sold	(a)
Gross profit	(b)
Operating expenses	1,600,000
Profit from operations	(c)
Interest expense	(d)
Profit before income taxes	(e)
Income tax expense	707,000
Profit	$ (f)

VIEUX CORPORATION Balance Sheet December 31, 2014	
Assets	
Current assets	
Cash	$ (g)
Accounts receivable	(h)
Inventory	(i)
Total current assets	(j)
Long-term investments	430,000
Property, plant, and equipment	4,420,000
Total assets	$ (k)
Liabilities	
Current liabilities	$ (l)
Non-current liabilities	(m)
Total liabilities	(n)
Shareholders' Equity	
Common shares	1,500,000
Retained earnings	1,900,000
Total shareholders' equity	3,400,000
Total liabilities and shareholders' equity	$ (o)

Additional information:
1. The gross profit margin is 40%.
2. The profit margin is 15%.
3. The receivables turnover is 10 times and all sales are on account.
4. The inventory turnover is 8 times.
5. The current ratio is 2:1.
6. The return on assets is 22%.

Instructions

Calculate the missing information using the ratios. Use ending balances instead of average balances, where averages are required for ratio calculations. Show your calculations.

TAKING IT FURTHER   Why is it not possible to calculate the missing amounts in the same sequence (i.e., a, b, c, etc.) that they are presented above?

▶ Continuing Cookie Chronicle

(*Note:* This is a continuation of the Cookie Chronicle from Chapters 1 through 17.)

The Koebels have considered the offer extended by Coffee Beans Ltd. (see Chapter 17) and have turned it down. Instead, Brian, Janet, and Natalie have decided to continue operating Koebel's Family Bakery Ltd. and to expand the business.

Koebel's Family Bakery Ltd. has excess cash for the expansion but needs time to organize it. In the meantime, the cash could be invested. The Koebels have been approached by a family friend who works in the investment industry. This family friend has made a strong recommendation to buy shares in Cookies and Cream Ltd., a public company. Because Janet, Brian, and Natalie are familiar with the bakery business, they believe that investing in a public company that operates a bakery could be a good investment. The investment in Cookies and Cream Ltd. could provide a significant return on a short-term basis while the Koebels organize for the expansion.

In order to assess this investment, Natalie has calculated several ratios for both Cookies and Cream Ltd. and Koebel's Family Bakery as follows:

Ratio	Cookies and Cream Ltd. Year End 2014	Cookies and Cream Ltd. Year End 2013	Koebel's Family Bakery Ltd. Year End 2014
Current ratio	1.0:1.0	1.1:1.0	8.4:1:0
Receivables turnover	15.6 times	18.5 times	47.8 times
Inventory turnover	21.4 times	22.6 times	7.6 times
Debt to total assets	31%	30%	13%
Times interest earned	61 times	31 times	65 times
Return on common shareholders' equity	7.8%	8.1%	36.9%
Return on total assets	5.4%	5.7%	32%
Gross profit margin	19.5%	21%	75.3%
Profit margin	3.3%	3.9%	22.1%
Dividend payout	32%	9.8%	60%
Price-earnings ratio	24 times	19 times	n/a

Instructions

(a) Which company is more liquid? Explain.
(b) Which company is more solvent? Explain.
(c) Which company is more profitable? Explain.
(d) Are Cookies and Cream Ltd.'s ratios improving? Explain.
(e) Overall, why do you think that the ratios of Koebel's are stronger than those of Cookies and Cream Ltd.?
(f) What other considerations must the Koebels keep in mind before making an investment in any public company?

BROADENING YOUR PERSPECTIVE | CHAPTER 18

Financial Reporting and Analysis

Financial Reporting Problem

BYP18–1   The financial statements of **Reitmans (Canada)** are shown in Appendix A at the end of this textbook.

Instructions

(a) Using vertical analysis, calculate the vertical percentage of a base amount for Reitmans' balance sheets and income statements for 2012 and 2011.

(b) Identify any significant items or trends you observe from your vertical analysis in (a).

Interpreting Financial Statements

BYP18–2   Selected financial ratios for **Canadian National Railway (CN)** and **Canadian Pacific Railway (CP)** are presented here for a recent year.

	CN	CP
Liquidity		
Current ratio	1.1:1	0.7:1
Acid-test ratio	1.0:1	0.6:1
Receivables turnover	10.2 times	10.3 times
Inventory turnover	21.1	22.6
Solvency		
Debt to total assets	59.0%	67.1%
Interest coverage	8.4 times	4.3 times
Free cash flow	$1,247 million	$(532) million
Profitability		
Gross profit margin	46.4%	43.7%
Profit margin	27.2%	11.0%
Asset turnover	0.4 times	0.4 times
Return on assets	9.6%	4.1%
Return on equity	22.4%	12.0%

Instructions

(a) Comment on the relative liquidity of the two companies.

(b) Comment on the relative solvency of the two companies.

(c) Comment on the relative profitability of the two companies.

(d) A commonly cited ratio in the railway industry is the operating ratio. This ratio measures the percentage that total operating expenses is of total revenue. CN's operating ratio is 63.5%, compared with CP's of 81.3% for the same year as the ratios provided above.

   1. Do you believe that a lower or higher operating ratio is preferable? Explain.

   2. Given your answer in item (1) above, which company has the better operating ratio?

   3. Does the operating ratio provide additional information to assist your assessment of profitability in part (c)?

▶ Critical Thinking

Collaborative Learning Activity

Note to instructor: Additional instructions and material for this group activity can be found on the Instructor Resource Site and in *WileyPLUS*.

BYP18–3 In this group activity, you will analyze two companies on an intracompany, intercompany, and industry basis. Based on your analysis, you will recommend which company is a better investment. Your instructor will evaluate the groups based on their analysis and rationale for their recommendation.

Communication Activity

BYP18–4 You are a new member of the audit committee and board of directors of EasyMix Cement Inc. EasyMix was a private company using ASPE until last year, when it became a publicly traded company using IFRS. You are about to attend your first meeting of the audit committee, at which the year-end financial results, including key ratios, will be presented.

Instructions

Identify any of the limitations of financial statement analysis that you believe may apply to EasyMix. Prioritize your list and prepare questions that you should raise at the audit committee meeting to help you better understand the financial results and ratios presented.

Ethics Case

BYP18–5 Sabra Surkis, president of Surkis Industries, wants to issue a press release to improve her company's image and boost its share price, which has been gradually falling. As controller, you have been asked to provide a list of financial ratios along with some other operating statistics from Surkis Industries' first-quarter operations for the current year.

Two days after you provide the ratios and data requested, Carol Dunn, the public relations director of Surkis, asks you to review the financial and operating data contained in the press release written by the president and edited by Carol. In the news release, the president highlights the sales increase of 5.2% over last year's first quarter and the positive change in the current ratio from 1.1:1 last year to 1.5:1 this year. She also emphasizes that production was up 10.1% over the prior year's first quarter.

You note that the release contains only positive or improved ratios, and none of the negative or weakened ratios. For instance, there is no mention that the debt to total assets ratio has increased from 35.1% to 44.9%. Nor is it mentioned that the operating cycle has increased by 19%. There is also no indication that the reported profit for the quarter would have been a loss if the estimated lives of Surkis's machinery had not been increased by 20%.

Instructions

(a) Who are the stakeholders in this situation?
(b) Is there anything unethical in president Surkis's actions?
(c) Should you as controller remain silent? Does Carol have any responsibility?

"All About You" Activity

BYP18–6 In the "All About You" feature, you learned that there are on-line investment services that provide advice to investors. These services offer stock quotes, company research reports, personal finance information, news, on-line seminars, and message boards. However, it is also important that as an investor you differentiate good information from bad information. Reading the financial statements and preparing a ratio analysis is one step in evaluating an investment. You have recently inherited $10,000 cash and you are considering investing in **Canadian Tire Corporation, Limited's** shares.

Instructions

Go to Canadian Tire's website at http://corp.canadiantire.ca and click on "Investors", Then click on "Annual Reports", and go to the 2012 annual report. [*Note:* It is also available on SEDAR. See part (h) of BYP14-6 for instructions on how to access information on SEDAR.]

(a) Included in the annual report is Management's Discussion and Analysis (MD&A), which provides highlights of the company's operations, explanations for changes in the company's financial position and strategic plans for the future. How might the MD&A provide useful information in your evaluation of the financial statement ratios?

(b) Calculate the following ratios for the 2012 fiscal year. Compare these to the 2011 ratios shown in the Ratio Analysis section of the chapter for Canadian Tire and reproduced in parentheses after each ratio below. For each ratio, has it improved or deteriorated from 2011?

    1. Current ratio (1.7:1)   6. Profit margin (4.5%)
    2. Inventory turnover (6.2 times)   7. Return on assets (4.0%)

3. Debt to total assets (64.3%)
4. Interest coverage (5.1 times)
5. Gross profit margin (29.5%)

8. Return on equity (11.1%)
9. Price-earnings ratio (12.7 times)
10. Payout ratio (19.6%)

(c) On the "Investors" section of Canadian Tire's website, click on "Shareholders" and then click "Historical Price Lookup." What were Canadian Tire's shares trading at on the following dates?

1. December 30, 2011
2. December 28, 2012

(d) Under "Shareholders" click on "Stock Chart" and input "5 years" into the time range. Comment on the changes in the price of Canadian Tire's shares over the five years.

(e) Based on your brief analysis of Canadian Tire's ratios and share prices, do you think buying Canadian Tire's shares is a good investment for you? Explain.

(f) If you are investing in the stock market, will you rely solely on your analysis of the financial statements? The history of Canadian Tire's stock price? Or do you think you might rely on both your financial statement analysis and the history of the stock price? Explain.

(g) In the "All About You" feature, we learned that critics of message boards on investment services' sites say that message boards can intensify the rumour mill. Do you think that you should ignore message boards when making investment decisions? Explain.

ANSWERS TO CHAPTER QUESTIONS

ANSWERS TO ACCOUNTING IN ACTION INSIGHT QUESTIONS

Across the Organization, p. 951

Q: What other liquidity ratios should be monitored, and by what department(s), across the organization?

A: The inventory turnover and days sales in inventory ratios would be monitored closely by both the purchasing and sales departments to make sure that the inventory is saleable. The finance department will also monitor these ratios to ensure that the cost of carrying the inventory is not unreasonable. The finance department would also watch the acid-test ratio in order to assess its cash flow requirements.

All About You, p. 963

Q: Suppose you are thinking about investing in shares of Tim Hortons. You scanned a variety of investor websites and found messages posted by two different investors. One says it's time to buy Tim Hortons shares; the other says it isn't. How should you decide whether to buy the shares or not?

A: Before purchasing any shares, you must ensure that you can differentiate the good information from the bad and don't get carried away by rumours. You should read the company's financial statements and calculate and review any relevant ratios (e.g., liquidity, solvency, profitability). You should also consider non-financial factors (e.g., the economy) in your decision.

ANSWERS TO SELF-STUDY QUESTION

1. a   2. d   3. c   4. c   5. a   6. b   7. d   8. c   9. d   10. a

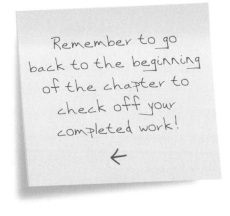

Photo Credits

Logos are registered trademarks of the respective companies and are reprinted with permission.

Chapter 1 Opener: The Canadian Press Images-Mario Beauregard; Page 5: © istockphoto.com/Andreas Rodriguez; Page 26: © istockphoto.com/Jacob Wackerhausen. **Chapter 2** Opener: Courtesy Prestige Dance Academy; Page 63: ©iStockPhoto.com/NevinGiesbrecht; Page 76: ©iStockPhoto.com/mihalec. **Chapter 3** Opener: Courtesy Seneca College of Applied Arts and Technology; Page 114: ©iStockPhoto.com/Ashwin82; Page 122: ©iStockPhoto.com/spxChrome. **Chapter 4** Opener: Courtesy Laurel Hyatt; Page 186: Copied with the permission of Canada Post Corporation; Page 187: Adapted and reprinted with the permission of Empire Company Limited; Page 188: BlackBerry®, RIM®, Research In Motion® and related trademarks, names and logos are the property of Research In Motion Limited and are registered and/or used in the U.S. and countries around the world. Used under license from Research In Motion Limited; Page 188: Tim Hortons is a registered trademark of the TDL Marks Corporation. Used with permission; Page 189: Used with permission of Sears Canada Inc; Page 189: Canadian National Railway Company ("CN"), reproduced by authorization of CN; Page 192: © iStockPhoto.com/WillSelarep. **Chapter 5** Opener: Courtesy Moulé; Page 249: © iStockPhoto.com/Leah-Anne Thompson. **Chapter 6** Opener: Courtesy Gravitypope/Louise Dirks; Page 304: ©istockphoto.com/SimplyCreativePhotography; Page 319: © istockphoto.com/Lewis Wright. **Chapter 7** Opener: © Barrett & MacKay Photo; Page 365: © istockphoto.com/Peter Garbet; Page 368: © istockphoto.comARICAN; Page 382: Tim Hortons is a registered trademark of the TDL Marks Corporation. Used with permission. **Chapter 8** Opener: Cindy Wilson/Telegraph-Journal; Page 419: ©iStockPhoto.com/Marcus Clackson; Page 434: AP/Charles Krupa/The Canadian Press. **Chapter 9** Opener: Courtesy George Brown College; Page 474: ©istockphoto/DNY59; Page 490: ©istockphoto/Chris Reed. **Chapter 10** Page 524: © istockphoto.com/GRAZVYDAS; Page 535: The Canadian Press/Marcos Townsend; Page 543: istockphoto.com/Morgan Lane Studios; Pages 544 and 555: Shoppers Drug Mart Corporation. **Chapter 11** Opener: Photo shows Rebecca Villmann, Principal, Accounting Standards Board. Photo courtesy of Accounting Standards Board, 2012; Page 584: © istockphoto.com/DNY59; Page 591: Frank Gunn/The Canadian Press. **Chapter 12** Opener: Courtesy Harris & Chong LLP; Page 628: © istockphoto.com/Aldo Murillo; Page 644: The Canadian Press/Ben Margot. **Chapter 13** Opener: Courtesy Doxsee & Co.; Page 676: © istockphoto.com/George Paul; Page 681: istockphoto.com/Björn Meyer. **Chapter 14** Opener: Photo courtesy of Tim Hortons. Tim Hortons is a registered trademark of the TDL Marks Corporation. Used with permission; Page 721: © istockphoto.com/Aaliya Landholt; Page 737: © Sheriar Hirjikaka, 2012. **Chapter 15** Opener: Photo Hydro-Québec; Page 768: © istockphoto.com/DNY59; Page 784: © istockphoto.com/ozlemonal. **Chapter 16** Opener: Kevin Frayer/The Canadian Press; Page 837: © istockphoto.com/Maria Toutoudaki. **Chapter 17** Opener: Courtesy Clearwater Seafoods; Page 871: © istockphoto.com/Pawel Gaul; Page 901: © istockphoto.com/wsfurlan. **Chapter 18** Opener: Courtesy of the Canadian Institute of Chartered Accountants (CICA); Page 951: © istockphoto.com/Kyu Oh; Page 963: CD1 WENN Photos/Newscom.

Reitmans (Canada) Limited

In this appendix, we illustrate current financial reporting with a comprehensive set of corporate financial statements that are prepared in accordance with International Financial Reporting Standards (IFRS). We are grateful for permission to use the actual financial statements of Reitmans (Canada) Ltd.—Canada's largest women's specialty clothing retailer.

Reitman's financial statement package features a statement of earnings, statement of comprehensive income, balance sheets, statement of changes in shareholders' equity, statement of cash flows, and notes to the financial statements. The financial statements are preceded by two reports: a statement of management's responsibilities for financial reporting and the independent auditors' report.

We encourage students to use these financial statements in conjunction with the relevant material in the textbook. As well, these statements can be used to solve the Financial Reporting Problem in the Broadening Your Perspective section of the end-of-chapter material.

Annual reports, including the financial statements, are reviewed in detail in *WileyPLUS* and on the companion website to this textbook.

MANAGEMENT'S RESPONSIBILITY FOR FINANCIAL STATEMENTS

The accompanying financial statements and all the information in the annual report are the responsibility of management and have been approved by the Board of Directors of Reitmans (Canada) Limited.

These financial statements have been prepared by management in conformity with International Financial Reporting Standards and include amounts that are based on best estimates and judgments. The financial information used elsewhere in the annual report is consistent with that in the financial statements.

Management of the Company has developed and maintains a system of internal accounting controls. Management believes that this system of internal accounting controls provides reasonable assurances that financial records are reliable and form a proper basis for the preparation of the financial statements and that assets are properly accounted for and safeguarded.

The Board of Directors carries out its responsibility for the financial statements in this annual report principally through its Audit Committee, consisting of all outside directors. The Audit Committee reviews the Company's annual financial statements and recommends their approval to the Board of Directors. The auditors appointed by the shareholders have full access to the Audit Committee, with and without management being present.

These financial statements have been examined by the auditors appointed by the shareholders, KPMG LLP, Chartered Accountants and their report is presented hereafter.

(signed) Jeremy H. Reitman
Chairman and
Chief Executive Officer

(signed) Eric Williams, CA
Vice-President, Finance and
Chief Financial Officer

March 28, 2012

INDEPENDENT AUDITORS' REPORT

To the Shareholders of Reitmans (Canada) Limited

We have audited the accompanying financial statements of Reitmans (Canada) Limited, which comprise the balance sheets as at January 28, 2012, January 29, 2011 and January 31, 2010, the statements of earnings, comprehensive income, changes in shareholders' equity and cash flows for the years ended January 28, 2012 and January 29, 2011, and notes, comprising a summary of significant accounting policies and other explanatory information.

Management's Responsibility for the Financial Statements

Management is responsible for the preparation and fair presentation of these financial statements in accordance with International Financial Reporting Standards, and for such internal control as management determines is necessary to enable the preparation of financial statements that are free from material misstatement, whether due to fraud or error.

Auditors' Responsibility

Our responsibility is to express an opinion on these financial statements based on our audits. We conducted our audits in accordance with Canadian generally accepted auditing standards. Those standards require that we comply with ethical requirements and plan and perform the audit to obtain reasonable assurance about whether the financial statements are free from material misstatement.

An audit involves performing procedures to obtain audit evidence about the amounts and disclosures in the financial statements. The procedures selected depend on our judgment, including the assessment of the risks of material misstatement of the financial statements, whether due to fraud or error. In making those risk assessments, we consider internal control relevant to the entity's preparation and fair presentation of the financial statements in order to design audit procedures that are appropriate in the circumstances, but not for the purpose of expressing an opinion on the effectiveness of the entity's internal control. An audit also includes evaluating the appropriateness of accounting policies used and the reasonableness of accounting estimates made by management, as well as evaluating the overall presentation of the financial statements.

We believe that the audit evidence we have obtained in our audits is sufficient and appropriate to provide a basis for our audit opinion.

Opinion

In our opinion, the financial statements present fairly, in all material respects, the financial position of Reitmans (Canada) Limited as at January 28, 2012, January 29, 2011 and January 31, 2010, and its financial performance and its cash flows for the years ended January 28, 2012 and January 29, 2011 in accordance with International Financial Reporting Standards.

KPMG LLP*

Chartered Accountants

Montréal, Canada
March 28, 2012

* CA Auditor Permit no. 23443

KPMG LLP is a Canadian limited liability partnership and a member firm of the KPMG network of independent member firms affiliated with KPMG International Cooperative ("KPMG International"), a Swiss entity.
KPMG Canada provides services to KPMG LLP.

REITMANS (CANADA) LIMITED
STATEMENTS OF EARNINGS
(in thousands of Canadian dollars except per share amounts)

	For the years ended	
	January 28, 2012	**January 29, 2011**
Sales	**$ 1,019,397**	$ 1,059,000
Cost of goods sold (note 7)	**363,333**	350,671
Gross profit	**656,064**	708,329
Selling and distribution expenses	**547,367**	528,676
Administrative expenses	**46,878**	55,511
Results from operating activities	**61,819**	124,142
Finance income (note 19)	**5,562**	4,505
Finance costs (note 19)	**1,509**	845
Earnings before income taxes	**65,872**	127,802
Income taxes (note 11)	**18,333**	38,817
Net earnings	**$ 47,539**	$ 88,985
Earnings per share (note 20):		
Basic	**$ 0.72**	$ 1.33
Diluted	**0.72**	1.32

The accompanying notes are an integral part of these financial statements.

REITMANS (CANADA) LIMITED
STATEMENTS OF COMPREHENSIVE INCOME
(in thousands of Canadian dollars)

| | For the years ended | |
	January 28, 2012	January 29, 2011
Net earnings	$ 47,539	$ 88,985
Other comprehensive income:		
Net change in fair value of available-for-sale financial assets (net of tax of $79; 2011 - $427) (note 19)	530	2,866
Reclassification of realized gains on available-for-sale financial assets to net earnings (net of tax of $22) (note 19)	-	(145)
Reclassification of impairment loss on available-for-sale financial assets to net earnings (net of tax of $9; 2011 - $11) (note 19)	64	67
Defined benefit actuarial losses (net of tax of $1,041; 2011 - $272) (note 15)	(2,965)	(777)
Total comprehensive income	$ 45,168	$ 90,996

The accompanying notes are an integral part of these financial statements.

REITMANS (CANADA) LIMITED
BALANCE SHEETS
(in thousands of Canadian dollars)

	January 28, 2012	January 29, 2011	January 31, 2010
ASSETS			
CURRENT ASSETS			
Cash and cash equivalents (note 5)	$ 196,835	$ 230,034	$ 228,577
Marketable securities	71,442	70,413	48,026
Trade and other receivables	3,033	2,866	2,926
Derivative financial asset (note 6)	751	-	-
Income taxes recoverable	4,735	-	-
Inventories (note 7)	78,285	73,201	63,127
Prepaid expenses	11,902	12,491	11,010
Total Current Assets	366,983	389,005	353,666
NON-CURRENT ASSETS			
Property and equipment (note 8)	184,221	193,064	208,362
Intangible assets (note 9)	17,057	13,841	9,964
Goodwill (note 10)	42,426	42,426	42,426
Deferred income taxes (note 11)	23,174	21,021	18,313
Total Non-Current Assets	266,878	270,352	279,065
TOTAL ASSETS	$ 633,861	$ 659,357	$ 632,731
LIABILITIES AND SHAREHOLDERS' EQUITY			
CURRENT LIABILITIES			
Trade and other payables (note 12)	$ 63,875	$ 64,093	$ 54,684
Derivative financial liability (note 6)	1,505	-	-
Deferred revenue (note 13)	22,278	19,834	18,122
Income taxes payable	-	5,998	4,677
Current portion of long-term debt (note 14)	1,474	1,384	1,300
Total Current Liabilities	89,132	91,309	78,783
NON-CURRENT LIABILITIES			
Other payables (note 12)	11,110	10,180	9,105
Deferred revenue (note 13)	-	2,384	2,686
Deferred lease credits	17,317	19,011	20,609
Long-term debt (note 14)	8,573	10,047	11,431
Pension liability (note 15)	14,877	13,626	11,865
Total Non-Current Liabilities	51,877	55,248	55,696
SHAREHOLDERS' EQUITY			
Share capital (note 16)	39,890	29,614	25,888
Contributed surplus	5,158	6,266	5,164
Retained earnings	439,067	468,777	461,845
Accumulated other comprehensive income (note 16)	8,737	8,143	5,355
Total Shareholders' Equity	492,852	512,800	498,252
TOTAL LIABILITIES AND **SHAREHOLDERS' EQUITY**	$ 633,861	$ 659,357	$ 632,731

Commitments (note 18)

The accompanying notes are an integral part of these financial statements.

On behalf of the Board,

(signed) Jeremy H. Reitman, Director   (signed) Stephen J. Kauser, Director

REITMANS (CANADA) LIMITED
STATEMENTS OF CHANGES IN SHAREHOLDERS' EQUITY
(in thousands of Canadian dollars)

	For the years ended	
	January 28, 2012	**January 29, 2011**
SHARE CAPITAL		
Balance, beginning of the year	$ **29,614**	$ 25,888
Cash consideration on exercise of share options (note 16)	**8,828**	3,569
Ascribed value credited to share capital from exercise of share options (note 16)	**2,228**	888
Cancellation of shares pursuant to share repurchase program (note 16)	**(780)**	(731)
Balance, end of the year	**39,890**	29,614
CONTRIBUTED SURPLUS		
Balance, beginning of the year	**6,266**	5,164
Share-based compensation costs (note 17)	**1,120**	1,990
Ascribed value credited to share capital from exercise of share options (note 16)	**(2,228)**	(888)
Balance, end of the year	**5,158**	6,266
RETAINED EARNINGS		
Balance, beginning of the year	**468,777**	461,845
Net earnings	**47,539**	88,985
Dividends (note 16)	**(52,654)**	(51,895)
Premium on repurchase of Class A non-voting shares (note 16)	**(21,630)**	(29,381)
Defined benefit actuarial losses (net of tax of $1,041; 2011 - $272) (note 15)	**(2,965)**	(777)
Balance, end of the year	**439,067**	468,777
ACCUMULATED OTHER COMPREHENSIVE INCOME		
Balance, beginning of the year	**8,143**	5,355
Net change in fair value of available-for-sale financial assets (net of tax of $79; 2011 - $427) (note 19)	**530**	2,866
Reclassification of realized gains on available-for-sale financial assets to net earnings (net of tax of $22) (note 19)	**-**	(145)
Reclassification of impairment loss on available-for-sale financial assets to net earnings (net of tax of $9; 2011 - $11) (note 19)	**64**	67
Balance, end of the year (note 16)	**8,737**	8,143
Total Shareholders' Equity	$ **492,852**	$ 512,800

The accompanying notes are an integral part of these financial statements.

REITMANS (CANADA) LIMITED
STATEMENTS OF CASH FLOWS
(in thousands of Canadian dollars)

	For the years ended	
	January 28, 2012	January 29, 2011
CASH FLOWS FROM (USED IN) OPERATING ACTIVITIES		
Net earnings	$ 47,539	$ 88,985
Adjustments for:		
Depreciation, amortization and impairment losses	64,990	59,754
Share-based compensation costs	1,120	1,990
Amortization of deferred lease credits	(4,635)	(4,956)
Deferred lease credits	2,941	3,358
Pension contribution	(4,245)	(629)
Pension expense	1,490	1,341
Realized gain on sale of marketable securities	-	(167)
Impairment loss on available-for-sale financial assets	73	78
Net change in fair value of derivatives	754	-
Foreign exchange loss (gain)	2,942	(31)
Interest and dividend income, net	(4,147)	(3,068)
Interest paid	(682)	(797)
Interest received	1,316	1,273
Dividends received	3,460	2,546
Income taxes	18,333	38,817
	131,249	188,494
Changes in:		
Trade and other receivables	(114)	106
Inventories	(5,084)	(10,074)
Prepaid expenses	589	(1,481)
Trade and other payables	504	9,073
Deferred revenue	60	1,410
Cash generated from operating activities	127,204	187,528
Income taxes received	793	6,040
Income taxes paid	(31,060)	(46,388)
Net cash flows from operating activities	96,937	147,180
CASH FLOWS (USED IN) FROM INVESTING ACTIVITIES		
Purchases of marketable securities	(420)	(20,803)
Proceeds on sale of marketable securities	-	1,709
Additions to property and equipment and intangible assets	(59,154)	(46,922)
Cash flows used in investing activities	(59,574)	(66,016)
CASH FLOWS (USED IN) FROM FINANCING ACTIVITIES		
Dividends paid	(52,654)	(51,895)
Purchase of Class A non-voting shares for cancellation	(22,410)	(30,112)
Repayment of long-term debt	(1,384)	(1,300)
Proceeds from exercise of share options	8,828	3,569
Cash flows used in financing activities	(67,620)	(79,738)
FOREIGN EXCHANGE (LOSS) GAIN ON CASH HELD IN FOREIGN CURRENCY	(2,942)	31
NET (DECREASE) INCREASE IN CASH AND CASH EQUIVALENTS	(33,199)	1,457
CASH AND CASH EQUIVALENTS, BEGINNING OF THE YEAR	230,034	228,577
CASH AND CASH EQUIVALENTS, END OF THE YEAR	$ 196,835	$ 230,034

Supplementary cash flow information (note 25)
The accompanying notes are an integral part of these financial statements.

REITMANS (CANADA) LIMITED
NOTES TO THE FINANCIAL STATEMENTS
(all amounts in thousands of Canadian dollars except per share amounts)

1. REPORTING ENTITY

Reitmans (Canada) Limited (the "Company") is a company domiciled in Canada and is incorporated under the Canada Business Corporations Act. The address of the Company's registered office is 3300 Highway #7 West, Suite 702, Vaughan, Ontario L4K 4M3. The principal business activity of the Company is the sale of women's wear at retail.

2. BASIS OF PRESENTATION

a) Statement of Compliance

These financial statements have been prepared in accordance with International Financial Reporting Standards ("IFRS") as issued by the International Accounting Standards Board ("IASB"). These are the Company's first annual financial statements prepared under IFRS in accordance with IFRS 1, *First-time adoption of IFRS*. The first date at which IFRS was applied was January 31, 2010 ("Transition Date"). In accordance with IFRS 1, the Company has:

- Provided comparative financial information
- Applied the same accounting policies throughout all periods presented
- Retroactively applied all effective IFRS standards as at January 28, 2012, as required; and
- Applied certain optional exemptions and certain mandatory exceptions as applicable for first-time IFRS adopters.

The Company's financial statements were previously prepared in accordance with accounting principles generally accepted in Canada ("Canadian GAAP"). An explanation of how the transition from Canadian GAAP to IFRS as at the transition date has affected the reported earnings, balance sheet and cash flows for the Company, including the mandatory exception and optional exemptions under IFRS 1, is provided in note 29.

These financial statements were authorized for issue by the Board of Directors on March 28, 2012.

b) Basis of Measurement

These financial statements have been prepared on the historical cost basis except for the following material items:

- available-for-sale financial assets are measured at fair value through other comprehensive income;
- the pension liability is recognized as the present value of the defined benefit obligation less the total of the fair value of the plan assets and the unrecognized past service cost; and
- derivative financial instruments are measured at fair value.

c) Functional and Presentation Currency

These financial statements are presented in Canadian dollars, which is the Company's functional currency. All financial information presented in Canadian dollars has been rounded to the nearest thousand, except per share amounts.

d) Estimates, Judgments and Assumptions

The preparation of the financial statements in accordance with IFRS requires management to make judgments, estimates and assumptions that affect the application of accounting policies and the reported amounts of assets, liabilities, the disclosure of contingent assets and contingent liabilities at the date of the financial statements and reported amounts of revenues and expenses during the period. These estimates and assumptions are based on historical experience, other relevant factors and expectations of the future and are reviewed regularly. Revisions to accounting estimates are recognized in the period in which the estimates are revised and in any future periods affected. Actual results may differ from these estimates.

The following is a summary of areas involving a higher degree of judgment or complexity, or areas where assumptions and estimates are significant to the financial statements:

Deferred Income Tax Assets

Management is required to make subjective assessments to determine the amount of deferred income tax assets to be recognized. Deferred income tax assets are recorded to the extent that it is probable that there will be adequate taxable income in the future against which they can be utilized.

Pension Plans

The cost of defined benefit pension plans is determined by means of actuarial valuations, which involve making assumptions about discount rates, the expected long-term rate of return on plan assets, future salary increases, mortality rates and the future increases in pensions. Because of the long-term nature of the plans, such estimates are subject to a high degree of uncertainty.

Sales Returns

The Company provides for the possibility that merchandise already sold may be returned by customers. To this end, the Company has made certain assumptions based on the quantity of merchandise returned in the past.

Share-Based Compensation

In computing the compensation cost related to share option awards under the fair value based method, various assumptions are used to determine the expected option life, risk-free interest rate, expected share price volatility and average dividend yield. The use of different assumptions could result in a share compensation expense that differs from that which the Company has recorded.

Gift Cards / Loyalty Points and Awards

Gift cards sold are recorded as deferred revenue and revenue is recognized when the gift cards are redeemed. An estimate is made of gift cards not expected to be redeemed based on the terms of the gift cards and historical redemption patterns. Loyalty points and awards granted under customer loyalty programs are recognized as a separate component of revenue and are deferred at the date of initial sale. Revenue is recognized when the loyalty points and awards are redeemed and the Company has fulfilled its obligation. The amount of revenue deferred is measured based on the fair value of loyalty points and awards granted, taking into consideration the estimated redemption percentage.

Slow-Moving Inventory

The Company has set up provisions for merchandise in inventory that may have to be sold below cost. For this purpose, the Company has developed assumptions regarding the quantity of merchandise sold below cost.

Asset Impairment

The Company must assess the possibility that the carrying amounts of tangible and intangible assets may not be recoverable. Management is required to make significant judgments related to future cash flows to determine the amount of asset impairment that should be recognized.

Fair value of derivative financial instruments

Derivative financial instruments are carried in the balance sheet at fair value estimated by using valuation techniques.

3. SIGNIFICANT ACCOUNTING POLICIES

The accounting policies set out below have been applied consistently to all periods presented in these financial statements.

a) Foreign Currency Translation

Monetary assets and liabilities denominated in foreign currencies at the reporting date are translated into the functional currency at the exchange rate at that date. Other balance sheet items denominated in foreign currencies are translated into Canadian dollars at the exchange rates prevailing at the respective transaction dates. Revenues and expenses denominated in foreign currencies are translated into Canadian dollars at average rates of exchange prevailing during the period. The resulting gains or losses on translation are included in the determination of net earnings.

b) Cash and Cash Equivalents

Cash and cash equivalents consist of cash on hand, bank balances and short-term deposits with original maturities of three months or less.

c) Financial Instruments

All financial instruments are classified into one of the following five categories: financial assets and financial liabilities at fair value through profit or loss, held-to-maturity investments, loans and receivables, available-for-sale financial assets or other financial liabilities. All financial instruments, including derivatives, are included on the balance sheet and are initially measured at fair value. The Company accounts for transaction costs related to financial instruments, other than those classified as fair value through profit or loss and for derivative instruments, in the initial measurement of the instrument. Subsequent measurement depends on their initial classification. Financial instruments and financial liabilities classified as financial assets and liabilities at fair value through profit or loss are subsequently measured at fair value and all gains and losses are included in net earnings in the period in which they arise. Available-for-sale financial instruments are subsequently measured at fair value and changes therein, other than impairment losses, are recognized in other comprehensive income. When an investment is derecognized, the cumulative gain or loss in other comprehensive income is transferred to net earnings. Loans and receivables, held-to-maturity investments and other financial liabilities, are subsequently measured at amortized cost using the effective interest rate method, less impairment losses.

Financial assets and liabilities measured at fair value use a fair value hierarchy to prioritize the inputs used in measuring fair value. Level 1, defined as observable inputs such as quoted prices in active markets; Level 2, defined as inputs other than quoted prices in active markets that are either directly or indirectly observable; and Level 3, defined as unobservable inputs in which little or no market data exists, therefore requiring an entity to develop its own assumptions.

The Company has classified its cash and cash equivalents and its trade and other receivables as loans and receivables and its marketable securities as available-for-sale financial assets. Trade and other payables and long-term debt have been classified as other financial liabilities and are measured at amortized cost.

Financial assets and liabilities are offset and the net amount is presented in the balance sheet when, and only when, the Company has a legal right to offset the amounts and intends either to settle on a net basis or to realize the asset and settle the liability simultaneously.

Derivative instruments are recorded at their fair value except under the own use exemption. Certain derivatives embedded in other contracts must also be measured at fair value. All changes in the fair value of derivatives are recognized in net earnings unless specific hedge criteria are met, which requires that a company must formally document, designate and assess the effectiveness of transactions that receive hedge accounting.

The Company considers the use of foreign currency option contracts, with maturities not exceeding six months, to manage its US dollar exposure. Foreign currency option contracts are not designated as hedges. Derivative financial instruments are not used for trading or speculative purposes.

d) Property and Equipment

Items of property and equipment are measured at cost less accumulated depreciation and accumulated impairment losses. Cost includes expenditures that are directly attributable to the acquisition of the asset, including any costs directly attributable to bringing the asset to a working condition for its intended use. Purchased software that is integral to the functionality of the related equipment is capitalized as part of that equipment.

When parts of an item of property and equipment have different useful lives, they are accounted for as separate items (major components) of property and equipment.

Depreciation is recognized in net earnings on a straight-line basis over the estimated useful lives of each component of an item of property and equipment. Land is not depreciated. Leasehold improvements are depreciated over the lesser of the estimated useful life of the asset and the lease term. Assets not in service include expenditures incurred to-date for equipment not yet available for use. Depreciation of assets not in service begins when they are ready for their intended use. Depreciation is calculated over the depreciable amount, which is the cost of an asset, less its residual value.

The estimated useful lives for the current and comparative periods are as follows:

- Buildings — 10 to 50 years
- Fixtures and equipment — 3 to 20 years
- Leasehold improvements — 6.7 to 10 years

estimated costs necessary to make the sale, taking into consideration fluctuations of retail prices due to seasonality.

i) Impairment

(i) Non-Financial Assets

All non-financial assets are reviewed at each reporting date for indications that the carrying amount may not be recoverable. When there is evidence of impairment, an impairment test is carried out. Goodwill is tested for impairment at least annually at the year-end reporting date, and whenever there is an indication that the asset may be impaired. For the purpose of impairment testing, assets that cannot be tested individually are grouped together into the smallest group of assets that generates cash inflows from continuing use that are largely independent of the cash inflows of other assets or groups of assets (defined as "cash-generating unit" or "CGU"). Impairment losses recognized in respect of CGUs are allocated first to reduce the carrying amount of any goodwill allocated to the CGU, and then to reduce the carrying amount of the other assets in the CGU.

An impairment loss is recognized in net earnings if the carrying amount of an asset or its related CGU exceeds its estimated recoverable amount. The recoverable amount is the higher of the value-in-use and the fair value less costs to sell. The value-in-use is the present value of estimated future cash flows, using a pre-tax discount rate that reflects current market assessments of the time value of money and the risks specific to the asset or CGU. The fair value less costs to sell is the amount for which an asset or CGU can be sold in a transaction under normal market conditions between knowledgeable and willing contracting parties, less costs to sell.

For the purposes of impairment testing, goodwill acquired in a business combination is allocated to the CGUs that are expected to benefit from the synergies of the combination. This allocation reflects the lowest level at which goodwill is monitored for internal reporting purposes.

The Company's corporate assets do not generate separate cash inflows. If there is an indication that a corporate asset may be impaired, then the recoverable amount is determined for the CGUs to which the corporate asset belongs.

An impairment loss in respect of goodwill is not reversed. In respect of other assets, an impairment loss is reversed if there has been a change in the estimates used to determine the recoverable amount. An impairment loss is reversed only to the extent that the asset's carrying amount does not exceed the carrying amount that would have been determined, net of depreciation or amortization, if no impairment loss had been recognized.

(ii) Financial Assets

For an investment in an equity security, a significant or prolonged decline in its fair value below cost is objective evidence of impairment. Impairment losses on available-for-sale financial assets are recognized by reclassifying losses accumulated in accumulated other comprehensive income to net earnings. The cumulative loss that is reclassified from accumulated other comprehensive income is the difference between the acquisition cost and the current fair value, less any impairment losses recognized previously in net earnings.

Depreciation methods, useful lives and residual values are reviewed at each annual reporting date and adjusted prospectively, if appropriate.

Gains and losses on disposal of items of property and equipment are recognized in net earnings.

e) Goodwill

Goodwill is measured at the acquisition date as the fair value of the consideration transferred less the net identifiable assets of the acquired company or business activities. Goodwill is not amortized and is carried at cost less accumulated impairment losses.

f) Intangible Assets

Intangible assets that are acquired by the Company and have finite useful lives are measured at cost less accumulated amortization and accumulated impairment losses.

Amortization is calculated over the cost of the asset less its residual value. Amortization is recognized in net earnings on a straight-line basis over the estimated useful lives of the intangible assets. Amortization of intangible assets not in service begins when they are ready for their intended use.

The estimated useful lives for the current and comparative periods are as follows:

Software   3 to 5 years

Amortization methods, useful lives and residual values are reviewed at each annual reporting date and adjusted prospectively, if appropriate.

g) Leased Assets

Leases are classified as either operating or finance, based on the substance of the transaction at inception of the lease. Classification is re-assessed if the terms of the lease are changed.

Leases in which a significant portion of the risks and rewards of ownership are not assumed by the Company are classified as operating leases. The Company carries on its operations in premises under leases of varying terms, which are accounted for as operating leases. Payments under an operating lease are recognized in net earnings on a straight-line basis over the term of the lease. When a lease contains a predetermined fixed escalation of the minimum rent, the Company recognizes the related rent expense on a straight-line basis and, consequently, records the difference between the recognized rental expense and the amounts payable under the lease as deferred rent, which is included in trade and other payables on the balance sheet. Contingent (sales-based) rentals are recognized in net earnings in the period in which they are incurred.

Tenant allowances are recorded as deferred lease credits and amortized as a reduction of rent expense over the term of the related leases.

h) Inventories

Merchandise inventories are measured at the lower of cost, determined on an average basis using the retail inventory method, and net realizable value. Costs include the cost of purchase, transportation costs that are directly incurred to bring inventories to their present location and condition, and certain distribution centre costs related to inventories. The Company estimates net realizable value as the amount that inventories are expected to be sold, in the ordinary course of business, less the

Any subsequent recovery in the fair value of an impaired available-for-sale equity security is recognized in other comprehensive income.

j) Employee Benefits

(i) Pension Benefit Plans

The Company maintains a contributory defined benefit plan ("Plan") that provides benefits to employees based on length of service and average earnings in the best five consecutive years of employment. The Company also sponsors a Supplemental Executive Retirement Plan ("SERP"), which is neither registered nor pre-funded. The costs of these retirement benefit plans are determined periodically by independent actuaries.

Benefits are also given to employees through defined contribution plans administered by the Federal and Québec governments. Company contributions to these plans are recognized in the periods when the services are rendered.

Pension expense/income is included in the determination of net earnings according to the following policies:

• The present value of the defined benefit obligation is actuarially determined using the projected unit credit method.

• For the purpose of calculating expected return on plan assets, the valuation of those assets is based on quoted market values at the year-end date.

• The discount rate used to value the defined benefit obligation is the yield at the reporting date on AA credit-rated bonds that have maturity dates approximating the terms of the Company's obligations and that are denominated in the same currency in which the benefits are expected to be paid.

• Unrecognized past service costs related to benefits are amortized on a straight-line basis over the average period until vesting. To the extent that the benefits vest immediately, the expense is recognized immediately in net earnings.

The Company recognizes all actuarial gains and losses from the Plan and SERP immediately in other comprehensive income, and reports them in retained earnings. Expenses related to defined contribution plans are recognized in net earnings in the periods in which they occur. The net obligation in respect of the Plan and SERP is the amount of future benefits that members have earned in return for their service in the current and prior periods discounted to its present value, less any unrecognized past service costs and the fair value of the plan assets.

(ii) Short-Term Employee Benefits

Short-term employee benefit obligations, which include wages, salaries, compensated absences and bonuses, are measured on an undiscounted basis and are expensed as the related service is provided.

A liability is recognized for the amount expected to be paid under short-term cash bonus or profit sharing plans if the Company has a present legal or constructive obligation to pay this amount as a result of past service provided by the employee, and the obligation can be estimated reliably.

(iii) Share-Based Compensation

Some employees receive part of their compensation in the form of share-based payments which are recognised as an employee expense, with a corresponding increase in equity, over the period that the employees unconditionally become entitled to the awards. The Company accounts for share-based compensation using the fair value based method. Compensation expense is measured at the fair value at the date of grant and the fair value of each award is recognized over its respective vesting period, which is normally five years. The amount recognized as an expense is adjusted to reflect the number of awards for which the related service conditions are expected to be met.

k) Provisions

A provision is recognized if, as a result of a past event, the Company has a present legal or constructive obligation that can be estimated reliably, and it is probable that an outflow of economic benefits will be required to settle the obligation. If the effect of the time value of money is material, provisions are determined by discounting the expected future cash flows at a pre-tax rate that reflects current market assessments of the time value of money and the risks specific to the liability. Where discounting is used, the unwinding of the discount is recognized as finance cost.

l) Revenue

Revenue is recognized from the sale of merchandise when a customer purchases and takes delivery of the merchandise. Reported sales are net of returns and estimated possible returns and exclude sales taxes.

Gift cards sold are recorded as deferred revenue and revenue is recognized when the gift cards are redeemed. An estimate is made of gift cards not expected to be redeemed based on the terms of the gift cards and historical redemption patterns.

Loyalty points and awards granted under customer loyalty programs are recognized as a separate component of revenue, and are deferred at the date of initial sale. Revenue is recognized when the loyalty points and awards are redeemed and the Company has fulfilled its obligation. The amount of revenue deferred is measured based on the fair value of loyalty points and awards granted, taking into consideration the estimated redemption percentage.

m) Finance Income and Finance Costs

Finance income comprises interest and dividend income, realized gains on sale of marketable securities, changes in the fair value of derivatives as well as foreign exchange gains. Finance costs comprise interest expense, realized losses on sale of marketable securities, changes in the fair value of derivatives as well as foreign exchange losses. Interest income is recognized on an accrual basis and interest expense is recorded using the effective interest method. Dividend income is recognized when the right to receive payment is established. Foreign exchange gains and losses and changes in the fair value of derivatives are reported on a net basis.

n) Income Tax

Income tax expense comprises current and deferred taxes. Current income taxes and deferred income taxes are recognized in net earnings except for items recognized directly in equity or in other comprehensive income.

The Company's income tax expense is based on tax rules and regulations that are subject to interpretation and require estimates and assumptions that may be challenged by taxation authorities. Current income tax is the expected tax payable or receivable on the taxable income or loss for the period, using tax rates enacted or substantively enacted at the reporting date, and any adjustment to taxes payable in respect of previous years. The Company's estimates of current income tax assets and liabilities are periodically reviewed and adjusted as circumstances warrant, such as for changes to tax laws and administrative guidance, and the resolution of uncertainties through either the final conclusion of tax audits or expiration of prescribed time limits within the relevant statutes. The final results of government tax audits and other events may vary materially compared to estimates and assumptions used by management in determining the income tax expense and in measuring current income tax assets and liabilities.

Deferred income tax is recognized in respect of temporary differences between the carrying amounts of assets and liabilities for financial reporting purposes and the amounts used for taxation purposes. Deferred income tax assets and liabilities are measured using enacted or substantively enacted income tax rates expected to apply to taxable income in the years in which temporary differences are expected to be recovered or settled. The effect on deferred income tax assets and liabilities of a change in tax rates is included in net earnings in the period that includes the enactment date, except to the extent that it relates to an item recognized either in other comprehensive income or directly in equity in the current or in a previous period.

The Company only offsets income tax assets and liabilities if it has a legally enforceable right to offset the recognized amounts and intends either to settle on a net basis, or to realize the asset and settle the liability simultaneously.

A deferred income tax asset is recognized to the extent that it is probable that future taxable profits will be available against which they can be utilized. Deferred income tax assets are reviewed at each reporting date and are reduced to the extent that it is no longer probable that the related tax benefit will be realized.

Deferred income tax assets and liabilities are recognized on the balance sheet under non-current assets or liabilities, irrespective of the expected date of realization or settlement.

o) Earnings per Share

The Company presents basic and diluted earnings per share ("EPS") data for its shares.

Basic EPS is calculated by dividing the net earnings of the Company by the weighted average number of Class A non-voting and Common shares outstanding during the period.

Diluted EPS is determined by adjusting the weighted average number of shares outstanding to include additional shares issued from the assumed exercise of share options, if dilutive. The number of additional shares is calculated by assuming that the proceeds from such exercises, as well as the amount of unrecognized share-based compensation, are used to purchase Class A non-voting shares at the average market share price during the reporting period.

p) Share Capital

Class A non-voting shares and Common shares are classified as equity. Incremental costs directly attributable to the issue of these shares and share options are recognized as a deduction from equity, net of any tax effects.

When share capital recognized as equity is purchased for cancellation, the amount of the consideration paid, which includes directly attributable costs, net of any tax effects, is recognized as a deduction from equity. The excess of the purchase price over the carrying amount of the shares is charged to retained earnings.

q) New Standards and Interpretations Not Yet Adopted

A number of new standards, and amendments to standards and interpretations, are not yet effective for the year ended January 28, 2012 and have not been applied in preparing these financial statements. New standards and amendments to standards and interpretations that are currently under review include:

IFRS 9 - Financial Instruments

This standard becomes mandatory for the years commencing on or after January 1, 2015 with earlier application permitted. IFRS 9 is a new standard which will ultimately replace IAS 39, *Financial Instruments: Recognition and Measurement*.

IFRS 13 – Fair Value Measurement

This standard provides new guidance on fair value measurement and disclosure requirements, which becomes effective for annual periods commencing on or after January 1, 2013.

IAS 1 - Presentation of Financial Statements

Amendments to IAS 1, *Presentation of Financial Statements* enhance the presentation of Other Comprehensive Income ("OCI") in the financial statements, primarily by requiring the components of OCI to be presented separately for items that may be reclassified to the statement of earnings in the future from those that would never be reclassified to the statement of earnings. The amendments are effective for annual periods beginning on or after July 1, 2012

IAS 19 - Employee Benefits

Amendments to IAS 19, Employee Benefits include the elimination of the option to defer the recognition of gains and losses, enhancing the guidance around measurement of plan assets and defined benefit obligations, streamlining the presentation of changes in assets and liabilities arising from defined benefit plans and the introduction of enhanced disclosures for defined benefit plans. The amendments are effective for annual periods beginning on or after January 1, 2013.

The extent of the impact of adoption of the above noted standards and interpretations on the financial statements of the Company has not yet been determined.

4. DETERMINATION OF FAIR VALUES

A number of the Company's accounting policies and disclosures require the determination of fair value, for both financial and non-financial assets and liabilities. Fair value estimates are made at a specific point in time, using available information about the asset or liability. These estimates are subjective in nature and often cannot be determined with precision. Fair values have been determined for measurement and/or disclosure purposes based on the following methods. When applicable, further information about the assumptions made in determining fair values is disclosed in the notes specific to that asset or liability.

a) Financial Assets

The Company has determined that the carrying amount of its short-term financial assets approximates fair value at the reporting date due to the short-term maturity of these instruments. The fair value of the Company's available-for-sale financial assets is determined by reference to their quoted closing prices in active markets at the reporting date, which is considered Level 1 input in the fair value hierarchy.

b) Non-Derivative Financial Liabilities

The fair value of the Company's long-term debt bearing interest at a fixed rate, which is determined for disclosure purposes, is calculated using the present value of future payments of principal and interest discounted at the current market rates of interest available to the Company for the same or similar debt instruments with the same remaining maturity.

c) Deferred Revenue

The amount of revenue deferred with respect to the Company's customer loyalty reward programs is estimated by reference to the fair value of the merchandise for which the loyalty rewards could be redeemed. The fair value takes into account the expected redemption rate and the timing of such expected redemptions.

d) Derivative Financial Instruments

The fair value of foreign currency option contracts is determined through a standard option valuation technique used by the counterparty based on Level 2 inputs.

e) Share-based Payment Transactions

The fair values of the employee share options are measured based on the Black-Scholes valuation model. Measurement inputs include share price on measurement date, exercise price of the share option, expected volatility (based on weighted average historic volatility adjusted for changes expected due to publicly available information), weighted average expected life of the share option (based on historic experience and general option holder behaviour), expected dividends, and risk-free interest rate (based on government bonds).

5. CASH AND CASH EQUIVALENTS

	January 28, 2012	January 29, 2011	January 31, 2010
Cash on hand and with banks	$ 12,563	$ 4,634	$ 4,677
Short-term deposits, bearing interest at 0.9% (January 29, 2011- 0.7%; January 31, 2010 - 0.3%)	184,272	225,400	223,900
	$ 196,835	$ 230,034	$ 228,577

6. FINANCIAL INSTRUMENTS

Derivative financial instruments

During the year, the Company entered into transactions with its bank whereby it purchased call options and sold put options, both on the US dollar ("USD"). These option contracts extend over a period of six months. Purchased call options and sold put options expiring on the same date have the same strike price.

Details of the foreign currency option contracts outstanding as at January 28, 2012 are as follow:

	Notional Amount in USD	Derivative Asset	Derivative Liability	Net
Put options sold	$ 44,000	$ 751	$ -	$ 751
Call options purchased	(100,000)	-	(1,505)	(1,505)
	$ (56,000)	$ 751	$ (1,505)	$ (754)

As at January 29, 2011 and January 31, 2010, there were no foreign currency option contracts outstanding.

7. INVENTORIES

During the year ended January 28, 2012, inventories recognized as cost of goods sold amounted to $361,319 (January 29, 2011 - $348,716). In addition, $2,014 (January 29, 2011 - $1,955) of write-downs of inventory as a result of net realizable value being lower than cost was recognized in cost of goods sold, and no inventory write-downs recognized in previous periods were reversed.

Property and equipment includes an amount of $8,414 (January 29, 2011 - $3,548) that is not being depreciated. Depreciation will begin when the assets have been available for use.

9. INTANGIBLE ASSETS

	Cost	Accumulated amortization	Net carrying amounts
Balance at January 31, 2010	$ 17,072	$ 7,108	$ 9,964
Additions / amortization	7,506	3,629	3,877
Disposals	(2,394)	(2,394)	-
Balance at January 29, 2011	$ 22,184	$ 8,343	$ 13,841
Balance at January 30, 2011	$ 22,184	$ 8,343	$ 13,841
Additions / amortization	7,175	3,959	3,216
Disposals	(1,105)	(1,105)	-
Balance at January 28, 2012	$ 28,254	$ 11,197	$ 17,057

The amortization of intangibles has been recorded in selling and distribution expenses and administrative expenses in the statements of earnings.

Software includes an amount of $10,846 (January 29, 2011 - $6,930) that is not being amortized. Amortization will begin when the software has been put into service.

10. GOODWILL

Goodwill is tested for impairment as described in note 3(i). For impairment testing purposes the Company uses the value-in-use approach. Value-in-use is determined by discounting the future cash flows generated from the continuing use of the respective CGU.

Management's key assumptions for cash flow projections are based on the most recent annualized operating results, assuming a series of cash flows in perpetuity. Projected cash flows are discounted using a pre-tax rate of 10% (January 29, 2011 - 11%) which reflects the specific risks and weighted average cost of capital for a company of similar size and industry.

Based upon the impairment tests as at January 28, 2012, January 29, 2011 and January 31, 2010, the value-in-use was determined to be higher than the carrying values. As a result, no impairment losses were recognized.

8. PROPERTY AND EQUIPMENT

	Land	Buildings	Fixtures and Equipment	Leasehold Improvements	Total
Cost					
Balance at January 31, 2010	$ 5,860	$ 52,411	$ 177,874	$ 194,782	$430,927
Additions	-	400	19,107	21,591	41,098
Disposals	-	(886)	(21,595)	(21,468)	(43,949)
Balance at January 29, 2011	$ 5,860	$ 51,925	$ 175,386	$ 194,905	$428,076
Balance at January 30, 2011	$ 5,860	$ 51,925	$ 175,386	$ 194,905	$428,076
Additions	-	2,291	25,079	24,818	52,188
Disposals	-	(53)	(37,346)	(37,650)	(75,049)
Balance at January 28, 2012	$ 5,860	$ 54,163	$ 163,119	$ 182,073	$405,215
Accumulated depreciation and impairment losses					
Balance at January 31, 2010	$ -	$ 17,946	$ 97,398	$ 107,221	$222,565
Depreciation	-	2,410	26,062	26,708	55,180
Impairment loss	-	-	-	1,724	1,724
Reversal of impairment loss	-	-	-	(779)	(779)
Disposals	-	(886)	(21,580)	(21,212)	(43,678)
Balance at January 29, 2011	$ -	$ 19,470	$ 101,880	$ 113,662	$235,012
Balance at January 30, 2011	$ -	$ 19,470	$ 101,880	$ 113,662	$235,012
Depreciation	-	2,601	25,599	26,699	54,899
Impairment loss	-	-	2,296	4,427	6,723
Reversal of impairment loss	-	-	-	(591)	(591)
Disposals	-	(53)	(37,346)	(37,650)	(75,049)
Balance at January 28, 2012	$ -	$ 22,018	$ 92,429	$ 106,547	$220,994
Net carrying amounts					
At January 31, 2010	$ 5,860	$ 34,465	$ 80,476	$ 87,561	$208,362
At January 29, 2011	$ 5,860	$ 32,455	$ 73,506	$ 81,243	$193,064
At January 28, 2012	$ 5,860	$ 32,145	$ 70,690	$ 75,526	$184,221

During the year, the Company tested for impairment certain items of property and equipment for which there were indications that their carrying amounts may not be recoverable and recognized an impairment loss of $6,723 (January 29, 2011 - $1,724). The recoverable amounts of the CGUs tested for impairment were based on their value-in-use which was determined using a pre-tax discount rate of 11% (January 29, 2011 - 12%). During the year, $591 of impairment losses were reversed following an improvement in the profitability of certain CGUs (January 29, 2011 - $779).

Depreciation expense and net impairment losses for the year have been recorded in selling and distribution expenses and administrative expenses in the statements of earnings.

11. INCOME TAX

Income tax expense

The Company's income tax expense is comprised as follows:

	For the years ended	
	January 28, 2012	January 29, 2011
Current tax expense		
Current period	$ 19,840	$ 42,409
Adjustment for prior years	(307)	(740)
Current tax expense	19,533	41,669
Deferred tax expense		
Recognition and reversal of temporary differences	(1,771)	(3,990)
Changes in tax rates	319	494
Adjustment for prior years	252	644
Deferred tax expense	(1,200)	(2,852)
Total income tax expense	$ 18,333	$ 38,817

Income tax recognized in other comprehensive income

	For the year ended January 28, 2012			For the year ended January 29, 2011		
	Before Tax	Tax (expense) benefit	Net of Tax (expense)	Before Tax	Tax (expense) benefit	Net of Tax (expense)
Available-for-sale financial assets	$ 682	$ (88)	$ 594	$ 3,204	$ (416)	$ 2,788
Defined benefit plan actuarial losses	(4,006)	1,041	(2,965)	(1,049)	272	(777)
	$ (3,324)	$ 953	$ (2,371)	$ 2,155	$ (144)	$ 2,011

Reconciliation of effective tax rate

	For the years ended			
	January 28, 2012		January 29, 2011	
Earnings before income taxes	$ 65,872		$127,802	
Income tax using the Company's statutory tax rate	18,642	28.30%	38,583	30.19%
Changes in tax rates	319	0.48%	391	0.31%
Non-deductible expenses and other adjustments	393	0.60%	658	0.51%
Tax exempt income	(966)	(1.47%)	(719)	(0.56%)
Over provided in prior periods	(55)	(0.08%)	(96)	(0.08%)
	$ 18,333	27.83%	$ 38,817	30.37%

Recognized deferred tax assets and liabilities

Deferred tax assets and liabilities are attributable to the following:

	Assets		Liabilities		Net	
	January 28, 2012	January 29, 2011	January 28, 2012	January 29, 2011	January 28, 2012	January 29, 2011
Property, equipment and intangible assets	$ 17,364	$ 12,984	$ -	$ -	$ 17,364	$ 12,984
Prepaid expenses		214			-	214
Marketable securities			379	299	(379)	(299)
Inventories			1,144	1,082	(1,144)	(1,082)
Trade and other payables	3,461	5,644			3,461	5,644
Pension liability	3,868	3,534			3,868	3,534
Other	42	46	38	20	4	26
	$ 24,735	$ 22,422	$ 1,561	$ 1,401	$ 23,174	$ 21,021

Changes in deferred tax balances during the year

	Balance January 31, 2010	Recognized in Net Earnings	Recognized in Other Comprehensive Income	Balance January 29, 2011	Recognized in Net Earnings	Recognized in Other Comprehensive Income	Balance January 28, 2012
Property, equipment and intangible assets	$ 10,626	$ 2,358	$ -	$ 12,984	$ 4,380	$ -	$ 17,364
Prepaid expenses	257	(43)	-	214	(214)	-	-
Marketable securities	121	(4)	(416)	(299)	8	(88)	(379)
Inventories	(1,039)	(43)	-	(1,082)	(62)	-	(1,144)
Trade and other payables	5,260	384	-	5,644	(2,183)	-	3,461
Pension liability	3,076	186	272	3,534	(707)	1,041	3,868
Other	12	14	-	26	(22)	-	4
	$ 18,313	$ 2,852	$ (144)	$ 21,021	$ 1,200	$ 953	$ 23,174

12. TRADE AND OTHER PAYABLES

	January 28, 2012	January 29, 2011	January 31, 2010
Trade payables	$ 26,155	$ 16,457	$ 15,148
Non-trade payables due to related parties	56	66	90
Other non-trade payables	10,553	11,817	4,437
Personnel liabilities	23,053	31,457	30,615
Payables relating to premises	14,398	13,630	12,630
Provision for sales returns	770	846	869
	74,985	74,273	63,789
Less non-current portion	11,110	10,180	9,105
	$ 63,875	$ 64,093	$ 54,684

The non-current portion of trade and other payables, which is included in payables relating to premises, represents the portion of deferred rent to be amortized beyond the next twelve months.

15. PENSION LIABILITY

The following tables present reconciliations of the pension obligations, the plan assets and the funded status of the retirement benefit plans:

Funded Status

	Fair value of plan assets	Defined benefit obligation	Funded status	Unamortized non-vested past service cost	Pension asset (liability)
As at January 28, 2012					
Plan	$ 15,727	$ 15,318	$ 409	$ -	$ 409
SERP	-	15,540	(15,540)	254	(15,286)
Total	$ 15,727	$ 30,858	$ (15,131)	$ 254	$ (14,877)
As at January 29, 2011					
Plan	$ 11,936	$ 12,717	$ (781)	$ -	$ (781)
SERP	-	13,184	(13,184)	339	(12,845)
Total	$ 11,936	$ 25,901	$ (13,965)	$ 339	$ (13,626)
As at January 31, 2010					
Plan	$ 10,369	$ 11,399	$ (1,030)	$ -	$ (1,030)
SERP	-	11,259	(11,259)	424	(10,835)
Total	$ 10,369	$ 22,658	$ (12,289)	$ 424	$ (11,865)

13. DEFERRED REVENUE

Deferred revenue consists of the following:

	January 28, 2012	January 29, 2011	January 31, 2010
Loyalty points and awards granted under loyalty programs	$ 10,979	$ 10,984	$ 10,142
Unredeemed gift cards	11,299	11,234	10,666
	22,278	22,218	20,808
Less amounts expected to be redeemed in the next twelve months	22,278	19,834	18,122
Deferred revenue – non-current	$ -	$ 2,384	$ 2,686

14. LONG-TERM DEBT

	January 28, 2012	January 29, 2011	January 31, 2010
Mortgage payable	$ 10,047	$ 11,431	$ 12,731
Less current portion	1,474	1,384	1,300
	$ 8,573	$ 10,047	$ 11,431

The mortgage, bearing interest at 6.40%, is payable in monthly instalments of principal and interest of $172. It is due November 2017 and is secured by the Company's distribution centre having a carrying value of $18,306 (January 29, 2011 - $19,282; January 31, 2010 - $20,304).

As at January 28, 2012, principal repayments on long-term debt are as follows:

Within 1 year	$ 1,474
Within 2 years	1,570
Within 3 years	1,672
Within 4 years	1,780
Within 5 years	1,896
Subsequent years	1,655
	$ 10,047

As at January 28, 2012, the fair value of long-term debt was $10,882 (January 29, 2011 - $12,247; January 31, 2010 - $13,045) compared to its carrying value of $10,047 (January 29, 2011 - $11,431; January 31, 2010 - $12,731).

The asset allocation of the major asset categories in the Plan for each of the years was as follows:

	January 28, 2012	January 29, 2011	January 31, 2010
Equity securities	60%	62%	61%
Debt securities	38%	36%	37%
Cash and cash equivalents	2%	2%	2%
	100%	100%	100%

The Company's pension expense was as follows:

	For the year ended January 28, 2012			For the year ended January 29, 2011		
Pension costs recognized in net earnings	**Plan**	**SERP**	**Total**	Plan	SERP	Total
Current service cost	$ 596	$ 239	$ 835	$ 480	$ 232	$ 712
Interest cost	684	695	1,379	646	628	1,274
Expected return on plan assets	(808)	-	(808)	(729)	-	(729)
Past service cost	-	84	84	-	84	84
Pension expense	$ 472	$ 1,018	$ 1,490	$ 397	$ 944	$ 1,341

Pension expense is recognized in administration expenses in the statements of earnings.

The following table presents the change in the actuarial gains and losses recognized in other comprehensive income:

	For the year ended January 28, 2012			For the year ended January 29, 2011		
	Plan	**SERP**	**Total**	Plan	SERP	Total
Cumulative amount in retained earnings at the beginning of the year	$ (144)	$ 1,193	$ 1,049	$ (144)	$ 1,193	$ 1,049
Recognized during the year	2,456	1,550	4,006		1,193	
Cumulative amount in retained earnings at the end of the year	$ 2,312	$ 2,743	$ 5,055	$ (144)	$ 1,193	$ 1,049
Recognized during the year net of tax			$ 2,965			$ 777

	For the year ended January 28, 2012		For the year ended January 29, 2011	
	Plan	**SERP**	**Total**	Plan	SERP	Total
Movement in the present value of the defined benefit obligation						
Defined benefit obligation, beginning of year	$ 12,717	$ 13,184	$ 25,901	$ 11,399	$ 11,259	$ 22,658
Current service cost	596	239	835	480	232	712
Interest cost	684	695	1,379	646	628	1,274
Employee contributions	144	-	144	140	-	140
Actuarial losses	1,778	1,550	3,328	567	1,193	1,760
Benefits paid	(601)	(128)	(729)	(515)	(128)	(643)
Defined benefit obligation, end of year	$ 15,318	$ 15,540	$ 30,858	$ 12,717	$ 13,184	$ 25,901
Movement in the fair value of plan assets						
Fair value of plan assets, beginning of year	$ 11,936	-	$ 11,936	$ 10,369	$ -	$ 10,369
Expected return on assets	808	-	808	729	-	729
Investment (loss) gain	(677)	-	(677)	712	-	712
Employer contributions	4,117	128	4,245	501	128	629
Employee contributions	144	-	144	140	-	140
Benefits paid	(601)	(128)	(729)	(515)	(128)	(643)
Fair value of plan assets, end of year	$ 15,727	$ -	$ 15,727	$ 11,936	$ -	$ 11,936

The Company has determined that, in accordance with the terms and conditions of the defined benefit plan, and in accordance with statutory requirements (such as minimum funding requirements) of the plans of the respective jurisdictions, the present value of refunds or reductions in the future contributions is not lower than the balance of the total fair value of the plan assets less the total present value of the obligations. As such, no decrease in the defined benefit plan asset is necessary at January 28, 2012 (January 29, 2011 and January 31, 2010 - no decrease in defined benefit asset).

Actuarial assumptions

Principal actuarial assumptions used were as follows:

	For the years ended	
	January 28, 2012	**January 29, 2011**
Accrued benefit obligation:		
Discount rate	**4.30%**	5.20%
Salary increase	**5.00%**	3.00%
Employee benefit expense:		
Discount rate	**5.20%**	5.50%
Expected return on plan assets	**6.50%**	7.00%
Salary increase	**3.00%**	3.00%

Expected rates of return on plan assets are based on external historical and forecast market information.

The Company expects $1,046 in employer contributions to be paid to the Plan and SERP in the year ending February 2, 2013.

The Company measures its accrued benefit obligations and the fair value of plan assets for accounting purposes at year-end. The most recent actuarial valuation for funding purposes was as of December 31, 2010 and the next required valuation will be as of December 31, 2011.

16. SHARE CAPITAL AND OTHER COMPONENTS OF EQUITY

The change in share capital for each of the periods listed was as follows:

	For the years ended			
	January 28, 2012		**January 29, 2011**	
	Number of shares	**Carrying amount**	**Number of shares**	**Carrying amount**
Common shares				
Balance at beginning and end of the year	13,440	$ 482	13,440	$ 482
Class A non-voting shares				
Balance at beginning of the year	52,869	$29,132	54,160	$25,406
Shares issued pursuant to exercise of share options	722	11,056	292	4,457
Shares purchased under issuer bid	(1,445)	(780)	(1,583)	(731)
Balance at end of the year	52,146	$39,408	52,869	$29,132
Total share capital	65,586	$39,890	66,309	$29,614

Authorized Share Capital

The Company has authorized for issuance an unlimited number of Common shares and Class A non-voting shares. Both Common shares and Class A non-voting shares have no par value. All issued shares are fully paid.

The Common shares and Class A non-voting shares of the Company rank equally and pari passu with respect to the right to receive dividends and upon any distribution of the assets of the Company. However, in the case of share dividends, the holders of Class A non-voting shares shall have the right to receive Class A non-voting shares and the holders of Common shares shall have the right to receive Common shares.

Issuance of Class A Non-Voting Shares

During the year ended January 28, 2012, a total of 722 (January 29, 2011- 292) Class A non-voting shares were issued as a result of the exercise of vested options arising from the Company's share option program. The amounts credited to share capital from the exercise of share options include a cash consideration of $8,828 (January 29, 2011- $3,569), as well as an ascribed value from contributed surplus of $2,228 (January 29, 2011- $888).

Purchase of Shares for Cancellation

For the year ended January 28, 2012, the Company purchased, under the prior year's normal course issuer bid, 1,445 (January 29, 2011 – 1,583) Class A non-voting shares having a book value of $780 (January 29, 2011 - $731) for a total cash consideration of $22,410 (January 29, 2011 - $30,112). The excess of the purchase price over the book value of the shares in the amount of $21,630 (January 29, 2011 - $29,381) was charged to retained earnings.

In November 2011, the Company received approval from the Toronto Stock Exchange to proceed with a normal course issuer bid. Under the bid, the Company may purchase up to 2,580 Class A non-voting shares of the Company, representing 5% of the issued and outstanding Class A non-voting shares as at November 14, 2011. The bid commenced on November 28, 2011 and may continue to November 27, 2012. No Class A non-voting shares were purchased under this new program.

Accumulated Other Comprehensive Income ("AOCI")

AOCI is comprised of the following:

	January 28, 2012	January 29, 2011	January 31, 2010
Net change in fair value of available-for-sale financial assets, net of taxes	$ 8,737	$ 8,143	$ 5,355

Dividends

The following dividends were declared and paid by the Company:

	For the years ended	
	January 28, 2012	**January 29, 2011**
Common shares and Class A non-voting shares	$ 52,654	$ 51,895

17. SHARE-BASED PAYMENTS

a) Description of the Share-Based Payment Arrangements

The Company has a share option plan that provides that up to 10% of the Class A non-voting shares outstanding, from time to time, may be issued pursuant to the exercise of options granted under the plan to key management and employees. The granting of options and the related vesting period, which is normally up to 5 years, are at the discretion of the Board of Directors and the options have a maximum term of 10 years. The exercise price payable for each Class A non-voting share covered by a share option is determined by the Board of Directors at the date of grant, but may not be less than the closing price of the Company's shares on the trading day immediately preceding the effective date of the grant.

b) Disclosure of Equity-settled Share Option Plan

Changes in outstanding share options were as follows:

| | For the years ended | | | |
| | January 28, 2012 | | January 29, 2011 | |
	Options	Weighted Average Exercise Price	Options	Weighted Average Exercise Price
Outstanding, at beginning of year	3,095	$ 14.58	3,207	$ 14.14
Granted	-	-	215	18.02
Exercised	(722)	12.23	(292)	12.23
Forfeited	(428)	16.33	(35)	14.50
Outstanding, at end of year	1,945	$ 15.07	3,095	$ 14.58
Options exercisable, at end of year	238	$ 18.81	935	$ 13.74

The weighted average share price at the date of exercise for share options exercised in the year was $15.44 (January 29, 2011 - $18.21)

There were no share option awards granted during the year ended January 28, 2012. Compensation cost related to share option awards granted during the year ended January 29, 2011 under the fair value based approach was calculated using the following assumptions:

| | For the year ended January 29, 2011 | | |
	100 Options Granted April 7, 2010	15 Options Granted June 2, 2010	100 Options Granted January 14, 2011
Expected option life	6.5 years	4.9 years	6.5 years
Risk-free interest rate	3.59%	2.44%	2.90%
Expected stock price volatility	47.18%	37.40%	33.52%
Average dividend yield	4.00%	4.38%	4.44%
Weighted average fair value of options granted	$6.22	$4.25	$4.05
Share price at grant date	$18.00	$18.26	$18.00

The following table summarizes information about share options outstanding at January 28, 2012:

| | Options Outstanding | | | Options Exercisable | |
Range of Exercise Prices	Number Outstanding	Weighted Average Remaining Contractual Life	Weighted Average Exercise Price	Number Exercisable	Weighted Average Exercise Price
$14.50	1,675	5.0 years	$ 14.50	-	$ -
$15.90 - $18.26	115	2.4	16.75	83	16.58
$19.23 - $22.02	155	0.7	20.00	155	20.00
	1,945	4.5 years	$ 15.07	238	$ 18.81

c) Employee Expense

For the year ended January 28, 2012, the Company recognized compensation costs of $1,120 relating to share-based payment arrangements ($1,990 for the year ended January 29, 2011), with a corresponding credit to contributed surplus.

18. COMMITMENTS

As at January 28, 2012, financial commitments for minimum lease payments under operating leases for retail stores, offices, automobiles and equipment, as well as amounts pertaining to agreements to purchase goods or services that are enforceable and legally binding on the Company, exclusive of additional amounts based on sales, taxes and other costs are payable as follows:

	Store and Office Operating Leases	Purchases Obligations	Other Operating Leases	Total
Within 1 year	$ 99,202	$102,637	$ 4,498	$ 206,337
Within 2 years	88,467	326	3,723	92,516
Within 3 years	77,563	117	2,672	80,352
Within 4 years	66,012	-	2,477	68,489
Within 5 years	49,802	-	8	49,810
Subsequent years	89,873	-	-	89,873
Total	$ 470,919	$103,080	$ 13,378	$ 587,377

The Company leases retail stores and offices under operating leases. The Company does not sublet any of its leased properties. The leases have varying terms, escalation clauses and renewal rights. Generally, the leases run for a period that does not exceed 10 years, with options to renew that do not exceed 5 years, if at all. The majority of the leases require additional payments for the cost of insurance, taxes, maintenance and utilities. Certain rental agreements include contingent rent, which is generally based on revenue exceeding a minimum amount.

For the year ended January 28, 2012, $181,998 was recognized as an expense in net earnings with respect to operating leases ($181,868 for the year ended January 29, 2011), of which $179,149 ($179,328 for the year ended January 29, 2011) represents minimum lease payments and $2,849 ($2,540 for the year ended January 29, 2011) represents contingent rents.

As at January 28, 2012, a total of 1,945 (January 29, 2011– 398) share options were excluded from the calculation of diluted earnings per share as these options were deemed to be anti-dilutive, because the exercise prices were greater than the average market price of the shares during the period.

The average market value of the Company's shares for purposes of calculating the dilutive effect of share options was based on quoted market prices for the period during which the options were outstanding.

21. RELATED PARTIES

Transactions with Key Management Personnel

Only members of the Board of Directors are deemed to be key management personnel. It is the Board who has the responsibility for planning, directing and controlling the activities of the Company. The Directors participate in the share option plan, as described in note 17. Compensation expense for key management personnel is as follows:

	For the years ended	
	January 28, 2012	January 29, 2011
Salaries and short-term benefits	$ 2,088	$ 2,899
Post-employment benefits	(63)	178
Share-based compensation costs	190	200
	$ 2,215	$ 3,277

Further information about the remuneration of individual Directors is provided in the annual Management Proxy Circular.

Other Related-Party Transactions

The Company leases two retail locations which are owned by companies controlled by the major shareholders of the Company. For the year ended January 28, 2012, the rent expense under these leases was, in the aggregate, approximately $198 (January 29, 2011- $190).

The Company incurred $584 in the year ended January 28, 2012 (January 29, 2011- $606) with professional service firms connected to outside directors of the Company for fees in conjunction with general legal advice and other consultation.

These transactions are recorded at the amount of consideration paid as established and agreed to by the related parties.

19. FINANCE INCOME AND FINANCE COSTS

Recognized in Net Earnings

	For the years ended	
	January 28, 2012	January 29, 2011
Dividend income from available-for-sale financial assets	$ 3,462	$ 2,640
Interest income from loans and receivables	1,367	1,225
Realized gain on disposal of available-for-sale financial assets	-	167
Foreign exchange gain	733	473
Finance income	5,562	4,505
Interest expense - mortgage	682	767
Net change in fair value of derivatives (note 6)	754	-
Impairment loss on available-for-sale financial assets	73	78
Finance costs	1,509	845
Net finance income recognized in net earnings	$ 4,053	$ 3,660

Recognized in Other Comprehensive Income

	For the years ended	
	January 28, 2012	January 29, 2011
Net change in fair value of available-for-sale financial assets arising during the year (net of tax of $ 79; 2011 - $427)	$ 530	$ 2,866
Finance income recognized in other comprehensive income (net of tax)	$ 530	$ 2,866

20. EARNINGS PER SHARE

The calculation of basic and diluted earnings per share is based on net earnings for the year ended January 28, 2012 of $47,539 ($88,985 for the year ended January 29, 2011).

The number of shares used in the earnings per share calculation is as follows:

	For the years ended	
	January 28, 2012	January 29, 2011
Weighted average number of shares per basic earnings per share calculations	65,975	66,771
Effect of dilutive share options outstanding	126	484
Weighted average number of shares per diluted earnings per share calculations	66,101	67,255

22. PERSONNEL EXPENSES

	For the years ended	
	January 28, 2012	January 29, 2011
Wages, salaries and employee benefits	$ 248,208	$ 251,702
Expenses related to defined benefit plans	1,490	1,341
Share-based compensation costs	1,120	1,990
	$ 250,818	$ 255,033

23. CREDIT FACILITY

At January 28, 2012, the Company had unsecured operating lines of credit available with Canadian chartered banks to a maximum of $125,000 or its US dollar equivalent. As at January 28, 2012, $52,187 (January 29, 2011 - $60,888) of the operating lines of credit were committed for documentary and standby letters of credit.

24. GUARANTEES

The Company has granted irrevocable standby letters of credit, issued by highly-rated financial institutions, to third parties to indemnify them in the event the Company does not perform its contractual obligations. As at January 28, 2012, the maximum potential liability under these guarantees was $5,083 (January 29, 2011 - $5,060). The standby letters of credit mature at various dates during year ending February 2, 2013. The contingent portion of the guarantee is recorded when the Company considers it probable that a payment relating to the guarantee has to be made to the other party of the contract or guarantee. The Company has recorded no liability with respect to these guarantees as the Company does not expect to make any payments for these items. Management believes that the fair value of the non-contingent obligations requiring performance under the guarantees in the event that specified triggering events or conditions occur approximates the cost of obtaining the standby letters of credit.

25. SUPPLEMENTARY CASH FLOW INFORMATION

	January 28, 2012	January 29, 2011
Non-cash transactions:		
Additions to property and equipment and intangible assets included in trade and other payables	$ 3,028	$ 2,819
Ascribed value credited to share capital from exercise of share options	$ 2,228	$ 888

26. FINANCIAL RISK MANAGEMENT

The Company's risk management policies are established to identify and analyze the risks faced by the Company, to set appropriate risk limits and controls, and to monitor risks and adherence to limits. Risk management policies and systems are reviewed regularly to reflect changes in market conditions and the Company's activities. Disclosures relating to the Company's exposure to risks, in particular credit risk, liquidity risk, foreign currency risk, interest rate risk and equity price risk are provided below.

Credit Risk

Credit risk is the risk of an unexpected loss if a customer or counterparty to a financial instrument fails to meet its contractual obligations. The Company's financial instruments that are exposed to concentrations of credit risk are primarily cash and cash equivalents, marketable securities, trade and other receivables and foreign currency option contracts. The Company limits its exposure to credit risk with respect to cash and cash equivalents by investing available cash in short-term deposits with Canadian financial institutions and commercial paper with a rating not less than R1. Marketable securities consist primarily of preferred shares of highly-rated Canadian public companies. The Company's trade and other receivables consist primarily of credit card receivables from the last few days of the fiscal year, which are settled within the first days of the next fiscal year.

As at January 28, 2012, the Company's maximum exposure to credit risk for these financial instruments was as follows:

Cash and cash equivalents	$ 196,835
Marketable securities	71,442
Trade and other receivables	3,033
	$ 271,310

Liquidity Risk

Liquidity risk is the risk that the Company will not be able to meet its financial obligations as they fall due. The Company's approach to managing liquidity risk is to ensure, as far as possible, that it will always have sufficient liquidity to meet liabilities when due. The contractual maturity of the majority of trade and other payables is within six months. As at January 28, 2012, the Company had a high degree of liquidity with $268,277 in cash and cash equivalents, and marketable securities. In addition, the Company has unsecured credit facilities of $125,000 subject to annual renewals. The Company has financed its store expansion through internally-generated funds and its unsecured credit facilities are used to finance seasonal working capital requirements for US dollar merchandise purchases. The Company's long-term debt consists of a mortgage bearing interest at 6.40%, due November 2017, which is secured by the Company's distribution centre.

Foreign Currency Risk

The Company purchases a significant amount of its merchandise with US dollars and as such significant volatility in the US dollar vis-à-vis the Canadian dollar can have an adverse impact on the Company's gross margin. The Company has a variety of alternatives that it considers to manage its foreign currency exposure on cash flows related to these purchases. This includes, but is not limited to, various styles of foreign currency option or forward contracts, not to exceed six months, and spot rate purchases. A foreign currency option contract represents an option or obligation to buy a foreign currency from a counterparty. Credit risks exist in the event of failure by a counterparty to fulfill its

Equity Price Risk

Equity price risk arises from available-for-sale equity securities. The Company monitors the mix of equity securities in its investment portfolio based on market expectations. Material investments within the portfolio are managed on an individual basis and all buy and sell decisions are approved by the Chief Executive Officer.

The Company has performed a sensitivity analysis on equity price risk at January 28, 2012, to determine how a change in the market price of the Company's marketable securities would impact equity and other comprehensive income. The Company's equity investments consist principally of preferred shares of Canadian public companies. The Company believes that changes in interest rates influence the market price of these securities. A 5% increase or decrease in the market price of the securities at January 28, 2012, would result in a $3,036 increase or decrease, respectively, in equity and other comprehensive income for the year ended January 28, 2012. The Company's equity securities are subject to market risk and, as a result, the impact on equity and other comprehensive income may ultimately be greater than that indicated above.

27. CAPITAL MANAGEMENT

The Company's objectives in managing capital are:

- to ensure sufficient liquidity to enable the internal financing of capital projects thereby facilitating its expansion;
- to maintain a strong capital base so as to maintain investor, creditor and market confidence;
- to provide an adequate return to shareholders.

The Company's capital is composed of long-term debt, including the current portion and shareholders' equity. The Company's primary uses of capital are to finance increases in non-cash working capital along with capital expenditures for new store additions, existing store renovation projects and office and distribution centre improvements. The Company currently funds these requirements out of its internally-generated cash flows. The Company's long-term debt constitutes a mortgage on the distribution centre facility. The Company maintains unsecured operating lines of credit that it uses to satisfy commitments for US dollar denominated merchandise purchases. The Company does not have any long-term debt, other than the mortgage related to the distribution centre, and therefore net earnings generated from operations are available for reinvestment in the Company or distribution to the Company's shareholders. The Board of Directors does not establish quantitative return on capital criteria for management, but rather promotes year over year sustainable profitable growth. On a quarterly basis, the Board of Directors also reviews the level of dividends paid to the Company's shareholders and monitors the share repurchase program activities. The Company does not have a defined share repurchase plan and decisions are made on a specific transaction basis and depend on market prices and regulatory restrictions. The Company is not subject to any externally imposed capital requirements.

---

obligations. The Company reduces this risk by dealing only with highly-rated counterparties, normally major Canadian financial institutions. For the year ended January 28, 2012, the Company satisfied its US dollar requirements primarily through spot rate purchases.

The Company has performed a sensitivity analysis on its US dollar denominated financial instruments, which consist principally of cash and cash equivalents of $27,547 and trade payables of $3,840 to determine how a change in the US dollar exchange rate would impact net earnings. On January 28, 2012, a 1% rise or fall in the Canadian dollar against the US dollar, assuming that all other variables, in particular interest rates, had remained the same, would have resulted in a $166 decrease or increase, respectively, in the Company's net earnings for the year ended January 28, 2012.

The Company has performed a sensitivity analysis on its derivative financial instruments, a series of call and put options on US dollars, to determine how a change in the US dollar exchange rate would impact net earnings. On January 28, 2012, a 1% rise or fall in the Canadian dollar against the US dollar, assuming that all other variables had remained the same, would have resulted in a $580 decrease or increase, respectively, in the Company's net earnings for the year ended January 28, 2012.

Interest Rate Risk

Interest rate risk exists in relation to the Company's cash and cash equivalents, defined benefit pension plan and SERP. Market fluctuations in interest rates impacts the Company's earnings with respect to interest earned on cash and cash equivalents that are invested in bank bearer deposit notes and bank term deposits with major Canadian financial institutions and commercial paper with a rating not less than R1. Overall return in the capital markets and the level of interest rates affect the funded status of the Company's pension plans. Adverse changes with respect to pension plan returns and the level of interest rates from the date of the last actuarial valuation may have a material adverse effect on the funded status of the retirement benefit plans and on the Company's results of operations. The Company has unsecured borrowing and working capital credit facilities available up to an amount of $125,000 or its US dollar equivalent that it utilizes for documentary and standby letters of credit, and the Company funds the drawings on these facilities as the payments are due.

The Company has performed a sensitivity analysis on interest rate risk at January 28, 2012 to determine how a change in interest rates would impact equity and net earnings. For the year ended January 28, 2012, the Company earned interest income of $1,367 on its cash and cash equivalents. An increase or decrease of 25 basis points in the average interest rate earned during the year would have increased equity and net earnings by $321 or decreased equity and net earnings by $235, respectively. This analysis assumes that all other variables, in particular foreign currency rates, remain constant.

The Company has performed a sensitivity analysis at January 28, 2012 to determine how a change in interest rates, in relation to the Company's retirement benefit plans, would impact the benefit costs included in other comprehensive income. A one percentage point decrease in the year-end discount rate would have resulted in an increase of approximately $4,300 in benefit costs included in other comprehensive income for the year ended January 28, 2012, whereas a one percentage point increase would have resulted in a decrease of approximately $3,800. The Company's expected long-term rate of return on Plan assets reflects management's view of long-term investment returns. The effect of a 1% variation in such rate of return would have a nominal impact on the total benefit costs included in net earnings and total comprehensive income.

28. COMPARATIVE FIGURES

Certain comparative figures have been reclassified to conform to the current year's presentation.

29. EXPLANATION OF TRANSITION TO IFRS

As stated in note 2 (a), these are the Company's first annual financial statements prepared in accordance with IFRS. The Company has applied IFRS 1 and the accounting policies set out in note 3 have been applied in preparing the financial statements for the year ended January 28, 2012, the comparative information presented in these financial statements for the year ended January 29, 2011 and in the preparation of the opening IFRS balance sheet at January 31, 2010, which is the Company's date of transition.

In preparing these financial statements in accordance with IFRS 1, the Company has adjusted amounts reported previously in the financial statements prepared in accordance with Canadian GAAP. An explanation of how the transition from Canadian GAAP to IFRS has affected the Company's previously published financial statements as at and for the year ended January 29, 2011 and as at January 31, 2010 is set out in the following tables and the notes that accompany the tables.

IFRS 1 requires first-time adopters to retrospectively apply all effective IFRS standards as of the reporting date of its first annual financial statements. However, it also provides for certain optional exemptions and prescribes certain mandatory exceptions for first-time adopters. Set forth below are the IFRS 1 applicable exemptions and exceptions applied in the Company's conversion from Canadian GAAP to IFRS.

a) IFRS Exemption Options

(i)   Business Combinations

The Company elected not to retrospectively apply IFRS 3 *Business Combinations* to business combinations that occurred prior to its Transition Date and such business combinations have not been restated. Under the business combinations exemption, the carrying amounts of the assets acquired and liabilities assumed under Canadian GAAP at the date of the acquisition became their deemed carrying amounts under IFRS at that date.

Notwithstanding this exemption, the Company was required at the Transition Date, to evaluate whether the assets acquired and liabilities assumed meet the recognition criteria in the relevant IFRS, and whether there are any assets acquired or liabilities assumed that were not recognized under Canadian GAAP for which recognition would be required under IFRS. The requirements of IFRS were then applied to the assets acquired and liabilities assumed from the date of acquisition of this exemption did not result in an IFRS transition adjustment to the opening balance sheet at January 31, 2010. In addition, under the business combinations exemption, the Company tested goodwill for impairment at the Transition Date and determined that there was no impairment of the carrying value of goodwill as of that date.

(ii)   Employee Benefits

IFRS 1 provides the option to apply IAS 19 *Employee Benefits* paragraph 120A(p), retrospectively or prospectively from the Transition Date. The retrospective basis would require the disclosure of selected information of the defined benefit plans for the current annual period and previous four annual periods. The Company elected to disclose the amounts required by paragraph 120A(p) of IAS 19 as the amounts are determined for each accounting period prospectively from the Transition Date to IFRS.

Present value concepts are widely used by accountants in the preparation of financial statements. Under IFRS, these concepts are more widely applied than under ASPE. This appendix will explain the basics that you must be aware of to understand related topics in this text.

Interest and Calculating Present Values

Interest is payment for the use of money. It is the difference between the amount borrowed or invested (the principal) and the amount repaid or collected. The amount of interest to be paid or collected is usually stated as a percentage rate over a specific period of time. The rate of interest is generally stated as an annual rate to allow for easier comparison between loan alternatives with different terms.

The amount of interest involved in any financing transaction is based on three elements:

1. **Principal** (p): The original amount borrowed or invested
2. **Interest rate** (i): An annual percentage of the principal
3. **Number of periods** (n): The time period that the principal is borrowed or invested

» **STUDY OBJECTIVE 1**

Calculate simple and compound interest, and the present value of a single future amount.

SIMPLE AND COMPOUND INTEREST

When calculating interest, it is important to know when and how to use simple or compound interest.

Simple Interest

Simple interest is calculated on the principal amount only. In accounting, simple interest is used in accrual accounting to record the amount of interest revenue earned or expense incurred on a loan. Accruals for interest can be easily calculated at the end of each accounting period and prorated for partial periods where appropriate.

Simple interest is usually expressed as shown in Illustration PV-1.

$$\boxed{\text{Interest}} = \boxed{\begin{array}{c}\text{Principal}\\(p)\end{array}} \times \boxed{\begin{array}{c}\text{Interest Rate}\\(i)\end{array}} \times \boxed{\begin{array}{c}\text{Number of Periods}\\(n)\end{array}}$$

▶ **ILLUSTRATION PV-1**
Simple interest formula

For example, if you borrowed $1,000 for three years at a simple interest rate of 9% annually, you would pay $270 in total interest, calculated as follows:

Interest = $p \times i \times n$	Year 1		Year 2		Year 3		
= $1,000 × 9% × 3	$90	+	$90	+	$90	=	$270
= $270							

Compound Interest

Compound interest is the return on (or growth of) the principal for two or more time periods. Compounding calculates interest not only on the principal but also on the interest earned to date on that principal, assuming the interest is left on deposit (that is, it is added to the original principal amount).

To illustrate the difference between simple and compound interest, assume that you deposit $1,000 in the Last Canadian Bank, where it will earn simple interest of 9% per year, and you deposit another $1,000 in the First Canadian Bank, where it will earn interest of 9% per year compounded annually. Also assume that in both cases you will not withdraw any interest until three years from the date of deposit. The calculations of interest to be received and the accumulated year-end balances are given in Illustration PV-2.

LAST CANADIAN BANK					FIRST CANADIAN BANK		
Simple Interest Calculation	Simple Interest	Accumulated Year-End Balance			Compound Interest Calculation	Compound Interest	Accumulated Year-End Balance
Year 1 $1,000.00 × 9%	$ 90.00	$1,090.00			Year 1 $1,000.00 × 9%	$ 90.00	$1,090.00
Year 2 $1,000.00 × 9%	90.00	$1,180.00			Year 2 $1,090.00 × 9%	98.10	$1,188.10
Year 3 $1,000.00 × 9%	90.00 $270.00	$1,270.00	$25.03 Difference		Year 3 $1,188.10 × 9%	106.93 $295.03	$1,295.03

▶ **ILLUSTRATION PV-2**
Simple versus
compound interest

Note in Illustration PV-2 that simple interest uses the initial principal of $1,000 to calculate the interest in all three years. Compound interest uses the accumulated balance (principal plus interest to date) at each year end to calculate interest in the following year. This explains why your compound interest account is larger: you are earning interest on interest. For practical purposes, compounding assumes that unpaid interest earned becomes a part of the principal. The accumulated balance at the end of each year becomes the new principal on which interest is earned during the next year. Assuming all else is equal (especially risk), if you had a choice between investing your money at simple interest or at compound interest, you would choose compound interest. In the example, compounding provides $25.03 of additional interest income.

When borrowing or lending money, the lending agreement should always state whether interest will be calculated using the simple or compound method. If the compound method is used, the frequency of compounding must also be stated. The shorter the amount of time between compounding calculations (that is, the more frequent the compounding), the more interest will be earned.

Compound interest is used in most business transactions. Simple interest is generally applicable only to short-term loans of one year or less. The shorter the term of the loan, the smaller the difference between simple and compound interest and therefore the parties will agree to use simple interest. Present value concepts use compound interest.

PRESENT VALUE OF A SINGLE FUTURE AMOUNT

In the previous example on compound and simple interest, the initial principal was given. It was used to calculate the interest earned and the value of the investment at the end of three years. **The initial principal, invested at the beginning of year one, is the present value (PV) of the investment. The value of the investment at the end of three years is the future value (FV) of the investment.**

You are probably more accustomed to being given the present value and then calculating the future value. But in business, there are many situations in which the future value (the cash flows that will occur in the future) is known, and it is necessary to calculate the present value (the value of those future cash flows at the beginning). For example, we determine the market price of a bond by calculating the present value of the future principal and interest payments. Calculating the amount to be reported for fixed and intangible assets, notes payable, pensions, and finance lease liabilities can also involve present value calculations.

Present value calculations are always based on three variables:

1. The *dollar amount* to be received (the future amount or future value)
2. The *length of time* until the amount is received (the number of periods)
3. The *interest rate* (the discount rate) per period

Alternative terminology The discount rate is also referred to as the *effective rate*, or the *imputed rate*.

The process of determining the present value is often referred to as **discounting the future cash flows**. The word "discount" has many meanings in accounting, each of which varies with the context in which it is being used. Be careful not to confuse the use of this term.

In the following section, we will show four methods of calculating the present value of a single future amount: present value formula, present value tables, financial calculators, and Excel.

Present Value Formula

To illustrate present value concepts, assume that you want to invest a sum of money at 5% in order to have $1,000 at the end of one year. The amount that you would need to invest today is called the present value of $1,000 discounted for one year at 5%.

The variables in this example are shown in the time diagram in Illustration PV-3.

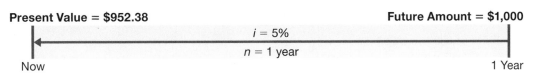

Present Value = $952.38   **Future Amount = $1,000**

$i = 5\%$

$n = 1$ year

Now   1 Year

▶ **ILLUSTRATION** PV-3
Time diagram for the present value of $1,000 discounted for one period at 5%

The formula used to determine the present value for any interest (discount) rate (i), number of periods (n), and future amount (FV) is shown in Illustration PV-4.

$$\text{Present value } (PV) = \frac{\text{Future value } (FV)}{(1 + i)^n}$$
$$= FV \div (1 + i)^n$$

▶ **ILLUSTRATION** PV-4
Present value of a single future amount formula

In applying this formula to calculate the present value (PV) for the above example, the future value (FV) of $1,000, the interest (discount) rate (i) of 5%, and the number of periods (n) of 1 are used as follows:

Alternative terminology The present value of a single future amount formula is also called the *present value of 1 formula.*

$$PV = \$1,000 \div (1 + 5\%)^1$$
$$= \$1,000 \div 1.05$$
$$= \$952.38$$

If the single future cash flow of $1,000 is to be received in two years and discounted at 5%, its present value is calculated as follows:

$$PV = \$1,000 \div (1 + 5\%)^2$$
$$= \$1,000 \div 1.05^2 \text{ or } [(\$1,000 \div 1.05) \div 1.05]$$
$$= \$907.03$$

The time diagram in Illustration PV-5 shows the variables used to calculate the present value when cash is received in two years.

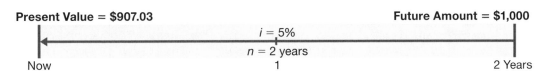

Present Value = $907.03   **Future Amount = $1,000**

$i = 5\%$

$n = 2$ years

Now   2 Years
1

▶ **ILLUSTRATION** PV-5
Time diagram for present value of $1,000 discounted for two periods at 5%

Present Value Tables

The present value may also be determined through tables that show the present value of 1 for n periods for different periodic interest rates or discount rates. In Table PV-1, the rows represent the number of discounting periods and the columns represent the periodic interest or discount rates. The five-digit decimal numbers in the respective rows and columns are the factors for the present value of 1.

When present value tables are used, the present value is calculated by multiplying the future cash amount by the present value factor specified at the intersection of the number of periods and the discount rate. For example, if the discount rate is 5% and the number of periods is 1, Table PV-1 shows that the present value factor is 0.95238. Then the present value of $1,000 discounted at 5% for one period is calculated as follows:

$$PV = \$1,000 \times 0.95238$$
$$= \$952.38$$

For two periods at a discount rate of 5%, the present value factor is 0.90703. The present value of $1,000 discounted at 5% for two periods is calculated as follows:

$$PV = \$1,000 \times 0.90703$$
$$= \$907.03$$

Note that the present values in these two examples are identical to the amounts determined previously when using the present value formula. This is because the factors in a present value table have been calculated using the present value formula. The benefit of using a present value table is that it can be quicker than using the formula. If you are using a simple calculator (not a financial calculator) or doing the calculations by hand, there are more calculations involved as the number of periods increases, making it more tedious than using the present value tables.

Table PV-1 can also be used if you know the present value and wish to determine the future cash flow. The present value amount is divided by the present value factor specified at the intersection of the number of periods and the discount rate in Table PV-1. For example, it can easily be determined that an initial investment of $907.03 will grow to yield a future amount of $1,000 in two periods, at an annual discount rate of 5% ($1,000 = $907.03 ÷ 0.90703).

TABLE PV-1
PRESENT VALUE OF 1

$$PV = \frac{1}{(1 + i)^n}$$

(n) Periods	2%	2½%	3%	4%	5%	6%	7%	8%	9%	10%	11%	12%	15%
1	0.98039	0.97561	0.97087	0.96154	0.95238	0.94340	0.93458	0.92593	0.91743	0.90909	0.90090	0.89286	0.86957
2	0.96117	0.95181	0.94260	0.92456	0.90703	0.89000	0.87344	0.85734	0.84168	0.82645	0.81162	0.79719	0.75614
3	0.94232	0.92860	0.91514	0.88900	0.86384	0.83962	0.81630	0.79383	0.77218	0.75131	0.73119	0.71178	0.65752
4	0.92385	0.90595	0.88849	0.85480	0.82270	0.79209	0.76290	0.73503	0.70843	0.68301	0.65873	0.63552	0.57175
5	0.90573	0.88385	0.86261	0.82193	0.78353	0.74726	0.71299	0.68058	0.64993	0.62092	0.59345	0.56743	0.49718
6	0.88797	0.86230	0.83748	0.79031	0.74622	0.70496	0.66634	0.63017	0.59627	0.56447	0.53464	0.50663	0.43233
7	0.87056	0.84127	0.81309	0.75992	0.71068	0.66506	0.62275	0.58349	0.54703	0.51316	0.48166	0.45235	0.37594
8	0.85349	0.82075	0.78941	0.73069	0.67684	0.62741	0.58201	0.54027	0.50187	0.46651	0.43393	0.40388	0.32690
9	0.83676	0.80073	0.76642	0.70259	0.64461	0.59190	0.54393	0.50025	0.46043	0.42410	0.39092	0.36061	0.28426
10	0.82035	0.78120	0.74409	0.67556	0.61391	0.55839	0.50835	0.46319	0.42241	0.38554	0.35218	0.32197	0.24718
11	0.80426	0.76214	0.72242	0.64958	0.58468	0.52679	0.47509	0.42888	0.38753	0.35049	0.31728	0.28748	0.21494
12	0.78849	0.74356	0.70138	0.62460	0.55684	0.49697	0.44401	0.39711	0.35553	0.31863	0.28584	0.25668	0.18691
13	0.77303	0.72542	0.68095	0.60057	0.53032	0.46884	0.41496	0.36770	0.32618	0.28966	0.25751	0.22917	0.16253
14	0.75788	0.70773	0.66112	0.57748	0.50507	0.44230	0.38782	0.34046	0.29925	0.26333	0.23199	0.20462	0.14133
15	0.74301	0.69047	0.64186	0.55526	0.48102	0.41727	0.36245	0.31524	0.27454	0.23939	0.20900	0.18270	0.12289
16	0.72845	0.67362	0.62317	0.53391	0.45811	0.39365	0.33873	0.29189	0.25187	0.21763	0.18829	0.16312	0.10686
17	0.71416	0.65720	0.60502	0.51337	0.43630	0.37136	0.31657	0.27027	0.23107	0.19784	0.16963	0.14564	0.09293
18	0.70016	0.64117	0.58739	0.49363	0.41552	0.35034	0.29586	0.25025	0.21199	0.17986	0.15282	0.13004	0.08081
19	0.68643	0.62553	0.57029	0.47464	0.39573	0.33051	0.27651	0.23171	0.19449	0.16351	0.13768	0.11611	0.07027
20	0.67297	0.61027	0.55368	0.45639	0.37689	0.31180	0.25842	0.21455	0.17843	0.14864	0.12403	0.10367	0.06110

Financial Calculators

Present values can also be calculated using financial calculators. Financial calculators have five distinctive keys on the numeric pad, usually in a row and in a different colour than other keys on the pad. The five keys correspond to the five possible variables that could be used in a present value calculation, as shown in Illustration PV-6.

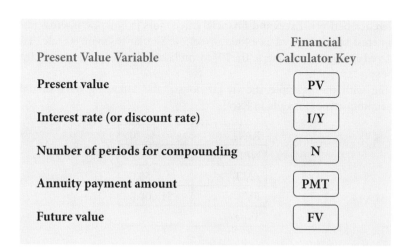

▶ **ILLUSTRATION** **PV-6**
Financial calculator
keys

To calculate the present value, **enter each of the other variable amounts followed by pressing the corresponding key for that variable amount**. If an amount represents an outflow of cash, a negative value for the amount must be entered. Once the four known variables are entered, in any order, press the CPT (compute or equivalent key) and the PV variable key and the answer will appear on screen. When calculating the present value of a single future amount, enter zero for the annuity payment amount, followed by the PMT key. We will learn about annuity payments in the next section of the appendix.

Helpful hint Always begin by clearing the calculator.

For example, if you are calculating the present value of a single future cash flow of $1,000 to be received in two years and discounted at 5%, the data are entered into the financial calculator as follows:

Enter:	5	2	0	1000			Result
Press:	I/Y	N	PMT	FV	CPT	PV	$(907.03)

Note that the result is the same as with the present value formula and tables except the calculator shows $907.03 as a negative number. The reason the present value is a negative number is to demonstrate that an outflow (negative) of cash today of $907.03 will provide a future inflow (positive) of cash of $1,000.00 in two years using an annual interest rate of 5%.

Helpful hint The interest rate is entered as a whole number, not as a percentage. In this example, the 5% interest rate is entered as "5" and not ".05" or "5%".

The present value amounts calculated with a financial calculator can be slightly different than those calculated with present value tables. That is because the numbers in a present value table are rounded. For example, in Table PV-1 the factors are rounded to five digits. In a financial calculator, only the final answer is rounded to the number of digits you have specified in the viewing screen.

Computer Spreadsheets

Present value calculations can also be prepared very easily using a computer spreadsheet. For example, in Excel, use the insert function (*fx*) icon (commonly found at the top of the screen or near the cell content bar). Click on this icon and a pop-up screen will appear, allowing you to select a function. Select the category Financial then select the PV function. Another pop-up box will appear, allowing you to enter the necessary information. The terms are very similar to a financial calculator. A comparison is shown in the table below.

Present Value Variable	Excel variable	Financial calculator key
Present value	PV	PV
Interest rate (or discount rate)	RATE	I/Y
Number of periods	NPER	N
Annuity payment amount	PMT	PMT
Future value	FV	FV

Excel will also ask for the type of annuity. For all of the calculations in this textbook, you should enter "0," which indicates that the payment is at the end of the period. You will learn about annuities with payments at the beginning of the period in other courses.

One difference between Excel and financial calculators is how the interest rate is entered. With Excel, a 5% interest rate is entered as either .05 or 5%. Similar to financial calculators, cash outflows should be entered as negative numbers. The PV formula can also be typed directly into a cell as follows: =PV(rate,nper,pmt,fv,type).

Continuing with the example shown previously, the following data should be used in the =PV(rate,nper,pmt,fv,type) formula in Excel:

RATE	.05
NPER	2
PMT	$0.00
FV	$1,000.00
Type	0

The result is a PV of $(907.03), which is the same as the result obtained using the financial calculator.

Summary of Methods

A major benefit of using a financial calculator or a spreadsheet is that you are not restricted to the interest rates or numbers of periods on a present value table. In Table PV-1, present value factors have been calculated for 13 interest rates (there are 13 columns in that table) and the maximum number of periods is 20. With a financial calculator, you could, for example, calculate the present value of a future amount to be received in 25 periods using any discount rate not in a present value table, such as 5.75%.

Regardless of the method used in calculating present values, **a higher discount rate produces a smaller present value**. For example, using an 8% discount rate, the present value of $1,000 due one year from now is $925.93 versus $952.38 at 5%. You should also realize that **the further away from the present the future cash flow is, the smaller the present value**. For example, using the discount rate of 5%, the present value of $1,000 due in five years is 783.53 compared to $952.38 in one year.

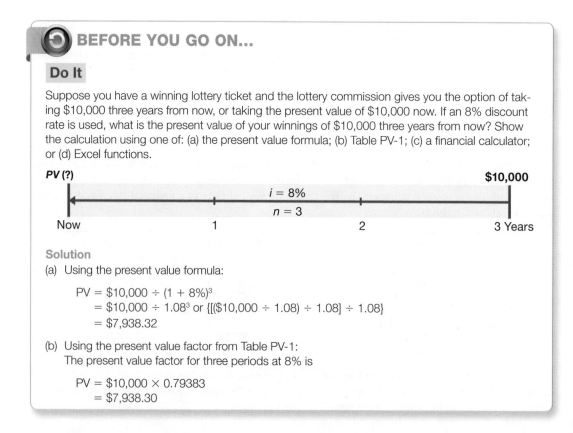

BEFORE YOU GO ON...

Do It

Suppose you have a winning lottery ticket and the lottery commission gives you the option of taking $10,000 three years from now, or taking the present value of $10,000 now. If an 8% discount rate is used, what is the present value of your winnings of $10,000 three years from now? Show the calculation using one of: (a) the present value formula; (b) Table PV-1; (c) a financial calculator; or (d) Excel functions.

PV (?)   **$10,000**

Now   1 $i = 8\%$ 2   3 Years
                          $n = 3$

Solution

(a) Using the present value formula:

$$PV = \$10,000 \div (1 + 8\%)^3$$
$$= \$10,000 \div 1.08^3 \text{ or } \{[(\$10,000 \div 1.08) \div 1.08] \div 1.08\}$$
$$= \$7,938.32$$

(b) Using the present value factor from Table PV-1:
The present value factor for three periods at 8% is

$$PV = \$10,000 \times 0.79383$$
$$= \$7,938.30$$

(c) Using a financial calculator:

Enter:	8	3	0	10000			Result
Press:	I/Y	N	PMT	FV	CPT	PV	$(7,938.32)

(d) Using the Excel PV function, the data used in the =PV(rate,nper,pmt,fv,type) formula are:

RATE	.08
NPER	3
PMT	$0.00
FV	$10,000.00
Type	0

PV = $ (7,938.32)

Do It Again

Determine the amount you must deposit now in your savings account, paying 3% interest, in order to accumulate $5,000 for a down payment on a hybrid electric car four years from now, when you graduate. Show the calculation using one of (a) present value formula, (b) Table PV-1, (c) financial calculator, or (d) Excel functions.

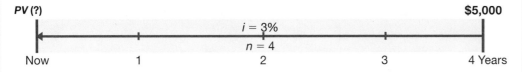

PV (?) $i = 3\%$ **$5,000**

$n = 4$

Now   1   2   3   4 Years

Solution

The amount you must deposit now in your savings account is the present value calculated as follows:

(a) Using the present value formula:

$$PV = \$5,000 \div (1 + 3\%)^4$$
$$= \$5,000 \div 1.03^4 \text{ or } (\{[(\$5,000 \div 1.03) \div 1.03] \div 1.03\} \div 1.03)$$
$$= \$4,442.44$$

(b) Using the present value factor from Table PV-1:
The present value factor for four periods at 3% is 0.88849.

$$PV = \$5,000 \times 0.88849$$
$$PV = \$4,442.45$$

(c) Using a financial calculator:

Enter:	3	4	0	5000			Result
Press:	I/Y	N	PMT	FV	CPT	PV	$(4,442.44)

(d) Using the Excel PV function, the data used in the =PV(rate,nper,pmt,fv,type) formula are:

RATE	.03
NPER	4
PMT	$0.00
FV	$5,000.00
Type	0

PV = $(4,442.44)

Related exercise material: BEPV–1, BEPV–2, BEPV–3, BEPV–4, and BEPV–5.

Action Plan
- Note that $10,000 is the future value, the number of periods is 3, and the discount rate is 8%.
- Recall that the present value of $10,000 to be received in three years is less than $10,000 because interest can be earned on an amount invested today (that is, the present value) over the next three years.
- Understand that the discount rate used to calculate the present value is the compound interest rate that would be used to earn $10,000 in three years if the present value is invested today.
- Remember that the answer obtained from the different methods will be slightly different due to rounding of the PV factors.
- Draw a time diagram showing when the future value will be received, the discount rate, and the number of periods.

Action Plan (Do It Again)
- Note that $5,000 is the future value, $n = 4$, and $i = 3\%$.

THE NAVIGATOR

Present Value of a Series of Future Cash Flows (Annuities)

» **STUDY OBJECTIVE 2**

Calculate the present value of a series of future cash flows (annuities).

The preceding discussion was for the discounting of only a single future amount. Businesses and individuals frequently engage in transactions in which a series of equal dollar amounts are to be received or paid periodically. Examples of a series of periodic receipts or payments are loan agreements, instalment sales, mortgage notes, lease (rental) contracts, and pension obligations. These series of periodic receipts or payments are called **annuities**. In calculating the present value of an annuity, it is necessary to know (1) the discount rate (i), (2) the number of discount periods (n), and (3) the amount of the periodic receipts or payments (PMT).

CALCULATING THE PRESENT VALUE OF AN ANNUITY

To illustrate the calculation of the present value of an annuity, assume that you will receive $1,000 cash annually for three years, and that the discount rate is 4%. This situation is shown in the time diagram in Illustration PV-7.

▶ **ILLUSTRATION** PV-7
Time diagram for a three-year annuity

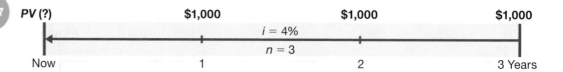

One method of calculating the present value of this annuity is to use the present value formula to determine the present value of each of the three $1,000 payments and then add those amounts as follows:

$$PV = [\$1,000 \div (1 + 4\%)^1] + [\$1,000 \div (1 + 4\%)^2] + [\$1,000 \div (1 + 4\%)^3]$$
$$= \$961.54 + \$924.56 + \$889.00$$
$$= \$2,775.10$$

The same result is achieved by using present value factors from Table PV-1, as shown in Illustration PV-8.

▶ **ILLUSTRATION** PV-8
Present value of a series of cash flows

Future Value	×	Present Value of 1 Factor at 4%	=	Present Value
$1,000 (one year away)		0.96154		$ 961.54
1,000 (two years away)		0.92456		924.56
1,000 (three years away)		0.88900		889.00
		2.77510		$2,775.10

Determining the present value of each single future cash flow, and then adding the present values, is required when the periodic cash flows are not the same in each period. But when the future receipts are the same in each period, there are other ways to calculate present value.

Present Value of an Annuity Formula

One way to calculate present value of a series of periodic payments is to use the present value of an ordinary annuity formula, as shown in Illustration PV-9.

▸ **ILLUSTRATION** **PV-9**
Present value of an
ordinary annuity of 1 formula

$$\text{Present value } (PV) = \text{Future value } (FV) \times \cfrac{1 - \cfrac{1}{(1 + i)^n}}{i}$$

$$= \$1{,}000 \times \left[(1 - (1 \div (1 + 4\%)^3)) \div 4\%\right]$$
$$= \$1{,}000 \times \left[(1 - (1 \div (1.04)^3)) \div 0.04\right]$$
$$= \$1{,}000 \times \left[(1 - (1 \div 1.124864)) \div 0.04\right]$$
$$= \$1{,}000 \times \left[(1 - 0.888996359) \div 0.04\right]$$
$$= \$1{,}000 \times 2.77509$$
$$= \$2{,}775.09$$

Present Value Tables

The second way to calculate the present value of a series of periodic payments is to use a present value of an annuity table. Table PV-2 shows the present value of 1 to be received periodically for a given number of periods at different discount rates. You can see in Table PV-2 that the present value factor of an annuity of 1 for three periods at 4% is 2.77509. This present value factor is the total of the three individual present value factors, as shown in Illustration PV-8.[1] Applying this present value factor to the annual cash flow of $1,000 produces a present value of $2,775.09 ($1,000 × 2.77509).

TABLE PV-2
PRESENT VALUE OF AN ANNUITY OF 1

$$PV = \cfrac{1 - \cfrac{1}{(1 + i)^n}}{i}$$

(n) Periods	2%	2½%	3%	4%	5%	6%	7%	8%	9%	10%	11%	12%	15%
1	0.98039	0.97561	0.97087	0.96154	0.95238	0.94340	0.93458	0.92593	0.91743	0.90909	0.90090	0.89286	0.86957
2	1.94156	1.92742	1.91347	1.88609	1.85941	1.83339	1.80802	1.78326	1.75911	1.73554	1.71252	1.69005	1.62571
3	2.88388	2.85602	2.82861	2.77509	2.72325	2.67301	2.62432	2.57710	2.53129	2.48685	2.44371	2.40183	2.28323
4	3.80773	3.76197	3.71710	3.62990	3.54595	3.46511	3.38721	3.31213	3.23972	3.16987	3.10245	3.03735	2.85498
5	4.71346	4.64583	4.57971	4.45182	4.32948	4.21236	4.10020	3.99271	3.88965	3.79079	3.69590	3.60478	3.35216
6	5.60143	5.50813	5.41719	5.24214	5.07569	4.91732	4.76654	4.62288	4.48592	4.35526	4.23054	4.11141	3.78448
7	6.47199	6.34939	6.23028	6.00205	5.78637	5.58238	5.38929	5.20637	5.03295	4.86842	4.71220	4.56376	4.16042
8	7.32548	7.17014	7.01969	6.73274	6.46321	6.20979	5.97130	5.74664	5.53482	5.33493	5.14612	4.96764	4.48732
9	8.16224	7.97087	7.78611	7.43533	7.10782	6.80169	6.51523	6.24689	5.99525	5.75902	5.53705	5.32825	4.77158
10	8.98259	8.75206	8.53020	8.11090	7.72173	7.36009	7.02358	6.71008	6.41766	6.14457	5.88923	5.65022	5.01877
11	9.78685	9.51421	9.25262	8.76048	8.30641	7.88687	7.49867	7.13896	6.80519	6.49506	6.20652	5.93770	5.23371
12	10.57534	10.25776	9.95400	9.38507	8.86325	8.38384	7.94269	7.53608	7.16073	6.81369	6.49236	6.19437	5.42062
13	11.34837	10.98319	10.63496	9.98565	9.39357	8.85268	8.35765	7.90378	7.48690	7.10336	6.74987	6.42355	5.58315
14	12.10625	11.69091	11.29607	10.56312	9.89864	9.29498	8.74547	8.24424	7.78615	7.36669	6.98187	6.62817	5.72448
15	12.84926	12.38138	11.93794	11.11839	10.37966	9.71225	9.10791	8.55948	8.06069	7.60608	7.19087	6.81086	5.84737
16	13.57771	13.05500	12.56110	11.65230	10.83777	10.10590	9.44665	8.85137	8.31256	7.82371	7.37916	6.97399	5.95423
17	14.29187	13.71220	13.16612	12.16567	11.27407	10.47726	9.76322	9.12164	8.54363	8.02155	7.54879	7.11963	6.04716
18	14.99203	14.35336	13.75351	12.65930	11.68959	10.82760	10.05909	9.37189	8.75563	8.20141	7.70162	7.24967	6.12797
19	15.67846	14.97889	14.32380	13.13394	12.08532	11.15812	10.33560	9.60360	8.95011	8.36492	7.83929	7.36578	6.19823
20	16.35143	15.58916	14.87747	13.59033	12.46221	11.46992	10.59401	9.81815	9.12855	8.51356	7.96333	7.46944	6.25933

Financial Calculators

The third method of calculating present value of a series of periodic payments is to use a financial calculator and input the variables as follows:

Enter:	4	3	1000	0		Result
Press:	I/Y	N	PMT	FV	CPT PV	$(2,775.09)

[1] The difference of 0.00001 between 2.77509 and 2.77510 is due to rounding.

When using a financial calculator to calculate the present value of an annuity, it is also necessary to specify if the annual cash flow is at the end of each period or the beginning. In **an ordinary annuity, the payments are at the end of each period**, as in our example. In **an annuity in arrears, the first payment starts immediately, at the beginning of the first period**. In this appendix and textbook, all of the annuity examples are ordinary annuities with the payments at the end of each period. Generally this is also the default setting on new calculators. But you should learn how to set your calculator for the two types of annuities. This will be slightly different for different calculators so you may need to check your calculator's user manual to learn how to switch between the two types of annuities.

Computer Spreadsheets

Using the Excel PV function, the data used in the =PV(rate,nper,pmt,fv,type) formula and the result for this example are:

RATE	.04
NPER	3
PMT	$1,000.00
FV	$0.00
Type	0

The result is a PV of $(2,775.09).

INTEREST RATES AND TIME PERIODS

In the preceding calculations, the discounting has been done on an annual basis using an annual interest rate. There are situations where adjustments may be required to the interest rate, the time period, or both.

Using Time Periods of Less Than One Year

Discounting, or compounding, may be done over shorter periods of time than one year, such as monthly, quarterly, or semi-annually. When the time frame is less than one year, it is necessary to convert the annual interest rate to the applicable time frame. Assume, for example, that the investor in Illustration PV-7 received $500 semi-annually for three years instead of $1,000 annually. In this case, the number of periods (n) becomes six (three annual periods × 2), and the discount rate (i) is 2% (4% × $6/12$ months).

If present value tables are used to determine the present value, the appropriate present value factor from Table PV-2 is 5.60143. The present value of the future cash flows is $2,800.72 (5.60143 × $500). This amount is slightly higher than the $2,775.09 calculated in Illustration PV-9 because interest is calculated twice during the same year. Thus, interest is compounded on the first half-year's interest.

Limitations of Present Value Tables

As previously discussed, one of the limitations of the present value tables is that the tables contain a limited number of interest rates. This is particularly a problem when time periods of less than one year are used. For example, if the annual interest rate was 7% and the payments were semi-annual, you would need to use the present value factor for 3.5%, which has not been included in Tables PV-1 or PV-2 in this textbook due to space limitations. If the payments were quarterly, you would need to use 1.75%, which is also not in the PV tables.

You will likely find PV tables to be of very limited value in other courses or in your own life. Consequently, we highly recommend you learn how to use either a financial calculator or a computer spreadsheet to perform these calculations.

 BEFORE YOU GO ON...

Do It

Corkum Company has just signed a capital lease contract for equipment that requires rental payments of $6,000 each, to be paid at the end of each of the next five years. The appropriate discount rate is 6%. What is the present value of the rental payments; that is, the amount used to capitalize the leased equipment? Show the calculation using one of (a) the present value of an annuity formula; (b) Table PV-2; (c) a financial calculator; or (d) Excel functions.

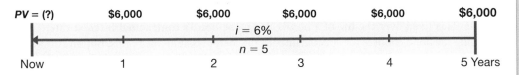

Action Plan

• Draw a time diagram showing when the future value will be received, the discount rate, and the number of periods.

• Note that each of the future payments is the same amount paid at even intervals; therefore, use present value of an annuity calculations to determine the present value ($i = 6\%$ and $n = 5$).

Solution

The present value of lease rental payments of $6,000 paid at the end of each year for five years, discounted at 6%, is calculated as follows:

(a) Using the present value of an annuity formula:

$$PV = \$6,000 \times [(1 - (1 \div (1 + 6\%)^5)) \div 6\%]$$
$$= \$6,000 \times [(1 - (1 \div (1.06)^5)) \div 0.06]$$
$$= \$6,000 \times [(1 - (1 \div 1.33823)) \div 0.06]$$
$$= \$6,000 \times [(1 - .747258) \div 0.06]$$
$$= \$6,000 \times 4.21236$$
$$= \$25,274.16$$

(b) Using the present value factor from Table PV-2:
The present value factor from Table PV-2 is 4.21236 (five periods at 6%).

$$PV = \$6,000 \times 4.21236$$
$$PV = \$25,274.16$$

(c) Using a financial calculator:

Enter:	6	5	6000	0			Result
Press:	I/Y	N	PMT	FV	CPT	PV	$(25,274.18)

(d) Using Excel functions and the PV formula =PV(rate,nper,pmt,fv,type):

RATE	.06
NPER	5
PMT	$6,000.00
FV	$0.00
Type	0

PV = $ (25,274.18)

Related exercise material: BEPV–6 and BEPV–7.

THE **NAVIGATOR**

Applying Present Value Concepts

CALCULATING THE MARKET PRICE OR PRESENT VALUE OF A BOND

» **STUDY OBJECTIVE 3**

Calculate the present value of a bond.

The present value (or market price) of a bond is a function of three variables: (1) the payment amounts, (2) the length of time until the amounts are paid, and (3) the market interest rate, also known as the discount rate.

The first variable (dollars to be paid) is made up of two elements: (1) the principal amount (a single sum), and (2) a series of interest payments (an annuity). To calculate the present value of the bond, both the principal amount and the interest payments must be discounted, which requires two different calculations. The present value of a bond can be calculated using present value formulas, factors from the two present value tables, a financial calculator, or Excel.

It is important to note that **the interest rate used to determine the annual or semi-annual interest payments is fixed over the life of a bond**. This is the **bond's contractual interest rate**. The company issuing the bond chooses the specific interest rate before issuing the bonds. But investors may use a different interest rate when determining how much they are willing to pay (the present value) for the bonds. Investors are influenced by both general economic conditions and their assessment of the company issuing the bonds. **Investors use the market interest rate to determine the present value of the bonds**. In the following sections, we will illustrate how to calculate the present value of the bonds using a market interest rate that is equal to, greater than, or less than the contractual interest rate.

Market Interest Rate Equals the Contractual Interest Rate

When the investor's market interest rate is equal to the bond's contractual interest rate, the bonds' present value will equal their face value. To illustrate, assume there is a bond issue of five-year, 6% bonds with a face value of $100,000. Interest is payable **semi-annually** on January 1 and July 1. In this case, the investor will receive (1) $100,000 at maturity, and (2) a series of 10 $3,000 interest payments [($100,000 × 6%) × $\frac{6}{12}$ months] over the term of the bonds. The length of time (n) is the total number of interest periods (10 periods = 5 years × 2 payments per year), and the discount rate (i) is the rate per semi-annual interest period (3% = 6% × $\frac{6}{12}$ months). The time diagram in Illustration PV-10 shows the variables involved in this discounting situation.

▶ **ILLUSTRATION PV-10**
Time diagram for the present value of a five-year, 6% bond paying interest semi-annually

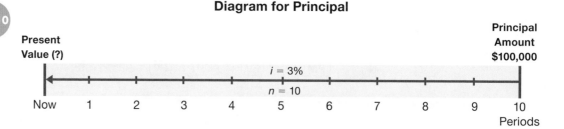

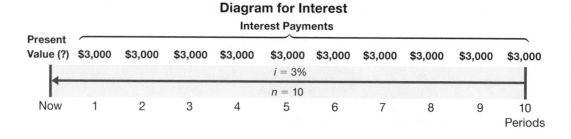

The calculation of the present value of these bonds using factors from the appropriate present value tables is shown in Illustration PV-11.

▶ILLUSTRATION PV-11
Present value of bonds
(market rate equals contractual
rate)

6% Contractual Rate and 6% Market Rate	
Present value of principal to be received at maturity	
$100,000 × PV of 1 due in 10 periods (n) at 3% (i)	
$100,000 × 0.74409 (Table PV-1)	$ 74,409
Present value of interest to be received periodically over the term of the bonds	
$3,000 × PV of 1 due periodically for 10 periods (n) at 3% (i)	
$3,000 × 8.53020 (Table PV-2)	25,591*
Present value of bonds	$100,000
* Rounded	

Using a financial calculator or Excel functions would yield the same result. Thus, when the market rate is the same as the contractual rate, the bonds will sell at face value.

Market Interest Rate Is Greater Than the Contractual Interest Rate

Now assume that the investor's market rate of return is 8%, not 6%. The future cash flows are again $100,000 and $3,000, respectively. **These cash flows are based on the bond contract and do not vary with the investor's rate of return**. But the investor's rate of return can vary, depending on available rates in the marketplace. If the market interest rate is 8%, then the present value is calculated using this rate. In this case, 4% (8% × ⁶⁄₁₂ months) will be used because the bonds pay interest semi-annually. The present value of the bonds is $91,889, as calculated in Illustration PV-12.

▶ILLUSTRATION PV-12
Present value of bonds
(market rate greater than
contractual rate)

6% Contractual Rate and 8% Market Rate	
Present value of principal to be received at maturity	
$100,000 × PV of 1 due in 10 periods (n) at 4% (i)	
$100,000 × 0.67556 (Table PV-1)	$67,556
Present value of interest to be received periodically over the term of the bonds	
$3,000 × PV of 1 due periodically for 10 periods (n) at 4% (i)	
$3,000 × 8.11090 (Table PV-2)	24,333*
Present value of bonds	$91,889
* Rounded	

While it was necessary to use both PV tables (one for the semi-annual interest payment and one for the final payment of the bond principal) in the previous calculation, the financial calculator and Excel can both handle the two sources of cash flows in a single calculation. This is another major benefit of using a financial calculator or Excel compared with using present value tables or formulas.

If using a financial calculator, the interest payments and future repayment of principal should both be entered as negative numbers because they represent cash outflows. The result shown for the present value will then be a positive number, which is consistent with the fact that the company will receive cash when it issues a bond. The data entered for this example and the result are as follows:

Enter:	4	10	−3000	−100000		Result
Press:	(I/Y)	(N)	(PMT)	(FV)	(CPT) (PV)	$91,889.10

Similarly, if using Excel functions, the interest payments and future repayment of principal are entered as negative numbers in the PV formula =PV(rate,nper,pmt,fv,type). The data entered and the result are as follows:

RATE	.04
NPER	10
PMT	$(3,000.00)
FV	$(100,000.00)
Type	0

Result: PV = $ 91,889.10

In this situation, the bonds will sell for $91,889, at a discount of $8,111. **If the market interest rate is greater than the contract interest rate, the bonds will always sell at a discount.** If investors determine that the bond's contract interest rate is too low, they will compensate by paying less for the bonds. Note that they will still collect the full $100,000 at the maturity date.

Market Interest Rate Is Less Than the Contractual Interest Rate

On the other hand, the market rate might be lower than the contractual interest rate. In this case, the interest paid on the bonds is higher than what investors expected to earn. As a result, they will compensate by paying more for the bonds. If the market interest rate is 5%, the present value will be calculated using 2.5% (5% × $\frac{6}{12}$ months) as the discount rate. The cash payments and number of periods remain the same. In this case, the present value of the bonds is $104,376, calculated as in Illustration PV-13.

▶**ILLUSTRATION** PV-13
Present value of bonds (market rate less than contractual rate)

6% Contractual Rate and 5% Market Rate	
Present value of principal to be received at maturity	
$100,000 × PV of 1 due in 10 periods (*n*) at 2.5% (*i*)	
$100,000 × 0.78120 (Table PV-1)	$ 78,120
Present value of interest to be received periodically over the term of the bonds	
$3,000 × PV of 1 due periodically for 10 periods (*n*) at 2.5% (*i*)	
$3,000 × 8.75206 (Table PV-2)	26,256*
Present value of bonds	$104,376
*Rounded	

If using a financial calculator, the data entered and the result are as follows:

Enter:	2.5	10	−3000	−100000			Result
Press:	I/Y	N	PMT	FV	CPT	PV	$104,376.03

If using Excel functions and the PV formula =PV(rate,nper,pmt,fv,type), the data entered and the result are as follows:

RATE	.025
NPER	10
PMT	$(3,000.00)
FV	$(100,000.00)
Type	0

Result: PV = $104,376.03

These bonds will sell for $104,376, at a premium of $4,376. **If the market interest rate is less than the contractual interest rate, the bonds will always sell at a premium.**

BEFORE YOU GO ON...

Do It

Forest Lake Enterprises issued $1 million of six-year, 4.5% bonds that pay interest semi-annually. The market rate of interest for the bonds at the issue date is 4%. What cash proceeds did Forest Lake Enterprises receive from the issue of the bonds?

Solution

1. Amount to be received at maturity is the face value of the bonds, $1,000,000
2. Semi-annual interest payment = $22,500 ($1,000,000 × 4.5% × 6/12 months)
3. Number of periods n = 12 (6 years × 2 payments a year)
4. Discount rate i = 2% (4% ÷ 2 payments a year)

The cash proceeds that Forest Lake will receive from issuing the bonds is the present value of principal to be received at maturity plus the present value of the interest received periodically, calculated as follows:

Present value of principal to be received at maturity:

$1,000,000 × 0.78849 (PV of $1 due in 12 periods at 2% from Table PV-1) .... $ 788,490

Present value of interest to be received periodically over the term of the bonds:

$22,500 × 10.57534 (PV of $1 due each period for 12 periods at 2% from Table PV-2) 237,945

Present value of bonds .... $1,026,435[2]

If using a financial calculator, the data entered and the result are as follows:

Enter:	2	12	−22500	−1000000		Result
Press:	I/Y	N	PMT	FV	CPT PV	$1,026,438.35

If using Excel functions and the PV formula =PV(rate,nper,pmt,fv,type), the data entered and the result are as follows:

RATE	.02
NPER	12
PMT	$(22,500.00)
FV	$(1,000,000.00)
Type	0

Result: PV = $1,026,438.35

[2] Note the financial calculator and Excel results are the same amount but they are slightly different than the PV table calculation because the factors in the PV tables are rounded.

Related exercise material: BEPV–8 and BEPV–9.

Action Plan

- Note that Forest Lake will be able to sell these bonds at a premium because the bonds pay higher interest (4.5%) than the current market interest rate (4%).
- Recall that the contractual interest rate is used to determine the interest payment; the market rate is used to determine the present value.
- Adjust the interest rates and number of periods for the effect of the semi-annual periods.
- Use Table PV-1 to determine the present value of the principal and Table PV-2 to determine the present value of the interest payments.
- You can instead use a financial calculator, remembering to enter the interest and principal payments as negative numbers.
- You can instead use Excel functions, entering the interest and principal payments as negative numbers.

THE **NAVIGATOR**

USING PRESENT VALUE CONCEPTS WITH NOTES PAYABLE

» **STUDY OBJECTIVE 4**

Apply present value concepts to notes payable to calculate the periodic payments, the interest rate, or the number of periods.

Long-term notes payable are normally repayable in a series of periodic payments. Examples of long-term notes payable include unsecured notes, mortgages (which are secured notes on real property, such as a house), and loans (for example, student or car).

The present value of the note payable is the amount borrowed and thus typically doesn't need to be calculated as in the case of a bond payable. The future value of a note payable is zero because the note will be paid in full through the periodic payments, which include both interest and principal. Instead, present value concepts are often used with notes payable to determine one of the following three variables: (1) the payment amount, (2) the length of time until the amounts are paid (time to maturity date), or (3) the market interest rate.

Calculating the Periodic Payment for a Note Payable

Payments for a long-term note payable may be fixed principal payments plus interest, or blended principal and interest payments. To illustrate these two types of payments, we will assume that Heathcote Company obtains a five-year note payable, with an 8% interest rate, to purchase a piece of equipment costing $25,000.

Fixed Principal Payments Plus Interest. If we first assume that repayment is to be in fixed principal payments plus interest, paid annually, then the payment amount would be $5,000 ($25,000 ÷ 5 years) for principal plus 8% interest on the outstanding balance. Illustration PV-14 shows how the interest and periodic cash payment are determined for this note.

▶ **ILLUSTRATION PV-14**
Note payable amortization table with fixed principal payments plus interest

Interest Period	(A) Cash Payment (B) + (C)	(B) Interest Expense (D) × 8%	(C) Fixed Reduction of Principal $25,000 ÷ 5	(D) Principal Balance (D) − (C)
Start of Year 1				$25,000
End of Year 1	$ 7,000	$2,000	$ 5,000	20,000
End of Year 2	6,600	1,600	5,000	15,000
End of Year 3	6,200	1,200	5,000	10,000
End of Year 4	5,800	800	5,000	5,000
End of Year 5	5,400	400	5,000	0
Totals	$31,000	$6,000	$25,000	

Note that the periodic cash payment is a different amount each period because the interest is a different amount each month. Recall that an annuity, by definition, is an equal payment each period. That means we cannot use present value concepts, as they have been introduced in this appendix, to analyze the note. Instead we will focus on notes payable with blended payments, which are the same amount each period, in the following section of this appendix.

Blended Principal Plus Interest Payments. In the case of blended principal and interest payments, the periodic payment is an annuity and thus present value concepts can be used to calculate the amount of the annual payment. As long as four of the five present value amounts (present value, interest rate, number of periods, payments, and future value) are known, they can be used to calculate the one unknown.

Present Value Tables. If we divide the total loan amount of $25,000 by the present value factor for an annuity from Table PV-2 for i = 8% and n = 5, then we can determine that the annual payment is $6,261.41 ($25,000 ÷ 3.99271). Illustration PV-15 shows the note payable amortization table using the annuity of $6,262.41 as the annual cash payment.

	(A)	(B)	(C)	(D)
			Reduction of Principal	
		Interest Expense	Principal	Principal Balance
Interest Period	Cash Payment	(D) × 8%	(A) − (B)	(D) − (C)
Start of Year 1				$25,000.00
End of Year 1	$ 6,261.41	$2,000.00	$ 4,261.41	20,738.59
End of Year 2	6,261.41	1,659.09	4,602.32	16,136.27
End of Year 3	6,261.41	1,290.90	4,970.51	11,165.76
End of Year 4	6,261.41	893.26	5,368.15	5,797.61
End of Year 5	6,261.41	463.80	5,797.61	0
Totals	$31,307.05	$6,307.05	$25,000.00	

▸ **ILLUSTRATION PV-15**
Note payable amortization table with blended principal plus interest payments

We can see from this illustration that the periodic blended payment of $6,261.41 is exactly the amount needed to pay the required interest plus the note in full by the end of year 5. Recall that the balance of zero at the end of year 5 is also the future value of the note payable.

Financial Calculators. If using a financial calculator to determine the periodic payment, the data entered and the result are as follows:

Enter:	8	5	25000	0			Result
Press:	I/Y	N	PV	FV	CPT	PMT	$(6,261.41)

Excel Functions. If using the Excel PMT formula =PMT(rate,nper,pv,fv,type), the data entered and the result are as follows:

RATE	.08
NPER	5
PV	$25,000.00
FV	$0.00
Type	0

Result: PMT = $(6,261.41)

While the above three methods all provided the same periodic payment, the financial calculator and Excel functions are more useful as they can be used for any interest rate and any number of periods, not just those included in the PV table.

Calculating the Interest Rate for a Note Payable

There are several situations in which it may be necessary to calculate the effective interest rate. For example, sometimes businesses offer financing with stated interest rates below market interest rates to stimulate sales. Examples of notes with stated interest rates below market are seen in advertisements offering no payment for two years. As we have seen in the case of bonds, if the contractual or stated interest rate is less than the market or effective interest rate, then the present value of the loan will be less than the face value. With a zero-interest-rate note, the market or effective interest rate in the transaction must be imputed using present value calculations.

As an example, assume that a furniture retailer is offering "No payment for two years, or $150 off on items with a sticker price of $2,000." The implicit interest cost over the two years is $150, and the present value of the asset is then $1,850 ($2,000 − $150). From Table PV-1, the effective interest rate can be determined as follows:

$$PV \div FV = \text{discount factor} \qquad \$1,850 \div \$2,000 = 0.925$$

Looking at the $n = 2$ row, this would represent an interest rate of approximately 4%. Most notes have an interest cost, whether explicitly stated or not.

Using a financial calculator will result in a more precise interest rate calculation. In this example, the data entered and the result are as follows:

Enter:	2	1850	0	−2000			Result
Press:	N	PV	PMT	FV	CPT	I/Y	3.975%

Helpful hint Remember to correctly enter cash inflows as positive numbers and cash outflows as negative numbers or the financial calculator will give an error message when calculating the interest rate.

In the Excel RATE formula =RATE(nper,pmt,pv,fv,type), the data entered and the result are as follows:

NPER	2
PMT	$0.00
PV	$1,850.00
FV	$(2,000.00)
Type	0

Result: RATE = 3.975%

Also note that the purchaser should record the furniture at a cost of $1,850 even if the purchaser chose the option of no payment for two years. In this case, the purchaser will recognize interest expense of $73.54 ($1,850 × 3.975%) in the first year and $76.46 [($1,850 + $73.54) × 3.975%] in the second year.

Canada Student Loans: Calculation of Time to Pay

The Canadian federal government, in an effort to encourage post-secondary education, offers loans to eligible students with no interest accruing while they maintain their full-time student status. When schooling is complete, the entire Canada Student Loan must be repaid within 10 years. Repayment of the loan can be at a fixed rate of prime plus 5%, or a floating rate of prime plus 2.5%. One calculation you might be interested in is how long it will take to repay your Canada Student Loan if you have a certain amount of money available to make monthly payments.

Let's assume that you attend school for four years and borrow $2,500 per year. Upon graduation, because there was no interest while you were a student, you have a total debt of $10,000. Also assume you have opted for a fixed rate of interest of 8% while repaying the loan. If you can pay $150 a month, will you be able to repay the loan within the 120 months (10 years × 12 months per year) allowed? To determine the answer to this question, you need to know in how many months the loan will be repaid.

Using a financial calculator, the data entered and the result are as follows:

	8 ÷ 12 or						
Enter:	0.6667	10,000	−150	0			Result
Press:	I/Y	PV	PMT	FV	CPT	N	88.46

Note that, because you are making monthly payments, the annual interest rate of 8% must be adjusted to a monthly rate of 0.6667%. Also note that the payments are a negative number because they are a cash outflow. The present value is a positive number because it is equal to the amount borrowed, which was a cash inflow. The future value is zero because the loan will be fully paid at maturity.

The result of 88.46 means that you would need to make 89 monthly payments: the first 88 months at $150 per month, and the last month at a lesser amount for the remaining balance. This is less than 120 months, which means that you will be able to pay your student loan in the allowed period.

The same result can be obtained using the Excel NPER formula =NPER(rate,pmt,pv,fv,type). The data entered and the result are as follows:

RATE	.08/12 = .006667
PMT	$(150.00)
PV	$10,000.00
FV	$0.00
Type	0

Result: NPER = 88.46 periods

This particular example could not be done with the PV tables in this textbook because of the interest rate. Since we are making monthly payments, we must also use a monthly interest rate. The monthly interest rate of 0.6667% is less than the lowest percentage on the table and thus the table cannot be used.

 BEFORE YOU GO ON...

Do It

You are about to purchase your first car for $25,000. You pay $1,000 cash and finance the remaining amount at an annual interest rate of 7% over a period of 48 months. How much is your monthly payment, assuming you make equal blended principal and interest payments each month?

Solution

1. The monthly payment is equal to the present value divided by the PV factor:

   $24,000 ÷ 41.76019 = $574.71

2. Using a financial calculator, the data entered and the result are as follows:

Enter:	7 ÷ 12 or 0.5833	48	24000	0			Result
Press:	(I/Y)	(N)	(PV)	(FV)	(CPT) (PMT)		$(574.71)

3. Using Excel functions, the formula is: =PMT(rate,nper,pv,fv,type).

RATE	.07 ÷ 12 = .005833
NPER	48
PV	$24,000.00
FV	$0.00
Type	0

Result: PMT = $(574.71)

Related exercise material: BEPV–10, BEPV–11, BEPV–12, BEPV–13, BEPV–14, BEPV–15, BEPV–16, BEPV–17, and BEPV–18.

Action Plan
- Use $n = 48$ and $i = 0.5833\%$ (7% ÷ 12 months), PV = $24,000, and FV = $0.
- If using present value factors, this number is 41.76019.
- Alternatively, you may use a financial calculator or Excel functions to calculate the payment.

THE **NAVIGATOR**

ASSETS: ESTIMATING VALUE IN USE USING FUTURE CASH FLOWS

 **STUDY OBJECTIVE 5**

Estimate the value of an asset using future cash flows.

As we have learned in a previous section, a bond can be valued based on future cash flows. So too can an asset. In Chapter 9, you learned that companies are required to regularly determine whether the value of property, plant, and equipment has been impaired. Recall that an asset is impaired if the carrying amount reported on the balance sheet is greater than its recoverable amount. The recoverable amount is either the asset's fair value or its *value in use*. Determining the value in use requires the application of present value concepts. The calculation of value in use is a two-step process: (1) estimate future cash flows, and (2) calculate the present value of these cash flows.

For example, assume JB Company owns a specialized piece of equipment used in its manufacturing process. JB needs to determine the asset's value in use to test for impairment. As the first step in determining value in use, JB's management estimates that the equipment will last for another five years and that it will generate the following future cash flows at the end of each year:

Year 1	Year 2	Year 3	Year 4	Year 5
$9,000	$10,000	$13,000	$10,000	$7,000

In the second step of determining value in use, JB calculates the present value of each of these future cash flows. Using a discount rate of 8%, the present value of each future cash flow is shown in Illustration PV-16.

▶ **ILLUSTRATION PV-16**
Present value of estimated future cash flows of specialized equipment

	Year 1	Year 2	Year 3	Year 4	Year 5
Future cash flows	$9,000	$10,000	$13,000	$10,000	$7,000
Present value factor[3]	0.92593	0.85734	0.79383	0.73503	0.68058
Present value amount	$8,333	$ 8,573	$10,320	$ 7,350	$4,764

The value in use of JB's specialized equipment is the sum of the present value of each year's cash flow, $39,340 ($8,333 + $8,573 + $10,320 + $7,350 + $4,764). A financial calculator or Excel functions could also be used in this calculation, although there would have to be five different calculations made because of the irregular amounts for the annual future cash flows. If this amount is less than the asset's carrying amount, JB will be required to record an impairment, as shown in Chapter 9.

The present value method of estimating the value in use of an asset can also be used for intangible assets. For example, assume JB purchases a licence from Redo Industries for the right to manufacture and sell products using Redo's processes and technologies. JB estimates it will earn $6,000 per year from this licence over the next 10 years. What is the value in use to JB of this licence?

Since JB expects to earn the same amount each year, Table PV-2 is used to find the present value factor of the annuity after determining the appropriate discount rate. As pointed out in the previous example, JB should choose a rate based on current market rates; however, adjustments for uncertainties related to the specific asset may be required. Assuming JB uses 8% as the discount rate, the present value factor from Table PV-2 for 10 periods is 6.71008. The value in use of the licence is $40,260 ($6,000 × 6.71008).

If using a financial calculator, the data entered and the result are as follows:

Enter:	8	10	6000	0			Result
Press:	I/Y	N	PMT	FV	CPT	PV	$(40,260.49)

If using Excel functions and the PV formula =PV(rate,nper,pmt,fv,type), the data entered and the result are as follows:

RATE	.08
NPER	10
PMT	$6,000.00
FV	$0.00
Type	0

Result: PV = $(40,260.49)

---

[3] The appropriate interest rate to be used is based on current market rates; however, adjustments for uncertainties related to the specific asset may be made. Further discussion on this topic is covered in more advanced texts.

The results using the financial calculator and Excel functions are negative as they represent the amount you should be willing to pay today to receive $6,000 per year for 10 years if the discount rate is 8%.

 BEFORE YOU GO ON...

Do It

You are attempting to estimate the value in use of your company's production equipment, which you estimate will be used in operations for another eight years. You estimate that the equipment will generate annual cash flows of $16,000, at the end of each year, for the remainder of its productive life, and that 9% is the appropriate discount rate. What is the value in use of this equipment?

Solution

The value in use is equal to the present value of the estimated annual future cash flows for the remaining life of the asset discounted at an appropriate discount rate.

Future annual cash flows:	$16,000
Number of periods:	8
Discount rate:	9%
Present value annuity factor ($n = 8$, $i = 9\%$):	5.53482
Present value:	$88,557 = $16,000 × 5.53482

If using a financial calculator, the data entered and the result are as follows:

Enter:	9	8	16000	0		Result
Press:	I/Y	N	PMT	FV	CPT PV	$(88,557.11)

If using Excel functions and the PV formula =PV(rate,nper,pmt,fv,type), the data entered and the result are as follows:

RATE	.09
NPER	8
PMT	$16,000.00
FV	$0.00
Type	0

Result PV = $(88,557.11)

Action Plan
- Identify future cash flows.
- Use Table PV-2 to determine the present value of an annuity factor for $n = 8$ and $i = 9\%$ and calculate the present value.
- Alternatively, use a financial calculator or Excel functions to solve.

Related exercise material: BEPV–19, BEPV–20, and BEPV–21.

THE **NAVIGATOR**

▶ Brief Exercises

BEPV–1 Determine the amount of interest that will be earned on each of the following investments:

	Investment	(*i*) Interest Rate	(*n*) Number of Periods	Type of Interest
(a)	$1,000	5%	1	Simple
(b)	$500	4%	2	Simple
(c)	$500	4%	2	Compound

Calculate simple and compound interest. (SO 1)

BEPV–2 Wong Ltd. is considering an investment that will return a lump sum of $600,000 five years from now. What amount should Wong Ltd. pay for this investment in order to earn a 4% return?

Calculate present value of a single-sum investment. (SO 1)

BEPV–3 Mohammed's parents invest $8,000 in a 10-year guaranteed investment certificate (GIC) in his name. The investment pays 4% annually. How much will the GIC yield when it matures? Compare the interest earned in the first and second five-year periods, and provide an explanation for the difference.

Calculate future value of a single-sum investment and demonstrate the effect of compounding. (SO 1)

Calculate number of periods of a single investment sum. (SO 1)

BEPV–4   Xin Su has been offered the opportunity to invest $44,401 now. The investment will earn 7% per year, and at the end of that time will return Xin $100,000. How many years must Xin wait to receive $100,000?

Calculate interest rate on single sum. (SO 1)

BEPV–5   If Jin Fei invests $3,152 now, she will receive $10,000 at the end of 15 years. What annual rate of interest will Jin earn on her investment? Round your answer to the nearest whole number.

Calculate present value of an annuity investment. (SO 2)

BEPV–6   Tarzwell Ltd. is considering investing in an annuity contract that will return $25,000 at the end of each year for 15 years. What amount should Tarzwell Ltd. pay for this investment if it earns a 6% return?

Determine number of periods and discount rate. (SO 2)

BEPV–7   For each of the following cases, indicate in the chart below the appropriate discount rate (i) and the appropriate number of periods (n) to be used in present value calculations. Show calculations. The first one has been completed as an example.

	Annual Interest Rate	Number of Years	Frequency of Payments	(n) Number of periods	(i) Discount Rate
1.	6%	2	Quarterly	$2 \times 4 = 8$	$6\% \div 4 = 1.5\%$
2.	5%	8	Semi-annually		
3.	7%	5	Annually		
4.	4%	3	Quarterly		
5.	2%	6	Semi-annually		
6.	6%	9	Monthly		

Calculate present value of bonds. (SO 3)

BEPV–8   New Line Railroad Co. is about to issue $100,000 of 10-year bonds that pay a 5.5% annual interest rate, with interest payable semi-annually. The market interest rate is 5%. How much can New Line expect to receive for the sale of these bonds?

Calculate present value of bonds. (SO 3)

BEPV–9   Assume the same information as in BEPV–8, except that the market interest rate is 6% instead of 5%. In this case, how much can New Line expect to receive from the sale of these bonds?

Calculate payment on note. (SO 4)

BEPV–10   Marsdon Company receives a six-year, $50,000 note that bears interest at 8% from a customer. The customer will make annual blended principal plus interest payments at the end of each year. What is the annual payment that Marsdon will receive from its customer?

Calculate payment on note. (SO 4)

BEPV–11   Assume the same information as in BEPV–10, except that the interest rate is 9% instead of 8%. What is the annual payment that Marsdon will receive from its customer?

Calculate effective interest rate on note (SO 4)

BEPV–12   Phang Ltd. issues a six-year, $1,058,871 mortgage note on January 1, 2014, to obtain financing for new equipment. The terms provide for semi-annual instalment payments of $112,825. What is the effective interest rate on the mortgage note payable?

Calculate quarterly payments on note payable. (SO 4)

BEPV–13   The municipality of Lansdown issued a three-year, 5% mortgage note payable for $185,000 to finance the purchase of three salt trucks. The terms provide for equal quarterly blended principal plus interest payments. What are the quarterly payments on the note?

Determine how long to repay note. (SO 4)

BEPV–14   You have borrowed $18,000. If the annual rate of interest is 4%, how long will it take you to repay the note if you are making semi-annual blended principal plus interest payments of $1,702?

Calculate annual payments. (SO 4)

BEPV–15   You would like to purchase a car that costs $32,000, and the dealer offers financing over a five-year period at 3%. If repayments are to be made annually, what would your annual payments be?

Calculate trade-in value of car. (SO 4)

BEPV–16   Assume the same information as in BEPV–15, except that you can only afford to make annual payments of $6,500. If you decide to trade in your present car to help reduce the amount of financing required, what trade-in value would you need to negotiate to ensure your annual payment is $6,500?

Compare financing options. (SO 4)

BEPV–17   As CFO of a small manufacturing firm, you have been asked to determine the best financing for the purchase of a new piece of equipment. If the vendor is offering repayment options of $10,000 per year for five years, or only one payment of $46,000 at the end of two years, which option would you recommend? The current market rate of interest is 8%.

Compare financing options. (SO 4)

BEPV–18   If the market rate of interest in BEPV–17 was 10%, would you choose the same option?

BEPV–19   Sam Waterston owns a garage and is contemplating purchasing a tire retreading machine for $16,100. After estimating costs and revenues, Sam projects a net cash flow from the retreading machine of $2,690 annually for eight years. Sam hopes to earn a return of 11% on such investments. What is the present value of the retreading operation? Should Sam Waterston purchase the retreading machine?

Calculate value of machine for purchase decision. (SO 5)

BEPV–20   Lee Company must perform an impairment test on its equipment. The equipment will produce the following cash flows: Year 1, $35,000; Year 2, $45,000; Year 3, $55,000. Lee requires a minimum rate of return of 10%. What is the value in use for this equipment?

Calculate value in use for a machine. (SO 5)

BEPV–21   Tsung Company signs a contract to sell the use of its patented manufacturing technology to Herlitz Corp. for 12 years. The contract for this transaction stipulates that Herlitz Corp. pays Tsung $21,000 at the end of each year for the use of this technology. Using a discount rate of 4%, what is the value in use of the patented manufacturing technology?

Calculate value in use of a patent. (SO 5)

Company Index

Subject Index